ESCAPE FROM EVIL'S DARKNESS

Robert J. Spitzer, S.J., Ph.D.

ESCAPE FROM EVIL'S DARKNESS

The Light of Christ in the Church, Spiritual Conversion, and Moral Conversion

Volume Two of the Trilogy:
Called Out of Darkness: Contending with
Evil through the Church, Virtue, and Prayer

IGNATIUS PRESS   SAN FRANCISCO

Nihil Obstat: Reverend Joseph Son Nguyen, M.Div., M.A., B.C.C., S.T.D.

Imprimatur: + The Most Reverend Kevin J. Vann, J.C.D., O.D.
　　　　　 Bishop, Diocese of Orange
　　　　　 August 26, 2020

Cover art:
Detail from *The Descent from the Cross*,
etching by Rembrandt van Rijn, 1633.
Image in the public domain.

Cover design by John Herreid

© 2021 by Ignatius Press, San Francisco
All rights reserved
ISBN 978-1-62164-418-7 (PB)
ISBN 978-1-64229-160-5 (eBook)
Library of Congress Catalogue number 2020938409
Printed in the United States of America ∞

*In loving memory of my mother and father, who showed me
the path out of darkness through faith and virtue.*

*And to my many mentors—for example, Father Thomas King;
Father Gordon Moreland; Father Gerard Steckler; Dr. Paul Weiss;
Lou Tice; Timothy Busch; Michael Patterson; Dan Brajcich; and
David Lau—as well as the board and leadership staff of the
Magis Institute and the Spitzer Center, and the board and cabinet
of Gonzaga University, who provided wisdom, practical know-how,
and invaluable support through their friendship and generosity.*

CONTENTS

ACKNOWLEDGMENTS

I am most grateful to Joan Jacoby, whose invaluable work brought mere thoughts into reality through her excellent editing suggestions and research. It is not easy to do research for a blind scholar, transcribe multiple copies of his dictation, clean up the manuscript, and endure his many edits, but she did so with great patience, care, competence, and contribution—a true manifestation of her virtue and dedication.

I am also grateful to Gabriella Negrete for her input and considerable assistance in preparing the manuscript.

I would also like to express my appreciation to the board and benefactors of the Magis Institute who gave me the time and resources to complete these publications.

INTRODUCTION TO THIS VOLUME

In the introduction to Volume I of this Trilogy,[1] we explained three kinds of conversion formally articulated by Bernard Lonergan—intellectual conversion, religious/spiritual conversion, and moral conversion.[2] We dedicated the majority of the Quartet to intellectual conversion (in the whole of Volumes II and III and parts of Volumes I and IV).[3] We showed there that God has not left us bereft of exterior evidence upon which to ground, both reasonably and responsibly, our interior awareness of Him and the desires He awakens.

As we have seen in Volumes I through III of the Quartet, God has provided significant evidence from science to validate our interior awareness of Him—for example, the Borde-Vilenkin-Guth proof for a beginning of physical reality,[4] the evidence of entropy for a beginning of the universe,[5] the fine-tuning of universal constants implying supernatural intelligence,[6] medical studies of near-death experiences validating our transphysical soul,[7] scientific evidence from the Shroud of Turin for Jesus' Resurrection,[8] and dozens of contemporary,

---

[1] *Christ versus Satan in Our Daily Lives: The Cosmic Struggle between Good and Evil* (forthcoming).

[2] See Bernard Lonergan, *Method in Theology*, ed. Robert M. Doran and John D. Dadosky, vol. 14 of *The Collected Works of Bernard Lonergan*, ed. Frederick E. Crowe and Robert M. Doran (Toronto: University of Toronto Press, 1990), pp. 144–45, 153–54, 204–5, 220–39.

[3] The Quartet is entitled *Happiness, Suffering, and Transcendence* (2015–2017): Volume I is entitled *Finding True Happiness: Satisfying Our Restless Hearts* (2015); Volume II, *The Soul's Upward Yearning: Clues to Our Transcendent Nature from Experience and Reason* (2015); Volume III, *God So Loved the World: Clues to Our Transcendent Destiny from the Revelation of Jesus* (2016); and Volume IV, *The Light Shines on in the Darkness: Transforming Suffering through Faith* (2017).

[4] See Robert Spitzer, *New Proofs for the Existence of God: Contributions of Contemporary Physics and Philosophy* (Grand Rapids, Mich.: Eerdmans, 2010), Chapter 1. See also Volume II, Appendix I, of the Quartet.

[5] See ibid.

[6] See Robert Spitzer and James Sinclair, "Fine-Tuning and Indications of Transcendent Intelligence", in *Theism and Atheism: Opposing Arguments in Philosophy*, ed. Joseph Koterski, S.J., and Graham Oppy (New York: Macmillan Reference, 2019), pp. 331–63. See also Spitzer, *New Proofs*, Chapter 2, and Volume II, Appendix I, of the Quartet.

[7] See Volume II, Chapter 5, of the Quartet.

[8] See Volume III, Appendix I, of the Quartet.

scientifically validated miracles through the name of Jesus or the agency of the Blessed Virgin.[9]

Furthermore, there are several proofs of God from metaphysics, logic, and mathematics—Lonergan's proof of God,[10] contemporary metaphysical proofs of God,[11] and a Hilbertian mathematical-logical proof of the beginning of all past time.[12] Additionally, new historical studies of the New Testament have added probative force to previous studies—particularly N. T. Wright's study of the historicity of Jesus' Resurrection,[13] John P. Meier's study of the historicity of Jesus' miracles,[14] and James Dunn's study of the charismatic manifestations of the Holy Spirit in the apostolic age.[15]

When we combine this external evidence for God, the soul, and Jesus with the interior call that the Lord gives to all of us through the numinous experience,[16] the intuition of the sacred,[17] our five transcendental desires,[18] conscience,[19] and the universal archetypes of cosmic good and evil,[20] we can reasonably and responsibly affirm our

---

[9] See the appendix to Volume I of this Trilogy.

[10] See Spitzer, New Proofs, Chapter 4. See also Robert Spitzer, "Philosophical Proof of God: Derived from Principles in Bernard Lonergan's Insight", MagisCenter.com, July 25, 2016, https://magiscenter.com/philosophical-proof-of-god-derived-from-principles-in-bernard-lonergans-insight/.

[11] For a recent metaphysical proof, see Robert Spitzer, "A Contemporary Metaphysical Proof for the Existence of God", International Philosophical Quarterly 59, no. 4 (December 2019): 427–66. For another metaphysical proof, see Spitzer, New Proofs, Chapter 3. For a contemporary Thomistic proof, see Volume II, Appendix II, of the Quartet. See also Robert Spitzer, "A Contemporary Thomistic Metaphysical Proof of God", MagisCenter.com, July 25, 2016, https://magiscenter.com/a-contemporary-thomistic-metaphysical-proof-of-god-with-a-response-to-richard-dawkins-the-god-delusion/.

[12] See Spitzer, New Proofs, Chapter 5.

[13] See N. T. Wright, The Resurrection of the Son of God (Minneapolis: Fortress Press, 2003). For a summary, see Volume III, Chapter 4, of the Quartet.

[14] See John P. Meier, A Marginal Jew: Rethinking the Historical Jesus, vol. 2, Mentor, Message, and Miracles (New York: Doubleday, 1994). For a summary, see Volume III, Chapter 5, of the Quartet.

[15] See James Dunn, Jesus and the Spirit: A Study of the Religious and Charismatic Experience of Jesus and the First Christians as Reflected in the New Testament (Philadelphia: Westminster Press, 1975). See also Volume III, Chapter 5, of the Quartet.

[16] See Volume II, Chapter 1, of the Quartet.

[17] See Volume II, Chapter 2, of the Quartet.

[18] See Volume II, Chapter 4, of the Quartet.

[19] See Volume II, Chapter 2, of the Quartet.

[20] Ibid.

call from the Lord to enter into a deepening relationship with Him that will bring us to the ultimate and eternal fulfillment of our nature, dignity, and destiny.

This brings us to religious/spiritual conversion and moral conversion, because they are essential to our battle with evil and our progress in appropriating and living ever deeper authenticity and love. In other words, they are integral to our eternal salvation with the Lord of unconditional love.

As will become clear, the surest way to moral conversion is a strong religious/spiritual conversion, and the surest way to a strong religious/spiritual conversion is the Catholic Church. Though this may sound terribly biased, I am convinced that this is precisely what Jesus intended for all of us when He initiated the Church in His commissioning to Saint Peter. To be sure, the Lord speaks to people of every faith. We have already seen this in the numinous experience, the intuition of the sacred, the universality of conscience, our awareness of the cosmic struggle between good and evil, the natural religiosity of most of the world, and Friedrich Heiler's seven common characteristics of most religions (see Volume II of the Quartet, Chapters 1–2). Furthermore, the Second Vatican Council proclaimed in its dogmatic constitution (*Lumen Gentium*):

> Those who, through no fault of their own, do not know the Gospel of Christ or his Church, but who nevertheless seek God with a sincere heart, and, moved by grace, try in their actions to do his will as they know it through the dictates of their conscience—those too may achieve eternal salvation.[21]

The Church further proclaimed in its pastoral constitution (*Gaudium et Spes*):

> The Christian is certainly bound both by need and by duty to struggle with evil through many afflictions and to suffer death; but, as one who has been made a partner in the paschal mystery, and as one who has

---

[21] Vatican Council II, Dogmatic Constitution on the Church *Lumen Gentium* (November 21, 1964), no. 16, in *Vatican Council II: The Conciliar and Postconciliar Documents*, new rev. ed., ed. Austin Flannery, O.P. (Collegeville, Minn.: Liturgical Press, 2014), p. 367.

been configured to the death of Christ, he will go forward, strengthened by hope, to the resurrection.

All this holds true not for Christians only but also for all men of
good will in whose hearts grace is active invisibly. For since *Christ
died for all*, and since all men are in fact called to one and the same
destiny, which is divine, we must hold that the Holy Spirit offers to
all the possibility of being made partners, in a way known to God, in
the paschal mystery.[22]

Beyond this, people of all *Christian* faiths are inspired by the Holy
Spirit through the name of Jesus, and the Catholic Church recognizes
the authenticity of their Baptism in the name of the Triune God.

Nevertheless, the Catholic Church provides five indispensable
graces that most other Christian churches (and all non-Christian
churches) do not provide—at least to the extent of the Church initiated by Jesus in His commission to Peter:

1. The Holy Eucharist, understood as the real transubstantiated
   crucified and risen Body and Blood of Jesus.
2. A Magisterium (teaching authority), to keep the People of God
   in unity while providing an authentic interpretation of the
   teaching of Jesus in faith and morals.
3. A rich sacramental life that includes not only Baptism, but Confirmation, Reconciliation (so important for moral conversion),
   Matrimony, Holy Orders, and the Anointing of the Sick.
4. The gifts of the "inner Church" (coming from integration into
   Christ's Mystical Body), particularly the *sensus fidei, sensus fidelium*,
   and *Koinōnia*, which unite us mystically to the heart of Jesus.
5. A vast spiritual tradition—from the Church Fathers to Saint Benedict, Saint Francis, Saint Dominic, Saint Ignatius, and so many
   more—as well as a rich mystical tradition articulated so beau-
   tifully by Saint Teresa of Avila, Saint John of the Cross, Saint
   Thérèse of Lisieux, and others.

These indispensable gifts of guidance and grace—along with the
Catholic theological, philosophical, and intellectual tradition—allow

---

[22] Vatican Council II, Pastoral Constitution on the Church in the Modern World *Gaudium et Spes* (December 7, 1965), no. 22, in Flannery, *Conciliar and Postconciliar Documents*,
pp. 923–24 (italics added).

us the surest way to reach a deep religious/spiritual conversion to ground and support our moral conversion made according to the teaching of Christ as faithfully interpreted by the Catholic Church throughout the ages.

There is one important condition: we must try faithfully to follow the truth and inspiration given us by Christ through the Church, and when we fail, avail ourselves of the mercy that He offers through our prayers of forgiveness and the Sacrament of Reconciliation.

No doubt, there have been real failures on the part of Church leadership throughout the centuries to live up to the religious/spiritual and moral conversion offered by Christ through the Catholic Church; but this does not reflect on the nature of the Church herself as a sure pathway to religious/spiritual and moral conversion intended by Jesus. It only reflects the moral failings of particular individuals who, either intentionally or through some weakness of mind or spirit, allowed themselves to let go of the grace that they had been offered by Jesus through the Church.

I in no way mean these comments to be disparaging to any other church, but say them only to inform readers of the tremendous treasure of grace offered to us by Jesus through His Holy Spirit and the Catholic Church from the day that He commissioned Peter to the present. If some readers do not know what I am talking about, particularly with respect to the five indispensable gifts of guidance and grace, I would ask them to read the following chapters with an open mind, to discover what could be for them a sure path to religious/ spiritual conversion, leading to a sure path, through many challenges, to moral conversion in the heart of Christ.

Since this volume is devoted to both religious/spiritual conversion and moral conversion, in Part I (Chapters 1–3) we examine the Catholic Church as a primary vehicle for religious/spiritual conversion (hereafter, "spiritual conversion"), and in Part II (Chapters 4–7) we explore the path from spiritual conversion to moral conversion.

As will be seen, spiritual conversion is concerned with grounding and deepening our relationship with the Triune God, through prayer and worship as well as the graces and guidance Jesus bestowed on us through the sacramental life, spiritual life, and teaching authority of the Catholic Church that He initiated two thousand years ago.

Moral conversion focuses specifically on the discipline of transformation through the appropriation of moral teaching, virtue, and what we shall call "higher identity". Though there are *natural* atti-tudes and habits for becoming virtuous (such as those suggested by classical and medieval philosophers as well as contemporary psychol-ogists), they are greatly strengthened and augmented by spiritual con-version (particularly a deep relationship with the Lord, the graces of the sacramental life, and the freeing power of prayer and religious self-examination). If we want "a fighting chance" to move beyond the powers of darkness into the light of Christ—and to stay within that salvific light—we will begin the process of moral conversion with a concerted effort to engage in spiritual conversion through the Catholic Church.

In Chapter 7, we examine the Sacrament of Reconciliation, which is the essential means for us to continue faithfully in moral conversion. The process of moral conversion is complex, has many ups and downs, and sometimes radical reversals and reversions. In the Sacrament of Reconciliation, the Lord offers us the opportunity of complete absolution, healing of the damage of sin, the power to break the grip of the evil spirit, and the grace of continued resolve in moral conversion.

We conclude this Volume with an Appendix (I) summarizing the four levels of happiness to which we refer throughout this Volume, and a list of spontaneous and common prayers to help us initiate and deepen our spiritual conversion (Appendix II).

PART ONE:

The Catholic Church and Spiritual Conversion

INTRODUCTION TO PART ONE

Where do we start the process of spiritual conversion? We must first seek out the most efficacious path to knowledge and relationship with the Lord. In Volume III of the Quartet, I made a case for Jesus as "the way, and the truth, and the life" (Jn 14:6), by appealing to His message about love as the highest virtue and the true meaning of life. We there considered Jesus' unique definition of love; His identification of love as the highest commandment; His revelation of God as unconditional love; His personal love of sinners, the sick, and the suffering; His self-sacrificial love for all people in His Passion and death; and the huge impact His teaching had on world culture through the Catholic Church. I supplemented this revelation of Jesus, which I considered to be the foremost truth of the heart, with the evidence for His Resurrection and glory; gift of the Holy Spirit; miracles by His own authority; and self-revelation—all of which validate His claim to be Emmanuel, the reality of God come to be with us.

If we accept that Jesus is Emmanuel, then we might surmise that He would have wanted to institute a Church that would perpetuate His teaching and graces throughout history and the world. If He did not, it would have been a catastrophic oversight wholly uncharacteristic of His otherwise inspired and prophetic power of mind and heart. Evidently, Jesus gave His divine spirit to His apostles—not merely as individuals, but also as official leaders of a Church community, a Church community that He established under the supreme leadership of Saint Peter and his successors. This is the subject of Chapter 1 of this volume.

Once we have validated the historicity and authenticity of the Church of Peter and his successors (the Catholic Church) as the official Church of Jesus Christ—the official interpreters of His Word and administrator of His grace—we then turn to the elements of spiritual conversion through that Church. In Chapter 2, we explore the grace given through what we will call "the outer Church", particularly manifest in the sacramental life, the Divine Liturgy, and the proclamation of God's Word. In Chapter 3, we probe the mystery of the "inner Church", particularly the gifts of the Mystical Body, the contemplative life (i.e., prayer leading to deep relationship with the Lord), and the devotional life. If readers enter into the sacramental graces, contemplative life, and Mystical Body within the Catholic Church, they will have built on rock the next stage of conversion—moral conversion. When challenges to moral conversion arise—and they *will* arise—this guidance, grace, and relationship with the Lord will help them immeasurably. The stage will then be set for Part II of this volume, concerned with moral conversion.

Chapter One

The Heart of Spiritual Conversion:
The Catholic Church

Introduction

Inasmuch as moral conversion depends on spiritual conversion, and spiritual conversion depends on a Church community, we will want to have as strong a conviction as possible about the Church community that will best serve the purpose of spiritual and moral conversion. This will entail a brief examination of the need for a Church community (Section I) and the importance of a supreme teaching and juridical authority within a Church community (Section II), as well as a justification of why the Catholic Church under the leadership of Saint Peter's successors is the Church established by Jesus as that supreme authority (Sections III–VII). This should provide the rational and spiritual framework underlying our conviction about the presence of Jesus and the Holy Spirit in the Catholic Church—the church best suited to our spiritual and moral conversion.

I. Why Do We Need a Church Community and Even a *Christian* Church Community?

In Volume II of the Quartet (Chapters 1–2), we explained that God is present to every human being through the numinous experience and the intuition of the sacred. So it would seem that our most fundamental way of relating to God would be a "one on one" relationship with Him in prayer. Though this is possible, it is highly unusual, because most people explicitize their initial relationship with God through a church—a religious community sharing common belief, common ritual and tradition, and common worship. This is true for two major reasons.

First, the numinous experience and the intuition of the sacred—though interiorly powerful and mysterious—are not explicit. They require discursive interpretation from religious authorities in order to be meaningful and specific. The early Church Fathers recognized this and held that the "inner Word" (the numinous experience and the intuition of the sacred—God's interior presence to us) had to be complemented by the "outer Word" (the explicit, discursive, self-revelation of God through religious authorities within a community). Conversely, the outer Word would be "dry"—devoid of sacredness, mysteriousness, fascination, and power—without the inner Word (see Lonergan's explanation below in Section VIII).

The second reason why a religious community is so fundamental is that human beings are *interpersonal and communitarian* by nature. From the moment we are born into the world, we are in relationship with our parents and extended families. Our initial sense of ourselves is not as solitary and autonomous individuals, but rather as beloved and familial—that is, in relationship. It is difficult to imagine that God did not take this into account when revealing Himself to us, and so would provide a means to mediate His initial relationship with us through our families and church communities.

The communitarian dimension of religion is not restricted to the exterior domain—that is, to the world outside of us. It seems that God brings a sense of religious community into our *interior* lives through His presence to our souls. In so doing, He gives us a sense of belonging to a spiritual family and community as a vital part of His presence to us.

The Christian poet John Donne expressed his intuitive awareness of this "spiritual relationship with humanity" in a famous poem:

> No man is an island,
> Entire of itself;
> Every man is a piece of the continent,
> A part of the main.
> If a clod be washed away by the sea,
> Europe is the less,
> As well as if a promontory were,

> As well as if a manor of thy friend's
> Or of thine own were:
> Any man's death diminishes me,
> Because I am involved in mankind,
> And therefore never send to know for whom the
>   bell tolls;
> It tolls for thee.[1]

Donne expresses a profound awareness that his relationship with God ties Him into the whole of humanity. We are all interinvolved with one another (which is mutually enhancing) within a spiritual fabric that unites us. Human beings are not only interpersonal; they are transcendentally and spiritually interrelated—*everyone* is intertwined with *everyone* else. If Donne's intuition is correct, then the enlightenment ideal of human autonomy is not only false, but a radical underestimation of the significance and value of every human being.

Recall from Volume I of this Trilogy that we have an implicit sense of being caught up in a cosmic struggle between good and evil, reflected in the popular contemporary epics of J. R. R. Tolkien (*The Lord of the Rings*), J. K. Rowling (*Harry Potter*), and George Lucas (*Star Wars*). This cosmic struggle between good and evil entails our universal involvement with the whole of humanity. Our actions and decisions affect this cosmic struggle (for better or for worse), which in turn affects the whole of humanity.

Saint Paul, inspired by Jesus, had a deep awareness of this universal spiritual relationship among human beings, and said that it is significantly enhanced when we become members of the Christian Church through Baptism. For him, Baptism initiates us into a deeper and more intimate level of spiritual interrelationship that he called "the Body of Christ"

> so that the members may have the same care for one another. If one member suffers, all suffer together; if one member is honored, all rejoice together. Now you are the body of Christ and individually members of it. (1 Cor 12:25–27)

---

[1] John Donne, "Meditation XVII", in *Devotions upon Emergent Occasions Together with Death's Duel* (University of Michigan Press, 1959; Project Gutenberg, 2011), http://www .gutenberg.org/cache/epub/23772/pg23772.txt.

Saint Paul implies here that the glorified body of the risen Christ is the unifying fabric among members of the Church community, which has the effect of relating us to one another in joy and suffering. We need one another, contribute to one another, and support one another through our Baptism into spiritual communion in Christ. Saint Paul calls this spiritual communion in Christ "*Koinōnia*", which carries with it a connotation of intimacy, deep feeling, and love (see Chapter 3, Section I).

He also saw an even deeper level of spiritual interrelationship within the "Body of Christ" that occurs through the ritual that Jesus gave at the Last Supper—His Body and Blood given through bread and wine:

> The cup of blessing which we bless, is it not the communion [*Koinōnia*] of the blood of Christ? The bread which we break, is it not the communion [*Koinōnia*] of the body of Christ? For we being many are one bread, and one body: for we are all partakers of that one bread. (1 Cor 10:16–17, KJV)

We are an integral part of a unity of humanity through God whose lives are tied up with one another, such that we can contribute to or diminish happiness, love, and goodness through our words and actions. If this is the case, then we are not called only to an *individual* relationship with a transcendent personal Being, but also to a relationship with the whole of humanity through that transcendent Being. We are called not only to individual prayer but to *Koinōnia*—Church community and spiritual communion. Therefore, Church community is indispensable to our spiritual nature, fulfillment, and destiny.

The idea that one can be a "spiritual person" (on an individual basis with God) without a Church community fails to recognize that we are interpersonal persons and communitarian beings. It also misunderstands the will of the Creator who wants our faith and relationship with Him to *include* others who are also in relationship with Him. The idea that our relationship with God can be isolated from others whom the Lord dearly loves and wants *us* to love, misunderstands the purpose of life in this world. The Lord created us as imperfect beings in need of one another to call us to serve and be served—that is, to care and love as He has loved us. This entails *Koinōnia*—community belief, worship, and service.

Beyond the need for spiritual community (both interiorly and exteriorly) there are four other reasons we need a church to actualize our true nature, dignity, and destiny:

1. A source of revelation
2. A forum for sacred ritual, worship, and symbol
3. A teaching authority to help us interpret sacred doctrines in light of the practical requirements of living in an ever-changing world
4. A source of spiritual teaching and guidance to help us in our relationship with God through prayer

We will discuss all of these needs for a Church community throughout this volume. For the moment, we will begin with a discussion of the first point concerning our need for God's self-revelation.

Though reason and science can give significant evidence for the existence of God understood as "a unique unrestricted uncaused reality existing through itself as an unrestricted act of thinking, which is the creator of everything else that exists" (see Volume II of the Quartet), it is restricted to "*what* God is". However, they cannot tell us much about "*who* God is"—that is, the heart of God. Is He loving? Is there a Heaven? If there is a Heaven, how does one get there? Does God redeem suffering; does He guide, inspire, and protect us? All such questions require the self-revelation of God—and this in turn requires prophets and other religious authorities to mediate the revelatory Word of God to the community. This normally entails a Church community to which the prophets and religious authorities belong. Since we need a source of revelation, we naturally turn to a Church community with religious authority to attain it.

There are many differences among world religions, but God has also been quite consistent in His revelation to all of them—which is reflected in the seven common characteristics elucidated by Friedrich Heiler:[2]

---

[2] Friedrich Heiler, "The History of Religions as a Preparation for the Cooperation of Religions", in *The History of Religions*, ed. Mircea Eliade and J. Kitagawa (Chicago: Chicago University Press, 1959), pp. 142–53.

1. The transcendent, the holy, the divine, the Other is real.
2. The transcendent reality is immanent in human awareness.
3. This transcendent reality is the highest truth, highest good, and highest beauty.
4. This transcendent reality is loving and compassionate—and seeks to reveal its love to human beings.
5. The way to God requires prayer, ethical self-discipline, purgation of self-centeredness, asceticism, and redressing of offenses.
6. The way to God also includes service and responsibility to people.
7. The highest way to eternal bliss in the transcendent reality is through love.

This leads us to the question of whether God would give a definitive revelation of Himself—an ultimate, personal, self-revelation to help us actualize our true dignity and destiny. In Volume III (Chapters 1–3) of the Quartet, we showed that Jesus Christ revealed five unique dimensions of God and human potential that not only changed the history of religions, but also world culture and history:

1. Love as the highest commandment to which all other virtues and commandments are subordinated
2. His definition of "love" (*agapē*) through the Beatitudes
3. His revelation of the unconditional love of God through the Parable of the Prodigal Son (Lk 15:11–32) and His distinctive address of God as "Abba".
4. His revelation of His unconditional love through His love of sinners, the sick, the poor, and the world—manifest supremely in His self-sacrificial death (which showed the similarity between Himself and His Father as unconditional love).
5. His identification of Himself with the poorest of the poor and with the slaves that constituted such a large part of ancient society—"as you did it to one of the least of these my brethren, you did it to me" (Mt 25:40)

If we believe that these five distinguishing marks of Jesus' revelation are the fulfillment of truth and meaning for us and the world, and we believe in the veracity of Jesus' Resurrection in glory, gift of the Spirit of God, and miracles by His own authority (discussed extensively in Volume III, Chapters 4–6, of the Quartet), then we will *want* to put our faith in the *revelation of Jesus*.

Though revelation comes through the Person of Jesus Christ, it is mediated through religious texts (i.e., the New Testament) and the religious authorities and churches that formulated and continued to interpret those texts. This leads us to the question concerning which religious authority—which church—we will want to choose as the true interpreter of the revelation of Jesus. Since there are many Christian churches, we will want to select the one that best conforms to the intention of the historical Jesus—the Son of God, who came to be with us.

As noted above, spiritual conversion begins with the selection of a Church community needed to interpret the words of Jesus, to give doctrinal and moral guidance, to administer sacraments, and to adjudicate disputes. In light of the evidence for the Catholic Church (given below) and the contemporary scientifically validated miracles specifically associated with the Catholic Church— that is, Mary, the saints, and the Holy Eucharist (see the appendix to Volume I of this Trilogy)—spiritual conversion can reasonably and responsibly be vested in the Catholic Church. Yet, spiritual conversion goes far beyond joining the Catholic Church and even participating in Mass on Sundays. It involves exploring the graces and ministries of the Church (and participating in them) as well as understanding the Church's theology and developing a personal and communal life of prayer. The purpose of Part I of this volume is to give an overview of the information needed to begin this process of deep spiritual conversion. As will be seen, spiritual conversion is brought to fruition through moral conversion, which will be discussed in Part II (Chapters 4–7 of this volume).

In this and the following two chapters, we will address the best means to know, choose, and live our true identity—that is, redeemed creatures made in the image of God. As we shall see, this is best done through faith in Jesus and participation in the Church initiated by Him, built on the rock of Saint Peter and his successors. The more we participate in the services and sacraments of that Church, the more we draw closer to the heart of Christ; and the more we draw closer to the heart of Christ, the more we can know, choose, and live the truth about ourselves—our creatureliness, our transcendence, our sinfulness, and our redemption by the Son of God.

II. The Need for a Supreme Teaching Authority and Jesus' Intention to Initiate One

If Jesus had not initiated the Church by creating a supreme teaching and juridical office on the foundation of Saint Peter and his successors (Mt 16:17–19), then we would have to wonder why He did not, because the Church, as Jesus created it (with its supreme teaching and juridical authority), is precisely what we need—not only to prevent a needless proliferation of distinct Christian churches,[3] but also to help us form our consciences. As we shall see, the Church is indispensable in our deepening conversion and our struggle against spiritual evil through its charism and authority to give a definitive interpretation of the Word of Jesus Christ (in the New Testament). The true meaning of the New Testament is not self-evident to every believer at every level of theological education and spiritual development. It is not even self-evident to individual believers at the highest level of theological and spiritual development, because we have limited perspective, limited experience, limitations of mind and heart, and we are subject to sinfulness and egocentricity, leading to every form of self-serving rationalization and hypocrisy. The idea that Jesus gave the Holy Spirit to individuals alone to sort all of this out and give every person a clear and definitive interpretation of the Bible, is erroneous, for we would have to be freely and perfectly open to the Holy Spirit to obtain this definitive interpretation—and I would submit that none of us can possibly make such a claim. Speaking for myself, I can see a myriad of ways in which my egocentricity, inauthenticity, human weaknesses, and proclivities toward sin can obscure, block, or even undermine a proper interpretation of Scripture. I have a

---

[3] This has been demonstrated over the last five hundred years since the Protestant Reformation, which opened the way to the creation of approximately 47,000 Protestant denominations, according to the Center for Global Christianity at Gordon-Conwell Theological Seminary (Stephen Beale, "Just How Many Protestant Denominations Are There?", *National Catholic Register*, October 31, 2017, https://www.ncregister.com/blog/just-how-many-protestant-denominations-are-there).

principle that I teach frequently to my students called "Spitzer's principle of infinite rationalization"—"Give me five minutes and enough reason to *want* to bend the truth to fit my strongest egotistical desires, and I will find an appropriate rationalization for it."

If our personal limitations are not enough to persuade us that we all need an objective definitive interpretation of Scripture, then the aforementioned proliferation of Protestant denominations in five hundred years should provide ample reason for subscribing to this need—and if that is not enough, then we might ask ourselves how we are going to resolve consistently all of the seeming conflicts among hundreds of Scripture passages in an objective way. Does anyone really believe that he has discovered the definitive hermeneutic for the objective resolution of all the seemingly conflictual passages in the Scriptures? If so, how can you be so sure that you haven't left out anything, or let your personal preferences be your guide, or are limited in your rational capabilities? I don't think anyone can achieve such certitude without gross overestimation of personal and human potential.

So if a definitive interpretation of Scripture and an objective resolution to seeming conflicts among scriptural passages is beyond any one person's spiritual, intellectual, scholarly, and moral capacities, then how will we ever be able to guide ourselves into deepening intellectual, moral, and spiritual conversion? Will we rely on a large group of really, really smart and seemingly spiritual and honest individuals? That has never worked in the past, for immediately upon gathering together as a group of intelligent, scholarly, and spiritual people they find themselves vehemently disagreeing with one another, which has led historically not only to the proliferation of scriptural interpretations, but the proliferation of denominations, congregations, and churches. Since my collegiate days, I have not been able to believe that Jesus, His Father, and the Holy Spirit left us victims of our own personal limitations, inauthenticity, and moral and spiritual immaturity—not to mention the limitations of our historical time and culture. I cannot believe that the Triune God would leave us bereft of a way to discover the definitive *truth* about how we are to conduct and develop our moral and spiritual lives—and so I cannot believe that Jesus did not anticipate the need to establish a Church that would give a definitive interpretation to His teachings, as well as the written documents communicating them (i.e., the

New Testament). Furthermore, I cannot believe that Jesus would not have anticipated what would be required to give a definitive interpretation of His words not only in the immediate aftermath of His Resurrection, but also for the decades and centuries of Christian history, which He would have anticipated. There is ample reason to believe from the New Testament that Jesus did in fact anticipate the need for a definitive interpretation of His teachings as well as a succession of definitive interpreters of those teachings (see below, Section III).

So what kind of church and church authority would be needed to give a definitive interpretation of Scripture for many generations beyond Jesus' immediate one? At least two conditions could be easily foreseen by any student of history having far less wisdom, divine inspiration, and spiritual authenticity than Jesus:

1. A supreme and definitive juridical and teaching authority ultimately invested in a *single* person having a special charism for this definitive authority
2. An *office* of highest juridical and teaching authority, guaranteeing that successors of the first office holder would be able to carry on this function until the end of the world

It can scarcely be believed that Jesus did not anticipate the first condition because He would have seen it manifest in Judaism—not only in His own time, but throughout the course of history. The many factions—Pharisees, Sadducees, Essenes, and others—and the factions within the factions would not have failed to impress on Jesus the need for a supreme authority to resolve the inevitable disagreements, disputes, and outright conflicts that would naturally follow upon His death and Resurrection. Indeed He saw this at the beginning of His ministry, which motivated Him to give Peter a special place among the other disciples again and again—not only to receive privileged teachings and revelations, but to be a successor to Him as definitive authority. True, Jesus was *the* definitive teaching authority, but Peter was clearly being groomed as a definitive interpreter of that teaching and a definitive resolver of disputes. In all New Testament accounts, Peter is mentioned more often than the other apostles, is given more time and attention, is singled out for more special revelations, and is

given more responsibility for the mission.[4] V
unless He was grooming Peter for a leader:
would He be grooming Peter for a leadersh'
well of His impending death, unless He ir
leader of the Church that was to succee(
appears to point to Jesus' intention to ir
tive interpretive teaching authority after His death a...
This inference is confirmed by the logion in Matthew 16:17–19:

> You are Peter, and on this rock I will build my Church, and the gates
> of Hades shall not prevail against it. I will give you the keys of the
> kingdom of heaven, and whatever you bind on earth shall be bound
> in heaven, and whatever you loose on earth shall be loosed in heaven.

In Section IV below, I show that this special commissioning of Peter
is not limited to Matthew's Gospel; it is also found in the Gospel of
John, the Acts of the Apostles, and Paul's Letter to the Galatians. Furthermore, the reference "the keys of the kingdom of heaven" very
probably refers to an *office* of definitive authority (such as prime minister), implying that Jesus is creating an office with definitive teaching and juridical authority not only for Peter, but for his successors
(see below, Section IV). This is confirmed by the likelihood that Jesus
expected the Church to last far beyond Peter (see the interpretation
of the eschatological discourses below in Section III) and that He foresaw the need to have a definitive authority to resolve doctrinal and
juridical disputes in the post-Petrine era.

Peter exhibits definitive and universal authority in the Council
of Jerusalem (Acts 15:1–12),[5] and Pope Clement of Rome (the second or fourth pope after Peter—depending on the source) believed
himself to have authority over all other bishops and to order them
under pain of sin (see below, Section VII). Likewise, Saint Ignatius
of Antioch and Saint Irenaeus believed that the bishop of the Roman
See had definitive authority over other bishops to resolve doctrinal
and juridical disputes (see below, Section VII). How would it be possible for Pope Clement and these early Church Fathers to declare the

---

[4] See John L. McKenzie, S.J., *Dictionary of the Bible* (New York: Macmillan, 1965), p. 663.
[5] See below, Section VI.

of Peter as supreme if there were no strong apostolic tradition back to Jesus Himself? Can it be believed that Matthew, John, ul, Pope Clement, Saint Ignatius of Antioch, and Saint Irenaeus simply made it up—and the Church and the other bishops simply acceded to it? If this is unreasonable, then it is likely that Jesus created an office of definitive doctrinal and juridical authority in Peter, with the intention of conveying this authority to his successors. If He did, then the promise made to Peter would also apply to them throughout the remaining life of the Church: "and the gates of Hades shall not prevail against it." The last two thousand years has borne out the veracity of this promise throughout countless persecutions, conflicts, doctrinal heresies, and foreign invasions.

The famous historian of culture and civilization Arnold Toynbee changed his personal position from agnosticism to Christian faith on the basis of his study of the effects of religion on civilization, and the enduring paramount effect of Christianity on world civilization. He even declared that "the greatest new event in history was the Crucifixion and the Crucifixion's spiritual consequences."[6] In his essay "Christianity and Civilization" (from his book *Civilization on Trial*), he points to the remarkable enduring character of the Catholic Church, implying that it has a providential character enabling it to do what no other institution or civilization has been able to do, and to influence the world in ways that no secular institution could do:

> The Church in its traditional form thus stands forth armed with the spear of the Mass, the shield of the Hierarchy, and the helmet of the Papacy; and perhaps the subconscious purpose—or the divine intention, if you prefer that language—of this heavy panoply of institutions in which the Church has clad herself is the very practical one of outlasting the toughest of the secular institutions of this world, including all the civilizations. If we survey all the institutions of which we have knowledge in the present and in the past, I think that the institutions created, or adopted and adapted, by Christianity are the toughest and the most enduring of any that we know and are therefore the most likely to last—and outlast all the rest.[7]

[6]John Wendon, "Christianity, History, and Mr. Toynbee", *The Journal of Religion* 36, no. 3 (July 1956): 147.

[7]Arnold Toynbee, "Christianity and Civilization", in *Civilization on Trial* (New York: Oxford University Press, 1948), http://www.myriobiblos.gr/texts/english/toynbee.html.

We might ask ourselves why the Catholic Church as an institution has outlasted every other institution in human history. Was this because of the administrative expertise, flexible structures, and impeccable wisdom of her leaders? I do not think anyone is willing to concede this or any other human cause for this remarkable historical persistence, continuous growth, and adaptability to multiple cultures and historical epics, and so we might infer, as did Toynbee, that there is very likely a supernatural agency behind it. Jesus identified this supernatural agency with His own risen body (the new universal temple) and the Holy Spirit (see Section IV). It seems that Jesus' promise to protect the Church that He built upon the rock of Saint Peter and his successors from the gates of Hades has been continuously kept—and still holds true today. Given all of this, it is reasonable and responsible to conclude that the Church truly is the community built upon the risen body of Christ and the Holy Spirit, and that it holds the key not only to the interpretation of Jesus' Word, but also to the administration of the sacraments and the graces that He gave us to deepen our spiritual and moral lives.

History has shown that the only Christian church to have maintained unity throughout the centuries is the Catholic Church. The apparent reason for this is that definitive juridical and teaching authority is vested in the holder of the office first occupied by Saint Peter. No other Christian church has such a definitive teaching and juridical office—and no other can trace their office holders back to the first one, Saint Peter, who was appointed by Jesus at the very inception of the office itself. Yes, there were deliberate breaks from this Church, but those breaks occurred because an individual or group of individuals deliberately broke with the supreme teaching and juridical authority of the holder of the office of Peter that had been initiated by Jesus.

In light of the above, it is reasonable and responsible to conclude the following:

- We need a church for moral guidance, and therefore for moral conversion.
- The Catholic Church was initiated by Jesus, who bestowed a definitive teaching and juridical authority upon Saint Peter and his successors to guide her until the end of the world.

- Historical evidence strongly suggests that Jesus kept His promise to be with the Church and to protect her from error and spiritual evil.

Some people may be disturbed by three spiritual and doctrinal contentions of the Catholic Church rejected by the Reformers—the Blessed Virgin Mary, intercessory prayer of the saints, and the Real Presence of Christ in the Eucharist (all of which are discussed in the appendix of Volume I). A myriad of books have been written on the appropriateness of the Catholic Church's teaching on these beliefs and spiritual practices,[8] but for those who want a validation of them through scientifically assessed miracles, you may want to refer back to the appendix of the previous volume. This appendix covers the scientific assessment of miracles themselves and presents five Marian miracles, three miracles associated with contemporary saints, and one Eucharistic miracle overseen by Archbishop Jorge Bergoglio (now Pope Francis).

In view of all this, it is highly likely that Jesus intended to initiate His Church under the supreme teaching and juridical authority of Saint Peter and his successors, and that this Church has legitimate magisterial authority in all areas pertaining to virtue, human rights, and the salvation of souls. The *Catechism of the Catholic Church* summarizes this as follows:

The Church, the "pillar and bulwark of the truth," "has received this solemn command of Christ from the apostles to announce the saving truth" (1 Tim 3:15; *Lumen Gentium* 17). "To the Church belongs the right always and everywhere to announce moral principles, including those pertaining to the social order, and to make judgments on any human affairs to the extent that they are required by the fundamental rights of the human person or the salvation of souls (CIC, can. 747 § 2)."[9]

If we hold that Jesus is (as the Son of God) the ultimate source of God's revelation and also hold that the religious authorities who formulated the texts of the New Testament did so in a manner consistent with Jesus' teaching, then we will also hold that the New

[8] See the recommended book lists from Catholic Answers at Catholic.com.
[9] *Catechism of the Catholic Church*, no. 2032 (hereafter cited as *CCC*).

Testament Scriptures are the Word of God. Though they can never be augmented, they can be interpreted for every age and culture. Scripture interpretation is not a simple matter—it is transmitted to us through oral traditions, literary genre, and the interpretive lenses of the Gospel and Epistle writers. When Scripture passages appear to conflict with one another, or different interpretations appear to conflict with one another, the faithful can be caught in confusion, and seriously deceived. This means that there will have to be some kind of teaching authority within the Church. If there were not, the Church community would be divided into factions, each having different interpretations of the same basic books of Scripture. One does not have to look too deeply into history to find such factions in the earliest years of the Church and throughout her history—the early Gnostic movements, the Arian and Monophysite movements, and the proliferation of thousands of denominations within the Reformation movement.

Did Jesus anticipate the possibility of such divisions within the Christian community? Did He intend to initiate a church in order to perpetuate His Word and maintain unity among her members? Did He appoint Saint Peter as the head of the Church (as indicated by the well-known logion in Mt 16:17–19)? If He did appoint Peter as head of the Church, did He also intend that not only Peter but his successors hold the same office as head of the Church? If so, then this would indicate Jesus' intention to start one Church that was to be governed by Peter and his successors until the end of the world—that is, the Catholic Church (governed by the successors of Peter). I believe that there is significant evidence to give an affirmative answer to all the above questions and therefore believe that it is reasonable and responsible to hold that the Catholic Church is the one church intended by Jesus to perpetuate His Word, His ministry, and His worldwide call to salvation. Let us take each of these questions in turn.

III. Did Jesus Think the Church Would Endure beyond the Apostles?

Did Jesus think that the Church would last only one generation—just to the end of the apostles' lives? This is unlikely for two reasons:

1. Jesus intended to be the new universal temple for all nations through His risen body.
2. The eschatological discourse in Mark implies that Jesus thought that the Church would last until the second tribulation (likely beyond the lives of the apostles).

Let us consider each in turn.

A. Jesus as the New Temple for All Nations through His Risen Body

The Gospel accounts of Jesus cleansing the Temple indicate that He intended to become the new universal temple for all nations through His risen body (Mt 21:12–16; Mk 11:15–18; Lk 19:45–48; Jn 2:13–16). As will be shown below, it is unlikely that Jesus would have foreclosed the possibility that the Church's post-Resurrection missionary activity would take more than a single generation. If this is the case, then Jesus would likely have initiated the supreme office given first to Peter with the intention that the office might continue for multiple generations through Peter's successors. Before considering this, we must first explore the meaning and significance of the Temple cleansing for Jesus.

In the Gospel accounts of the Temple cleansing, Jesus judged the current Temple administration as corrupt, foretold the destruction of the Jerusalem Temple, and revealed that He intended to replace the Jerusalem Temple with His risen body as the new universal temple for all nations. N. T. Wright provides the incisive clue to Jesus' intention in this prophetic action, which is reminiscent of Nehemiah's prophetic action five centuries earlier. According to Wright[10] and his student Nicholas Perrin,[11] Jesus believed that part of His mission was to supersede the Temple—to replace the static brick and mortar Temple in Jerusalem with His living Word and living presence throughout the world. Many groups within Israel (e.g., the Essenes) believed that the Temple was already defunct and that it was being run by wicked priests. Jesus goes beyond these groups by saying that

---

[10] See N. T. Wright, *Jesus and the Victory of God* (Minneapolis: Fortress Press), pp. 490–501.
[11] See Nicholas Perrin, *Jesus the Temple* (Ada, Mich.: Baker Academic, 2010).

even if the Temple were not run by a corrupt administration, it would still have to be replaced by a dynamic redemptive eschatological power transcending space and time—namely, *Himself.*

When Jesus entered the Temple precincts, He was very *well prepared* to initiate the time of His Passion and Resurrection leading to the New Jerusalem, which would be worldwide ("for all nations" [Mk 11:17]). When He drove out the merchants and buyers and disallowed people from carrying anything in the Temple area, He established His authority over the old Temple and its administration. When He overturned the tables and seats of the moneychangers and sellers, He prophetically initiated the impending destruction of the old Temple. His action is more than a prediction—as a prophetic gesture, it sets history on an inevitable course that is brought to completion only when the Temple is destroyed (in A.D. 70). He renders judgment against the Temple and its administration when He subsequently declares, "Is it not written, 'My house shall be called a house of prayer for all the nations'? But you have made it a den of robbers" (Mk 11:17). Instead of making the Temple a house of prayer for all nations, the Temple administration had corrupted it and mired it in the things of this world. When Jesus' judgment against the Temple administration was combined with His prophetic action of overturning the moneychangers' tables and chairs, it signified and anticipated not only the destruction of the Temple, but something new that would become a "house of prayer for *all* the nations" (italics added).[12]

Later, Jesus interprets His prophetic actions in the Temple cleansing. He tells the Parable of the Wicked Tenants (Mt 21:33–46; Mk 12:1–12; Lk 20:9–19), which allegorically describes the persecution of Israel's prophets, culminating with the murder of the vineyard owner's (God's) beloved Son. The owner then comes back, destroys the tenants, and gives the vineyard to others. Though Jesus does not directly say that He is the beloved Son of the vineyard owner (God), He implies it when He declares, "Have you not read this Scripture: 'The stone which the builders rejected has become the cornerstone; this was the Lord's doing, and it is marvelous in our eyes'?" (Mk 12:10–11; cf. Mt 21:42; Lk 20:17).[13] Notice what Jesus has done—if

---

[12] See Wright, *Jesus and the Victory of God*, pp. 490–501.
[13] The Scripture that Jesus is quoting is Psalm 118:22–23.

He really is the beloved Son in the parable, and the beloved Son is the "stone which the builders rejected [that] has become the cornerstone", then Jesus is the cornerstone of the New Temple—indeed, He is the New Temple; He is the "something new that will become a house of prayer for *all* nations". These actions will find their completion first in the rejection of Jesus, then in His subsequent torture and death, His Resurrection, the gift of the Holy Spirit, the establishment of the Christian Church, and the destruction of the Temple and its administration.

Did Jesus really intend to make His risen body the new universal temple for all peoples and nations? The Gospel of John states this plainly within the context of the Temple cleansing:

> The Jews then said to him, "What sign have you to show us for doing this [cleansing the Temple]?" Jesus answered them, "Destroy this temple, and in three days I will raise it up." The Jews then said, "It has taken forty-six years to build this temple, and will you raise it up in three days?" But he spoke of the temple of his body. When therefore he was raised from the dead, his disciples remembered that he had said this; and they believed the Scripture and the word which Jesus had spoken. (2:18–22)

John's account of Jesus' association of the New Temple with His risen body is also implicitly attested by Mark's, which recounts witnesses during Jesus' trial, making the claim that Jesus said He would destroy the Temple and rebuild it in three days:

> We heard him say, "I will destroy this temple that is made with hands, and in three days I will build another, not made with hands." (14:58)

Evidently, Jesus made such a claim, and John interprets it within the context of the Temple cleansing as referring to "the temple of His body" (2:21). This dovetails precisely with Jesus' words in Mark's Gospel (11:17), implying that the Temple is meant for all nations—and that Jesus is the cornerstone of that New Temple (12:10).

Saint Paul was apparently aware of Jesus' proclamation about being the new universal temple for all nations through His risen body, and he applies it to the new Christian Church (1 Cor 6:15; 12:27). In

Romans 12:4–5, Paul summarizes his view that the Christian Church is the new universal "temple" in Christ's body through which we are interrelated to one another:

> For as in one body we have many members, and all the members do not have the same function, so we, though many, are one body in Christ, and individually members one of another.

We may now return to the question of whether Jesus believed that His Church would last only until the death of the apostles. If Jesus intended, as His cleansing action prophetically indicated, that He would become the new universal temple *for all nations* after His Resurrection and gift of the Spirit (and the destruction of the Jerusalem Temple), did He believe this would occur in a generation? Evidently, the worldwide Church membership that He foretold would have to occur through the missionary activity of His apostles. Did He believe that His apostles could reach out and incorporate *all* nations into the Church in one generation—or would He have anticipated the possibility that this might take multiple generations? Given the internal resistance of the Jewish religious leaders and the Roman government as well as the difficulty and time required for missionary journeys, it is unlikely that Jesus foreclosed the possibility of missionary activities going beyond the apostolic generation to multiple generations of apostolic successors. This is borne out by Jesus' prophecy in the Marcan eschatological discourse.

B. The Second Tribulation in Mark's Eschatological Discourse

The second indication that Jesus anticipated the Church lasting beyond the lives of the apostles comes from Mark's eschatological discourse, which reflects Jesus' view about not only the destruction of the Temple, but also the final tribulation and the coming of the Son of man (the glorified Jesus) at the end of time. The discourse speaks about two tribulations—the first tribulation that will culminate in the destruction of the Temple and the death of the apostles (Mk 13:1–13), and the second tribulation that will occur later (after an undisclosed period of time) in which the entire world will be caught

final teaching authority and final resolution of doctrinal and juridical disputes? To answer this we will want to address three subsidiary questions: Why is this central logion mentioned only in the Gospel of Matthew, or is it? If this logion reflects a very early tradition of the Church (also recognized by Paul and John), then does it give Peter an extraordinary and supreme authority not given to the other apostles? If so, was it Jesus' intention to give this authority to the successors of Peter? As noted above, we might infer Jesus' intention to convey this authority on Peter's successors because of His openness to the possibility that the Church would endure beyond Peter. Is there evidence in the *text itself* that Jesus intended to bestow this authority on those successors—to create a highest juridical and teaching *office*? Let us begin with the logion itself:

> Blessed are you, Simon Bar-Jona! For flesh and blood has not revealed this to you, but my Father who is in heaven. And I tell you, you are Peter [*Petros*], and on this rock [*petra*] I will build my Church, and the gates of Hades shall not prevail against it. I will give you the keys of the kingdom of heaven, and whatever you bind on earth shall be bound in heaven, and whatever you loose on earth shall be loosed in heaven. (Mt 16:17–19)

This text is so important to the future of the Church that it provokes the question of why it is only to be found in Matthew. One possible explanation for why it is not to be found in Mark or Luke is that it comes from Matthew's special sources, and therefore was not in Mark or in the common source shared by Matthew and Luke called "Q" (referring to *Quelle*, meaning "source" in German).[17] Luke's omission of the commission may be attributable to his neat division between his Gospel (the story of *Jesus*) and the Acts of the Apostles (the story of the Holy Spirit working through *Peter*, in the first half of Acts, and Paul in the second half). Luke evidently recognized Peter's primacy—not only because of his centrality in the first part of Acts (Chapters 1–15), but also because of Peter's implied superiority to Paul, particularly at the Council of Jerusalem, in Chapter 15.

---

[17] Q is an early collection of Jesus' sayings translated into Greek. Most scholars believe that Q is a single written source, though some hold that it is a plurality of sources. We do not know who the editor or editors were.

Though the commissioning is absent in Mark and Luke, an earlier tradition underlying the commission in Matthew is very probably known to Paul and John. Before looking at those texts, we will want to determine whether there is a primitive Aramaic tradition standing behind the commissioning logion in Matthew. This would indicate that the logion was not a Matthean redaction, but rather a pre-Matthean tradition probably originating with Jesus. What is the evidence for this?

The logion is filled with Semitisms—literal translations of an Aramaic original into Greek (which can be detected by their peculiar words and structures). These Semitisms indicate an early Aramaic origin before Matthew's Greek rendition of the Gospel, which likely has its origin in Jesus.[18] Some of these Semitisms are the following:

1. Jesus' expression "blessed are you" (*makarios eimi*) is typically Semitic.
2. The use of "Bar-Jona" is also typically Semitic.
3. "Flesh and blood" in reference to human beings is also typically Semitic.
4. Jesus' renaming of Peter was meant to be a pun in Aramaic— "You are Peter [*Cephas*], and on this rock [*Cephas*] I will build my Church." However, in order to translate Jesus' Aramaic pun into Greek, Matthew had to make the feminine noun *petra* (rock) into a masculine proper name *Petros*.
5. "Gates of Hades [netherworld]" is sometimes used by pagans, but is typically Jewish.
6. There are several parallel expressions to those used in the commissioning logion in the scrolls of Qumran, indicating typicality in Jewish culture.

In view of the above, it is unlikely that this text was a redaction of Matthew or a creation of the later Church.[19] It very likely represents an early Aramaic tradition of which both Paul (in the first two chapters of the Letter to the Galatians) and John (Chapters 20 and 21) were apparently aware (see below in this section).

[18] See W. D. Davies and Dale C. Allison, *International Critical Commentary*, vol. 2, *Matthew 8–18* (New York: T&T Clark, 1991), pp. 626–29.
[19] Ibid.

Furthermore, the renaming of Peter (Mt 16:18) indicates the logion's probable origin in Jesus. It requires a very high authority to rename a person in Semitic culture. The name chosen by the parents is almost sacrosanct. Jesus not only changes Peter's *first* name from "Simon" to *Cephas*; He also changes his *last* name from Bar-John to Bar-Jona (associating him with that biblical figure). Who besides Jesus would have the authority to do this, and have it accepted by the renamed person?[20] Additionally, Paul is aware of the renaming of Peter, and refers to it in the context of associating his commissioning to that of Peter (see below in this section).

So what is the evidence that both Paul and John knew of the primitive Aramaic tradition standing behind Matthew's commissioning logion? With respect to Paul, the first two chapters of the Letter to the Galatians have five parallels between Peter's commissioning (in the above logion) and Paul's commissioning as an apostle:[21]

1. After three years in Arabia, Paul goes to Jerusalem to meet with *Peter alone* for fifteen days—presumably to integrate himself *officially* within the Church of Jesus Christ. After a seeming approbation from Peter, Paul considers himself to be missioned to the Gentile church (see Gal 1:18). This implies that Paul believed Peter to have had the highest authority within the Church, which would have been required to accept another person into apostolic status (ranking second only to Peter).

2. In Galatians 2:7–8, Paul compares his commissioning (to be entrusted with the gospel to the Gentiles) to Peter's commissioning *by Jesus* (to be entrusted with the gospel to the circumcised).

3. In connecting his commissioning with Peter's commissioning, Paul translates the name *Cephas* as *Petros*, which is the Greek translation of the Aramaic *Cephas*, meaning "Rock". Evidently, this parallels the commissioning logion in Matthew 16:17–19. This is the *only* time Paul translates the name *Cephas* in his corpus. Is it mere coincidence that he uses this unusual expression only in the context of paralleling his commission with that of Peter's?

---

[20] Ibid.
[21] Ibid.

4. In Galatians 1:16, Paul uses the unusual Semitic expression "flesh and blood" to refer to "human", which, as noted above, is also used in the commissioning logion in Matthew. This is the only time that he uses this expression in his corpus. Is it mere coincidence that his unique use of this expression—which precisely parallels Matthew's commissioning logion—occurs in a passage referring to Paul's own commissioning?

5. Paul refers to "James and Cephas and John" as pillars of the Church, which has overtones of Jesus' commissioning of Peter as the foundation rock (Gal 2:9).

In view of these parallels, it is possible that Paul was aware of a primitive Aramaic tradition underlying Matthew's commissioning logion—and used these parallels to shore up his own commissioning by Jesus as apostle to the Gentiles.[22] At the very least, Paul seems to have been aware of a special commissioning of Peter by Jesus as head of the Church, which enables him to legitimize his own commissioning by Jesus (Gal 2:7–9)—with tacit approbation from Peter (Gal 1:18)—as apostle to the Gentiles.

Is there evidence that John was also aware of Jesus' special commissioning of Peter as head of the Church? We must assume that he was aware of it because of the central passage on Peter's commissioning in the Johannine appendix (Jn 21:15–19) and Jesus' conferral of the power to bind and loose on the apostles (Jn 20:21–23). Though John does not mention Peter's change of name in the commissioning passage (Jn 21:15–19), he acknowledges it at the beginning of the Gospel (1:42), translating the Aramaic *Cephas* to *Petros* for his Greek readers: "He [Andrew] brought [Simon] to Jesus. Jesus looked at him, and said, 'So you are Simon the son of John? You shall be called Cephas' (which means Peter)." Let us now examine John's account of Peter's commissioning after the Resurrection:

> When they had finished breakfast, Jesus said to Simon Peter, "Simon, son of John, do you love me more than these?" He said to him, "Yes, Lord; you know that I love you." He said to him, "Feed my lambs." A second time he said to him, "Simon, son of John, do you love me?"

---

[22] Ibid.

He said to him, "Yes, Lord; you know that I love you." He said to him, "Tend my sheep." He said to him the third time, "Simon, son of John, do you love me?" Peter was grieved because he said to him the third time, "Do you love me?" And he said to him, "Lord, you know everything; you know that I love you." Jesus said to him, "Feed my sheep. Truly, truly, I say to you, when you were young, you fastened your own belt and walked where you would; but when you are old, you will stretch out your hands, and another will fasten your belt for you and carry you where you do not wish to go." (This he said to show by what death he was to glorify God.) And after this he said to him, "Follow me." (21:15–19)

There are three aspects of this passage indicating Jesus' intention to set Peter apart as head of the Church:

1. Jesus speaks *only* to Peter in the special commission—which takes place in front of the other apostles who are witnesses to it.
2. Jesus asks Peter, "Do you love me more than these?" (Jn 21:15). The intention here is to indicate Peter's heightened fidelity and loyalty to Jesus—which indicates why Jesus has chosen him to occupy his office as "shepherd".
3. After each of Peter's three responses, Jesus commissions Peter either to feed or to tend His sheep. In these words Jesus gives the *exclusive* commission to Peter to take over His office as "primary shepherd". Inasmuch as the other disciples are not given this special commission, we can infer that it is consistent with the one set out in Matthew 16:17–19.

When we consider both John's awareness of Simon's change of name by Jesus and his awareness of an exclusive commission given to Peter to take Jesus' place as primary shepherd, it is reasonable to infer that John was aware of an exclusive commissioning of Peter as head of the apostles and head of the Church.

There is one more key historical indication of Peter's primacy that is embedded in the order of the Resurrection appearances given in the Pauline list in 1 Corinthians 15:5–7. Reginald H. Fuller (an Anglican priest) believes that the order of this list—and the order of the appearances themselves—is not arbitrary. Rather, it is "Church founding" and establishes the primacy of Peter in the "eschatological community".[23] Fuller believes that the use of the name *Cephas* (instead of "Simon") indicates Peter's designated role to be the rock or foundation of the Church:

> The theological significance of the appearances to Peter, we find ... [as indicated in 1 Corinthians 15:5] by the use of the name Cephas.... Simon Bar-Jonah receives the name Cephas ... appointing him to be the foundation upon which the eschatological community is built.[24]

Apparently, Jesus' ordering of His appearances to the disciples confirms the order that He indicated in His ministry—namely, that Peter be the head of the apostles and the Church herself.

So what might we conclude about the historicity of Jesus' special commission to Peter to be head of the apostles and head of the Church? First, the tradition is not exclusive to Matthew 16:17–19. It occurs in different form in John 21 and by implication in Galatians 1–2. The Semitisms in Matthew 16:17–19 (two of which are borrowed by Saint Paul to refer to his own commission in parallel with Peter's) indicate an earlier Aramaic tradition that was known not only by Matthew, but probably by Saint Paul, and perhaps by John.

We may now proceed to the important question of whether the above early Aramaic version of the commissioning logion had its origin in Jesus. There are five indicators of this that collectively point to Jesus as the source of the logion:

1. The change of name (which only a person of Jesus' stature could have done), bringing about the commissioning of Peter
2. The heavy use of Semitisms that are consistent with Jesus' "style" (e.g., "blessed are you" and "flesh and blood")
3. The multiple attestation of the power to bind (retain) and loose (forgive) in both Matthew's special sources (Mt 16:19) and John

---

[23] See Reginald H. Fuller, *The Formation of the Resurrection Narratives* (New York: Macmillan, 1971), p. 35.
[24] Ibid.

(20:21), which gives to Peter a divine or heavenly power that only Jesus could legitimately bestow

4. The use of "Pater Mou" (Mt 16:17), which likely refers to Jesus' address to the Father—"Abba".[25] Joachim Jeremias shows that this address is almost exclusive to Jesus.[26]

5. The use of the emphatic "ego" (i.e., "I")—"I say to you" (Mt 16:18, NAB[27])—where the unnecessary first-person pronoun "I" ("ego") is used with "say" ("lego"), which is almost exclusive to Jesus, according to Jeremias[28]

These five indicators show the likelihood of Jesus as the origin of the early Aramaic tradition behind the Matthew commissioning logion.

In view of all this, it is highly likely that Peter was given a special commission by Jesus to be head of the Church. Furthermore, if Matthew or John had invented this special commissioning, it would have been hotly disputed in the apostolic Church, whose leadership would have been acutely aware of the falsity of such an important claim were it not true. In view of the historical likelihood of Peter's commissioning as chief shepherd and teacher by Jesus, we must now examine what the logion means—specifically whether it refers not just to Peter, but also to the office of "primary shepherd", which Peter is the first to occupy. Let us now turn to the passage in question.

---

[25] Joachim Jeremias notes in this regard, "We have every reason to suppose that an *Abba* underlies every instance of *pater (mou)* or *ho patēr* in his words of prayer." Joachim Jeremias, *New Testament Theology* (London: SCM Press, 1971), 1:65.

[26] Jeremias notes, "In the literature of Palestinian Judaism no evidence has yet been found of 'my Father' being used by an individual as an address to God.... It is quite unusual that Jesus should have addressed God as 'my Father'; it is even more so that he should have used the Aramaic form '*Abba*'" (ibid., 1:64).

Though a few rare references of *pater mou* and "Abba" have been found since Jeremias' claim, it is still exceedingly rare and is therefore a good indicator of the ipsissima verba (i.e., the very words of Jesus).

[27] Gk: "kagō de soi legō" ("and I say to you"). In Greek, the verb already has the subject in it, and therefore does not need a pronoun, such as "I". This usage is highly unusual and almost exclusive to Jesus in New Testament and intertestamental literature. See ibid., 1:252–54.

[28] Jeremias indicates that Jesus' virtually exclusive use of the emphatic "ego" is used as a solemn command to expel demons, to make modifications to the law, to make a new law, and to commission His disciples. This expression translates Jesus' unique Aramaic expression, "Amen, I say to you." See ibid., 1:252–54.

V. Did Jesus' Commission of Peter Include His Successors?

Blessed are you, Simon Bar-Jona! For flesh and blood has not revealed this to you, but my Father who is in heaven. And I tell you, you are Peter, and on this *rock* I will build *my Church*, and *the gates of Hades* shall not prevail against it. I will give you the *keys of the kingdom of heaven*, and whatever you *bind* on earth shall be bound in heaven, and whatever you *loose* on earth shall be loosed in heaven. (Mt 16:17–19; italics added)

There are six italicized terms in the above passage that require explanation:

1. "rock",
2. "my Church",
3. "the gates of Hades",
4. "keys of the kingdom of heaven",
5. "bind", and
6. "loose".

An explanation of each, particularly the "keys of the kingdom of heaven", will indicate the strong likelihood that Jesus was not only commissioning Peter to be head of the Church, but rather, He was creating an office of "prime minister", of which Peter was to be the first holder. We will examine each phrase in turn.

"Rock" refers to the "foundation rock" upon which *Jesus' Church* is to be built. The context is so clear that it does not warrant other interpretations.[29] Why does Jesus use this particular image to rename Peter at the commission? W. D. Davies and Dale C. Allison see a parallel between Abraham (the initial leader of the People of God, who is called a "rock" in Isaiah 51:1) and Peter (the initial leader of the new People of God). They note in this regard:

Here the new people of God is brought into being, hewed not from the rock Abraham but instead founded on the rock Peter.[30]

[29] Davies and Allison, *Matthew 8–18*, p. 614.
[30] Ibid., p. 624.

A name in first-century Jewish thought represents the core identity of a person as well as his purpose in life. Thus, the renaming of Simon as *Cephas* (which is unique to Peter) indicates that his *raison d'etre* is to be the foundation of Jesus' Church and the foundational leader of the new People of God.

The term "my Church" (*mou Ekklesia*) very probably refers to the new universal Church, not a particular local assembly. Davies and Allison hold that the future tense ("I *will* build") refers to that universal Church, and that the concept "church of Jesus" ("my church") does not refer to a particular assembly in Hebrew, but rather to *qehal-YHWH*—"the congregation of God".[31] This interpretation is accepted by most New Testament exegetes, including Rudolf Bultmann.[32] Given this, Jesus is very probably establishing Peter as the head of the new universal Church that is to come through His Passion, death, Resurrection, and gift of the Holy Spirit.

Recall from above that, in both the Gospels of Mark and John, Jesus proclaims that *He* will be the new universal temple to replace the old Jerusalem Temple built by human hands (Mk 14:58; Jn 2:19). John interprets this text by noting, "He spoke of the temple of his body" (Jn 2:21). This interpretation reflects the early Church's view of Jesus' body as the foundation of the new universal Church, which is borne out in Jesus' interpretation of the Temple cleansing. Recall from above that in Mark's version of the cleansing (as well as Matthew and Luke), when Jesus' authority is questioned, He responds to the Pharisees by telling the Parable of the Wicked Tenants (Mt 21:33–46; Mk 12:1–12; Lk 20:9–19), in which He indirectly associates Himself with "the beloved son" (Mk 12:6; Lk 20:13; cf. Mt 21:37). After predicting the beating and death of the Son (Himself), He then asks, "Have you not read this Scripture: 'The very stone which the builders rejected has become the cornerstone; this was the Lord's doing, and it is marvelous in our eyes'?" (Mk 12:10–11; cf. Mt 21:42; Lk 20:17).[33] According to N. T. Wright, Jesus portraying Himself as the cornerstone of the new universal temple to be built in place of the old Temple.[34] Thus, it seems that Mark's interpretation is

---

[31] Ibid., p. 629.

[32] Ibid.

[33] Recall from the discussion above that the Scripture being quoted is Psalm 118:22–23.

[34] Wright, *Jesus and the Victory of God*, pp. 497–501.

the same as John's: Jesus is making His body the new universal temple for everyone in all future generations through His forthcoming death and Resurrection.

Did Jesus have this in mind when He declared to Peter, "You are Peter [Rock] and on this rock I will build *my Church*, and the gates of Hades shall not prevail against it"? It is likely that He did because He seems to have had this idea in mind *before* He predicts and interprets His Passion, death, and Resurrection (Mt 16:21–28; Mk 8:31—9:1; Lk 9:22–27). This interpretation explains why He is knowingly going to Jerusalem to encounter His painful destiny. Jerusalem is the place of the Temple—where the cleansing action must take place, and where His prophetic claim to become the new universal temple will be initiated and fulfilled.

This brings us to our next expression: "the gates of Hades". Though this may seem like a pagan expression (because of the term "Hades"), it is not. As Davies and Allison indicate, it is a very common Semitic expression—and the Greek translation of it is very likely a Semitism.[35] The expression "the gates of Hades shall not prevail against it" has an obvious ring of permanence or ongoingness—not limited to the current time or any specific time. Since Peter is the foundation rock of Jesus' Church—the universal temple constituted through His risen body—it will last forever, and it will never be overcome by evil or the domain of evil.

How does the above analysis help us with our question about whether Jesus is referring to only Peter or to Peter and all his successors? If the above interpretation of Matthew 16:18 is correct, and Jesus intended to start a universal and permanent Church through His own body on the foundation rock of Peter, it follows that if Jesus believed that the Church would last longer than Peter, then the commission to Peter would apply to all his successors until the end of time. As noted above with respect to Mark's eschatological discourse (Section III), Jesus was at least open to the possibility of a lengthy period of time between the first tribulation (culminating in the destruction of the Temple) and the second tribulation (the coming of the Son of man at the end of the world). In view of this, it is likely that Jesus intended to start a universal Church (through His own risen body) that would

---

[35] Davies and Allison, *Matthew 8–18*, p. 623.

be able to last beyond the apostles until the end of the age—and that He appointed Peter as the first individual to hold the highest teaching and juridical office in that Church. This is further validated by Jesus' expression "I will give you the keys of the kingdom of heaven" (see below in this section).

Before discussing the "keys of the kingdom", it will be helpful to discuss what is meant by the authority to "bind" and "loose". Benedict Viviano describes Peter's power as follows:

> God shall bind and loose what Peter binds and looses. This verse gives enormous authority to Peter. What is the nature of this authority? Binding and loosing are rabbinic technical terms that can refer to binding the devil in exorcism, to the juridical acts of excommunication and of definitive decision making (a form of teaching through legislation, policy setting). See J. Jeremias, *TDNT* 3 744–53. The authority to bind and loose is given to the disciples in 18:18, but to Peter alone are accorded the revelation, the role of the rock of foundation (Eph 2:20), and especially the keys.[36]

Viviano and J. Jeremias interpret Peter's "authority to bind and loose" as a supreme teaching and juridical authority. The reason for such authority is first and foremost to lead the People of God in the truth of Jesus Himself. Yet, there is another very important reason for these two kinds of authority: to resolve doctrinal (teaching) disputes and juridical (Church governance) disputes. Later in Matthew's Gospel (18:18), Jesus gives this same authority to bind and loose to all the apostles, but He does not do so in the same way that He gives it to Peter. Before giving this authority to the other apostles, Jesus first gives it to Peter in the context of the foundation rock as well as the keys to the kingdom (see below). Both of these images indicate *ultimate* or *highest* authority to resolve doctrinal and juridical disputes. After establishing Peter's supreme authority, He then bestows the nonsupreme authority on the other apostles. We are now in a position to analyze "the keys of the kingdom of heaven".

The phrase "keys of the kingdom of heaven" has a rich history filling it with meaning, not only for Jesus and Peter, but for the modern

---

[36] Benedict Viviano, "The Gospel according to Matthew", in Brown, Fitzmyer, and Murphy, *New Jerome Biblical Commentary*, p. 630.

Church. Timothy Gray presents a compelling interpretation of this phrase in light of several Old Testament texts in his book *Peter: Keys to Following Jesus*.[37] The most striking Old Testament parallel to Jesus' commission occurs in Isaiah 22:18–22.[38] In this passage, Isaiah delivers an oracle to Shebna, who was appointed prime minister of the house (the kingdom) of Judah by King Hezekiah. Shebna proved himself unfaithful by not trusting in God, anticipating Israel's fall to the Assyrians. Assuming he would die at the hands of the Assyrians, he constructed an elaborate tomb for himself. Since Shebna had not trusted God, God replaced him as prime minister by sending Isaiah the prophet with an oracle against Shebna and appointing Eliakim as his replacement:

> In that day I will call my servant Eli'akim the son of Hilki'ah, and I will clothe him with your robe, and will bind your belt on him, and will commit your authority to his hand; and he shall be a father to the inhabitants of Jerusalem and to the house of Judah. *And I will place on his shoulder the key of the house of David; he shall open, and none shall shut; and he shall shut, and none shall open.* (Is 22:20–22; italics added)

Now compare the last line from the above oracle of Isaiah ("I will place on his [Eliakim's] shoulder the key of the house of David; he shall open, and none shall shut; and he shall shut, and none shall open") with the words of Jesus to appoint Peter as head of the Church: "I will give you the keys of the kingdom of heaven, and whatever you bind on earth shall be bound in heaven, and whatever you loose on earth shall be loosed in heaven" (Mt 16:19). The parallelism between the two passages is sufficiently close to imply a relationship between them in the mind of Jesus.

If we accept that Jesus had this passage in mind, then we will want to examine the full context of the Isaiah passage. Notice that Isaiah's words were used to appoint Eliakim as *prime minister* over the kingdom of Judah. Isaiah's use of the word "key" along with

---

[37] Timothy Gray, *Peter: Keys to Following Jesus* (San Francisco: Ignatius Press; Greenwood Village, Colo.: Augustine Institute, 2016), pp. 70–76.

[38] See also John L. McKenzie, "The Gospel according to Matthew", in *The Jerome Biblical Commentary*, ed. Raymond Brown, Joseph A. Fitzmyer, and Roland E. Murphy (Englewood Cliffs, N.J.: Prentice-Hall, 1968), p. 92.

the description of the authority to open and shut were words of installation—to make Eliakim the new prime minister over the house of Judah. In the previous line, Isaiah deposes Shebna from his *office* and takes away his *authority over the kingdom*. Thus, when he gives Eliakim the *key along with the authority to open and shut*, he is installing him in the *office* held by Shebna (prime minister), giving him the full authority of that office.

If Jesus had this passage from Isaiah in mind, then He likely viewed His declaration to Peter, using the word "keys" (with the authority to bind and loose), in a similar way to that of Isaiah—that is, as words of *installation*. If so, then He intended to install Peter into an *office* of *highest authority* (like that of prime minister in the case of Eliakim). So what does this mean? If giving the *keys* means "to appoint or install someone as chief administrator of a kingdom", then Jesus likely meant to install Peter in that office. The term "keys" implies administrative authority over a kingdom—the highest office. If Jesus did not intend to initiate an office with high administrative authority, why would He have used the image of "keys" in conjunction with the authority to bind and loose? Why use an expression that implies such an office with such striking parallels to Isaiah's oracle, if He did not have the creation of a supreme office of His Church in mind? If He was at least open to the possibility that His Church would last beyond the death of Peter until the end of time (which is likely, given the Marcan eschatological discourse), why wouldn't He have foreseen the need for other individuals, after Peter, to occupy that highest administrative office with the same keys and the supreme power of "binding and loosing"?

Evidently, there are some differences between Isaiah's oracle and Jesus' commissioning of Peter. First, Jesus is giving Peter the keys of the supreme office of the Church, which pertains to the *heavenly* Kingdom, while Isaiah gives the keys to Eliakim to the supreme office over the *earthly* kingdom of Judah. Second, Jesus gives Peter the power to "bind and loose" over *heavenly* matters (consistent with the supreme *heavenly* office that he has been given), while Isaiah gives Eliakim only the earthly power to open and shut with respect to the kingdom of Judah.

Inasmuch as Jesus' conferral of the divine power to bind and loose is the ultimate authority to resolve doctrinal and juridical disputes (that could lead to fractioning and division)—that is, the ultimate authority to preserve unity within the Church—and inasmuch as Jesus foresaw the possibility of such disputes and disunity beyond the life of Peter (between the first and second tribulation), it is reasonable to conclude that His use of "keys of the kingdom of heaven" refers to an office of supreme authority (needed to preserve Church unity) that would be held by the successors to Saint Peter. As we shall see below (Section VII), the immediate successors to Saint Peter (in the See of Rome) as well as early Church Fathers believed this to be the case.

VI. Peter in the Acts of the Apostles and at the Council of Jerusalem

Peter plays a central a role in the Acts of the Apostles. If he did not have supreme doctrinal and juridical authority, the roles he plays in the early Church would be inexplicable. As John McKenzie notes:

> In the first Christian community of Jerusalem, Peter appears as the leader immediately after the ascension of Jesus and retains this position through Acts 1–12. He proposes the election of a successor to Judas in the Twelve (Acts 1:15–26). He is the spokesman of the disciples at Pentecost (Acts 2), after the cure of the lame man (Acts 3), and before the council (Acts 4; 5:29). He more than any other exhibits the healing power of Jesus (Acts 3; 5:15; 9:32–43). In the episode of Ananias and Sapphira he is the spokesman of the community (Acts 5:1–11) and he rejects the proposal of Simon Magus (Acts 8:20–24).... He is the first to preach the gospel to Gentiles (Acts 10) and explains this as the result of a heavenly revelation (Acts 11:1–18). The same attitude is shown in his discourse at the council of Jerusalem (Acts 15:7–11). Paul likewise attests his importance in the primitive Church both in Jerusalem and elsewhere.... Paul sets him apart as a witness of the resurrection (1 Cor 15:5). On Paul's first visit to Jerusalem he conferred with Peter but saw no other apostle except James (Gal 1:18).[39]

The role of Peter in the Council of Jerusalem is particularly important (Acts 15:1–21). Apparently, a strong faction of Jewish Christians

---

[39] McKenzie, *Dictionary of the Bible*, pp. 663–64.

(seemingly from the Jerusalem Church) were trying to impose the Jewish law upon Gentile converts. Paul and Barnabas traveled to Jerusalem to appeal to the apostles (who are evidently regarded as having a higher authority than he) to resolve the matter before it caused serious division within the Church.

The apostles convene the first council of the Church (the Council of Jerusalem) to resolve the matter. Luke presents the conclusions of the council in two steps:

- The decree of Peter (Acts 15:1–12)
- The decree of James (Acts 15:13–21)

Scholars are divided about whether Luke telescoped two different councils in his account of the Council of Jerusalem—one led by Peter and concerned with circumcision (Acts 15:1–12), and the other led by James, concerned with dietary proscriptions and unlawful marriage (Acts 15:13–21). Whatever the case, Luke indicates that Peter's authority is greater than that of James; it comes directly from God and is *universal*—applicable to the whole Church. James, in contrast, does not claim authority from God himself. Instead, he appeals to Moses and the prophets and restricts his decree to Jewish Christians, probably in the church that he oversees—the Church of Jerusalem. A brief discussion of these points will show that in the early Church, Peter's authority is precisely what we would expect in light of Jesus' commissioning—the highest universal authority.

After the council was convened, Peter—speaking on behalf of the *Church herself*—read the decree concerning circumcision, and perhaps dietary proscriptions (Acts 15:7). Notice that Peter claims that his authority comes from God Himself:

> Brethren, you know that in the early days *God* made choice among you, that by *my* mouth the Gentiles should hear the word of the gospel and believe. (Acts 15:7; italics added)

Peter's commissioning by Jesus and his witness of the Holy Spirit descending upon Cornelius and his household (Gentiles), without being subject to the Law of Moses (Acts 10:44–48), convinces Peter that *God Himself* has given him authority to resolve the dispute within the Church. Since Peter speaks with divinely conferred authority (from Jesus), he does not have to make an appeal to Jewish Scripture or the Mosaic Law (unlike James, who takes great pains to do so).

Notice too that Peter's decree is universal and definitive. After he shows how God bore witness to the authenticity of the Gentiles' conversion (without being subject to the Law of Moses) by sending the Holy Spirit upon them, he gives his theological justification— that the Gentiles are saved in the same way as Jewish Christians—that is, "by faith [and] ... through the grace of the Lord Jesus" (Acts 15:9, 11). After he presents the justification and theological explanation of his decision, the assembly falls silent (Acts 15:12), meaning that Peter's word put an end to all debate and discussion—it was definitive.

Peter's decree stands in stark contrast to that of James. James enjoys no direct authority from God (or special commission from Jesus). Therefore, he must find another ground of authority for his primarily Jewish audience (in the Church of Jerusalem, which he leads). To do this, he makes an appeal to Jewish Scripture— first to the prophet Amos (Amos 9:11–12 in Acts 15:16–18), and then to Moses (Acts 15:21). James' responsibility is to give the detailed information to the Jewish Christians about the three dietary proscriptions from which the Gentiles are excused. These three dietary proscriptions were considered very important to his audience, and the Gentiles' violation of them was offensive to James' audience. James' decree would therefore have had a calming effect. James appears to have no authority beyond this subsidiary role.

What might we conclude from Luke's presentation of the Council of Jerusalem? In around A.D. 50 (the time of the council), Peter was already acknowledged as the head of the Church who could claim special commission from Jesus and direct authority from God. James and Paul both implicitly acknowledge this—James in his acknowledged secondary role and Paul in referring the matter to the apostles whose spokesman is Peter. Peter can speak on his own authority and does not need to make recourse to the Mosaic Law or to the Old Testament Scriptures, and his decree is universal—that is, for the whole Church, not for one part of the Church (i.e., Jerusalem). It can scarcely be believed that Peter would have this authority if it were not given to him explicitly by Jesus.

VII. Were Peter's Successors Accorded Primacy in the Post-Petrine Church?

One explicit way of determining whether Petrine primacy was conveyed to Peter's successors (the bishops of Rome) is to examine what the early popes and the bishops acknowledged. Unfortunately, letters and texts of the popes succeeding Saint Peter are rare indeed, but four texts pertaining to Petrine primacy from early sources still survive today:

1. Pope Saint Clement of Rome's Letter to the Corinthian Church (A.D. 80)
2. Bishop Saint Ignatius of Antioch's Letter to the Church of Rome (around A.D. 100)
3. Saint Irenaeus, from his work *Adversus Haereses* (A.D. 180)
4. Bishop Cyprian of Carthage, from *On the Unity of the Catholic Church* (A.D. 250)

These texts confirm an unbroken line of thought from the death of Saint Peter to the writings of Cyprian of Carthage that the successors of Saint Peter maintained his primacy over the universal Church in matters of teaching and the resolution of juridical disputes. We will examine each text in turn.

A. Pope Clement I

Pope Clement of Rome (papacy, A.D. 88–99) is considered as either the second or fourth pope, depending on how we view Peter's consecration of Linus and Cletus.[40] Tertullian viewed Clement as the immediate successor to Peter, while Saint Irenaeus viewed him as

---

[40] According to Tertullian (ca. A.D. 199), Clement was consecrated by Peter himself, and he believed that Clement was the immediate successor to Peter with care for the universal Church (*De Praescript* 32). In Tertullian's view, Peter's consecration of Linus and Cletus was for the purpose of service to the people of Rome, as distinct from Clement, who had custody over the universal Church (ibid.). An earlier account from Saint Irenaeus (ca. 180) declares that Clement was the fourth pope (*Adv. Haer.* 3, 3). Eusebius of Caesarea (ca. 314) followed Irenaeus' ordering in his *Ecclesiastical History*. In any case, Clement's witness to Petrine supremacy is quite early, probably around A.D. 95 (see the text below in this section).

the third successor to Peter, after Linus and Cletus. The confusion comes from the fact that Peter apparently consecrated both Linus and Cletus for priestly service to the Church, while consecrating Clement as leader of the universal Church (according to Tertullian). In view of the twenty-four-year gap between the death of Saint Peter (ca. A.D. 64, during the persecution of Nero) and the beginning of Clement's papacy (ca. A.D. 88), it is likely that Peter consecrated Linus as his successor while possibly expressing a preference to have Cletus succeed Linus. Clement evidently succeeds Cletus, but we cannot be certain how his ascendency to the See of Rome occurred. Nevertheless, as successor to the See of Saint Peter (the Diocese of Rome), Pope Clement held that he had the authority to order the *Corinthian* Church under *obedience* to reconstitute her leaders after they were deposed:

> The Church of God which sojourneth at Rome, to the Church of God which sojourneth at Corinth, to them that are called and sanctified in the will of God through our Lord Jesus Christ: Grace and peace be multiplied unto you from Almighty God through Jesus Christ.
>
> On account of the sudden and repeated calamities and mischances, brethren, that have come upon us, we suppose that we have the more slowly given heed to the things that are disputed among you, beloved, and to the foul and unholy sedition, alien and foreign to the elect of God, which a few headstrong and self-willed persons have kindled to such a degree of madness, that your venerable and famous name, worthy to be loved of all men, is greatly blasphemed....
>
> Let us, therefore, submit to his all-holy and glorious name, and escape the threats that have been before spoken by Wisdom against the disobedient, that we may abide trusting in the most holy name of his greatness.
>
> Accept this our advice, and it will not be repented of by you. For as God liveth, and as the Lord Jesus Christ liveth, and the Holy Spirit, the confidence and hope of the elect, he who observeth in humility with earnest obedience, and repining not, the ordinances and commands given by God, he shall be reckoned and counted in the number of them that are saved by Jesus Christ, through whom is there to him glory, world without end. Amen.
>
> But if some should be *disobedient to the things spoken by him through us* [italics added], let them know that they will entangle themselves in no small transgression and danger....

It is right, therefore, that those who have attended to so great and so many examples should submit their necks, and fill the place of obedience, so that being at peace from the vain sedition we may attain, without any blame, to the end set before us in truth.

For joy and rejoicing will ye afford us if, becoming obedient to the things that have been written by us, ye put an end, by the suggestion of the Holy Spirit, to the unlawful wrath of your discord, according to the supplication which we have made concerning peace and unity in this epistle.[41]

As the above letter indicates, Clement was certain that he possessed the authority of God (as Peter's successor) to resolve disputes for the *whole* Church beyond the See of Rome. He also believed that he had the authority to order the leaders of the Corinthian Church, under obedience and pain of sin, to follow his orders. He asserts that he is inspired by the Holy Spirit to order the Corinthian Church to desist from their seditious behavior. If Clement's universal and supreme authority as successor to Peter at the See of Rome were not well known and accepted, his letter, enjoining the Corinthian Church to obey under pain of sin, would have seemed at best unintelligible, and at worst, ludicrous. Apparently, the Corinthian Church obeyed his command and restored the original clergy to their proper place.

Henry Chadwick interprets Clement's letter as follows:

Towards the latter part of the 1st century, Rome's presiding cleric named Clement wrote on behalf of his church to remonstrate with the Corinthian Christians who had ejected clergy without either financial or charismatic endowment in favor of a fresh lot; Clement apologized not for intervening but for not having acted sooner.... Roman bishops were already conscious of being custodians of the authentic tradition of true interpretation of the apostolic writings. In the conflict with Gnosticism, Rome played a decisive role, and likewise in the deep division in Asia Minor created by the claims of the Montanist prophets.[42]

---

[41] Clement of Rome, "The First Epistle of Clement to the Corinthians", introduction; 1, 1; 58, 1; 58, 2; 59, 1; 63, 1; 63, 2; trans. Charles H. Hoole, 1885, *Early Christian Writings* (website), 2020, http://www.earlychristianwritings.com/text/1clement-hoole.html.

[42] Henry Chadwick, "The Early Christian Community", in *The Oxford Illustrated History of the Christian Church*, ed. John McManners (New York: Oxford University Press, 2001), p. 36.

Clement (and other early successors to Peter in the See of Rome) couldn't have claimed this universal authority on his own. There must have been some recognition on the part of bishops and Church leaders in the first century that Clement possessed the same universal authority over the Church as Peter. The certainty with which Clement holds this supreme power (as well as the implicit acknowledgment of it by the Corinthian Church) suggests some well-known justification and authentication (prior to Clement's papacy) of supreme power vested in Peter's successors at the See of Rome. It is not unreasonable to believe that this justification and authentication came from Saint Peter himself. We have no written record of such a clarification, but it would be difficult to believe that Peter would have consecrated bishops for the See of Rome without attending to such an important matter of succession, particularly as he anticipated his martyrdom.

B. Saint Ignatius of Antioch

Saint Ignatius of Antioch, bishop of Antioch (ca. A.D. 100) wrote a letter to the Church of Rome, acknowledging that she was superior to, and presided over, all other Christian churches:

> Ignatius, who is also Theophorus, unto her that
> hath found mercy in the bountifulness of the Father
> Most High and of Jesus Christ His only Son; to the
> church that is beloved and enlightened through the
> will of Him who willed all things that are, by faith
> and love towards Jesus Christ our God; even unto her
> *that hath the presidency in the country of the region*
> *of the Romans*, being worthy of God, worthy of honour,
> worthy of felicitation, worthy of praise, worthy of
> success, worthy in purity, and having the *presidency*
> *of love*, walking in the law of Christ and bearing the
> Father's name; which church also I salute in the name
> of Jesus Christ the Son of the Father; unto them that
> in flesh and spirit are united unto His every
> commandment, being filled with the grace of God

without wavering, and filtered clear from every foreign stain; abundant greeting in Jesus Christ our God in blamelessness.[43]

According to Ludwig Ott:

> Clear recognition of the consciousness of the Primacy of the Roman Bishops, and of the recognition of the Primacy by the other churches appears at the end of the 1st Century.... St. Ignatius elevated the Roman community over all the communities using his epistle as a solemn form of address. Twice he says of it that it is the presiding community, which expresses a relationship of superiority.[44]

Charles Belmonte makes a comparative analysis of the tone of Ignatius' many letters to other bishops and of the above letter to the Church of Rome:

> When one compares the tone of the epistles of St Ignatius, one notices that the epistle addressed to the church of Rome is different. There is no doubt that the bishop of Antioch is writing to a superior. He greets the church that is "presiding in the chief place of the Roman territory;" evidently, presiding not over itself but over the other Christian communities. He calls her "the one presiding in charity," or "presiding in the bond of love." This is his way of saying "presiding over the Church universal." St Ignatius will be the first writer to use the expression "Catholic Church" (Cf. Ep. to the Smyrnaeans, 8) to designate the Church founded by Christ.[45]

We now have two sources at the end of the first century indicating that the successors to Peter in the See of Rome have supreme authority over other Christian churches: one from the vantage point of Pope Clement to the Church of Corinth (ordering obedience under

---

[43] Saint Ignatius of Antioch, "Ignatius to the Romans", introduction, trans. J.B. Lightfoot and J.R. Harmer, in *Apostolic Fathers*, 1891, *Early Christian Writings* (website), 2020 (italics added), http://www.earlychristianwritings.com/text/ignatius-romans-lightfoot.html.

[44] Ludwig Ott, *Fundamentals of Catholic Dogma* (Rockford, Ill.: Tan Books, 2009), p. 283.

[45] Charles Belmonte, commentary to "Letter of St. Ignatius of Antioch to the Romans", in *Faith Seeking Understanding* (Metro Manila, Philippines: Cobrin Publishing, 2012), http://fsubelmonte.weebly.com/letter-of-st-ignatius-of-antioch-to-the-romans.html.

pain of sin), and one from the bishop of Antioch to the Church of Rome, recognizing superiority and the authority to preside over other Christian churches. This means that the view of the primacy of Peter's successors was widespread among the Church's leaders, twenty-five to thirty-five years after Peter's death—and beyond.

C. Saint Irenaeus

About eighty years after Ignatius of Antioch (ca. A.D. 180), Saint Irenaeus declares that the Church of Rome (whose presiding bishop is the pope) is owed obedience in matters of teaching by all other Christian churches. He declares that all other churches, and therefore all the faithful, must agree with this church. This means that all other churches must obey and consent to the head of the Roman Church:

> But since it would be too long to enumerate in such a volume as this the succession of all the churches, we shall confound all those who, in whatever manner, whether through self-satisfaction or vainglory, or through blindness and wicked opinion, assemble other than where it is proper, by pointing out here the successions of the bishops of the *greatest* and most ancient church known to all, founded and organized at Rome by the two most glorious apostles, Peter and Paul, that church which has the tradition and the faith which comes down to us after having been announced to men by the apostles. With that church, because of its *superior origin, all the churches must agree*, that is, all the faithful in the whole world, and it is in her that the faithful everywhere have maintained the apostolic tradition.[46]

There appears to be an unbroken line of acknowledgment among the churches' leadership from Saint Peter to Clement I, to Saint Ignatius of Antioch, and to Saint Irenaeus that the successor to Peter at the See of Rome has authority over all other churches—and is the final arbiter over all doctrinal and juridical disputes. This is confirmed sixty years later by Cyprian of Carthage.

---

[46] Saint Irenaeus, *Against Heresies* 3, 3, 2, in "Catholic Biblical Apologetics: Post-Apostolic Fathers of the Church", under "The Authority of the Pope", ed. Robert Schihl and Paul Flanagan, FreeRepublic.com, 2010 (italics added), http://www.freerepublic.com/focus/religion/2476599/posts?page=1.

D. Saint Cyprian of Carthage

Cyprian of Carthage, one of the greatest Latin apostolic Fathers and bishop of Carthage, wrote an important treatise entitled *On the Unity of the Catholic Church* in A.D. 250. In a central passage, he notes:

> The Lord says to Peter: "you are Peter, and upon this rock I will build my Church, and the gates of hell will not overcome it. And to you I will give the keys of the kingdom of heaven; and whatever things you bind on earth shall be bound also in heaven, and whatever you loose on earth, they shall be loosed also in heaven." ... On him [Peter] he builds the Church, and to him he gives the command to feed the sheep [Jn 21:17], and although he assigns a like power to all the apostles, yet he founded a single chair [*cathedra*], and he established by his own authority a source and an intrinsic reason for that unity. Indeed, the others were also what Peter was [i.e., apostles], but a primacy is given to Peter, whereby it is made clear that there is but one Church and one chair. So too, all [the apostles] are shepherds, and the flock is shown to be one, fed by all the apostles in single-minded accord. If someone does not hold fast to this unity of Peter, can he imagine that he still holds the faith? If he [should] desert the chair of Peter upon whom the Church was built, can he still be confident that he is in the Church?[47]

Approximately two hundred years after the death of Peter, we have a juridical declaration and a theological explanation of the doctrine of the primacy of the Bishop of Rome. This follows the unbroken chain of acknowledgment of the doctrine by popes, bishops, and theologians—Saint Peter, Pope Clement, Saint Ignatius of Antioch, and Saint Irenaeus. In this work, Cyprian confidently declares that anyone who does not acknowledge and submit to the Bishop of Rome as his superior does not belong to the Church of Rome. They

---

[47] Cyprian of Carthage, *On the Unity of the Catholic Church* 4. Though this text was hotly disputed by some Protestant scholars in the late nineteenth and early twentieth centuries, several scholars have since shown that it is very probably the authentic text of Cyprian of Carthage. The matter is explained in an important article by Dom John Chapman (who has provided the translation in my text). See Dom John Chapman, "St. Cyprian on the Church and the Papacy", in *Studies on the Early Papacy* (Port Washington, N.Y.: Kennikat Press, 1971). It is reprinted with a brief introduction at Philvaz.com, http://philvaz.com/apologetics/num44.htm.

are the equivalent of excommunicated heretics. He also gives a theological explanation of why Jesus committed this highest authority to Saint Peter and his successors: for the sake of the unity of the whole Christian Church. Cyprian here is merely recapitulating what Jesus, Saint Peter, Saint Ignatius of Antioch, and Saint Irenaeus have acknowledged and practiced, but gives it a theological and juridical clarity as he looks back on the history of Church leadership.

If we suppose that the above four texts represent the general view of the leadership of the Catholic Church throughout two and a half centuries—since the time of Saint Peter—then it is highly likely that the Church (in the first three centuries) both implicitly and explicitly submitted herself to the primacy of the successor to Saint Peter, occupying his chair at the Roman See in matters of doctrine. Local churches also submitted themselves to the See of Peter (Rome) for the resolution of doctrinal and juridical disputes. Though there were many heresies and challenges facing the young Church, the primacy of Peter's successors safeguarded the teaching of Jesus and maintained the unity of the Church. Given the above, this one Church, unified under the leadership of Peter's successors, should be viewed as the true Church initiated by Jesus—the Church to which Jesus bestowed His Spirit and the promise that the gates of Hades would not prevail against it. To the successors of Peter, He gave the same keys to the Kingdom of Heaven so that whatever they declared bound on earth would be bound in Heaven and whatever they declared loosed on earth would be loosed in Heaven. This prime "binding and loosing" authority bound all bishops, clergy, and laity to obedience for the sake of unity and peace.

VIII. The Evidence for the Catholic Church as the True Church of Jesus

We may now review the evidence for Peter and his successors as the head of the Church that Jesus chose to be His authentic interpreter. As noted above, there is considerable evidence showing that Jesus intended to establish a Church through Peter, to make Peter's primary authority extend to his successors, and to be present to Peter and his successors through His risen body and the Holy Spirit until the end of time. We addressed the following five areas:

1. In Sections I–II, we discussed why a Church community is essential, focusing on the need for an authentic interpretation of Jesus' revelation lest differences of opinion lead to an accelerating proliferation of churches and denominations. We showed how this was manifest in the Protestant Reformation, where a multitude of denominations were started over the last five hundred years because of differences in the interpretation of Jesus' words and actions. We noted there that Jesus must have foreseen this possibility in starting His Church, and that He would have responded to this challenge by instituting a *supreme* (primary) teaching and juridical authority to be the final word on all such disputes.

2. In Sections III–VI, we discussed the evidence for Jesus initiating and authenticating the Catholic Church through the office of Peter and his successors.

   • In Section III, we examined the likelihood that Jesus was open to multiple generations of successors to Peter and the apostles, focusing specifically on His creation of the new universal temple for all nations through His risen body (Section III.A) and His teaching that the end of the world would come only after a second tribulation whose time was not known by anyone including Himself (Section III.B). In view of this it is reasonable to infer that Jesus was open to the possibility of multiple generations of the Church that the office of Peter might have to serve.

   • In Section IV, we examined the historicity of Matthew's commissioning logion (Mt 16:17–19), showing that it was very probably not a Matthean redaction, but rather traces back to an earlier Aramaic tradition likely known to both Saint Paul and Saint John. This is evidenced by the formula of Peter's exclusive threefold commissioning as chief shepherd by Jesus in John 21:15–17, as well as the many similarities in formula and Semitisms between Matthew's commissioning and Paul's comparison of his commissioning to Peter's in Galatians 2:7–9. We also showed five textual indications that this earlier tradition originated with Jesus Himself.

- In Section V, we gave an extensive exegesis of Jesus' commission to Peter in Matthew 16:17–19, and noted there the preponderance of evidence for Jesus indicating His intention to start a primary teaching and juridical *office* through Peter and his successors. This interpretation turns on the preponderance of exegetical interpretation of the words "rock", "my Church", "keys of the kingdom of heaven", and the power to "bind" and "loose".

3. In Section VI, we showed how Peter's relationship to the other apostles in Acts 1–15 indicates his supreme authority within the new Church. This is particularly evident in his primary and universal role at the Council of Jerusalem (Acts 15), which shows him to have a higher and more pervasive authority than that of James (head of the Jerusalem Church) and Saint Paul (head of the Gentile Church).

4. In Section VII, we showed that Saint Clement of Rome (third successor to Saint Peter at the See of Rome A.D. 88–99) believed himself to have supreme authority over other bishops, even demanding obedience of them under pain of sin. We also showed that Saint Ignatius of Antioch (bishop of Antioch, ca. A.D. 100) acknowledged to the pope in Rome that he held the presidency over all churches (dioceses outside of Rome). Additionally, we presented texts of Saint Irenaeus and Cyprian of Carthage (early Church Fathers) that advocated the primacy of the successor to Peter at Rome, as well as his supreme authority required to maintain the unity of the universal (Catholic) Church.

5. The above historical evidence is further corroborated by the nine contemporary scientifically validated miracles discussed in the appendix to Volume I of this Trilogy. These miracles are directly connected with Mary (the Mother of Jesus), contemporary saints, and the Real Presence of Jesus' Body in the Holy Eucharist. Inasmuch as all three of these doctrines are challenged by non-Catholic Christian churches, we might ask why God (the Father of Jesus Christ) would be working His supernatural power through these intermediaries toward ends that are specifically Catholic, if Jesus had not intended to invest Peter and his successors with the ultimate authority to interpret His revelation and oversee the community (juridical authority).

When we combine all of the above evidence summarized in numbers 1–5 above, it is highly likely that Jesus did commission Peter, and through him, his successors, to have ultimate teaching and juridical authority, implying that the Catholic Church is the authentic interpreter of the words and actions of Jesus.

IX. Conclusion

Up to this point, we have been addressing the question of Jesus' intention to establish His Church on the foundation of Saint Peter and his successors as supreme teaching and juridical authorities. This authority is guaranteed by Jesus in order to withstand the forces of evil until the end of time. Thus, this authority will be able to discern the truth in matters of doctrine and maintain the unity of the Church. As we shall see in Chapter 2, Jesus and the apostolic Fathers established a Church structure, the sacraments, and the basic doctrinal framework behind the Creed through the Gospels, the New Testament epistles, and decisions of the first councils and successors to Peter. Essential as all this was and is, Jesus intended that the new universal Church be even more than the *external* structure, Scriptures, sacraments, liturgy, and traditions that He established. He also intended to make this Church an *interior* reality within every baptized member—an interior reality grounded in His risen Mystical Body and the Holy Spirit (see above Section III.A).

We might rephrase the above reflection by noting that Jesus intended to give us not only His "outer Word" (His teaching interpreted by the Church that comes to us, as it were, from outside of us), but also His "inner Word" (the intuitions, feelings, and inspirations guided by the Holy Spirit and His mystical presence within us that encourage us, incline us, guide us, and deepen us through participation in the Church).[48] We might at first think that the inner Word

---

[48] This distinction is made implicitly in the Gospel of John where Christ is portrayed at once as "the Word" and the inner light of man (1:1–7); this is taken up by the Church Fathers and explicitized by Saint Augustine in *Tolle Lege*, where he says, "The sound of our word strikes your ears, but the Master is within you." The distinction then becomes a touchstone for medieval theology and spirituality, particularly in Saint Catherine of Siena, Saint Thomas à Kempis, and Jan van Ruysbroeck.

is at best vague and obscure, and at worst, nonexistent, but nothing could be further from the truth. The inner Word takes us into the domain of the heart—the domain of love, goodness, beauty, spirit, and transcendence that goes far beyond the domain of the mind (what can be grasped through concepts, logic, and empirical verification).[49] Bernard Lonergan describes the distinction as follows:

> The outer word of the Gospel and the inner word of the Spirit— the word that took flesh in Jesus Christ and was expressed in the public world of human history in his words and deeds, death and resurrection, and the word that is spoken in the silent depths of our hearts, where what is most personal, most distinctive, most defining about ourselves is determined.[50]

We need the inner Word as much as the outer Word, because we are not reducible to our minds. Indeed our higher nature is characterized more markedly by our hearts—the various intuitions, desires, feelings, and decisions related to love, goodness/morality, beauty, spirituality, and transcendence, which factor prominently in our faith, relationship with God, struggle with evil, and sharing of faith with others. This is why Lonergan (following Aquinas) contends that we need not only intellectual conversion (the mind's reasons), but also spiritual conversion[51] and moral conversion.[52] If we in our transcendent nature are called to these three kinds of conversion, then

---

[49] The great mathematician and spiritual writer Blaise Pascal recognized this when he asserted that "the heart has its reasons that the mind knows not of." See Blaise Pascal, *Pensées* 277, trans. W. F. Trotter (New York: E. P. Dutton, 1958), p. 78.

[50] Bernard Lonergan, *Verbum: Word and Idea in Aquinas*, ed. Frederick Crowe and Robert M. Doran (Toronto: University of Toronto Press, 1967), p. 13.

[51] Bernard Lonergan, *Method in Theology*, ed. Robert M. Doran and John D. Dadosky, vol. 14 of *The Collected Works of Bernard Lonergan*, ed. Frederick E. Crowe and Robert M. Doran (Toronto: University of Toronto Press, 1990), pp. 150, 161, 217–35. For an excellent analysis of the progression of Lonergan's thought in this area, see Robert Doran, "What Does Bernard Lonergan Mean by 'Conversion'?", LonerganResource.com, 2011, http://www .lonerganresource.com/pdf/lectures/What%20Does%20Bernard%20Lonergan%20Mean %20by%20Conversion.pdf.

[52] Lonergan sees moral conversion as not only a conversion of conscience and adherence to principles ("the good" or "the just"), but also a conversion in the distinctive kind of love that Jesus identified with the highest commandment and virtue: *agapē* (see Lonergan, *Method in Theology*). We give an extensive interpretation of moral conversion in Chapters 4–6 of this volume.

Jesus would want to give us more than His outer Word; He would also want to help us in the deepest domains of our hearts—to be present to us as the inner Word. He provided for this in two ways—through the gift of the Holy Spirit, who clearly works within the inner recesses of our hearts, and by incorporating us into His risen Mystical Body that unifies all believers with one another through Him (see above, Section III). With respect to the inner Word of the Holy Spirit, Saint Paul writes:

> God has revealed to us through the Spirit. For the Spirit searches everything, even the depths of God. For what person knows a man's thoughts except the spirit of the man which is in him? So also no one comprehends the thoughts of God except the Spirit of God. Now we have received not the spirit of the world, but the Spirit which is from God, that we might understand the gifts bestowed on us by God. And we impart this in words not taught by human wisdom but taught by the Spirit, interpreting spiritual truths to those who possess the Spirit. (1 Cor 2:10–13)

Yet, the Lord has given us more than His Spirit (which is at once the Spirit of His Father); He has also brought us into His risen body, which refers not merely to His external form, but to everything He is: His mind, and above all, His heart. That is why Saint Paul insists that the Spirit of God works in and through the risen body of Christ:

> For just as the body is one and has many members, and all the members of the body, though many, are one body, so it is with Christ. For by one Spirit we were all baptized into one body—Jews or Greeks, slaves or free—and all were made to drink of one Spirit. For the body does not consist of one member but of many.... If one member suffers, all suffer together; if one member is honored, all rejoice together. Now you are the body of Christ and individually members of it. (1 Cor 12:12–14, 26–27)

The Holy Spirit works in us individually *and* through our unity with one another in the risen body of Christ. The activity of the Holy Spirit cannot be reduced to His work within individuals alone because He does so much more through the Mystical Body of Christ—the Church.

Why did Jesus provide both of these gifts—the Holy Spirit and His own risen body—to convey His inner Word to us? Wouldn't the Holy Spirit alone have been sufficient? This question arises frequently within our culture, which tends to emphasize autonomy and individualism instead of our interpersonal and societal (communitarian) nature. Yet, we are not mere individuals—our own islands in the midst of a vast ocean; we are inescapably interpersonal (requiring complementarity from others, naturally empathizing with others, and desiring deep friendships with others), and we are also social and communitarian (desiring participation, the exchange of ideas, and common cause within community and societal groups for the common good). In sum, we are interpersonal, social, and interdependent by both nature and necessity. Jesus recognized this and bestowed His inner Word on us, not only individually, but in unity with one another—not only giving each individual His Holy Spirit, but giving us His risen body through which the Holy Spirit can work through the whole Church to us, and through us to the whole Church.

One last point deserves consideration. We sometimes think that being integrated into Christ's risen body is simply being integrated into an interior unifying fabric or substrate, but Jesus' risen body (soma[53]) is far more than an interior unifying substrate. It refers to everything He is in His risen state—that is, not only His glorified body (flesh—sarx), but also His glorified heart, mind, and spirit. When we are incorporated into Christ's risen body through Baptism, we share directly in His heart and mind—the beginning point of what John Henry Newman called cor ad cor loquitur (heart speaking to heart).

If the gospel and explicit Church teaching provide the outer Word of Jesus, how does the inner Word of Jesus come to us? Initially it comes to all religious believers through the numinous experience, the intuition of the sacred, and our sense of transcendence, religious mystery, and the cosmic struggle between good and evil (discussed

---

[53] Saint Paul uses soma to refer to Jesus' risen body in both 1 Corinthians 12:26–27 and Romans 12:4–5, the passages where he refers to Jesus' risen body as the unity of the Church. It should be noted that soma in the New Testament often refers to the whole person (like "body" in the English words "everybody" and "somebody"), while sarx generally refers to the flesh or the physical form of the body. See Strong's Concordance, s.v. "4983: sóma", http://biblehub.com/greek/4983.htm, and s.v. "4561: sarx", https://biblehub.com/greek/4561.htm.

in detail in Volume II, Chapters 1–2, of the Quartet). After Baptism, Christians receive the Holy Spirit and are incorporated into the Mystical Body of Christ. When this occurs, we are introduced into a whole new domain of God's consciousness going far beyond the numinous experience and the intuition of the sacred—being brought into the heart and risen body of Christ and the collective heart of the communion of saints as well as all members of the Church throughout the world.

We may now proceed to the two interrelated essential elements of the Church—the outer Church and the inner Church. Extending the analogy of the outer Word and the inner Word given above, we might define the "outer Church" as the sacraments and other services offered to the faithful through the ministry of the *visible* Church. Using the same analogy, we might define the "inner Church" as the inspiration of the Holy Spirit working through the Mystical Body of Christ to deepen our relationship with Him through prayer and devotion. We will first discuss the outer Church (Chapter 2) and then the inner Church (Chapter 3), showing how each assists us in spiritual and moral conversion.

Chapter Two

Spiritual Conversion and the
"Outer Church"—the Sacramental Life

Introduction

As noted in the previous chapter, the "outer Church" refers to the sacraments and services of the visible Church that lead to deepened intellectual, spiritual, and moral conversion. The *Catechism of the Catholic Church* summarizes the importance of these services in both spiritual and moral conversion:

> It is in the Church, in communion with all the baptized, that the Christian fulfills his vocation. From the Church he receives the Word of God containing the teachings of "the law of Christ" (Gal 6:2). From the Church he receives the grace of the sacraments that sustains him on the "way." From the Church he learns the *example of holiness* and recognizes its model and source in the all-holy Virgin Mary; he discerns it in the authentic witness of those who live it; he discovers it in the spiritual tradition and long history of the saints who have gone before him and whom the liturgy celebrates in the rhythms of the sanctoral cycle.[1]

The following eight outer Church services and gifts are among the most important for our intellectual, spiritual, and moral development:

1. The grace and power of the sacraments made present through priests and other qualified ministers
2. Celebration of the sacred liturgy—the *mysterium* of Christ— filled with diverse prayers, symbols, and proclamations

---

[1] *CCC* 2030 (italics in original).

3. Proclamation of the Word of God for purposes of conversion, catechetical and doctrinal education, and evangelization
4. Moral instruction and sacraments of forgiveness and reconciliation to deepen moral conversion
5. The sacred community not only for purposes of worship and teaching, but also for service and support
6. Custodian of the sacred tradition and its development, as well as inspiration of spirituality, theology, sacred art, architecture, music, and poetry
7. Provider of assistance to those who are sick, mourning, and in need
8. Inspiration of the Catholic intellectual tradition, integrating not only philosophy, theology, and spirituality, but also the sciences, social sciences, humanities, and the arts to deepen our intellectual and spiritual conversion

When believers avail themselves of the above outer Church services, they awaken and deepen the inner Church—the Holy Spirit working through the Mystical Body of Christ. The more believers avail themselves of the services of the outer Church, the more explicit the heart of Christ (the inner Word) becomes. When this occurs, we become free to grow in our trust and love of the Lord, which in turn gives the freedom to deepen our spiritual and moral conversion.

We sometimes think that moral conversion is merely a matter of studying the virtues and then disciplining ourselves to make them habitual through a stoic act of will; but this is far from the truth of Christ and the Catholic Church, which is not stoic and has never recommended willing oneself to virtue like a shot out of a cannon. Jesus Christ, first and foremost, is concerned with *freedom*—not simply "freedom from", but "freedom for". Freedom for what? The freedom to grow in trust and love of Him. In order to do this, we will have to let go of our fears (that make us trust only in ourselves), our egocentricity (that makes us act only for ourselves), our resentments (which compel us to seek retribution), and our pride (which makes us want to dominate others). Now that's a tall order! How in the world will we achieve the freedom to let go of our fears, anxieties, egocentricity, resentments, and pride? The "world" will provide very little help here, but with God all things are not only possible, but highly probable.

So how does God help us to let go of these negative states that hold our psyches captive and block the inner Word (the heart of Christ) from speaking to our hearts? The answer given implicitly by Christ and explicitly by the Catholic Church for two thousand years is really quite simple: to avail ourselves as much as possible of the sacraments and other services provided by the outer Church (given in the list above).

Woody Allen once said that "80 percent of success in life is just showing up."[2] Though this is not exactly the case with spiritual and moral conversion, we might say that much of our conversion does not come from heroic efforts, but by sincerely availing ourselves of the above-mentioned church services. "Showing up" requires effort and some sacrifice, but not onerous burdens—for Christ's "yoke is easy", and His "burden is light" (Mt 11:30). What happens when we avail ourselves of the above services of the Church? In a phrase, the *freedom* to let go of the above-mentioned fears, anxieties, egocentricity, resentments, and pride, which almost immediately opens the way to another freedom: to trust and love the Lord more deeply. When we deepen our trust and love of the Lord, we awaken the heart of Christ within us—and then His heart begins to speak eloquently to our hearts; this brings with it yet another level of freedom: the freedom not only to deepen our moral and spiritual conversion, but to follow the path of a heroic self-sacrificial love for God, His Kingdom, and His people that moved the great saints before us.

Thus, the above eight sacraments and services provide three levels of freedom:

1. Freedom to let go of our fears, anxieties, egocentricity, resentments, and pride
2. Freedom to trust and love the Lord more deeply
3. Freedom for moral and spiritual conversion opening upon heroic self-sacrificial love in imitation of Jesus, His Mother, and the saints

When we have removed the obstacles to the inner Word's capacity to dialogue with our hearts, the most amazing things can

---

[2] "Showing Up Is 80 Percent of Life", QuoteInvestigator.com, accessed July 15, 2020, http://quoteinvestigator.com/2013/06/10/showing-up/.

happen—not only for the acquisition of virtue and the resistance to deadly sin, but also for the awakening of heroic self-sacrificial love and mystical prayer.

We might adduce from the above that spiritual and moral conversion are intertwined, because spiritual conversion leads us to greater detachment from our fears, anxieties, worldly goods, power, and prestige that facilitates our capacity to choose virtue over the deadly sins for the sake of Christ and the good itself (see Chapter 5, Section I). The natural virtues of temperance (saying no to the deadly sins) and fortitude (saying yes in a courageous and committed way to virtue) are important to moral conversion, but they are not enough. Their power is limited by the effects of our attachments, fears, and anxieties within our psyche. Spiritual conversion (coming from participation in the major services of the Church) gradually frees us from these attachments, fears, and anxieties, allowing us to say no to the deadly sins and yes to Christ and virtue with ever greater facility. The greater our spiritual conversion, the greater our spiritual freedom, and the greater our spiritual freedom, the greater our facility to reject vice and embrace virtue. Yet, spiritual conversion is not enough. We must apply the above fruits of detachment (freedom) to specifically moral objectives—that is, to specific decisions of saying no to the deadly sins and yes to virtue and ethical actions. We might say that spiritual conversion plus increased virtue and resistance to sin equals moral conversion. When spiritual freedom (detachment from the world) leads to moral freedom (increased virtue and resistance to sin), then spiritual conversion (greater love of and attachment to Christ) leads to moral conversion (the capacity to imitate the heart of Christ in our attitudes and actions).

If spiritual conversion does not move toward moral conversion, it does not achieve its natural and supernatural objective. It is like a person with exceptionally high intelligence refusing to go to school to learn how to use this gift for himself and others—or a remarkable athlete who refuses to train and practice a particular sport. The ability lies fallow, and great potential is wasted. As the Lord frequently notes, belief is important but it is not enough; it must be used to follow His commands:

> Every one then who hears these words of mine and does them will be like a wise man who built his house upon the rock; and the rain fell,

and the floods came, and the winds blew and beat upon that house, but it did not fall, because it had been founded on the rock. And every one who hears these words of mine and does not do them will be like a foolish man who built his house upon the sand; and the rain fell, and the floods came, and the winds blew and beat against that house, and it fell; and great was the fall of it. (Mt 7:24–27)

Let us now return to the services of the outer Church mentioned above. There are four foundational ways to facilitate spiritual conversion through those services:

1. Receiving the Holy Eucharist (Section I.A and I.C)
2. Participation in the sacred liturgy (Section I.B)
3. Listening to the proclamation of the Word of God (Section I.B)
4. Participation in the sacramental life (Section II)

There are two foundational ways to facilitate the movement from spiritual to moral conversion through the above services:

1. Learning the moral teaching of the Church (Volume III of this Trilogy)
2. Participating in the Sacrament of Reconciliation (Chapter 7 of this volume)

Since spiritual conversion should ideally precede moral conversion to fill the latter with the grace and power of the Holy Spirit and the teaching of Christ, we will first examine how the sacraments and liturgy facilitate spiritual conversion (in this chapter), then how the interior gifts of the Mystical Body and contemplative prayer facilitate spiritual conversion (Chapter 3), and finally how spiritual conversion strengthens and deepens moral conversion (Chapters 4–7).

I. The Holy Eucharist and the Mass

The first and most important habit for deepening our spiritual conversion is participation in the Eucharistic liturgy and reception of the Real Presence of the Lord at Communion. The Eucharist connects us directly with the heart of Christ and galvanizes five special graces within our souls (see below, Section I.C). The more we receive the Holy Eucharist with prayerful attentiveness, the more manifest and powerful these gifts become in our interior lives. As implied above, being intimately connected with the heart of Christ and experiencing these five spiritual gifts builds a strong foundation for moral freedom. The closer we are to Christ in our hearts and the greater our sense of divine peace, guidance, and community, the more cognizant we will be of Christ's loving presence, and the more confident we will be in His desire to forgive, heal, and save us. This strong interior grace is what enables us to detach from fear, anxiety, and reliance on our own power and resources, which frees us to abandon ourselves to His care and to pursue His teaching and path to salvation. Jesus makes this promise explicit in the Gospel of John:

> He who eats my flesh and drinks my blood has eternal life, and I will raise him up at the last day. For my flesh is food indeed, and my blood is drink indeed. He who eats my flesh and drinks my blood abides in me, and I in him. As the living Father sent me, and I live because of the Father, so he who eats me will live because of me. (6:54–57)

Even though it is difficult to see or feel the graces at the time we receive the Eucharist, they are evident when we look back on our lives over the long term. This miracle of connection to and transformation in the heart of Christ through the Holy Eucharist is available to anyone who receives the Eucharist, confidently believing that it is really the crucified and risen body of Christ. Much of the grace of this sacrament occurs simply from receiving it sincerely in faith. Yet, it must also be stressed that *conscientious* and *reverent* reception (involving our intentionality) enhances the efficacy of the Eucharist's power of peace and transformation through the heart of Christ.

Daily reception of the Holy Eucharist builds a very strong foundation for moral freedom, but as we shall see in Part II, it must be accompanied by a concerted effort to apply this deeper connection with the heart of Christ to moral conversion.

In order to explain the power and love intrinsic to this great sacrament—the Lord's gift of His whole self—we will first need to explain what Jesus intended at the Last Supper and why it points to His Real Presence in the Eucharist (Section I.A). We will then proceed to look at the sacred Eucharistic liturgy (the Mass) that developed around the ritual reliving of Jesus' Last Supper (Section I.B). After this we will discuss five specific graces of the Holy Eucharist integral to our spiritual and moral conversion (Section I.C).We will then conclude with some recommendations for Eucharistic devotion that can help to catalyze and deepen our interior life (Section I.D).

A. Jesus' Intention in Instituting the Holy Eucharist

In Volume III (Chapter 3) of the Quartet, I gave a detailed explanation of Jesus' intention in establishing the Eucharistic gift of His Body and Blood at the Last Supper. I will give a brief review of that explanation here, but readers seeking a deeper understanding should return to that volume. As noted there, Jesus placed Himself at the center of a ritual self-sacrificial act, separating His Body (given before the supper) and His Blood (given after the supper), precisely as would be done with a sacrificial animal offered for the forgiveness of sins. His intention is not only to give us His Body and Blood, but also His whole self—crucified and risen in an act of unconditional love that redeems our sins, heals and transforms our hearts, and leads us to eternal life with Him.

If we are to enter into this celebration of unconditional love more fully, we will first want to understand His Eucharistic words. When He said, "This is my body which is given for you" (Lk 22:19; see 1 Cor 11:24), the Greek word used to translate His Hebrew (*zeh baśari*) or Aramaic (*den bisri*) was *sōma* instead of *sarx*. *Sarx* means "flesh" and would certainly refer to Jesus' *corporeal* body given on the Cross, while *sōma* is much broader and refers to the *whole* person (mind, soul, and will, as well as corporeal body). Thus, *sōma* is much like the word "body" in "everybody" or "somebody" in English. It might, therefore, be roughly translated as "person" or "self". If we substitute the word "self" for "body" in the Eucharistic words, we obtain "This is myself which is given for you." This is remarkably close to Jesus' definition of love ("gift of self") given in the Gospel of John—"greater love has no man than this, that a man lay down his life for his friends" (Jn 15:13). Thus, in the Eucharist, Jesus is not only giving us His whole self—that is, His whole person; He is also giving us His love, indeed, His *unconditional* love—that is, a love that cannot be exceeded.

This unconditional love is confirmed by the gift of His blood (which, according to Jewish custom, is separated from the body of the sacrificial offering). When Jesus offered His Blood separately from His Body, He showed Himself to be an intentional self-sacrifice that He interpreted to be an offering of unconditional love.

Blood (the principle of life for the Israelites) was the vehicle through which atonement occurred in sin or guilt offerings. Jesus' reference to His sacrificial blood would almost inevitably be seen as the blood of a sin offering—with the notable exception that the sin offering is no longer an animal, but rather, Jesus Himself, the Beloved One of Abba. Jesus humbled Himself (taking the place of an animal—a sacrificial sin offering) as the Beloved One of the Father, to take away the sin of the world forever.

Jesus goes beyond this by associating Himself with the Paschal Lamb. His use of blood within the context of the Passover supper shows that He also intended to take the place of the Passover lamb. He loved us so much that He desired to become the new Passover sacrifice, replacing an unblemished lamb with His own divine presence.

Recall that the blood of the Passover lamb (put on the doorposts of every Israelite household) was the instrument through which the Israelite people were protected from death (the angel of death passing over those houses), which enabled them to move out of slavery in Egypt to freedom in the Promised Land. When Jesus (the Son of God) took the place of a sacrificial lamb, He transformed a merely temporal and conditional freedom (given through the Passover ritual) into a *trans*temporal freedom from slavery to sin and death, which is the entryway into an eternal life of unconditional love. Thus, He made His self-sacrifice the new vehicle for protection from death itself (for all eternity) by outshining sin and darkness with His unconditionally loving eternal light.

There is yet a third dimension of Jesus' use of blood that He explicitly states as "the blood of the covenant". A covenant was a solemn promise that bound parties to an unbreakable agreement. When Jesus associates His blood with the covenant, He is *guaranteeing* the covenant with His life (because blood is the principle of life). When He sheds His blood on the Cross (the following day), He elevates His guarantee from the status of word-based to action-based. By shedding His blood, He has guaranteed His covenant absolutely—there can be no higher proof of the guarantee.

So what is this covenant or contract about? It is a guarantee of His unconditional love (by giving us His whole self), a guarantee of the forgiveness of our sins (by making Himself a sin offering), a guarantee of freedom from darkness, emptiness, and slavery to sin and evil (by taking the place of the Pascal lamb), and a guarantee of eternal life (by giving us the blood of the New Covenant).

How do we know that Jesus intended to give us His *real* Body and Blood—His *real* crucified and risen self—rather than a merely symbolic presence in the bread and wine? First, there are the obvious implications of John's Eucharistic discourse (6:22–59). Consider the following:

> I am the bread of life. Your fathers ate the manna in the wilderness, and they died. This is the bread which comes down from heaven, that a man may eat of it and not die. I am the living bread which came down from heaven; if any one eats of this bread, he will live forever; *and the bread which I shall give for the life of the world is my flesh....* Truly, truly, I say to you, unless you eat the flesh of the Son of man and drink his blood, you have no life in you; he who eats my flesh and drinks my blood has eternal life, and I will raise him up at the last day. For my flesh is food indeed, and my blood is drink indeed. He who eats my flesh and drinks my blood abides in me, and I in him. (Jn 6:48–51, 53–56; italics added)

Second, Jesus' action at the Last Supper is prophetic—that is, it reaches into the future toward its fulfillment, and in accordance with Jesus' intention, brings the future fulfillment into the present. Recall from Volume III (Chapter 3) of the Quartet that the first-century Jewish view of time is quite different from our physical view of time. While *we* view time as physical, objectively determinant and measurable, first-century Judaism viewed it as sacred, malleable, and collapsible, particularly with respect to prophetic utterances about the future and ritual reenactments of past events.[3]

---

[3] See Volume III, Chapter 3, Section IV.A–C. There are several references to historical studies justifying this view of "malleable and collapsible sacred time" in both Jewish culture and other ancient cultures. For studies concerned with Jewish culture, see Johannes Betz,

With respect to prophetic utterances, the prophetic word was understood to move into the future, collapsing the time between the prophetic utterance and its future fulfillment. Thus, when Jesus says, "Take, eat; this is my body" (Mt 26:26; see Mk 14:22; Lk 22:19; 1 Cor 11:23–24), He means it *is* really His Body *right now* though it is to be given on the Cross in the future. He intends through His prophetic word and action to bring His future sacrificed Body into the bread He is giving to His disciples in the present. The same holds true for the blood. When He says, "This is my blood of the covenant" (Mt 26:28; Mk 14:24; see Lk 22:20; 1 Cor 11:25), He intends to collapse the future Blood shed on the Cross into the cup of wine given to His disciples. In sum, when Jesus uttered His prophetic words at the table, He made present His *real* future Body and Blood sacrificed in love for mankind on the Cross. For Him, the separation of time was transcended and overcome by His divine power—and therefore the reality of His future body sacrificed on the Cross was just as real in the present moment as it would be in the future.

It is important to note here that first-century Judaism did not have a view of a merely symbolic (abstract) prophetic utterance. Beyond the fact that Judaism did not make a strict separation between mind and body, there is no precedent for reducing a prophetic utterance to merely symbolic (nonreal) significance. In view of this, we should interpret Jesus' words as He very probably meant them—that the bread was His real crucified Body, and that the wine was His real blood poured out for us on the Cross.

Jesus did not expect the bread to turn into the appearance of His flesh—or the wine to turn into the appearance of His blood. Though these appearances are very important to our scientific mindset, they were seen only as incidental by the first-century Jewish mindset that

"Eucharist", in *Sacramentum Mundi*, ed. Karl Rahner (London: Burns & Oates, 1968), 2:260–61. See also Joachim Jeremias, *The Eucharistic Words of Jesus* (London: SCM Press, 1966), pp. 223–24.

For an explanation of the ancient Jewish view of the collapse of time in the reenactment of the Passover, see Gerhard von Rad, *Old Testament Theology*, vol. 2, *The Theology of Israel's Prophetic Traditions* (London: Westminster John Knox Press, 1965), pp. 104–8. For studies concerned with "collapsible sacred time" in other ancient cultures, see Mircea Eliade, *The Sacred and the Profane: The Nature of Religion* (New York: Harcourt Brace Jovanovich, 1987), pp. 40–45. See also Mircea Eliade, *The Myth of the Eternal Return: Or Cosmos and History* (Princeton, N.J.: Princeton University Press, 1971), the entire volume.

saw the bread as the medium through which the future salvific event is present—really present—irrespective of what it looked like to them. This is why John's Eucharistic discourse can be so explicit—"and the bread which I shall give for the life of the world *is* my flesh" (6:51; italics added).

It might be objected that "time really doesn't work in the way Jesus expected—scientific explanation implies that time does not collapse with prophetic utterances so that the future can become present." While it is true that *physical* time does not work the same way as sacred time, sacred time works because God wills it to be so. If God is beyond all time (and that time exists through the mind of God), then God can do anything He wants—He can bring a future event into the present (as Jesus expects He will in His prophetic utterance), and He can bring the reality of a past event into the future, which is what Jesus expects He will do when He commands His disciples to "Do this in remembrance of me" (Lk 22:19; 1 Cor 11:24).

So what did Jesus mean by His command to the apostles, "Do this in remembrance [memory] of me"? In Volume III (Chapter 3) of the Quartet, we discussed the notion of memory in Jewish culture. We will briefly review it here because of its importance in the development of the Mass and to correct misunderstandings of it that have occurred throughout the centuries. Readers interested in the scholarly studies justifying the following synopsis should again consult the previously mentioned references to Johannes Betz, Joachim Jeremias, Gerhard von Rad, and Mircea Eliade cited above.[4]

As noted above, "memory" does not mean "calling to mind"—a merely cognitive recollection. It means a ritualistic reliving of the salvific event that brings the *reality* of God's grace and power into the present in the same way it occurred in the past. Recall that first-century Judaism did not make a separation between mind and body (a Greek distinction). Thus, a ritualistic reliving was a representation of a *real*—not merely an abstract—event in which God's real saving grace and power are present.

Recall further that first-century Judaism shared with other contemporary cultures the view of sacred time in which the reliving or reenactment of a sacred event causes time between the past event and

---

[4] See references in the previous note.

the present to collapse.[5] Thus, the reenactment brings the grace and power of the past event into the present moment. So when Jesus said, "Do this in remembrance [memory] of me," He meant that the apostles (and their followers) should engage in a ritual reenactment of His Eucharistic words (which would make His real Body and Blood—His whole Person—really present in the bread and wine). Thus, when a priest reenacts Jesus' words and actions at the Last Supper, the time between the Last Supper and the present reenactment collapses. This reenactment makes His Body and Blood present to every generation until the end of time.

Johannes Betz summarizes the positions of Eliade, Jeremias, and von Rad, as follows:

> *Anamnesis* [remembrance] in the biblical sense means not only the subjective representation of something in the consciousness and as an act of the remembering mind. It is also the objective effectiveness and presence of one reality in another, especially the effectiveness and presence of the salvific actions of God, in the liturgical worship. Even in the Old Testament, the liturgy is the privileged medium in which the covenant attains *actuality*. The meaning of the logion ["Do this in remembrance of me"] may perhaps be paraphrased as follows: "do this (what I have done) in order *to bring about my presence*, to make really present the salvation wrought in me."[6]

In sum, the reality of Jesus' crucified Body and Blood in the bread and wine is a result of a double collapse of time that God effects through prophetic utterance and ritualistic reenactment:

- First collapse of time: Jesus' prophetic utterance brings His real crucified Body and Blood (in the future) into the present bread and wine in the ritual during the Passover supper.
- Second collapse of time: Future priests collapse the time between the Last Supper (in which Jesus' Body and Blood are really present in the bread and wine He offered to His disciples) into the present moment through the Consecration at Mass, the ritual reenactment of Jesus' Eucharistic words.

[5] See the references to Betz, Jeremias, von Rad, and Eliade cited above.
[6] Betz, "Eucharist", p. 260 (italics added).

It may be difficult for us in the present day to conceive of the Eucharistic gift (Jesus' real Body and Blood) being made present through a double collapse of time by prophetic utterance and ritual reenactment. However, this difficulty can be mitigated by refusing to absolutize the physical notion of time, effectively precluding Jesus' sacred view of time. Jesus' collapsible view of time is metaphysically justifiable in view of the fact that time must exist within the unrestricted mind of God—allowing Him to abrogate temporal separation however He wishes.[7] Why wouldn't sacred time be as real—if not more real—than physical time, if God is in control of time? It should be noted that this interpretation of collapsible time is acknowledged by both Catholics (e.g., Johannes Betz) and Protestants (e.g., Joachim Jeremias and Gerhard von Rad).[8]

B. The Sacred Eucharistic Liturgy (the Mass)

As can be seen from the above, reception of the Holy Eucharist is intensely individual, intimate, and transformative, as well as intensely communal (in the Mystical Body of Christ—see below, Section I.C). This double dimension of individual and communal grace (referred to as "Holy *Communion*") is also reflected in the sacred liturgy (the Mass). Since the apostolic period, the celebration and reception of the Holy Eucharist was not limited to the reenactment of the Last Supper and the reception of Communion—though this certainly lay at its center. It was a communal liturgy that incorporated a rite of preparation and a Eucharistic (thanksgiving) prayer into this central rite.[9] At the

---

[7] For the requirement that time exists through a transcendent mentative state, see Henri Bergson, *Duration in Simultaneity: Bergson and the Einsteinian Universe*, trans. Leon Jacobson (Clinamen Press, 1991). See also Robert Spitzer, *New Proofs for the Existence of God: Contributions of Contemporary Physics and Philosophy* (Grand Rapids, Mich.: Eerdmans, 2010), pp. 183–97. See also Robert Spitzer, "Definitions of Real Time and Ultimate Reality", *Journal of Ultimate Reality and Meaning: Interdisciplinary Studies in the Philosophy of Understanding* 23, no. 3 (September 2000): 260–76.

[8] See the above citations.

[9] Josef Jungmann, *The Mass: An Historical, Theological, and Pastoral Survey* (St. Paul, Minn.: North Central Publishing, 2006), p. 20. I summarize Jungmann's account of the development of the Mass in Robert Spitzer, *Credible Catholic Big Book*, Volume 9, *The Sacraments, Part 1—The Sacred Eucharistic Liturgy* (Magis Center, 2017), CredibleCatholic.com, Chapters 2–4, https://www.crediblecatholic.com/pdf/M9/BB9.pdf#P1V9.

end of the first century and in the early second century, the liturgy was expanded again to incorporate a penitential rite and an enhanced Eucharistic prayer. There are several historical sources of this progression, beginning with the *Didache*.[10]

1. A Brief History of the Development of the Mass

The *Didache* (*The Teaching of the Twelve Apostles*)—an early work (written toward the end of the first century, ca. A.D. 90)—is the first complete catechism of the Catholic Church. It contains a wealth of information about Church rituals, authority, ethical norms, disciplinary practices (e.g., fasting), and Church organization. It contains two full, early Eucharistic prayers, an identification of the Eucharist with sacrifice, and a specification of those who were appointed to celebrate the reenactment of the Last Supper.[11]

With respect to the identification of the Eucharistic (thanksgiving) commemoration with sacrifice, the *Didache* notes:

> But every Lord's day gather yourselves together, and break bread, and give thanksgiving after having confessed your transgressions, that your *sacrifice* may be pure.[12]

The *Didache* not only uses the word "sacrifice" to describe the commemoration; it tells how important this interpretation of the commemoration was—for it required the early Christians to insert a penitential rite (a confession of sins) to ensure that the celebration of the sacrifice by the congregation was pure—not defiled—in conformity with the pure sacrifice of Malachi (see Mal 1:11, 14).[13]

The *Didache* also tells us *who* was celebrating the Eucharistic commemoration in the earliest times—apostles and prophets.[14] The

---

[10] For an expanded history of the development of the Mass of the Roman Rite, see Spitzer, *Credible Catholic Big Book*, Volume 9, *The Sacred Eucharistic Liturgy*, Chapters 1–4, https://www.crediblecatholic.com/pdf/M9/BB9.pdf#P1V9.

[11] For a digital English translation, see *Didache*, trans. M.B. Riddle, from *Ante-Nicene Fathers*, vol. 7, ed. Alexander Roberts, James Donaldson, and A. Cleveland Coxe (Buffalo, N.Y.: Christian Literature Publishing, 1886); revised and edited for New Advent (website) by Kevin Knight, 2020, http://www.newadvent.org/fathers/0714.htm.

[12] *Didache* 14 (italics added).

[13] Ibid.

[14] See *Didache* 10: "But permit the prophets to make Thanksgiving as much as they desire."

twelve apostles were given authority by Jesus to preside over the Eucharistic commemoration. But why does the *Didache* mention prophets? In pre-Christian Israel, the prophets were not limited to foretelling the future; they were appointed by Yahweh to speak on His behalf (Ex 7:1–2). Sometimes, this involved foretelling future events if Israel did not obey Yahweh's commands; sometimes, it involved initiating a direction of the future, and still other times it involved speaking on behalf of Yahweh. This last charism of Old Testament prophets was taken up by the early Church, in which prophets were appointed by the apostles through the laying on of hands. Prophets were designated as those having a charism of the Holy Spirit to speak for God, delivering messages and teachings for the good of the Church. Inasmuch as Jesus is the Son of God,[15] the early Church held that prophets had the charism to speak on behalf of Him as well, particularly in reenacting His Eucharistic words (see above, Section I.A). In Paul's ranking in 1 Corinthians 12, they are listed as second in authority, immediately after the apostles (see 1 Cor 12:28). Given their charism to speak in place of God, they were naturally thought to have the charism to speak the words of commemoration on behalf of Christ (along with the apostles). Thus, they were viewed as acting *in the place of Christ* in the reenactment of Christ's self-sacrificial words.

As noted above, the *Didache* indicates that in missionary territories, itinerant apostles *and prophets* celebrated the Eucharistic commemoration.[16] However, as churches became more stable, they had their own local authority structure that replaced itinerant apostles and prophets.[17] These local authorities having the power of apostles and prophets—by ordination—were called *episcopoi* (overseers) and *presbyteroi* (elders).

---

[15] See Volume III of the Quartet (Chapter 6), which is dedicated to elucidating the evidence used by the early Church to ground her belief in Jesus' proclamation to be the exclusive Son of the Father (see especially the Q logion in Mt 11:26–27 and Lk 10:21–22). This evidence includes not only Jesus' preaching, but also His Resurrection in glory, gift of the Holy Spirit, His miracles by His own authority, and the power of His name after the Resurrection (see Chapters 4–6 of Volume III of the Quartet).

[16] In *Didache* 11, a set of rules is given to distinguish true apostles and prophets from false apostles and prophets, with the implication being that there were itinerant apostles and prophets who had to be tested before they would be allowed to celebrate the Eucharist and instruct the faithful.

[17] See Jungmann, *Mass*, p. 20.

Later, *episcopoi* were given the role and function of bishops and *presbyteroi* the role and function of priests.[18]

The transition from *presbyteroi* to priests has created confusion, because there is no clear mention of a ministerial priesthood in the New Testament. Though there is reference to the priesthood of Jesus Christ (Heb 7) and the royal priesthood of the faithful (1 Pet 2:9), there is no clear expression of priesthood with respect to Christian ministry. Why didn't the early Church clearly associate prophets and presbyters with "priests" who were designated as "offerors of sacrifice" in the Old Testament? It would seem to have been appropriate since Jesus[19] (and His followers[20]) clearly associated the Eucharist with His self-sacrifice, and designated the authority to celebrate that Eucharistic sacrifice to the apostles and prophets, who were later called *presbyteroi*. The basic reason is that the early Church did not want to confuse the priesthood of Jesus with the Jewish priesthood (see below, Section II.E). Around A.D. 180, this confusion was no longer a major issue in the Church, and the terms "priest" and "priesthood" were used by the Church Fathers, such as Saint Irenaeus (A.D. 180)[21] and Origen. Writing in about A.D. 232–235, Origen noted:

> So, too, the apostles, and those who have become like apostles, being priests according to the Great High Priest and having received knowledge of the service of God, know under the Spirit's teaching for which sins, and when, and how they ought to offer sacrifices, and recognize for which they ought not to do so.[22]

We may now return to the development of the Mass. In about A.D. 150, Justin Martyr indicates that the early Church also incorporated

---

[18] Ibid.

[19] See Section I.A, above.

[20] See *Didache* 14, as explained above in this section.

[21] Saint Irenaeus states that "all the apostles of the Lord are priests, who do inherit here neither lands nor houses, but serve God and the altar continually" (*Against Heresies* 4, 8, 3).

[22] Saint Justin Martyr, *First Apology* and *Second Apology*; available at New Advent's website at https://www.newadvent.org/fathers/0126.htm and http://www.newadvent.org/fathers /0127.htm, respectively (trans. Marcus Dods and George Reith, from *Ante-Nicene Fathers*, vol. 1, Alexander Roberts, James Donaldson, and A. Cleveland Coxe, eds. (Buffalo, N.Y.: Christian Literature Publishing, 1885); revised and edited for New Advent (website) by Kevin Knight, 2020.

a Scripture service—in imitation of synagogue custom—before the Eucharistic prayers.[23] Old Testament passages (including Psalms) were an essential part of the Scripture service, and as the Christian canon became better known and disseminated, New Testament Scriptures were incorporated as well.[24]

After the time of Justin Martyr, the Church added other prayers and rites to the early central rite discussed above. These additions (particularly expansions of the Eucharistic prayers) are discussed in multiple sources throughout the centuries, most notably:

- Saint Irenaeus (*Against Heresies*), A.D. 180
- Tertullianus (*De Oratione*), A.D. 190
- Origen (*On Prayer*), A.D. 235
- The Council of Nicaea, A.D. 325
- The Canons of Hippolytus (anonymous; detailed liturgical instructions), A.D. 336
- Apostolic Constitutions (anonymous; detailed liturgical instructions), A.D. 375
- The Council of Constantinople, A.D. 381
- The Council of Chalcedon, A.D. 451
- The Fourth Lateran Council (definition of transubstantiation), A.D. 1215
- The Council of Trent (Tridentine Mass), A.D. 1570
- Second Vatican Council (Constitution on the Sacred Liturgy; contemporary Mass), 1963

2. Prayerfully Entering into Holy Mass

Today, the Holy Mass weaves together ten "symphonic" movements around the central rite of the reenactment of Jesus' Eucharistic words and the reception of the Lord's Body and Blood:

1. The *Introductory Rites*, which generally begin with a procession and processional hymn, the sign of the cross, and an introduction from the priest, inviting the congregants into the Penitential Rite

[23] See Jungmann, *Mass*, p. 156.
[24] Ibid.

2. The *Penitential Rite*, which is meant to bring the Lord's for-giveness and reconciliation to the congregation before enter-ing into the celebration of the Eucharist. It recites the ancient Greek formula "*Kyrie, eleison* (Lord, have mercy), *Christi, eleison* (Christ, have mercy), *Kyrie, eleison* (Lord, have mercy)." It then concludes with a virtual rite of absolution—that was a real rite of absolution prior to high scholasticism[25]—"May Almighty God have mercy on us, forgive us our sins, and bring us to everlasting life."

3. The *Gloria*, a hymn to the Trinity with special emphasis on the redeeming glory of Christ that is generally sung and is meant to convey majesty, joy, and praise for the salvation brought through the love of the Trinity, particularly Christ, the incarnate Savior

4. The *Liturgy of the Word*, which generally proclaims passages from the Old Testament, the Psalms, the New Testament Epistles, and the Gospels so that congregants might celebrate God's work in salvation history and embrace the Lord's words of hope, encouragement, and instruction. This is followed by a homily, based on the Scripture readings and aimed at edifica-tion and instruction—mostly the former.

5. The *General Intercessions*, which are prayers for the Church, the world, and the congregation, bringing contemporary concerns into the offering that will take place through the Eucharistic Prayer, which is about to be offered

6. The *Offertory*, which uses the ancient Jewish formula: "Blessed are you, Lord God, of all creation", was part of Jesus' words and actions at the Last Supper. It was meant to introduce the Eucharistic Prayer that would lead to Jesus' words in the Rite of Institution. Sometimes it is solemnized by additional prayers and incensing, but it is meant to be a pathway into the Liturgy of the Eucharist.

7. The *Rite of Institution*, which is the reenactment of Jesus' Eucha-ristic words giving rise to the Real Presence of His Body and Blood on the altar (the Consecration)

8. The *Eucharistic Prayer* that surrounds the *Rite of Institution*, including the Sanctus (the "Holy, holy, holy . . .", a first-century

[25] See ibid, p. 164.

hymn combining words from Isaiah's vision and Jesus' entrance into Jerusalem), as well as praise and thanksgiving for creation and Christ's redemption and prayers for the Church, the deceased, and the congregants. It concludes with the traditional doxology: "Through Him, with Him, and in Him, O God, Almighty Father, in the unity of the Holy Spirit, all glory and honor is Yours, forever and ever. Amen."

9. The *Communion Rite*, during which the Lord's Body and Blood are shared with the congregants. This rite begins with the Lord's Prayer, proceeds to the sign of peace, and continues with the traditional prayer Agnes Dei: "Lamb of God,..." After the second elevation where the congregants address their unworthiness, the priest and extraordinary ministers of Holy Communion distribute the Lord's Body and Blood to the congregants.

10. The *Concluding Rite* and *Benediction*

Recognizing that many readers select a liturgy that best suits their families, and that family participants can present a myriad of distractions, and recognizing that some priests may be less interesting homilists or less prayerful celebrants and that some congregants may have experienced or are about to experience incredible stresses in their lives, the Holy Mass still provides a rich variety of prayers, music, Scripture readings, and above all, the very Body and Blood of Christ, which will allow even the most distracted congregant to enter, at least superficially, into prayerful relationship with the Lord. Sometimes, the Penitential Rite or the reception of Holy Communion can break through the fog of stress, anxiety, and distraction, bringing peace, reconciliation, and hope. This breakthrough makes participation in Sunday Mass worthwhile—not only for the practical benefit of restoring calm and hope, but also for reconnecting the congregant with the Lord in ways that will not become apparent until later in the week, or in the long term. Those who drift away from the Mass for superficial reasons (e.g., boring homilies or "the same old prayers") do themselves a terrible disservice by disconnecting themselves from an immense source of peace, reconciliation, hope, and relationship with the Lord. I would ask any reader who is on the brink of giving in to apathy to reconsider any such move, to trust in the Lord's promise to bring gifts of peace, reconciliation, transformation, and consolation through His Body and Blood, and to resist the false teachings of the current culture that "if you don't get a benefit now, it doesn't matter." There is a benefit even if we can't feel it, a benefit perhaps throughout the week, and throughout our lives.

I once had a student at Georgetown University who indicated that he no longer found the Mass interesting because homilies had limited intellectual content and the prayers seemed quite repetitive. I asked if he saw anything at all in the Mass that might be beneficial to him or the people around him. He obviously had not thought about this question because he looked somewhat startled and at a loss for words. I tried to give him a quick course on how spiritual consolation works—that it can be quite subtle at first, that its effects are frequently not felt, but manifest themselves in our psychic outlook and the quality of our actions. I also emphasized that spiritual consolations (e.g., peace, hope, reconciliation, and relationship with God) had a cumulative effect—that is, they increase over the course of time, over the course of faithfully participating in many Masses. He responded that this explanation seemed ethereal, to which I responded that the only way he could verify that this ethereal explanation was true is if he trusted the Lord and me, and put it into practice. I assured him that if he tried it, he would discover that my ethereal response was far more real than the tangible sports program on television that he was substituting for the Mass.

He asked if there was some way of enhancing his participation in the Mass, to which I responded that the Mass has the above ten movements, and if he opened himself to each of those movements as they were occurring—that is, if he reflectively thought about what was going on in those movements (and the effects that they had on two millennia of saints and ordinary congregants)—he would "get" far more out of the Mass. I would recommend this to every reader. Allow me to explain.

As the Mass begins, prepare yourself to enter into the Penitential Rite, considering sins of the past week or areas in which you need reconciliation and healing—then as you recite the words "Lord have mercy, Christ have mercy ..." and hear the words of virtual absolution, "May Almighty God have mercy on us, forgive us our sins, and bring us to everlasting life," you will receive that reconciliation more profoundly, taking it with you into the rest of the Mass and into the rest of the week.

Similarly, when you hear the cantor sing, "Glory to God in the highest and peace to His people on earth ...," enter into the Spirit of giving praise to the Father for creation, including the creation of your soul; to the Son of God for His redemption, including your redemption unto eternal life. There is no better way of loving the Lord who has loved you than to express thanks and praise for that love in the beautiful words provided by this hymn.

Again, prepare yourself for the Liturgy of the Word. Try to shake off the stresses and distractions of the week and try to understand the passages of Scripture being proclaimed. There is something truly marvelous about having the Word of God read to us almost like listening to our parents reading to us our Catholic picture Bibles. We can simply relax and put ourselves on "absorb". Of course, all kinds of questions will come up about how to interpret the passage. Sometimes the priest will cover these difficult issues in his homily, but if he doesn't, let this be an occasion to study the passages in question *after* the Mass. There are all kinds of resources that can be used to obtain a deeper understanding of these passages. I would recommend a good study Bible, such as *The Catholic Study Bible*, edited by Donald Senior, which contains excellent introductions to each book and explanatory footnotes for difficult passages.[26] If you have questions about particular readings, simply go to the USCCB (United States Conference of Catholic Bishops) website and click on the readings of the day. This will give you the precise citations for the Scripture passages that you heard during Mass; then go to *The Catholic Study Bible* and look up the footnotes for those passages. There is a fairly good chance that you will find at least a partial answer to your questions. There are also several smartphone apps providing explanations and meditations on the readings of the day.[27] The more you study Scripture, the more it embeds itself in your conscious and unconscious psyche.

Preparation for the General Intercessions is quite simple: in addition to participating in the prayers read by the lector, add your special prayers of petition in your mind; for these will all be added into the prayer of the congregation by the priest when he concludes the

---

[26] Donald Senior, ed., *The Catholic Study Bible* (New York: Oxford University Press, 1990).

[27] Go to the App Store and get the free app "Catholic Daily Mass Readings", or do a Google search for "smartphone apps daily Scripture readings" and you will discover several excellent resources. Additionally, you may want to get the free app "Laudate", which will also provide the daily Mass readings and will also include the saint of the day and reflections.

rite by saying, "Grant these petitions and those unmentioned within our hearts through Jesus Christ, our Lord."

As you listen to the Offertory, recognize that you are entering into the Liturgy of the Eucharist, and position yourself within the tradition going back over two thousand years, starting with the Jewish table blessings before Jesus' Eucharistic blessing. As you proceed to the Sanctus, recognize the majesty and the glory of the angels and the heavenly chorus in Isaiah's vision (Is 6:2–3) and the crowd acclaiming Jesus' entrance into Jerusalem on a donkey: "Blessed is he who comes in the name of the Lord! Hosanna in the highest!" (Mt 21:9). This ancient hymn is a preparation and invitation to adore the Lord in the Holy Eucharist, which is about to become present in the words of the Rite of Institution (the Consecration).

Now, prepare yourself for the central rite of the Mass: the reenactment of Jesus' Eucharistic words. If possible, recall what He intended in His Eucharistic words: to give us His crucified Body, risen Body, and unconditional love. Recall also the significance of the blood, that He intended to become a sin offering for us, the Blood of the Paschal Lamb (leading to definitive liberation from evil and death), and to provide the Blood of the New Covenant, guaranteeing eternal life for those who are trying to follow God in sincerity and true repentance. As the priest raises the Host, consider that this really is Jesus' crucified and risen Body that will lead to forgiveness, freedom from evil, and eternal life (see Jn 6). If it helps, you may want to read about the Eucharistic miracle overseen by Jorge Bergoglio (now Pope Francis) in Buenos Aires in 1996. It is summarized near the end of the appendix of Volume I of this Trilogy. This Eucharistic Host was transformed into a piece of flesh from the left ventricle wall with an abundance of white blood cells still present (indicating that the tissue was taken from a living, beating heart). Moreover, there were several signs that the heart was under severe stress, seemingly from torture.[28] Try to imagine that the Host you are seeing, which is substantially changed,

---

[28] The famous cardiologist and forensic pathologist Dr. Frederick Zugibe, a member of the team assembled to examine the tissue, and unaware of where the tissue sample originated, concluded, "The analyzed material is a fragment of the heart muscle found in the wall of the left ventricle close to the valves. This muscle is responsible for the contraction of the heart. It should be borne in mind that the left cardiac ventricle pumps blood to all parts of the body. The heart muscle is in an inflammatory condition and contains a large number of white blood

is in fact the crucified and risen Body and Blood of our Lord. As the priest raises the Host, it is appropriate to adore and give thanks to the Lord of unconditional love. When we really know what is going on in the Mass, it is difficult to claim, as my student did, that it is boring. It is the unfolding and reality of the drama of salvation through the self-sacrificial love of God—nothing less.

Again, we need to prepare ourselves for the other parts of the Eucharistic Prayer: participating in the priest's proclamation of praise and thanksgiving for creation and redemption, and entering into the prayers for the Church, the deceased, and the congregants, including ourselves.

As we prepare to receive Holy Communion, we will want to pay special attention to the Our Father and the three petitions of the Agnus Dei: "Lamb of God, you take away the sins of the world, have mercy on us ... have mercy on us ... grant us peace." As you see the Body and Blood of Christ raised up again with the priest's words, "Look, this truly is the Lamb of God, who takes away the sins of the world; happy are we to be called to His supper," consider the Lord of love that you will be receiving—the Lord who will grant you mercy, peace, healing, and transformation in His own image—then meaningfully pray, "Lord, I am not worthy that you should enter under my roof, but only say the word, and my soul shall be healed."

As you return to your seats after receiving the Lord's Body and Blood, pray for the graces intrinsic to this precious sacrament (given below in Section I.C). This will bring you into an intimate and close relationship with the Lord of love, which will transform and console you after Mass, and perhaps during the Mass itself.

The special celebrations for the four liturgical seasons outside of Ordinary Time—Advent, Christmas, Lent, and Easter—can also

---

cells. This indicates that the heart was alive at the time the sample was taken. It is my contention that the heart was alive, since white blood cells die outside a living organism. They require a living organism to sustain them. Thus, their presence indicates that the heart was alive when the sample was taken. What is more, these white blood cells had penetrated the tissue, which further indicates that the heart had been under severe stress, as if the owner had been beaten severely about the chest." Quoted in Mieczyslaw Piotrowski, "Eucharistic Miracle in Buenos Aires", *Love One Another!*, 2010; the quotation and a summary of this article can be found in "Eucharistic Miracle Beheld by Pope Francis?", Aleteia.org, April 22, 2016, https://aleteia.org/2016/04/22/eucharistic-miracle-beheld-by-pope-francis/.

enhance our participation in Holy Mass. The Advent season (four weeks before Christmas) combines the sense of excited anticipation of redemption with repentance and contrition. The Christmas season (from Christmas Day to the Feast of the Baptism of the Lord) celebrates the Son of God's entrance into the world with complete humble love to redeem us. The Lenten season (from Ash Wednesday to Holy Saturday) provides opportunities beyond the liturgy to examine our conscience, seek forgiveness, improve our lives, make sacrifices, and increase in prayer and virtue. This Lenten ethos can't help but become part of our experience of Holy Mass during that season. Finally, the Easter season (fifty days following Easter Sunday, ending on Pentecost) is a season of joy celebrating Christ's victory over Satan, sin, and death, which anticipates our resurrection with Him into glory. The ethos of each special season is infused within the hymns, prayers, readings, homilies, and blessings of the liturgy, which in turn colors the liturgy with distinctive movements of the heart, affecting our prayer, personal attitudes, and relationship with the Lord.

As if this were not enough, the Church tradition weaves in a panoply of special celebrations for Sunday Mass, such as the celebration of the Trinity, the Holy Eucharist (*Corpus Christi*), the Holy Family, and the Blessed Virgin Mary. For weekday Masses, the Church integrates a panoply of feasts and memorials for the Blessed Virgin Mary, the saints, special occasions (such as the conversion of Saint Paul), and special churches (such as Saint John Lateran). The richness of the liturgical celebration is enhanced by these special lights within Church history and tradition. This complex of ten liturgical movements with the specialness of the liturgical seasons, special celebrations, and memorials of the saints blends together so masterfully that it can raise the prepared heart into the hearts of the Trinity themselves.

Even if we do not feel moved during the liturgy itself, our concerted attempts to participate in it will bear much fruit in the long term, a strengthening of confidence, peace, hope, healing, and reconciliation, as well as loving transformation leading us more surely on the path to eternal salvation. Even if the homilies are less than scintillating and the music less than symphonic, we will still derive eternal benefit, dispel the darkness that may be in our hearts, put the

Evil One to flight, and enter more resolutely on the road to salvation. We will be connected to and transformed by the Son of God, who came to be with us, to enter into us, and to love us into His eternity. We now turn to an explanation of these effects of the Holy Eucharist and the Mass.

C. Five Eucharistic Graces toward Spiritual and Moral Conversion

The Catholic Church, since the time of Jesus, made the ritual celebration of the Eucharist the center not only of its worship but of its spiritual life precisely as Jesus instructed: "Do this in remembrance of me" (Lk 22:19; 1 Cor 11:24). For centuries, Catholics have experienced the fulfillment of Jesus' promises through the reception of His Body and Blood. They have experienced a deep peace beyond themselves, a healing of their inner being reflecting Jesus' act of forgiveness, a gradual transformation of their hearts toward the heart of Christ, and a unity with others in the Mystical Body of Christ.[29] These transformative graces are sometimes incisive and powerful, and sometimes subtle and gradual. In my case, they have been mostly the latter, but over the course of time, they have become radically transformative. I interpret this to be God respecting my freedom to go along with His loving plan—at my pace. He is careful not to push me beyond where I am able to go. Slowly but surely He entices me into imitating His heart ever more deeply, which brings about peace, healing, and greater unity with other believers. For this reason the Church, and certainly I, recommend receiving the Eucharist as often as possible. For some, this might mean daily Mass and for others it might mean Sunday Mass. Whatever we can do, the Lord will honor us with His presence and grace—and in the long run, it will be transformative, leading to His loving eternity.

What did Jesus intend this total gift of Himself to bring?

1. Spiritual peace
2. Forgiveness and healing

---

[29] See Robert Spitzer, *Five Pillars of the Spiritual Life: A Practical Guide for Active People* (San Francisco: Ignatius Press, 2008), pp. 15–19.

3. Transformation in His image (heart)
4. Unity within the Mystical Body
5. Everlasting life (eternal salvation)

Let us briefly examine each.

With respect to the first gift (spiritual peace), the prayers of the Mass petition the Lord to grant us this grace along with His grace of mercy (forgiveness):

Lamb of God, you take away the sins of the world, *grant us peace.*

This association of Jesus' Body and Blood with the gift of peace is also found implicitly in the Gospel of John. During Jesus' final discourse, Jesus explains the purpose of His Passion and the gift of the Spirit that will come through it. He then tells the disciples the specific gift or fruit of His Passion, Resurrection, and the Spirit:

Peace I leave with you; my peace I give to you; not as the world gives do I give to you. Do not let your hearts be troubled, neither let them be afraid. (Jn 14:27)

I can certainly attest to this gift of peace in my own life. I can remember going to Mass with very disturbing thoughts in my mind (having received bad news, or having been criticized or irritated by someone's actions). I carried the "tape-playing" and emotional discharge associated with those things right into the Mass with me. This sometimes provoked an intensification of internal disturbance during the Mass. Yet, many have been the times when a deep calm (beyond myself) replaced that disturbance as I anticipated and received the Holy Eucharist. I have difficulty attributing this change of condition to mere self-delusion, because wishful thinking has never overcome "intense disturbance" in other circumstances in my life.

The crucified and risen Body and Blood of our Lord places us in intimate relationship with Him, which, if we allow it, brings an increased trust in the Lord—a capacity to let go of our worries by giving them to Him. This, in turn, enables us to accept the peace given to us by the Holy Spirit, even in times of abject fear and deep grief. I have experienced this many times and can assure the reader that there is no better time to pray Saint Teresa's prayer for peace than after trustingly receiving the Lord in the Holy Eucharist:

> Let nothing disturb you
> Let nothing frighten you
> All things are passing
> God never changes
> Patience obtains all things
> He who possesses God lacks nothing
> God alone suffices.[30]

With respect to the second gift (forgiveness and healing), Jesus taught that His Body and Blood was for *the forgiveness of sins* (Mt 26:28). He meant this not only in a general sense—the forgiveness of the sinfulness of people throughout the world for all time—but also in an individual sense, the forgiveness of the recipient of His Body and Blood. Jesus made Himself a sin offering for all people, and specifically for those who would participate in the reenactment of His Eucharistic meal. Therefore, it seems likely that He intended to bring about reconciliation and healing through the consumption of His Body and Blood.

The Church continues to proclaim this grace of forgiveness and healing in the Liturgy. At the minor elevation of the Host, the priest proclaims, "Behold the Lamb of God, behold Him who *takes away the sins of the world*. Blessed are those called to the supper of the Lamb." The priest here clearly associates the Host with the One who takes away the sins of the world. This is not meant in a general sense alone. It also pertains to the individuals who are to receive Holy Communion. This is evident from the priest's further proclamation, "Blessed are those called to the supper of the Lamb." Hence, this proclamation anticipates the congregation receiving the grace of Christ's forgiving love in the Holy Eucharist.

The same Communion Rite also acknowledges the *healing* power of the Holy Eucharist. After the priest proclaims the forgiving power of the Lord during the minor elevation, the congregation responds,

---

[30] Saint Teresa of Avila, "Let Nothing Disturb You", Order of Carmelites (website), 2020, http://ocarm.org/en/content/let-nothing-disturb-you.

"Lord, I am not worthy that you should enter under my roof, but only say the word, and my soul shall be *healed*." This prayer, which recounts the centurion's act of faith (Mt 8:8; Lk 7:6–7), asks the Lord to heal our souls through the grace of His Body and Blood. The above scriptural and liturgical references make clear the forgiving and healing power of the Holy Eucharist.

How does this square with Paul's admonition not to receive the Holy Eucharist unworthily? Paul is concerned about the Corinthians' conduct toward each other prior to and during the Eucharistic meal. In the early Church there was a meal between the rite of the bread-body and the rite of the wine-blood—and during this meal, some of the Corinthians were getting drunk and others would not share their lavish portions with the poor who had next to nothing for the meal (1 Cor 11:17–21). Since the Eucharistic sacrifice is a sacrament of unity, Paul believed that the conduct of the Corinthians during the meal was scandalous—and therefore that the Corinthians were receiving the Lord's Body and Blood unworthily.[31] He tells them that they must repent and act like true disciples of Jesus—refraining from drunkenness at the meal and sharing their goods with the poor.

Beyond the problem addressed by Saint Paul, the *Catechism of the Catholic Church* teaches that we should not receive Communion after we have committed a mortal sin.[32] If we have committed such a sin, we should go to the Sacrament of Reconciliation before receiving Communion. It should be noted that mortal sin requires sufficient reflection and full consent of the will (no impediments to the free use of the will). There are many such impediments that would mitigate culpability, thereby negating the occurrence of a mortal sin endangering our salvation. Impediments may be external (such as being constrained, forced, or threatened to do something against one's will) or internal (such as strong passions or feelings,[33] strong unconscious motivations, psychological disorders,[34] addictions, deeply

---

[31] See Jerome Murphy-O'Connor, "The First Letter of Paul to the Corinthians", in *The New Jerome Biblical Commentary*, ed. Raymond E. Brown, Joseph A. Fitzmyer, and Roland E. Murphy (Englewood Cliffs, N.J.: Prentice-Hall, 1990), p. 810.

[32] *CCC* 1385.

[33] According to the *Catechism of the Catholic Church*, "The promptings of feelings and passions can also diminish the voluntary and free character of the offense, as can external pressures or pathological disorders" (*CCC* 1860).

[34] Psychological disorders may include psychosis, schizophrenia, bipolar disorder, obsessive-compulsive disorder, and long-standing neuroses—among other disorders.

engrained habits, and strong situational fear, duress, and depression). Though there are many conditions required for the commission of a mortal sin, we must be aware that we have sufficient freedom to commit one; and if we really do commit such a sin without impediment to the free use of our will, we should refrain from Holy Communion until we have received absolution at the Sacrament of Reconciliation.

In view of the above, how might we say that the Holy Eucharist forgives our sins? When we receive the Holy Eucharist with sincere contrition, the Lord will forgive and heal sins that are not mortal. This would include not only venial sins, but also actions classified as grave matter, but committed without sufficient knowledge and/or full consent of the will. With respect to the latter, we may be unsure of whether sufficient knowledge and full consent of the will were present, and so it is best to plan on going to confession to obtain absolution and to ask the priest for clarification on this matter (see Chapter 7, Section II, for a further explanation of this).

Saint Ambrose (A.D. 375) in his work on the sacraments emphasizes this grace of forgiveness:

> As often as we receive [Holy Communion], we show the Lord's death; if we show his death, we show remission of sins. If, as often as blood is poured forth, it is poured for remission of sins, I ought always to receive it, that my sins may always be forgiven me. I, who am always sinning, ought always to have a remedy.[35]

This theological viewpoint has been reinforced throughout the last two thousand years and is found today in the *Catechism of the Catholic Church*:

> The body of Christ we receive in Holy Communion is "given up for us," and the blood we drink "shed for the forgiveness of sins." For this reason the Eucharist cannot unite us to Christ without at the same time cleansing us from past sins and preserving us from future sins.[36]

---

[35] Saint Ambrose, *Treatise on the Sacraments* 4, 6, 28, in *"On the Mysteries" and the Treatise on the Sacraments by an Unknown Author*, ed. J. H. Strawley and trans. T. Thompson, B.D. (New York: Macmillan, 1919), http://oll.libertyfund.org/titles/ambrose-on-the-mysteries-and-the-treatise-on-the-sacraments.

[36] CCC 1393.

Yet, the reconciling power of Christ's Body and Blood is not limited to forgiveness and cleansing of sin. It also heals souls that have been adversely affected by sin. It is as if Christ's healing power (manifest in his extensive ministry of healing) is personally present within us, helping us to overcome the habits and effects of past darkness.

The healing power of the Eucharist has been long attested by those who have benefited from it emotionally, physically, and spiritually.[37] This healing power has truly helped the sick, the depressed, and the anxious, as well as those who are recovering from addictions and those who are recovering from spiritual illness, particularly those who have been away from God, Christ, and the Church.[38] I would recommend reading the many online testimonials to this healing power.[39] The key to healing through the Holy Eucharist is our awareness of the presence and power of the Lord's Body and Blood accompanied by fervent prayer for healing.

With respect to the third gift (transformation in the Lord's image), Jesus says:

> He who eats my flesh and drinks my blood abides in me, and I in him. (Jn 6:56)

The term "abiding" (*menei/menó*) in Greek means "remaining" or "staying" or "dwelling"; "to take up one's abode"; "to live".[40] The more typical preposition to combine with *menei* would be "with", which would signify "staying with", "living with", or "abiding with". But Jesus uses a somewhat unusual preposition with *menei*— "in" ("en" in Greek). This would signify "living in" or "taking up one's abode in".[41]

The idea of one person living *in* another is the highest possible form of intimacy—far exceeding living *with* another. Jesus intended

---

[37] See, for example, John Hampsch, *The Healing Power of the Eucharist* (Welland, Ontario: Servant Book Publications, 1999).

[38] See ibid.

[39] See, for example, the many Eucharistic healings recounted in "Healing through Communion", SidRoth.org, March 1, 2006, http://sidroth.org/articles/healing-through-communion/.

[40] See *Strong's Exhaustive Concordance Online*, s.v. "3306: menó", BibleHub.com, 2020, https://biblehub.com/greek/3306.htm.

[41] See BillMounce.com, s.v. "meno", accessed July 6, 2020, https://billmounce.com/greek-dictionary/meno.

that we enter into this highest possible intimate relationship with Him by receiving Him in His Body and Blood—the Holy Eucharist. If He did not intend this, the expression "living in" would be virtually inexplicable.

Why did Jesus use this expression of highest intimacy? He wanted to signify not only the highest unitive state we could have with another, but also the *transformative effects* that come from this intimate union. For example, when we live with another person whom we respect, like, and love, it is quite typical for that person to "rub off on us". We can't help it—we assimilate not only his good characteristics, but also some of his personality attributes, his feelings, and even his mindset. If this can occur by merely living *with* another, we can only imagine what could happen when we live *in* another, and another lives *in* us. Perhaps the best way of conveying this is through the mottoes of Saint Francis de Sales and Saint John Henry Newman—*cor ad cor loquitor*—"heart speaking to heart".

When we receive the Holy Eucharist and call to mind that Jesus has entered into this most intimate relationship with us and in us, His heart will begin to affect—indeed transform—our hearts. He will not do this in a way that undermines or overpowers our freedom, but in a way that respects our freedom, seizing every opportunity He can to transform our hearts, ever so patiently, into the unconditionally loving heart He has for us. Sometimes this is so subtle that we barely notice the transition taking place within us. This happened to me.

I decided in my sophomore year of college to begin attending daily Mass because of the challenge of a friend during Lent, and additional encouragement by other friends. I was not at the same level of humility and generosity as those friends. Indeed, I had some deep-seated utilitarian, egotistical, and materialistic tendencies. Nevertheless, I felt attracted to the prospect through my faith. After about a year of attending daily Mass, my friends began to comment that I "had really changed". I told them (quite sincerely) that I had not—I was "the same old utilitarian, self-interested person". It seemed I was the only one who had not noticed the gradual but cumulative change that had occurred in my heart. I had always said that rationality could be trusted but the emotions could not. This had the unfortunate effect of delaying affective and emotional maturity. In retrospect, I attribute my discovery and re-appropriation of my heart to the gradual transformative influence of the Lord through the Holy Eucharist. I do not consider this incredible life-giving discovery to have arisen out of normal maturation (I was anything but normal)—nor do I attribute it to something desired or willed, because I was really not aware of the goodness of my heart, for I did not trust my emotions. Furthermore, I do not attribute this transformation to appropriating the emotional conditions of the people around me. Rather, I believe that the Eucharist prepared my heart for the simple exposure to the Word of God, and to the love of God manifest through others at Mass. Slowly but surely Christ's presence and love turned me toward the grace to which I could not bring myself. I received a heart, not a completed heart, but a "foundational heart" opening upon a deeper and deeper appropriation of the unconditional love of God, which is the purpose of my life.

With respect to the fourth gift of the Holy Eucharist (unity with the Mystical Body), Saint Paul taught that we are all united in the Mystical Body of Christ:

> If one member suffers, all suffer together; if one member is honored, all rejoice together. Now you are the body of Christ and individually members of it. (1 Cor 12:26–27)

Saint Paul is telling us that we share in and derive strength from the grace, love, and joy of the whole communion of saints, both past and present—and that we also share in the tribulations of the Mystical Body on earth. The more we receive the Body of Christ, the more we become unified with Him and every member of the Church and the communion of saints. As we receive the Eucharist, we become more tightly bound to the community living in and through Christ. This has a twofold effect. First, the joy, love, strength, tribulation, and challenge of the Church community affects our minds and hearts—our conscious and subconscious psyche. Second, we affect and contribute our gifts and challenges to the same community. It is like living with family members—the more time we spend with them, the more their joys, loves, and concerns and sufferings affect us, and our joys, concerns, and sufferings affect them. We can feel—or perhaps better, sense—the liturgical seasons, the sorrow and repentances of Lent, the joy and redemption of Christmas and Easter, and the joyful expectation of Advent. We become more attuned to the ways that the Spirit is working—not just in our lives, but in the lives of members of our local Church, and even in the universal Church. I have had several concrete experiences of this, but the most memorable one occurred on Christmas Eve when I was about twelve or thirteen years old.

On that Christmas, my family had just finished our "present opening" and my siblings and I were going to Mass with my mother. I felt an unusually pronounced happiness that I could not ignore, and so I told my mother, "Mom, I'm feeling very happy, but I'm not sure why." She said in reply, "Well, you probably received all the presents you wanted." For some reason, I knew that it was not material happiness (coming from possession of a gift, consumption of food, playing games, etc.), and so I told her, "Mom, I did get all the presents I wanted, but that's not what's making me *this* happy." She thought about that for a while, and then, with a great deal of hope, said, "Well, maybe you're growing up and thinking of things beyond presents. Maybe you're happy because you've grown to appreciate your family and you had a really intense experience of them this evening." I said in reply, "Uhhh, family?—Well I really love our family, but I don't think that's it." So my mother thought about it some more, and then said, as if inspired, "Well, maybe it's the joy of the whole communion of saints on this Christmastide coursing through your veins." I have no idea why she said this, or why I knew it was true, but I said, "Yep, that's why I think I'm happy."

To this day, that childlike response to my mother's deeply insightful remark seems to me to be truth. It is the truth about the communion of saints and the truth about the unifying power of the Eucharist. It is the truth about the love and joy of the whole communion of saints, past and present, coursing through our spiritual veins (see Chapter 3, Section I.B, on *Koinōnia*).

Years later, I had a flashback to that Christmas when I was sitting with my family at my sister's house on Easter. My little niece Kristen was slightly more than a year old, and she was sitting in a bouncy seat in the middle of a large dining-room table at which about twelve of us were seated. Someone told a humorous story that made everybody laugh, and Kristen (who did not understand a word of it) began to laugh as well. It occurred to me that she was sharing in the delight of everyone else that she empathetically sensed—and that her union with us was so pronounced that our laughter induced her laughter; our happiness induced hers. I flashed back to the Christmas of the "joy of the communion of saints" many years before, and thought, "Her unconscious empathy with all of us was like my unconscious empathy with the Mystical Body of Christ at Christmas." How did I have such a strong sense of unconscious empathy with the Mystical Body of Christ at such a young age? I think it was because of the Holy Eucharist—unquestionably, the Holy Eucharist.

The unifying aspect of the Holy Eucharist is not limited to the enhancement of individual believers who receive it; it is a way for each believer to participate in the universal Church—both in this world and in the Kingdom of Heaven (the communion of saints).

There can be little doubt that Jesus intended the Eucharist to be both a universal and unifying gift. The themes of "unity of believers" and "life for the world" were picked up by the early Church Fathers, where the Eucharist was considered to be the communion between the faithful and their bishop. Saint Ignatius of Antioch, for example, exhorts his followers in multiple letters to maintain unity among themselves, meeting together in the Eucharist under the bishop as their head.[42] This theme was further emphasized in later encyclicals—for example, Pope Pius XII, *Mystici Corporis Christi*,[43] Pope Paul VI, *Mysterium Fidei*,[44] and Pope John Paul II, *Ecclesia de Eucharistia*.[45] Thus, the Eucharist is the occasion to pray for the local Church community, the worldwide Church community, and the life of the world.

As noted above, the Eucharist is a remarkably beautiful and efficacious gift of *personal* transformation and life. Yet, It cannot be held to

[42] See Saint Ignatius of Antioch, *Letter to the Ephesians* 4, 2. See also Raymond Johanny, "Ignatius of Antioch", in *The Eucharist of the Early Christians*, trans. Matthew J. O'Connell (New York: Pueblo, 1978), p. 59.

[43] Pope Pius XII, *Mystici Corporis Christi* (June 29, 1943), nos. 19, 51, http://w2.vatican.va/content/pius-xii/en/encyclicals/documents/hf_p-xii_enc_29061943_mystici-corporis-christi.html.

[44] Pope Paul VI, *Mysterium Fidei* (September 3, 1965), no. 70, http://w2.vatican.va/content/paul-vi/en/encyclicals/documents/hf_p-vi_enc_03091965_mysterium.html.

[45] Pope John Paul II, *Ecclesia de Eucharistia* (April 17, 2003), http://www.vatican.va/holy_father/special_features/encyclicals/documents/hf_jp-ii_enc_20030417_ecclesia_eucharistia_en.html.

the domain of the personal. By the intention of Jesus, and therefore by Its nature (unconditional love), It reaches out to the whole world. It gives life to those in spiritual and temporal need, It unifies the Church in its life-giving nature and mission, and It moves through the Church to the rest of the world.

Thus, when we receive the Holy Eucharist, we not only pray for personal transformation; we pray for the Church, the unity of the Church, the life of the world, and the Church reaching out to the world in its spiritual and temporal need. This is why the General Intercessions (prayers of the faithful during Mass) and the intercessions in the Eucharistic Prayer specify the needs of the Church, the local community, and the world.

The fifth grace of the Eucharist (eternal salvation) is the central focus of the Eucharistic discourse in the Gospel of John. The repetition of "eternal life" shows not only the importance of this grace, but its centrality in John's Eucharistic theology:

> I am the bread of life. Your fathers ate the manna in the wilderness, and they died. This is the bread which comes down from heaven, that a man may eat of it and not die. I am the living bread which came down from heaven; if any one eats of this bread, he will live for ever; and the bread which I shall give for the life of the world is my flesh.... Truly, truly, I say to you, unless you eat the flesh of the Son of man and drink his blood, you have no life in you; he who eats my flesh and drinks my blood has eternal life, and I will raise him up at the last day. For my flesh is food indeed, and my blood is drink indeed. He who eats my flesh and drinks my blood abides in me, and I in him. As the living Father sent me, and I live because of the Father, so he who eats me will live because of me. This is the bread which came down from heaven, not such as the fathers ate and died; he who eats this bread will live for ever. (6:48–51, 53–58)

This Gospel passage summarizes Jesus' primary intention at the Last Supper—to secure the eternal salvation of all who receive His Body and Blood in faith. The words of Consecration say, "The new and *everlasting* covenant which will be poured out for you and many [all] for the forgiveness of sins." This formula very likely comes from Jesus Himself, even though the word "everlasting" is not used in either the Matthew-Mark or Luke-Paul formulas (see Mt 26:28; Mk

14:24; Lk 22:20; 1 Cor 11:25). With the words of Jeremiah in mind,[46] Jesus intended to establish an everlasting covenant that would lead to the permanent and everlasting forgiveness of sins through eternal life (resurrection) with Him and the Father. This is the reason that Jesus took the place of a sin offering (for the forgiveness of sins) and the Paschal Lamb—to liberate us from slavery to evil (see above, Section I.A). After Jesus gave His life in complete self-sacrifice (unconditional love) and rose from the dead clothed in the glory of God, the early Church had no doubt about the significance of His Body and Blood. They knew that continuous faithful reception of this gift would lead to everlasting life:

> If any one eats of this bread, he will live for ever; and the bread which I shall give for the life of the world is my flesh.... He who eats my flesh and drinks my blood has eternal life, and I will raise him up at the last day. (Jn 6:51, 54)

Jesus' strategy now becomes clear: the first four gifts of the Holy Eucharist—peace, forgiveness of sins/healing, transformation in his heart, and unity with the Church through His Mystical Body—all lead to everlasting life and love in Him with His Father. Ultimately, this gift is the reason not only for the Eucharist, but for the Mass itself, which has as its center the truth, goodness, beauty, and love of the complete self-sacrifice of Jesus leading us to eternal life.

As can be seen from Sections I.A through I.C above, there can be no greater prayer, no greater grace, no greater transformative power, and no greater path to salvation than the faithful reception of the Holy Eucharist, in which we focus intently on the Real Presence of our Lord and Savior, Jesus Christ, in His crucified, risen, and Mystical Body. This is the central act of spiritual conversion within Christianity

---

[46] The word "everlasting" very probably comes from Jeremiah because there are only two passages about the "everlasting covenant" in the Old Testament—both of which come from the book of Jeremiah—32:39–41 and 50:5. It is reasonable to assume that Jesus himself used these words of Jeremiah to express his own intention, because the early Church would not have made it up without certain knowledge of its origin in Jesus. These are the most sacred of words invoking the most precious of gifts—the Lord himself. The apostolic traditions about Jesus are not limited to what is in specific Gospel texts or the New Testament epistles, and this is probably an instance in which there is a tradition not captured by the Mark-Matthew source or the Luke-Paul source.

itself. The denial of the Real Presence of Jesus in the Eucharist under-mines not only His intention for all His followers, but also the most powerful and loving grace available to us for communion with Him (spiritual conversion), moral conversion, and the path to salvation.

D. Eucharistic Devotion

Inasmuch as the Holy Eucharist is the real crucified and risen pres-ence of our Lord, it should not be surprising to learn that the early Church Fathers encouraged prayerful devotion to the Holy Eucha-rist. When the Holy Eucharist is reserved (e.g., in a tabernacle in a Church) or presented for adoration (e.g., in a monstrance during benediction), the Real Presence of the Lord—body, mind, spirit, and divinity—flows from the tabernacle or monstrance into the entire devotional space or church. As believers gather in adoration, their faith awakens Jesus' Real Presence within their hearts, focusing them in prayer, deepening their communion with Him, inciting a sincere desire for deeper conversion, and calling them to the life of loving charity in communion with the Christian faithful. Though Jesus' pri-mary motive for instituting the Holy Eucharist was to dwell within us, and for us to dwell within Him (when we sincerely receive His Body and Blood), Eucharistic devotion can enhance this central grace and path to salvation by intensifying our prayer and devotion to His Real Presence, which we then bring back to our sincere reception of Him at Holy Mass.

Eucharistic devotion goes back to the custom of *fermentum* begin-ning in A.D. 120. A portion of the consecrated Host was put in a con-tainer and carried from one diocese to another when a new bishop was appointed—to show unity of the dioceses (and the Church) in the One Body of Christ.[47] The devotion developed and flourished in the monasteries and hermitages of both the Eastern and Western churches from the third century to the present day.[48]

---

[47] See John Hardon, S.J., *The History of Eucharistic Adoration: Development of Doctrine in the Catholic Church* (Oak Lawn, Ill.: CMJ Marian Publishers, 2003), http://www.therealpresence.org/archives/Eucharist/Eucharist_017.htm.

[48] For a history of this devotion, see Spitzer, *Credible Catholic Big Book*, Volume 12, *The Church and Spiritual Conversion*, Chapter 4, https://www.crediblecatholic.com/pdf/M12/BB12.pdf.

Saint John Chrysostom spoke of the joy, consolation, and hope that comes from reverencing the Sacrament of the Eucharist:

> When you see It [the body of Christ in the Holy Eucharist] set before you, say thou to yourself, "Because of this Body am I no longer earth and ashes, no longer a prisoner, but free: because of this I hope for heaven, and to receive the good things therein, immortal life, the portion of angels, converse with Christ; this Body, nailed and scourged, was more than death could stand against; this Body the very sun saw sacrificed, and turned aside his beams; for this both the veil was rent in that moment, and rocks were burst asunder, and all the earth was shaken. This is even that Body, the blood-stained, the pierced, and that out of which gushed the saving fountains, the one of blood, the other of water, for all the world."[49]

Saint John Chrysostom's faith in the Real Presence of Jesus in the Eucharist moved him to a state of consolation and hope by simply coming into the presence of the exposed sacrament for reverence and adoration. His experience of Christ in the sacrament led him to conviction about his liberation from slavery to sin and death, and his imminent resurrection with the Lord. This experience of Christ in the Sacrament of the Eucharist has been recounted by dozens of other saints, such as Saint Thomas Aquinas, Saint Francis de Sales, Saint Margaret Mary, Saint Claude de la Colombière, and Saint Pope John Paul II—to mention but a few.[50] Pope Paul VI clarified and enhanced this experience of consolation and inner strength coming from the reception and adoration of Christ in the Eucharist:

> Anyone who has a special devotion to the sacred Eucharist and who tries to repay Christ's infinite love for us with an eager and unselfish love of his own, will experience and fully understand—and this will bring great delight and benefit to his soul—just how precious is a life hidden with Christ in God and just how worthwhile it is to carry on a conversation with Christ, for there is nothing more consoling

---

[49] Saint John Chrysostom, "Homily 24 on First Corinthians", under "1 Corinthians 10:23–24", trans. Talbot W. Chambers, from *Nicene and Post-Nicene Fathers*, 1st series, vol. 12, ed. Philip Schaff (Buffalo, N.Y.: Christian Literature Publishing, 1889); revised and edited for New Advent (website) by Kevin Knight, 2020, http://www.newadvent.org/fathers/220124.htm.

[50] See Hardon, *History of Eucharistic Adoration*, Chapter 2.

here on earth, nothing more efficacious for progress along the paths of holiness.[51]

When we approach the exposed Eucharist on the altar (or in the tabernacle), we will want to recall the words of the Council of Trent identifying Jesus in the Eucharistic species with the historical Jesus in Galilee and on the Cross,

who, finally, as the Scriptures testify, was adored by the apostles in Galilee.[52]

When we go to a holy hour for adoration in benediction, we will want to look upon the Host in the same way that the apostles looked upon the historical Jesus in His exorcisms, miracles, raising the dead, teaching, forgiveness of sinners, Passion, death, and Resurrection. When we do this—and open ourselves to the presence of the One whom the apostles saw—His consolation, peace, warmth, and love begin to fill the room, and can sometimes be quite palpable.

In addition to the consolation and spiritual growth coming from the adoration of the Lord in the Eucharist (looking upon Him as the apostles did in Galilee), Pope Paul VI promises several specific additional graces leading to spiritual growth and conviction:

For it is not just while the Sacrifice is being offered and the Sacrament is being confected, but also *after* the Sacrifice has been offered and the Sacrament confected—while the Eucharist is reserved in churches or oratories—that Christ is truly Emmanuel, which means "God with us." For He is in the midst of us day and night; He dwells in us with the fullness of grace and of truth. He raises the level of morals, fosters virtue, comforts the sorrowful, strengthens the weak and stirs up all those who draw near to Him to imitate Him, so that they may learn from His example to be meek and humble of heart, and to seek not their own interests but those of God.[53]

[51] *Mysterium Fidei*, no. 67.

[52] Council of Trent, Thirteenth Session, "Decree concerning the Most Holy Sacrament of the Eucharist", Chapter 5, "The Worship and Veneration to Be Shown to This Most Holy Sacrament", EWTN.com, 2020, https://www.ewtn.com/catholicism/library/thirteenth-session-of-the-council-of-trent-1479.

[53] *Mysterium Fidei*, no. 67 (italics added).

The pope here summarizes many works of previous monks, saints, and popes about the graces intrinsic to reverencing or adoring the Eucharist. The first grace, raising the level of morals, refers to a kind of heightening of both consciousness and conscience about the moral life to which we aspire. The recognized presence of the Lord, and reverence for Him, enables Him to reach into the deepest recesses of our hearts to make a high moral life attractive—and a lower moral life frightening and repulsive. As we spend time with the Lord in the Eucharist, asking to be transformed by Him, we can feel a power beyond ourselves drawing our desire to be like Him and to shun a lifestyle leading us away from Him.

The pope mentions a second grace—the strengthening of virtue— which is similar to the first grace, raising the level of morals. Once again, our abiding and conversing with Christ in the Holy Eucharist enables Him to draw our desires closer to His desires (our hearts closer to His heart). This has the effect not only of *enlightening* us about a higher moral life, but also of strengthening our resolve to imitate him in interior attitudes and virtues. We don't have to be like stoics—willing ourselves to greater virtue. We can simply converse with Him and enjoy His presence, which enables *His* heart to "rub off" on ours. When we spend time with a friend—simply conversing with him and enjoying him—he tends to "rub off" on us, and so it is with our companionship with Jesus in the Eucharist. As we identify more and more with the heart of Jesus, we will also grow in the desire for His virtues—temperance (contra gluttony); chastity (contra lust); zeal for souls (contra sloth); patience and forgiveness (contra anger); generosity (contra greed); gratitude (contra envy); humility (contra pride and vanity). All of these virtues serve the key virtue of love (*caritas* in Latin; *agapē* in Greek)—the highest virtue for Jesus.[54] The main point to remember is that the more we spend time with Jesus in the Eucharist, the more we become transformed in His heart and virtue.

Pope Paul VI goes on to speak of two additional graces coming from Eucharistic reverence and adoration—comfort for the sorrowful and strength for the weak. It may at first seem strange to think that spending time before the Lord in the Holy Eucharist can bring comfort or strength, but this, in fact, has been the experience of thousands

---

[54] For a full explanation of this, see Chapter 4, Section II, of this volume.

of people throughout the world. When we feel overwhelmed, and at the point where we cannot control the negative events in our lives, we can be sure that prayer will help. Some of these prayers are mentioned in Appendix II of this volume: "Lord, snatch victory from the jaws of defeat." "I give up, Lord. You take care of it." "Lord, make optimal good come out of this suffering." If we say these prayers in faith, we *will* receive the grace of calm and peace, and as will be explained, this enables us to be rational—to think about "back-up" plans, who we should consult, how to do damage control, etc. It is really quite amazing how grace coming from our brief spontaneous prayers can induce this kind of calm and rational reflection.

Yet, if we want even deeper peace, peace that helps us see how our sufferings can purify our hearts, lead us to new opportunities, and ultimately usher us into our salvation, I would recommend prayer before the Holy Eucharist—either in the tabernacle or, if possible, before the exposed Eucharist at a holy hour or adoration. As noted earlier, the presence of Jesus in the Holy Eucharist—the same Jesus that the apostles adored in Galilee—not only sanctifies a church sanctuary, but also fills it with His warmth, peace, and consoling presence. If the Eucharist is exposed and we gaze upon Him with faith, the effects of consolation and strength are even more palpable than prayer alone. The spiritual and heart-felt demeanor of Christ emanating from the Holy Eucharist brings deep calm, hope, and consolation, enabling us to increase our trust and seek the opportunities of suffering to do His will.

II. The Sacramental Life

The six other sacraments ground and complement the central gift of the Holy Eucharist and are integral to our spiritual and moral conversion. The Sacrament of Reconciliation is central to moral conversion, and so we will take it up briefly in this chapter (Section II.C) and then dedicate the whole of Chapter 7 to it. Thus, we will here discuss

- The grace of Baptism (Section II.A)
- The grace of Confirmation (Section II.B)
- A brief overview of the Sacrament of Reconciliation (Section II.C)

- The grace of Matrimony (Section II.D)
- The grace of Holy Orders (Section II.E)
- The grace of the Anointing of the Sick (Section II.F)[55]

A. The Grace of Baptism

The Sacrament of Baptism is the entryway into Christian life and the Catholic Church, the source of regeneration, and the gateway to all other sacraments. The *Catechism of the Catholic Church* describes it as follows:

> Holy Baptism is the basis of the whole Christian life, the gateway to life in the Spirit (*vitae spiritualis ianua*) (cf. Council of Florence: DS 1314: *vitae spiritualis ianua*), and the door which gives access to the other sacraments. Through Baptism we are freed from sin and reborn as sons of God; we become members of Christ, are incorporated into the Church and made sharers in her mission: "Baptism is the sacrament of regeneration through water and in the word" (*Roman Catechism* II, 2, 5; cf. Council of Florence: DS 1314; CIC, cann. 204 § 1; 849; CCEO, can. 675 § 1).[56]

Inasmuch as Baptism integrates us into the Mystical Body of Christ, it is the means by which the Holy Spirit works in us through the Church. This brings with it inspiration, protection from the Evil One, and a variety of charisms and graces.

As a young seminarian, I reflected back on my early life and recognized the influence and power of the many graces I received through the Sacrament of Baptism. Realizing that the Lord gives inspiration and grace to all children of many faiths,[57] I discern the specifically

---

[55] For an extended explanation of Baptism, Confirmation, Holy Orders, and Anointing of the Sick, see Spitzer, *Credible Catholic Big Book*, Volume 10, *The Sacraments, Part 2—Baptism, Confirmation, Reconciliation, Orders, Sacrament of the Sick*, https://www.crediblecatholic.com/pdf/M10/BB10.pdf. For an extended explanation of Matrimony, see Spitzer, *Credible Catholic Big Book*, Volume 11, *The Sacraments, Part 3—Marriage*, https://www.crediblecatholic.com/pdf/M11/BB11.pdf.

[56] *CCC* 1213.

[57] The Harvard psychologist Robert Coles assembled case studies of children from five faiths that showed inspiration, guidance, theological interest, and a sense of the sacred in children of all faiths—though it manifested itself quite differently in their life's meaning and actions according to their faith tradition. The case studies of the Catholic and Christian children had remarkable similarities to my own religious awareness as a child. See Robert Coles, *The Spiritual Life of Children* (Boston: Houghton-Mifflin, 1990).

Christian inspiration and guidance that I supposed came from the Holy Spirit (and the Mystical Body of Christ) received at Baptism.

As far back as I can remember, I was fascinated by the Mass, religious art, and the special feasts of the Church, such as Ash Wednesday, Good Friday, Easter, and Christmas. I would stare at the pictures in my Catholic picture Bible, the stained-glass windows at church, the crèche scene at my home—becoming absorbed in the ethos of sacredness, goodness, and transcendence that they evoked. Using my children's missal to translate the Latin Mass, I tried to pray the prayers along with the priests, and on Good Friday, I felt deeply sincere contrition and identification with Christ. I have tried to explain this by appealing to my mother's faith, my subconscious symbolism, and childlike need, but the combination of these potential causes has never been able to explain fully my sense of specifically Christian sacredness or my sense of being loved by Jesus. I do not think that my sense of Jesus' presence, sacredness, and love was a figment of my imagination, because I would not have been able to conjure up those specific feelings and states of mind without having first experienced them. Besides, I experienced Jesus as a distinct transcendent subjectivity—not as an imaginary playmate.[58]

Additionally, I was fascinated by religious instruction. I looked forward to catechism class—not because the teachers were particularly interesting and loving, but because the content evoked the same uniquely Christian sacred feelings and states of mind, the same distinctly transcendent presence and love of Jesus. I not only loved catechism, but also serving at Mass—even the early Mass. I even loved hanging around the church and the rectory, which seemed to evoke the same sense of Christian sacredness, particularly the Holy Family and Christ Himself (see the more expanded description of this in Chapter 5, Section III.B). I have no better explanation for this sense of Christian holiness—this being at home with Christ—than *the grace of Baptism*, being incorporated into Christ's Mystical Body and receiving the Holy Spirit, who knows and communicates the heart of Jesus and His Father:

---

[58] Most children, as well as myself, during the ages of five through nine, have sufficient ego-functioning to know that an imaginary playmate is not completely real. See Craig Isaacs, *Revelations and Possession: Distinguishing Spiritual from Psychological Experiences* (Kearney, Neb.: Morris Publishing, 2009), pp. 60–63. I believe I had sufficient ego-functioning to make a distinction between an imaginary playmate and my sense of the distinct transcendent presence of Jesus.

No one comprehends the thoughts of God except the Spirit of God. Now we have received not the spirit of the world, but the Spirit which is from God, that we might understand the gifts bestowed on us by God. And we impart this in words not taught by human wisdom but taught by the Spirit, interpreting spiritual truths to those who possess the Spirit. (1 Cor 2:11–13)

Saint Paul speaks about four graces of Baptism integral to life in the Church as well as to spiritual conversion and moral conversion. He associates all four graces with salvation and integration into the Mystical Body of Christ. The four graces are as follows:

1. The forgiveness of sins
2. The grace or power to put off the life of sin (contra-concupiscence)
3. Entrance into the light and risen life of Christ, which will find its completion in His eternal Kingdom
4. Integration into Christ's Mystical Body so as to be one with all the members of the Church living in the world and in the Kingdom.

In Romans 6:4 and Colossians 2:11–12, Saint Paul articulates the first three graces of Baptism—the forgiveness of our sins (which is preached repeatedly by Peter and the other disciples in the Acts of the Apostles), the grace to resist the life of sin (the "pull" of sin), and integration into Christ's risen life that will lead ultimately to eternal life with Him (if we remain faithful to Him and sincerely ask for His forgiveness when we fail). These three graces form the basis for Saint Augustine's theology of Baptism;[59] he grounds his argument for infant Baptism in the second grace—the grace to put off the life of sin, contra-concupiscence.[60] Augustine's views on Baptism, particularly with respect to concupiscence and original sin, form the foundation for later Church theology.

---

[59] See Saint Augustine, *Merits and Remission of Sin, and Infant Baptism* 1, 6, 6; *Patrologia Latina* 44:112–13; cf. *The Literal Meaning of Genesis* (De Genesi ad litteram) 9, 6, 11, trans. John Hammond Taylor, S.J. (Mahwah, N.J.: Paulist Press, 1982), 2:76–77; *Patrologia Latina* 34:397. See also Saint Augustine, *On Baptism, against the Donatists* 1. This treatise is devoted to refuting the Donatists' use of Cyprian's theology of Baptism to advance certain heresies. In it, Augustine articulates the graces of Baptism. An electronic version of this treatise can be found on New Advent's website at https://www.newadvent.org/fathers/14081.htm.

[60] See Saint Augustine, *Merits and Remission of Sin, and Infant Baptism* 1, 6, 6; PL 44, 112–13.

With respect to the first grace, Saint Paul and Saint Augustine held that the cleansing of Baptism washed away both original sin and, in adults, actual sin. With this forgiveness comes healing and consolation—a way out of evil's darkness and emptiness.

With respect to the second grace (contra-concupiscence), life in the Holy Spirit gives us the wisdom, inspiration, guidance, protection, and strength to recognize and resist our inclination toward what we have called the eight deadly sins. These inclinations (experienced even to some small degree by children) are the residual effects of original sin. We cannot underestimate how important the gift of the Holy Spirit (at Baptism) is in our daily struggle with these concupiscent desires. The Spirit works invisibly within us to heighten our natural sense of conscience, to recognize the darkness of these aberrant desires, and to fight against them. Without this foundational gift of the outer Church, we are left with a weakened conscience and are consigned to fight against the deadly sins with at least one arm tied behind our backs.

The gift of the Holy Spirit must be accompanied by our free choice to follow His inspiration and guidance. If we do not choose to resist sin, the Spirit cannot help us, for He will not violate our freedom. However, if we make even a weak resolve to struggle against temptation and sin, the Holy Spirit can rush into us and fortify that weak resolve, giving us enough strength to resist the deadly sins with greater effectiveness.

The Holy Spirit does far more than increase our ability to recognize and fight concupiscent desires. He heightens the presence of God within our consciousness, and fills our sense of God's presence with the love and trustworthiness of Jesus Christ and His Father. Thus, the indwelling of the Holy Spirit and the presence of Jesus (given in Baptism) fills the mysteriousness and sacredness of the numinous experience with a heightened sense of love, joy, home, and peace. This infuses our initial fear of the numinous wholly Other with love, trust, and delight, which makes the inviting presence of God quite powerful. As I will indicate in Chapter 5 (Section III.B), this foundational gift of Baptism had a huge effect in my spiritual life and conversion from the time of my childhood to the present.

An important condition must be fulfilled in order for the Spirit to inspire and help us to resist temptation—namely, education by parents and the Church. The Spirit's presence within children (after

Baptism) is the inner Word, infusing the numinous mystery with love, joy, and home. Though the child can experience this quite profoundly (as both C. S. Lewis[61] and I[62] did in our childhood), the inner Word can be greatly enhanced by the clarity and explanatory power of the outer Word given in catechetical and parental teaching. If parents fulfill their duty and make certain that children are given proper catechesis, it will have a profound effect on them. Though this effect may lose some of its efficacy during adolescence and young adulthood, it can be resurrected in many cases after maturation and adult education.

The third grace of Baptism (entry into the risen life and light of Jesus) brings the light of Christ into our souls. This light, symbolized by the light of the Easter candle at Baptism, overwhelms the darkness of the Evil One and draws us like a beacon toward itself. As we freely move toward the light of Christ drawing us to itself, we are motivated to deepen our spiritual and moral conversion. The light is so desirable that we will make sacrifices to resist evil's seductions and to reinforce our higher spiritual nature.[63] When we do not move toward the light of Christ, we sense a deep emptiness, alienation, and guilt. However, when we do follow it, we sense a transcendent peace, confidence, and love that draws us ever more closely toward the source of the light—Jesus Christ Himself. If we try to follow His light to its ultimate conclusion, we will be united with Him forever in the Kingdom of Heaven.

The fourth grace of Baptism is integration into the Mystical Body of Christ. In Galatians 3:27–29 and 1 Corinthians 12:12–14, 26–27, Saint Paul incorporates this vital gift into his theology of Baptism—a gift that unites us with Christ and all the members of the Christian community, both in Heaven and on earth. This integration into the Mystical Body of Christ enables us to live as a family with all members of the Church (suffering what they suffer and being honored when they are honored), and also enables us to contribute the grace of our sufferings and honorable deeds to every other member (see

[61] See C. S. Lewis, *Surprised by Joy: The Story of My Early Life* (New York: HarperCollins, 1955).

[62] See Chapter 5, Section III.B, of this volume.

[63] I discuss what I call the "higher self" (the new man/nature) and the "lower self" (the lower man/nature) in Chapter 5, Section III, of this volume.

Col 1:24). Thus, Baptism into Christ's Mystical Body is the foundation for the five graces of the Eucharist (see above Section I.C).

This integration into the Mystical Body brings with it several additional graces that will be addressed in the next chapter—the *sensus fidei*, the *sensus fidelium*, and the sense of *Koinōnia*. For the moment, suffice to say that the gifts of the inner Church (coming from integration into Christ's Mystical Body) gives us a palpable sense of the sacredness of the communion of saints, the history and tradition of the Church, and the Church's doctrinal and moral teachings. This sense of deep holiness and truth not only protects us from error, but inspires us with a rich sacredness intrinsic to the wide range of personalities and life histories, manifest in the saints and leaders of the Church throughout her history. Through Baptism, we are given spiritual fervor and wisdom for our pursuit of interior holiness and external evangelization and service that helps us in tough circumstances to persevere and grow in holiness amid challenges.

As may now be evident, all the graces of Baptism are needed to facilitate and strengthen our spiritual and moral conversion. Without it, we would not be integrated into Christ's Mystical Body or have the life of the Holy Spirit, which enhances our experience of God and our sense of His loving will. We would not have the inspiration, guidance, and protection of the Holy Spirit in our pursuit of spiritual and moral conversion, and our defense against the Evil One would be severely weakened. As such, Baptism is truly rebirth into the life of the Divine—the life of Christ through the Holy Spirit, which helps us immeasurably on the road to eternal salvation.

B. The Grace of Confirmation

The apostolic Church's view of a distinction between Baptism by water (called "Baptism of Jesus") and Baptism by the Holy Spirit (conferred through the laying on of hands) is articulated in Acts 8:

> Now when the apostles at Jerusalem heard that Sama'ria had received the word of God, they sent to them Peter and John, who came down and prayed for them that they might receive the Holy Spirit; for the Spirit had not yet fallen on any of them, but they had only been

baptized in the name of the Lord Jesus. Then they laid their hands on them and they received the Holy Spirit. (8:14–17)

Evidently, Baptism by water (in the name of Jesus) could be separated from Baptism by the Holy Spirit, which was conferred by a distinct rite of the laying on of hands.

This second rite confers powers from the Holy Spirit on the recipient that are oriented toward evangelization and missionary activity—teaching, prophecy, preaching, healing, miracle working, administration, corporal works of mercy, and speaking in tongues (see Paul's explanation below). Since the rite of the laying on of hands (associated with the powers of evangelization) was seen to be distinct from and complementary to the rite of Baptism by water, we may adduce how it later became known as the distinct but complementary Sacrament of Confirmation.[64]

Quoting *Lumen Gentium*, the *Catechism of the Catholic Church* summarizes the grace of Confirmation as follows:

"By the sacrament of Confirmation, [the baptized] are more perfectly bound to the Church and are enriched with a special strength of the Holy Spirit. Hence they are, as true witnesses of Christ, more strictly obliged to spread and defend the faith by word and deed" (*Lumen Gentium* 11; cf. *Ordo Confirmationis*).[65]

Throughout 1 Corinthians 12, Paul speaks of the charismatic gifts of the Holy Spirit that come through the laying on of hands, which later becomes the Sacrament of Confirmation. These gifts give us additional inspiration and power to evangelize and engage in missionary activities. Some are interior gifts—for example, wisdom, faith, knowledge, and understanding. Some are external charisms—for example, teaching, prophecy, healing, miracle working, charisms for corporal works of mercy, and speaking in tongues. All of us have proclivities toward some of these gifts, but generally not toward all of them. It is our responsibility to discern our gifts and to use them not only to build the Kingdom of God, but also

[64] For a history of this development, see Spitzer, *Credible Catholic Big Book*, Volume 10, *The Sacraments, Part 2—Baptism, Confirmation, Reconciliation, Orders, Sacrament of the Sick*, Chapter 2, https://www.crediblecatholic.com/pdf/M10/BB10.pdf#P1V10C2T1.

[65] *CCC* 1285.

to develop our faith—for as Jesus said, "To every one who has will more be given, and he will have abundance; but from him who has not, even what he has will be taken away" (see Mt 25:29).

The underlying implication of Paul's and Jesus' words are that the more we evangelize by using the particular gifts we are given through the spirit in Confirmation, the more we will grow in faith and love—that is, in spiritual and moral conversion. In sum, the effect of Confirmation, as indicated by the rite and its symbols, is a special outpouring of the Holy Spirit that brings about an increase and deepening of baptismal grace for inspiring, strengthening, and defending the Church as well as for evangelization and missionary activity.

The seal of the Holy Spirit completes the conferral of universal priesthood on the newly confirmed, which authorizes them to evangelize and witness to their faith officially—"*quasi ex officio*".[66]

I can personally testify to this grace of evangelization coming through Confirmation. When I was in seventh grade preparing to receive the sacrament, I had a few special classes that explained the sacrament as becoming "a soldier of God", but I did not fully understand the significance of the sacrament. After receiving the sacrament, despite my ignorance, I began to act according to the effects of the sacrament almost immediately. As explained in Chapter 5 (Section III.B), I became more curious about the reasons underlying the Catholic faith, and I became the "local religious authority" at my school in Honolulu. When I went to high school, one of my colleagues told his friends and fellow classmates, "If you have any religious questions, go ask Spitzer—he's the religion guy." I honestly can say that I never did anything consciously to develop this intense desire to know and defend the faith or to develop the charism to explain and protect it. As noted above, I had an interest in the faith from the time of my childhood, but something happened at Confirmation to enhance my desire and passion to understand and defend it. The source of that "inspiration" seems to have been the sacrament itself.

What can we do to best utilize the special graces given us in the Sacrament of Confirmation? First and foremost, *start* using them! Even if we have delayed using these graces for several years (throughout the distracted period of our adolescence and young adulthood),

---

[66] CCC 1305, quoting Saint Thomas Aquinas, *STh* III, 72, 5, ad 2.

all we need do is begin the process of educating ourselves in our faith, which will, in turn, incite the special graces of the Holy Spirit within us. We do not have to go to adult education classes in our parish (though this would be great); we can begin with using some of the free Internet resources available online. I would seriously recommend going to my website CredibleCatholic.com and reading the Big Book explanations of the first six modules.[67] If this is too overwhelming or scientific, I would recommend going to the same website, and then clicking on "7 Essential Modules", choosing the module whose topic interests you most. This would give you the same material in a voiceover PowerPoint with plenty of graphics and embedded videos. Adult education, especially in apologetics and fundamental theology, will catalyze the gifts of the Holy Spirit conferred through Confirmation within you, because the Spirit will impel you to share what you have learned and to seek the salvation of your family, friends, colleagues, and even total strangers.

The graces of Confirmation will also impel you to share your other special gifts—beyond apologetical information and evangelization. As Saint Paul implies (in 1 Cor 12), some of us have gifts of teaching, while others have gifts of preaching, healing, administration, service to youth, service to the poor, financial expertise, organizational expertise, prayer and devotion, and much more. To the extent that we recognize our gifts and share them with others both inside and outside the Church community, the Spirit will encourage us to do even more. When we follow the urgings of the Spirit, He provides us with the inspiration, the words, the courage, the energy, the guidance, and the protection we need to optimize the use of our gifts as well as our passion for evangelization. As noted above, the more we use our gifts, the more we get in return, particularly in spiritual and moral conversion. Our converted heart, in turn, enables us to follow the inspiration of the Holy Spirit even more fully and deeply. This brings to mind the Parable of the Mustard Seed, in which Jesus

---

[67] Go to CredibleCatholic.com and click on the Big Book, and then click on the volume you want, for example, Volume 1, *The Existence of God*. You will be given a huge amount of information showing the scientific, medical, and logical evidence for God. You can also do the same for Volume 2, to get the scientific, medical, and logical evidence for a transphysical soul that will survive bodily death. There are twenty volumes with over two thousand pages of footnoted material.

compares the Kingdom of God to the smallest of seeds, which when planted in good soil (i.e., using our gifts) becomes the largest of shrubs that can be a home for the birds of the air (Mt 13:31–32; Mk 4:30–32; Lk 13:18–19; cf. Mt 17:20). However, the opposite is also true—if we do not use our gifts, and we bury our talents in the sand, we will lose what little we have, as taught by Jesus in the Parable of the Talents (Mt 25:14–30; Lk 19:12–28). Jesus sums up His teaching on this matter by noting, as stated above, "For to every one who has [i.e., who uses his gifts], will more be given, and he will have abundance; but from him who has not [i.e., who does not use his gifts], even what he has will be taken away" (Mt 25:29).

C. A Brief Overview of the Sacrament of Reconciliation

Though the Sacrament of Reconciliation will be explained in detail in Chapter 7, its importance in the process of spiritual and moral conversion requires a brief overview of the powerful graces it brings to believers. Readers interested in a detailed explanation of this important sacrament may want to read Chapter 7, and then return to this chapter.

Though the Sacrament of Reconciliation is frequently minimized and even overlooked in today's Church culture, its power to catalyze a change of heart, the call of God, and moral conversion makes it essential in a culture steeped in materialism, sensuality, and egoism on the Internet, traditional media, the workplace, social settings and associations, and even educational institutions. In the upcoming chapters, we will address the importance of this sacrament in many areas of our spiritual and moral life. In order to understand the significance of this sacrament in these areas, I will briefly address six key graces explained throughout this book and in Chapter 7.

1. *Definitive absolution for mortal and venial sins.* When penitents are sincerely contrite (perfectly or imperfectly) and express firm purpose of amendment, the forgiving and merciful power of Jesus Christ is given definitively to them through the absolving action of the priest. At this juncture, they are no longer held bound by their sins and can start their spiritual and moral lives anew.

2. *Reconciliation with the Church community.* As will be explained, a life of sinfulness affects the entire Mystical Body of Christ. Instead of bringing our light to the Mystical Body, we bring a darkness, sadness, and emptiness to it. Sometimes our sins are known and associated with the Church community, which may bring ridicule or shame to it. This vital sacrament provides reconciliation with and restoration to the Church community so that penitents can resume their Church lives with a "clean slate".

3. *Spiritual solidification of a turning point in life.* Countless are the number of people who have lost their way—or were in the process of losing their way from the Church, the moral teaching of Jesus, and a moral life. As will be explained, the Lord will try to call this wayward person back to his light and life through feelings of deep spiritual emptiness, alienation, and loneliness; through disturbing dreams and wake-up calls at three o'clock in the morning that reveal the darkness into which a person is moving; and by sending signs of the consequences of the evil that they are pursuing, through thoughts in the back of the mind, friends and family members, books and films, and so forth. If the wayward person acts on these "big hints", he will need a solid grace-filled foundation on which to ground his turning point and change of heart. As anyone who has turned his life around can attest, the Sacrament of Reconciliation is indispensable for filling one's desire to change with the grace, power, and love of God so that he will not be held bound by his past failures and enslavement to sin (and sin's master, the Evil One). The grace and power of this important sacrament is like God snatching Goethe's *Faust* out of the hands of Mephistopheles (the devil). The grace of the Sacrament of Reconciliation gives substance to the act of conversion, removes the bondage of the person to the Evil One, decreases the influence of the Evil One on his life, and fills him with a renewed sense of light and hope in Christ. Given that many will have several "turning point" moments throughout life, this sacrament is essential for bringing the needed substance and reinforcement to the penitent's intentions, liberating him from the bondage and influence of the Evil One, and filling him with the light of Christ.

4. *Healing of the damage of sin.* As will be explained, a sinful life can cause considerable damage to one's emotional, intellectual, and spiritual life. Sin can cause us to feel hostility toward the truth, healthy loving relationships, religion, the Church, and even Christ himself. We need the grace of Jesus Christ to help us return to the light of truth, love, goodness, and faith, not only to break with our old proclivities, but to rekindle the desire for new proclivities in Christ. The power and grace of the Sacrament of Reconciliation catalyzes the light and love of Christ within our hearts, and if we receive the sacrament several times per year, it continues to help us, building on itself as "grace upon grace" (Jn 1:16). As healing continues through our efforts and the grace of this sacrament, sanity, truth, love, goodness, and faith in Jesus Christ return and grow stronger.

5. *Graced resolve for continued conversion.* Many of the benefits of this sacrament occur *after* receiving it. If we continue to bring our firm purpose of amendment to daily prayer after the sacrament, its grace fills our intention with a kind of supernatural strength that reinforces our Examen Prayer (see Chapter 6, Section II), facilitating progress in our moral conversion.

6. *The peace of Christ.* When we recognize the harm our sins have done to others and the spiritual jeopardy to which they have subjected us, we may suffer a deep sense of emptiness, alienation, loneliness, and guilt from which it is difficult to find relief. Most human solutions, such as counseling or conversation with friends, do not seem to get at the heart of the alienation and guilt. Even our best friends cannot take it away. In my experience, the one truly freeing breakthrough moment that transforms deep self-alienation and guilt into supernatural peace is the Sacrament of Reconciliation. After absolution and the priest's farewell—"Go in peace"—dozens of penitents have reported to me after the fact that they finally felt peace, sometimes after several years of avoiding this sacrament. If anyone wants evidence of the power of supernatural grace helping us beyond mere natural and human causation, the grace of this sacrament which is a "peace beyond all understanding" (see Phil 4:7) may well provide it. It is as if the Lord's light and peace breaks through the darkness into which the Evil One has

lured and mired us—yet another instance of Christ's victory over Satan manifest in our lives.

As can be seen from the above six graces (to be explained more fully in Chapter 7), the Sacrament of Reconciliation is one of the very best gifts that God has given to us through the Church that He founded on Peter and his successors. It is so powerful in liberating us from the darkness of evil into which we may have become mired, in healing the residual damage from it, and in filling us with peace and continuing resolve, that it may well be called "evil's spell breaker" or "the continued victory of Christ over Satan in our lives". Though some Catholics question the need for this sacrament because it can be challenging or they think that a human mediator is unnecessary, they are terribly mistaken, for it is one of the very best ways of authentically examining our conscience and bringing the definitive absolving and healing presence of Christ into our lives. If someone offers you a definitive means of unshackling yourself from the Evil One, separating yourself from him, and bringing you a peace beyond all understanding for the mere request of authentically acknowledging and being contrite for your sins, wouldn't you accept it?

From a personal point of view, this has been one of the greatest gifts I have ever received, one of the reasons I am so privileged to be a Catholic, and one of the principal vehicles for my moral conversion. I thank the Lord so much for the wonderfully challenging, grace-filled Sacrament of Reconciliation that He continually bestows upon me.

D. The Grace of Sacramental Marriage

What does the grace of sacramental marriage have to do with spiritual and moral conversion? Just about everything. This is revealed in a question that all potential spouses will want to ask themselves, a question that reflects the heart of Jesus' and the Catholic Church's teaching on marriage: "Is this the person I wish to *serve* for the rest of my life?" Christian marriage is not about "What's in it for me?" but rather "What's in it for us, our children, and the good we can do together for the world and God's Kingdom?"—and this requires faith-filled, generative, intimate, and self-sacrificial love for spouse and children unto the salvation of all. This is precisely the objective of spiritual and moral conversion.

If we enter marriage with the illusion that we will now be set for life—that it will not require disciplined and loving service to the other—our expectations will be dashed sooner rather than later. However, if we enter marriage with the desire to serve the good of the other, we will find deep happiness, meaning, dignity, fulfillment, and salvation through it. As Jesus taught, "Whoever humbles himself will be exalted" (Mt 23:12; cf. Lk 14:11; 18:14).

Protestant churches deny the sacramentality of marriage. However, there is abundant scriptural evidence to show that the medieval Church's inclusion of marriage in the seven sacraments was justified.[68] As we shall see, Jesus elevated the Sacrament of Matrimony from a virtually social custom (in the Old Testament) to a sacred covenant leading toward the sanctification of a couple and their children.

The Church discerned that Jesus had elevated the marriage commitment to the level of a sacrament (an outward and visible sign of an inward and spiritual grace) by His words in the Gospels:

> And Pharisees came up to him and tested him by asking, "Is it lawful to divorce one's wife for any cause?" He answered, "Have you not read that he who made them from the beginning made them male and female, and said, 'For this reason a man shall leave his father and mother and be joined to his wife, and the two shall become one'? So

---

[68] For a history of the sacramental theology underlying Matrimony, see Spitzer, *Credible Catholic Big Book*, Volume 11, *The Sacraments, Part 3—Marriage*, https://www.crediblecatholic .com/pdf/M11/BB11.pdf#P1V11C1T1. Jesus implicitly declared marriage to be a sacrament when He elevated it to an indissoluble relationship created by God Himself—a divine grace—in Matthew 5:31–32; 19:6. Saint Augustine laid the systematic groundwork for this sacramentality in his work *On the Good of Marriage* (A.D. 401). He distinguished three values in marriage: fidelity, which is more than sexual; offspring, which "entails the acceptance of children in love, their nurturance in affection, and their upbringing in the Christian religion"; and sacrament, in that its indissolubility is a sign of the eternal unity of the blessed. Eight hundred years later, four Church councils formally declared marriage to be a sacrament—the Council of Verona (A.D. 1184), the Fourth Lateran Council (A.D. 1215), the Second Council of Lyons (A.D. 1274), and the Council of Florence (A.D. 1439). Though Saint Augustine wrote about the sacramentality of marriage, the Church delayed her formal declaration of it until she had formulated her definition of "sacrament" as "an outward and visible sign of an inward and spiritual grace" at the Council of Verona in 1184.

they are no longer two but one. *What therefore God has joined together,*
let no man put asunder." They said to him, "Why then did Moses
command one to give a certificate of divorce, and to put her away?"
He said to them, "For your hardness of heart Moses allowed you to
divorce your wives, but *from the beginning* it was not so. And I say
to you: whoever divorces his wife, except for unchastity, and marries
another, commits adultery." (Mt 19:3–9; italics added)[69]

Jesus' declaration that *God* has joined the man and woman together
reveals His conviction that marriage is a spiritual/divine reality. This
spiritual/divine reality was God's original intention "from the beginning". Here Jesus harkens back to Genesis 2:21–24,[70] interpreting
God's intention to be a divine blessing not only for Adam, but also
for Eve and the relationship between them. The medieval Church
recognized in these words that Jesus' teaching showed the marriage
covenant to be an outward visible sign of a divine and sacred reality,
which is truly a spiritual grace.

This interpretation of Mark 10:1–12 and Matthew 19:3–9 is borne
out in 1 Corinthians 7:13–14:

> If any woman has a husband who is an unbeliever, and he consents
> to live with her, she should not divorce him. For the unbelieving
> husband is consecrated [i.e., sanctified] through his wife, and the
> unbelieving wife is consecrated [i.e., sanctified] through her husband.
> Otherwise, your children would be unclean, but as it is they are holy.

In this passage Saint Paul recognizes a grace—an agency of consecration (i.e., sanctification)—in the marriage union. Some of Paul's
readers are worried that they will be defiled by being married to an
unbeliever, but Paul assures them that their belief, the willingness of
the pagan partner to stay in the marriage, and the marital union itself

---

[69] The Markan version of this passage (Mk 10:1–12) includes an additional verse for the
Gentile Church, which was not necessary for the Jewish Church: "And if she divorces her
husband and marries another, she commits adultery" (Mk 10:12).

[70] "So the LORD God caused a deep sleep to fall upon the man, and while he slept took
one of his ribs and closed up its place with flesh; and the rib which the LORD God had taken
from the man he made into a woman and brought her to the man. Then the man said, 'This
at last is bone of my bones and flesh of my flesh; she shall be called Woman, because she was
taken out of Man.' Therefore a man leaves his father and his mother and cleaves to his wife,
and they become one flesh."

will "sanctify" (hegiastai—"make holy") them. Not only that, but the marital union will also sanctify their children. Though there is difference of opinion on the interpretation of hegiastai, it would be a real stretch to interpret Paul's meaning as precluding a sanctifying power of the marital union—for both the pagan partner and the children. In view of this, the medieval Church had good scriptural grounds for including marriage among the seven accepted sacraments. In the view of Saint Paul, marriage really is an inward spiritual grace (leading toward sanctification) conveyed through an outward visible sign.

As we shall see in Chapters 4–6, one of the primary objectives of spiritual and moral conversion is to have the heart of Jesus—a purified desire and capability to love in accordance with the Beatitudes: humble-heartedness ("poor in spirit"), gentle-heartedness (meekness), desire for righteousness (to be purified so as to be saved), merciful (to be forgiving and compassionate to the marginalized), pure of heart, to be a peacemaker, and to sacrifice oneself for the Kingdom of God (see Mt 5:1–12). Readers may recognize that these qualities of love given in the Beatitudes are precisely those needed in a successful marriage for the sake of both the spouse and the children. Inasmuch as the grace of Matrimony (in the Church) helps couples to achieve this kind of love, it must be efficacious in bringing about real spiritual and moral conversion.

When Catholics proceed toward marriage (or are already involved in a marriage), they should be aware of six major intentions that help to make their marriage and family strong, committed, holy, and efficacious for the common good, the Kingdom of God, and salvation. The grace of the Sacrament of Matrimony works through these six intentions, and when spouses concertedly try to actualize them, matrimonial grace is abundant, which helps them (and their children) to progress in spiritual and moral conversion. The six intentions are

1. Commitment to fidelity
2. Commitment to indissolubility
3. Commitment to exclusivity
4. Seeking common cause
5. Forgiving and transforming weakness into strong covenant love
6. Being open to children and forming them according to the Catholic faith

Though the commitments to fidelity, indissolubility, and exclusivity (nos. 1–3 above) are the primary commitments required for marriage, they are complemented by other intentions (such as nos. 4–6 above) to sustain and foster it as Christ conceived it.

1. The Three Solemn Commitments of Fidelity, Exclusivity, and Indissolubility

The solemn vow of exclusivity and indissolubility enables each spouse to have the radical trust and freedom to relinquish the "me" in favor of the "us". This is what creates a new reality—a new unity and relationship. We will here briefly discuss the theological and spiritual underpinnings of these three commitments.

Eros (romantic love viewed as a support for the highest level of person-to-person commitment) builds on *philia* (friendship). When a man and woman become attracted romantically to each other, the natural course for this romance is not to jump immediately to sexual expression, but to grow in friendship—reciprocal commitment and love—which in the context of romance finds its expression first in deep care, intimacy, tenderness, generativity, and understanding, which awakens the desire to support the other in their need and to seek out ways of contributing to the other and helping the other toward salvation. Within this high level of commitment and friendship, romance reaches its proper end—the highest level of human commitment, intimacy, and mutual care that will be necessary for raising children and maintaining a high level of familial care and bondedness—that is, a caring home.

Why must romantic love be within an exclusive relationship with one person only? Can romantic love and sexual expression be an end in itself? Or is its proper end to support and ground the highest level of friendship and "human to human" commitment? When sexual "love" becomes an end in itself, it becomes separated from the highest level of commitment to another person. This results in an "objectification" or "thingafication" of the other—the other as mere "physical body" or "mere cause of physical arousal" or mere "instrument of physical pleasure". Divorcing sexuality from genuine commitment to the good of others de-humanizes and de-spiritualizes them. It implicitly says that we care more about the arousal, pleasure, and ego-satisfaction they bring to us than we care about *them*.

We now return to the question about why *eros* must be exclusive—with one person only. If the natural end of *eros* is to support the highest level of friendship—the highest level of commitment, of self and future, to the care, support, and salvation of another for the purpose of raising children destined for eternal salvation—then *eros* (romantic and sexual expression) is meant to support that highest level of committed love in which children deserve to be raised, the kind of commitment that will give rise to a truly loving home destined for our eternal home. Only in this context can *eros* reach its ideal fulfillment. If this is the true end of *eros*, then it is meant to support a "first priority commitment". Inasmuch as the marital commitment is the first priority of human commitments, there can be no other priority of equal importance. After all, how many highest level ("first priority") commitments can you have? Evidently, only one—logically. Therefore, *eros* and marriage must be exclusive.

We now move to the commitment of indissolubility. The reason why the marital commitment is called a "vow" instead of a "promise" is not only because of the religious character of a Catholic marriage, but also because it reflects the indissolubility intrinsic to the highest commitment of self for the good of the other and the family. This commitment enables each person to *trust* that there will be no abrogation of the relationship—even under the most challenging circumstances. This solemn trust on the part of both parties is absolutely necessary if they are to change their identities, purpose, and lives completely, which is precisely what a loving home and family require. Such a home and family cannot be grounded in autonomy ("me first"). It must be given over to mutuality and reciprocity. Similarly, a loving home and family cannot be grounded in domination, but only in submissiveness, listening, and solicitude. Again, a loving home and family cannot be grounded in the expectation of simply being gratified and fulfilled. Rather, it requires the intention to receive gratification by first gratifying and fulfilling spouse and children. Again, a loving home and family cannot be grounded in keeping one's time, priorities, and happiness for oneself—it requires subordinating "my time" to "our time", "my priorities" to "our priorities", and "my happiness" to "our happiness".

All of these radical changes in identity, meaning, and fulfillment require radical trust—a conviction grounded not just in a guarantee, but in a *solemn* guarantee before God, family, friends, and the public.

The solemnity of this vow that grounds each person's radical trust creates the necessary freedom to make the radical changes needed to transform two "me's" into an indissoluble "us", which is the ideal ground of a loving home and family. Yes, there will be many other requirements for this loving home and family, such as daily sacrifices, honesty, charity, forgiveness, faith, and God's grace working through it all; but all of these are dependent upon the radical trust needed to change one's identity, meaning, and life—a radical trust that is dependent on the solemnity of the marriage vow. If this is understood by each party from the beginning, a loving home and family have a solid foundation "built on rock", which can survive the buffeting of winds, rain, and every form of challenge. Without this solemn intention of highest commitment, indissolubility, and exclusivity, the marriage is "built on sand", and in today's world with its ever-challenging surrogates for "highest life priority", it is almost doomed to failure. The solemnity of the marriage vow is freedom for the other to commit and love completely—to give up the "me" for the "us", and to create a new relationship that will become the loving home needed to protect, nurture, educate, and raise children who will in turn be capable of virtue, committed love, and faith.

A violation of the marriage vow, such as infidelity, or an abrogation of it in divorce is so hurtful and demoralizing that it can literally ruin the other spouse and undermine the identity and stability of the children. For this reason, the Church insists at the inception of marriage on what Jesus declared long ago—the pure intention and solemn vow of complete fidelity, indissolubility, and exclusivity to the other party. This requires adequate preparation before marriage so that the kind of love and the solemnity of the vow are completely understood—for without such understanding, the intention of indissolubility and exclusivity is meaningless.

Before proceeding to the next three intentions aimed at common cause, forgiveness, and children, it may prove helpful to address three fundamental attitudes and practices that foster sacramental marriage.

2. Three Disciplines for Fostering Sacramental Marriage

Christian theologians from Saint Augustine and Saint Ignatius of Loyola to C. S. Lewis and Gabriel Marcel have implicitly taught that three disciplines practiced by both spouses can foster the above three commitments to fidelity, exclusivity, and indissolubility as well as the three intentions toward common cause, transformation through weakness, and children:

1. Looking for the good news in the other
2. Never asking the question "whether" again, but only the question "how"
3. Praying together to stay together

We will briefly discuss each as a support to sacramental marriage.

a. Looking for the Good News in the Other

Empathy is a necessary condition of care for others, and care for others, a necessary condition of love. By "love" here we are speaking at once of *philia* (friendship), *eros* (the highest form of friendship and commitment through which romance and sexuality are expressed), and *agapē* (the recognition of the intrinsic and unique goodness and lovability of the other that elicits the desire to sacrifice oneself for the other—irrespective of reciprocity or reward of any kind)—see above Section II.D.1. As implied above, marital relationships require all three kinds of love: *philia*, which ultimately develops into the desire for highest friendship and commitment, *eros* (the romantic and sexual expression of that friendship and commitment oriented toward children), and *agapē* (sacrifice of self for the good of the other without expectation of reciprocity).

The state of consciousness and emotion necessary for these three kinds of love is care, which is a direct result of empathy. When empathy occurs, an individual is in a state of unity with the other, whereby doing the good for the other is just as easy, if not easier, than doing the good for oneself. So empathy—this strong feeling of attraction and being drawn to the other, this feeling of unity with the other—mitigates the more primitive desire for self-interest. Though empathy is a natural feeling—a very powerful one capable of mitigating self-interest—it must be awakened.

Perhaps the quickest, easiest, and most powerful way to awaken empathy is to look for the good news in the other. The problem is that the bad news is more immediately riveting than the good news. When we are irritated, insulted, frustrated, or hurt, we cannot focus on anything else. We seem to fix our gaze on our irritation and the shortcomings of others that arouse it. Thankfully, we cannot focus on both the good news and the bad news simultaneously. If we are focused on the bad news, the good news melts away into the background, almost eliminating the possibility of empathy. Fortunately, the reverse is also the case. When we are focusing on the good news, the bad news, though still recognized, is contextualized and mitigated by the more prominent good news. This reawakens empathy, which, in turn, incites us to care and love.

So what does this mean? When we are looking for the bad news in the other (mitigating the possibility of empathy, care, and love), we must intentionally shift our focus to the good news in him—looking for the little good things he tries to do, the great good things to which he aspires, his gratuitous acts of kindness, his virtues, strengths, and faith, and even his delightful idiosyncrasies and transcendent mystery. As we consider the specific features of the good news, the bad news will gradually loosen its grip, restoring the possibility of empathy and care. As this occurs, the possibility of gratitude, compassion, and forgiveness come back to the fore, and our relationship with that person gains new life.

Try it for yourself when you are obsessing on the bad news—what is irritating, unkind, stupid, or weak. Now, shift your focus to the good news—looking for the little good things the other tries to do; his gratuitous acts of kindness (especially when we don't deserve them); the great things to which he aspires; his principles, ideals, and faith; and so forth. Notice what happens as you bring the good news into closer focus—the bad news begins to fade into the background, and so also the aversion and hostility accompanying it. Note also that as the good news proceeds to the foreground (and the bad news to the background), empathy—the feelings of natural attraction to and unity with the other—becomes stronger. Soon, a genuine unity with the other begins to form—a bond through which our minds and hearts are interrelated and even intertwined. All we need do now is choose to make these feelings and this state of empathy endure—choose to make it prevail over the bad news. As you make this choice, notice that your care for the other increases, and so also the capacity for *philia, eros, and agapē*.

It is quite difficult to stop looking at the bad news when we are not looking for the good news. Even the most self-controlled stoics will find it difficult to break with the riveting power of the bad news by an act of the will. However, if we simply shift our intentional focus to the good news by looking for the good qualities, virtues, kindness, and faith of the other, we will not have to fight off the bad news. It will be put into its proper place by the good news, which will weaken it to the point where empathy can overcome it.

The above technique holds true for all friendships, acquaintances, and business relationships, but it is especially true for spouses and children. Marriage requires empathy, care, gratitude, compassion, and forgiveness more than any other relationship, for it entails spending large amounts of time, psychic energy, physical energy, and dedication to spouse and children. If empathy and care break down, this shared time and focus can become a frustration and torment rather than mutual reinforcement and support. So it is incumbent on spouses to make a concerted decision and effort to incorporate the discipline of looking for the good news in the other at the beginning and end of every day.

Frustration, disagreements, and conflicts are a virtual inevitability in any friendship or close relationship. We can't be perfect all the time. We get preoccupied, stressed, tired, and sometimes overwhelmed, and when we do, we say things, do things, or fail to do things that cause frustration, irritation, hurt feelings, and anger. It is precisely on these occasions when we will want to make immediate recourse to the good news in the other. Even though we may be hurt or justifiably angry, we need not follow those feelings into resentment and conflict. All we need do is reawaken our feelings of empathy—attraction to and unity with the other—by focusing on the good news: past kindnesses, high aspirations, strengths, faith, unique goodness and lovability, delightful idiosyncrasies, and so forth. The goodness intrinsic to the other will naturally awaken our empathy, which will in turn awaken forgiveness, compassion, and care. Strangely, the other can become quite irresistible only moments after he was annoying, hurtful, or antagonistic.

One final point: it is always a good idea to reflect on the good news in our spouses when we are not in conflict—and have some time and space to reflect contemplatively on them. Bringing these attributes before God in prayer can help to deepen our appreciation of them. This will prove quite helpful when inevitable conflicts arise, for we will then avert the difficult task of thinking about the good news when we are unprepared and in a conflictual situation. Our prepared mind need only refocus on the good qualities we have already discerned. This is a more manageable and potentially successful approach. When the good news in the other is ready at hand, it can connect with our goodwill and God's grace, and that can make all the difference for a good sacramental marriage.

b. Never Ask the Question "Whether" but Only the Question "How"

The exclusivity and indissolubility of marital commitments require that we be vigilantly intentional about maintaining our solemn vows. This requires going beyond our pronouncement during our wedding to refocusing our purpose whenever even implicit temptations arise. One incisive way of doing this is to make the pledge that whenever frustration, conflict, difficulty, or anger arises, I will never ask the question "whether" again, but only the question "how". The question "whether"—"whether I should have entered into a lifetime commitment"—is destined to undermine permanent commitment, because it throws it into abeyance. The moment this occurs, we are given a false sense of "availability", which implicitly abandons our spouse. This inauthentic sense of availability, in turn, causes the mind and heart to wander—"perhaps this other person would have been a better match" or, more threateningly, "perhaps that person would have been a better spouse." The moment our imagination takes hold of this inauthentic "possibility", our resolve to remain committed to our spouse is weakened—whether we act on these fantasies or not. If we do act on these fantasies, our weakened resolve can easily turn into betrayal—with its terrible consequences for spouse, children, and the marriage itself.

It is difficult to keep a purely negative resolve at the forefront of our consciousness—"I will never ask the question 'whether' again—I really, really won't—really." The negativity of the resolve makes it hard to imagine and choose. It is much easier to substitute a negative resolve with a positive resolve that will engage our imagination and will—"I will never ask the question 'whether' again, but only the question 'how'." The question "how" is filled with positive possibilities. When problems or conflicts arise or spirits droop, we do not have to succumb to the destructive question of "whether we should have entered into a lifetime commitment with this person". Instead we can replace it with the positive question "how", which fills the imagination with positive ways of making the relationship work—"How can we use our mutual strengths, our faith, our families, our friends, and our mutual resolve to make the best out of this challenging situation and our drooping spirits?" Notice that the minute we engage in this positive question, the negative question of "whether" is pushed into the background, and the products of our positive imagination come into the foreground, rekindling the commitment and the relationship.

As we practice this discipline throughout the multiple temptations and challenges of long-term marriage, the question "how" becomes habitual—indeed virtuous—which makes the destructive question "whether" recessive and impotent. Potential spouses will want to agree before marriage to integrate this discipline into their individual and collective lives to support their promise of exclusivity and indissolubility—sacramental marriage—for the sake of themselves, the family, the children, and all the friends supported by them.

c. Pray Together to Stay Together

The charismatic "Rosary priest", Father Patrick Peyton, popularized a Christian-Catholic truism about marriage—"The family that prays together, stays together." His contention has been borne out by study after study, and it embraces the truth that grace (through prayer) lies at the heart of truly blessed Christian marriages. For example, four major longitudinal studies at seven universities—Florida State University, University of Georgia, Bowling Green State University, University of Auburn, East Carolina University, University of North Texas, and University of Calgary—show that couples who participate together at church services, pray together, and integrate faith attitudes within the family are much more likely to be happy in marriage, remain married for a lifetime, and raise children who will also participate in church and prayer in their adult lives.[71] In view of this, engaged and married couples should plan on integrating church services, daily prayer, and faith attitudes into their marriages, for family prayer is one of the very highest predictors of marital success, family stability, and long-term faith and success of children. There are dozens of good Catholic resources for family prayer that could prove helpful.[72]

3. Three Additional Intentions for a Successful Sacramental Marriage

Bearing the above three disciplines in mind, we now proceed to three additional intentions that foster sacramental marriages, loving homes, and faith-filled children:

1. The Intention toward Common Cause (Section II.D.3.a)
2. The Intention to Transform Weakness into Covenant Love (Section II.D.3.b)
3. The Intention toward Children and Family (Section II.D.3.c)

a. The Intention toward Common Cause

It is not enough that a couple *become* a new reality (and "us"); they must act like one. Sometimes couples believe that being in love is focused on the other partner alone. Though intimate, affectionate, generative, understanding, and forgiving love are absolutely essential to marriage, it is not enough; for such a marriage would only be inward looking. Yet, we must remember that love always goes beyond itself—not just one partner's love for the other partner, but the two partners' united love for the people beyond and around them. A loving couple is not meant to serve the other person alone, but their united love is meant

[71] For a summary of these studies' conclusions, see David Briggs, "5 Ways Faith Contributes to Strong Marriages, New Studies Suggest", *Huff Post*, February 8, 2015, http://www.huffingtonpost.com/david-briggs/5-ways-faith-contributes_b_6294716.

For a summary of the Swiss study correlating fathers' church attendance with the likelihood of adult children participating in church, see Robbie Low, "The Truth about Men and Church", *Touchstone: A Journal of Mere Christianity*, June 2003, http://www.touchstonemag.com/archives/article.php?id=16-05-024-v#ixzz4RjWtmadF.

[72] See, for example, Dominican Sisters of Saint Cecilia Congregation, *A Short Guide to Praying as a Family: Growing Together in Faith and Love Each Day* (Charlotte, N.C.: Saint Benedict Press, 2015). See also Donald F. X. Connolly, *Family Prayer Book* (Melville, N.Y.: Regina Press, 1967).

to serve the people around them. Just as each individual must seek the good of the other, so also the union itself—united love of the couple—must seek the good of others beyond themselves.

Christian wisdom has consistently held that an exclusively inward-looking marital love is nothing more than another pool of Narcissus. Recall that Narcissus was so enamored by his reflection in the pool that he could not tear himself away from it. Unable to do anything else except stare at himself, he withered away from unfulfilled yearning and lack of sustenance.[73] The same thing occurs with the couple that looks into one another's eyes and is so enamored by the "just us" that they see no purpose beyond themselves. They simply isolate their purpose in one another's finitude—and wither away. "Just us" is "just wrong" and is doomed to failure.

The union arising out of marital love must go beyond itself—first and foremost to the children of the marriage, then to ideals that a couple can and want to fulfill together—for example, religion (participation in a church); cultural, social, and political ideals (e.g., attempts to influence the culture or politics in a positive direction); service or educational ideals (helping the poor, assisting in a school, etc.). So long as a couple finds common cause in their children, their family and friends, their religion, and the greater community, their union will flourish—much like an individual who flourishes by doing the good beyond himself.

This does not mean that a couple should not do things independently of one another. Each partner still has an autonomous life—with different friends, different job responsibilities, and even different causes or ideals they intend to support. Yet, autonomous activity alone is not enough, for the union constituted by their mutual love must also serve a positive purpose beyond itself. Naturally, children are the primary common good and common cause of any marital union, but there are many other activities in which a couple can participate to serve the greater community through their union with one another. The more they invest their common effort and idealism in children, friends, relatives, community service, religion, religious service, and so forth, the more their union will grow in strength, for as Christ intimated long ago, the one who dies to himself will find

---

[73] See Ovid, *Metamorphoses* 3.

himself and be raised anew. Therefore, it is incumbent upon the couple to find not only autonomous ways of serving a good beyond themselves, but also united ways to serve their children and the good beyond their family.

b. The Intention to Transform Weakness into Covenant Love

Let us proceed to the second intention—the commitment to grow in intimacy, understanding, forgiveness and respect through one another's weakness and through collective challenges. Engaged couples should be aware of the fact that growth in intimate relationships is by no means steady and unhindered. Even if a couple has agreed on important potentially conflictual issues before the marriage (such as religious practice, spending, finances, the raising of children, and so forth), relationships go through stages of decompression, disinterest, and even resentments. This means that both parties will likely experience a range of negative emotions that become expressed when there are stresses from weaknesses and insensitivities in the relationship and from the workplace, as well as from children. The best marriages make provision for these natural decompressions, stresses, weaknesses, and their resultant emotional negativity. Ironically, if handled well, these negative influences on the marriage can lead to growth in intimacy, understanding, compassionate love, and marital love.

The following threefold plan of action can transform these "negatives" into long-term "positives":

- Realism and Planning
- Prayer and Grace
- Understanding and Forgiveness (through Grace)

Realism and Planning. The first step in what might be called "transformational love" is to give up naïve assumptions, such as, "I never thought xxx could happen!" or "I never bargained for this!" or "I thought God would work everything out perfectly." These and similar thoughts have absolutely no basis in any relationship in reality. Their presumption by either party—or the couples themselves—can only lead to disappointment and dashed expectations. Yes, we want to enter a marriage hoping for the best and expecting high standards of ourselves and our spouse, but we cannot build a psychological expectation of perfection on the part of the other—or ourselves. Such expectations lead in the beginning to subtle irritation, then to frustration, then to blatant anger, and then to some form of rejection.

A more successful strategy is to hope for the best and make a realistic plan of action when things do not go as well as might be expected. Plan ahead of time *not* to move into "silent resentment mode". Agree as a couple before the marriage on how you want to *communicate charitably* about points of disagreement, irritation, and frustration where the offended party will have to give as much to the remedy as the offender. Resolve ahead of time to make backup plans for how to live through difficult times in the relationship in a nonideal, but workable way. Above all, plan to engage in the next two steps—prayer and forgiveness. Louis Pasteur observed that "chance favors the prepared mind." Chance also favors the patient and benevolent heart.

Prayer and Grace. Individual faith and the grace that results from it are integral to dealing with the deep emotional hurts that can occur in romantic marital relationships. As noted above (Section II.D.2.c), shared faith is even more powerful in patiently contending with insensitivity, frustration, hurt feelings, and resentments. The deeper one's love and commitment, the more deeply insensitivity, being ignored, being taken for granted, being marginalized, and being insulted will be felt. As noted above, realism and planning help to mitigate these negative feelings, but we cannot underestimate how powerful individual prayer—and especially shared prayer—can be in finding a solution to a problem. Shared prayer (e.g., "Lord, help us to understand and respect one another more") can bring a problem to light while calling us to *authenticity before God* at the time of prayer.

It truly amazes me how praying about a problem with a person helps me to be honest in my own imaginative conception of the problem, honest about my role in it, understanding and forgiving of the other in his weakness, and revealing of my hidden hypocrisies in communicating my side of the problem. By praying together about a difficulty, we invite God into our individual conscience as well as the collective ethos of the relationship. God's presence (and grace) calls us to a higher level of honesty, authenticity, respect for the other, and forgiveness of the other, which is precisely the call of Jesus in the Beatitudes.

In this moment of shared grace, a couple may take the opportunity to write some of the things that they need to help the relationship move forward. This must be a two-sided *charitable* exercise—in which there is dialogue about each point that each partner brings up. The objective would be to find some way of accommodating a needed change so that it is not overly burdensome to one of the parties and does not require a complete change in personality or nature. When the couple is finished communicating about these changes, it is helpful to conclude with a prayer, asking the Lord for the resolve to succeed in accommodating them. Including this petition in nightly shared prayer over the course of several weeks helps to make it a reality.

Understanding and Forgiveness. As might be expected, prayer and shared faith are integral to understanding and forgiveness. Prayer calls us not only to greater authenticity, but also to Jesus' precepts of refraining from negative judgment, profoundly respecting the other, and forgiving the other from the heart "seventy times seven" times (Mt 18:22). It is easy to jump to judgment when one is tired, irritated, or "fed up". Caught up in the emotion of the moment, our imagination begins to work overtime with remarkable creativity. We want to justify our impatience or anger, and so we prepare a set of statements that sounds like the concluding speech of a prosecuting attorney at a criminal trial. Somehow we conceive of ourselves as an innocent offended party, and the other as an aggressive criminal. Furthermore, the characterization of the offensive actions seems to originate and proceed from the offending party alone. I would not mention this so bluntly if I hadn't done it so many times myself. I want to excuse myself for the negative conduct I am about to display.

The best part about faith—particularly shared faith—is that it becomes increasingly hard to believe my skewed story when my heart is open to the Lord. Somehow the Parable of the Unmerciful Servant (Mt 18:23–35) keeps creeping into my prayer. After being forgiven thousands of times for greater offenses by the Lord, I am throttling my fellow servant by saying, "Pay me what you owe!" It's not that this parable makes me feel fearful—it really does not, because I believe in God's unconditional love for me. Rather, it makes me feel like a complete hypocrite before the perfectly authentic and loving Lord. This implicit call to "authenticity" has been indispensable in every deep friendship I have experienced. I have to stop, question my motive before the Lord, and realign myself to the reality around me. This tends to dispel the irritation and negative emotion as well as the mythologizing of the other's negative traits. Once done, I can get about doing the hard spiritual work of understanding, excusing, and forgiving.

Understanding, putting ourselves in the other's situation, is much easier to accomplish when we acknowledge that we and the other are loved by God. When we recognize God's benevolent gaze upon us, it is difficult to blind ourselves to the good news in the other (see above Section II.D.2.a). As we allow the unique goodness, lovability, and mystery of the other to penetrate our consciousness, appreciation, respect, and compassion begin to arise naturally in our psyche. When this occurs, we must seize the opportunity to put ourselves into the other's situation—to look upon the other with the kind of love with which the Lord looks upon us. At this juncture, seeing the other through the compassionate eyes of Christ, we will want to make an intentional act of forgiveness.

Forgiveness should be distinguished from forgetting. The former can be done immediately by simply using the prayer, "Lord, You are the just judge—You take care of it, or him." When we let an offense go—by putting it into the Lord's hands and then praying for the offending party—we let go of the just penalty we might want to exact in vengeance upon the other. We give that just penalty to the Lord, trusting that He will take care of the needed nuances of heart that are beyond our power. As I pray this prayer, I notice a freedom and peace coming over me, which becomes the first step to forgetting. I have told generations of classes that "forgetting takes at least six months longer than forgiving—and if the offense is great, up to several years longer!" How true this is, but truer still is the fact that failure to forgive the other will result in the complete incapacity to forget. Indeed, the opposite will occur—vengeance will beget vengeance, and violence will beget violence, until the unforgiven and unforgotten offense drives us and the other to a breaking point. Thus, we must do everything in our power to see the Lord's love for us and the other, to look benevolently at the other through His eyes, and to make the all-important prayer that begins the process of forgiveness: "Lord, You are the just judge—You take care of it." Slowly but surely, our grip will loosen; we will no longer have to hold onto anger in indignation of the offense that has seared into our memory—and we can begin the natural process of forgetting through continual forgiveness and prayer for the offender.

One final point should be made about forgiveness. Forgiveness is the intention to let go of the just penalty for an unjust offense into the Lord's hands, but this does not mean we have to endure continual abuse without seeking remediation or defending ourselves. In Christian theology, we have every right to protect ourselves and to stipulate better conduct toward ourselves in the future. We can be sure Christ wants us to achieve better ways to be respectful and understanding within the relationship, while at the same time assuring that we are not continuously abused.

So where does forgiveness come in? It affects the way we redress intolerable issues or offenses. Christ asks us to redress injustices and seek protection from abuses, but *not* with anger, hatred, and vengeance. Nothing good will come of that. Rather, we must seek redressing and protection with peace, understanding, and compassion—though seek it persistently, diligently, and, if need be, with *hard love*, if the offending party is not willing to listen. The Lord is not against us requesting love and understanding—or redressing intolerable offenses in repeated conduct. Rather, He is against anger, hatred, and vengeance in the heart—all of which are interrelated (see Mt 5:21–22). Since this is best achieved through grace, our second step of bringing God, prayer, and grace into the picture is absolutely essential.

We return now to our original point—namely, that when we make a firm resolve to understand and forgive one another from the heart "seventy times seven" times, weaknesses, stresses, insensitivity, insults, and challenges of every kind can actually *help* us to grow in intimacy, compassion, and relational bonding rather than undermining them. As noted above, the best way of achieving this understanding and forgiveness is to prepare ahead of time, to be realistic, to formulate backup plans, to be prayerful, to invite the other into shared prayer, and to allow God into the process of forgiveness ("Lord, You are the just judge—You take care of it"). No doubt the above three-step plan requires discipline and diligence, but in the end it will not only save marriages but help the couple achieve their highest fulfillment in covenant love and in Heaven.

c. The Intention toward Children and Family

Our final intention for a sound Catholic marriage is openness to children and family. In his remarkably insightful encyclical letter *Familiaris Consortio*, Saint John Paul expresses how children and the covenant of family bring *eros*—exclusive indissoluble conjugal love—to its fruition:

> In its most profound reality, love is essentially a gift; and conjugal love, while leading the spouses to the reciprocal "knowledge" which makes them "one flesh" (cf. Gn 2, 24), does not end with the couple, because it makes them capable of the greatest possible gift, the gift by which they become cooperators with God for giving life to a new human person. Thus the couple, while giving themselves to one another, give not just themselves but also the reality of children, who are a living reflection of their love, a permanent sign of conjugal unity and a living and inseparable synthesis of their being a father and a mother.[74]

Children and family raise the dignity of marriage to a supreme height by the creation of two new loving and transcendent realities:

1. Children whose transcendent and eternal nature is brought into existence by God's creation of their unique transphysical soul
2. A familial bond and home that will bring the parent's and children's love to heightened fulfillment

The objective of conjugal love, from a natural-biological point of view, is procreation. This procreative act goes far beyond a merely biological activity, for it brings a transcendent and eternal soul into existence through God's creative act. Parents provide the occasion for the creation of this transcendent soul by creating not only a body to which the soul will be united, but also a loving, spiritual covenant

[74]John Paul II, *Familiaris Consortio* (November 22, 1981), no. 14, www.vatican.va/content /john-paul-ii/en/apost_exhortations/documents/hf_jp-ii_exh_19811122_familiaris-consortio .html.

in which the child's spirit will be awakened and fed by faith, religion, love, moral goodness, wisdom, and education.

Recall from Volume II of the Quartet that God's creation of a unique, transcendental soul gives rise not only to our capacity to survive bodily death, but also to five kinds of transcendental awareness and desire—the desire for perfect truth, love, goodness-justice, beauty, and home, a profoundly spiritual awareness and yearning that finds its culmination not only in the perfection of these attributes, but in communion with the unconditionally loving Trinity themselves. There can be no higher calling in human life than this—except perhaps the actual care and guidance of souls toward their fulfillment in God. Parents have both roles—being the instruments through which God creates a soul (or souls) as well as the ground of a faithful family through which that soul can be guided to eternal life.

The immense dignity of the parental vocation does not eclipse the dignity of the married vocation addressed above—they complement one another. Though a single parent can raise a child well, the ideal for the child is to have the love, support, faith, and guidance of both parents, individually and collectively, so that they may benefit from the distinct contributions and the unitive love coming from the couple. This underlies Jesus' admonition to intend marriage indissolubly.

Evidently, this ideal parental contribution may be interrupted or undermined because of negative challenges along life's way, such as unanticipated stresses and difficulties that seriously undermine the individuals or the relationship, or endangerment of the children (arising out of drugs, alcohol, or unforeseen psychological disorders). However, when mitigating factors can be managed through faith, charity, and virtue, God's will is that we continue to solemnly intend the indissolubility of the marriage for the sake of the couple, the relationship, and above all, the children. If we do this, the children will be the beneficiaries of the spouses' unity, stability, and synergistic and complementary action, as well as their spiritual life, moral principles, wisdom, and education. If divorce or death of a spouse should occur, spouses must do their best to ensure that the children see the dignity of the other spouse and learn the common principles of their parents—despite their separated condition.

The vocation of parenthood is not only one of the highest possible meanings of life that brings the union of marriage to its fulfillment and highest dignity; children themselves also enhance the lives of their parents as well as the marital union itself. We do not have to look very far to see how much the love of children means to the identity, dignity, and meaning of the parents. Children impart this kind of meaning and fulfillment to their parents on a daily basis by simply expressing natural affection and need. Yes, temper tantrums, bad behavior, and life's discouragements punctuate the parent-child relationship, but the bond of love between generative parents and their children is so strong that parents naturally transform these challenges into occasions of self-sacrificial love (*agapē*). This seems to happen almost universally even in families that are severely challenged by environmental and economic stresses. This natural bond—this natural manifestation of self-sacrificial love—is most often undermined when parents are cruel, unloving, or uncaring, or when children have severe psychological difficulties brought on by physical challenges (brain and nervous system disorders), severe trauma, inherited addictions from parents, physiological problems arising out of maturation, friendships with unstable or troubled children, or an absence of hope (from lack of religion and significant friendships). The challenges, emotions, independence, mischievousness, and tensions of adolescence are generally overcome if parents remain patient, loving, and firm in guidance and support, showing dignity, love, and faith. When parents remain steady and committed to their children, children will eventually return their love, in gifts of appreciation, faithfulness, love, meaning in life, and when they are older, physical and psychological support. This loving and life-giving relationship will endure throughout eternity—complemented by the divine parental love of the Trinity.

The family is a reflection of the Holy Trinity itself. The Trinity's love is not complete when the Father loves the Son and the Son, receiving the love of the Father, loves Him in return. They form a union with one another—and this loving union goes beyond itself just as the love of both individuals must go beyond themselves. Thus when the union between the parents moves beyond itself to the good of the children, it replicates the union between the Father and the Son moving beyond itself to the Holy Spirit.

Yet, familial love does not end there. When children receive this unitive love from their parents, they return love to their parents in a way that makes their *parents'* love and bondedness come alive and solidify. This is very similar to the fourth loving procession of the Holy Trinity. The Spirit does not simply receive the love of the Father and Son—He returns His love to the Father and Son, which completes (fulfills) their love for one another.[75] In this sense, the family—imitating the Trinity—gives rise to the highest and most complete manifestation of interpersonal human love.

Insofar as the grace of the Sacrament of Matrimony supports all of the above intentions (when couples act on them), it also supports, actualizes, and enhances spiritual and moral conversion. For many families, the sacred covenant of marriage (and the grace coming through it) is the most profoundly felt pathway to these two kinds of conversion—and therefore to the actualization of committed love and to salvation.

E. The Grace of Holy Orders

Priesthood in the Catholic Church is the priesthood of Jesus Christ. It is one of the most vital sacramental gifts given by the Lord to the Church for spiritual and moral conversion, and, ultimately, for redemption. The extraordinary grace of this sacrament, enabling the priest to act in the place and Person of Christ, transforms him in the image of Christ through his service to the faithful. We will discuss the sacrament in three sections:

1. Priesthood in the Teaching of Jesus (Section II.E.1)
2. Doctrine and Practice of the Priesthood (Section II.E.2)
3. A Spirituality of the Priesthood (Section II.E.3)

---

[75] There is an important difference between the Holy Trinity and the interpersonal relationship within a family. The love of the parents creates the embodiment of the child through which God *creates* the child's soul. In contrast, the Holy Spirit is not created by the love of the Father and the Son—He is naturally generated from the one unrestricted power and nature of God from all eternity, just as the Father and the Son. We do not know *how* this eternal generation of the three Persons occurs from the one unrestricted power–nature of God; we only know *that* it can occur through this unrestricted power because there is no limit to what can be timelessly generated through an unrestricted power timelessly existing through itself. See the metaphysical proof of God in Volume II (Appendix II) of the Quartet and the explanation of the Holy Trinity in Volume III (Appendix II) of the Quartet.

1. Priesthood in the Teaching of Jesus

As noted above (Section I.B), the New Testament does not speak about the ministerial priesthood arising out of the Sacrament of Holy Orders, but rather about apostles, prophets, and presbyters who are responsible for celebrating the Eucharistic commemoration. The apostolic Church did not want to confuse their ordained ministers (apostles and prophets) with the Jewish priesthood, and so she shied away from using the term "priest" of her ordained ministers. Nevertheless, New Testament sources reveal that the successors to the apostles became known as "bishops" (*episcopoi*) and successors to the prophets became *presbyteroi*. Later, in the second century, *presbyteroi* were called "priests", because of the association of the Eucharistic celebration with the sacrifice of Jesus. Let's examine some of these New Testament texts.

We have four primary texts showing Jesus' intention to initiate a special ministerial office (having special powers) within the Church. The first is with respect to Jesus' institution of the Holy Eucharist, the second with respect to the Sacrament of Penance (or Reconciliation), the third with respect to the juridical authority to excommunicate and restore membership within the community, and the fourth with respect to Baptism. Let us examine each passage.

In all three Synoptic Gospels, Jesus concludes His Eucharistic commemoration with the words of anamnesis: "Do this in remembrance of me" (Lk 22:19; see Mt 26:17–30; Mk 14:12–26; Lk 7–30). These words are addressed to the apostles who are being directed by Jesus to commemorate His Eucharistic words after His Passion and Resurrection. Recall that this commemoration produces a collapse of time that brings the grace of the past (Jesus' whole self given in complete self-offering—unconditional love) into the present through the reliving of the Eucharistic event by designated presiders of the ritual (see above, Section I.A). The apostolic Church interpreted Jesus' words to mean that not only the apostles would be official presiders over the Eucharistic commemoration, but also their successors and a second tier of leaders—the prophets.

The second passage concerned with Jesus' intention to initiate a special ministerial office for the apostles and their successors is John 20:21–23:

Jesus said to them again, "Peace be with you. As the Father has sent me, even so I send you." And when he had said this, he breathed on them, and said to them, "Receive the Holy Spirit. If you forgive the sins of any, they are forgiven; if you retain the sins of any, they are retained."

Jesus imparted the Holy Spirit on the apostles to give them the power to forgive sins in His place. He is calling them to a special ministerial status through these special powers—and this special indwelling of the Holy Spirit. Again, the apostolic Church interpreted Jesus' intention in this action to be not only for the apostles, but also for their successors and the prophets (the second rung of Church leadership).

The third passage indicating Jesus' intention to create a special ministerial office is Matthew 18:18.

Truly, I say to you, whatever you bind on earth shall be bound in heaven, and whatever you loose on earth shall be loosed in heaven.

This passage refers to the apostles' power to excommunicate (exclude) a person from the community, as well as the power to restore a person to the community after excommunication. This is a juridical power that complements the power to forgive sins imparted by Jesus in John 20:23.[76] This juridical power implies a juridical office within the new Church to be founded on the rock of Peter (Mt 16:17–19). Evidently, this juridical office of binding and loosing was not reserved by Jesus to Peter alone, but to all the apostles (as indicated in Mt 18:18) and their successors (who would later be known as *episcopoi*—"bishops").

The fourth passage concerned with Jesus' intention to start a special ministerial office is Matthew 28:18–19:

Go therefore and make disciples of all nations, baptizing them in the name of the Father and of the Son and of the Holy Spirit, teaching them to observe all that I have commanded you; and behold, I am with you always, to the close of the age.

After the Resurrection, the disciples saw the risen Jesus in His glory, at which point He commissioned them to evangelize all nations and to baptize them, in the name of the Father, the Son, and the Holy

---

[76] See Benedict Viviano, "The Gospel according to Matthew", in Brown, Fitzmyer, and Murphy, *New Jerome Biblical Commentary*, p. 662.

Spirit. Though there is disagreement about whether Jesus would have used the Trinitarian formula of Baptism, the matter is really a moot point with respect to the institution of the Sacrament of Baptism. Matthew reveals that the apostolic Church clearly believed that the apostles and their successors were infused with the power to baptize all peoples not only in the name of Jesus and the Holy Spirit, but also in the name of the Father (see above, Section II.A).

What can we conclude from these four Gospel passages? It is clear that Jesus intended to give a special ministerial office to the apostles by imparting four ministerial powers (authority) upon them.[77]

As will be seen below, the apostles understood themselves to have one other ministerial power—the power to convey the ministerial office (and its four powers) to other worthy disciples to carry out the work of evangelization to which Jesus had commissioned them. The Acts of the Apostles and the letters of Paul speak of this additional power as belonging to the apostles and their successors alone.

In the Acts of the Apostles, Saint Luke indicates that Paul and Barnabas appointed elders (presbyters) by the laying on of hands in the missionary regions that they visited:

> And when they had appointed [ordained through the laying on of hands[78]] elders [presbyters] for them in every church, with prayer and fasting, they committed them to the Lord in whom they believed. (14:23)

What is the office of elder (presbyter)? In the Old Testament, "elders" have considerable authority—tantamount to scribes and priests—and their authority to interpret Torah was significant.[79] In the early Church, elders were accorded similar authority to teach, preach, and minister to the people. They were commissioned in the same way

---

[77] The term "apostle" means "one who is sent away" or "one who is sent on mission". When Jesus gave the apostles the four powers described above, He advances the meaning of the term from "one who is sent" to "one who has a ministerial office instituted by Jesus who imparted His ministerial power and authority on them".

[78] The Greek words *ceirotonhsantes cheirotonesantes* (literally, "hand-outstretching selecting") mean more than "appointment". The term refers directly to the laying on of hands, which refers to ordination to the presbyterate (see 1 Tim 4:14).

[79] John L. McKenzie, S.J., *Dictionary of the Bible* (New York: Macmillan, 1965), p. 226.

as elders in the Old Testament—by the laying on of hands (Num 27:18–23; Deut 34:9). Robert Wild suggests that the discernment of worthy candidates occurred through the community's prophets who discerned the charism of possible candidates. When they were selected, the apostles and elders laid hands on them, conveying special charisms of the Holy Spirit for their ministerial office.[80]

The elders (presbyters) are associated with the apostles and had authority similar to them during the Council of Jerusalem (see Acts 15).[81] Though the powers of the elders are not explicitly listed in the New Testament, we can infer from passages in the Pastoral Letters and the Letter of James that they had the power to teach, preach (1 Tim 5:17), and minister to the sick (Jas 5:14–15). We might also infer from 1 Timothy 4:14 that elders were given the charism of prophecy through the laying on of hands.

Prophecy is second only to the office of apostle in the early Church (see 1 Cor 12:28). It may seem strange to refer to the prophetic charism as indicative of a ministerial office, but this seems to be the understanding of Saint Paul and the apostolic Church. Moreover, this ministerial office seems to have an authority attached to it similar to that of the apostles (see Rom 12:6; 1 Cor 12:10; Eph 2:20; 3:5; 4:11).[82] Prophets had not only the charism to speak on behalf of God (as in the Old Testament), but also a cultic charism (to carry out the ministries assigned to the apostles—to celebrate the Eucharist, Baptism, forgiveness of sins, and to determine membership or exclusion from the Christian community).[83] This cultic function of the prophets is confirmed in the *Didache* (written ca. A.D. 95), which explicitly mentions the roles of the apostles and the prophets in the Eucharist: "but suffer the prophets to hold Eucharist as they will".[84] The *Didache* also indicates that there were itinerant apostles and prophets in missionary territories who celebrated the Eucharistic commemoration.[85]

---

[80] Robert Wild, "The Pastoral Letters", in Brown, Fitzmyer, and Murphy, *New Jerome Biblical Commentary*, p. 898.

[81] See McKenzie, *Dictionary of the Bible*, p. 226.

[82] See ibid., p. 699.

[83] See ibid.

[84] See *Didache* 10, 7.

[85] In *Didache* 11, a set of rules is given to distinguish true apostles and prophets from false apostles and prophets, with the implication being that there were itinerant apostles and prophets who had to be tested before they would be allowed to celebrate the Eucharist (see *Didache* 10, 7) and instruct the faithful.

The prophetic office—and its special authority and power within the Church—closely parallels the later-mentioned office of elders (presbyters) in the Acts of the Apostles (written ca. A.D. 85) and the Pastoral Letters (written ca. A.D. 100).[86] Apparently, in the twenty or so years between the writing of Paul's letters and the completion of the Acts of the Apostles, the ministerial and leadership office of prophet is gradually referred to as the "office of presbyter". They are essentially the same office with similar authority and power to lead the Church in a particular region (or a part of a region) as well as to preach, teach, and celebrate the Eucharist and other cultic activities. By A.D. 100 (the writing of the Letter to Titus), the office of prophet has transitioned almost fully into the office of presbyter, and presbyters are being appointed (through the laying on of hands) by bishops (*episcopoi*) in every missionary region:

> This is why I left you in Crete, that you amend what was defective, and appoint presbyters in every town as I directed you. (1:5)

How did the office of bishop (*episcopoi*) develop? By the year A.D. 100 (the writing of the Pastoral Letters) all the apostles had passed away, and so the office of apostle had no membership. The new office of the successors to the apostles was eventually called *episcopoi* (overseers or guardians). *Episcopoi* were already recognized as a group of trusted leaders in Paul's Letter to the Philippians (see 1:1). By the writing of the Pastoral Letters, *episcopoi* had two functions:

- Leaders of household churches in which a local community congregated (for the Eucharistic commemoration and other ministries)
- A regional leader (succeeding the apostles) with the power to appoint presbyters and to monitor, correct, and discipline other bishops (leaders of household churches)

The final stage of conceptual development for *presbyteroi* occurred in the late second century. As noted above, by that time, there was little chance for confusing *presbyteroi* (elders) with the Jewish priesthood of

---

[86] Wild, "Pastoral Letters", in Brown, Fitzmyer, and Murphy, *New Jerome Biblical Commentary*, p. 893.

Aaron and Levi. Furthermore, the celebration of the Holy Eucharist (within the Holy Mass) was associated with Jesus' self-sacrificial act in His Passion, death, and Resurrection. Hence, the office of *presbyteroi* became known as "priests" sometime around A.D. 180, when Saint Irenaeus recognized that the successors to the apostles were all priests.[87] This is later confirmed by Origen in A.D. 232,[88] after which the association of the presbyterate with "priests" becomes virtually commonplace.

2. Doctrine and Practice of the Priesthood

From the above explanation of the New Testament and early history of prophets, presbyters, and priests, we can infer the definition of Holy Orders given in the *Catechism of the Catholic Church*:

> Holy Orders is the sacrament through which the mission entrusted by Christ to his apostles continues to be exercised in the Church until the end of time: thus it is the sacrament of apostolic ministry. It includes three degrees: episcopate, presbyterate, and diaconate.[89]

Ordination is an integration into one of the three ministerial offices ("ordo") instituted by Jesus—bishop, presbyter, or deacon. It confers special powers of the Holy Spirit upon the ordinand through the laying on of hands and a special blessing of consecration by the bishop. Thus, ordination imparts a special gift of the Holy Spirit that gives a sacramental power and sets the man apart as a successor of the apostles.

The priest, by virtue of his ordination, acts in the Person of Christ Himself, who is the one and only high priest. In *Mediator Dei*, Pius XII explains:

> It is the same priest, Christ Jesus, whose sacred person his minister truly represents. Now the minister, by reason of the sacerdotal

---

[87] Saint Irenaeus states that "all the apostles of the Lord are priests, who do inherit here neither lands nor houses, but serve God and the altar continually" (*Against Heresies* 4, 8, 3).

[88] As quoted above in Section I.B.1, Origen states, "So, too, the apostles, and those who have become like apostles, being priests according to the Great High Priest and having received knowledge of the service of God, know under the Spirit's teaching for which sins, and when, and how they ought to offer sacrifices, and recognize for which they ought not to do so" (*On Prayer* 18).

[89] CCC 1536.

consecration which he has received, is truly made like to the high priest and possesses the authority to act in the power and place of the person of Christ himself (*virtute ac persona ipsius Christi*).[90]

The "authority to act in the power and place of the person of Christ" was given to the apostles and their successors by Jesus Himself when He gave them the same four sacred powers He exercised throughout His ministry:

- The power to stand in His Person in the celebration of the Eucharist—"Do this in remembrance of me" (Lk 22:19; see Mt 26:17–30; Mk 14:12–26; Lk 22:7–30).
- The power to forgive sins—"If you forgive the sins of any, they are forgiven" (Jn 20:22).
- The power to excommunicate from and restore membership to the Church community—"Whatever you bind on earth shall be bound in heaven, and whatever you loose on earth shall be loosed in heaven" (Mt 16:19; 18:18; cf. Jn 20:23).
- The power to baptize and teach—"Go therefore and make disciples of all nations, baptizing them in the name of the Father the Son and the Holy Spirit, teaching them to observe all that I have commanded you" (Mt 28:19–20). These ministerial commissions given to the apostles and their successors impart the power of Christ Himself—to take the place of Christ, the high priest.

The power to "act in the place of the Person of Christ" is ministerial; it does not mean that a priest is always a reflection of the Person of Christ. Priests can make theological errors and misleading statements; they can sin, be imprudent, and make poor judgments, though they are called to do their best to imitate Christ, whose Person they represent (see below, Section II.E.3). Since the priest acts in place of the Person of Christ during his sacramental service, his sinfulness and imperfection cannot impede the power and perfection of Christ's presence in the sacramental action.[91]

---

[90] Pope Pius XII, encyclical *Mediator Dei* (November 20, 1947): AAS 39 (1947), p. 548.
[91] See *CCC* 1550.

As noted above, there are three degrees of Holy Orders: bishops (the fullness of Holy Orders), presbyters (who share in the ministerial priesthood with the bishops, but are subordinate to them), and deacons (who are in service to the bishop and presbyters in the administration of the Church, but do not share in the ministerial priesthood). Thus, there are two degrees of orders within ministerial priesthood (bishops and presbyters), and one nonpriestly degree of orders (deacons). Each degree of orders has specific powers and authority that are imparted by the laying on of hands and the specific blessing of consecration.

In conclusion, through the Sacrament of Baptism, the faithful are integrated into the common priesthood of the body of Christ (1 Pet 2:9). Yet, Christ also instituted a ministerial priesthood by giving the apostles and their successors the commission, authority, and special ministerial powers to preside over the sacraments and the governance of the Church. Thus, ordained ministers, whether they be bishops, presbyters, or deacons, are the unifying and governing fabric of the Church, without which it would not exist. The Sacrament of Holy Orders confers a special, indelible, sacred character upon the ordained minister that cannot be repeated or removed. It configures him to the Person of Christ and enables priests (bishops and presbyters) to act in the power and place of his Person. Thus, the integral hierarchical structure of the Church results from Christ's institution of ordained ministry to the apostles and their successors.

The Sacrament of Holy Orders (in all three of its degrees) is essential to spiritual and moral conversion. Bishops and priests (and to some extent deacons) are representatives of the Magisterium of the Church, and so provide the guidance needed by the faithful to grow more deeply in Christ and to avoid errors that could jeopardize their faith and moral conversion. Jesus foresaw the need for this hierarchically instituted teaching and guidance ministry within the role of shepherd. Furthermore, bishops and priests confect all of the sacraments except Matrimony (which is contracted by the parties themselves before a bishop, priest, or deacon within the Church). Deacons can perform the Sacrament of Baptism (and in emergencies, laypeople can baptize). Deacons can also officiate at marriages. As explained above, the grace and power of these sacraments is essential to supporting and strengthening our faith as well as spiritual and moral conversion.[92] Jesus foresaw the need to have these sacraments available to the faithful not only for their spiritual and moral conversion, but also for the purposes of strengthening marriage, evangelization, and serving the most needy. In short, the Sacrament of Holy Orders is the font (source) from which the Church disseminates the sacramental grace of Jesus Christ (through the Holy Spirit) as well as the teaching and guiding functions so necessary to keep the faithful on the path to salvation. What could be more important for our spiritual and moral conversion? In view of this we must follow Jesus' request to pray for more priests and deacons:

> When he saw the crowds, he had compassion for them, because they were harassed and helpless, like sheep without a shepherd. Then he said to his disciples, "The harvest is plentiful, but the laborers are few; pray therefore the Lord of the harvest to send out laborers into his harvest" (Mt 9:36–38)

3. A Spirituality of the Priesthood

Ordination to the priesthood is at once a transformative grace and an acceptance of tremendous responsibility. The grace is an ontological transformation—being allowed to stand in the Person of Christ (*in persona Christi*), which demands a spiritual and moral transformation on the part of the priest to conform as best he can to the heart and spirit of the incarnate Lord He represents. Additionally, the priest must try to present the face and heart of Jesus to the people around him—not only to his particular flock, but also to those outside the parish, the Church, and even his culture. Though standing in the Person of Christ occurs formally in the celebration of the Holy Eucharist, the Sacrament of Reconciliation, and other sacraments, the priest brings the face and heart of the Lord to every Church meeting, community outreach, social occasion, and encounter with the People of God.

If the priest is to represent and present Christ to the community and the world, he must first know Him—know His heart, mind, and desire to save. He must know the Lord's love for the faithful, sinners, the marginalized, the powerful, the poor, the rich, Christians,

---

[92] The Sacrament of Reconciliation is particularly important for moral conversion. This will be explained in Chapter 7 after the explanation of moral conversion.

non-Christians—indeed, everyone made in the image and likeness of God. He must identify with Christ's compassion for the sick, the poor, the suffering, and sinners; Christ's joy in relating to His followers; Christ's firmness and courage in dealing with adversaries; and His resoluteness in confronting evil and the Evil One. A priest must be devoted to the truth of Christ's teaching as interpreted by the Church, and must find pastorally sensitive ways of presenting that truth to those who are seeking it. He must also follow the Lord in evangelizing those who are not part of the faithful or seekers, and protect His flock from those who are deceivers and adversaries. He must at once present the face of mercy and compassion as well as the truth about sin and darkness, and be simple in heart and nuanced in mind.

Thus, the charism of standing *in persona Christi* requires not only philosophical and theological education, but also prayer—contemplative prayer—that appropriates the heart of Jesus in the Scriptures, the tradition, our own hearts, and the lives of those around us. The prayer life of a priest is grounded first and foremost in the celebration and reception of the Holy Eucharist, which conforms his heart to the One for whom he stands in mysterious and deliberate ways. This transformation is reinforced and protected from the Evil One by frequently participating in the Sacrament of Reconciliation (see Chapter 7) and through the daily recitation of the Divine Office (the Breviary—see Chapter 3, Section III.B.2), as well as contemplative prayer. The Breviary is the prayer of the Church and the bedrock of priestly prayer, but it must be complemented by additional contemplative prayer aimed at deepening the priest's relationship with the Lord. Contemplative prayer has two dimensions. The first is a deep appropriation of the Person and heart of Jesus in the Gospels, which can be enhanced significantly by the practice of Ignatian contemplation and *lectio divina* (see Chapter 3, Section II). The second dimension of contemplative prayer is the prayer of companionship (see Chapter 3, Section III.C.2).

The prayer of companionship is particularly important because we open ourselves to Christ's heart coming close to us, influencing us, leading us, and transforming us as we seek His mercy for our weakness and His inspiration for our progress. Through this we become aware of the many ways in which He has forgiven us, protected us, guided us, and called us from our darkness into His light of truth and love. As this occurs, we are inspired to express our sincere and deep gratitude for His love, followed by our exclamation "and I love you too." Sometimes, His voice pops into the back of our minds, expressing His call to us and His love for us (see Chapter 3, Section V).

These intimate encounters in contemplative prayer galvanize the grace of the Holy Eucharist (see above, Section I.C), the Sacrament of Reconciliation, and the Breviary, which opens the way to showing the authentic heart of Jesus to the Church community and the world. They also open the way to standing authentically in the Person of Christ during the celebration of the Holy Eucharist, the preaching of the Word, and the celebration of the other sacraments. Without this contemplative prayer, a priest can quickly lose his authenticity and bearing in representing the Lord to the world.

In sum, a priest must, as Saint Ignatius noted, be a contemplative in action. He must appropriate the heart of Christ in the Holy Eucharist, his contemplative prayer, and the Sacrament of Reconciliation, then bring that heart to the community he serves, filled with compassion, love, truth, joy, firmness, gentleness, and faith. If he is genuine about manifesting the Lord's heart to others, they will recognize it right away, thank him, feed him, and contribute to his sanctification. As a priest manifests Christ to his flock, they will manifest Christ back to him. Their gratitude, growth in faith, and indispensable support express the Lord's love for him, his work, and the community around him. Contemplation purifies action, and authentic action enhances contemplation.

Thus, the priest's appropriation of the Lord's love in prayer, his sharing of it *in persona Christi*, and his reception of it from the community forms his identity and spirit, filled with the heart of Christ—an identity and spirit that can faithfully lead the community, face challenges, and protect and be fed by the community. It is precisely what Jesus asked the Father for His apostles as He approached His Passion, death, and Resurrection:

> [Father,] I have manifested your name to the men whom you gave me from out of the world; they were yours, and you gave them to me, and they have kept your word. Now they know that everything that you have given me is from you; for I have given them the words which you gave me, and they have received them and know in truth

that I came from you.... I do not pray that you should take them out of the world, but that you should keep them from the evil one. They are not of the world, even as I am not of the world. Sanctify them in the truth; your word is truth. As you sent me into the world, so I have sent them into the world. And for their sake I consecrate myself, that they also may be consecrated in truth.... O righteous Father, the world has not known you, but I have known you; and these know that you have sent me. I made known to them your name, and I will make it known, that the love with which you have loved me may be in them, and I in them. (Jn 17:6–8, 15–19, 25–26)

As a priest encounters the Lord in contemplative prayer, seeking to know His heart, he puts himself in the place of the apostles in Jesus' priestly prayer. At this point, Jesus can reveal to him the "name" (the heart and essence) of His Father. As the priest comes closer to Jesus, he knows more intimately the heart of His Father, which allows the Lord to protect him from the Evil One, to sanctify him in truth, and to fill him with the very love with which the Father loves Jesus. Being filled with that love enables the priest to bring the Person of Jesus authentically to the world. He becomes less vulnerable to the temptations of the Evil One and the allurements of the world, preferring the light, truth, and love of his master, Jesus, who has brought the heart of His Father to the world.

As a follower of Jesus, a priest will invariably encounter the cross in his own life, the sufferings of his flock, and hostility to Jesus' truth from the secular culture, fierce adversaries, the Evil One, and even his own faith community. From his prayerful identity and serenity, the priest will instinctively know how to show his flock the presence, guidance, redemption, and salvation of the Lord to help them move beyond their suffering and darkness into the hope and light of Christ. His prayerful identity in the Lord will also help him encourage his community to be countercultural and to confront the sophisticated sophistry and omnipresent allurements of materialism, egoism, and the eight deadly sins. By being true to the teachings and mercy of Jesus, he will open and guide his flock to the light of Truth and Love itself—the heart of the Father. This will galvanize the grace of the Eucharist, the Sacrament of Reconciliation, and other sacraments within the individual and collective heart of the Church community—the Mystical Body of Christ.

The stronger the priest's prayerful identity in Christ, the more authentically he stands in the Person of Christ in the Holy Eucharist, the Sacrament of Reconciliation, and the other sacraments, as well as in preaching and teaching. His identification with Christ in celebrating the sacraments intensifies his love for the One whom he represents. The priest takes this love back to contemplative prayer, which enables the Lord to transform his heart to even closer conformity with His own. This not only affects the way the priest celebrates Mass and the other sacraments, but also deepens his trust in God, his reverence for the teachings of Jesus, and his love for the people he serves. As a result, the priest takes on a close affinity with the Lord, enabling him to bring Christ's truth to the people in the ways they need to hear it. As they grow in faith, the priest finds fulfillment in his priestly identity and ministry, for he is not simply carrying out the function of an office, but is substantializing his priestly character and identity (received at ordination) through the heart of Jesus Christ.

F. The Grace of the Sacrament of the Sick

We can see how the above six sacraments are foundational and integral to spiritual and moral conversion, but what about the Sacrament of the Anointing of the Sick? As Jesus and the Church have taught, suffering is an integral part of our lives, and one of the best ways to incite spiritual and moral conversion—particularly when we are faced with the prospect of imminent death. As we shall see, the five graces of the Sacrament of the Anointing of the Sick (explained below) help to convert the experiences of suffering and dying into both conversion and loving service to the Kingdom of God.

It should be noted that God does not want anyone to suffer any more than parents want their children to suffer, yet they allow their children to engage in school, sports, and challenging situations that may cause suffering and pain. They do this because they know that their children will benefit from these challenging activities and even from the moments of suffering and pain arising out of them. The Lord is the same way—He allows us to live in an imperfect and challenging world that will have suffering and pain, but He works through the Holy Spirit, especially the graces of this sacrament, to bring about deep spiritual and moral conversion leading to salvation. Before discussing this, we will first look at the origins of this sacrament in the New Testament.

The Anointing of the Sick has a strong foundation in both the Gospels and the Letter of James (ca. A.D. 63). Inasmuch as this apostolic ritual effects grace through the laying on of hands and the sign of blessed oil, and confers not only the forgiveness of sins, but also the healing power of Jesus Christ through the Holy Spirit (as shown in the Letter of James cited below), it is considered a sacrament.[93] This sacramental view of anointing is implicit in Jesus' conferral of the power to heal through anointing during His ministry:

> [The Apostles] cast out many demons, and anointed with oil many that were sick and healed them. (Mk 6:13)

It seems that the apostles referred back to the power of healing through anointing given to them by Jesus when they integrated it into their earliest ritual celebrations, which gave rise to the exhortation in the Letter of James.

Though the Acts of the Apostles addresses healing only through the ritual of laying on of hands (8:17–18; 19:6), the Letter of James speaks of the apostles' praying over the sick and anointing them with oil:

> Is any among you sick? Let him call for the elders [*presbyters*] of the Church, and let them pray over him, anointing him with oil in the name of the Lord; and the prayer of faith will save the sick man, and the Lord will raise him up; and if he has committed sins, he will be forgiven. (Jas 5:14–15)

Perhaps praying over the sick (in the above passage) refers to laying on of hands, but it is unclear. What is clear is that prior to James' letter, there was a strong ritual tradition (that James presupposes) of praying over and anointing the sick in the name of the Lord for the forgiveness of sins, restoration to physical health, and restoration to spiritual health.

---

[93] The formal declaration of the sacramentality of this sacred anointing by a priest was declared at the Council of Trent (Session 14).

The *Catechism of the Catholic Church* describes five graces of the Sacrament of the Anointing of the Sick as follows:

> The special grace of the sacrament of the Anointing of the Sick has as its effects:
>
> —the uniting of the sick person to the passion of Christ, for his own good and that of the whole Church;
> —the strengthening, peace, and courage to endure in a Christian manner the sufferings of illness or old age;
> —the forgiveness of sins, if the sick person was not able to obtain it through the sacrament of Penance;
> —the restoration of health, if it is conducive to the salvation of his soul;
> —the preparation for passing over to eternal life.[94]

We will consider each of these graces in turn.

The first grace—the uniting of the sick person to the Passion of Christ—joins the sufferings of the sick person to the self-sacrifice of Jesus on the Cross. As explained in Volume IV (Chapter 8) of the Quartet, Jesus transformed His suffering and death into an act of voluntary self-sacrifice to the Father, making Himself a sin offering for the forgiveness of sins and the eternal salvation of all people in the world. Recall that Jesus viewed self-sacrifice (gift of self) as an act of unconditional love that has the power to forgive sins, transform hearts, and help us to enter into eternal life with Him. Saint Paul invites us to join our sufferings to Jesus' sufferings to transform them into the same loving grace that the Father will use to help the Church and redeem the world (see Col 1:24). The Sacrament of the Anointing of the Sick helps us to make this offering of ourselves in imitation of Jesus so that our sufferings may have an optimally good effect on our families, friends, strangers, and the whole Kingdom of God. Hence, it facilitates and strengthens our spiritual conversion through suffering.

The second grace of the sacrament is the peace and courage to endure suffering through our Christian faith. We may recall times when we have lost a loved one or suffered a setback, and in the midst of feeling grief and loss, we also feel an overwhelming sense of peace—that everything is going to be alright, that God is taking care of everything. Even though we have no idea why this would be the case, or how it might come to pass—we have a strong sense of conviction and peace that we do not have to be in charge, because God is already taking care of us and the ones we love. Sometimes the Lord gives us this peace, conviction, and courage gratuitously; nevertheless, He likes to be asked, and this sacrament is the ideal way to do so, because His Son has provided us with the Holy Spirit, who brings to us "the peace of God, which passes all understanding" (Phil 4:7), through the laying on of hands and the anointing with sacred oil (see Mk 6:12–13; 16:17–18). Many have been the times I have seen this peace flow through the recipients of holy anointing before surgeries, extensive medical treatments, and passing from this world to the next. Inasmuch as peace enables us to see better the spiritual benefits of our suffering, to trust in the Lord, and to offer that suffering for the sake of souls in the Church, it greatly assists our spiritual conversion.

The third grace—the forgiveness of sins—is given through the Sacrament of the Anointing of the Sick, as James proclaims—"and if he has committed sins, he will be forgiven" (Jas 5:15). As we shall see (Chapter 7), the Sacrament of Reconciliation has several distinct graces that make it the ideal way to obtain the forgiveness of sins, reunification with the Mystical Body of Christ, and graced resolve to do better in the future. Nevertheless, there are many occasions in which a sick person will not be able to receive the Sacrament of Reconciliation before receiving the Sacrament of the Anointing of the Sick, because time may be short and/or the sick person may not be able to prepare for Reconciliation due to cognitive impairment from injury or illness, inability to concentrate for long-enough periods of time to examine conscience and confess sins, and so forth. In all such cases, the Sacrament of the Anointing of the Sick, by itself, is sufficient to mediate (through the bishop or priest) Christ's gift of the forgiveness of sins. Evidently, this gift, along with Viaticum (Holy Communion at the time of passing), is tremendously efficacious and helpful for a dying person as well as those who are seriously ill. In view of this, the grace of the Sacrament of the Anointing of the Sick is integral to moral conversion.

The fourth grace—restoration to health—is a grace of the s effected by both the laying on of hands and the anointing wi oil. Recall that there are many opportunities in sickness and s that help us toward salvation (and also help us to help others toward salvation)—shocking us out of superficial or dark lives, strengthening our reliance on God, helping us to be humble, deepening our empathy and compassion, and helping us to live in the light of faith and the Holy Spirit so that we can become true spiritual leaders, imitating Jesus in His self-offering to the Father (unconditional love) for the world. If sickness and suffering are having these important good effects on us, then the Lord will not remedy our illness through the Sacrament of the Anointing of the Sick. His first priority is to *save us*, His second priority to help us lead others to salvation, and His third priority to alleviate sickness and suffering. Hence, this fourth grace—restoration to health through the supernatural power of God—will only occur if it does not interrupt the more important graces of salvation, and spiritual and moral conversion. However, if our sickness or suffering is not needed for these more important purposes, then we can be sure, in faith, that God's supernatural power will help us to regain our health.

This does not mean that we should rely solely on supernatural power through the grace of the sacrament to heal us. We should avail ourselves of every feasible and ethical medical treatment to restore our health, and then complement these treatments with the supernatural power of God. Grace builds on nature—not only in our spiritual lives, but also in our physical bodies.

The fifth grace of the sacrament is preparation to pass over into eternal life. It is really a combination of the previous four graces— forgiveness to reconcile us with God, peace to settle our minds and hearts amid apprehensions at the time of passing, the endurance of suffering during the time of transition, and the grace to unite our sufferings with those of Christ. Following are the words of the sacramental formula:

"Through this holy anointing may the Lord in his love and mercy help you with the grace of the Holy Spirit. May the Lord who frees you from sin save you and raise you up" (cf. CIC, can. 847 § 1).[95]

[95] Ibid., 1513.

As we listen to the words of the sacramental formula, the Spirit galvanizes our sense of peace, endurance, and confidence so that when we receive Christ's Body and Blood, we will meet Him in our hearts as He prepares us to leave this world and go to His Kingdom. This is a catalyzing and concluding dimension of spiritual conversion.

III. Conclusion

By now it may be evident that the outer Church is concerned with two major areas of our spiritual and moral conversion:

1. The provision of a supreme authority to guide and teach the faithful in matters of faith and morals (see Chapter 1)
2. The administration and dissemination of the seven sacraments, giving us the grace needed to support and strengthen our spiritual and moral conversion, marriages, evangelization efforts, service efforts, and community life

Without the grace and guidance of the outer Church, the interior life (the inner Church) would be dependent on our own interpretation of Scripture and bereft of the special grace of the Holy Spirit manifest through the sacraments instituted by Jesus. Yet, the guidance and graces of the outer Church are not enough, for as we have noted several times above, the faithful must cooperate with that guidance and grace, and when they do, they can deepen their faith (spiritual conversion) as well as their moral conversion (toward holiness) in the imitation of Jesus.

The gifts of the inner Church, complementing the grace of the outer Church, will lead the faithful on a remarkable journey through the Holy Spirit and the Mystical Body of Christ (into which they are integrated through Baptism). The inner journey occurs through the spiritual gifts of the inner Church—the sense of the heart of Jesus, the *sensus fidelium*, and the sense of the Church community throughout the ages (*Koinōnia*). This divine presence within us is deepened and solidified by contemplative prayer—contemplation on the Word of God, building a contemplative spiritual life, and devotion to Blessed Mary and the saints. This will be the subject of Chapter 3.

Chapter Three

Spiritual Conversion and the "Inner Church"—the Life of Prayer

Introduction

We have already addressed spiritual conversion and the outer Church—the Church of the Magisterium, Holy Eucharist, sacramental grace, and worldwide spiritual community. Yet, there is a whole other interior dimension of spiritual conversion underlying moral conversion—the Church of Christ's Mystical Body, the indwelling of the Holy Spirit, and the inner Word speaking to our hearts—the inner Church that supports, deepens, and strengthens contemplative life. For Christians, contemplative prayer is the means through which we allow the Lord to love us, heal us, and encourage us on the most intimate level, which elicits from us gratitude, sorrow for sin, and above all, love in return. This process occurs intimately through the indwelling of the Holy Spirit, who knows the mind and heart of the Father and Jesus:

> As it is written, "No eye has seen, nor ear heard, nor the heart of man conceived, what God has prepared for those who love him," God has revealed to us through the Spirit. For the Spirit searches everything, even the depths of God. For what person knows a man's thoughts except the spirit of the man which is in him? So also no one comprehends the thoughts of God except the Spirit of God. Now we have received not the spirit of the world, but the Spirit which is from God, that we might understand the gifts bestowed on us by God. And we impart this in words not taught by human wisdom but taught by the Spirit, interpreting spiritual truths to those who possess the Spirit. (1 Cor 2:9–13)

Our incorporation into Christ's Mystical Body (through Baptism) brings with it the indwelling of the Holy Spirit, who imbues us with the mind and heart of God Himself. The Divine Heart gradually becomes more manifest to us when we enter into a life of prayer and contemplation and receive the graces of the sacraments (explained in the previous chapter). But how do we enter into a life of contemplation? We will explore this in seven sections:

1. The Gifts of the Inner Church (Section I)
2. Contemplating on the Word of God (Section II)
3. Contemplation and Personal Relationship with the Lord (Section III)
4. Holiness and the School of the Cross (Section IV)
5. Some Ways in Which the Lord May Speak (Section V)
6. Marian Devotion (Section VI)
7. The Saints and Hagiography (Section VII)

When we combine these dimensions of the contemplative life with the faithful reception of the Holy Eucharist and the grace of the other sacraments, our love for the Lord cannot help but deepen, which not only leads us closer to our salvation in Him, but also enables us to help others do the same.

I. The Gifts of the Inner Church

When we are baptized we become part of the Mystical Body of Christ and are thereby connected with the heart of Christ through the Holy Spirit. When we are united with the heart of Christ, His heart speaks to our heart—at first subconsciously with desires, feelings, symbols, and notions, but as we make our faith more explicit, discursive, and conscious, His heart becomes progressively more manifest. What we first understand as mere feelings and desires becomes enhanced by a nuanced and discursive awareness of His love and goodness, the direction in which He is leading, and the way to deepen our conversion intellectually, morally, and spiritually.

Before proceeding to the specific spiritual gifts given to us in Baptism, we should recall that all people—baptized and unbaptized—are given three interior spiritual powers by God that invite them into communion with God through religious community, religious worship, sacred truths, and universal moral teachings:

1. The numinous experience (see Volume II, Chapter 1, of the Quartet)
2. The intuition of the sacred that draws all people to religious community, sacred worship, and sacred truths (see Volume II, Chapter 2, of the Quartet)
3. The sense of moral rectitude manifest in conscience as well as an awareness of the cosmic struggle between good and evil (see Volume II, Chapter 2 of the Quartet)

The gifts of the inner Church imparted through Baptism build upon the above spiritual gifts given to all people. Reviewing them here is beyond the scope of this Trilogy. However, since we are here concerned with moral conversion, it will be helpful to give a brief review of some of the points made about *conscience* in Volume II, Chapter 2, of the Quartet.

Recall that Plato believed that the highest reality was the good itself, and that the good itself was present to all, and that we could know it through questioning and dialectic.[1] Saint Paul brought these considerations to a whole new level by showing that all individuals could know the good (as well as evil) through their *conscience*. In the Letter to the Romans, he reflects on the Gentile's ability to know God's law without having the benefit of Judeo-Christian revelation:

> When Gentiles who not have the law do by nature what the law requires, they are a law to themselves, even though they do not have the law. They show that what the law requires is written on their hearts, while their conscience [συνειδησις] also bears witness and their conflicting thoughts accuse or perhaps excuse them. (2:14–15)

For Saint Paul, "the law" is *God's law*, and he asserts that God writes this law on the hearts of all people so distinctly that it accuses and defends them.

---

[1] See Plato, *The Republic* 7.

Saint Thomas Aquinas concurred with Saint Paul and formulated a general explanation of conscience that has become a cornerstone of philosophy up to the present time. Recall from Volume II (Chapter 2) that conscience has two components:

1. What Aquinas called *synderesis* (an attraction to and love of the good and a fear of and repulsion toward evil)
2. Awareness of certain *general* precepts of the good

With respect to *synderesis*, our attraction to and love of the good leads to feelings of nobility and fulfillment when we do good (or contemplate doing it). Conversely, our fear of and repulsion toward evil leads to feelings of guilt and alienation when we do evil (or contemplate doing it).[2]

Conscience not only has the above emotional and personal component; it also has an intellectual one. We have a sense of *what* is good or evil (in a general way). These precepts might include do good, avoid evil; do not kill an innocent person; do not unnecessarily injure another, steal from another, or otherwise unnecessarily harm another; give everyone what is owed to him in justice; and be truthful to yourself and others. This general "natural law" is explained in Volume III, Chapter 1, of this Trilogy.[3]

Aquinas associated these precepts of conscience with the natural law, holding that the natural law is part of God's eternal law:

> Now among all others, the rational creature is subject to Divine providence in the most excellent way, in so far as it partakes of a share of providence, by being provident both for itself and for others. Wherefore it has a share of the Eternal Reason, whereby it has a natural inclination to its proper act and end: *and this participation of the eternal law in the rational creature is called the natural law.*[4]

---

[2] "It is fitting that we have bestowed on us *by nature* not only speculative principles but also practical principles.... The first practical principles bestowed on us by nature, do not belong to a special power but to a special *natural* habit, which we call *synderesis*. Thus *synderesis* is said to incite to good and to murmur at evil, inasmuch as we proceed from first principles to discover and judge of what we have discovered." *The Summa Theologica of St. Thomas Aquinas*, trans. Fathers of the English Dominican Province, vol. 1 (New York: Benziger Brothers, 1947), I, q. 79, art. 12, p. 407 (italics added).

[3] For a lucid explanation of this "natural law" in all major religions, see C.S. Lewis, *The Abolition of Man* (New York: HarperCollins, 1974).

[4] *Summa Theologica* I–II, q. 91, art. 2 (italics added).

Immanuel Kant and John Henry Newman use conscience as a basis for inferring the presence (and therefore the existence) of a divine authority (God) within it. Newman shifts Kant's emphasis from an "obligation-imposing Subject outside ourselves" to an "interpersonal, caring, fatherly authority who is the source of goodness and law". He uses five existential inferences to move from the subjective feelings of conscience to the presence of God within it.[5] Given at least partial veracity of Newman's inference and the Catholic philosophical tradition from Saint Paul to Saint Thomas Aquinas, we can reasonably conclude that God is quite active in in our transphysical soul through our conscience.

The grace of the sacraments (outer Church) as well as the six *interior* gifts of the Holy Spirit (inner Church) make the general precepts of conscience come alive, leading them to their fulfillment. At Baptism, the Spirit heightens the function of our conscience by connecting it with the heart of Christ. The more we open ourselves to Christ in faith, the more His heart can speak to our conscience—awakening it with greater intuitions of God's love, knowledge, wisdom, and will. This has effects beyond the ordinary functions of conscience, helping us to sense or intuit the appropriateness or inappropriateness of theological ideas and interpretations of doctrines, as well as moral and spiritual advice and direction.

There are a myriad of interior gifts from the Holy Spirit that come with this integration into Christ's Mystical Body. We might classify them into six areas:[6]

1. The guidance, inspiration, and protection of the Holy Spirit, arising out of what we call "the conspiracy of divine providence" (discussed in Volume I, Chapter 1, of this Trilogy)
2. Peace beyond all understanding during times of tribulation and suffering (discussed in Volume I, Chapter 1, of this Trilogy)
3. The *sensus fidei*—interior sense of truth within the individual believer (discussed in Volume I, Chapter 1, of this Trilogy)

---

[5] See Adrian J. Boekraad and Henry Tristram, eds., *The Argument from Conscience to the Existence of God according to J. H. Newman* [with the text of an unpublished essay by Newman, entitled "Proof of Theism"] (Louvain: Editions Nauwelaerts, 1961).

[6] Saint Paul discusses these gifts within the Mystical Body in 1 Corinthians 6 and 12, and in Romans 12. See also the discussion in Pope Pius XII, *Mystici Corporis Christi* (June 29, 1943), http://w2.vatican.va/content/pius-xii/en/encyclicals/documents/hf_p-xii_enc_29061943 _mystici-corporis-christi.html.

4. The *sensus fidelium*—the sense of truth within the community of believers, the Church (discussed below in Section I.A)
5. The sense of spiritual community—*Koinōnia* (discussed below in Section I.B)
6. Interior transformation in the heart of Christ through our assent to Church teaching and our attempt to follow His moral and spiritual precepts genuinely (discussed later in this volume, Chapters 4–6)

A. The Sensus Fidelium

The *sensus fidelium* (sense of the faithful) is a consensus of the faithful—from the pope through the laity—about the truth of a particular doctrine, interpretation of a doctrine, or extension of a doctrine. According to *Lumen Gentium*,

> The entire body of the faithful, anointed as they are by the Holy One, cannot err in matters of belief. They manifest this special property by means of the whole peoples' supernatural discernment in matters of faith when "from the Bishops down to the last of the lay faithful" they show universal agreement in matters of faith and morals. That discernment in matters of faith is aroused and sustained by the Spirit of truth. It is exercised under the guidance of the sacred teaching authority, in faithful and respectful obedience to which the people of God accepts that which is not just the word of men but truly the word of God. Through it, the people of God adheres unwaveringly to the faith given once and for all to the saints, penetrates it more deeply with right thinking, and applies it more fully in its life.[7]

The Vatican Council declared that the whole People of God, when guided by the Holy Spirit, the Magisterium, and previous tradition, can as a whole discern matters of faith and morals more extensively than might be found in Scripture and previous Church doctrine. Thus, the whole faithful—from the bishops to the last

[7]Vatican Council II, Dogmatic Constitution on the Church *Lumen Gentium* (November 21, 1964), no. 12, quoting S. Augustinus, D Praed. Sanct. 14, 27: PL 44, 980, http://www .vatican.va/archive/hist_councils/ii_vatican_council/documents/vat-ii_const_19641121 _lumen-gentium_en.html.

layperson—through their common agreement and consent can declare the truth of a particular teaching that is not properly found either in sacred Scripture or previous tradition (doctrine). In order to do this, the faithful—from the bishops to the last layperson—must have substantial agreement, adhere to the Magisterium, be faithful to all past tradition (doctrine), and listen attentively to the Holy Spirit moving through the Church as a whole. If these conditions are met, a truth like that of the Immaculate Conception can be discerned, and then declared a doctrine infallibly by a pope or an ecumenical council. Without this infallible declaration by a pope or ecumenical council, the people's discernment is only a strong consensus. In order to be defined as a dogma, it must be declared infallibly by a pope or ecumenical council.

B. The Sense of Spiritual Community (Koinōnia)

The Church's view of spiritual community (*Koinōnia*) may well be lost on contemporary culture, but a brief overview of this interior gift may help readers recognize more deeply the profound reality into which they have been incorporated at their Baptism. This will help us understand how spiritual community can protect us from the deadly sins and spiritual evil.

The term *Koinōnia* is used in the New Testament to refer not simply to the gathering of Christian believers, but to the spiritual gift that each believer contributes to the group and receives from the group when two or more are gathered together (see Acts 2:42; Rom 15:26; 1 Cor 1:9; 10:16; 2 Cor 6:4; 8:4; 9:13; 13:13; Gal 2:9; Eph 3:9; Phil 2:1; 3:10). When believers are baptized and then gathered together to practice their faith (in Mass, prayer, study, service, etc.), the Holy Spirit conveys not only a sense of unity through the Mystical Body of Christ, but also a sense of increased faith, peace, encouragement, inspiration, and belovedness through that communion. The more we are gathered together with believers to practice our faith, the stronger the sense of unity and the spiritual gifts accompanying it.

These spiritual gifts were quite palpable in the early Church, which had an overtly charismatic character; however, they might seem quite intangible to believers in our less charismatic and more secular, materialistic world. We can reclaim and rebuild them by recalling simple experiences we may have taken for granted. Have you ever felt a deeper-than-usual closeness with people who are your friends from church? When you are gathered together with friends to practice your faith (in prayer, study, or service), have you experienced a deep sense of Christ's presence—or the presence of a saint (e.g., the Blessed Virgin Mary)—within the community gathering? Again, have you had the experience of praying, for example, a group Rosary when you were quite troubled by one of life's challenges, mentioned your problem to no one, and walked away from that Rosary far less troubled and with a strong sense of peace? Have you ever been present at a gathering of believers and found yourself feeling encouraged and inspired when you were trying to help somebody else? Again, have you ever had the experience of "being bombarded" with a myriad of ideas and inspirations—one following upon another—while participating in a group devotion or Bible study? The list could go on and on, but the point is that gathering together to practice faith frequently leads to an unexpected and somewhat mystical sense of peace, security, consolation in times of trouble, edification and inspiration of faith, a sense of being at home—in our true home—and an increased resolve to strengthen our moral life and character and to deepen our conversion.

These kinds of experiences are so common among believers who practice the faith that we can scarcely call into question Jesus' promise that "if two of you agree on earth about anything they ask, it will be done for them by my Father in heaven. For where two or three are gathered in my name, there am I in the midst of them" (Mt 18:19–20).

This sense of unity, peace, spiritual camaraderie, true home, inspiration, edification, and resolve toward deeper conversion occurs not only on a personal level, but also on a universal one. Strange as it may seem, we have a tacit awareness that our personal spiritual edification or decline involves everybody else in the Church—including the whole communion of saints. Catholics may seem peculiar to the modern world, because we naturally believe that Heaven is not simply "God and me alone", but a family—starting with the Holy Family at Christmas and burgeoning into a huge family, having saints of every kind, personality, apostolic strength, and historical background in its membership. We not only naturally feel this diverse richness within the Mystical Body of Christ; we feel close to many of the individuals within it. I must admit that I naturally believed this since my earliest memories of childhood when I gazed upon a Christmas crèche scene and felt right at home in it as well as when I looked at my little book of saints and felt almost mystically at home with so many of them, sensing a mystical familial relationship with them going far beyond mere identification with a character in a story. I would then go to church and feel that same sense of "true home and spiritual friendship" by simply walking into the building or in the courtyard. I still have this experience of spiritual home, holiness, and friendship with the saints when I read about particular saints, visit older churches and monasteries, and remember my childhood feelings, but I really don't need to arouse this awareness by doing these things. They simply occur at random times when I'm saying my Rosary, praying a psalm, or going to the chapel. It is almost as if the Blessed Virgin or particular saints are tapping me on the shoulder, reminding me that they are here. If Catholics don't drum this natural sense of the Mystical Body and the communion of saints out of themselves, and if they are trying to stay on the path to salvation, they are likely to become reacquainted with what they naturally knew as children. But I must get back to the main point.

How does our unity with the communion of saints and the universal Church affect our moral conversion and struggle against spiritual evil? When we are feeling strengthened, inspired, and resolute toward conversion, we feel like the whole Church is strengthened by it, producing a feeling of closeness to Christ and the communion of saints, like being in our true spiritual home. Conversely, if we begin to lessen the practice of our faith, we feel not only a sense of personal emptiness and alienation, but also the emptiness and alienation of the wider Church. Though our culture encourages us to believe that our destiny is our own, it is certainly not the case. The whole Church and communion of saints longs for the salvation of all of us—and if we are Christian, longs for our participation and edification with *them*. Thus, we should not be surprised if our feelings of spiritual closeness and camaraderie have "intimations" of the communion of saints and the universal Church beyond the group of believers with whom we are gathered—nor surprised that the feelings of emptiness and alienation arising out of our spiritual decline would have intimations of emptiness and alienation experienced by the communion of saints and the universal Church.

It is difficult to describe what these intimations of spiritual closeness and camaraderie with the communion of saints feels like. Perhaps we might compare the feelings of spiritual camaraderie and closeness to being at home with beloved holy friends and family members—and conversely, the feelings associated with spiritual decline to losing connection with friends and family members in our true home.

I would not blame anyone in our culture for doubting the above-mentioned tacit awareness and feelings of the communion of saints and the universal Church within our feelings of spiritual camaraderie and spiritual alienation, for we have been trained to eschew such mysterious and subjective states of mind—particularly if they are not reducible to specific brain functions or the physical processes constituting them. However, if you, the reader, have had even a glimmer of this universal spiritual awareness associated with the communion of saints and the universal Church, then fasten onto it and remember it, because I guarantee that it will occur again, and when it does you will begin to recognize it more easily until it becomes like an old friend who has been silently accompanying you throughout your spiritual journey.

We cannot underestimate the importance of the communion of saints' presence to us in our struggle against the deadly sins and spiritual evil, for as we begin to recognize easily the feelings of spiritual home and spiritual camaraderie when we are progressing in the spiritual life, we will also easily recognize the feelings of spiritual alienation (the loss of connection with our true home) when we are falling off the path of conversion. These feelings of spiritual alienation act like an alarm bell—alerting us to the increased power of spiritual evil in our lives as well as the decreased presence of the communion of saints within our hearts. These feelings can be so poignant that we are immediately inclined to reverse our decline and return to our path of conversion. Most spiritual writers mention the importance of these changes in our spiritual state and feelings, because they play such an important part in our spiritual development.[8]

---

[8] Spiritual writers, such as Saint Ignatius of Loyola, speak about these feelings under the general categories of spiritual consolation and desolation (see *Spiritual Exercises*, "Rules for Perceiving and Knowing in Some Manner the Different Movements Which Are Caused in the Soul" and "Rules for the Same Effect with Greater Discernment of Spirits"). With respect to *Koinōnia* we might nuance these categories by using the terms of spiritual camaraderie, communion, and closeness (in relationship to consolation), and spiritual alienation from the communion of saints (in relationship to desolation).

II. Contemplating on the Word of God

Jesus gave us His outer Word when He became incarnate and lived among us, and the evangelists transformed His words into the text of the four Gospels, which are complemented by the letters of Saints Paul, Peter, John, James, and others. When we attentively read and reflect on the outer Word of God, the Holy Spirit dwelling within us guides us toward inner transformation leading toward spiritual and moral conversion. We have already discussed the outer Word and the inner Word (in Chapter 1, Section I), noting how the outer Word gives a discursive understanding of the mind while the inner Word (coming through Christ's Mystical Body and the Holy Spirit) gives an intuitive awareness of the love, goodness, beauty, and holiness of the Lord who is the source of that word.

Reading the Word of God transforms our hearts even if we do not fully understand the methods of exegesis, such as form and redaction criticism, biblical Greek, literary genre, and hermeneutics. There is something about the way Jesus preached and the way the New Testament was written that hits us directly in the heart, if we want to hear it. If we do desire to understand it, then the Holy Spirit will make certain that its significance will, as it were, leap off the page. As Jesus said:

> Ask, and it will be given you; seek, and you will find; knock, and it will be opened to you. For every one who asks receives, and he who seeks finds, and to him who knocks it will be opened. (Mt 7:7–8)

The one condition needed to receive the fruit of the Gospels within our hearts is to *desire* to understand Jesus' meaning. If we really want to know what He means and we really want to follow Him and His words, then they will transform our hearts according to His heart, even if we do not know how this is occurring within us. It is sufficient to read the Scriptures attentively (as interpreted by the Church) while desiring to understand and follow the Lord, for then *He* will begin the process of transforming our hearts. Just as we unconsciously imitate those whom we love and admire, so also we unconsciously imitate the Lord, whom we love by reflecting on His Word. If we are hesitant about trusting or following the Lord, or fearful of changing our ways, then the Word of God will have very little effect on us consciously or subconsciously.

In sum, if we desire to understand God's Word in the Gospels (as interpreted by the Church), and trust in His providential plan, the Holy Spirit will give us sufficient understanding to be transformed in the heart of Jesus. However, if we do not trust in the Lord or desire to be transformed by Him, then the Holy Spirit will not be able to move us much—if at all. As this word sinks into our hearts and transforms us, it will assure us of the love of Christ and His Father and inspire us to imitate them, which in turn will free us to detach ourselves from the fears, anxieties, and "things" of the world.

Though contemplating on the Word of God can be very effective in the process of spiritual conversion, those who do not have long periods of time to devote to it should know that transformative benefits can be obtained from even short reflections on the Lord's Word. If we spend a short amount of time, say, on the Gospel of the day, sincerely opening ourselves to the Word and will of Christ within it, then we will connect more deeply with Him and become transformed by Him, which will help us to be detached from worldly fears, goods, power, and prestige (the beginning of moral freedom). For those who cannot attend daily Mass, I recommend using the Gospel reading of the day from the USCCB's website, which is free of charge.[9]

Those who have more time to devote to contemplation on the Word of God will want to acquaint themselves with two major methods for doing so—Ignatian meditation and *lectio divina*. The former originated with Saint Ignatius of Loyola, who formalized the methods of previous spiritual masters in his *Spiritual Exercises*. The latter was developed by Saint Benedict, and is practiced not only in most Benedictine monasteries, but also by clergy and laity in every walk of life. A brief explanation of these methods is given below with recommendations for further reading in Sections II.A (Ignatian Contemplation) and II.B (*Lectio Divina*).

---

[9] As suggested in Chapter 1, go to the website for the USCCB, and click on the calendar for the readings of the day. This will give you the precise citations for the Scripture passages heard during daily Mass. There are also the free apps "Catholic Daily Mass Readings" and "Laudate".

A. Ignatian Contemplation

Ignatian contemplation uses imagination to enter into scenes from the life of Christ. Saint Ignatius made this kind of imaginative contemplation the center of the *Spiritual Exercises* because it had such a profound effect on his life. When he entered the various scenes of Jesus' childhood, ministry, Passion, and Resurrection, the Holy Spirit enabled him to feel a friendship, even an intimate kinship, with Jesus and the other disciples. When he put himself in a scene with Jesus, and saw how Jesus interacted with the other "characters" and how they were interacting with Him, he began to get a sense, through the power of the Holy Spirit, of what Jesus was like—His authority and love, His call to repentance and His gift of forgiveness, His arguments with the Pharisees and love of sinners, His respect for human freedom, and His call to companionship. These descriptions are mere conceptual abstractions of what Saint Ignatius experienced in his contemplation. He was aware of much more than these abstractions. He *experienced* empathy, *felt* love and sympathy, and entered into *relationship* and *friendship* with Christ. His imagination, inspired by the Holy Spirit, imparted a knowledge of the heart—not merely a knowledge of the mind.

Father Kevin O'Brien describes Ignatian contemplation as follows:

> Let the events of Jesus' life be present to you right now. Visualize the event as if you were making a movie. Pay attention to the details: sights, sounds, tastes, smells, and feelings of the event. Lose yourself in the story; don't worry if your imagination is running too wild. At some point, place yourself *in the scene.*... Contemplating a Gospel scene is not simply remembering it or going back in time. Through the act of contemplation, the Holy Spirit makes present a mystery of Jesus' life in a way that is meaningful for you now. Use your imagination to dig deeper into the story so that God may communicate with you in a personal, evocative way.[10]

It helps to have a sense of the sights, sounds, and characters in the Gospel scene before moving into the meditation. If you are

---

[10] Kevin O'Brien, S.J., "Ignatian Contemplation: Imaginative Prayer", in *The Ignatian Adventure* (Chicago: Loyola Press, 2011), pp. 141–42. See also www.ignatianspirituality.com /ignatian-prayer/the-spiritual-exercises/.

unacquainted with this background knowledge, you may benefit from one of the popular versions of the life of Christ. Pope Benedict XVI has written three volumes that give important historical and cultural background to the Gospel accounts.[11] Archbishop Alban Goodier has written an excellent traditional life of Christ in two volumes,[12] and Fulton J. Sheen has also written a life of Christ that has contemporary significance.[13]

Ask the Holy Spirit to move your imagination in a way that will help to reveal the heart of Jesus to *you*. When you become accustomed to doing this kind of prayer, you will be amazed at how the Holy Spirit can introduce something of great relevance to you through a part of the Gospel scene that is *not* articulated by the evangelists. This normally leads to an appreciation of how much the Lord loves you, which leads, in turn, to a response of appreciation and love. For those seeking a more detailed explanation, see Volume I (Chapter 7, Section IV) of the Quartet.

B. Lectio Divina

The traditional Benedictine practice of *lectio divina* has been adapted to contemporary needs and audiences in many ways. In all its adaptations it retains four major steps: (1) reading a passage of Scripture, (2) reflecting on that passage to see how it affects *our hearts*, (3) praying about how this passage speaks to *our lives*, and (4) contemplatively entering into the call of Christ in the passage. Notice that *lectio divina* is not concerned with exegesis and hermeneutics (a scholarly theological approach), but rather with how a passage of

---

[11] See Pope Benedict XVI, *Jesus of Nazareth: The Infancy Narratives* (San Francisco: Ignatius Press, 2018); Pope Benedict XVI, *Jesus of Nazareth: Holy Week; From the Entrance into Jerusalem to the Resurrection* (San Francisco: Ignatius Press, 2011); and Pope Benedict XVI, *Jesus of Nazareth: From the Baptism in the Jordan to the Transfiguration* (San Francisco: Ignatius Press, 2008).

[12] See Alban Goodier, *The Public Life of Our Lord Jesus Christ* (New York: P.J. Kenedy & Sons, 1944), and *The Passion and Death of Our Lord Jesus Christ* (New York: P.J. Kenedy & Sons, 1944).

[13] See Fulton J. Sheen, *Life of Christ* (Garden City, N.Y.: Image Books, 1977; originally, New York: McGraw-Hill, 1953).

Scripture challenges us to become more like Christ, and to enter into that challenge with Christ ("the school of the heart"). In it, we want to hear the call of Christ in our *hearts*, to discover where He might be *calling* us.[14]

III. Contemplation and Personal Relationship with the Lord

I am using "contemplative prayer" here in the most general sense—that is, any form of prayer open to direct connection with the Lord for enough time to establish intimacy. In my view, this would have to be for more than fifteen minutes continuously per day. By "intimacy" here, I mean personal familiarity, closeness, and caring, but not necessarily the tender feelings intrinsic to some forms of Christian spirituality and mysticism.

Though God enters into deep relationships with people of all faiths, the large number of Catholic spiritual masters and mystics as well as Catholic spiritual traditions and disciplines shows how the Church, the sacraments, and the six gifts of the Holy Spirit are for the development and deepening of contemplative prayer, the spiritual life, and mystical union. Evidently, the more we participate in the sacraments and other gifts of the Church, the more deeply we will grow in the contemplative life, growing closer and closer to the Lord in love and holiness.

I cannot exaggerate the importance of personal contemplative prayer because it complements the public forms of prayer (e.g., the sacraments, liturgy, and penance services) by opening our hearts to the Lord in deep and close personal relationship. This relationship brings freedom, peace, and wisdom into our active lives, which ultimately transforms us in virtue and holiness. The *Catechism of the Catholic Church*, citing Saint John Chrysostom, states this precept as follows:

---

[14] Many excellent books are devoted to this practice. I recommend the following two volumes to get started: Basil Pennington, *Lectio Divina: Renewing the Ancient Practice of Praying the Scriptures* (New York: Crossroad Publishing, 1998), and Timothy Gray, *Praying Scripture for a Change: An Introduction to Lectio Divina* (West Chester, Penn.: Ascension Press, 2009).

"Nothing is equal to prayer; for what is impossible it makes possible, what is difficult, easy.... For it is impossible, utterly impossible, for the man who prays eagerly and invokes God ceaselessly ever to sin."[15]

We might restate Saint John Chrysostom's principle as follows: a person can live for a while both praying and sinning, but eventually he will get rid of one of them. Contemplative prayer (closeness to the Lord) is so antithetical to sin that it will either move us away from sin or sin will move us away from prayer. There is no long-term middle ground. This shows the power of personal prayer in our active lives, for fervent prayer—along with the Holy Eucharist and the Sacrament of Reconciliation—is the foundation and most important dimensions of spiritual conversion leading to moral conversion. As such, a life of sincere and constant contemplative prayer in conjunction with the Holy Eucharist and the Sacrament of Reconciliation is *the* vital foundation for moral conversion. When combined with the four steps of moral conversion (in Chapters 5–6), it will root out sinfulness from our hearts by strengthening the presence of Jesus within us (see 2 Cor 12:9–10).

We will address contemplative prayer in three sections:

1. Getting Started on Personal Contemplative Prayer (Section III.A)
2. The Second Stage of Contemplative Prayer: Extended Discursive Prayer (Section III.B)
3. The Third Stage of Contemplative Prayer from Discursive to Meditative and Silent Prayer (Section III.C)

A. Getting Started on Personal Contemplative Prayer

My purpose is to give a simple overview of how to get started on personal contemplative prayer. There are three major principles of the spiritual life that are essential to doing this. I will briefly discuss each in turn.

---

[15] *CCC* 2744, quoting Saint John Chrysostom, *De Anna* [Sermons on Hannah] 4, 5: PG 54, 666.

1. Constancy and consistency (Section III.A.1)
2. Freedom and grace for moral conversion (Section III.A.2)
3. Selecting times and prayers (Section III.A.3)

1. The First Principle of Contemplative Prayer: Constancy and Consistency

Constancy and consistency is the most important dimension of forming a personal relationship with the Lord. In this respect it resembles all personal relationships. We need dedicated time and presence to others to get to know and appreciate them better. Normally, this brings us closer to them, and we begin to commit ourselves more fully to them. Eventually our commitment becomes strong enough to prioritize them in our lives, to care about their welfare, to care for them, and ultimately to sacrifice ourselves for them. The more time and presence we consistently bring to our relationships, the stronger our bond in friendship and love become. The same holds true for our relationship with God. The more time we spend with Him in contemplative prayer, the more attractive and familiar He will become, making His presence, love, and truth integral to our mind and heart.

One might object that our human friends are visible and responsive, but the Lord is invisible and frequently silent, so there must be some difference between the dynamics of divine and human friendship. True enough, but make no mistake about it—the Lord's presence, though invisible, can be quite palpable. As we acknowledge His presence and love to us and proceed to our contemplative prayers, we might feel relief from emptiness, loneliness, and alienation, or feel a subtle sense of peace that calms us and leads to trust. We might also have a subtle awareness of God's sacredness and love. These are some indications that we are not alone, and that another profoundly transcendent interpersonal consciousness has drawn close to us in His compassion and peace. If we remain close to Him for the set time of our prayer, day after day, we can be sure that He will make His presence more profoundly felt, and above all, He will transform us through our relationship with Him.

Now, take a few moments to consider what a good time might be for consistently committing yourself to a minimum of fifteen minutes of personal prayer every day. It is just as important to avoid making your prayer time too long as making it too short. Fifteen minutes is a great starting time for those who are beginning personal contemplative prayer, but avoid any time period that is too long to be sustained over the course of time. If you select an initial prayer time of say thirty minutes, and you suddenly find yourself bored, distracted, or sensing that it is unmanageable, then back away from this, and go to twenty minutes, and then test it. Consistency and manageability is far more important than the initial length of time given to prayer. Don't worry—your prayer period will grow over the course of time (see below).

If you are anything like me, there is no substitute for the morning—immediately after getting out of bed. Be sure to wake up early enough so that you will not feel rushed by the impending requirements of the day, and if possible leave a little extra time for your prayer to go longer than you might have thought. Slip away to a place where you have some privacy, and then *stick to it every day*. There may be some days when this will be difficult, because of early morning commitments, such as plane travel at early hours. If you do have to sacrifice this time for such occasions, provide some way of making up for it during the day. If we are to be contemplatives in action—the ideal of Christian life—we must protect the time to be with the Lord in prayer so that our activities won't eclipse the contemplation that will bring us closer to Him in love and transformation.

Before proceeding to the next subsection, we must address the matter of distraction. As we are getting started in contemplative prayer, the silence can lead to an almost deafening series of distractions. One reason for this is that there is so little silence in our contemporary lives. If we are not glued to our smartphones or computers, then we are listening to a television program or the radio in the background. Hence, when we quiet ourselves to enter into communion with the Lord, we feel a sense of alienation—thrown, as it were, out of our normal element. As we become accustomed to the silence, our subconscious mind seizes the opportunity to bring a myriad of items forward to the conscious mind—items that we may have kept under the surface for weeks, months, or even years. Some of these items are unpleasant and so we want to reach for the smartphone or the television to re-distract ourselves. Some items may be curiosities that cause us to think about answers—or how to get answers. Some may be pleasant memories causing us to reminisce at great length. Some of these distractions come from our subconscious mind, while others are engendered by the Evil One, who wants to prevent us from coming into communion with the Lord, knowing precisely how to distract us, particularly with anxieties about the past and fears about the future.

As we begin the contemplative life, these distractions can be quite frustrating because we may find it difficult to pray even three Hail Marys with devotion and connection to our Blessed Mother without drifting off into anxious, fearful, pleasant, and curious distractions. It will take a little work to improve the situation, but I recommend the following. When a distraction of any kind comes up—for example, in the middle of a Hail Mary or other prayer—simply pray to the Lord, "Lord Jesus, I turn everything over to You", then pray a petition such as the following: "Please help me to resolve this problem after prayer"; "Please help me to remember this item after prayer"; "Please bless the person who is angering me"; or "Please help my son or daughter." Try to keep this prayer as short as possible—for example, "Lord Jesus, I trust You and I turn this over to You." At first you may have to use this prayer once or twice per minute. Don't worry about it—you are not alone. Everyone in the current time who has started a contemplative prayer life has had to deal with these distractions.

One last point: if your intention is really to enter into communion with the Lord, to praise Him, to engage Him through common prayers or Scripture, or simply to be in His loving and caring presence, then no matter how bad the distraction, do not reach for the smartphone, the television, the radio, or any other visible distraction. If you resist distractions and turn your thoughts and concerns over to the Lord, then over the long term, distractions will become less frequent and intense. Think of prayer as consecrating your time to the Lord, giving it to Him to bless and make holy.

2. The Second Principle of Contemplative Prayer: Freedom and Grace for Moral Conversion

We might begin with the adage that the majority of the positive effects of prayer will occur outside of prayer. Sometimes, people who initiate personal contemplative prayer expect to feel intimacy with the Lord almost immediately during their time of prayer. Though this certainly can and does occur, it frequently does not. Instead of feeling the Lord's presence, we become more familiar with Him, at ease with Him, and more comfortable with His healing hand amid our sin and imperfection.

Sometimes when we begin the contemplative life we might have a sense of shame, guilt, or fear that makes us very uncomfortable— even ready to bolt—when we allow the Lord to draw close to us. Though shame, guilt, or fear might be appropriate from the vantage point of our actions or lifestyle, do not avoid being in personal relationship with the Lord. When He comes close, He means only to heal us and save us—to draw us away from our enemy, the Evil One, who will use every suggestion of your unworthiness to incite shame so that you will want to avoid the One who can save you. Remember, it is not the Lord who is screaming, "You unworthy wretch—I'm disgusted with you." This is the accuser—your enemy, the Evil One.

If you allow the Lord to draw close to you in your sin and imperfection, you will feel a sense of shame that will no doubt be uncomfortable, but this is not because the Lord is angry or disgusted with you, but only because He wants to heal you and rescue you from your enemy. Instead of avoiding the Lord or finding some way of distracting yourself from your prayers, make an act of trust, such as, "Lord Jesus, I place my trust in you", or "Have mercy on me, Lord, for I am a sinful man/woman." Repeat it again and again until the urge to flee or find a distraction lessens. When you can sense God's benevolent, loving, and healing presence, consider what He is suggesting to you. Be sure of this—He will suggest something to you in a very nonaccusatory way that is quite manageable. It may seem like a hurdle, but it will be a manageable one. This is the critical moment of free choice. Inasmuch as the suggestion is manageable, then ask the Lord for the grace to undertake it. Don't worry—the Lord does not expect you to be perfect. He knows you will likely fall many times, but the important thing is to try to accommodate His suggestion. I assure you that if you stay faithful to your contemplative prayer, and try to accommodate the Lord's suggestion, *it will* get easier and easier to the point where you will find yourself becoming freer and freer from the sinful proclivity that was undermining your relationship with Him.

The reader might be thinking, "I have a hundred questions about that last paragraph." I cannot answer all the questions now, but I must address one question whose answer must be correct if we are to advance in contemplative prayer and moral life—what do I mean by "the Lord making a suggestion"? Will the Lord be, as it were, standing outside of me saying, "Bob, here is what I am suggesting to you"? Obviously not. Instead, the Lord is likely to incite a thinking process that culminates in a *desirable* course of action—"*I would really like* to be more patient or compassionate or generous or chaste in certain specific situations." Notice that this is quite different from "I *should* be more compassionate", or "I better be more compassionate", which implies threat and accusation by the Lord.

The Lord is not interested in threatening you, and then pushing you or forcing you to obey lest He bring down the hammer. Any such suggestion is from the Evil One. Rather, the Lord wants you to see that some mode of conduct is leading you into darkness and endangering your soul—even to the point where you would actually choose the darkness over the light of love and even over the light of His heavenly Kingdom. He wants you to sense the danger posed by your enemy's grip on your freedom, and after recognizing it, to call to Him for help to lead you out of the darkness. At this juncture *you* will desire to change your conduct precisely because it is so dangerous to your state of being and even your salvation. If you resolve to follow your desire to get out of the darkness, the Lord will give you the grace to keep that resolve going. Yes, you might fail many, many times, but if you get up, ask for forgiveness, make an act of trust in the Lord, and continue to follow your resolve (all the while maintaining your daily practice of contemplative prayer), then I guarantee that you will get better at what the Lord is suggesting to the point where you will be able to leave the darkness behind and enter more fully into His light.

I recall my novice master, Father Gordon Moreland, telling this sage story about how the Lord feels as we begin the process of personal contemplative prayer, spiritual conversion, and moral conversion. As we begin, the Evil One sweeps in immediately and plants the image of a really angry parent who discovers that we have habituated ourselves to some form of darkness and sin, and screams at us that we better get our act together right now or he will abandon us or even condemn us. In contrast to this, the Lord—through the Holy Spirit—presents the image of a parent who walks into a room and sees a snake lying in the bassinet next to us—His beloved, precious, and fragile child. Instead of being angry and condemnatory, the parent is terrified by the impending danger lying next to us and has only one thought in mind: to remove the danger. This is precisely how the Lord of unconditional love feels, just like the father of the prodigal son. Yet, in the case of our moral lives, He must operate within the contours of our freedom. He can't simply pick up the snake and get rid of it; He has to show us how dangerous the snake is so that we *will want* to avoid it, even though the snake has convinced us that he is quite harmless and wants only to make us happy and fulfilled.

Does the Lord always present such suggestions to us during our contemplative prayer? Sometimes, but by no means always. Sometimes, the Lord will influence a dream in which an image or a narrative informs us of the mortal danger of a specific kind (or kinds) of conduct or attitude. When we awaken from that dream, we will likely remember it and be quite disturbed by it. Notice that we are disturbed not by the Lord's anger or threat, but by the impending danger and darkness into which we have entered by our conduct or attitude. When the Lord has made the point about the danger, it is incumbent upon us to recognize the gift we have been given (even though it is disturbing), and then to pray the prayer of Saint Peter as he sank into the water while attempting to walk: "Lord, save me" (Mt 14:30). If we recognize the danger (instead of running from the Lord) and ask the Lord for help to overcome a destructive form of conduct, He will help us by *gradually* leading us to little improvements in our attitude or conduct. If we really follow through on these small steps, away from the sin and danger, our desire for that sin becomes tempered—and eventually we will lose interest in what had formerly fascinated us, and even transfixed us. Again, it may take many attempts and subsequent failures, but eventually the desire for the sin will lessen to the point where it is no longer desirable.

When I began this discussion above, I mentioned that the majority of the positive effects of prayer occur outside of prayer. The above discussion shows how the Lord accomplishes this. So long as we remain faithful to our daily contemplative prayer and follow through on the suggestions from the Lord that come to us during prayer, in our dreams, when we are awakened at three o'clock in the morning, or by the voices of other people, we can be sure that our desire for the darkness (of sin) will gradually subside, while our desire for the light will intensify. When this occurs, our love for the Lord will also intensify, and we will want to draw near Him in contemplative prayer for additional time, which in turn will motivate us to separate ourselves from the darkness even more—and the cycle will continue. Contemplation leads to reform in our moral lives, while reform of our moral lives leads to deeper contemplation and love of the Lord. We might conclude this discussion by reiterating three points. First, the above life of grace and sanctity begins with fidelity to contemplative prayer every day—even if it is for only fifteen minutes. Second, we should expect that the majority of the fruit of prayer will occur outside of prayer. Finally, as we begin the contemplative life, contending with feelings of shame, guilt, or fear, we must trust that the Lord's sole intention is to love and heal us, and then make acts of trust in Him so that we can remain faithful to our contemplative prayer (instead of fleeing or finding a distraction). We must then be alert to the suggestions the Lord will make through our contemplative prayer, our dreams, our feelings of cosmic emptiness, loneliness, and alienation, and through the voices of others. When we sense the impending danger and darkness of our conduct or attitudes, we will want to respond with the plea "Lord, save me", and the Lord will infuse His grace into our desire to flee the danger of our sin. If we remain constant in prayer and implement our small steps to reform our conduct, we will ultimately succeed, because the Lord's grace will not be insufficient to flee from the darkness.

3. The Third Principle of Contemplative Prayer: Selecting Times and Prayers

The third principle of the spiritual life is more practical than the previous one. It concerns setting out the kinds of prayers you will want to say as you begin the spiritual life, and progress in it. As you begin your contemplative prayer life, you might find that praying an entire Rosary or the Divine Office is difficult to complete in a time period of fifteen to twenty minutes. Since the objective of contemplative prayer is to come into loving connection with the Lord and open ourselves to His suggestions, I would recommend, as you are getting started, shorter prayers that can do this in a relatively short time. Therefore, I would recommend five kinds of "short prayers":

1. Parts of the Rosary (see below, Section III.B.1)
2. Spontaneous prayers (see the list in Appendix II, Section I, of this volume)
3. Common Catholic prayers (see the list in Appendix II, Section III)
4. Some profound, well-known psalms of praise, thanksgiving, petition, and repentance (see the list in Appendix II, Section II)
5. The prayer of gratitude for all blessings (see below in this section)

I would recommend using combinations of these prayers and psalms sufficient to fill about 75 percent of your allotted time of contemplation. Leave 25 percent of your time for conversation with the Lord about some concerns of the day or week as well as for responding to some of the suggestions you sense He is giving to you.

As you can see, beginning a contemplative life requires a bit of homework, because you will want to familiarize yourself with the spontaneous prayers, psalms, and common prayers on the lists in Appendix II, and then make a selection of an appropriate number corresponding to the time you have allotted for contemplative prayer. Stay with the same prayers during the week. If you want to change them every week, feel free to do so. But staying with the same prayers means that you can devote yourself to connecting with the Lord in prayer instead of spending time and psychic energy on deciding what and how to pray.

Before starting your selected prayers, you will want to begin with the first step of all contemplative prayer—recognizing the presence of the Lord or the Blessed Virgin. I typically use the prayer "Lord, I know You are here, and I know You love me" (or if praying to the Blessed Mother: "Mother Mary, I know you are here, and I know you love me."). I repeat this prayer until my consciousness is open to His (or her) presence, and He is filling me with it. This "being filled" with the Lord's presence need not have any emotional content, but oftentimes does—a feeling of peace or the sense of being near a profound friend. At the very least, I have a tacit awareness that I am not alone. When you are in this connected interpersonal state, proceed to your selection of psalms and prayers. Remember, the point is not to get through all of them, but rather to say them deliberately and lovingly while recalling His presence and love for you.

As noted above, most of the grace of prayer occurs after your prayer session is completed. Keep alert to clues about where the Lord might be leading, interior clues as well as exterior ones. If you sense new freedom to detach from the world or one of the eight deadly sins, take note of it and bring it back to your contemplative prayer to ask for the grace to increase that freedom until the attachment has subsided.[16]

a. Prayer Blocks and Expansion of Prayer

Some people may find themselves in a state of "prayer block" (much like writer's block). The reason for this might stem from sinful proclivities or habits that may have been a problem in the past and continue to be so in the present. This may require a turning moment *to begin* the process of opposing those sinful proclivities or habits. The best way of doing this is to avail ourselves of the Sacrament of Reconciliation (confession), which has the particular grace of quickening our resolve to oppose a sinful proclivity—though such opposition may only be partially or even minimally successful at the outset (see Chapter 7, Sections II.B–C, of this volume). If you go to confession with the intention of beginning a process of opposition to a sinful proclivity, and find that you have only a little success in contending with it, do not grow discouraged, but instead resolve to go to confession on a monthly basis. The combination of the Sacrament of Reconciliation (confession) and the contemplative prayer life you are initiating will help you to break the spell and the habit of that particular sin, which will in turn decrease its influence in your life. Confession tends to lessen the "prayer block", which in turn enables you to initiate a habit of contemplative prayer; in combination with the grace of confession,

---

[16] In Chapter 6 (Section II), we will discuss a special form of prayer, related to an examination of conscience, recommended by Saint Ignatius of Loyola—the Examen Prayer. You may want to incorporate this prayer into your spiritual life in the evening for the reasons mentioned in Chapter 6.

this tends to lessen the influence of sinful proclivity. Repeated confessions, fidelity to contemplative prayer, and speaking to the Lord
about your struggles during contemplative prayer, all weaken sinful
proclivities and habits. The longer we engage in this process, the more
we gain freedom in resisting the proclivity.

There are some other complementary steps that we can take from
contemporary psychology—namely, visualizations and affirmations,
which have proven to be quite successful in changing our subconscious identity (discussed in detail in Chapter 6, Section I, of this
volume). When these are combined with the Sacrament of Reconciliation, the Examen Prayer (see the previous note), and a contemplative prayer life, success in breaking the spell of the proclivity
is likely to occur, though it may be a long process. As the proclivity weakens, your relationship with the Lord through contemplation will strengthen; and as a result, you will bring that relationship
into your active life—for example, in your apostolate, your family,
and your workplace. At this point, you will be progressing toward
the Ignatian ideal of being a contemplative in action.

If you are anything like me, the time of your contemplative prayer
will begin to expand *naturally*. If you start off with, say, fifteen minutes,
you may notice that it takes twenty or twenty-five minutes to finish
your desired prayers. Frequently, you do not even notice that you have
added extra time to your prayer. When this begins to happen consistently, add an extra five or ten minutes to your allotted prayer time to
accommodate what you desire—to be lovingly in the presence of the
Lord. Do not force yourself to move to twenty-five minutes. Wait
until the twenty-five minutes happens naturally. If you force yourself,
you will turn your "*wanting* to pray" into "*having* to pray", which will
undermine the relationship with the Lord that you are trying to cultivate. Remember—when you have completed your selection of psalms,
spontaneous prayers, and common prayers, devote at least five minutes
to loving conversation with the Lord, asking Him what His desires are
for you, your spiritual development, and your moral development, as
well as your life and relationship issues. When your conversation is
complete, conclude with an Our Father and a Glory Be.

As noted above, when your life of contemplation becomes more
habitual, you will naturally desire to spend more time in prayer. Sometimes affective desolation may cause dryness, which may increase

distractions. (This is explained in Volume I, Chapter 1, Section III, of this Trilogy.) Prescinding from affective desolation, the desire to be with the Lord in contemplative prayer tends to increase (along with detachment from sinful proclivities). As this occurs, you will probably experience little moments of affective consolation (see below, Section III.A.3.b) and will be drawn to additional spontaneous and common prayers.

Let us now return to the subject of selecting particular prayers. The saints of the Catholic Church throughout the centuries—such as Saint Paul, Saint Augustine, Saint Francis of Assisi, Saint Thomas Aquinas, Saint Ignatius Loyola, and many more—have written literally hundreds of prayers and litanies that constitute the vast repertoire of Catholic devotional prayers available today. There are many excellent prayer books that provide a large number of these prayers at a reasonable cost.[17] I recommend that readers purchase one or two of these prayer books and mark the pages of prayers that have potential to connect you intimately with the Lord during your daily prayer session. I have provided several of these prayers in Appendix II (Section III) to get you started, but these barely scratch the surface of our huge Catholic repertoire.

b. The Prayer of Gratitude

The prayer of gratitude is particularly important and has been recognized by virtually every spiritual master as foundational to the contemplative life. Gratitude is an acknowledgment that we have been blessed by the Lord, which makes us aware of His presence and love in our lives. When we say, "Thank You, Lord," it is generally infused with the recognition of His love as well as our love for Him. When we are grateful, we take nothing for granted, which frees us from the entitlement mentality and from resentment toward others and God for what we do not have. There is much for which to be grateful in our lives if we focus on what we have (rather than what we do not have)—our families, friends, opportunities at work and in community, and above all, for our creation, redemption by Jesus, and

---

[17] A simple web search for "Catholic Prayer Books Amazon" will give at least forty excellent, reasonably priced prayer books from which to choose. The descriptions given indicate fairly clearly whether these are more traditional or contemporary prayer books.

the Church community. Though suffering can reach critical points in our lives, this too can become a blessing to help us toward our salvation—and even to help others toward their salvation (see Volume IV, Chapter 7, of the Quartet).

It is best to begin the prayer of gratitude with recent blessings, perhaps the success of a child at home or an accomplishment at work or a new opportunity in the community or work, or a spiritual insight from church or from a book. We can also be thankful for natural beauty or the weather or little acts of friendship and love.

You might also see the blessings in some of the challenges of life, particularly how those challenges led to detachment from a sinful proclivity or caused a change in life's meaning or direction. Don't force yourself to think of things for which to be grateful if nothing is coming to mind. Instead, focus on some more general dimensions of your life, such as your spouse, children, friends, gifts and talents, faith, home, and even the blessings you have received in the past. I recommend making a little "Book of Gratitude" that details the many areas where you may find the Lord's providential hand helping us. Volume I (Chapter 9) of the Quartet has a detailed explanation of both the prayer of gratitude and Book of Gratitude that will help readers engage in this practice on a regular basis.

When you become accustomed to some of these prayers (common prayers, spontaneous prayers, psalms, and the prayer of gratitude), you may notice little lucid moments of the Lord's (or the Blessed Virgin's) presence and love (called "affective consolation"). This presence may be quite subtle—like a tacit awareness or a memory of a past moment when His presence was evident. Sometimes His presence will be more than tacit, and you will be aware of a sense of peace or "being at home" that goes beyond purely natural manifestations of these feelings. Sometimes you may feel a sense of holiness, sacredness, and unity that is quite otherworldly, and sometimes you may feel a combination of these feelings along with a sense of supernatural love and joy. You may also notice that when these feelings occur, they incite desire for more within you—and when they fade, you are left longing for the divine presence that so animated and fulfilled you. C. S. Lewis described this profound combination of feelings, filled with intense desire for the divine presence, as "a stab of joy", using the following words:

As I stood beside a flowering currant bush on a summer day there suddenly arose in me without warning, as if from a depth not of years but of centuries, the memory of that earlier morning at the Old House when my brother had brought his toy garden into the nursery. It is difficult to find words strong enough for the sensation which came over me; Milton's "enormous bliss" of Eden (giving the full, ancient meaning to enormous) comes somewhere near it. It was a sensation, of course, of desire; but of desire for what? Not, certainly, for a biscuit tin filled with moss, nor even (though that came into it) for my own past—and before I knew what I desired, the desire itself was gone, the whole glimpse withdrawn, the world turned commonplace again, or only stirred by a longing for the longing which had just ceased. It had taken only a moment of time; and in a certain sense everything else that had ever happened to me was insignificant in comparison.[18]

Most of the time, our contemplative prayer will not elicit this type of profound feeling, but it is not unusual for the Lord to provide a tacit awareness of His presence and love when we recall His presence and pray in the words that the saints have given us. Though this feeling can be quite subtle, it deepens our conscious and subconscious sense of the divine presence that carries over into the rest of our day, and provides the basis for detaching ourselves from the things of this world (moral freedom). It might be helpful to scrutinize one or more Catholic prayer books and study some of the prayers given there until you land upon one or more that resonates with you. Remember, before praying, call to mind the presence of the Lord or our Blessed Mother and affirm their love for you, using a prayer similar to this—"Lord, I know you are here, and I know you love me." Do not think about your feelings or how the Lord might be interacting with you during the prayer; simply pray it, trying to intend what its saintly author meant to express. Even if we do not notice the above feelings or effects on a daily basis, we may be sure that we will notice them over the long term, for contemplative prayer provides a very powerful foundation for transformation in the heart of Christ, catalyzing the transformative power of the Holy Eucharist.

[18] C. S. Lewis, *Surprised by Joy: The Shape of My Early Life* (New York: Harcourt, Brace, Jovanovich, 1966), pp. 22–23.

If you remain faithful to this contemplative prayer life, whether it be fifteen minutes or forty-five minutes, you will begin to make spiritual progress—more aware of the Lord's love for you and even your love for Him, a greater sense of freedom to detach oneself from the world and deadly sins, a greater sense of the Lord's presence to you during the day, and a transformation in the quality of your actions, most especially with the virtues of love mentioned by Saint Paul in 1 Corinthians 13: greater patience, kindness, and compassion as well as greater control over anger, boasting, rejoicing in evil, and so forth. Regular contemplative prayer is a game changer, because simply being present to the Lord or the Blessed Virgin makes their presence "rub off" on us. Their presence and love transform our hearts precisely in the manner described by John Henry Cardinal Newman: *cor ad cor loquitur*—"heart speaking to heart".

As your contemplative prayer life expands, you may want to move into one of the more lengthy forms of contemplative prayer listed below.

B. The Second Stage of Contemplative Prayer: Extended Discursive Prayer

As we advance in contemplative prayer, we become progressively more aware of the loving presence of the Father, Jesus, the Holy Spirit, and the Blessed Virgin to the point where we desire (are drawn into) deeper prayer—beyond fifteen to twenty minutes. At this juncture, we will probably want to add a more extended form of prayer and meditation to the spontaneous prayers, common prayers, and familiar psalms mentioned above. What kinds of prayer can lead to an intimate (close and caring) connection with the Lord? There are literally dozens of such prayer forms, but I will address two that have been particularly helpful to me: the Rosary (Section III.B.1) and the Divine Office, the Liturgy of the Hours (Section III.B.2).

1. The Rosary

The Rosary is one of the most powerful vehicles for initiating and maintaining contemplative prayer. Every recent pope and canonized saint has recommended it repeatedly, and it has been part of every major Marian apparition of the nineteenth and twentieth centuries—for example, Lourdes, Fatima, and Medjugorje. The Catholic spiritual tradition has, since its inception, integrated Marian spirituality into the foundation of its prayer—both communally and individually (see below, Section VI). Icons and prayers to Mary are found in the art and inscriptions of the catacombs, and in every artistic era since that time. The Rosary does not exhaust Marian spirituality in the Catholic Church. There is a richness of Marian reflection (Mariology), Marian feast days, litanies, novenas, hymns, special prayers, and extraliturgical celebrations. Several of the Marian pilgrimage sites, particularly Lourdes, Fatima, and Guadalupe, have miracles associated with them; Lourdes has a medical-scientific commission (the Lourdes Medical Bureau) permanently set up to assess and archive those miracles (see the Appendix to Volume I, Section I.B).

In the midst of this plentitude, the Rosary still stands out as spiritually significant, because it is so helpful for initiating and maintaining a contemplative life. It incorporates the motherly love of the Blessed Virgin into praise and prayers to the three Persons of the Holy Trinity in a simple, repetitive, and diverse way (see below, Section VI). The presence, love, and assistance of the Divine Persons and the Blessed Mother are evident, which makes it an ideal foundation for contemplative prayer.

The Rosary is also an invitation into meditation on the major events in the life of Jesus and the Blessed Virgin. There are four major sets of meditations, called "mysteries", that most of us are familiar with and can focus on while reciting the Hail Mary:

1. The Joyful Mysteries—the Annunciation, the Visitation, the Birth of Jesus, the Presentation of Jesus in the Temple, and the Finding of the Child Jesus in the Temple
2. The Luminous Mysteries—the Baptism of Jesus in the Jordan, the Wedding Feast at Cana, the Proclamation of the Kingdom of God, the Transfiguration, and the Institution of the Holy Eucharist
3. The Sorrowful Mysteries—the Agony in the Garden, the Scourging of Jesus at the Pillar, the Crowning with Thorns, the Carrying of the Cross, and the Crucifixion

4. The Glorious Mysteries—the Resurrection, the Ascension, the Descent of the Holy Spirit, the Assumption of Mary, and the Coronation of Mary[19]

It is more important to pray the Rosary thoughtfully and intentionally than to "get it all done". Though meditating on the mysteries can be an excellent complement to the prayers of the Rosary, the prayers themselves are more than sufficient to establish intimate connection with the Father, Jesus, and the Blessed Virgin. As I am praying the well-known words of the Our Father, the Hail Mary, and the Glory Be, all kinds of other words, feelings, and intuitions seem to pop up through inspiration of the Holy Spirit. Thus, it is not unusual for me when I am saying, "Hail Mary, full of grace," to be thinking or feeling, "Gentle Mary, full of grace," or when I am praying, "The Lord is with thee," to be thinking or feeling that the Lord is with *me* through her. Similarly, I can be saying or feeling that "I love you" or "I thank you" or "I am happy to be with you" as I am saying the seemingly unrelated words, "Blessed are you among women and blessed is the fruit of your womb." The point I am trying to make here is that we need not focus on the precise discursive words of the prayer, but on the spirit of giving praise to the Lord or the Blessed Virgin through the prayer that opens us to her presence or the presence of the Father or Jesus. As we are praying these prayers with the intention of praising and petitioning the Lord and Mary, they will frequently grace us with a sense of consolation, which is unmistakably heavenly and personal. Most of the time, this sense of the Lord's or Mary's presence is not overwhelming, but distinctive and uplifting, inviting us into deeper communion with them. Though subtle, their presence shows that we are loved by them, which induces a response of thanks—an expression of our love. We do not have to do much more than conscientiously

---

[19] There is much to be said about meditating on these mysteries and familiarizing yourself with them, but that is beyond the scope of this short explanation. Therefore, I would recommend getting one of the many books written on this, such as the following: Christianica Center, *Scriptural Rosary* (Glenview, Ill.: Christianica Center Publishing, 1989); Connie Rossini and Dan Burke, *The Contemplative Rosary with St. John Paul II and St. Teresa of Avila* (Irondale, Ala.: EWTN Publishing, 2017); and Rev. J. M. Lelen, *Pray the Rosary* (Totowa, N.J.: Catholic Book Publishing, 1999).

pray these common prayers repeatedly to give the Lord or Mary an opportunity to make their presence, support, and care subtly felt—and this is why the Rosary has become such an important part of contemplative prayer in the lives of the saints.

Sometimes contemplative prayer goes beyond the feelings and intuitions of intimate connection with the Lord or the Blessed Virgin, because *they* make their presence felt in a more evident way than the subtle sense of their presence mentioned above. Occasionally they make the immensity of their presence felt—the beauty of their holiness and virtue—and the joy of the ultimate home to which they are drawing us. Sometimes we can feel the intensity of their love filled with unity, joy, mystery, and holiness. These more intense experiences are rarer than the more subtle manifestations of the divine presence mentioned above, but their occasional occurrence assures us of the Lord's deep love and care for us. Though these more intense experiences are important for our close connection with the Lord, they are not necessary for moral freedom and action. The simpler and subtler kinds of awareness are sufficient for this.

The Rosary is not the only way to make an intimate connection with the Lord in contemplative prayer. The Divine Office (Section III.B.2) and nondiscursive contemplative prayer (Section III.C) also provide a meeting space for the Lord to manifest His familiar caring presence. Just as the words of prayer in the Rosary incite words, feelings, and intuitions of God's mysterious, holy, and loving presence, so also the words of the psalms and devotional prayers go beyond themselves. Though we can concentrate on the words of these psalms and devotional prayers, they will frequently lead—thanks to the presence of the Lord and the Blessed Mother as well as the inspirations of the Holy Spirit—to new layers of awareness of the Lord's love that elicit expressions of our gratitude and love in return.

2. The Divine Office and Psalms of Praise

Though the Divine Office (sometimes called the Breviary or Liturgy of the Hours) is a part of the Church's official public worship, it can also be prayed individually and can be used as a part of our contemplative life.[20] The Divine Office has been an integral part of the Church since the first century and took its inspiration from the Jewish division of a day into "hours of prayer". Though priests are obligated to pray the Office, and most monastic religious communities pray it in common, laity are not so obliged, but are invited to do so if they wish.

The Divine Office is split into four seasonal parts: (1) Advent and Christmas, (2) Ordinary Time I, (3) Lent and Easter, and (4) Ordinary Time II. It is a terrific resource for seasonal readings, antiphons, and prayers. It is organized into a four-week cycle called the Psalter, but the prayers for the season can be substituted by psalms, prayers, and antiphons for feasts, the memorial of saints, and other occasions. The majority of the prayers are psalms with some Old Testament canticles and New Testament canticles interspersed throughout. For readers who do not have the time to pray the Divine Office, there are a few publications that provide an abridged psalm-based resource with seasonal antiphons and reflections, the most popular of which is the *Magnificat*.[21] For readers seeking a non-psalm-based prayer cycle based on the Mass readings and meditations on them, see *The Word among Us*.[22]

Since the Divine Office is psalm-based, I recommend that readers learn how to read the psalms in their historical context, and to "update" some of the images of ancient Israel in the psalms to reflect the reality of the modern Christian Church.[23] For example, you can

---

[20] The complete Breviary is online, free of charge on iBreviary.com: http://www.ibreviary.com/m2/breviario.php. Simply click on the Hour of the Day—say, the Office of Readings or Morning Prayer, and pray or print. There is a free app for the daily Breviary. Go to the App Store on your smartphone and subscribe to the Breviary app. Simply put in the date and the rest is automatic.

You may also purchase the full four-volume set used by priests and religious (by Catholic Book Publishing). It is popularly available as a vinyl-bound set and can be ordered on any search engine under "Christian Prayer, Liturgy of the Hours Four Volumes".

For those who do not have the time to pray the Office of Readings, there is a one-volume version of the Breviary containing Morning and Evening Prayer. You can order this by putting "One-Volume Christian Prayer, Liturgy of the Hours" into any search engine.

[21] See the home page for *Magnificat* subscriptions: https://us.magnificat.net/.

[22] Go to *The Word among Us* subscription page to order either a print edition or a digital edition: https://wau.org/subscribe/.

[23] See, for example, Charles Miller, *Together in Prayer: Learning to Love the Liturgy of the Hours* (Eugene, Ore.: Wipf and Stock Publishers, 2004).

substitute "Catholic Church" or "Mystical Body of Christ" for the many references to the city of Jerusalem or to the nation of Israel.

Why does the Church still use these ancient psalms as the basis for her official public and private prayer? Beyond the fact that the psalms are part of Divine Revelation and the Catholic Canon of the Old Testament, they are truly inspired hymns of praise, gratitude, and trust. The psalmists almost always seem to be in a state of wonder and awe at God's creation, His providential care for Israel (and the Church), and His desire to lead all of us to justice, virtue, and piety. It is not important (from the vantage point of prayer) that the psalmists' view of nature is nonscientific and his view of God's providential care is unnuanced. The revelation and view of creation he does have is marked by wonder and awe, which is precisely the view we should all have of nature and human beings, especially seen through the lens of modern science. Furthermore, the psalmists' view of God's providential care is intimate and filled with thanks, which again is precisely the view we all ought to have. In light of the many documented and undocumented miracles and healings that are quite prevalent, I am unbothered by the psalmists' unscientific view of nature, because I know that God is the Creator of nature and can transform it in any way that He wishes. Additionally, I am overwhelmed by the psalmists' passionate correct view of nature and human beings as mysterious, wonderful, and crafted with love. If readers can overlook some of these anachronistic features and update the psalmists' images of Israel, the Temple, and Jerusalem, the experience of praying the psalms will likely be significantly enhanced.

I tend to personalize the psalms (when I say the Breviary by myself) by changing the impersonal "the Lord" into the personal "You, Lord". Hence, when the psalm says, "The Lord is my rock and my shield," I substitute, "You, Lord, are my rock and my shield." I have been doing this so long that I don't have to think about it anymore, and it helps me to make a personal connection with the Lord by speaking my praises directly to Him. As noted above, it does not take long for certain phrases of the psalms to leap off the page as personally meaningful; and sometimes, I feel the Lord's presence and consolation welling up through my prayer. These feelings of consolation may or may not be related to the words of the psalms, because they are caused by the Lord, who chooses to make His presence felt on the basis of many factors beyond the words of the psalms and my capacity to understand. Invariably, when I feel His loving presence—even if it be as slight as a gentle breeze—I respond with closeness, trust, and love.

For those who are not accustomed to praying the psalms, it is important to recognize that some parts and phrases in the psalms were constructed during the time when Israel was a warrior society, and so there might be stanzas that appear to be quite violent and incongruent with the teachings of Jesus. These phrases probably *are* incongruent with the teachings of Jesus because they were formulated within a cultural context that did not know the fullness of Jesus' revelation of the unconditional love of His Father or His unconditional self-sacrificial love for the world.

There is a principle of New Testament interpretation that we might call "asymmetrical hermeneutics" ("one-directional interpretation"). This principle recognizes the development of doctrine from the Patriarchal period to the Mosaic period to the period of the Judges to the Davidic kingdom to the major prophets (preexilic and postexilic) and finally to the fullness of revelation in Jesus. It declares that we can look *backward* from the fullness of New Testament revelation (in Jesus) to the incomplete revelation of the Old Testament, but not vice versa. There is no problem with seeing the Old Testament within the much fuller framework and categories of the New Testament, because the New Testament categories can tell us how to interpret Old Testament passages that seem to be at variance with Jesus' fuller teaching. However, we cannot do the opposite—that is, interpret the fullness of revelation in the New Testament through the much narrower framework and categories of the Old Testament. This would be like putting new wine into old wineskins. The old wineskins cannot hold it, and the new wine will burst the old wineskins, leading to the loss of both (see Mt 9:14–17).

For example, Psalm 139 is one of the most beautiful, spiritual, loving psalms in the Old Testament Psalmody. However, one stanza appears incongruent with the teaching of Jesus and the rest of the psalm:

> O that you would slay the wicked, O God, and that men of blood would depart from me, men who maliciously defy you, who lift themselves up against you for evil! Do I not hate them that hate you, O LORD? And do I not loathe them that rise up against you? I hate them with perfect hatred; I count them my enemies. (139:19–22)

How can we reconcile this stanza of the psalm with Jesus' command to love our enemies and do good for those who hate us in imitation of His heavenly Father (Mt 5:43–48)? We must give priority of interpretation to Jesus' commandment and deemphasize the hatred in this stanza accordingly. I use this principle when I encounter these kinds of stanzas not only in the psalms, but in other Old Testament passages that are clearly in tension with Jesus' fuller teaching. The Breviary and the *Magnificat* frequently do most of this editing work for us, but occasionally some phrases stand out as dissonant. When this occurs, I deemphasize them and proceed to the next stanza of the psalm.

For the most part, the psalms are inspired prayers that manifest a pure love and trust of God, an honest portrayal of emotion, and a beautiful insight into His providential care. This is why the Church still uses them as the foundation for priestly and religious prayer, and recommends them wholeheartedly to the faithful. If you are not accustomed to the psalms, you might want to start with a few psalms that are familiar and can be said on a daily basis, such as Psalm 8, Psalm 23, Psalm 51, Psalm 103, and Psalm 139. I have provided these "starter psalms" for your convenience in Appendix II (Section II) of this volume.

The important thing to remember is that the Lord can speak quite powerfully through this ancient vehicle of prayer. If we pray the psalms conscientiously and with the desire to praise, give thanks, and petition God earnestly, the Lord will make His presence felt subtly, but quite distinctly. As with the Rosary, His presence sometimes manifests itself as a sense of holiness, heavenly home, intense joy and desire, loving mystery, and unity with the whole of reality. Irrespective of the subtly or intensity, or the kinds of feelings-desires aroused, there is always a personal dimension embedded within the experience—generally, the presence of the Father or His Son, Jesus Christ. As such, the psalms and the Breviary are a vehicle through which the Lord can come to us in contemplative prayer.

3. Conversation with the Lord

It is not uncommon for the Lord to initiate a conversation with us in the midst of praying the Rosary or the Breviary (see below, Section V). Sometimes, He does this by a little voice in the back of our heads calling attention to some matter that requires improvement or something for which we would want to be thankful. Sometimes, He gives us a fleeting moment of affective consolation or an extended experience of it. Sometimes, He gives us insight into theological or spiritual matters—and sometimes, deep insights into our personal lives and history.

When these invitations occur, I suspend praying the Rosary or Breviary, because I do not want to miss an opportunity to listen to and converse with the Lord, who is my teacher, protector, caring Father, and companion. I do not worry about having to finish the whole Rosary or the Breviary entry. After all, the objective of prayer is communion with the Lord. What better way to do this than listen to and converse with the One who loves us? When an invitation pops up, we might respond with the prayer of Eli and Samuel: "Speak, Lord; your servant is listening" (1 Sam 3:10). Sometimes He will respond immediately by giving us a recognition of His presence in our past life hitherto unnoticed for which we will want to thank and praise Him immediately—or He might give us an insight into a spiritual or personal matter that we will want to explore with Him. In these latter cases, I follow where the Lord's inspiration seems to be leading, and I frequently ask Him questions—"Is this what You are saying?" or "Is this what You have been doing?" or "Is this where You're leading me?" Frequently, He gives me a sense of affirmation, and sometimes He suggests something that changes the track of the conversation. Much of the time, I have a fairly good sense of what He is communicating—though not always.

Sometimes when the Lord gives me an insight into His love or protection or a brief moment of affective consolation, I simply thank Him and tell Him, "I love you too." Sometimes when the Lord is communicating a matter for improvement or repentance, I try to attend to what He is suggesting, and then commit to a modest first step, the Sacrament of Reconciliation, or even a modest first and second step. Why modest? Because modest "small" steps are doable, while gigantic steps normally wind up in failure and discouragement. Remember—the Lord who created us and knows us through and through does not inspire us to do the undoable. Rather, our enemy, Satan, is likely to do this in order to provoke us to discouragement and despair (see below, Section IV.B).

If our conversation with the Lord is short in duration, we will probably be able to return to some part of the Rosary or Breviary. If it is more extended, it may be best to conclude with a prayer of thanks and praise, followed by the Our Father. This theme of conversation with the Lord is developed below in Sections III.C.2, IV, and V.

Contemplative prayer brings us close to the Lord and to the Blessed Virgin, assuring us of the fact that we are loved and cared for by an affectionate, humble, gentle, compassionate, and forgiving Lord and Mother. This is essential for letting go of our fears, need for control, and obsession with establishing "our place in the world" (moral freedom). It should be noted that contemplative prayer and the Eucharist go hand in hand. The Eucharist connects us with the love of Christ in the depths of our hearts, transforming us and filling us with spiritual gifts (see Chapter 2, Section I.C), while contemplative prayer explicitizes this connection with the heart of Christ, making conscious (or at least tacitly conscious) the profound reality of Christ lying in the depths of our hearts. As such, contemplative prayer explicitizes the profound loving and transforming power of Christ in the Eucharist, while the Eucharist deepens the intimate loving presence of the Lord coming from contemplative prayer. When the Eucharist and contemplative prayer complement one another, they provide a strong foundation for the detachment needed for moral freedom. It should be remembered that spiritual conversion—even this very powerful kind of spiritual conversion—is not enough for detachment and moral freedom. We must also concertedly direct our awareness of Christ and His loving way to the process of detaching ourselves from sensuality, egoism, and their manifestation in the eight deadly sins (see Chapters 5–6).

C. The Third Stage of Contemplative Prayer from Discursive to Meditative and Silent Prayer

The third stage of contemplation is constituted by one of the following three prayer forms:

- Meditation/contemplation on the Gospels (e.g., Ignatian meditation) or other suggested themes from spiritual masters (Section III.C.1)
- The prayer of companionship with the Trinity and the Blessed Virgin (Section III.C.2)

- The prayer of silence (listening and intimate connection) (Section III.C.3)

1. Ignatian Meditation

As explained above in Section II.A, Ignatian meditation provides a good method for entering into an encounter with Jesus in the Gospels. The point of the contemplation is to be with Jesus in the scene, to recognize the quality of His love for others (as manifest through their reaction to Him), and to love Him in return. His love for us is infectious and induces us to imitate Him, because we enjoy being like the one we love. This form of meditative prayer can be quite powerful in connecting us to the Lord in an intimate and serious way (as generations of Jesuits can attest), and it can provide an excellent pathway to moving from discursive prayer to the prayer of companionship and then to the prayer of silence.[24]

It might be best to ease your way into the third stage of contemplation by retaining some of the more discursive prayers from the second stage, and then adding a time for Ignatian meditation. Stay with this combination of discursive and nondiscursive prayers until you sense a distinctive call from the Lord to move further away from discursive prayer to more meditative or silent prayer. Some of the signs of the Lord's call to do this are discussed in Volume I (Chapter 1, Section III) of this Trilogy.

One way of initiating a less discursive, more meditative kind of prayer through Ignatian meditation is to focus on the Passion of Jesus. This meditation has been central to Christian spirituality since the apostolic age, because it manifests clearly the unconditional love that the Lord has for each of us, and His desire to save us. When we personalize the Passion, it is one of the most intimate communions we can have with the One who spared nothing to rescue us from evil and bring us into the light of His salvation.

---

[24] There are several excellent books on this subject that help beginners enter into several Gospel narratives through the Ignatian method of meditation, such as the following: Timothy M. Gallagher, O.M.V., *Meditation and Contemplation: An Ignatian Guide to Praying with Scripture* (New York: Crossroad Publishing, 2008), and Timothy M. Gallagher, O.M.V., *An Ignatian Introduction to Prayer: Scriptural Reflections according to the Spiritual Exercises* (New York: Crossroad Publishing, 2007).

The Passion accounts are by far the most detailed narratives in all four Gospels (Mt 26:36—27:66; Mk 14:32—15:47; Lk 22:39—23:56; Jn 18:1—19:42); and the Passion itself lies at the heart of the Pauline and Petrine letters. Reverence for the crucified Christ is expressed not only in the New Testament, but in practically every form of religious art from the crucifix (positioned at the center of the church) to the stations of the cross that adorn its walls. During the Middle Ages, Christ's Passion was fixed at the center of art and iconography, and the wounds of Christ factor prominently into every image of the Sacred Heart. Christ's complete self-sacrificial love manifest in the Passion lies at the center of the spirituality of almost every Catholic saint, providing the impetus to follow and love Him out of sheer gratitude. When we realize that He truly is the Son of God, and that He truly wanted to completely sacrifice Himself in love for us, it is difficult to resist His call to follow. Each dimension of the Passion accounts reveals yet another length to which the Lord was willing to go to reveal His love and salvific intent. As we consider what He was thinking and feeling as He endured the pain and humiliation to give Himself totally to us, we are moved to respond with thanks and love.

The centrality of the Passion is not restricted to the saints. It is everywhere present in the Church herself. There are so many devotions to the Cross, the Sacred Heart, the crucifix, and the stations of the cross that an outside observer could not help but notice it. Why is this? As implied above, the Passion is not only the ultimate symbol, but the ultimate reality of the love of Jesus—which is unconditional and totally self-sacrificial. If we want to know how much we are loved by God, we need only gaze upon the crucifix or a picture of the Sacred Heart. As we do this, His love for *us* leaps out of the symbol upon which we are gazing. The time between the actual event and the current age seems to collapse as the crucified Christ gazes on us—as He did to Saint Francis in the Church of St. Damiano. The symbol connects us with His actual Crucifixion two thousand years ago, and if we attend to it, we are almost like the women and the beloved disciple standing at the foot of the Cross. It is not difficult to hear Him saying to us that He is willingly doing this for us because He loves us. We can hear echoes of the mystical vision of Saint John of the Cross in which Christ makes known to him the love He has for us:

Since He is the virtue of supreme *humility*, He *loves you* with supreme humility and esteem and *makes you His equal*, gladly revealing Himself to you in these ways of knowledge, in this His countenance is filled with graces, and telling you in this His union, not without great rejoicing: "*I am yours and for you* and *delighted* to be what I am so as to be yours *and give myself to you.*"[25]

The meditation on the Passion of Christ is so central to my own spirituality that I would recommend it to anyone as the subject of prayer at least one time per month. Some people believe that the place to start is contemplation on the Sorrowful Mysteries of the Rosary. If this helps to galvanize the momentousness of the Passion event and the love of the Lord within it, then by all means do it. I have also derived great benefit from slowly reading the Passion account in one of the Gospels.[26] I take only one scene at a time, starting with the Garden of Gethsemane, and as I slowly reflect on what is taking place, I pause to give thanks to the Lord who did this for me and all humanity. I then proceed to the betrayal by Judas, pausing once again to thank the Lord for enduring this humiliation and betrayal. I don't rush to finish the whole account but take only as much as I can to contemplate fruitfully within one session of prayer. When my prayer session is completed, I express my love for His self-sacrificial redemptive love for me, and then pick up the Passion account where I left off in my next prayer session. If you are anything like me, this meditation will bear fruit in connecting you to the Lord, helping you to sense His loving presence, moving you to gratitude and love, and inspiring you to imitate and follow Him. This will provide a strong basis from which to pursue detachment from the world (moral freedom), which will in turn provide the foundation on which to ground resistance to the deadly sins and the pursuit of moral action.

---

[25] Saint John of the Cross, "The Living Flame of Love", in *The Collected Works of St. John of the Cross*, ed. and trans. Kieran Kavanaugh, O.C.D., and Otilio Rodriguez, O.C.D. (Washington, D.C.: ICS Publications, 1979), p. 613 (italics added).

[26] Some of you might know that I am nearly blind and may be wondering, how does he meditate on the Gospel narratives? Simple answer is, I have audible recordings of the New Testament that I can easily access.

2. The Prayer of Companionship

The prayer of companionship might be described as resting in the mysterious and loving company of the three Persons of the Holy Trinity and the Blessed Virgin Mary. This kind of prayer presumes that individuals can sense and recognize the presence of the three Divine Persons and the Blessed Virgin Mary when they make themselves manifest. This normally arises out of practicing the first two stages of contemplative prayer for a period of time, which varies from person to person. As one develops in the contemplative life, the three Divine Persons and the Blessed Virgin make themselves subtly yet distinctly present. This experience may be an intense feeling of joy-filled consolation (see Volume I, Chapter 4, Section V.A of this Trilogy), but much of the time it is more subtle—like a distinct sense of the Divine Persons and the Blessed Virgin welcoming us into their presence. As we develop in the contemplative life, the Divine Persons' and Blessed Mary's distinctive presence becomes more apparent and recognizable, and so when we enter into the prayer of companionship with them, we frequently sense and recognize them in their distinctive sacredness.

Though the Divine Persons and Blessed Mary can often make their presence manifest, they do not always do so. When they do, their presence may be quite faint or profound. Even when their presence is at its faintest, it is enough to hold us, captivate us, and sometimes even fill us with their consciousness, holiness, and love. If the Divine Persons and Blessed Mary make their presence manifest, and we are open to it, we need do nothing more than enjoy being with the ones who love us and who we in turn love. This experience of being captivated and filled transforms us by a process of spiritual assimilation.

Why don't the Divine Persons and Blessed Mary make themselves manifest every time we open ourselves to their presence and companionship? If being in their company is transformative, why wouldn't they want us to be transformed every time we pray? The brief answer is sensuality and egocentricity particularly as manifest in the eight deadly sins (see Volume I, Chapters 5–6 of this Trilogy). Recall what has been said in Volume I about human freedom. The Lord will not melt away our sensuality and egocentricity if we do not choose to give it over to Him. If He did, He would destroy our freedom. This means that the Lord will have to find other ways to help us *choose* to detach from sensuality and egocentricity, which can be quite addictive. This usually entails "the school of the cross" (see below, Section IV).

The Divine Persons veil their presence and make recourse to the school of the cross when purification is needed to turn us from sinful lifestyles, keep us on the path to salvation, and deepen our religious and moral conversion. So, for example, if we have become acquainted with the presence of the Divine Persons and Blessed Mary by practicing the first two stages of contemplative prayer for a reasonable period of time, and find that they are not manifesting themselves during prayer for several days or more, we will want to examine what kind of purification they may be attempting to actualize. The following questions will prove helpful:

1. Am I doing something in my spiritual life that is causing me to backslide in the areas of sensuality and/or egocentricity? If so, when will I go to confession, and how should I rectify these problems?

2. If I am not backsliding, are the Divine Persons trying to help me deepen my religious and/or moral conversion? Have they been trying to connect with me in the early morning hours to guide me to a deeper state of holiness? If so, what kinds of initial small steps will I take to facilitate this process? (See below, Section IV.B.)

3. If I am not backsliding, and my spiritual director and I[27] cannot detect the Lord leading me to deeper religious and moral conversion, then is the Lord leading me to a deeper form of purification (through the dark night of the soul) to move from, say, the purgative way to the illuminative way—or from the illuminative way to the unitive way? (See below, Section IV.C.) If I am entering a "dark night", how do I best trust in and follow the Divine Persons?

---

[27] Many priests and religious have spiritual directors, but oftentimes, laypeople are not able to find one. I would recommend trying to find a committed spiritually mature friend or perhaps an available religious sister, priest, or trained lay spiritual director to help you at times when you are perplexed by the absence of the Divine Persons' presence or affective consolation for long periods of time. There are some good books on discernment, but having a spiritually mature interlocutor can be quite helpful in breaking through our subconscious screens and scotomas (self-blindings).

This process of purgation and inspiration through the school of the cross (complemented by the Sacrament of Reconciliation) helps us choose detachment from sensuality and egocentricity, which enables the Divine Persons and Blessed Mary to make their presence felt more frequently and intensely. Their purpose in using these purgative methods is solely to help us stay on the path to salvation and grow in holiness (agapē—generous, nonegocentric, and even self-sacrificial love; see Chapter 4, Section II).

So how can we initiate the prayer of companionship? Beginners, including myself, are frequently aided by discursive prayers that focus on *who* the Divine Persons and Blessed Mary are in their heart of hearts—their unrestricted goodness, love, sanctity, and sacred beauty (glory). These discursive prayers incite awareness of the presence of the Divine Persons and Blessed Mary as well as their deep love for us individually and collectively. The forthcoming prayers (below in this section) are helpful to me, but readers may want to adjust and adapt them to their own preferences. If you do this, remember that the prayers are meant to incite us to an awareness of *who* the Divine Persons and Blessed Mary are in their heart of hearts—not so much to emphasize *what* they are in power, intellect, attributes, and Being.

I enter this kind of prayer by holding onto my own crucifix, which has a very pronounced corpus of Jesus. This helps me to focus on the "who" and "heart" of the Lord. Readers may also want to use a picture of the Sacred Heart, an icon of Jesus or the Trinity, a statue of Mary, or some other image that helps them focus on the heart of the Divine Persons and Blessed Mary, who are *really* present with them (whether manifest or not).

I begin my prayer by recognizing the presence of *the Father* by praying something like, "Oh profound mystery of unrestricted being and love in whose thought I exist that surrounds me, imbues me, knows me, and loves me,[28] I thank You for Your unconditional care and love that You and Your Son have revealed to me interiorly and exteriorly. Thank You for wanting to be with me and for wanting

---

[28] I believe that we are all thoughts in the unrestricted intelligence of the one God, and give a proof for this in Volume II, Appendix II, of the Quartet. I give another metaphysical proof of this in "A Contemporary Metaphysical Proof for the Existence of God", *International Philosophical Quarterly* 59, no. 4 (December 2019): 427–66. I also give two additional proofs of this in Robert Spitzer, *New Proofs for the Existence of God: Contributions of Contemporary Physics and Philosophy* (Grand Rapids, Mich.: Eerdmans, 2010), Chapters 3–4.

me to be with You this day despite my sinfulness and many imperfections. I place myself in Your mysterious midst. I praise You for Your glorious creative, fatherly love that has fashioned my soul and sent Your only Son to redeem, rescue, and teach me Your way of love. Thank You for sharing Yourself with me and being present to me—I love You and I want to be closer to You."

Though this prayer is quite "wordy", parts of it may be useful for inciting the goodness, beauty, and love of the Father. If they are helpful, then use them. If not, ignore them or find a substitute. The main point is to enter into loving communion with the Father (and the other Divine Persons and Blessed Mary), sensing His presence as He makes Himself manifest. Thus, the most important part of the prayer is the one that helps us maintain loving communion with Him—such as "Thank You. I love You. Help me to grow closer to You." As we enter more deeply into the heart of the Father, it is frequently not necessary to say even these shorter prayers, but only to say the pronoun "You" lovingly and knowingly as we call to mind our loving Father. These very short prayers can lead naturally into the prayer of silence (see the following subsection).

I then shift my focus to *Jesus*, very conscious of the corpus on the crucifix I am holding. I say a similar prayer as the one addressed to the Father:

> Lord Jesus, I know that I exist in and through Your divine thought You share with Your Father, and I am grateful that You, who are the divine beloved Son, would want to sacrifice Yourself completely for me and the world in an act of unconditional love—being scourged, crowned with thorns, humiliated, and crucified. I cannot begin to grasp the breadth and depth of Your self-emptying love for me and all others, and I am honored that You would want to be with me and that You would welcome me to be in Your company. I place myself in Your unconditionally loving, caring, and healing presence. Thank You for being the gentle, humble Lamb of God who spared nothing to save me and humanity, and for being the compassionate, forgiving teacher and reconciler who leads me on the true path to salvation while rescuing me from my mortal enemy Satan. I love You and desire to grow ever closer to You through your loving grace.

Again, it is not necessary to use this "wordy" prayer unless it is truly helpful for placing you in loving communion with the Lord Jesus.

As with praying to the Father, you may want to reduce the words in the above prayer to something like, "Lord Jesus—beloved Son, divine Teacher, and gentle and humble Lamb of God—I thank You and love You; thank You and love You; thank You and love You ..." As you become habituated to this prayer, you will likely shorten the prayer even more to "Lord Jesus, I love You" or to knowingly and lovingly reciting the pronoun referring to the corpus on the crucifix, "You".

I then turn my attention to the *Holy Spirit* with this prayer:

Holy Spirit, I know who Jesus has revealed You to be: the recipient of the united love of Him and His Father who returns that love to them while bestowing it on the whole of humanity. I am so grateful for the way You inspire me, guide me, and protect me at every moment, and honored by the fact that you welcome me into Your company—Your very relationship with Jesus and His Father. I place myself in Your loving, inspiring, and protective presence. Thank You for searching my heart and sharing the hearts of the Father and Jesus with me; for revealing the goodness and lovability of the people around me; for inspiring me within the Church toward greater depths of holiness, and for protecting me from my enemy, Satan. I thank You and I love You; thank You and love You; thank You and love You ...

This prayer can be shortened in the same way as those given above toward the Father and Jesus.

Finally, I turn my attention to Blessed Mary, the Mother of God, with the following prayer:

Mother Mary, I know that your love for your Son radiates out to the whole of humanity, particularly to believers who open themselves to your maternal, gentle, instructive love, which has guided and helped me throughout my life. I am so honored that you would not only want to be my own sacred Mother, but would welcome me into your loving company with your Son, His Father, and the Holy Spirit. I place myself in your good and gentle presence. Thank you for coming to me during my times of failing, for calling me back to your Son, and for never giving up on me. Thank you for your example of purity and goodness and for your consoling presence in times of suffering. I thank you and love you; thank you and love you; thank you and love you.

It is not necessary to do all four prayers in any given session. You may want to focus on only one of the Divine Persons or on Blessed

Mary—or on two of the Divine Persons, say, the Father and Jesus. After reciting the prayers to the Divine Persons and/or Blessed Mary, you can continue to awaken your openness to them by praying, "Heavenly Father, I thank You and love You," adding similar prayers to Jesus, the Holy Spirit, or Blessed Mary as you feel called. You may also feel called to stop reciting these short prayers—or, if the Divine Persons or Blessed Mary make their presence manifest, simply to enjoy and assimilate their holiness and goodness in silence. This leads to our next topic.

3. The Prayer of Silence

The prayer of silence is described in the *Catechism of the Catholic Church* as follows:

> Contemplation is a *gaze* of faith, fixed on Jesus. "I look at him and he looks at me": this is what a certain peasant of Ars in the time of his holy curé used to say while praying before the tabernacle. This focus on Jesus is a renunciation of self. His gaze purifies our heart; the light of the countenance of Jesus illumines the eyes of our heart and teaches us to see everything in the light of his truth and his compassion for all men.[29]

Since this prayer form is virtually nondiscursive, few books are written about it. One notable exception is the fourteenth-century classic of Christian mysticism by an anonymous author—*The Cloud of Unknowing*. The author, counseling a young student, advises him to detach himself completely from any intellectual thought about God or His attributes, and to focus solely on the love of God by uniting himself intensely with the Lord, on whom he is contemplating:

> For He can well be loved, but he cannot be thought. By love he can be grasped and held, but by thought, neither grasped nor held. And therefore, though it may be good at times to think specifically of the kindness and excellence of God, and though this may be a light and a part of contemplation, all the same, in the work of contemplation itself, it must be cast down and covered with a cloud of forgetting.

---

[29] *CCC* 2715 (italics in original).

And you must step above it stoutly but deftly, with a devout and delightful stirring of love, and struggle to pierce that darkness above you; and beat on that thick cloud of unknowing with a sharp dart of longing love, and do not give up, whatever happens.[30]

The only way to penetrate the cloud of unknowing is to unite oneself firmly to the Lord in love. The objective of this kind of prayer is simply loving and trusting communion with the Lord, which opens us to an infusion of His loving self, carrying with it an awareness of His love and holiness, and His peace and unity.

Sometimes our attempts to find and connect with Him in love is greeted by more silence. The Lord's silence should not be interpreted in any way as rejection by Him or indifference to us, but rather as a call to trust Him radically as He leads us and purifies us of our ego-centricity and self-concern so that we can enter more fully into the mystery of His love, holiness, and home.

There are several doorways into the Divine Mystery through silent prayer—simply resting with the Lord; adoring Him in the Blessed Sacrament through Eucharistic devotion (see Chapter 2, Section I.D); adoring the Lord on the crucifix, in an image of the Sacred Heart, or a sacred icon; or simply sitting in a sacred place to sense the Holy Mystery of the One who comes to us. These doorways lead us to the Lord, who can manifest Himself in many affective and intuitive ways—both subtly and explicitly. As we rest in His presence, we open ourselves to Him in an act of self-surrender and attentiveness.

As we rest in the Lord and open ourselves to Him through self-surrender, we let Him come to us and lead us to where we cannot lead ourselves. Sometimes we will have a subtle experience of His loving holiness and sometimes a powerful one; sometimes a sense of His call or guidance, and sometimes mere silence. As noted above, the Lord's silence does not mean indifference or rejection, but instead, purification of our egos, in order to enter more fully into His loving mystery. Christian mysticism is focused on this journey into the mysteriously loving heart of the Lord through the fluctuations between silence and the experience of loving holiness, between desolation

---

[30] Anonymous, *The Cloud of Unknowing and Other Works*, trans. A. C. Spearing (New York: Penguin Classics, 2001), p. 27.

and consolation, being emptied and being filled, and being alone and being at home. We gave an explanation of this process in Volume I (Chapter 1, Section III) of this Trilogy by summarizing the works of two great Carmelite mystics—Saint John of the Cross and Saint Teresa of Avila.

Let us now return to the subject of the third stage of contemplative prayer. This kind of prayer places the focus on companionship with the Divine Persons and Blessed Mary. Most laypeople who are constrained by family and work commitments may find it challenging to move into this stage of contemplative prayer, because it requires additional time and private space. If laypeople are serious about making this kind of commitment, they might want to do it on a retreat or devote some time to it on a weekend once per month, or whatever may work in their schedule.

Those who embark on the third stage of contemplation—whether priest, religious, or lay—will benefit greatly by a directed retreat with at least three or four hours devoted to one or more of the three prayer forms in the third stage of contemplation. Directed retreats are especially important for those beginning the third stage of contemplation, to help them recognize the presence of the Divine Persons and Blessed Mary and to help them discern between movements of the Lord and those by our enemy, Satan. These retreats do not have to be completely silent, but long hours of silence between meals will help retreatants to open themselves to the presence of the Divine Persons and Blessed Mary. We now proceed to a very important topic concerned with progress in the contemplative life and spiritual and moral conversion—the school of the cross.

IV. Holiness and the School of the Cross

In this section, we will introduce the topic of moral conversion, which has been on the horizon of spiritual conversion throughout the previous chapters. As may now be clear, spiritual conversion provides a foundation for moral conversion. As our relationship with the Lord deepens through the sacraments, contemplative prayer, and devotion (spiritual conversion), we become more familiar with Him, which enables us to recognize when and how He is guiding us. This familiarity enables us to recognize the Lord's providential presence (even in our suffering) as well as His guiding hand helping us in our moral conversion—the way He communicates with us at three o'clock in the morning, or through the Sacrament of Reconciliation, or through spiritual and affective consolation and desolation. This recognition of the Lord's presence and guiding hand (arising out of spiritual conversion) is indispensable for moral conversion, because it enables the Lord to guide us—mostly through challenges, suffering, and desolation—to initial and ever deepening moral conversion. As I have noted in Volume IV (Chapter 7) of the Quartet, suffering viewed through the eyes of faith can shock us out of superficiality, cause us to ask about the deeper meaning of life, reveal the presence of darkness and evil in our lives, increase our faith (trust) in the Lord, and incite us to greater empathy and compassion. These spiritual insights are magnified considerably when we have the benefit of deep spiritual conversion (grounded in contemplative prayer and devotion), which enables us to recognize how the Lord works through our sufferings (past and present) and what and how He is communicating to us (oftentimes in the early hours of the morning) through that suffering. This communication by the Lord is a key means (along with the Sacrament of Reconciliation and the Examen Prayer) for actualizing moral conversion (discussed in Chapters 4–7 of this volume).

As will become clear, moral conversion is the most difficult part of the conversion process, because it requires breaking though sensuality and egocentricity (and even addictions to them), breaking with ingrained bad habits, confronting previously held beliefs leading us into darkness, and helping us to pursue previously avoided teachings of the Lord and the Church. Though a strong sacramental and contemplative prayer life are essential for initiating and deepening moral conversion, they are frequently not enough. Something else is needed—something that will break the spell of sensuality, egocentricity, bad habits, and false beliefs. Much of the time, the "spellbreaker" is suffering—challenges, deprivation, physical and emotional pain, insecurity, contentious relationships, insults and injury, grief, and affective desolation and spiritual desolation—to mention but a few manifestations. This will come as no surprise to Christians who have deeply embraced the word of Jesus in the Gospels, particularly

His oft-repeated teaching that His followers must deny themselves, take up their cross, and follow Him (see, for example, Mt 16:24).

Evidently, Jesus held that the Cross was an essential path to the Resurrection—an essential part of spiritual and moral conversion. He taught that His Father would never leave us in challenging and painful times, but rather would give us insight, grace, and providential direction to help us through these challenges. Saint Paul and Church tradition have consistently taught that the Lord would use our sufferings to detach us from our sensuality and egocentricity, enhance our empathy and compassion, and ultimately bring us closer to Him and our salvation. Though the Lord does not directly cause suffering (except in rare cases such as Saint Paul's conversion), He uses suffering (caused by ourselves, other people, and nature) to break the spell of sensuality, egocentricity, bad habits, and false beliefs, to deepen our spiritual and moral conversion. The sacraments, contemplative prayer, and devotion to Mary and the saints are essential for giving purpose and direction to our crosses so that they will not cause resentment, anxiety, and hopelessness, but instead incite us to deeper levels of faith and love. This is fully explained in Volume IV of the Quartet.

So how does the Lord combine the cross with the sacraments, contemplative prayer, and devotion to break the spell of our baser and egotistical nature to guide us to greater holiness (faith and love)? He uses three methods, each of which involves a form of difficulty or spiritual pain:

1. He gives inspiration and insight into the spiritual opportunities in our suffering (Section IV.A).
2. He communicates to us (frequently, at early hours of the morning) a need for change through a sense of guilt or profound awareness of past failings (Section IV.B).
3. He uses affective desolation to communicate a need for change and a new path to follow (Section IV.C).

A. First Method of Inspiring Moral Conversion through the Cross

The first method concerns inspiration toward the spiritual opportunities of suffering. We will want to remember that the deeper our relationship is with the Lord, the more we will be able to intuit and understand the ways that the Lord is using our suffering to purify us and lead us to salvation. If our relationship with Him is quite close, we will have considerable insight into the spiritual opportunities of our suffering—particularly sinful or destructive paths that need to be changed, superficiality that needs to be overcome, patience and compassion that need to be cultivated, prayer or devotion that need to be deepened, relationships that need to be healed, forgiveness that needs to be asked, and attitudes that need to be adjusted. Suffering has a remarkable way of challenging old beliefs and habits, opening us to new insights, asking the Lord for help, and resolving to follow a new path.

When we are suffering and vulnerable, we are likely to pray earnestly for help, and open ourselves to where the Lord is leading. When the Lord sees our openness, He rushes in with insight and grace to help us. The more we open ourselves to that insight and grace, and the more we look for it, the more He can help us. I recommend this little prayer—"Dear Lord, help me to know what I should do to use this cross to bring about my purification, salvation, and ministry to your people—show me the way." This little prayer disposes our free will to the Lord's inspirational love, and He responds quite quickly with little intuitions, urgings, cajolings, and inspirations of our desire to grow closer to Him.

Sometimes we will get an insight into something that requires change in our attitude or life direction as well as a quickening of our resolve to make that change, but other times we will be greeted by what we perceive to be silence. Do not be disturbed; silence is not necessarily from the Lord. It could be attributable to our inability to understand or even a subconscious blocking of what the Lord is saying. When we are seemingly greeted by silence, the best response is to offer up our sufferings in unity with those of Jesus on the Cross for the salvation of souls, reparation of sins, the souls in Purgatory, and the needs of the Church. After this, ask the Lord to give you His insights when you are capable of listening to and understanding them. I assure you, if you really mean this, the Lord will guide you toward the needed change and the opportunities for new purpose and direction in life. Countless have been the times when I resisted what the Lord was trying to say to me because something inside my conscious or subconscious psyche was too afraid or too intransigent to listen to it. I have always found that the Lord will try and try again to communicate where I need to go—and when I ask Him to lead me and help me, I find out much sooner where His benevolent and loving hand is pointing.

The Lord does not limit Himself to interior inspirations when guiding and communicating with us during times of suffering. He also uses His grand providential conspiracy, sending people to us who give us much-needed guidance, opening doors to new opportunities, inspiring us to read an article, or view a video, and combinations of these and many other "communication techniques". When these exterior signs are synthesized with His interior inspirations, they show us a path to using our challenges and sufferings to break the spell of sensuality, egocentricity, bad habits, and false beliefs, which frees us to follow a path to deeper holiness—increased faith, hope, and love through the Church and Her teachings. Remember, the Lord's objective for us in this life is to help us choose salvation over darkness, to purify us now rather than in the life to come (Purgatory), and to help us help others toward their salvation.

B. Second Method of Inspiring Moral Conversion through the Cross

The Lord's second method of inspiring moral conversion occurs through a sense of guilt or a profound awareness of past failings. Frequently, He inspires these states when we are not besieged by the clutter of our very active lives. For me, this is between two o'clock and three o'clock in the morning. We may wake up and perhaps be a little perplexed as to why we cannot sleep. As we lie there, we may find that there is a strong suggestion coming to us—perhaps a feeling of guilt about a relationship that needs to be healed or something about which we should ask for forgiveness; perhaps a sense of remorse for some action or actions done long ago; or perhaps a penetrating recognition of how destructive a particular course of action is to our lives or the Kingdom of God. At the same time, we might recognize the presence of the Lord, the Blessed Virgin, or other holy beings trying to help and inspire us toward a resolution or course of action. Recall that as our contemplative prayer life develops it becomes easier to recognize the presence of these divine and sacred beings. When this combination of events occurs—for example, a profound sense of guilt followed by an awareness of the Lord's presence—we might also sense a call to a change of life in a particular way and even in a particular direction. This is very likely to be a direct communication from the Lord.

Sometimes, the Lord will come with an incisive insight into a bad habit or pattern that has developed in our lives. It generally comes in the form of a feeling of alienation (not being "at home") followed by a message of gentle correction or chastisement. It is not an audible message, but one that nonetheless is clear to the mind. Much of the time, it takes the form of a question, such as, "Why are you going in this destructive direction?" or "Why are you so hard on this person?" Sometimes it can be more admonitional, such as, "You are going down a path of darkness" or "You need to make a change." Sometimes, it can be an image, such as the Blessed Virgin crying or a sense of darkness. These messages will also be accompanied by a sense of the Lord's caring and loving presence, sometimes accompanied by other heavenly beings, such as the Blessed Virgin or the saints.

When you receive these communications from the Lord, it is essential to respond with sorrow or even remorse for the harm done to others, self, and the Kingdom of God. After expressing this sorrow and remorse, make a resolution to begin moving out of the destructive path by developing a *few* doable steps to reverse it (see below). After expressing this sense of resolve and your "doable steps" to the Lord, give thanks—sincere thanks—to the Lord for caring so much about *you*, your salvation, and for guiding you in your life. Tell Him that your firm desire is to be with Him, to turn your life around, and to follow Him as best you can, asking for His grace to help you.

The most efficacious way of galvanizing your resolve and obtaining the grace to follow the Lord better is through the Sacrament of Reconciliation. After you have had an experience similar to the one mentioned above, it is essential to arrange a time to receive this sacrament, bringing the insights given you by the Lord to it. By doing this, you will solidify your contrition and strengthen your resolve to do better in the future. Oftentimes, the Lord will seize upon your profound confession and give you yet another deeper experience of contrition the following night. When I experience this compounded sense of contrition through the Sacrament of Reconciliation, it generally provides a strong incentive to make and carry out doable resolutions for a change of life.

In the aftermath of your deep contrition, try to discern where the Lord's caring voice is leading you, and make a resolution to pursue the change in life or direction to which you are being led. Think of some practical steps you really can do—some first steps to change ingrained patterns of sensuality, egocentricity, and bad habits. When these first steps have been accomplished, then think about other doable steps that follow from them. Remember it is much better to accomplish "small steps" than to despair over failure to accomplish gigantic ones. Frequently, if you succeed in accomplishing your first doable resolutions, the Lord will come back to you again at a later lucid moment (e.g., three o'clock in the morning) with some other suggestions—perhaps a deeper sense of guilt or remorse or a more profound insight into your life and the path to salvation. The Lord is our best spiritual director—if we are listening. The stronger our relationship with the Lord (through faith and contemplative prayer), the more deeply He can lead us into moral conversion. As has been noted many times above, this movement toward moral conversion is made possible through a strong spiritual conversion (relationship with the Lord) that enables us to perceive, understand, and follow the Lord's voice and guiding hand.

The above profound experiences are a springboard out of the Evil One's grip, and so we should expect that he will try to put a stumbling block in our way to slow or reverse our progress in moral conversion. If we have listened and responded to the Lord's grace and call to sorrow, resolve, and planned action, then we will be in a state of spiritual fervor that the Evil One will not be able to refute easily. Therefore, he will try to deceive us. Normally, he will try to weave his way into our spiritual fervor by suggesting something that *appears* to be consistent with our experience of the Lord—something consistent with goodness and holiness. However, this suggestion will be filled with exaggeration delivered by a different noncaring, callous voice, exhorting us to unhealthy practices, overwhelming guilt, and a loss of hope. For example, "You see how much you have sinned; you wretch, you had better clean up your act ASAP or you will be in Hell!" Evidently, the Evil One's purpose is to discourage us—not to help us toward salvation, or to purify us in holiness, or to help us help others toward their salvation (the Lord's intention). Remember, the devil can quote Scripture and can inspire us to do what is morally correct; *however*, he will only lead us in a seemingly good direction to deceive us and lead us into discouragement and ultimately despair. This is what Saint Paul (2 Cor 11:14) and Saint Ignatius of Loyola meant by "the devil appearing as an angel of light".[31] In view of this, we must be careful to discern whether a communication that follows upon and seems similar to the Lord's call to conversion is really from the Lord and not from His enemy—the Evil One.

In Volume I (Chapter 4, Section V) of this Trilogy, we discussed discernment of spirits in some detail. For the moment, suffice it to say that if we sense "the accuser" in our experience of guilt, remorse, or insight, then it may well be the Evil One who is trying to use a seeming good suggestion in order to exaggerate it so much that we are tempted to give up, despair, and abandon trust in God. Recall from that chapter the signs of the accuser—a sense that God is more demanding than loving, a sense that God is calling you despicable or a wretch, a sense that the only thing in which God is interested is "harder, faster, and better" (instead of getting to a goal you are capable of accomplishing), and a sense of despondency, hopelessness, and despair. If these signs are present, it is likely that the Evil One has woven himself into your spiritual fervor and desire for moral conversion. Should you abandon your sense of guilt, remorse, and resolve altogether? No—unless those feelings are generated out of a sense of exaggerated scrupulosity. Though our sense of guilt may be justified, we must be careful not to follow the exaggerated direction and hostile voice of our enemy to its intended conclusion—despondency and despair. As your prayer life deepens, you will be able to discern the voice of the accuser proficiently. When you sense the voice of the accuser, simply *ignore* the exaggerations, the false notions of God, the "harder, faster, better", and the exaggerated sense of self-loathing. Bear in mind that the Lord loves you unconditionally, does not want you to have an exaggerated

---

[31] This deception can be so devious that Saint Ignatius of Loyola had to devote a section of the *Spiritual Exercises* to what he called "discernment in the Second Week". See Saint Ignatius of Loyola, *Spiritual Exercises*, trans. Elder Mullan, S.J. (New York: P.J. Kenedy & Sons, 1914), pp. 91–93.

sense of self-loathing, and certainly does not want you to give up or despair. Separate the wheat from the weeds.

Once you have sorted out the voice of the accuser, return to the sense of guilt or remorse and the presence of the loving and caring Lord (and the Blessed Mother) present in the experience. If your relationship with the Lord is quite strong (through the sacraments and contemplative prayer), your sense of remorse and resolve will lead to the first stage of a genuine change in life—moral conversion.

The above profound experience, grace, and movement toward moral conversion is foundational, and without it, moral conversion would be far more difficult. It can be complemented by other techniques, such as the Ignatian Examen Prayer or by psychological affirmation processes (described in Chapters 5–6); but these cannot replace the call of the Lord, the Sacrament of Reconciliation, and the school of the cross. This call originates from and is sustained by the Lord, and when complemented by the Sacrament of Reconciliation, it has the capacity to change our hearts profoundly and move us to abandon our self-interests to follow Him.

C. Third Method of Inspiring Moral Conversion through the Cross

The Lord's third method of inspiring moral conversion through the cross is called affective desolation. This concept was discussed in some detail in Volume I (Chapter 4, Section V) of this Trilogy, but I will give a brief overview of the salient points below.

Like the other two methods for inspiring moral conversion, the Lord uses suffering and spiritual pain to help us deepen our moral conversion and stay on track in the resolutions we have already made. Recall from Volume I (Chapter 4) that affective desolation is a felt sense of spiritual emptiness, loneliness, and alienation that can *feel* like a separation from God, an empty wasteland, and a detachment from ultimate meaning and love. Notice that these feelings directly resemble our state of being—that is, our state of soul. We cannot help but notice when it occurs, because we lose even our ordinary sense of spiritual peace, home, and belovedness. The Lord can cause this by simply toning down or withdrawing His affective presence to our consciousness. As noted in Volume I, He generally makes His affective presence felt, so when He tones it down or even withdraws it, we feel spiritually and cosmically alone, empty, and alienated. Why does the Lord do this? For two major reasons:

1. To keep us on the road to holiness and deeper moral conversion
2. To help us move from what is called the purgative way to the illuminative way and ultimately the unitive way through the dark night of the soul (see Volume I, Chapter 1, Section III of this Trilogy)

With respect to the first reason, all of us can grow weak in our resolutions, slip, and even fall. The Lord wants to prevent us from even starting on the path to weaken resolve, and when He perceives that this is happening (leading to a regression or a fall), He alerts us to our complacency by simply withdrawing His affective presence. This is readily noticeable, causing spiritual and affective distress. Once the Lord has my attention, I ask myself immediately why the Lord is doing this, which generally leads to my discovery of straying off the path or regressing from a previously better spiritual state. My reaction is generally swift. I immediately ask for forgiveness for my failings, seek the Sacrament of Reconciliation, and establish some steps to get back on the road to moral conversion and holiness. As I do so, the feelings of spiritual (cosmic) emptiness, alienation, and loneliness begin to subside, and the Lord again makes His affective presence felt. This reason for affective desolation is essential to sustaining and deepening moral conversion. There are other reasons for affective desolation, some of which are tied up with the Evil One appearing as an angel of light (a deceiver) as well as an accuser, discussed in Volume I (Chapter 4, Section V), and some of which are tied up with spiritual-moral progression through the dark night of the soul (discussed in Volume I, Chapter 1, Section III). We will here only briefly discuss the dark night of the soul.

As noted in Volume I (Chapter 1, Section III) of this Trilogy, the Lord can intensify the purification of individuals who are spiritually and morally capable of moving from what is called the purgative way to the illuminative way and ultimately to the unitive way. With respect to the purgative way, the Lord withdraws much of His affective consolation from individuals pursuing holiness in order to wean them off of dependence on it and help them detach themselves from sensuality. This allows them to move from the purgative to the illuminative way where affective consolation is restored at a much greater intensity. This is called "the dark night of the senses".

In the illuminative way, the individual is quite detached from sensuality and the world but is still vulnerable to "spiritual sins" of anger, envy, and particularly pride (spiritual pride). This requires another deprivation of affective consolation, called the "dark night of the spirit", to make purification complete. When this occurs, the individual reaches the unitive way, where affective consolation is restored at an even more intense level described by mystics as "ecstasy" or "overwhelming joy".

It is important to understand that the Lord is not using affective desolation to call these holy individuals back from regression or failure in the spiritual or moral life, but precisely the *opposite*—to help these holy individuals to progress in the purification of their sensuality and egocentricity.

D. Summary of the Lord's Use of the Cross in Spiritual and Moral Conversion

The Lord does not want anyone to suffer, but like a parent, He has to allow us to contend with challenge, deprivation, pain, and affective desolation to shock us out of superficiality and destructive paths; incite us to develop our strengths, courage, and fortitude; call us to humility, compassion, and deeper faith; and help us detach from sensuality and egocentricity—all of which are essential for our purification and, ultimately, for salvation. As noted above, when we encounter suffering, the Lord gives us inspiration and insight to help us attain optimal benefit for our salvation and to help others toward their salvation. He also can induce guilt, remorse, and insight into past failures (often in the early hours of the morning) to call us to the Sacrament of Reconciliation, and through it, to a positive change in attitudes and habits. Finally, He can use affective desolation to call us back to holiness if we are regressing, and to purify us in holiness when we are progressing in spiritual and moral conversion (the dark night of the soul). The Lord's action in all three of these painful or challenging conditions is not meant to be a punishment meted out in anger, but rather a loving call to help us detach from a destructive life, exaggerated sensuality, and egocentricity, which lead us toward darkness and evil—away from His loving presence. The Lord does not want to cause anyone pain or suffering, but He will use these means to call us back from the grip of the Evil One so that we will be able to choose His eternal light and love. This is why Saint John of the Cross calls these moments of suffering and desolation an integral part of the "living flame of love".

V. Some Ways in Which the Lord May Speak

We have already addressed several ways in which the Divine Persons communicate with us:

- Awakening us in the early morning with a sense of emptiness and guilt while pointing the way to reform and deeper conversion (Section IV.B)
- Inspiring us (beyond our limitations) to understand the meaning of suffering and deprivation, discern answers to theological questions, sense the presence of danger and Satan, sense a peace beyond all understanding, and guide us through their conspiracy of divine providence (see Volume I, Chapter 1, Section II of this Trilogy)
- Using affective desolation and consolation to guide us and deepen us in holiness and conversion (see Volume I, Chapter 4, Section V of this Trilogy)
- Making their presence subtly and distinctly manifest to captivate us, deepen us, fill us, transform us, and bring us ever more deeply into their lives (see above, Section III.C.2)
- Public apparitions and individual visions and revelations (see Volume I, Appendix, for public apparitions, and Volume I, Chapter 1, Section II, for individual visions and revelations)

There are other ways in which the Divine Persons and Blessed Mary can communicate and make themselves manifest. One way can occur during Ignatian meditation. It generally consists in a surprising twist occurring in the midst of a Gospel scene. I recall once doing a meditation on the call of Peter and Andrew at the Sea of Galilee. I was imagining the scene of Jesus passing by and saying, "Follow me, and I will make you fishers of men" (Mt 4:19). As I was imagining Peter hearing this, Jesus' voice very distinctly appeared in my mind, unmistakably addressing *me*. I was, to say the least, astonished, and was so certain about His personal presence that I was confirmed in my call to be a priest and avowed religious. I was not looking for such a confirmation and was not focused in any way on myself. I did not think that it was a subconscious projection into my conscious state of imagination, because the voice was filled with a divine authority and personality so different from my own; so I concluded that the Lord decided to reinforce His call to me to strengthen me at a time of growth and discernment.

I recall another time when I was meditating on the Nativity, and Mary was speaking to Jesus saying, "I love You," at which point she surprisingly looked up at me and said, "And I love you too." Despite my amazement, I managed to blurt out, "And I love you too!" I felt a very strong closeness and affirmation of her love and care, reflecting the disposition of her Son, at that moment, which has stayed with me to this day. These unexpected, personalized twists in the Gospel scene have all the markings of the Lord of love and His Blessed Mother. Since the voice and personality of the imagined characters were so distinct from and independent of my own, I cannot help but think that they are communications from the Lord and His Blessed Mother.

There are still other ways in which the Lord communicates. Many of these occur outside of prayer and are surprising twists within our ordinary lives. I recall once directing a retreatant on the Ignatian exercises who told me that his belief in God was only intellectual because he continuously felt that the world around him was cold, dark, and empty. I asked him to pray for a sign that the Lord was really present and cared for him, but he summarily ignored my request because he was convinced that God did not do such things. A day and a half later, he came to my room after midnight, knocked on my door, and told me that he had the most remarkable experience as he was walking along the road at about eleven o'clock in the evening. Completely contrary to his mindset as he walked along the cold dark road, he was filled with a sense of light and warmth and love. He was so surprised by the occurrence that he thought he might be hallucinating, but the sense of love embedded in the light and warmth was so strong and "insistent" that he opened himself to it, at which point he *knew* it was Jesus. His conviction and excitement was so great that he had to tell me about the incident immediately. I kept in touch with him for a few years thereafter, and he indicated that the experience had profoundly changed him, inciting him to prayer and causing him to change his career choice and way of life.

As noted above (Section IV.A), the Lord can inspire profound understanding of opportunities during times of suffering. He may also manifest Himself in a direct *affective* way during such times to give reassurance of His presence and love. For example, when Saint Thérèse of Lisieux's sickness was beginning to manifest itself seriously, she experienced tremors. She was placed in her sister Marie's room, which had a statue of the Blessed Virgin Mary; shortly thereafter, she had a profound experience of the Blessed Virgin smiling at her. On May 13, 1883, she reported:

> Our Blessed Lady has come to me, she has smiled upon me. How happy I am.[32]

Children frequently have visions of God, angels, and the Blessed Virgin during times of grave illness. Dr. Geni Bennetts (when hematologist and oncologist at Children's Hospital of Orange County, California) reported that a large number of children have visions of God or angels that reassure them about their life after death. The children report these visions to their parents, to assuage their parents' sadness and fears. Though Dr. Bennetts was appropriately skeptical, she indicated that she was certain these visions were not induced by narcotics or the result of hallucinations, because the information related by the children about the future time and nature of their deaths had never been in error.[33] These peaceful yet powerful visions

---

[32] Saint Thérèse of Lisieux, *The Story of a Soul*, trans. Thomas N. Taylor (Teddington, U.K.: Echo Library, 2006), p. 36.

[33] See Dianne Klein, "The Visions of Dying Children Seem to Bring God Alive", *Los Angeles Times*, April 22, 1990, http://articles.latimes.com/1990-04-22/local/me-518_1_fewer-children.

are common to children in both religious and nonreligious house-holds.[34] Dr. Bennetts' research was then confirmed by a much larger study carried out by Yale University's professor of pediatrics and oncology, Dr. Diane Komp,[35] and later confirmed by multiple stud-ies reported by David J. Bearison.[36]

Deathbed visions are by no means limited to children, occurring frequently in middle-aged and elderly adults.[37] My own grandfather experienced one such vision prior to his death. He was a very ratio-nal, objective man (formerly chief naval architect of the Pacific with headquarters at Pearl Harbor) who was not inclined to flights of fantasy. As he lay dying, surrounded by family members, he began to converse animatedly with beings in the room other than family members. My brother asked, "Granddaddy, who are you talking to?" and he calmly responded, "To the angels." His conversation continued for a good ten minutes, and everyone assumed he was "seeing things". He suddenly looked up and asked my mother, "Can I go now?" to which everyone responded, "Well, sure," at which point he died. Needless to say, the immediacy of his death gave everyone pause. I believe he reported precisely what he saw—a divine favor.

I conclude these reflections by discussing one of the most fre-quent and important ways in which the Lord communicates with us—namely, how He makes suggestions to do something completely out of the ordinary, which, if followed, cause a positive change in life's direction or meaning. The history of initial and deepening con-version is replete with these suggestions, which many people describe as a "little voice in the back of their heads". The little voice seems like an individual's own voice, but with a slightly different, persistent

---

[34] Ibid.

[35] See Diane Komp, *Images of Grace: A Pediatrician's Trilogy of Faith, Hope, and Love* (Grand Rapids, Mich.: Zondervan, 1996).

[36] David J. Bearison, *The Edge of Medicine: Stories of Dying Children and Their Parents* (New York: Oxford University Press, 2012).

[37] Though many in the medical community relegate deathbed visions to mere hallucination resulting from cerebral hypoxia, there is reason to believe in their veracity. The reason for this is the frequency with which dying people have visions of their relatives who they thought were still alive. Only after these visions were reported was it discovered that the relatives in fact had died. See, for example, Victor Zammit and Wendy Zammit, *A Lawyer Presents the Case for the Afterlife* (U.K.: White Crow Books, 2013).

tone, advocating for a change of conduct or attitude hitherto ignored or rejected.

Prior to these suggestions, many individuals find themselves in a sad, empty, or depressed state, frequently for no apparent reason. Though the cause is not apparent to unconverted individuals, there is good reason to believe that it arises out of their lack of a significant relationship with God needed to achieve fulfillment of their nature and purpose. As we have noted often, Saint Augustine phrased this succinctly with respect to his own life—"For Thou has made us for Thyself, and our hearts are restless until they rest in Thee." The American Psychiatric Association's 2004 study of the difference between religiously affiliated and nonreligiously affiliated people also confirms this view of human nature and fulfillment. The study showed that nonreligiously affiliated individuals have significantly higher rates of malaise, impulsivity, aggressivity, substance abuse, familial tensions, and suicide rates.[38]

Frequently, these sad or empty individuals would be going about their ordinary life's activities. Suddenly and surprisingly, they would sense a little voice in the back of their heads suggesting going into a church (which they had not done in decades) or picking up a book about God or religion (which they formerly would never have considered). Sometimes, there is no "little voice" at all, but rather a sudden sense of relief from sadness and alienation when they gaze upon a sacred image, hear a sacred song, or pass by a church. This little voice or sense of peace amid sadness is not overwhelming and does not force anyone against his will. It is simply presented to consciousness—often persistently—leaving the person free to choose the unfamiliar action, attitude, or behavior.

Readers may be thinking that the "little voice" is only a person's subconscious impression coming to the surface of consciousness when triggered by the sight of a church or sacred image. No doubt that may be true in a few cases, but I'm of the opinion that it is not true for most cases for two reasons. First, the "little voice" is making suggestions that are quite new and contrary to the inner voice

---

[38] See Kanita Dervic et al., "Religious Affiliation and Suicide Attempt", *American Journal of Psychiatry* 161, no. 12 (December 2004): 2303–8, https://ajp.psychiatryonline.org/doi/full /10.1176/appi.ajp.161.12.2303.

of these individuals in the past. Second, when individuals have not moved to any significant level of spiritual or moral conversion, their subconscious does not move them to a higher level of conversion, but rather to a decidedly lower one (see Chapters 5–6 of this volume). There may be a few inexplicable cases of the subconscious acting contrary to its nature, but it would be unreasonable to believe that this occurs frequently or most of the time in the many cases where the "little voice" is persistently advocating for a behavior or attitude leading toward spiritual or moral conversion in an individual who has hitherto ignored these considerations. Therefore, it seems reasonable to believe that the little voice is inspired by the Lord when it persistently advocates toward greater conversion among the virtually unconverted.

As noted above, the Lord subdues His voice to allow individuals the free choice to follow it. However, this gives rise to a problem—if individuals are completely unaccustomed to the behavior or attitude being advocated persistently but subtly, what are the odds that they will follow it? We must assume that the chances are high enough to warrant the Lord's course of action. Nevertheless, converted Christians should not sit idly by. If the occasion presents itself, we might want to mention to our unconverted friends that if they find themselves in an ongoing malaise, and then one day hear a persistent subtle voice in the back of their heads making a suggestion to pray, go to Church, or turn their lives around, then they should follow that voice because it is very likely the Lord of love who is trying to help them move from darkness to light, emptiness to fullness, malaise to peace, and alienation to being at home with Him. Your friends might look at you curiously or even critically, but if their malaise increases, your suggestion may be the most powerful moment of evangelization in their lives. It is truly worth a few moments of people rolling their eyes or even sneering, because your outer voice will have complemented the Lord's persistent inner voice to lead them toward peace and salvation.

Does the Lord's little inner voice also work in the lives of individuals who have reached at least a basic level of spiritual and moral conversion? Yes—the Lord never tires of using this technique in all of His beloved sons and daughters, irrespective of their level of conversion, because we all need His guiding hand to keep us out of darkness and on the road to salvation. We have already seen how He does this by awakening us in the early hours of the morning to call us out of darkness or to greater conversion (see Section IV.B).

The Lord does not reserve this technique to calling us out of darkness. He also uses it to call us into greater light—higher levels of spiritual and moral conversion. I and many of my friends have experienced the "little voice" doing this in our own lives. I will give two personal examples, but I would venture to say that most individuals in the process of conversion will remember multiple examples in their own lives if they chose to follow the little voice. If they did not do so, they would have probably forgotten it long ago.

One incident I have written about elsewhere occurred in my early years of university studies when a woman acquaintance asked me if I would teach a catechism class to ninth-grade boys. I was quite reticent, because I did not think I was "religious enough". When I refused, the woman provoked me by noting that I was making a less than optimal decision for the Lord and His Kingdom. I then indicated that I would be willing to teach *one* class on the relationship between faith and science, pointing to a creation of the universe. Though she was probably stunned by my choice of topic, she said that it would be fine.

When I began teaching, the students thought they were in the wrong class, because they had never heard a catechism teacher talk about physics and cosmology previously. I assured them that it was relevant and they would get something out of it. As the class progressed, students who had probably not paid attention to any religion class started taking notes. Then the Lord capitalized on the situation. The little voice kept suggesting that this would be something good to do beyond this one class because it was doing obvious good for the students. I tried to ignore the little voice as best I could, because I did not want to be inconvenienced in the future. However, at the end of the class, one student who was evidently one of the more interested ones quickly and excitedly came up to me and asked, "Are you going to be our catechism teacher for the rest of the year?" He was looking at me with expectant, almost pleading eyes, and the little voice suggested yes. The combination of the little voice, the pleading eyes, and the excited question made these unexpected words well up from within me—"Yes, I will be your teacher." The rest—at least with respect to my teaching career—is history.

The second incident concerns a series of little voices making suggestions to me in my later collegiate years with respect to being a Jesuit priest. Though I was quite convinced in my senior year that I should go to law school and follow in my father's footsteps, my increasing interest in philosophical theology, Scripture, and the Church had reached a point where I was also convinced that the most important dimension of my life was my relationship with God and my religion. The Lord had inflamed my heart with interest and desire to enter more fully into the Church and to build His Kingdom. This "inflaming of desire" is yet another way in which the Lord communicates with us. My desire was so strong that I set about looking for a way to increase my service to Him without giving up my plan to pursue law school and a corporate law career. My mother saw an article in a popular news magazine on the permanent deaconate, and the Lord once again capitalized on the situation. The little voice persistently echoed in my mind that this would be a terrific idea, enabling me to get married, have children, pursue a law career, and serve the Church as a deacon. I could not help myself. I then set about getting as much information as I could on the permanent deaconate, deciding to delay pursuing it until after I was married. I then fit it quite nicely into my long-term plan.

In the meantime, I was auditing as many theology classes as I could fit into my academic schedule, including classes on the Gospel of John, and the "love-justice dialectic". These classes stoked my desire to pursue theological studies and serve the Lord's Kingdom even before I was married and in a corporate law career. The little voice again started making suggestions, such as, "What's more important— building the Kingdom or pursuing a law career?" As usual, I was able to suppress the little voice for several weeks until I was leaving Sunday Mass.

As I walked past a stand with pamphlets and small books, I caught sight of a booklet on being a priest. The Lord again capitalized on the situation—"Pick that booklet up and take a look at it." Truly, this was the last thing on my mind, but moved with a sense of slight curiosity and desire by the suggestion, I picked it up and started looking at it. It was an older vocations brochure that was a bit outdated, but after looking at the pictures in that brochure and reading a few paragraphs, my heart once again became filled with the desire to serve the Lord and His Kingdom. I let the idea of being a priest cross my mind for a few minutes, and that's all it took. It stuck, and I could not shake the idea.

Nevertheless, I really wanted to be married and have children because my own experience of family was so positive and joy-filled. So I thought, "This has to be put to rest. I am not going to be a priest!" However, the Lord had other plans. Every time I went to Mass and saw a priest, the little voice would ask, "Is that not you?" I would then see priests teaching philosophy and theology, and then at the next moment giving retreats and spiritual direction, which I greatly admired. The little voice would again ask, "Is that not you?" For the first time, I began to have doubts about my cherished plan to get married and pursue corporate law.

I found myself getting pulled into more "Kingdom-building activities"—appearing on a local television program defending the Church's position against abortion, giving lectures at various local colleges on faith and science, and becoming a spokesman for Christianity and the Church. Suffice to say that a series of additional experiences, including a rainstorm, embedded with the little voice's suggestions brought me to a point where I had sufficient freedom to let go of my plans for marriage and a law career to consider actually being a priest. I followed the little voice, and again, the rest is history.

After multiple experiences of the little voice, I have come to believe that when it is directing me to deeper spiritual and moral conversion, while inflaming me with the desire to serve the Lord and His people, it is very likely to be the voice of the Lord guiding me toward salvation and the edification of His Kingdom. Why only "very likely"? As noted above (Sections IV.B–C), the devil can appear as an angel of light, making suggestions that *seem* to lead to spiritual and moral conversion and service of God's Kingdom. We can differentiate the voice of the wolf from the voice of the shepherd by looking for some telltale signs:

- The voice of the accuser filled with contempt and deprecation (e.g., "you wretch")

- A focus on "faster, harder, and better" rather than the Beatitudes (humble-heartedness, gentle-heartedness, compassion, forgiveness, and peacefulness)
- A sense of affective desolation and confusion immediately after the voice
- Long-term decrease in trust in the Lord, hope, and salvation, and the desire to be charitable and loving (see 1 Cor 13)

These telltale signs are discussed in greater detail with respect to Saint Ignatius of Loyola's rules for the discernment of spirits in Volume I (Chapter 4, Section V) of this Trilogy.

I assume most readers of this book are already in the process of spiritual and moral conversion. If so, then you will be able to become more "in-tune" with the Lord's little voice and His suggestions. In so doing, you will let the Lord help you on the path to conversion, evangelization, and salvation. As I have had to learn many times, one of the most important dimensions of spiritual and moral conversion is to be aware of the Lord's little voice, assuring me that it is not the voice of our enemy, Satan. When we discern that it really is the Lord, we will want to listen attentively and follow Him. We will not be disappointed.

VI. Marian Devotion

Since this chapter is primarily concerned with spiritual conversion and prayer, we will proceed directly to the topic of Marian devotion, without providing a scriptural and historical justification for it. Readers who are at home with Marian devotion will want to proceed to the following discussion.

Marian devotion is so deeply developed within the Catholic Church that literally thousands of books, articles, booklets, pamphlets, prayer cards, and websites are devoted to it. The Rosary, meditations for the Rosary, novenas, special prayers, and litanies are but a few expressions of this devotion. There is no possible way of summarizing these devotions nor the countless icons and paintings meant to inspire it in a relatively small section of a chapter. To do so would be to underdignify, undervalue, and underestimate tens of thousands of expressions of love and devotion throughout the centuries. What we *can* do is give a general sense of the importance of Mary's presence and voice in our spiritual lives and how she manifests herself to individuals, the public, and in the history of salvation.

We have already discussed the power of the Rosary in initiating a life of contemplative prayer (see above, Section III.B.1), and even a casual observer can recognize the prominent role of Mary in contemplation and Church life. It is hard to miss the sheer proliferation of icons, rosaries, and statues to Mary, not only in churches, but in most Catholic households. As we shall see, Catholics do not worship Mary; they call upon her in their prayer to bring her distinctive presence, love, and familial presence into their experience of the Trinity's grace, presence, and plan. In my view, this is precisely what the Triune God had in mind from the inception of time for all believers.

We now turn to a brief explication of the "voice of Mary" in our prayer and devotion. By "voice", I do not mean an audible voice present to our ears or mind or even an intense feeling (though this may occasionally occur). "Voice" refers to a subtle sense of peace or "being at home" that has the qualities of transcendence and feminine ethos. It is a sort of subtle peace and assurance that a transcendent Mother would offer. It is the kind of peace or sense of home that can occur while one is praying a Rosary or a few Hail Marys.

It might be helpful to begin our exploration of Mary's powerful yet gentle presence with the viewpoint of a secular historian commenting on the influence of Marian devotion in the development of European culture. William Lecky recognized Mary's civilizing influence within a harsh and benighted culture:

> The world is governed by its ideals, and seldom or never has there been one which has exercised a more salutary influence than the medieval concept of the Virgin. For the first time woman was elevated to her rightful position, and the sanctity of weakness was recognized, as well as the sanctity of sorrow.
>
> No longer the slave or toy of man, no longer associated only with ideas of degradation and of sensuality, woman rose, in the person of the Virgin Mother, into a new sphere, and became the object of reverential homage, of which antiquity had no conception. A new type of character was called into being; a new kind of admiration was fostered. Into a harsh and ignorant and benighted age, this ideal

type infused a conception of gentleness and purity, unknown to the proudest civilizations of the past. In the pages of living tenderness, which many a monkish writer has left in honor of his celestial patron; in the millions who, in many lands and in many ages, have sought to mold their characters into her image; in those holy maidens who, for love of Mary, have separated themselves from all glories and pleasure of the world, to seek in fastings and vigils and humble charity to render themselves worthy of her benedictions; in the new sense of honor, in the chivalrous respect, in the softening of manners, in the refinement of tastes displayed in all walks of society; in these and in many other ways we detect the influence of the Virgin. All that was best in Europe clustered around it, and it is the origin of many of the purest elements of our civilization.[39]

If a secular historian can recognize the power of Marian devotion in European culture, it is not a far stretch for Catholics and Christians to see the plan of God and the power of the Holy Spirit working through Mary's faith, humility, compassion, simplicity, and love of her Son throughout European and world history. Though Lecky would not have recognized God's providence (from the beginning of time) in the most remarkable free act of a human being in history—the *fiat* of Mary—Christians can see it clearly through the lens of Jesus' glorified Resurrection, miraculous power, and gift of the Holy Spirit. This certainly occurred in the early Church when the apostles included her in the gathering in the upper room at Pentecost (Acts 1: 14), when Saint Luke recognized her universal role in the history of salvation (Lk 1:39–56; 2:1–40), and when the author of Revelation (A.D. 90) recognized her eschatological role in the cosmic struggle between good and evil (12:1–6, 13–17).

Mary is at once Mother of the incarnate Word, Mother of the Church, and our own Mother; she is the model of purity and chastity who calls us to the same ideal manifest in her perpetual virginity; and she is the one who was assumed into Heaven to be a central intercessor and mediatrix of grace for the Church and for each believer. As such, she, bonded with her Son, is integral to the Divine Family and the communion of saints, which extends to the Mystical Body on

---

[39] William Lecky, quoted in John L. Stoddard, *Rebuilding a Lost Faith: By an American Agnostic* (Rockford, Ill.: Tan Books and Publishers, 1990), p. 247.

earth. She is the woman clothed with the sun—the divine radiance—who assists us against Satan, leads us toward her Son, and comforts us like a mother. We can call upon her presence, protection, and intercessory power by entering into the Rosary, which is a central element of Catholic contemplative life. Devotion to Mary will always lead us more deeply into the heart of her Son while bringing her motherly and familial presence into our contemplative lives. Like a mother, she is gentle, calming, and healing; yet she can also call us to the purity and continence that protects us from the empty promises of Satan and leads us ever more deeply into the communion of saints.

With the above in mind, we now ask the question of what Mary can and does bring to our prayers and spiritual development. Some people might think that Mary cannot add anything to the infinity of God. Though this is theoretically true, it is not God's *will* to exclude anyone from participating in the efficacious drama of salvation. He has prepared a part for each of us to play—through our prayers, faith, actions, words, compassion, self-sacrifice, virtue, and sufferings, because He exudes the "logic of love"—the more we give to others of our faith, hope, and loving service, the more we will receive, until we are transformed from the smallest of seeds to the largest of shrubs (Mt 13:31–32).

Through His loving will, He shares His mission of salvation with all of us—a sharing that knows no competition, no "zero sum game". On one occasion, Bishop Fulton Sheen was asked, "By praying to Mary aren't you taking away something from Jesus?" He responded, "Well, if I love your mother does that mean I love you any less?" We can extend Sheen's insight further by asking, "If I love your Mother, doesn't that enhance my love for you?" This is the logic of love out of which the Holy Trinity shares the mission of mediating grace with the Blessed Virgin Mary, and enables our prayers and the prayers of all the saints to be efficacious in actualizing the work of salvation.

Within the scope of their loving will, the Holy Trinity allows Mary to have a unique presence in the hearts of believers throughout the world. This presence has genuine feminine, motherly, and familial qualities. Yes, the Father of Jesus, whom He teaches us to address as "Abba" ("Daddy") and analogizes through the father of the prodigal son (see Chapter 7, Section I), has compassionate familial qualities, but He manifests those qualities as "fatherly". To be sure, those fatherly qualities are affectionate, gentle, trustworthy, and compassionate, but He manifests those qualities in a *fatherly* way. Jesus manifests those same qualities as Lord, master, and human companion. Though the Persons of the Trinity can manifest Their loving qualities in any way that They wish, They chose to make room for Mary to enter into her salvific role as Mother of the Church. Her voice is different from the Father and Jesus but complementary to Them in its particular feminine and motherly compassion, affection, gentleness, and guidance. We all know that a mother's guidance and affection feels and sounds different than that of a father or a Lord and companion.

One might think that this is raising Mary to an exalted, divine-like status—and that would be correct. The Trinity has not raised Mary to a *divine* status, but to a divine*like* status—higher than the angels. Just as Mary freely assented to the Incarnation of the second Person of the Trinity into her worldly embodiment, the Holy Trinity has exalted her into a heavenly status as the distinctively feminine-motherly voice and presence to all believers for whom she is Mother.

When we pray to Mary for protection, help, intercession, or simple companionship, she responds with her particular feminine motherly presence and voice. This particular presence elicits feelings of familial comfort, confidence, affection, and guidance that complement those of the Holy Trinity, enhancing our prayer and our communion with them. For this reason alone, I can see why the Trinity would have guided the whole of human history toward the Incarnation of the second Person through Mary, leading to her exaltation and heavenly role in prayer and salvation.

Interestingly, children seem to be able to sense her presence and differentiate it from the presence of the Father and Jesus. No doubt many will say that this is mere projection of the voice of their own mothers, fathers, and teachers onto their imaginary conception of Mary, the Father, and Jesus. I frankly do not believe this, because in my own childhood I was able to distinguish between the presence of a divine and human father, a divinelike and human mother, and a divine and human teacher. One presence was filled with the numinous divine mystery, while the other presence, though holy and grace-filled, was not filled with the numinous divine mystery. But I digress. The point is that for believers, Mary has a distinctive presence that elicits feelings and responses that adults, particularly those who have lived a life of faith and prayer for many years, can detect and differentiate from the presence of the Father, Jesus, and the Holy Spirit. This feminine motherly voice, this distinctive presence, is precisely what the Trinity wanted to make manifest when They exalted Mary to her heavenly status, making her Mother of the Church (see Lk 1:48–53; Rev 12:1–6).[40]

Yet, Mary brings more than her complementary feminine-motherly presence to our prayers; she also brings the presence of family—sacred family and sacred home—into our individual and collective prayer. As a child I used to look upon the big crèche scene displayed in our home at Christmas time, and it evoked for me a sense of peace, home, and family. The Holy Family's home, which was essentially a simple barn, *felt* like *my* home; and since Mary was integral to that home, I *felt* that *her* sacred home was *my* home, and *her* sacred family, *my* family. I look back on it now and consider this intuition of sacred peace-home-family to be more than a childhood insight. It was a grace, a conviction supported by the Holy Spirit—a *truth* emblazoned on my *heart*.

When such "graced truths" occur, we have a certitude and confidence going beyond the evidence of the mind—it *feels* so certain that we do not believe we have to question it. This is precisely how I felt about the sacred peace-home-family of both the Holy Family and Mary, which, in its turn, gave me confidence about her presence and care when I was in need. Later on, it occurred to me that God was not calling us as *autonomous individuals* to Himself alone (a sort of "one on one" relationship) but rather calling us as *interpersonal persons* into a huge family that had its origins in His Holy Family. If this was what God was doing, then He would want to select a human mother for the Incarnation of His Son;[41] and this mother would have to resemble Him in humility and compassion—with the exception that she would be a more feminine version of this kind of love. My

---

[40] The doctrine of *Theotokos* is explained in Spitzer, *Credible Catholic Big Book*, Volume 12, *The Church and Spiritual Conversion*, Chapter 4, Section III.B, https://www.crediblecatholic.com/pdf/M12/BB12.pdf#P1V12.

[41] See Volume III (Appendix II) of the Quartet for an explanation of the Trinity and the Incarnation of the Son—the second Person of the Trinity.

sense of the Blessed Mother's presence and care (as well as the biblical description of her) communicated this "feminine version of humble and compassionate familial love".

I truly sensed a harmony between mind and heart. I knew that what I *felt* when reading the Parable of the Prodigal Son (Lk 15:11–32) was quite similar to what I had *felt* while looking at the crèche scene—a sense of sacred *home*, a sense of sacred *belonging*, a sense of sacred *family* that presented to my heart an awareness of peace and love beyond the merely human.

This experience of sacred family-home is often elicited through prayers to and symbols of our Blessed Mother Mary. As noted above, I believe this sense of sacred "family-home" is a *special* grace given to us through the intercession of Jesus' Mother, who is our Mother, and this special grace imparts comfort, peace, and trust, particularly during times of suffering.

This last point is very important, because as noted above, we are not being called into a "one on one" relationship with God alone, but rather, to an interpersonal relationship with the Holy Trinity and the Holy Family. This means that we have to use the "logic" of *family* love to understand the dynamic of the heavenly home, to which we are called. This family logic is not exemplified by competition for love and sibling rivalry, but rather by co-responsibility for one another, sharing and compounding of love, and rejoicing in others' belovedness within the family.

I believe that the Trinity from the inception of time had this plan in mind for the woman who would become Mother of the incarnate second Person. Integral to Their plan was the role that she would play throughout the rest of human history to believers like ourselves. The Trinity planned that she would become for all believers this distinctive feminine-motherly presence and voice in our prayers, this distinctive gentleness, compassion, affection, and guiding light in our lives, and this manifestation of the sacred family-home into which we are called. They planned to bring her into full partnership with their salvific and spiritual plan, to allow her to bring a complementary voice and presence to their own, and even to accompany them in protecting believers from the darkness of Satan and his followers. To ignore this richness of complementary love and presence because of a false conviction that God would not have followed the plan of the *Magnificat* in sharing His salvific mission with Mary (Lk 1:46–55), is tantamount to excising a part of one's brain from a conviction that this part of the brain really doesn't add much to one's thinking capacity.

If the above points about Mary's presence in prayer and role in our salvation make sense, I would recommend that all readers read the appendix to Volume III of this Trilogy, to see why and how Mary became so prominent in the spiritual life of the Church from her very inception until today. Above all, begin to pray the Rosary— if only a decade, then two, or more. Familiarize yourself with some other Marian devotions that are inexpensively and widely available on the Internet.[42] I would also recommend memorizing the various Marian prayers given in Appendix II, and procuring a Marian icon or statue for your home.[43] Once you begin integrating devotion to the Blessed Virgin into your contemplative prayer, you will probably never give it up because it becomes an almost addictive "mainstay" filled with Mary's motherly transcendent peace and sense of home—a true port in life's storms.

VII. The Saints and Hagiography

The Church's encouragement of intercessory prayer went beyond the Blessed Virgin to the entire communion of saints and angels. The Book of Revelation (composed around A.D. 90) makes specific mention of prayers of the angels and saints in Heaven (Rev 5:8; 8:4). As noted in the appendix to Volume III of this Trilogy, prayers to the saints are also manifest in the second-century catacombs of Rome. The catacombs are filled with graffiti, asking for intercession or prayers from the saints—Saints Peter, Paul, and many of the Roman martyrs. Some of these graffiti originated in the second century, but the majority in several catacombs can be accurately dated to the persecution of Valerian between 253 and 260. These graffiti continued into the late third and early fourth centuries—at which point such

---

[42] Simply put "Marian devotion booklets" into your Internet search engine, and you will retrieve multiple results, most of which are excellent.

[43] Simply put "icons and statues of Virgin Mary" into your Internet search engine, and you will retrieve dozens of results with photographs of the various icons and statues that you can purchase online.

intercessory prayers could be spoken publicly (after Constantine's Edict of Toleration in A.D. 313).[44]

The practice of intercessory prayer was encouraged and promoted by early Church Fathers, such as Clement of Alexandria (A.D. 208),[45] Origen (A.D. 233),[46] and many others[47] (see the appendix to Volume III of this Trilogy). From that time on, the practice grew quite rapidly, inspiring generations of Catholics in faith, charity, holiness of life, and prayer.

Mary and the saints provide us with not only powerful intercessory prayers, but also profound examples of holiness that can help us in our spiritual and moral conversion. There are spiritual benefits in reading hagiographies (lives of the saints). We can be inspired by simply learning about the major events in a saint's life—actions to build faith, build the Church, serve the poor, and contemplative prayer. If readers are inspired by this basic level of hagiographical presentation, they may want to pursue a deeper level that goes beyond recounting major actions and words—and delve into greater detail in certain works, preaching, or reflections of a saint. It is important to make a selection about the level of detail, the level of scholarship, and the level of devotion that best fits one's spiritual life.

As you begin looking into the lives and spiritual practice of these extraordinary men and women, you might want to reflect on saints having charisms similar to your own. The following general breakdown might help you make a selection of saints and hagiographies to inspire your prayer and service to others. Those interested in *intellectual* and *educational* service may want to read about Saint Paul, Saint Augustine, Saint Thomas Aquinas, Saint Bonaventure, Saint Thomas

---

[44] See a summary of archaeological findings in Danilo Mazzoleni, "Ancient Graffiti in Roman Catacombs", EWTN.com, 2020, from *L'Osservatore Romano*, February 9, 2000, p. 6, https://www.ewtn.com/catholicism/library/ancient-graffiti-in-roman-catacombs-1642.

[45] "In this way is he [the true Christian] always pure for prayer. He also prays in the society of angels, as being already of angelic rank, and he is never out of their holy keeping; and though he pray alone, he has the choir of the saints standing with him [in prayer]." Clement of Alexandria, *Miscellanies* 7, 12 (A.D. 208), https://www.churchfathers.org/intercession-of-the-saints.

[46] Origen wrote: "But not the high priest [Christ] alone prays for those who pray sincerely, but also the angels ... as also the souls of the saints who have already fallen asleep." *Prayer* 11 (A.D. 233), https://www.churchfathers.org/intercession-of-the-saints.

[47] See the Shepherd of Hermas, *The Shepherd* 3, 5, 4 (A.D. 80); Cyprian of Carthage, *Letters* 56 (60), 5 (A.D. 253); Cyril of Jerusalem, *Catechetical Lectures* 23, 9 (A.D. 350), https://www.churchfathers.org/intercession-of-the-saints.

More, Jacques Maritain, Father Georges Lemaître (discoverer of the Big Bang theory), Saint Catherine of Sienna, Saint Hildegard of Bingen, and Edith Stein (Saint Teresa Benedicta of the Cross).

Those interested in pastoral ministries may want to read about holy popes, bishops, priests, and women religious who gave their lives to guiding their flocks, beginning with Saint Peter, Saint Paul, Saint Augustine, Leo the Great, Gregory the Great, Saint Dominic (founder of the Dominicans), Saint Ignatius Loyola (founder of the Jesuits), John XXIII, Saint John Paul II, Saint Katherine Drexel (founder of the Sisters of the Blessed Sacrament), Saint Frances Xavier Cabrini (founder of the Missionary Sisters of the Sacred Heart), Saint Jane Frances de Chantal (founder of the Visitation Sisters), and Saint Elizabeth Ann Seton (founder of the Sisters of Charity).

Those leaning toward prayer and spiritual ministries may want to look into the lives of Saint Anthony (the Desert Father), Saint Benedict, Saint John of the Cross, Saint Francis de Sales, Thomas à Kempis, Saint Alphonsus de' Liguori, Father Jean Pierre de Caussade, Blessed Charles de Foucauld, Julian of Norwich, Saint Teresa of Avila, Saint Margaret Mary Alacoque, Saint Bridget of Sweden, Saint Thérèse of Lisieux, and Catherine de Hueck Doherty.

Those leaning toward charitable ministries may want to study the lives of Saint Francis of Assisi, Saint John Bosco, Saint Vincent de Paul, Saint Peter Claver, Saint Elizabeth of Hungary, Saint Rose of Lima, Saint Frances Xavier Cabrini, and Saint Teresa of Calcutta (Mother Teresa).

Those inclined toward missionary vocations may want to read about Saint Paul, the eleven apostles (in Eusebius' *Ecclesiastical History*), Saint Francis Xavier, Bartolome de las Casas, Saint Isaac Jogues, Saint Junipero Serra, Matteo Ricci, and Father Eusebio Kino.

We may now turn our attention to the selection of hagiographies that will build our spiritual life and moral character. As we begin, we should bear in mind that no saint is equivalent to Christ, our Lord. All of them (with the exception of the Blessed Virgin Mary) had to contend with concupiscence—the negative effects of original sin—all of them had to go through a process of conversion, and all of them maintained their weakness and dependence on the Lord to the end of their lives. Saint Paul—toward the end of his life in the Letter to the Romans—laments:

I do not understand my own actions. For I do not do what I want, but I do the very thing I hate.... For I do not do the good I want, but the evil I do not want is what I do. Now if I do what I do not want, it is no longer I that do it, but sin which dwells within me.... For I delight in the law of God, in my inmost self, but I see in my members another law at war with the law of my mind and making me captive to the law of sin which dwells in my members. Wretched man that I am! Who will deliver me from this body of death? Thanks be to God through Jesus Christ our Lord! (7:15, 19–20, 22–25)

As noted above, there are spiritual benefits in reading most hagiographies. These saints can become both powerful examples and intercessors in the development of our spiritual lives.

A good place to begin is with spiritual autobiographies in which a saint writes about his life, including theological and spiritual viewpoints and relationship with God, others, and the Church. Such autobiographies range from a simple reflection to complex interior probings and theology.[48] There are also several spiritual autobiographies not written by canonized saints that have been helpful to general audiences[49] as well as spiritual biographies of saints by famous authors that may also prove to be a suitable place to begin the pursuit of hagiographical inspiration.

There are so many hagiographies by less-known authors available today that making a selection might seem overwhelming. For example, if you were to search Ignatius Press' website for "saints", you would get a few hundred biographies for adults and children. Again, if

[48] Five excellent spiritual autobiographies (ranked in order of simplicity to complexity) are as follows: Saint Ignatius Loyola, *A Pilgrim's Journey: The Autobiography of Ignatius of Loyola*, rev. ed., trans. Joseph N. Tylenda, S.J. (San Francisco: Ignatius Press, 2001); Saint Thérèse of Lisieux, *The Story of a Soul: The Autobiography of the Little Flower*, ed. Mother Agnes of Jesus, trans. Michael Day (Charlotte, N.C.: TAN Books, 2010); *St. Teresa of Avila: Her Life in Letters*, trans. Kieran Kavanaugh, O.C.D. (Notre Dame, Ind.: Christian Classics, 2018); John Henry Newman, *Apologia Pro Vita Sua*, ed. Maisie Ward (Eugene, Ore.: Wipf & Stock, 2017); Saint Augustine, *Confessions*, trans. and ed. Henry Chadwick (New York: Oxford University Press, 1991).

[49] Lewis, *Shape of My Early Life* (note that this is a partial autobiography, from Lewis' early childhood until his conversion to Christianity); Sheldon Vanauken, *A Severe Mercy* (New York: HarperCollins, 1987); Thomas Merton, *Seven Storey Mountain* (New York: Harcourt, 1998); G.K. Chesterton, *The Autobiography of G.K. Chesterton* (San Francisco: Ignatius Press, 2006); Henri Nouwen, *The Road to Daybreak: A Spiritual Journey* (New York: Doubleday, 1988); Walter Ciszek, S.J., *He Leadeth Me: An Extraordinary Testament of Faith* (New York: Image, 1973); Walter Ciszek, S.J., *With God in Russia* (San Francisco: Ignatius Press, 1997).

you made a restricted search for books about "Jesuit saints" or "Jesuit biographies" in Google, you would find hundreds of biographies or compendia of biographies. If you search only for "Saint Francis Xavier", you will discover many different English biographies—from children's stories to the four-volume work of Georg Schurhammer. So where might we begin?

One way of proceeding might be to look up the saint of the day from the annual liturgical calendar. This can be done by simply doing a Google search for "saint of the day". Click on Franciscan Media, and you will see the saint(s) for that particular day. Some saints are major and some minor. If you find a saint's life and teaching to be inspiring and edifying, you may want to do an Internet search for free articles on that saint. If that proves fruitful, you may want to go deeper and do a search for a book—a hagiography—that fits your interests and is helpful to your spiritual life. There are three dimensions about which to be conscientious:

1. What level of simplicity or complexity fits your needs or interests?
2. What level of historical scholarship are you interested in?
3. What kind of spiritual approach is most helpful to you—one that emphasizes the strengths and piety of the saints or one that addresses weaknesses and challenges as well?

With respect to the first dimension—simplicity or complexity—"know thyself". If you are the type that enjoys details and depth, find an extensive hagiography that provides it; however, if you are the type that "just likes the facts" or "bullet points", find a shorter hagiography that emphasizes general points in the life, doctrines, and spiritual works of the saint. Children obviously need works that are age-appropriate. If you do a brief search of the table of contents and the "Amazon reviews" of a particular hagiography, you can determine fairly quickly the author's intended level of detail and linguistic complexity. If you are not sure where your interests lie, start with simpler biographies and work your way up.

With respect to the second dimension of your search—level of scholarship—all you need do is search for the book on either Amazon's website or Google Books and see if you can look inside. If you can, simply go to the last page of the actual text and look at the footnote number. If there are twice as many footnotes as pages, the level of scholarship will probably be quite high, and the "Amazon reviews" are likely to mention a good scholarly apparatus. If the number of footnotes are about the same as the number of pages, you will probably find an adequate scholarly apparatus and attention to primary sources. Again, the "Amazon reviews" will indicate this. Finally, if you find there are only a few or no footnotes, the book was probably written on a "popular" level. This kind of volume is great if you are not interested in validation of data or primary sources. However, if sources and validation of data are important to you, you probably want to make recourse to the higher levels of historical scholarship.

The third dimension of your search—biographies that emphasize strengths and piety of a saint versus those that include weaknesses and challenges—is probably the most difficult to predetermine. Sometimes, the "Amazon reviews" give some good clues, but often enough, they do not. One general rule might be that the more complex and scholarly the work, the more likely it will contain weaknesses and challenges of a particular saint because these biographies tend toward a *complete* portrayal of the whole person in historical context.

This third characteristic is very important because the point of reading spiritual biographies—hagiographies—is to be inspired and edified. It is somewhat counterproductive to read a biography that portrays a saint's life in a fashion that emphasizes negativity rather than positivity. I'm not saying here that we should restrict ourselves to hagiographies that portray a saint and the Church through "rose-colored glasses". My point is really about the way in which the weaknesses and challenges of the saints and the Church are portrayed. Some authors are "respectful" and capable of seeing positivity amid weakness—while a few begin with a "less than respectful" and sometimes even a hypercritical point of view. Though I truly value complex and scholarly biographies, I always avoid those whose authors manifest disrespect, suspicion, negativity, or even "antispiritual" points of view.

VIII. Spiritual Reading

I am using "spiritual reading" here in a most general sense: to refer to the Church's collective approved writings in theology, philosophy, spirituality, history, and literature. The Catholic Church has a vast intellectual tradition, consisting not only of these five areas, but also literature, natural science, the social sciences, and fine arts. It is no exaggeration to say that there are tens of thousands of volumes devoted to these pursuits. As such, "spiritual reading" includes not only spiritual and moral conversion, but also intellectual conversion.

Some people must begin their spiritual reading with works devoted to intellectual conversion in order to break free from the physicalist and materialist perspectives of our culture. If they have this need, they should concentrate on obtaining evidence for God, the soul, and Jesus until they are satisfied (see Volumes 2–3 of the Quartet). Though some individuals do not need as much evidence to break free from the grip of cultural materialism, a large percentage of our culture really does. Without a thorough presentation of this evidence, a faith life is almost impossible for them since they have difficulty intuiting the presence of God from the numinous experience, their intuition of the sacred, their sense of beauty and elegance of creation, and even the remarkably creative and transcendent character of each individual person. Jesus and the Catholic Church (throughout her history) did not expect people to rely solely on these kinds of interior evidence. Jesus provided us with remarkable clues of His transcendence—in His Resurrection, miracles, and gift of the Spirit. Additionally, the Church since the first century has provided philosophical and theological apologists to overcome materialistic and naturalistic perspectives in every era.

Readers who are beset or bothered by doubts will want to devote at least thirty minutes every day to the pursuit of intellectual conversion. There is so much evidence for a theistic and Christian perspective that there is no real need to be beset by doubts if you are open to belief. Readers wishing additional information may want to first consult a free resource with voiceover PowerPoints giving essential evidence for God, the soul, Jesus, and the Church.[50] This resource covers a wide range of evidence, including peer-reviewed medical studies of near-death experiences and terminal lucidity, contemporary scientific evidence of an intelligent Creator, historical evidence of Jesus as well as evidence for His Resurrection from the Shroud of

---

[50] Go to www.crediblecatholic.com and click on the large red button, "7 Essential Modules".

Turin, contemporary scientifically validated miracles connected with the Catholic Church, the four levels of happiness/purpose in life, and why an all-loving God would allow suffering.

Those looking for a deeper and more scholarly approach to these topics may go to the same resource (CredibleCatholic.com) and click on "The Big Book". They may also consult the following four books by me that attempt to explain the above evidence comprehensively:

1. *New Proofs for the Existence of God: Contributions of Contemporary Physics and Philosophy*, concerning scientific evidence for an intelligent Creator and three contemporary philosophical proofs of God

2. Volume II of the Quartet, concerning contemporary peer-reviewed medical studies of near-death experiences, contemporary studies in the philosophy of mind concerning the transcendental nature of human mathematical intuition (Gödel's proof), self-consciousness (David Chalmers), the transcendental nature of conceptual ideas (Sir John Eccles), the transcendentality of our unrestricted desire to know (Bernard Lonergan), and our four other transcendental desires for perfect love, justice-goodness, beauty, and home (Karl Rahner, John Henry Newman, and C. S. Lewis)

3. Volume III of the Quartet, concerned with the historical investigation and validation of Jesus' Resurrection (N. T. Wright and the scientific examination of the Shroud of Turin), Jesus' miracles by His own authority (John P. Meier), the gift of the Holy Spirit in the early Church and today (James D. G. Dunn), and the preaching, Passion, and Eucharist of Jesus (Joachim Jeremias, N. T. Wright, and John P. Meier)

4. Volume IV of the Quartet, concerning why an all-loving God would allow suffering and how to suffer well through Christian faith

These books present a comprehensive array of footnotes and references, enabling the reader to access primary sources for this scientific, philosophical, historical, and medical evidence. Hence, they are a good place to begin the process of intellectual conversion in a contemporary light.

Readers who have a strong conviction about faith (with fe·
or reservations) will probably want to focus their spiritual reading on
spiritual or moral conversion. This could include a vast array of topics
in the areas of theology and spirituality such as the *Catechism of the
Catholic Church*, Scripture studies, systematic theology, spiritual theology, moral theology, Church history, philosophical theology, apologetics, and fundamental theology (such as the four books mentioned
above). Some readers will want to emphasize combinations of subjects, such as theology and culture, the Church and culture, theology
and science, theology and political theory, theological anthropology,
theology and psychology, spirituality and psychology, theology and
sociology, theology and social ethics, and so forth. There are many
books of various scholarly quality published annually in most of these
areas, and hundreds of books spanning the last ten years.

For those who are just getting started on nontheological and non-
spiritual parts of the Catholic intellectual tradition, you may want to
consider the authors described below near the end of the conclusion
to Part I.

Perhaps the easiest way to find theology, spirituality, philosophy,
and other books is to put one of the above subject areas into your
search engine along with a general book provider, such as Amazon or
Google Books, and consider the various options. Before purchasing
anything, you should do a search of the author, read the Amazon and
other reviews, and "look inside" to judge the scholarly apparatus
and the quality of the prose. Remember two points:

1. Not all published works are good quality or faithful to the
   teaching of Christ—so be a discerning reader.
2. Even though we live in a culture that emphasizes short videos
   and computer enhancements, books still provide the deepest
   and most scholarly approach to all major subject areas. They
   may not be as immediately engaging, but they will provide
   the most sourced and comprehensive presentation if done by a
   scholarly author of faith.

Though our days are so filled with family, work, activities, and traditional and social media, it is truly worthwhile to dedicate what time
you can to reading some of the excellent books coming from the

Catholic theological, spiritual, and intellectual tradition. They will not only enhance the depth and quality of your faith, but also your confidence in the presence and providence of the Lord of unconditional love manifest in Jesus Christ and in His Mystical Body, the Church.

IX. Conclusion

The Catholic spiritual tradition is remarkably deep and wide. Built on the foundation of Jesus' Mystical Body and the communion of saints and believers united through him, it provides frameworks for scriptural meditation, personal contemplative prayer, devotion to the Blessed Mother and the saints, and sacramentals, symbols, religious art, architecture, and music that probes the heights and depths of the Holy Spirit's movement within human imagination, intellect, and memory. The Church's many religious orders and spiritual traditions help us to enter into the mind and heart of the Triune God by providing guidance on the stages of contemplative life, the ways in which the Lord communicates, how to transform suffering into salvation (the school of the cross), how to contend with the forces of evil through the Holy Spirit, and how to allow the Lord to speak lovingly to our hearts. No other spiritual tradition can compare with the breadth and depth of this magnificent panoply of Christ's glory manifest through the hearts of hundreds of saints throughout the ages.

The only way to probe the richness of the Church's spiritual depth is to enter into her sacred doorway through contemplative prayer and the rich devotional tradition of her sacraments and saints imbued with the love of the Triune God and the Mother of Christ. Those who enter and strive concertedly toward spiritual conversion will not be disappointed. They will undoubtedly find themselves challenged by the cross, resisted by Satan, pressured by the secular world, and even ridiculed by friends and colleagues. Nevertheless, as Jesus promised, if we persevere in the sacraments, prayer, devotion, and moral conversion, we will grow ever closer to the light of Christ, which will purify our hearts and lead us to an incomprehensibly beautiful and glorious joy, love, and peace with the Lord of unconditional love.

CONCLUSION TO PART ONE

Why Be a Catholic?

What does the Catholic Church provide to believers *not* offered by any other Christian church? What graces, guidance, teachings, and spiritual depth are unique to the Catholic Church in helping believers to live in the truth and form a steadfast unity with other believers, leading to eternal salvation? Among many unique features, six are particularly important: (1) the Holy Eucharist, (2) Magisterium and Church unity, (3) Magisterium and doctrinal truth, (4) the Sacrament of Reconciliation, (5) the other five sacraments of the Church, and (6) the richness of Catholic spiritual life, moral life, and intellectual life.

1. *The Holy Eucharist.* Current historical exegesis strongly indicates that the Catholic Church has taught and actualized Jesus' true meaning of the *Holy Eucharist*—that is, to make Himself *really present* in the species of bread and wine, which, if true, is the most significant spiritual gift provided by any church at any time. This authentic interpretation of Jesus' intention in the Holy Eucharist—His Real Presence—is confirmed by current studies of the Jewish prophetic view of the "collapse of time" and Jesus' equation of unconditional self-sacrifice with unconditional love (self-gift). This belief in His Real Presence in the Eucharist is the universal view of the New Testament writers and the early Church Fathers (see Chapter 2, Section I, of this volume) on Jesus' intention in the Eucharist.[1]

---

[1] For an extended explanation and historical development of the Holy Eucharist in the first century, see Robert Spitzer, *Credible Catholic Big Book*, Volume 9, *The Sacraments, Part 1— The Sacred Eucharistic Liturgy* (Magis Center, 2017), CredibleCatholic.com, Chapter 2; see Chapter 3 for an explanation on transubstantiation, https://www.crediblecatholic.com/pdf /M9/BB9.pdf#P1V9.

2. *Magisterium and Church Unity.* The Church has maintained unity over the ages through the supreme magisterial authority invested in the unbroken line of successors given first to Peter and continuing to the present day. As noted above, without this supreme authority, there would be a huge number of distinct denominations within the Catholic Church, resembling the multitude of denominations within the Protestant church after five hundred years. Note that the Catholic Church has maintained her unity throughout two thousand years, lasting fifteen hundred years longer than any Protestant church. The absence of this fractioning—amid considerable disagreement and dispute—evidences the presence of the Holy Spirit and a fulfillment of Christ's promise to Peter that he (Peter) would be the rock upon which the Church would be built and that the gates of the netherworld would not prevail against it (Mt 16:18). (See Chapter 1, Sections I–II, of this volume.)

3. *Church Magisterium and Doctrinal Truth.* In addition to the Magisterium's role in maintaining unity within the Church, it also has the important function of guaranteeing the authentic interpretation of Jesus' doctrinal and moral teaching. As can be seen from Christian history (see Chapter 1, Sections II–VII), Jesus' words are not completely self-evident, so without an authentic interpreter of them, we are left to ourselves. Regrettably, our lack of scriptural and theological knowledge and our inclination toward self-interest and bias makes us less-than-ideal authentic interpreters of Jesus' true meaning in the Scriptures. The Protestant doctrinal pillar, *sola scriptura* (by scripture alone), has unfortunately led to tens of thousands of different doctrinal teachings. To say the least, this is not only confusing, but in many cases, terribly misleading.[2] Its shortcomings manifest our deep need for a supreme teaching authority. Given our need for an authentic interpretation of

---

[2] "Unless I am convinced by the testimony of the Scriptures or by clear reason (for I do not trust either in the pope or in councils alone, since it is well known that they have often erred and contradicted themselves), I am bound by the Scriptures I have quoted and my conscience is captive to the Word of God" (Martin Luther, "Reply to the Diet of Worms", April 18, 1521, in *Luther's Works*, vol. 32, *Career of the Reformer II*, ed. and trans. by George W. Forell (Philadelphia: Fortress Press, 1958), 112.

Jesus' words to pursue deep and genuine spiritual and moral conversion, we have to believe that Jesus would have anticipated both our need and our inability to do this for ourselves. To imagine that Jesus would not have foreseen this need and the problems that would arise without a supreme authority is inconceivable. For this reason it is reasonable to infer that the true interpretation of Jesus' doctrinal and moral teaching was provided by Jesus Himself when He commissioned Peter to be the rock upon which His Church would be built. Since that commission applied also to Peter's successors (see Chapter 1, Sections III–VII), we may infer that the authentic interpretation of Scripture is to be found in the Catholic Church. Its reliability is attested by the generations upon generations of recognized and unheralded saints who relied upon and benefited from its supreme authority to guide their spiritual and moral conversion.

4. *The Sacrament of Reconciliation.* The Sacrament of Reconciliation bestows a most powerful grace and light, severing our bondage to the Evil One, exposing his lies, substantializing our conversion, revealing the light of Christ, galvanizing our continued conversion with graced resolve, and keeping us on the path to salvation. It is one of the most precious gifts given to the apostles and the Church to wipe away our sins definitively and to secure us on the path to salvation and to grant the peace and light of Christ. Why would any Christian want to live without it if he understood the true reality of the cosmic struggle between good and evil in which we are living? (See Chapter 2, Section II.C, and Chapter 7, Section II.)

5. *The Other Five Sacraments of the Church.* With respect to sacramental life, most Christian congregations support Baptism, but do not support many, if not all, of the other six sacraments. As noted above, they do not have a doctrine of the Real Presence of Christ in the Holy Eucharist, their view of Confirmation and Matrimony is nonsacramental, and they do not recognize the Sacrament of Reconciliation, Sacrament of the Anointing of the Sick (last rites), and Sacrament of Holy Orders. These sacraments in the Catholic Church constitute a whole way of life with Christ through the Christian community that is

inspiring, edifying, and grace-filled (see Chapters 2 and 7 of this volume).

6. *Spiritual, Moral, and Intellectual Life.* There are several other benefits offered by the Catholic Church leading to spiritual and moral conversion:

- *Spiritual life*—The many developments of spirituality (through religious orders and lay associations), the development of Christian mysticism from the Desert Fathers through the current day, and the development of multiple modes of prayer from *lectio divina* to the discernment of spirits shows the presence of the Holy Spirit animating the Church's awareness and practice of deep, authentic, spiritual life. No other Christian church manifests anything close to this richness of spiritual depth and tradition. When we combine the spiritual traditions arising out of the Church Fathers, the Benedictines, the Franciscans, the Dominicans, the Jesuits, the Carmelites, and the many other religious and spiritual traditions in the Catholic Church, we must ask ourselves, "What is the font from which all of these rich spiritual traditions sprang?" We are led back to what Saint Irenaeus called "the *greatest* and most ancient church known to all.... It is in her that the faithful everywhere have maintained the apostolic tradition."[3] (See above in this chapter.)

- *Moral life*—The Catholic Church applied the teachings of Jesus to almost every aspect of moral, social, cultural, and political life, including the development of the notion of conscience (Saint Paul), the notion of free will (Saint Augustine), the development of systematic moral theology (Saint Thomas Aquinas and others), justice theory (Saint Augustine, Saint Thomas Aquinas, and others), natural law theory (Saint Thomas Aquinas), the universalization of personhood (Father Bartolomé de las Casas), inalienable rights theory (Father Francisco Suarez), and the social teaching of the Catholic

---

[3] Saint Irenaeus, *Against Heresies* 3, 3, 2, in "Catholic Biblical Apologetics: Post-Apostolic Fathers of the Church", under "The Authority of the Pope", ed. Robert Schihl and Paul Flanagan, FreeRepublic.com, 2010 (italics added), http://www.freerepublic.com/focus/religion/2476599/posts?page=1.

Church—from Pope Leo XIII to today (discussed in Volume III of this Trilogy).[4] There is nothing like this development, systemization, and socio-political application of moral thought in any other religion in world history. This again shows the action of the Holy Spirit in the life of the Church.

- *Intellectual life*—The Catholic Church applied Christian religious and theological thought to virtually every area of science and the humanities.
  - With respect to *science*, the Church's clergy made invaluable contributions to astronomy (Nicholas Copernicus, a Catholic cleric and the father of heliocentrism), biology-genetics (Abbott Gregor Mendel, the father of quantitative genetics), geology (Bishop Nicolas Steno, the father of contemporary geology and stratigraphy), and astrophysics-cosmology (Monsignor Georges Lemaître—the father of the Big Bang theory)—to mention but a few.[5]
  - With respect to *philosophy*, Saint Augustine, Saint Albertus Magnus, Saint Thomas Aquinas, Saint Bonaventure, Father Duns Scotus, Jacques Maritain, Father Joseph Marechal, Father Bernard Lonergan, Father Emerich Coreth, Father Karl Rahner, Josef Pieper, Gabriel Marcel, and Father John Courtney Murray provided the foundation and development of realist transcendental metaphysics, theodicy, integrated realist epistemology and ontology, and natural law and natural rights theory.
  - With respect to *literature*, Saint Augustine, Dante Alighieri, Father Desiderius Erasmus, Saint John Henry Newman, Father Gerard Manley Hopkins, G. K. Chesterton, Hilaire Belloc, Evelyn Waugh, François Mauriac, J. R. R. Tolkien, T. S. Eliot (Anglo-Catholic), Graham Greene, Flannery O'Connor, and Walker Percy (among others) made valuable contributions to the integration of theology/spirituality with literature.

---

[4] See also Robert Spitzer, *Ten Universal Principles: A Brief Philosophy of the Life Issues* (San Francisco: Ignatius Press, 2011), pp. 21–118.

[5] See Angelo Stagnaro, "A List of 244 Priest-Scientists (from Acosta to Zupi)", *National Catholic Register* (blog), November 29, 2016, https://www.ncregister.com/blog/astagnaro/a-list-of-244-priest-scientists-from-acosta-to-zupi.

○ With respect to *music and the fine arts*, there are literally hundreds of Catholic artists, musicians, and architects who made thousands of contributions to sacred art, architecture, and music. A brief perusal of the websites devoted to sacred art and music should provide significant evidence of the strong inspiration of the Holy Spirit to sacred beauty.

Given the above evidence from Scripture; the self-understanding of the early popes; the unity of the Church (despite many contentious moments); the authentic interpretation of Scripture; the unswerving proclamation of the reality of Jesus' Real Presence in the Eucharist; our deep need for the Sacrament of Reconciliation; the richness of spirituality; moral and political theory; and the integration of theology with all natural disciplines, there is more than adequate rational and experiential evidence of the Spirit of Christ working through the Catholic Church. Furthermore, every major doctrinal proclamation concerned with Blessed Mary, the saints, and the Real Presence of Christ in the Eucharist has been confirmed by contemporary scientifically validated miracles (see the appendix to Volume I of this Trilogy).

Though some leaders and individuals in the Church did not adhere to the moral teachings of Christ, the Church did not succumb to these influences, but rather, rectified them through her authentic teaching and juridical authority—and moved beyond them through the remarkable love and faith manifest through her thousands of canonized saints.[6] As we survey the enduring holy character of the Catholic Church amid the world's other institutions, we should again ponder the words of the famous historian of culture and civilization Arnold Toynbee, who observed:

The Church in its traditional form thus stands forth armed with the spear of the Mass, the shield of the Hierarchy, and the helmet of the Papacy; and perhaps the subconscious purpose—or the divine intention, if you prefer that language—of this heavy panoply of institutions

---

[6] Alban Butler, *Butler's Lives of the Saints*, 2nd ed., 4 vols., ed. Herbert J. Thurston and Donald Attwater (New York: Christian Classics, 1956).

in which the Church has clad herself is the very practical one of out-lasting the toughest of the secular institutions of this world, including all the civilizations. If we survey all the institutions of which we have knowledge in the present and in the past, I think that the institutions created, or adopted and adapted, by Christianity are the toughest and the most enduring of any that we know and are therefore the most likely to last—and outlast all the rest.[7]

As John Henry Newman might say, there is more than enough evidence throughout two thousand years of history to justify a pro-bative informal inference sufficient to ground rationally and inspire intellectual, spiritual, and moral conversion through the Catholic Church.[8] Given this, why would we not want to bring the spiritual power and love of the Catholic Church—both the inner Church and the outer Church—into the heart of our conversion?

We now proceed to Part II, concerned with the movement from spiritual conversion to moral conversion. As we proceed to enter into the domain of virtue, moral purification, and reconciliation, it will be essential to bear in mind the previous three chapters on spiritual conversion, lest we needlessly deprive ourselves of Jesus' Mystical Body and the power of the Holy Spirit coming to us through the Catholic Church.

---

[7] Arnold Toynbee, "Christianity and Civilization", in *Civilization on Trial* (New York: Oxford University Press, 1948), http://www.myriobiblos.gr/texts/english/toynbee.html.

[8] According to Newman, an informal inference occurs when multiple antecedently and independently probable sources of data corroborate and complement one another. See John Henry Newman, *An Essay in Aid of a Grammar of Assent* (Notre Dame, Ind.: University of Notre Dame Press, 2013), pp. 189–215.

PART TWO

From Spiritual Conversion
to Moral Conversion

INTRODUCTION TO PART TWO

In Part I we showed the essential benefit of the Catholic Church for grounding and deepening spiritual conversion—that is, developing a close relationship with the Divine Persons and Blessed Mary within Christ's Mystical Body. We now proceed to moral conversion— resistance to the deadly sins and evil, the appropriation of virtue, and our transformation into the "new nature" in imitation of Jesus Christ. Building on the foundation of Part I, we will now propose a method for entering into this transformational process through Jesus Christ and the Catholic Church. This will consist of four chapters:

Chapter 4—Virtue versus the Deadly Sins
Chapter 5—Moral Conversion and the "Higher Self"
Chapter 6—Moral Conversion and Resisting Temptation
Chapter 7—God's Mercy and Reconciliation

Chapter Four

Virtue versus the Deadly Sins

Introduction

The *Catechism of the Catholic Church* defines virtue as follows:

> A virtue is an habitual and firm disposition to do the good. It allows the person not only to perform good acts, but to give the best of himself. The virtuous person tends toward the good with all his sensory and spiritual powers; he pursues the good and chooses it in concrete actions.[1]

This definition is consistent with the whole of virtue theory in recognizing that virtue is an inner disposition formed by choice and habit that orients a person toward good ends and actions. As the history of philosophy and Christian theology recognizes, we are not created virtuous, but rather must choose to be virtuous over against opposed inner dispositions inclined toward sin and evil. The appropriation of virtue requires commitment and effort. We must first recognize virtue's goodness and power to orient us toward the good that moves us to prefer it to evil inclinations. We must then commit ourselves to choosing it repeatedly (over against evil inclinations) so that it becomes habitual or second nature. When a person makes a wide complementary spectrum of virtues habitual, he becomes a virtuous person, which, as the *Catechism* states, enables him "to tend toward the good with all his sensory and spiritual powers [so as to] pursue the good and choose it in concrete actions".

The *Catechism* goes on to describe the interior and behavioral state of a virtuous individual:

[1] *CCC* 1803.

Human virtues are firm attitudes, stable dispositions, habitual perfections of intellect and will that govern our actions, order our passions, and guide our conduct according to reason and faith. They make possible ease, self-mastery, and joy in leading a morally good life. The virtuous man is he who freely practices the good.[2]

The commitment, work, and faith to achieve a virtuous disposition enables us to reach the goal stated by Gregory of Nyssa—to become like God.[3] Reaching this goal through the mercy and grace of God prepares us to enter into the heavenly Kingdom of perfect love with the Lord and the blessed forever.

Christian theology from its inception has advocated seven virtues, which, when rightly understood in their interrelationship with one another, constitute a virtually complete set:

- The four cardinal natural virtues—prudence (wisdom), justice, temperance (self-control), and fortitude (courage)
- The three theological virtues—faith, hope, and love

The supreme virtue of love is constituted by several subvirtues mentioned in 1 Corinthians 13 and the Beatitudes (Mt 5:3–12), such as patience, kindness, forbearance, humble-heartedness ("poor in spirit"), gentle-heartedness ("meek"), mercy (constituted by compassion and forgiveness), peacemaking, and chastity (mentioned later in the Sermon on the Mount [Mt 5:27–28]). All of these virtues and subvirtues are discussed below in this chapter.

As implied above, virtues originate from our commitment to choose them repeatedly as well as our actual free choices. Though free choice is essential, it can be greatly assisted by appropriate formation (i.e., teaching and example), and supernatural grace (i.e., divine inspiration, guidance, and providential orchestration of events in our lives). The importance of good formation cannot be exaggerated because repeated teaching, good example, and firm discipline help to instill virtues in the immature mind of a child. As that child grows to maturity and independence, he will be impelled to make choices

---

[2] Ibid., 1804 (italics in original).
[3] Gregory of Nyssa, *De Beatitudinibus* 1 (*Patrologia Graecae* 44:1200D).

toward good or evil. If he knows what his parents, teachers, and religious authorities taught him about the good, if he respects those authorities, and if he has faith in the Lord Jesus, he will likely choose most and possibly all of those virtues. This does not mean that he will choose a virtuous path all the time when confronted with temptations toward the eight deadly sins (see Volume I, Chapters 5–6), because his *subconscious* predisposition will be strongly influenced by these deadly sins.[4] Though good formation can help a person to choose virtuous conduct over against the deadly sins, it can be greatly assisted and complemented by faith and grace.

The whole of Christian ethical reflection (from the New Testament to the present) is replete with explanations and practical teachings on how to use the supernatural gifts given us by Jesus to form our conscience, choose the good, and solidify a virtuous interior disposition. Some of these supernatural gifts include the Lord's moral teaching (interpreted by the Church), the grace of the sacraments, and the grace of prayer and divine inspiration and communication.

Speaking for myself and the vast majority of my friends, I can attest that my moral life would have been significantly diminished were it not for my faith in Jesus Christ, my commitment to the Church, my desire to appropriate Christ's moral teaching, my sacramental life (particularly the Holy Eucharist and the Sacrament of Reconciliation), and my commitment to prayer, because these religious commitments open the door to the Lord's immense supernatural grace, filled with mercy, reconciliation, healing, resolve, inspiration, protection, and guidance. Recognizing His love for me animated my love for Him, which in turn inspired me on the path to spiritual conversion and then to moral conversion. This brings us to our current place in this volume—the movement from spiritual to moral conversion.

Virtue constitutes a fruitful middle ground for the movement from spiritual to moral conversion. As the reader may have surmised, non-religious people can be virtuous. However, religious individuals, particularly those with significant depth of spiritual conversion, have much greater success in practicing virtue in the long term. This is evidenced in several recent comprehensive studies. For example, the

---

[4] See Chapters 5–6 of this volume on the subconscious mind's initial orientation toward the lower self (the "old man"), which is inclined toward the deadly sins.

empirical study of K. Praveen Parboteeah and others, in 2008,[5] used the religious typology of Marie Cornwall and others[6] to confirm the findings of previous studies,[7] showing that "belief in church authority, religiosity's affective component, and the behavioral component are negatively related to individuals' willingness to justify unethical behaviors".[8] Thus, religion influences—and frequently strongly influences—people's unwillingness to be unethical.

Furthermore, as the reader may have inferred from the previous chapters, the Lord's guidance, inspiration, communication, and grace (coming from the sacraments, prayer, and the school of the cross) help enormously in moral conversion (the appropriation of virtue, resistance to sin, and transformation of identity). This contention will be explained and deepened throughout the next three chapters. For the moment, suffice it to say that deep spiritual conversion significantly helps deep moral conversion.

Notwithstanding these strong correlations between spiritual and moral conversion, it should be noted that virtue is accessible and beneficial for nonreligious individuals, and has been the subject of considerable reflection in the areas of natural philosophy and law for centuries. Prominent natural philosophical adherence to virtue ethics are Plato (e.g., the *Republic* and the *Protagoras*), Aristotle (e.g., the *Nichomachean Ethics*), Cicero (e.g., *On the Ends of Good and Evil*), Saint Thomas Aquinas (e.g., the *Summa Theologica* and *The Commentary on Aristotle's Nichomachean Ethics*), Josef Pieper (e.g., *The Four Cardinal Virtues*), G. E. M. Anscombe (e.g., "Modern Moral Philosophy"), and Alasdair MacIntyre (e.g., *After Virtue*). A major contribution made by these thinkers is their reflection on the four cardinal virtues: prudence (wisdom), justice, temperance (self-control), and

---

[5] See K. Praveen Parboteeah, Martin Hoegl, John B. Cullen, "Ethics and Religion: An Empirical Test of a Multidimensional Model", *Journal of Business Ethics* 80, no. 2 (June 1, 2008): 387–98.

[6] See Marie Cornwall et al., "The Dimensions of Religiosity: A Conceptual Model with an Empirical Test", *Review of Religious Research* 27, no. 3 (1986): 226–44.

[7] See C. R. Tittle and M. R. Welch, "Religiosity and Deviance: Toward a Contingency Theory of Constraining Effect", *Social Forces* 61, no. 3 (1983): 653–82. See also G. R. Weaver and B. R. Agle, "Religiosity and Ethical Behavior in Organizations: A Symbolic Interactionist Perspective", *Academy of Management Review* 27, no. 1 (2002): 77–97; and J. H. Turner, *The Institutional Order* (New York: Addison-Wesley Educational Publishers, 1997).

[8] Paraboteeah, Hoegl, and Cullen, "Ethics and Religion", p. 393.

fortitude (courage). We discussed these virtues in Volume I (Chapter 4, Section IV.B) of this Trilogy and will briefly summarize this treatment below in Sections I.A–D.

Though these natural virtues are important for being a just, well-focused, disciplined, and effective person, they do not reach the heart of goodness, our transcendent nature, dignity, and destiny, the will of God, or our contribution to the cosmic struggle between good and evil (see Volume I, Chapter 3 of this Trilogy). To reach these supremely important objectives, we must make recourse to the three supernatural virtues—faith, hope, and love.

Faith is indispensable for actualizing our transcendent nature, for knowing the heart and will of God, for knowing the *summum bonum* (the highest good), and for calling upon the inspiration and grace of the Lord. As such, faith helps us to resist evil and darkness, to transform our identities (to conform with the Lord's), and to find and stay on the path to eternal salvation with Christ. We have discussed faith in considerable detail in our treatment of spiritual conversion above in Chapters 2 and 3. Indispensable as it is, faith is not enough to help us avoid the darkness of spiritual evil and stay on the path to salvation. We also need hope and love.

Hope is the desire for and expectation of eternal salvation arising out of the free gift of God through Jesus Christ and our concerted attempt to follow His teaching, call upon His mercy, and participate in the Church. Hope orients our will and life's purpose toward God. Without it, we would not only be subject to despair, but compelled to live for some purpose other than God and eternal salvation. Jesus has given us the deepest and most powerful foundation for hope not only through His teaching about eternal salvation, but also through His self-sacrificial Passion and death (revealing His desire to save all mankind) and His Resurrection in glory (revealing His and His Father's intention to bring us into His eternal glorified state). We discussed this in Volume IV (Chapter 1, Section II) of the Quartet. Like natural virtue and faith, hope is essential, but not enough. Moreover, natural virtue, faith, and hope together are still not enough. As Jesus and Saint Paul asserted, we require the supreme supernatural virtue of love (as revealed by Jesus) to animate and guide the natural virtues, faith, and hope to their ultimate objective—the heart of God. When we freely choose to imitate the Lord in love, it animates

and guides not only our behavior, but also the formation and transformation of our hearts (the intuitive, affective, transcendent dimension of our soul). This gives rise to empathy, compassion, humility,
forgiveness, self-giving, and self-sacrifice—the freedom to appreciate and interact with others for their own sake without the impediments of egocentricity. Thus, love brings all other virtues to their
highest end—perfect union with the Lord of unconditional love that
is at once the perfect embrace of goodness and the perfect shunning
of evil and darkness.

Evidently, the interplay among the four natural virtues and the
three theological virtues is essential for bringing moral conversion
to its fulfillment. So also is the interplay between nature and grace—
between natural habits and divine inspiration, guidance, protection,
and providential opportunity. By helping to bring moral conversion
to its fulfillment, this interplay among the virtues and between nature
and grace facilitates our purification and preparation to enter into the
Kingdom of Heaven, where our capacity for love will be unobscured
by ego to reflect the brilliant light and love of Jesus Christ. We will
take these issues up in the following two sections:

- Section I: The Four Cardinal Virtues
- Section II: The Supreme Virtue—Love

I. The Four Cardinal Virtues

Inasmuch as virtue is an interior disposition orienting the will to
choosing good actions, and inasmuch as these interior dispositions
arise out of both naturally cultivated habits and divine grace (some
of which is given to all individuals and some only to baptized Christians), then the ideal or optimal virtuous disposition must come from
an interplay among all seven virtues, which brings with it an interplay
between nature and grace.

Let us now proceed to the natural virtues. There is an interesting
coincidence between the philosophical reflection on natural virtue
in Plato and Divine Revelation in the Book of Wisdom. In Book 4
of *The Republic*, Plato implies that wisdom consists in allowing the
rational part of the soul, which knows what is good for the parts and
the whole, to rule the whole person; that courage (fortitude) is the

capacity to allow the rational part of the soul to maintain control amid pleasures, pains, and fears; and that temperance is agreement among the parts of the soul that the rational part should govern. All three of these personal virtues serve the end of justice (fairness).[9]

The Book of Wisdom does not define the various virtues, but probes the depths of wisdom (prudence) and shows how she is able to direct us to the other three cardinal virtues—justice, courage, and self-control:

> And if understanding is effective, who more than [Wisdom] is fashioner of what exists? And if any one loves righteousness, her labors are virtues; for she teaches self-control and prudence, justice and courage; nothing in life is more profitable for men than these. (8:6–7)

Both Plato and the author of Wisdom identify wisdom (prudence) as the font of understanding or reason, revealing wisdom to be the virtue from which the other three draw their strength. This confluence of reason and revelation indicate the degree to which the four cardinal virtues are interrelated within the mind and heart of the virtuous person. Before exploring this, we will first give a brief description of the four natural virtues as they have developed within Christian tradition. We will begin with wisdom (prudence) since this is the font from which the other virtues draw their strength (Section I.A). We will then examine the other two personal virtues—fortitude (courage) (Section I.B) and then temperance (self-control) (Section I.C). We will then discuss the interpersonal natural virtue—justice (Section I.D). We will conclude with a brief discussion on the interplay among the four cardinal virtues (Section I.E).

A. Prudence

Prudence guides all other virtues—natural and theological—toward proper actions.[10] In the Christian tradition, prudence receives its guiding light from conscience. Reason takes the light of conscience and determines it toward specific actions, judging which actions

---

[9] See Plato, The Republic 4, 442b–d.
[10] See Josef Pieper, The Four Cardinal Virtues (South Bend, Ind.: University of Notre Dame Press, 1966), pp. 12–67.

are good and evil as well as the best action in particular situations. Hence, prudence is said to guide the judgment of conscience. We have discussed conscience and its divine origin in Volumes I and II of the Quartet.[11]

Conscience is a divine gift given to all people, enabling them to have a profound sense of good and evil in particular actions as well as a sense of some general norms of conduct.[12] Christian faith can strengthen the influence of conscience and refine the principles of conscience through its teaching, the power of the sacraments, and spiritual-moral conversion. As conscience is strengthened and refined through faith, reason has more to guide it in its judgments of the kinds of actions to be pursued (and avoided).

Let us now return to the virtue of prudence or wisdom. If we are to grow in this virtue so that it may properly guide our actions toward optimal good, we will want to do the following:

1. Deepen our spiritual and moral conversion
2. Inform our conscience through the teaching of Jesus and the Church
3. Educate ourselves about the truest and fullest purpose in life (e.g., the four levels of happiness)[13]
4. Educate ourselves about how best to use the light of faith, conscience, and highest purpose to formulate the best set of life goals and intermediate goals, and to choose the optimally best course of action in particular situations

These four steps are essential for liberating the power of conscience and practical reason to achieve this optimal result, and so we have dedicated considerable space to them in the Quartet and this Trilogy:

---

[11] For an explanation of the interior obligation, principles, and feelings of conscience, see Volume I, Chapter 1, Section IV, of the Quartet. For an explanation of how conscience originates with God in the thought of Emmanuel Kant and John Henry Newman, see Volume II, Chapter 2, Section II, of the Quartet.

[12] See C. S. Lewis' excellent discussion of this in *The Abolition of Man* with respect to what he calls the "Tao". Lewis shows that all major religions hold to an inner moral guiding light as well as five general norms associated with that inner sense of good and evil. See C. S. Lewis, *The Abolition of Man* (New York: HarperCollins, 1974), pp. 19–55.

[13] For a summary of the four levels, see Appendix I of this volume. For an extensive explanation of the four levels and our movement from the lower to higher levels, see Volume I (Chapters 1–6) of the Quartet.

- For a discussion of spiritual conversion, see Chapters 2–3 of this volume.
- For a discussion of moral conversion, see Chapters 5–6 of this volume.
- For a discussion of the Christian formation of conscience, see the whole of Volume III of this Trilogy.
- For a discussion of the four levels of happiness, see Volume I (Chapters 1–5) of the Quartet, which is summarized in Appendix I of this volume.
- For a primer on setting goals, developing action plans, and making practical ethical decisions, see Stephen Covey's *7 Habits of Highly Effective People*.[14]

The virtue of prudence (wisdom) does not occur overnight. It deepens significantly over the course of time as one grows in spiritual and moral conversion, following the light of conscience and mastering the lessons of life experience. Some of these developments occur almost naturally, but the vast majority of them take place because we are seeking them, pursuing spiritual and moral conversion and preparing ourselves to learn the wisdom of the ages and the lessons of practical experience. We might say that this great virtue of oversight and guidance requires not only more time than the other virtues, but also more concerted effort to appropriate the light of God and practical experience. Readers who are serious about deepening virtue and moral conversion will want to make a plan for deepening the above four characteristics by using the resources mentioned above as well as complementary resources cited in the notes.

B. Fortitude (Courage)

The virtue of fortitude is oriented toward the pursuit of worthy principles, ideals, and goals. It is not so much concerned with identifying the principles, ideals, and goals (the domain of prudence), but

---

[14] See Stephen Covey, *The 7 Habits of Highly Effective People: Powerful Lessons in Personal Change* (Miami: Mango Publishing, 2017).

cultivating strong inner resolve, passion, and will to attain those principles, ideals, and goals, even at great self-sacrifice.[15] Thus, fortitude necessarily includes stamina and courage to endure pain, deprivation, and perhaps even death for the sake of the principle, ideal, or goal.

Fortitude is integral to commitment, for without strength of resolve and will, commitment would be based simply on the *intellectual* appropriateness of an ideal or goal to which one is committed. However, as is evident to most astute observers, intellectual awareness of the appropriateness of a goal without strength of will does almost nothing and goes almost nowhere. Yet, strength of will is not enough; we must also have courage—the capacity to accept pain and deprivation, to make sacrifices without counting the cost. The willingness to make sacrifices for the sake of a worthy or noble principle, ideal, or goal gives us remarkable freedom from fear and anxiety. History is replete with examples of people who could have been great and world-transforming, but settled for a mere fraction of their potential out of fear of hardship or reprisals.

So how can we cultivate the various aspects of fortitude—strength of will, resolve, and courage? The following five-step program may prove helpful:

1. Develop a set of worthy or noble principles, ideals, and goals that give your life optimal meaning and define the character you desire to have (focusing on Level Three and Level Four ideals and goals[16]).
2. Justify to yourself why these principles, ideals, and goals are the most worthy of your time, energy, commitment, and sacrifice. Are they, for example, for the sake of God, God's Kingdom, the common good, and the optimal actualizable good?
3. Create a realistic plan to actualize these ideals and goals, including who can help you, where to obtain necessary resources, and the message you will need to convince others to believe in your cause, particularly the worthiness of the cause.
4. *Visualize* your involvement in actualizing this plan so that your imagination incites passion for the plan as well as the cause.

---

[15] See Pieper, *Four Cardinal Virtues*, pp. 124–44.
[16] For a definition of Level Three and Four goals, please see Appendix I of this volume.

Visualize also your acceptance of effort and sacrifice to achieve the plan.[17]

5. Resolve ahead of time never to compromise your ethical principles or to use people (treat them like things) in moving toward your goals with passion.

The reader may have noticed that the first three steps in the above program are really the domain of prudence, revealing how important prudence is not only in guiding the other virtues, but also in initiating and strengthening them. If we have done our homework in the area of prudence—committing ourselves to higher purpose (e.g., building the Kingdom of God or optimizing the common good) and determining the principles, ideals, and goals corresponding to that higher purpose, then it will carry over into the virtue of fortitude; for if we consider these ideals and goals to be truly noble and worthy of us, they will enkindle our passion to make them a reality—even at the cost of considerable effort and sacrifice.

Pure rationality will not incite us to passion for a cause—this requires a movement of the heart arising out of a fundamental desire to live for the most worthy and noble purpose in life. Our intellects can determine what the highest purpose in life would be, which is the subject of the four levels of happiness (purpose in life) summarized in Appendix I of this volume. Those who have read through the four levels[18] will have noticed not only engagement of the intellect, but also engagement of the desire to be optimally contributive and noble—a desire that stems from conscience.[19] When this desire is combined with the intellectual awareness of what is most worthy, contributive, and noble, we are filled with a passion to actualize that noble objective. This leads to fortitude—resolve, courage, and willing self-sacrifice.

Prudence can also help us alleviate fears (be courageous) during times of setbacks, threats, and confrontation. When these things

---

[17] For an explanation of visualization, see Chapter 6 (Section I) of this volume.

[18] See Volume I (Chapters 1–5) of the Quartet for an extended version of the summary of Appendix I of this volume.

[19] Notice that the intuitions and feelings of conscience have two sides—the side of shame-guilt-alienation-aversion arising out of the anticipation or commission of evil, and the side of nobility-peace-satisfaction-desire arising out of the anticipation or commission of good deeds. See Volume I (Chapter 1, Section III) of the Quartet.

happen, fear can seize us, sometimes paralyzing us, until prudence comes to our rescue in the form of rational questions, such as, "What are some livable fallback plans?" "Who are some people that might be able to help?" "How do I mitigate the negative consequences of these problems or threats?" These kinds of strategic questions not only help us to find partial resolutions and a "softer landing", but also take our mind off the paralyzing fear we feel; for when we are focused on rational thought processes, we have to take our focus off of the emotion of the moment.

Let us now move to the fourth step of the above program. Are there other ways of fueling the passion and will of fortitude in addition to engaging our desire to actualize the most worthy, noble, and contributive ideals and goals? Contemporary psychology (e.g., the work of Dr. Albert Bandura—see Chapter 6, Section I) suggests a technique called visualization. When our desire to accomplish noble and worthy goals has been engaged, it is helpful to set out the practical steps needed to accomplish those goals, and then to visualize ourselves engaged in accomplishing those steps. As Bandura and others note, visualization (imagination) evokes additional emotion (passion) for the goal as well as belief in our imminent successful accomplishment of it. This, in turn, incites our will to action and relieves inhibitions arising out of nonrational self-doubt. This additional passion and self-assurance cannot help but strengthen our resolve and courage—building the virtue of fortitude.

With respect to the fifth step in the above program, we must resolve ahead of time not to compromise our ethical principles to accomplish even a most worthy goal; for as we shall discuss in Volume III of this Trilogy, the end does not justify the means. This well-known Christian principle[20] teaches that we cannot use an evil means to accomplish a good end. The evil of the means would undermine the goodness, worthiness, and nobility of the end. This principle alerts us to the fact that fortitude must be regulated and guided by virtues that prescribe the good to be sought and evil to be shunned. As important as fortitude is for doing the good, it does not determine from within itself what ends should be sought *and what means* should be used or avoided. Thus, fortitude must first be guided by the judgment of

---

[20] This principle is first codified by Saint Augustine in *Contra Mendacium* 7.

prudence, which seeks not only the most noble purpose in life, but also what means may be used to accomplish it.

We have already seen how to identify highest purpose in life (and goals or *ends* commensurate with it) in our exploration of the four levels of happiness (purpose in life; see Appendix I). But where would we turn to identify the *means* we should use and the ones to be avoided? Classical philosophers, such as Plato, Socrates, and Aristotle, taught that the virtue of justice would provide such a guiding light. In brief, justice is the habit of avoiding unnecessary harms and giving all individuals what belongs and is owed to them. Christian theologians, such as Saint Paul, Saint Augustine, and Saint Thomas Aquinas, also affirmed this role for justice. As we shall see below (Section I.D), the virtue of justice is integral to the natural law, which all people know to be true in their conscience, making it a bedrock for public law as well as public and political ethics.

Christian philosophers and theologians go beyond the virtue of justice to guide the passion of fortitude. They hold, along with Jesus Christ, that love (defined below in Section II) is the highest virtue. Love includes justice, but goes beyond it, by recommending mercy, compassion for the needy, and optimal good for one's neighbor (going beyond the prescripts of equity and nonmaleficence required by justice). We might conclude, then, that all people must look to justice and their conscience to guide fortitude's passion and will—and Christians should look also to love, in addition to justice and conscience, to guide the pursuit of their goals. Without the guidance of at least some of these beacons, fortitude could be turned into a most cruel vice—an unmitigated pursuit of power, an evil pursuit of a seemingly good goal, and an unregulated passion to achieve regardless of who gets in the way.

C. Temperance (Self-Control)

Temperance is the complement to fortitude. Whereas fortitude empowers the resolve and courage needed *to do* something, temperance empowers the will to resist—*not to do*—something. Like fortitude, temperance is an inner strength or resolve arising out of the will. It focuses the will to restrain our sensory appetites, instincts,

egotistical desires, and passions so that they will conform to prudence's determinations of highest purpose in life as well as the dictates
of conscience, justice, and love.[21] Just as fortitude focuses the will on
achieving a noble goal, temperance focuses the will on restraining our
sensory, instinctual, and ego-driven passions from undermining and
negating our good and noble principles, ideals, and goals.

As we saw with respect to fortitude, pure rationality or intellection is not enough to get us to the noble ideals and goals determined by prudence. So also, pure intellection is not enough to
restrain our passions from undermining what prudence knows to be
detrimental to our noble ideals and goals. Once again, we need
to involve our will—directing it to give precedence to our desire
for high purpose and the good, over our desires for base pleasures,
egoism, and false "loves". When we first focus our will on high and
good desires (over against base and egotistical ones), we have to be
very deliberate and insistent, calling to mind the reasons why these
higher and good desires are what we *really* want. Much of the time
these reasons include wanting to surrender to the Lord we love,
wanting eternal salvation, wanting high purpose in life, wanting to
be optimally contributive and respectful to others, and wanting
to be a positive influence (rather than a negative one) within society.
When we continue to direct our will toward our desire for higher
purpose and the good, it starts to become habitual—or second
nature—and we no longer have to think of our motives and insist on
them. At this point, we are beginning to inculcate the virtue (habit)
of temperance.

Though the above natural way to direct our will to give precedence
to high and good desires (by calling to mind our noble reasons and
choosing them in the midst of strong competitive base desires) can
be accomplished in theory, it oftentimes fails to reach its objective,
and sometimes even fails to reach first base in our hyperstimulated
culture of abundance and social license. For this reason, many in
our culture are powerless to restrain their passions and egocentric
desires on their own, returning to the dominance of those passions
against their best interest, time and time again. The only way that
many of these individuals will be able to move beyond their base

---

[21] See Pieper, *Four Cardinal Virtues*, pp. 145–90.

nature and passions is by making recourse to the Lord's grace manifest in His providential orchestration of events and His interior workings within their hearts. This makes a life of faith and deepening spiritual conversion essential for the virtue of temperance in our contemporary culture. As noted throughout the last chapter, deep spiritual conversion leads to deep moral conversion, particularly in the area of temperance and resistance to temptation.

Recall that virtues, like all habits, are cultivated by repeated free choices. This means that the Lord cannot simply instill virtue within us. Since He gave us freedom, He works with us to help us choose virtue. He does this in a variety of ways discussed in the previous chapter. Sometimes, He uses the suffering arising out of our intemperate choices—for example, a hangover, a jealous rage, physical illness as a result of not taking proper care of our health, and the terrible problems associated with addictions to alcohol, drugs, and pornography. When these consequences arise, He uses His "little voice in the back of our minds" to make suggestions about choosing more temperate actions in the future (see Chapter 3, Section V). Sometimes, when we are moving more deeply into the darkness by choosing more serious intemperate lifestyles, He will intervene at three o'clock in the morning with a sense of profound emptiness and alienation followed by a strong suggestion to turn our lives around before we destroy ourselves, others, and slip into the Evil One's deeper darkness (see Chapter 3, Section IV.B). Remember, He will not have the hateful voice of the accuser (Satan), but a gentle yet firm voice of a concerned parent who deeply loves and cares about us. In this insistent voice, He will probably call us to the Sacrament of Reconciliation and to take some first step in moving toward healing and temperance (e.g., reversing a destructive course of conduct or getting help from a program).

If we are not in serious trouble, but languishing in a moderately intemperate lifestyle that leaves us open to the near occasion of darker lifestyles, the Lord may use the voice of other people (say, family members or friends) or even a book or television program to make an external suggestion. When made, He follows it up with an interior suggestion, sometimes using the little voice in the back of our heads, mild affective desolation, or a sense of impending danger if we do not seek a more temperate lifestyle going forward. Much of the time, the Lord will call us to the Sacrament of Reconciliation, and suggest a deeper commitment to spiritual conversion, perhaps in the form of a little extra prayer, or occasional daily Masses, or adoration or a Rosary with friends, because the deeper our spiritual conversion, the more open we become to temperance, resistance to temptation, and moral conversion.

Though spiritual conversion is a huge first step in the cultivation of temperance (so necessary for moral conversion), we can take additional efficacious steps to developing it. I will explain three of these steps in the next two chapters:

1. Making recourse to the Sacrament of Reconciliation on a monthly basis with a focused examination of conscience (see Chapter 7, Section II)
2. The use of the Ignatian Examen Prayer on a daily basis (see Chapter 6, Section II)
3. Making use of two contemporary psychological techniques for reconditioning our subconscious identity—visualizations and affirmations. I suggest ways of integrating faith and prayer into these techniques to bring the power of grace to bear on this reconditioning process (see Chapter 6, Section I).

We will defer discussion of these recommendations to those later chapters.

The reader may be wondering why I'm spending so much time on temperance when it seems to be secondary to prudence, justice, and love. I do it because it is the Achilles' heel of this culture, and if we don't attend to it, it threatens to undermine all the other virtues. As we saw in the previous subsection, love, virtue, and prudence without fortitude (the power of the will to actualize the impetus of these primary virtues) goes nowhere. In like manner, love, justice, and prudence without temperance (the power of the will to restrain base appetites, instincts, and egocentric desires) are likely to be over-shadowed by those base desires and egocentricity—and even severely undermined by them. Sadly, this is the fate that so many face in our culture of materialism, superabundance, and social license. If we are to extricate ourselves from this personal and social decline, we will have to rehabilitate the classical virtue of temperance (self-control) while making use of every spiritual resource that the Lord bestows upon us through our spiritual conversion.

D. Justice

Justice has a long and deep tradition within natural philosophy. Plato devoted his great dialogue *The Republic* to it, initially defining it as "giving each person his due", which includes doing no unnecessary harm to friends and rendering to all citizens what is owed to them and taking nothing from them that they rightfully own.[22] He later enshrines it as an absolute excellence (in a metaphysical-ontological sense),[23] suggesting its origin in and closeness to divinity. As such, it is the principal virtue and excellence that guides the leaders (guardians) of the state, allowing it to be at harmony and peace (not at war within itself).

Aristotle follows Plato in holding that justice is a primary virtue that can rightly guide our relationships with one another, allowing for a good and peaceful community.[24] Aristotle takes a decidedly different approach from Plato, removing justice from the domain of metaphysical absolutes, and assessing it pragmatically through the lens of a merit-based system of equity—giving a person what is owed to him on the basis of his relative merit.[25]

These classical philosophers enabled later Christian thinkers to use justice as the basis for a common natural law (among all peoples— Christian and non-Christian) as well as a common guiding principle to judge legal cases fairly and even the legitimacy of political regimes. Saint Augustine seized upon justice as the guiding principle to determine the legitimacy of all laws and states, noting that "an unjust law is no law at all."[26] This became a virtual axiom among social-political theorists and social critics, including Francisco Suarez, John Locke,

[22] See Plato, *The Republic* 1, 331e.
[23] See ibid., 7, 516c–517e.
[24] See Aristotle, *Nicomachean Ethics* 5.
[25] See ibid., 5, 1131.
[26] See Saint Augustine, *On the Free Choice of the Will* 1, 5.

Thomas Jefferson, Edmund Burke, Mahatma Gandhi, and Martin Luther King.[27]

The principle of justice lies at the foundation of Saint Thomas Aquinas' natural law theory[28] and grounded Father Francisco Suarez's inalienable rights theory, which became the basis of inalienable rights in John Locke's seventeenth-century's *Second Treatise on Government*, the American Declaration of Independence, and even the 1948 United Nation's Declaration on Human Rights.[29]

Independent of its huge influence in public law, justice is also a virtue that governs our individual lives. It determines the right relationship among people (irrespective of their religion or formation). As Saint Paul implies, all individuals know by the light of reason certain general principles of right and wrong, sensing an attraction to the good, and revulsion toward evil:

> When Gentiles who have not the law do by nature what the law requires, they are a law to themselves, even though they do not have the law. They show that what the law requires is written on their hearts, while their conscience [συνειδησις] also bears witness and their conflicting thoughts accuse or perhaps excuse them. (Rom 2:14–15)

One of the major norms written in our hearts by the Lord (and manifest through our conscience) is justice, and this awareness of and attraction to justice embodies the two elements mentioned by Plato—"give every person his due" and "do no unnecessary harm".[30] In ethical theory we refer to the first principle as the "principle of equity" and the second principle as "the principle of nonmaleficence". The principle of nonmaleficence is the most basic principle of ethics and justice. It is found in every major religion and culture throughout the world, including the Old Testament (see Tob 4:15; Sir 31:15). This gives credence to Saint Paul's implication that it is written in our hearts. The basic expression of it with respect to our personal conduct is called "the Silver Rule": "Do not do unto others

---

[27] For the precise citations and references, see Robert Spitzer, *Ten Universal Principles* (San Francisco: Ignatius Press, 2011), pp. 72–74.

[28] See Pieper, *Four Cardinal Virtues*, pp. 68–123.

[29] See Spitzer, *Ten Universal Principles*, pp. 52–80.

[30] Plato, *The Republic* 1, 331e.

what you would not have them do unto you." In other words, do not do a harm to others that you would not want done to you. The modern formulation of this is "Do no unnecessary harm to others, and if a harm is unavoidable, minimize it."

This principle is the foundation of personal ethics and public law in virtually all cultures, because if it is delegitimized, then the whole objective foundation of ethics and law would likewise be delegitimized, leaving us completely unprotected from every form of arbitrary malevolence, cruelty, and tyranny, reducing us to the state of mere survival of the fittest. In view of this, we should be thankful to the Lord,[31] who inscribed this law in everyone's heart such that the majority of people would adhere to it and form communities and societies around it.

So how might we cultivate the virtue of justice? Do we need a program similar to the ones proposed above for prudence, fortitude, and temperance? No, we do not. All that is required to instill justice in our hearts is to listen to the light of conscience as interpreted by reason, and commit to refusing to compromise it for the sake of others, the society, and ourselves. Religiously inclined individuals will have the very powerful additional motivation of being obedient to the most fundamental of the Lord's commandments. Most of the time, it requires little sacrifice to be fair (equitable) in our dealings with others and to avoid unnecessary harms to them, so there is very little excuse for failure to cultivate this basic virtue of human relationships. Thus, those who do violate it in a serious way enter into a dangerous domain of interior darkness and evil, undermining individual rights, God's expectations for human dignity, and the peace and welfare of community, society, and state. The best program for implementing justice, then, is to attend to the dictates of our conscience, and consistently follow them. As with all the other virtues, deep spiritual conversion paves the way for consistently following this most fundamental precept.

We may now proceed to the relationship between justice and love. We might begin by saying that justice is required of every

---

[31] Emmanuel Kant and John Henry Newman attempted to show that this fundamental principle of conscience—and conscience itself—had to have its origin in a divine authority. For a summary of their arguments, see Volume II, Chapter 2, Section II, of the Quartet.

individual as the minimum they must do to be ethical, while love goes beyond—and sometimes far beyond—the dictates of justice, opening itself to the good of others irrespective of what is owed to them in justice (see below, Section II). When Jesus elevated love to the highest commandment (indicating that it characterized His and His Father's nature), He no doubt realized that it was a much higher calling than justice—one that would be difficult for people to understand and embrace through the light of *reason* alone. He knew that His *revelation* would have to be accepted in faith through the inspiration of the Holy Spirit in our hearts. To reinforce the interior movement of the spirit toward compassion, forgiveness, and self-sacrifice, He gave us signs of His divine mandate and nature—exorcisms and miracles performed by His own authority, His Resurrection in glory, and His gift of the Holy Spirit to the apostles who performed miracles in His name.[32] When these interior spiritual movements and exterior signs are combined and synthesized with Jesus' words and actions of love, particularly His love of sinners and His self-sacrificial Passion and death, we have a strong rationale for both mind and heart to affirm His teaching that love is the supreme virtue, going beyond the minimal requirements of justice. Those who follow it will inherit the unconditionally loving eternity prepared for us by His Father.

Jesus taught the supremacy of love by His word and example, but His most fundamental teaching is found in His formulation of the Golden Rule—"Do unto others as you would have them do unto you." We might say that the Silver Rule defines the minimal requirements of justice, while the Golden Rule points to the maximal ideal of love. When Jesus removed the "nots" from the Silver Rule, He converted it from "ethical minimalism (justice)" to "ethical maximalism (love)".[33]

---

[32] For a rational and scientific justification of these claims, see Volume III, Chapters 4–5 and Appendix I, of the Quartet. For an exploration of contemporary scientifically validated miracles, see the appendix to Volume I of this Trilogy.

[33] Explicit mentions of the Golden Rule are rare in non-Christian religions. Some authors classify non-Christian religious ethical texts as "proscriptive versions of the Golden Rule". However, this classification leads to a major misunderstanding of the Golden Rule, because the so-called proscriptive version is really the Silver Rule, the avoidance of harm (minimalistic ethics), while the so-called prescriptive version is the Golden Rule taught by Jesus, "optimal benefit to neighbor" (ethical maximalism). When this confusion is clarified, non-Christian citations of the Golden Rule are quite rare. The Old Testament references (Tob 4:15: "What

We might rephrase the Golden Rule as follows: "Do the good for others that you would want done to you." The emphasis is no longer on merely avoiding harm, but also on doing good (beyond the avoidance of harm). Evidently, doing the good for others entails avoiding harm, but it also entails much more—namely, any good that we would want done unto us. We will discuss what this means in both interior attitude and exterior action below in Section II. For the moment, we need only focus on our commitment not to compromise the dictates of justice as manifest through the light of conscience and reason, anticipating that Jesus will show us a more excellent way that holds out hope not only for salvation, but for continuous improvement in social welfare over the course of history.

The supremacy of love gives rise to a question. If love really does supersede justice, and Christians are drawn and called to it through Baptism and catechesis, then why do Christian believers need to cultivate justice? Can't Christian believers dispense with it, leaving only six fundamental virtues? There are two major reasons why justice should not be supplanted by the more excellent virtue of love.

First, justice is an uncompromisable requirement of all individuals—including Christians. Through the light of conscience and reason, it tells us precisely what we *should not* do to our neighbor. Though love must be built on the foundation of justice, it really focuses us on what we *should do* for our neighbor. Though Jesus asks us to seek love by imitating Him in our hearts and actions, we cannot equate a failure in love with a failure in justice. A failure in justice is much more severe, causing a harm to someone who does not deserve it—someone who is owed the minimum dignity of equitable treatment and the avoidance of unnecessary harm. Failures in love that are not failures in justice can certainly be hurtful, falling short of the service, compassion, and humility of Jesus, but they generally do not cause additional underserved harms and inequities. A failure in love (which is not a failure in justice) is generally a failure to improve the condition of one or more individuals, while a failure in justice leads to a decline

---

you hate, do not do to anyone"; Sir 31:15: "Judge your neighbor's feelings by your own, and in every matter be thoughtful") are clearly manifestations of the Silver Rule. For non-Christian citations of the Golden Rule, see Simon Blackburn, *Ethics: A Very Short Introduction* (Oxford: Oxford University Press, 2001), p. 101.

in the current condition of one or more individuals. Even though Christians try to act in accordance with the ideal of love, we need to be constantly aware of the requirements of justice to avoid causing unnecessary and undeserved personal and societal destruction.

We might restate it as follows: justice alerts us to what is *proscribed* (prohibited) by conscience, reason, and faith, and so warns us about lines that should *not* be crossed, while love, going beyond justice, reveals what is *prescribed* (recommended) by our affect (heart) guided by the teaching of Jesus and the inspiration of the Holy Spirit. Christians must focus not only on the good to be pursued, but also on the evil to be avoided—the lines that should not be crossed. If we take our eyes off the latter, we can fall into the easy trap of using an unjust means to accomplish a good and noble end. Love focuses us on the noble end, while justice focuses us on proscriptions—the dictates of conscience and the natural law—that help us discern the legitimacy of the means to that end. We need both.

The second reason Christians should appropriate the virtue of justice is to interact with our larger pluralistic society (with Christians and non-Christians). We cannot impose our ethical beliefs with respect to compassion, forgiveness, optimal contribution, and self-sacrifice on non-Christians, because these are not required by the light of conscience and the natural law. However, we can "impose" the requirements of justice on nonbelievers, because the universal dictates of conscience require us to respect our inherent obligations to others—namely, to refrain from violating their inalienable rights of life, liberty, property, and the pursuit of happiness. When Christians have a keen awareness of the requirements of justice, they not only defend the goodness of just laws, but also protect the inalienable rights of their neighbors.

E. The Interplay among the Seven Virtues

We are now in a position to explore the interplay among the seven virtues. Each of these virtues requires the others in order to become fully effective. Prudence without fortitude is powerless to actualize the good opportunities it recognizes. Fortitude without prudence is a nonrational exertion of the will that might be either good or evil.

Prudence without temperance is powerless to prevent the undermining of the good by our base desires and egoism. Temperance without prudence is self-control for its own sake (stoicism) without direction or purpose beyond itself. Prudence without justice is Machiavellian pragmatism without benefit of conscience or principle, which can be heartless and cruel. Justice without prudence is the felt awareness of conscience and principles without the ability to utilize them effectively in the world.

Likewise, justice without fortitude is the felt awareness of conscience and principles without the willpower to utilize them in the world. Justice without temperance is the felt awareness of conscience and principles without the willpower to prevent it being undermined by base desires and egoism.

Temperance without fortitude is self-control without the willpower to actualize good opportunities—and finally, fortitude without temperance is the willpower to achieve without control over our base desires and egoism. This commonly leads to bravado and blind ambition.

As can be seen, the four cardinal virtues are like a perfectly constructed jigsaw puzzle. Each piece enables the others to be more intelligible and connected—and therefore more effective. If one piece is missing, all the other pieces lose effectiveness, undermining our character and capacity to achieve the good. Hence, it is important for us to become proficient at all four cardinal virtues so that we might also be proficient at actualizing and defending the good in all that we do.

As we shall see, the three theological virtues take all four cardinal virtues to a whole new level—a level that was never dreamt by classical philosophers. This whole new level comes from the Incarnation, life, death, and Resurrection of Jesus, who gave us five life-transforming gifts—His teaching, the Holy Spirit, the promise of eternal salvation, the Church, and the sacraments. These gifts are precisely what make the theological virtues of faith, hope, and love possible, efficacious, and transformative. With the gifts of Jesus Christ working through our faith, hope, and love, we become new *supernatural* beings, seeking the high purposes of love beyond justice and becoming instruments of divine providence to bring the grace of divine healing, inspiration, protection, and hope to a world that would otherwise be deprived of it. When Christians allow the natural virtues to be brought to fulfillment by the theological virtues, they become

God's instruments of loving transformation to individuals and a world that would otherwise have remained stagnant.

Just as the theological virtues bring the natural virtues to a new level of supernatural and providential healing, hope, and transformation, so also the theological virtues need the natural virtues as their foundation. If a person has great faith without concomitant prudence, fortitude, temperance, and justice, he is likely to be an ineffective, uninformed, irrational, and intemperate enthusiast. If a person has great hope without the natural virtues, he is likely to be a naïve optimist and a directionless dreamer. If a person has great love without the natural virtues, that love would be reduced to mere feelings of goodwill and compassion without the rational competence and willpower to bring them into reality. Furthermore, that person's feelings of love are likely to be undermined by his uncontrolled base desires and egoism. Though love is the supreme end to which we are ordered by the faith and hope that makes us supernatural beings united to Jesus, it is almost powerless without the fortitude to actualize it, the courage to stand up for it, the prudence to guide it, the temperance to control what undermines it, and the justice to prevent our using unjust means to noble ends. With these four cardinal virtues in mind, we now proceed to the supreme virtue of love, which can bring the cardinal virtues to a supernatural end.

II. The Supreme Virtue—Love

As we begin our investigation of the virtue of love, we must first acknowledge that Jesus and the early Church advanced the concept and reality far beyond that of the classical philosophers and pre-Christian religions.[34] Plato's great dialogues on love—the *Phaedrus* and the *Symposium*—concentrate mostly on *eros* (romantic love) and some elements of *philia* (friendship), but do not begin to approach the Christian notion of love—good for the other without expectation of return (*agapē*; see below). Aristotle in his *Nichomachean Ethics* (Book 8—on friendship) focuses on *philia* (the love of friends), concentrating on friendships of utility, pleasure, and goodness. Friendships of utility

---

[34] Josef Pieper, *About Love* (Chicago: Franciscan Herald Press, 1974), pp. 95–118.

allow for mutual benefit; friendships of pleasure allow for enjoyment of another's pleasant qualities; and friendships of goodness allow for mutual striving toward greater goodness. The third is the only one that approaches Jesus' idea, but as we shall see, Jesus and the Christian Church go far beyond it.

Pre-Christian religions focused on the Silver Rule (avoiding harm), but Jesus goes further, advocating that we provide optimal good to our neighbor (see above, Section I.D). He then defines love through the Beatitudes that orients it toward interior attitudes leading toward forgiveness, compassion, humility, and gentleness of spirit. As will be explained in Volume III of this Trilogy, this change in the definition of love, accompanied by Jesus' example, Passion, death, Resurrection, and gift of the Spirit, led to a complete transformation of culture throughout the world, particularly in the areas of social welfare, health care, education, and decreased social stratification.[35]

Before examining this remarkable phenomenon, we must first examine Jesus' teaching on love (Section II.A) and how eight dimensions of love counteract the eight deadly sins (Section II.B).

A. Jesus' Teaching on Love

In Volume III of the Quartet, we discussed how Jesus advanced the idea and practice of love, and through it, transformed the history of religions and the world. We noted there that Friedrich Heiler discovered seven major similarities among the world's religions, in which love makes a twofold appearance.[36] In view of the fact that these religions had very distinct times, places, and cultures of origin, it is quite remarkable that they should all point to the importance of love within seven major similarities. I cannot help but believe that the Lord (through the numinous experience,[37] the intuition of the

[35] See Robert Spitzer, *Credible Catholic Big Book*, Volume 4, *The Significance of Jesus* (Magis Center, 2017), CredibleCatholic.com, Chapter 9, https://www.crediblecatholic.com/pdf/M4/BB4.pdf#P1V4C9.

[36] See Friedrich Heiler, "The History of Religions as a Preparation for the Cooperation of Religions", in *The History of Religions*, ed. Mircea Eliade and J. Kitagawa (Chicago: Chicago University Press, 1959), pp. 142–53.

[37] See Volume II, Chapter 1, of the Quartet.

sacred,[38] and divine inspiration[39]) engendered this common belief about His love in virtually every individual and culture.

The Lord went beyond this common revelation by first sending prophets to His chosen people, Israel. The prophet Hosea is the first to introduce God's passionate love for His people, a passion that could be cooled if Israel flagrantly violated His commands.[40] The Deuteronomic author speaks of God's special love for His people (though not for particular individuals), implying care and protection for them.[41] In view of God's love for Israel, the people were asked to love God with their whole heart, whole self, and whole strength (Deut 6:5). Some of the later psalms metaphorically manifest God's care, forgiveness, and protection, signs of His love for individuals (see, for example, Ps 23: "The LORD is my shepherd...."; Ps 51: "Have mercy on me, O God, according to your merciful love...."; and Ps 139: "O LORD, you have searched me and known me! ...").

Notwithstanding these developments, the Lord's revelation of His love was still vastly incomplete, for He had not yet revealed the true meaning of love, His unconditional love for us, or the love He intended to share with us throughout eternity. He reserved this fullness of revelation for His Son, who was sent to reveal it not only in word, but also in action, Resurrection, and gift of the Holy Spirit—and to share His divine loving nature with us as His adopted children. And so, Saint Paul tells us, "When the time had fully come, God sent forth his Son, born of woman, born under the law, to redeem those who were under the law, so that we might receive adoption as sons" (Gal 4:4–5).

Jesus proclaimed Himself to be the exclusive Son of the Father, by sharing in His divinity (see Mt 11:25–27; 16:15–17; Mk 14:61–62; Lk 10:21–22; Jn 8:58; 10:30; 14:9). As such, He was (and is) the fullness of God's self-revelation, speaking definitively about God's heart, purpose, intention, and love toward humanity. He gave substantial evidence for His remarkable claim, which we have assessed in Volume III of the Quartet (Chapters 4–6). Four major areas of evidence

---

[38] See Volume II, Chapter 2, of the Quartet.
[39] See Chapter 3, Sections III–V, of this volume.
[40] John L. McKenzie, S.J., *Dictionary of the Bible* (New York: Macmillan, 1965), pp. 520–21.
[41] Ibid.

were significant for the early Church that enabled them to preach His divine Sonship at great personal and communal sacrifice:

1. Jesus' Resurrection in glory, which is validatable in several compelling ways:
    a. The scientific investigation of the Shroud of Turin showing the need for a burst of light energy of several *billion* watts as well as a spiritual (physically transparent) body, in order to produce the precise, three-dimensional, perfect photographic negative image on the very surface of the fibrils of a non-photographically sensitive linen cloth. It is very probably a relic of a spiritual resurrection in light and glory similar to that described by the Gospels and Saint Paul (see Volume III, Appendix I, of the Quartet).
    b. Remarkable correlations between Jesus' resurrected appearance and qualities of the spiritual bodies reported by individuals during near-death experiences, given in studies published in peer-reviewed medical journals (see Volume II, Chapter 5, and Volume III, Chapter 4, of the Quartet).
    c. New historical-exegetical studies of the Resurrection appearances in both the Gospel narratives and Saint Paul, particularly those done by N. T. Wright[42] (see Volume III, Chapter 4, of the Quartet).
2. Jesus' gift of the Holy Spirit, enabling His disciples to perform similar miracles to His own through His name. The combination of new miraculous power with the name of Jesus gave significant evidence of Jesus' continuous resurrected presence as well as His Father's approval (see Volume III, Chapter 5, of the Quartet).
3. Jesus performed exorcisms, healing miracles, and raisings from the dead by His own authority and power (unlike any previous prophet), implying that this supernatural power belonged to Him as much as it did to His Father—a sign of divinity (see Volume III, Chapter 5, of the Quartet).
4. Contemporary scientifically validated miracles associated with Jesus—concerned with the Blessed Virgin Mary, the saints,

[42] See N. T. Wright, *The Resurrection of the Son of God* (Minneapolis: Fortress Press, 2003).

and the Holy Eucharist (see the appendix in Volume I of this Trilogy).

The remarkable scientific corroboration of these four kinds of evidence enables us in the twenty-first century to be nearly as confident as the early members of the Church in believing that Jesus was everything that He claimed to be—the exclusive Son of the Father, who knows the Father precisely as the Father knows Him (Mt 11:25–27; Lk 10:21–22), and who shares not only the Father's divinity, but also His heart of unconditional love. We will discuss this latter point below. For the moment, suffice to say that in sharing the Father's divinity, Jesus is the fullness of God's self-revelation. He not only brought to fullness the interior revelation given to all religions throughout the world, but also demonstrated in His actions the unconditional love He claimed characterized His and His Father's heart and nature. As we shall see, Jesus reveals His and His Father's unconditional love in several ways—in both word and action reported in the Gospel of John:

> As the Father has loved me, so have I loved you; abide in my love. If you keep my commandments, you will abide in my love, just as I have kept my Father's commandments and abide in his love. These things I have spoken to you, that my joy may be in you, and that your joy may be full.
>   This is my commandment, that you love one another as I have loved you. Greater love has no man than this, that a man lay down his life for his friends. (15:9–13)

So how did Jesus illustrate and validate His and His Father's unconditional love, the very love He calls us to imitate (which will become the joy of our eternal salvation with Him) and the very love with which He intends to transform the world? What was His plan to bring the history of religions, and even history itself, to the fullness of truth, sanctification, and joy? Before discussing His fourfold plan, it will be worth mentioning that His transformation of the idea and practice of love was so radical that it forced the Christian Church to search for a new word to describe this uniquely transformative virtue while keeping it distinct from the other three much more common

Greek words for love—*storgē* (feelings of affection), *philia* (friendship), and *eros* (romantic love).

The Christian community decided upon *agapē*, which was rare in profane Greek,[43] enabling them to transform the idea to conform to Jesus' teaching. This term was translated into Latin as *caritas* ("charity" in English) to keep it distinct from romantic love, feelings of affection, and friendship. To this day, *caritas* is still associated with the uniquely Christian view of love for all mankind.[44] In brief, *agapē* refers to love (care and charitable action) for others *for their own sake* without expectation of implicit or explicit reciprocity—even to the point of self-sacrifice. It extends to everybody—foreigners, strangers, and even enemies, all of whom are elevated to the status of neighbors, friends, or even family members. It provides the interior disposition to do the most difficult and unrewarded actions needed for peace, healing, and transformation of relationships, such as forgiveness of unwarranted transgressions against us, compassion for those who are not only destitute, but ungrateful, and service to those who do us harm. When the Christian community took Jesus' teaching and mandate seriously, it spread like wildfire and transformed the world even in the midst of persecution.[45]

So what was Jesus' fourfold plan to communicate His and His Father's *agapē* (charity) by word and action?

1. Sermons, teachings, and parables on the meaning and practice of love/charity
2. Sermons, teachings, and parables on His Father's unconditional love
3. Demonstrations of His love/charity for sinners, the sick, the spiritually distraught, and the poor

---

[43] McKenzie, *Dictionary of the Bible*, p. 521.

[44] For example, the *Oxford Dictionary*'s definition of *caritas* is "Christian love of humankind; charity", https://en.oxforddictionaries.com/definition/caritas.

[45] Helmut Koester, "The Great Appeal: What Did Christianity Offer Its Believers That Made It Worth Social Estrangement, Hostility from Neighbors, and Possible Persecution?" *Frontline* (New York: WGBH Educational Foundation, 1998), pbs.org/wgbh/pages/frontline/shows/religion/why/appeal.html. See also James M. Robinson and Helmut Koester, *Trajectories through Early Christianity* (Philadelphia: Fortress, 1971; repr., Eugene, Ore.: Wipf & Stock, 2006).

4. Demonstration of His most radical form of self-sacrificial love
in His Passion (and Holy Eucharist)

We will here briefly summarize what was more extensively explained
in Volume III, Chapters 1–3, of the Quartet.

1. Jesus' Teaching on the Meaning and Practice of Love

Let us begin with Jesus' teachings and parables about the meaning and
practice of love. As we begin, it should be noted that Jesus premised
His teaching on love with the most remarkable claim—that love is
the highest commandment and virtue. Never before in the history of
religions had any religious teacher or prophet proclaimed a specific
virtue or principle to be the highest. Jesus not only makes love the
highest commandment, but also *uniquely* ties together three kinds of
love—love of God, neighbor, and self. The idea that love of neighbor
is similar to love of God would have been radical indeed for any religion, in which the love of God would be more important than the
love of an individual.[46] After making this radical claim, Jesus goes on
to define "neighbor" to include even foreigners and sworn enemies
(see the Parable of the Good Samaritan [Lk 10:25–37]) as well as "the
least of these brothers and sisters of mine" (Mt 25:40, 45).

As if these transformations were not enough, Jesus then extends
the practice of love not only to behaviors, but also to interior attitudes. He specifies the interior attitudes in six of the eight Beatitudes
(Mt 5:3–12), after which He elucidates the exterior behaviors going
along with these attitudes throughout the rest of the Sermon on the
Mount (Mt 5:13–7:28).

This brief summary allows for only a listing of the interior attitudes
and concomitant behaviors that have come to transform the world.
Readers seeking a more extensive explanation will want to study
Volume III (Chapters 1–3) of the Quartet.

---

[46] This was certainly the case for Old Testament and intertestamental Judaism, which
viewed the Deuteronomic commandment "You shall love the LORD your God with all your
heart, and with all your soul, and with all your might" (Deut 6:5) as a "heavy" (very important) commandment by comparison to Jesus' second commandment from Leviticus, "You
shall love your neighbor as yourself" (Lev 19:18). See John L. McKenzie, "The Gospel
according to Matthew", in *The Jerome Biblical Commentary*, ed. Raymond Brown, Joseph A.
Fitzmyer, and Roland E. Murphy (Englewood Cliffs, N.J.: Prentice-Hall, 1968), 2:101.

The *interior attitudes* given in the Beatitudes are as follows:

- "Poor in spirit" (Mt 5:3), which may be understood as humble-heartedness
- "The meek" (Mt 5:5), which may be understood as gentle-heartedness
- "Those who hunger and thirst for righteousness" (Mt 5:6), which may be understood as those seeking the virtues and dispositions of faith, hope, and love/charity, leading to eternal salvation
- "The merciful" (Mt 5:7), which may be understood as those who are forgiving of others as well as compassionate to the least and marginalized
- "The pure in heart" (Mt 5:8), which may be understood as those who embrace the truth of Jesus Christ and try to define their own authenticity in terms of it
- "The peacemakers" (Mt 5:9), which may be understood as those who try to bring remediation and healing to disputes not only in their own lives, but in the lives of others they touch

I recall reading the Beatitudes when I was a young man, and thinking to myself, "I wish I could really believe in all that—let alone, do all that!" I am elated that I did not simply walk away from Jesus' call in a state of discouragement. I had an inkling that the Lord would help me inch toward these ideals over the course of time, and that He would give me the means to get to the first step—what Saint Ignatius called "the desire for the desire".[47] I would recommend that anyone who feels like I felt in those days to pray for that desire to want to be like the Lord in the Beatitudes. It was the beginning of my spiritual conversion and my long journey toward moral conversion.

Two other gifts from God really helped me in those days. First, I had a natural sense of compassion. I did not want to hurt, undermine, or insult anyone (except for the occasional public adversary in the hallowed halls of academe). After I started going to daily Mass, this natural sense of compassion increased considerably, and I followed it

[47] Saint Ignatius of Loyola, *Constitutions of the Society of Jesus and Their Complementary Norms* (St. Louis: The Institute of Jesuit Sources, 1996), par. 102, https://jesuitas.lat/uploads/the-constitutions-of-the-society-of-jesus-and-their-complementary-norms/Constitutions%20and%20Norms%20SJ%20ingls.pdf.

(thanks be to God). It was a rough-edged, but solid foundation upon which to build the virtue of love that had to fight against the vast egocentric wasteland within my life.

Second, as I grew in love of the Lord through daily Mass and study, I truly did not want to undermine Him, His Kingdom, or His Church in any way (because I loved Him). Though I tried to ignore thinking about my departures from several of the Lord's teachings—actions that invariably enhanced sensual and egocentric satisfaction—it was harder to ignore Him as His voice became more evident (see Chapter 3, Sections III–V).

Frequently enough, the Lord would combine these two initial gifts (my natural sense of compassion and my growing love for the Lord) to help me take some "small steps" toward transformation of my heart along the lines of the Beatitudes. One of His favorites was to suggest putting myself in the other person's situation. I knew how absolutely fortunate I had been in my upbringing, family, and education, and was well aware of being privileged beyond belief. The Lord levered this tiny dimension of authenticity in my psyche for all it was worth. When I began to have contemptuous or judgmental thoughts, I would get an incisive voice into that person's goodness amid his difficult upbringing—an awareness that he was acting out of some past challenge I could not possibly hope to understand. These little glimpses of understanding, sympathy, and compassion launched me on my way not only to great friendships, but also into the adventure of forgiveness and the rejection of impatience and anger.

As I noted in the previous chapter, the Lord works with us through His myriad forms of communication in *small steps*, counting on our acceptance of His lead even when it is highly inconvenient. In view of this, we should not think we are going to get to the Beatitudes like a shot out of a cannon. If you are anything like me, it will be a slow, arduous process filled with the Lord's patient instruction, and supported by the four dimensions of spiritual-moral conversion—the sacraments (particularly the Holy Eucharist and the Sacrament of Reconciliation), prayer (see Chapter 3, Sections III–V), the teaching of Jesus, and moral resolve (explained below). If we remain faithful to these four disciplines, and listen for the Lord's suggestions (in affective consolation and desolation as well as "little voices in the back of our heads"), He will lead us where we cannot take ourselves—into the heart of the Beatitudes—His and His Father's heart of compassion.

The main exterior *behaviors* (both proscriptive and prescriptive) characterizing Jesus' view of love in the Sermon on the Mount are as follows:

- Avoid spiritual sloth (*acedia*)—use the inner light, gifts, and grace you have been given to help others and build the Kingdom of God, lest you waste your life on mere self-aggrandizement, and become like flavorless salt and hidden light. Spiritual sloth is particularly deadly because it undermines a life of virtue (particularly love) at its very foundation (see Mt 5:13–16).
- Avoid anger, particularly insults and contempt for others (see Mt 5:21–26).
- Avoid retaliation in any of its forms, forgiving others from the heart (see Mt 5:38–42; 6:14–15).
- Avoid judging others, because you do not know their hearts— only God can judge (see Mt 7:1–5).
- Avoid adultery and even thoughts that could lead to adultery. Note that Jesus' teaching on chastity is particularly strong, because He knows that even adulterous thoughts open the door to the Evil One to corrupt our identity, virtuous intent, spiritual lives, and relationships with others; see below, Section II.B.8 (see Mt 5:27–30).
- Avoid divorce if there is not abuse of spouse and/or children. Jesus views marriage as a covenant relationship that includes God, oriented toward self-sacrificial contribution and high respect for the temporal and spiritual good of spouse and children. It is a high vocation toward salvation and co-responsibility—not a pragmatic relationship of convenience (see Mt 5:31–32).
- Love your enemies—pray for them and do good for them (see Mt 5:43–48).
- Live for contributive and transcendent purpose—avoid living for the things of this world: money, honors, and power, by replacing them with contributions and spiritual pursuits (see Mt 6:19–21, 24).

Throughout the Sermon on the Mount, there are several calls to spiritual conversion that is truly beneficial (and necessary) for moving more deeply into the practice of love/charity. If this dimension of faith and prayer is not well developed, we deprive ourselves of God's companionship, spiritual power (grace), protection, and inspiration as we try to detach from riches, honors, and pride to deepen our love/charity in imitation of the Lord we love. As we have noted several times above, attempting moral conversion without a life of prayer and devotion is like fighting with both hands tied behind our backs. Jesus' recommendations for spiritual conversion include:

- Commitment to prayer (see Mt 6:5–14)
- Authenticity in prayer—not for public accolades (see Mt 6:5–14)
- Openness to and trust in God's will (see Mt 7:7–12)
- Looking for His truth and will (a sound eye) rather than sensuality and egocentricity that fill us with darkness
- Continually trying to deepen our faith, hope, and love—"ask, seek, and knock" (see Mt 7:7–8)

We have discussed the recommendations made by Jesus with respect to spiritual conversion in Chapters 2–3.

The sheer height, depth, and breadth of Jesus' explanation of love/charity can be quite overwhelming, causing us to ask, "Where should we begin?" It could also open the door to the Evil One's suggestions of discouragement—"You will never be able to do this—it's way, way, way beyond you." Of course, the Evil One leaves out one major factor—it is not *just* about us; we are on a lifetime path with the Lord, the Church, our faith community, friends, and family. We are not going to have instant success, but rather a long journey of prayer, the sacraments, human interaction, and moral resolve filled with failings, reconciliation, communication from God, consolation, desolation, and much more. If we commit ourselves to the four dimensions of spiritual-moral conversion (the sacraments, prayer, Jesus' teaching, and moral resolve), over the long term, we will notice new little moments of freedom—little "successes" in detaching from the world and deadly sins—that constitute a transformation in Jesus' heart and love as we inch along the stages on life's way. We will address this gradual freedom and transformation below in this chapter and in the following three chapters. For the moment, please do not be overwhelmed! Rather, trust in the Lord of love who will lead you to that Promised Land if you commit yourself to spiritual-moral conversion.

2. Jesus' Teaching on the Unconditional Love of His Father

We may now proceed to the second part of Jesus' fourfold plan to transform the idea and practice of love/charity: sermons, teachings, and parables on His Father's unconditional love. Never before in the history of religions has anyone described God as unconditional love—let alone in the absolute terms Jesus used to do this. It is, of course, part of the "good news" that Jesus preaches from the very beginning of His ministry (Mk 1:15)—good news that we cannot take for granted. The unconditional love of the Lord is the solid foundation of our hope that He will forgive us, heal us, and work with us not only until the day we die but throughout the course of our purgation until He brings us into His Kingdom—so long as we try to follow Him by staying faithful to Him and His teaching. If we remain confident in His unconditional love and His promise to escort us continuously on our journey to His Kingdom (through spiritual-moral conversion), we will never fall prey to despair. Instead, we will be able to rest in the deep peace and trust arising out of His loving assurance and continued presence. So how did Jesus teach and demonstrate His and His Father's unconditional love? Before considering Jesus' demonstration of unconditional love, we will examine His teaching about His Father's unconditional love. The Synoptic Gospels emphasize three of Jesus' teachings on this central revelation that Saint Paul and Saint John use to ground faith and hope in the early Church:

1. Love as the highest commandment
2. The father of the prodigal son
3. Jesus' name for the Father—"Abba"

Let us begin with Jesus' first indication of His Father's love—the highest commandment. The three Synoptic Gospels attest that Jesus elevated love/charity to the highest commandment, which, as noted above, was unique in the history of religions (Mt 22:38–39; Mk 12:30–31; Lk 10:26–27). Matthew's Gospel points to the implications of Jesus' elevation of the commandment of love to this highest status—"On these two commandments depend all the law and the prophets" (Mt 22:40).

At first glance, this passage seems to be restricted to the centrality of the commandment to love, without saying anything about God. However, it should be noted that the rabbis taught that the law was a reflection of the heart, wisdom, and moral will of Yahweh.[48] When we combine this well-known rabbinical teaching with Matthew's observation that the entire law and prophets depend on the love of God and neighbor, we can see the implication for Matthew's audience: the commandment to love reflects the heart of God—or more precisely, the commandment to love is the best approximation we have to the heart and moral will of Yahweh. This implication may be summed up in Saint John's simple phrase "God is love" (1 Jn 4:8).

We now turn to Jesus' second and most pronounced illustration of His Father's unconditional love: the father of the prodigal son (see the parable in Lk 15:11–32). In Chapter 7 (Section I) of this volume, we give a more extended explanation of this parable, but because of its importance to Jesus' revelation of the highest virtue of love, we will provide a summary of it here. In sum, Jesus uses the parable to illustrate the heart of His Father, who is represented by the father in the parable. Jesus sets up the parable so that the younger son will have violated every major precept of goodness and righteousness in first-century Judaism. The younger son first betrays and shames his father and older brother by asking for his share of the inheritance before the proper time, then betrays and shames his country and election by going to the land of the Gentiles. He then betrays and shames God and the Torah by spending all the money on dissolute living, and finally finds himself on a Gentile farm tending the pigs, making him ritually impure. The son's sins were so egregious that his father had every right to disown him formally and reject him.

After experiencing the pain and wont of his condition, he hopes to obtain some mercy from his father by reducing himself to a household slave. No doubt Jesus' audience thought that this mercy would have been undeserved, and that total rejection by the father would be a just and fitting penalty; however, this is not what happens. The father (representing God) sees the boy coming from a distance, rushes out to meet him, and in a state of joy, throws his arms around him, and kisses him. He tells the servants to get a cloak (normally reserved for

---

[48] See McKenzie, *Dictionary of the Bible*, pp. 498–99.

aristocracy) and put it on him, essentially saying, "Treat my son like royalty." He then tells the servants to give him sandals, moving him from the status of a slave (who were barefoot) to a free man. Then he tells the servants to give him a ring that men wore to identify their familial lineage (like a signet ring with a coat of arms). By doing this, he pledges to his son that he now belongs to the family as a full-fledged member, without any conditions, and then kills the expensive fatted calf for a family celebration—such was his joy and love.

This parable is Jesus' consummate revelation of His Father's unconditional love, because the father in the parable was justified in disowning his son for so many breaches of loyalty, respect, goodness, and love. At the very least, the father could have established several onerous conditions for his son's return—but he did not. Instead, he lavishes everything he has as well as full family membership on the boy to bring him back into the household *unconditionally*. If you are a Christian, this is *your* God.

We now move to Jesus' third major indication of His Father's unconditional love—the name "Abba". In Semitic culture, a name signifies the heart or essence of the person named—as Jesus' name for Peter, "rock", or the Father's name for Jesus, "Beloved One". The name "Abba" (to this very day) is a child's name for his father, similar to "daddy" or "papa". It implies affection, gentleness, trustworthiness, and care of a father.[49] Using this very affectionate and familiar name for God—who is considered the master of the universe, the all-powerful one, the holy one, and the majestic and glorious one deserving of all praise and honor—is *truly extraordinary*, so much so that it is virtually unique to Jesus in the whole of Old Testament and intertestamental literature.[50] Why did Jesus use what would have been considered a presumptuous and even disrespectfully familiar name for His beloved Father? It was certainly not apologetically appealing to the religious authorities and pious Jews. So why did He teach His apostles to use this address? The obvious answer seems to be that He knew it to be *true*. This affectionate

---

[49] See McKenzie, *Dictionary of the Bible*, p. 1.

[50] Joachim Jeremias thought it was completely unique to Jesus (see Joachim Jeremias, *New Testament Theology* [London: SCM Press, 1971], 1:64–65). However, N. T. Wright has noted a few rare exceptions (see N. T. Wright, *Jesus and the Victory of God* [Minneapolis: Fortress Press, 1996], p. 649).

familiar name characterizes His Father's heart and essence—fatherly, trustworthy, and affectionate love.

When we examine the above three remarkable testimonies to the unconditional, affectionate, compassionate, and merciful Father, it is not surprising to read Saint Paul's characterization of that love, which he discovers through the risen Jesus:

> If God is for us, who is against us? He who did not spare his own Son but gave him up for us all, will he not also give us all things with him? Who shall bring any charge against God's elect? It is God who justifies; who is to condemn? Is it Christ Jesus, who died, yes, who was raised from the dead, who is at the right hand of God, who indeed intercedes for us? Who shall separate us from the love of Christ? Shall tribulation, or distress, or persecution, or famine, or nakedness, or peril, or sword? ... No, in all these things we are more than conquerors through him who loved us. For I am sure that neither death, nor life, nor angels, nor principalities, nor things present, nor things to come, nor powers, nor height, nor depth, nor anything else in all creation, will be able to separate us from the love of God in Christ Jesus our Lord. (Rom 8:31–35, 37–39)

Saint John emphasizes the same unconditional love of the Father, which is consummately manifest in His sending His only Beloved Son into the world to give Himself totally to us so that we might be redeemed:

> For God so loved the world that he gave his only-begotten Son, that whoever believes in him should not perish but have eternal life. For God sent the Son into the world, not to condemn the world, but that the world might be saved through him. (3:16–17)

Saint John recounts further that Jesus taught that the Father loves us as He loves His own Son (i.e., unconditionally). In His priestly prayer, Jesus says:

> [Father, I pray] that the world may know that you have sent me and have loved them [the apostles] even as you have loved me. (17:23)

There is no greater testimony to the Father's unconditional love than this.

3. Jesus' Demonstration of His Love for Sinners, the Sick, and the Poor

Jesus' unconditionally loving heart is powerfully manifest in His genuine care for sinners, the sick, and the poor. Jesus clearly intended His disciples to imitate His heart of compassion and to teach others to do so: "Love one another as I have loved you" (Jn 15:12). As we consider first Jesus' love of sinners, then His love of the sick, and finally, the poor, we may want to bring these reflections to our contemplative prayer so that we will be similarly moved to compassion and charitable love.

Jesus' love of sinners. There can be no doubt that much of Jesus' ministry was devoted to the healing and restoration (i.e., love) of sinners. As explained in Volume III (Chapter 3, Section II.C) of the Quartet, sinners were held in contempt and disgust not only by the Jewish religious authorities, but also by pious Jews who believed that sinners would get their just desserts at the time of judgment. Serious sinners (e.g., tax collectors) were not only rejected, but also treated like lepers by "more righteous" believers. As such, they were considered to be unlovable by God and the "righteous".

Jesus was well aware of what these groups were thinking, and knew that sinners had no possibility of justifying themselves or their conduct before God and others—but He did not reject them. Instead, He probed deeply into their hearts to find what goodness and piety there might be; and when He found it, moved with compassion, as in the case of Zacchaeus (Lk 19:1–10), He reached out to them in whatever way He could to get their attention. Beyond reaching out, Jesus counterculturally and counterreligiously went to their homes, enjoyed table fellowship with them (treating them like family) and ardently defended them against attacks from the religious authorities. His first tactic was to restore their dignity in public (even at the risk of being disdained by that same public), then to enter into close friendship with them to gain their trust, and finally, if they were willing, to forgive them, exorcise them, and heal them. Instead of treating them as "unlovables", He did the opposite—not only recognizing their lovability (amid their sinfulness), but doing everything possible, within the bounds of their freedom, to heal them and restore them to the fullness of spiritual health and justification before God.

Jesus did this at great personal and social cost to Himself, for it earned Him the contempt and disdain of the religious authorities, whose anger Jesus knew would one day lead to not only rejection, but persecution and death. Why did He make such sacrifices for these most marginalized and rejected of Jewish society? For one principal reason: He did not want one single intrinsically precious individual to be lost because of a false belief that God did not love or care about him. Seeing Himself as the voice of His Father, He lavishes the very care He knew His Father would give in order to bring them into the fullness of dignity, life, and eternal salvation. This motive alone made His sacrifice completely worthwhile, for if only one of these "least ones" turned to the Lord in repentance, there would be more joy, not only in His heart, but also in the whole Kingdom of Heaven, than if ninety-nine righteous people had entered by a less aberrant route (see Lk 15:4–5). If this is not enough evidence of the unconditionally loving heart of Jesus and His Father, what is? As we shall see, Jesus' Passion and death are the ultimate proof.

Jesus' love of the sick and spiritually distraught. The Gospel narratives are filled with brief descriptions of Jesus' healings, exorcisms, and raisings of the dead. Many of these narratives do not attempt to describe Jesus' interior state. However, three narratives break with their usual brief style to describe Jesus' disposition of heart—the healing of Bartimaeus, the blind beggar (Mk 10:46–52); the raising of the widow of Nain's son (Lk 7:11–17); and the raising of Lazarus (Jn 11:1–44). As we consider each, we discover not only Jesus' compassion for these individuals, but also His heart of compassion for us in our physical, emotional, and spiritual need. Please know that if we are not healed during our worldly life from these infirmities, it is for a good reason, affecting our or others' salvation, and that we will be completely healed and transformed when we are brought into His Resurrection.

Let us consider the first narrative—that of Bartimaeus, the blind beggar (Mk 10:46–52). In this narrative, we are presented with a scene in which Jesus attracts a large crowd as He enters into Jericho. A blind man on the side of the road, Bartimaeus, whom few respect because of his infirmity, discovers that Jesus is passing by. He has heard about Jesus' healing power, and uses an ancient Jewish term of respect, "Son of David" (Mk 10:47–48), to cry out to Jesus, asking Him to have pity on him. People in the crowd rebuke him and tell him to be quiet, while others barely notice him—*but Jesus hears his pleading*, which causes Him to stop. Much to the surprise of the crowd, Jesus asks that this seemingly insignificant invalid be given special attention, and be brought to Him. The crowd changes their attitude and tells him to "take heart; rise, he is calling you" (Mk 10:49). Jesus asks Bartimaeus what He can do for him, and using another Jewish term of respect, he says, "Master, let me receive my sight" (Mk 10:51). When Jesus sees Bartimaeus' belief, He has compassion on him, and heals him with these words, "Go your way; *your* faith has made you well" (Mk 10:52; italics added). Bartimaeus cannot help himself—he follows Jesus and His disciples.

Let us now turn to Jesus before the widow of Nain (Lk 7:11–17). We are here presented with Jesus coming into a very small (and insignificant) town with a large group of disciples. Coming out of the town gate is a funeral party with a young man on a bier who is the only son of his widowed mother. Jesus sees the scene and intuits the tragic turn of events in this woman's life. He recognizes her anguish at the loss of her son, and realizes that without the support of her son she is probably destined for a life of abject poverty. The woman is weeping, and once again, Jesus cannot help Himself. The story specifies that Jesus is moved by a visceral sense of compassion (*esplagchnisthē*, the same word used by Jesus in the Parable of the Good Samaritan—see below, Section II.B.6). This Greek word signifies "feelings of sympathy originating in the bowels, which were thought to be the seat of love and pity". Hence, it implies a deep movement of the heart (the seat of noble affections), which can cause interior emotional pain from sympathy.[51] He asks the woman to stop weeping because He intends to put an end to her pain by raising her son to life. Jesus touches the bier, and the bearers stop. Jesus does not touch the young man, but instead raises him by His authoritative word: "Young man, *I say* to you, arise" (Lk 7:14). Jesus then gives the young man back to his mother.

Finally, we turn to the passage of the raising of Lazarus, which probes deeply into the heart of Jesus. John gives such profound and deep consideration of Jesus' emotional state that it might be best to let the passage speak for itself. An abridged version will bring to light the heart and love of Jesus:

---

[51] See *Strong's Exhaustive Concordance Online*, s.v. "4697: splagchnizomai", BibleHub.com, 2020, https://biblehub.com/greek/4697.htm.

Now a certain man was ill, Laz´arus of Bethany.... [Lazarus'] sisters sent
to [Jesus], saying, "Lord, he whom you love is ill." ... Now Jesus loved
Martha and her sister and Laz´arus.... Now when Jesus came, he found
that Laz´arus had already been in the tomb four days.... When Martha
heard that Jesus was coming, she went and met him, while Mary sat
in the house. Martha said to Jesus, "Lord, if you had been here, my
brother would not have died. And even now I know that whatever you
ask from God, God will give you." Jesus said to her, "Your brother will
rise again...." She went and called her sister Mary, saying quietly, "The
Teacher is here and is calling for you." And when she heard it, she rose
quickly and went to him.... Then Mary, when she came where Jesus
was and saw him, fell at his feet, saying to him, "Lord, if you had been
here, my brother would not have died." When Jesus saw her weeping,
and the Jews who came with her also weeping, he was deeply moved
in spirit and troubled; and he said, "Where have you laid him?" They
said to him, "Lord, come and see." Jesus wept. So the Jews said, "See
how he loved him!" ... Then Jesus, deeply moved again, came to the
tomb; it was a cave, and a stone lay upon it. Jesus said, "Take away
the stone." ... So they took away the stone.... He cried with a loud
voice, "Laz´arus, come out." The dead man came out, his hands and
feet bound with bandages, and his face wrapped with a cloth. Jesus
said to them, "Unbind him, and let him go". (11:1, 3, 5, 17, 20–23,
28–29, 32–36, 38–39, 41, 43–44)

As can be seen from these three passages, Jesus very much heard
the cry of those in need and felt profound compassion for them—
even to the point of tears. Seeing their vulnerability, their need, and
their unique lovability, He found them irresistible, which moved
Him to heal them. At this point His deeds of power became deeds of
unconditional love, revealing that in God, love and power are one
and the same.

Jesus' love of the poor. Jesus also loved another marginalized group
in Jewish society—the poor. Whereas wealth was frequently seen as a
sign of God's favor, poverty was interpreted as "pointless suffering",
frequently indicating lack of favor from God.[52] Jesus not only reaches
out to the poor, but strongly implies that their poverty is not a sign
of disfavor from God, but rather an undeserved condition that, if not
remedied on earth, will be healed and rewarded in Heaven:

---

[52] See Ronald Eisenberg, *What the Rabbis Said: 250 Topics from the Talmud* (Santa Barbara,
Calif.: ABC-CLIO, 2010), pp. 20, 139–43.

Blessed are you poor, for yours is the kingdom of God. Blessed are you that hunger now, for you shall be satisfied. Blessed are you that weep now, for you shall laugh. (Lk 6:20–21)

Jesus feels the plight of the poor in precisely the same way He describes the Good Samaritan's feelings as He gazes upon the beaten and robbed Jewish enemy of His people—with deep compassion (see below, Section II.B.6).

Jesus felt that the salvation of the poor and the alleviation of their suffering was integral to the Kingdom of God, and promised that the consolation of the poor will come when the Kingdom of God is fully realized. He did not expect the suffering of the poor to be completely alleviated until His Kingdom was fully actualized. He encouraged His disciples to imitate His example and help the poor in their midst, particularly by giving alms to them (see Mt 5:42; 19:21; Lk 11:41).[53] In carrying out this key responsibility, Christians actualize His Kingdom in the present moment. Those who help the hungry, thirsty, stranger, naked, sick, and imprisoned will also "inherit the kingdom prepared for [them] from the foundation of the world" (Mt 25:34). Jesus also teaches that those who have no sympathy or compassion for the poor and marginalized must change their hearts lest they jeopardize their salvation (see Mt 25:41–46; Lk 16:19–31).

Once again, we see Jesus seeking out the marginalized and rejected, showing them compassion while elevating their dignity to that of His own (see Mt 25:40, 45). In so doing, He reveals His unconditional love for us, particularly in our need. Since He calls us to be like Him in this love, He asks that we form our own hearts through the power of His Spirit to reflect that same compassion, for it will lead to the fullness of joy in His presence (see Jn 15:9–13).

4. Jesus' Demonstration of His Unconditional Love in the Total Self-Sacrifice of His Passion

The enormity of the Passion and death of the Son of God cannot be exaggerated; for there can be no greater manifestation of love than for the Son of God to enter into a restricted nature and give Himself

---

[53] Jesus' command to alleviate the plight of the poor through service and almsgiving is taken up by all New Testament epistle writers. See, for example, 2 Cor 9:5–7, esp. v. 7; 1 Tim 6:18; Heb 13:16; 1 Jn 3:17.

completely—not only in death, but in extended torture, insult, abandonment, and rejection. In Jesus' mind and heart, this total self-sacrificial act was a consummate gift of self by God—that is, an unrestricted actualization of love that would become an unrestricted font of grace for the forgiveness of sins, the healing of hearts, and the overcoming of darkness and evil. By undergoing this consummate self-sacrifice as the divine Son of the Father, Jesus intended to actualize an infinite act of love in the world that would remain until the end of time to redeem all sins, defeat evil, initiate the Mystical Body of the Church, and nourish us through the Holy Eucharist. How do we know that Jesus intended this?

In Volume III (Chapter 3, Section IV) of the Quartet, we explained Jesus' choice of Psalm 22 for His final words to the Father and the world when He was on the Cross. The first line of that psalm, "My God, my God, why have you forsaken me?" (Mt 27:46; Mk 15:34; quoting Ps 21), cannot be interpreted independently of the psalm from which it was derived. In the first century, it was customary to refer to the *whole psalm* by its first line. Note that this psalm is not a psalm of abandonment, but of *trust in God*, and that it vividly describes a scene of torture and rejection very similar to what Jesus experienced more than five hundred years after the psalm's writing. The final stanzas of the psalm reveal the reason why the innocent man is unjustly undergoing this torture. He is transforming it into an act of self-sacrifice that will become the vehicle (the font of grace) to redeem not only the Jewish people, but also the Gentile peoples—not only in His generation, but in all past and future generations.

We also see this very same intention reflected in the Fourth Suffering Servant Song of Isaiah (Is 52:13—53:12), which Jesus explicitly refers to in His Eucharistic words "poured out for [the] many for the forgiveness of sins" (Mt 26:28).[54] This Suffering Servant Song, like

---

[54] Compare Is 53:12: "He *poured out his soul to death*, and was numbered with the transgressors; yet he *bore the sin of [the] many*, and made intercession for the transgressors" (italics added), with Mt 26:28—"This is my blood of the covenant, which is poured out for [the] many for the forgiveness of sins." Note that the strange expression "the many" (*to pollōn*), which is a literal Greek rendition of the Hebrew word for "all", occurs in both Isaiah 53:12 and Matthew 26:28. In view of the fact that the Mark-Matthew version of Jesus' Eucharistic words is more original than the Luke-Paul version (indicating closeness to Jesus' own words), it is quite likely that Jesus had Isaiah's Fourth Suffering Servant Song in mind when He was uttering His Eucharistic words. See Joachim Jeremias, *The Eucharistic Words of Jesus* (London: SCM Press, 1966), pp. 179–81.

Psalm 22, also speaks of an innocent victim who pours himself out through torture and death as a total self-sacrifice for the universal forgiveness of sins.[55] Furthermore, the Eucharistic words themselves also indicate Jesus' intention to use His forthcoming self-sacrifice on the Cross as the vehicle through which the sins of mankind would be forgiven.

When we put these references in the context of Jesus' declaration that "greater love has no man than this, that a man lay down his life for his friends" (Jn 15:13), it is difficult to deny that Jesus intended to create an unconditional and unrestricted gift of love through His complete self-sacrifice that would last to the end of time for the forgiveness of the sins of everyone who would accept it.

It is difficult for us to imagine that the Son of God would allow Himself to be sacrificed (like an animal) as a sin offering for all mankind for all time. Some of us may be inclined to think that He really didn't need to go that far—He could have found a "less extreme" way. Some of us might think that Jesus' self-sacrifice is simply too good to be true. These statements, however, do not reflect the intentions of an unconditionally and unrestrictedly loving God who would not do anything less than save us through an *unconditionally* and *unrestrictedly* loving act that entailed *complete* self-sacrifice. If God truly is *unconditionally* and *unrestrictedly* loving, then this is precisely what He would do to redeem us—nothing less. When Jesus sacrificed Himself completely, His action screamed out from the Cross, "I and my Father are unconditional and unrestricted love—and here is the proof! Place your faith in us!" When we see this act of unconditional and unrestricted love in light of Jesus' Resurrection, gift of the Spirit, and miracles (for which there is considerable scientific and historical evidence [see above, Section II.A]), we come face-to-face with the ultimate ground of hope for our salvation, face-to-face with the unconditionally and unrestrictedly loving God who saves us. Now we must make a decision: to put our faith in Him or not. If we put our faith in Him, then we must trust not only in His unconditional salvific intent but also in His words about *following Him*, not only in the way of compassion,

[55] As indicated in the previous note, *to pollōn* is very probably a Semitism (a literal Greek translation of a Hebrew or Aramaic expression, which almost never occurs in common Greek parlance). This means that it should be translated as "all" (the definite article [the prefix "he"] plus *Rabbim*). See Jeremias, *Eucharistic Words of Jesus*, pp. 179–81.

but even in taking up our cross. Jesus did not say that it would be easy to have faith. Rather, He indicated that it would entail challenge, purification, and the cross, but if we place our trust in Him, and try to stay on the path of His teaching through the Church, we will be purified in love, and be united with Him forever. The rest of this chapter will be devoted to exploring what it means to follow Jesus in this way of *agapē* (love/charity).

B. How Love Counters the Eight Deadly Sins

From the above description of Jesus' teaching on love, we can discern eight integral elements, which I call "subvirtues", that help to counter the eight deadly sins:

1. Contributive and Transcendent Identity (Section II.B.1).
2. Gratitude (Section II.B.2)
3. Respect and Care for Others and Their Salvation (Section II.B.3)
4. Humble-Heartedness (Section II.B.4)
5. Gentle-Heartedness (Section II.B.5)
6. Compassion (Section II.B.6)
7. Forgiveness (Section II.B.7)
8. Chastity and Covenant Romantic Love (Section II.B.8)

The following table outlines those subvirtues and the deadly sins they counter. Six of the deadly sins are primarily countered by love's subvirtues, while two of the deadly sins (gluttony and sloth) are countered primarily by two of the cardinal virtues (temperance and fortitude; discussed above in Sections I.C and I.B, respectively). Irrespective of which subvirtues are primary, it should be noted that love's subvirtues are complemented by the four cardinal virtues, and the cardinal virtues, in turn, by love's subvirtues. As noted in Chapters 1–3, the theological virtue of faith sustains and enhances love through the gifts of the Holy Spirit and the Church. Likewise, the theological virtue of hope focuses us on our salvation as well as the mercy of God (in times of failing) as we endeavor to progress along the difficult road to appropriate virtue and deepen moral conversion.

Eight Deadly Sins	Counteracting Virtues
Gluttony	Temperance and prudence
Greed	Contributive and transcendental identity and gratitude
Lust	Chastity, respect and care for others, and temperance
Sloth	Prudence, fortitude, and contributive-transcendental identity
Vanity	Contributive-transcendental identity, humble-heartedness, respect and care for others
Anger	Forgiveness, compassion, and gentle-heartedness
Envy	Gratitude, justice, and compassion
Pride	Humble-heartedness, justice, and compassion

The explanation of the eight subvirtues of love comes not only from Jesus' teaching and actions, but also from centuries of Christian reflection and action. I have tried to summarize below this rich tradition and complement it with insights from contemporary philosophy and psychology. We will now consider each subvirtue in turn.

1. Contributive and Transcendent Identity

In Appendix I, we briefly summarize Volume I of the Quartet, by providing a summary of the four levels of happiness. Readers who are not familiar with this material will want to read Appendix I before proceeding to the rest of this chapter, because it gives a self-motivating rationale for why one should move from the dominant identity of this culture (Level One, materialistic-sensual, and Level Two, ego-comparative) to the dominant identity taught by Jesus (Level Three, contributive-love, and Level Four, transcendent-faith). This will help readers to build a solid foundation for the seven other subvirtues discussed below, the first of which is forming a dominant identity grounded in contributive-love (Level Three) and transcendent-faith (Level Four).

As noted above, these two identity fulcrums lie at the foundation of the other seven subvirtues, and therefore at the foundation of Christian moral life and resistance to the deadly sins. As noted in

Appendix I, contributive identity is not enough for Christian love/ charity, because this virtue requires a relationship with God that opens upon a host of experiences, inspirations, revelations, and graces that enable us to love in imitation of Jesus Christ—a love that is unattainable without help from Him, His Father, and the Holy Spirit. If we are solid in our choice to move beyond ego-comparative identity through contribution and faith, and are reasonably convinced by the significant evidence for God, our soul, and Jesus as Emmanuel (intellectual conversion), and moved in our hearts by the words and actions of Jesus, and the inspirations of the Holy Spirit (spiritual conversion), then we will be in a position to pursue the following seven subvirtues of Christian love (Sections II.B.2–II.B.8), and through them the life of Christian virtue (moral conversion). This conversion into the love of Christ not only protects us from the darkness and death of the deadly sins, but also liberates our hearts to become like Jesus' heart and to experience His unrestricted joy in the Kingdom of Heaven. As He promised: "These things I have spoken to you, that my joy may be in you, and that your joy may be full. This is my commandment, that you love one another as I have loved you" (Jn 15:11–12).

The motivation for contributive and transcendental identity is within us, for we have an in-built desire to make an optimal positive difference with our lives (see Volume I, Chapters 1–4, of the Quartet), an in-built desire for the five transcendental perfections (see Volume II, Chapter 4, of the Quartet), and an invitation from God to be in relationship with Him through the numinous experience, the intuition of the sacred, and conscience (see Volume II, Chapters 1–2, of the Quartet). These desires and God's interior invitation to us are subtle; yet, if we fail to act on them, they will awaken within us a profound sense of emptiness, loneliness, and alienation (on both a human and cosmic level).

When we combine this interior call with the considerable contemporary scientific, logical, and empirical evidence for God, the soul, and Jesus given in Volumes I–III of the Quartet (summarized in the introduction to this volume), we can appreciate the very probative rational and intuitive foundation that the Lord has given us to secure our journey into the heart of love and gratitude.

As if this were not enough, He has also provided us with His Son to give us the concrete example of how to pursue this contributive and transcendental identity (see above, Section II.A.1–4). This gift has many dimensions—Jesus' words, His actions of self-sacrificial love, and His Holy Spirit to guide us interiorly in that love. Without these words, examples, and graces (given through the Holy Spirit) we would be left in a state of radical incompleteness in our pursuit of highest purpose and identity. Yet, with this supremely and unconditionally loving act of God, we have not only the awareness of how to pursue this highest purpose and identity, but also the spirit to help us and the unrestricted mercy of Christ to restore us when we fail. Provided with all of this, we are given the realistic hope and grace to enter into eternal and unrestricted love and joy in the Kingdom of Heaven.

Beyond this, Jesus gave us one more gift—the Church under the leadership of Saint Peter and his successors to guide and support us in our relationship with Him and to help us build a moral life (see Chapters 1–3 of this volume). The following seven subvirtues of love explain the ideal to which Jesus was calling us—the ideal built upon our contributive and transcendental identity, the ideal that will be our joy in Heaven.

2. Gratitude

Gratitude is the key not only to virtue, but also to happiness and prayer. There is an old expression that asserts the correlation between gratitude and happiness: "I never knew a person who was grateful and unhappy, or a person who was ungrateful and happy." The grateful person who takes nothing for granted sees his life as a blessing from God and others—undisturbed by issues of comparative disadvantage. However, the ungrateful person is continually beset by what he doesn't have, consumed by resentment, anger, and envy. The former cannot help but be happy, while the latter consigns himself and others around him to misery. Much of human happiness and generosity flows naturally out of gratitude to God and others, and so much of human misery and vice (particularly anger and envy) flows out of the ungrateful person's resentment.

We discussed in Chapter 2 (Section II.D.2.a) how looking for the good news in the other leads naturally to empathy, and how empathy leads naturally to contributive and even self-sacrificial love. The same starting point leads naturally to gratitude. If we look for the good news in others, we will be moved to gratitude for them; and if we look for the good news in our lives—for example, the gifts we have, the opportunities we have been given, and the times we have averted problems—we will be moved to gratitude to God and the people who provided these benefits. Looking for the good news helps us in another important way: it contextualizes and mitigates our vision of the bad news in life, and so mitigates resentment, anger, envy, depression, and inferiority.

It might be thought that intentionally focusing on the good news in life is a naïvely optimistic ("Pollyanna") view of life, and that we should have the guts and realism to look straightforwardly at all the bad news around us. But this "naïve" view of life is based on a false sense of realism that assumes that bad news is more real or more important than good news. I had a friend once who expressed this philosophy perfectly: "Bob, you're an optimist but I am a pessimist; you'll be happier than me, but I'll be right more often." True, he was more distrustful, suspicious, and critical—and far less hopeful than I was—but amid all of that, he was not right more often. Indeed, his suspicious worldview lost him many opportunities in life as well as good relationships with people he could not bring himself to trust. Regrettably, he grew increasingly frustrated when I was right more often. The optimistic or pessimistic lens we bring to the world forges very different paths through the "real world" like self-fulfilling prophesies. If we have a positive view of life, others, and the world, and see positivity in the future before us, we will follow the path to which those positive apperceptions lead us. The same holds true for emphasizing the negative in life, which causes us to focus on all the pitfalls and threats we will want to avoid. This prompts us to forge a future path around potential obstacles instead of a path toward a positive goal. The frequent result is that the pessimist has a far less efficacious, other-centered, and happy life than the optimist.[56]

Of course, optimists cannot afford to be unrealistic. They have to be conscious and even calculating about the obstacles they are likely

[56] See Martin Seligman, *Learned Optimism: How to Change Your Mind and Your Life* (New York: Vintage Books, 1990), pp. 3–16, 95–115, 185–204.

to encounter, and factor these into their plans and goals. Yet, optimists do not accentuate or exaggerate these problems, because they have an intuitive awareness that their goals are worthy and achievable— worthy enough to make the effort to overcome the obstacles toward them. Moreover, if they have faith, and sense the inspiration of the Holy Spirit toward these goals, they have great assurance that they will reach them if they proceed prudently (see above, Section I.A). This fundamental belief enables optimists (particularly optimists with faith) to move naturally toward their goals, to derive energy from the potential to actualize them, to convince others to work with them toward these goals, and to summon the energy and courage to overcome even unanticipated obstacles. As Martin Seligman notes, most of us are not brought into the world as realistic optimists; we have to learn this discipline and stick to it.[57] Now if we can learn the art and discipline of realistic optimism (particularly optimism inspired by the Holy Spirit), then we can also learn the art and discipline of realistically looking at and for the good news in our life. This is the first step toward a life of gratitude.

The second step in cultivating gratitude is another dimension of realism: the rejection of entitlement and the expectation of perfect fairness. Though we live in a culture and society of privilege, we cannot afford to use this uncritically to justify these expectations. In Heaven, we might expect perfect fairness, but we live in a world in which we will have to form our purpose and identity by our free choices. This means that some people with whom we live will make poor choices that lead to inequities and suffering. Moreover, the imperfections of the natural world that bring about inequities and suffering can be of great service to help us choose ideals, principles, purpose, and identity that will lead to greater equity, fairness, goodness, and love within the world (see Volume IV, Chapter 10, of the Quartet). Thus, the expectation of perfect fairness in this world is erroneous because it assumes that *we* can participate in a world of perfect fairness without any preparation or choices that would enable *us* to be perfectly fair. If we are to be able to participate in a perfectly fair world, then we and others must have the capacity to be perfectly fair, and this will require moving beyond

[57] Ibid.

egocentricity and the eight deadly sins it engenders. This requires a lifetime of vulnerability, learning from mistakes, acts of contrition, getting on the pathway to justice and love, as well as the mercy and grace of God. And so the freedom with which we have been created necessarily consigns us to live in an imperfect world with other human agents who will likely misuse their freedom along with us. This means living in a world of imperfect fairness. We should expect this in a realistic worldview.

The belief in entitlement is likewise unrealistic, for it not only expects perfect fairness in this world, but assumes that we deserve perfect fairness. The falsity and presumptuousness of this belief is revealed by the above reflection on the need for a world of imperfect fairness to develop the capacity to live in a world of perfect fairness. How can we deserve to live in a perfectly fair world if we are incapable of being perfectly fair? In order to deserve perfect fairness, we would at the very least have to be capable of being perfectly fair ourselves. Yet, this is clearly never the case. If we are to get beyond our egocentricity, we need the help of God and others—and we are dependent on countless gifts of forgiveness, mercy, healing, contribution, and love to sustain us on our journey. Can anyone realistically say he deserves perfect fairness? Those who make such a claim would demonstrate a hypocritical and egocentric self-assessment, revealing their incapacity to be perfectly fair and therefore to participate in a perfectly fair world.

The third step in cultivating gratitude is the recognition that our lives are not necessary, but rather a gift—a pure gift of the Creator. In Volume II of the Quartet, we gave eight kinds of evidence, including quite probative medical studies of near-death experiences, to show that each one of us has a unique transphysical soul capable of surviving bodily death. This evidence strongly implies that a transphysical cause (i.e., God) has created this unique soul. Why would He do so? We might infer from our five transcendental desires (see Volume II, Chapter 4, of the Quartet) that His purpose was to fulfill those desires completely and eternally through our unique acts of self-consciousness and freedom. Furthermore, as we saw in the same chapter, God alone can satisfy our desires for perfect truth, love, goodness, beauty, and home, because He is the one reality through whom these attributes can exist perfectly. As Saint Augustine noted while praying to God, "For thou hast made us for Thyself, and our hearts are restless until they rest in Thee."[58]

What does this mean? It means that not only our existence is a pure gift of the Creator, but also our transphysical soul, our five transcendental desires, and the eternal fulfillment of those five transcendental desires by God Himself. God did not have to create any of these things but He did so as a pure gift—to us—to share His very self with us. Why would He do this? Certainly not to reduce us to indentured servitude or unhappiness. If that were His intention, He would not have created us with our five transcendental desires capable of being satisfied only by Him. So why did He create us? He did so to fulfill those five transcendental desires which would bring us into complete union with Him in perfect love and joy. He does this through our acts of consent and free choice, and so He creates us in this imperfect world with other human agents capable of causing us suffering so that the collective human community can freely choose this loving communion with Him and others (with the help of His grace). We might infer from this not only that the Creator is a pure giver, but also that our lives and souls are His sublime gift to us. If we choose to love Him and others—transcending our egocentricity—He further intends to give Himself to us in loving fulfillment forever.

The affirmation of the above inferences constitutes the third step in cultivating gratitude. The fourth step is really quite simple—to allow ourselves to move toward our natural response, the exclamation "Thank you!"

These four steps for cultivating gratitude need not be daunting. If we allow our natural capacity for empathy and love to supersede egocentricity in even a minimal way (i.e., choosing Level Three, a contributive identity), and we allow the evidence for our transphysical soul and transcendental desires to solidify our interior awareness of the sacred spiritual mystery within us (i.e., choosing Level Four, a transcendental identity), then the above four steps of gratitude will almost naturally follow. Now let's review them:

1. Looking at and for the good news in our lives, others, and in the world around us

---

[58] Saint Augustine, *Confessions* I, I.

2. Rejecting belief in entitlement and the right to live in a world of perfect fairness
3. Affirming that our lives, souls, and the fulfillment of our souls are the pure gift of God out of love for us
4. To respond from the heart—"Thank you!"

When we sincerely thank the Lord for all that we have and are, and maintain that attitude of sincere gratitude, we no longer take everything for granted, but see everything as gift. This catalyzes and enhances a natural instinct that has its roots in our childhood—the recognition that our parents, like God, did not have to give us good things, or even give us existence; that our family members and friends did not always have to treat us kindly, encourage us, and help us beyond the proverbial call of duty; and that our parents and teachers did not have to forgive us countless times for misbehavior of every sort. They did so because they loved us; they were giving themselves to us, and this often incites the natural response—"Thank you!"

When Jesus gave us the highest commandment to love, He showed the complementarity of love of God and love of neighbor, implying that an increase in love of God would open the way to an increase in love of neighbor, and vice versa. The same holds true for gratitude. An increase in our gratitude to God opens the way to an increase in gratitude to others, and vice versa. When we are amazed by God's love and goodness (no longer taking it for granted, but seeing it as pure gift), it opens the way to recognize the gratuity of others' gifts of friendship, kindness, support, encouragement, and self-sacrifice. When we dispel the fog of taking these gifts for granted, it is almost breathtaking—looking at the sheer outpouring of gifts and self-sacrifice out of love for us. When we get to the point of appreciation and gratitude for purely gratuitous love from God and others, we frequently have the natural reaction to love them in return. As most of us know, the sincere exclamation "Thank you!" is another way of saying, "I love you!" and it is the key to the other six subvirtues of love (given below) as well as the key to Christian spiritual life.

As most Christian saints have recognized, gratitude is the catalyst for deepening our spiritual life (our relationship with God). When we realize the pure gift that we are (our unique transphysical soul, our five transcendental desires, and the perfect and eternal fulfillment of those desires to which we are called), the gratuitous love standing behind the creation and beauty of the world around us, and the gratuitous unconditional love of the Incarnation, ministry, Passion, and Resurrection of the Son of God, Jesus, we cannot help ourselves—we are naturally moved to give God thanks and praise, and to express our love to Him for everything He has freely and gratuitously given us. As we shall see, imitation of this love is not only the sincerest form of flattery; it is also the sincerest way in which to express our love to Him. As Ignatius of Loyola continuously noted, love is expressed more sincerely in actions than in words, and the sincerest of actions is the imitation of the Beloved who has loved us first.[59] As will be shown below, the sincere desire to imitate the heart of Christ—the Beloved who has loved us first—is the key to accepting the most difficult aspect of Jesus' way of love: the cross.

Now let us return specifically to prayer—particularly contemplative prayer (see Chapter 3, Sections III–V). When we are filled with gratitude to God for all we have and are, we become acutely aware of how the Lord has provided for us, protected us, guided us, and inspired us, which paves the way for increased trust. This trust not only dispels fear and anxiety, but also gives us the patience to wait for God's solutions to life's problems and challenges. This trust, in turn, brings peace and confidence not only into our active lives but also into our contemplative prayer. When we begin to pray the Rosary or the Breviary, we can put ourselves into the Lord's presence,

---

[59] In two of the meditations marking "Turning Points" in the *Spiritual Exercises* of Saint Ignatius Loyola—the Kingdom Meditation and the Meditation on the Two Standards—we are encouraged to imitate and follow the call of Christ the King and the standard of Christ (the way in which He expresses His love); see *The Spiritual Exercises of St. Ignatius of Loyola*, "The Twelfth Day", trans. Elder Mullan (New York: P.J. Kennedy & Sons, 1914), SacredTexts.com, http://sacred-texts.com/chr/seil/seil26.htm. In the final meditation—the Contemplation to Attain Divine Love—we are encouraged to imitate His heart of love, even unto self-sacrifice for the world. See ibid., http://sacred-texts.com/chr/seil/seil35.htm. Please note that though there are many excellent modern translations of Saint Ignatius of Loyola's *Spiritual Exercises* published, for example, the translation by George Ganss, S.J. (Chicago: Loyola Press, 1992), and the translation by Louis J. Puhl (Westminster, Md.: Newman Press, 1951), I will refer throughout to the older, but faithful, translation by Elder Mullan cited above, since it is offered online free of charge by the Internet Sacred Text Archive, where it can be readily accessed and searched by all readers at the following website: http://sacred-texts.com/chr/seil/index.htm.

decreasing the distractions about the problems that have occurred or are likely to occur in our active lives—the problems we are having with individuals or groups, and even the challenges of desolation and dryness in prayer. We can put ourselves in God's hands, tell Him to take the problems of the day or week, and ask simply to enjoy the time spent with Him and His Father.

The peace that comes with trust and gratitude also decreases resentments, jealousy, inferiority, superiority, anger, fear, and anxiety, which opens us to the direct experience of God's presence, companionship, friendship, delight, encouragement, and support. At this juncture the benefits of gratitude manifest themselves again. Recall from above that gratitude moves us to praise and love the One who has blessed us and gratuitously given us love beyond measure. Filled with peace, confidence, and gratitude, we once again cannot help ourselves—we are moved to praise Him for all that He has given us. The psalms are an ideal way of doing this, because so many of them are psalms of praise to God for His many gifts—and they are so effusive and palpable in that praise. The meditations of the Rosary are also ideal to give thanks to the Lord for the events of salvation history that have led to our redemption and the road to salvation. The peace and love coming from gratitude can even open us to other blessings and gifts for which to be grateful—such as the blessings of our families, the recent events of our life, and the friends and opportunities we have been given.

When we give praise to God or contemplate His goodness and gifts, He communicates to us. We receive insights not only into who He is and how He operates—insights into His goodness, love, and beauty—but also into His love for us. Sometimes these are *felt* insights—an experience of being loved by Him during prayer—and sometimes they are felt memories of having been loved by Him in the past. These felt insights and memories are sometimes quite subtle yet noticeably transcendent, and sometimes they are quite overwhelming, glorious, and beautiful. God also communicates by giving us words and ideas to help others. Countless have been the times when I have been working on a book or thinking about a presentation at the office, and then, when I am ready to retire at night praying my Rosary, I am suddenly filled with one idea after the next—really good ideas that I had not been thinking about before, ideas that would be helpful to listeners or readers, not just myself. I used to think that these ideas probably originated in my creative subconscious when I was in a relaxed state of mind during prayer, but I have come to conclude, after much experience, that the ideas are unrelated to my prayer and that my subconscious mind is simply not that smart or creative, leading me to the conclusion that the Lord is inspiring me through the Holy Spirit.

Are we to believe that gratitude gives rise to all of this—the desire to imitate Christ in action; the trust, peace, and praise of contemplation; and the multifold communication of God through it? Yes, this is precisely the fruit of gratitude, and the reason that it leads to the other six subvirtues of love. The saints are correct—where gratitude abounds, so also do trust, peace, praise, and love, not only our love for the Lord but also the Lord's love for us, communicated in insights, inspiration, guidance, and palpable experiences of His loving presence.[60]

Saint Ignatius had a saying that described not only Jesuit spirituality but Christian spirituality in general—we are to become contemplatives in action. We can now see why he believed that gratitude stood at the foundation of spiritual life. As noted above, gratitude stands at the foundation of active life and service, because it moves us not only to love the Lord in return for the love He has given to us, but even more importantly, to imitate His heart in our treatment of others—particularly in compassion, forgiveness, and service. Moreover, gratitude stands at the foundation of contemplation by opening the door to trust, peace, praise, and love. Thus, the fruit of gratitude is the ideal of Christian spirituality—contemplation in action, contemplation leading to the imitation of Christ in action, and loving actions leading back to increased trust, peace, and praise in contemplation.[61]

---

[60] Saint Thérèse of Lisieux sums up the wisdom of Saint Paul, Saint Benedict, Saint Augustine, Saint Francis of Assisi, Saint Dominic, Saint Thomas Aquinas, Saint Ignatius of Loyola, and Saint Teresa of Avila in a simple but powerful phrase: "With me prayer is an uplifting of the heart; a glance towards heaven; a *cry of gratitude* and love, uttered equally in sorrow and in joy. In a word, it is something noble, supernatural, which expands my soul and unites it to God." Thérèse of Lisieux, *The Story of a Soul*, ed. Thomas N. Taylor (Burns, Oates, and Washbourne, 1912; 8th ed., 1922; Project Gutenberg, 2009), Chapter 10, (italics added), http://www.gutenberg.org/cache/epub/16772/pg16772-images.html.

[61] See Joseph Conwell, *Contemplation in Action: A Study in Ignatian Prayer* (Spokane, Wash.: Gonzaga University Press, 1957).

Saint Ignatius was so convinced of the efficacy of gratitude in galvanizing contemplation in action that he formulated the Examen Prayer, which is devoted in great part to giving thanks to God for all that we have and are, the events of our daily lives, and Christ's acts of redemption. He considered this prayer to be so important that he instructed Jesuits that it should be said every day and should never be abandoned even if everything else had to be abandoned for the sake of the apostolate.[62] We will look at the prayer more closely in Chapter 6 (Section II).

3. Respect and Care for Others and Their Salvation

This subvirtue of love arises out of our natural power and desire for empathy. We can "switch on" this natural power and desire by simply looking for the good news in the other (see Chapter 2, Section II.D.2.a). When we do this we put the "bad news" within the context of the unique goodness and lovability of the other, which prevents the bad news from controlling our feelings about and relationship with the other. At the very moment we switch on empathy by looking for the good news in others, respect for them *in themselves* begins to arise naturally, and when this happens, we will not only treat them with respect, but also refrain from hurting or harming them. Furthermore, if we look for the full transcendent good news in them (Level Four), then we will also respect their eternal and transcendental dignity and destiny. As Christians, we will naturally desire not only their fulfillment in this finite, short, and sometimes painful life, but also their salvation with the God of unconditional love. This helps us not only to see the *full* nature, dignity, purpose, fulfillment, and destiny of others, but also to refrain from underestimating, undervaluing, and underappreciating their true transcendental goodness and mystery. This is the condition necessary for avoiding insult and injury.

Jesus not only preached the need for respect of others; He also practiced it unconditionally. He saw the unique goodness, lovability, and transcendent mystery in everyone He encountered—not just in His disciples and friends, but also in sinners, the sick, the possessed,

---

[62] See David L. Fleming, S.J., "Reflection and Our Active Lives", IgnatianSpirituality.com, 2020, https://www.ignatianspirituality.com/ignatian-prayer/the-examen/reflection-and-our -active-lives.

and the poor. As we saw above, sinners were disregarded by the religious authorities of Jesus' day, but Jesus did not follow this precedent. Indeed, He practiced the opposite, deliberately pursuing them, experiencing intimate friendship with them at meals, and defending them from the religious authorities. His forgiveness of Matthew (who was a tax collector—a very serious offense in first-century Judaism) is remarkable in itself; but when He calls Matthew into His closest company (the twelve apostles), then goes to his house for table fellowship with other sinners, and then defends them from the Pharisees, He introduces a whole new level of respect and care for sinners (Mt 9:9–13). The same may be evidenced in several pericopes in the Gospels of Luke and John. With respect to Luke, we see Jesus not only calling a chief tax collector—Zacchaeus—but also eating at his house (19:1–10), Jesus defending a repentant woman at the house of Simon the Pharisee (7:36–49), and even the call of a repentant thief on the cross (23:39–43). With respect to the Gospel of John, we see Jesus' defense of the Samaritan woman (4:1–42), His defense of the woman caught in adultery (8:1–11), and His forgiveness of Peter after his threefold denial (21:15–19). Why did He do this? Jesus was convinced of the intrinsic and unique goodness and lovability of *every* individual no matter what sins and mistakes they may have committed in their lives, and even if they were actively plotting against Him—even to kill Him. He still saw them as immeasurably valuable and worthy of being called into God's Kingdom. Yes, He called them to repent and reform their lives, but this did not impede His vision of their lovability and dignity.

Jesus' preaching is also focused on respect for the intrinsic and unique goodness of others. He exhorts us not to judge others, because we do not know either their goodness or the true reason for why they may have sinned (Mt 7:1–3), but to forgive others seventy times seven times—a way of signifying an innumerable number of times (Mt 18:21–22), and to love and do good for our enemies (Mt 5:43–48). He also tells us that His heavenly Father sees the goodness in others without limit or condition—as exemplified by the Father in the Parable of the Prodigal Son (Lk 15:11–32). Perhaps Jesus' most telling testimony to the inestimable value and goodness of every person is His identification with the seemingly lowliest individuals in society—not only the poor and slaves, but even prisoners (criminals):

"As you did it to one of the least of these my brethren, you did it to me" (Mt 25:40; see vv. 31–46).

Jesus asks us to conform our hearts to His own in seeing the intrinsic dignity and lovability of every individual, most especially the lowly, and even our enemies. As we noted above, this subvirtue can be cultivated by focusing on the good news in others, but it can be significantly enhanced through prayer and contemplation. The more we meditate on the example of Jesus, and the more we give thanks for the respect and love He has given to us (see above, II.B.2), the more He comes into our conscious and subconscious psyche, detaching us from egocentricity, pettiness, and vengefulness, by giving us spiritual freedom we could have hardly imagined or anticipated. The spiritual freedom coming from prayer and contemplation enhances our ability to look for the good news in others, which strengthens our empathy with them (even our enemies); this can in turn be strengthened more when we bring that empathy back to the Lord in contemplation and prayer. It is truly remarkable how these two simple disciplines can initiate a whole new kind of life filled with enhanced respect, empathy, and freedom from egocentricity. With rewards so great, and disciplines so simple, we would be remiss indeed if we did not try to actualize them through prayer to the Lord of love.

4. Humble-Heartedness

Humble-heartedness arises out of both Level Three and Level Four identity. As we saw in the previous volume (Chapter 6), it is one of the most important dimensions of love because it protects us from three of the most pernicious deadly sins—vanity, envy, and pride. Though Level Three and Four identity are conditions necessary for humble-heartedness, they are not enough—for this virtue must be specifically cultivated and prayed for. Humble-heartedness in the Christian context is the conviction that *every* individual is uniquely and equally good, worthy, lovable, and transcendent before God, who created each one with a unique transcendental and eternal soul.[63] The profound recognition that we are all equally transcendent and equally created—equally mysterious and equally lovable—provides the foundation for this conviction, for in the eyes of God none of us

---

[63] See the considerable evidence for our transcendent soul in Volume II (all chapters) of the Quartet.

is intrinsically better than another. Yes, we are transcendent creatures who are wonderfully made (Ps 139:14) in the very image and likeness of God (Gen 1:27), but we are not God, and we cannot attempt to be God for anyone, including ourselves. It is the consummate lie of the devil himself.[64]

Though levels of authority (which must be commensurate with responsibility) are needed for societal, commercial, educational, governmental, religious, and military organization, they do not indicate intrinsic superiority of one person over another, but only additional authority/responsibility in a particular social context.

Furthermore, people with higher brain functioning should not be considered superior to the developmentally disabled or those experiencing degeneration of the brain, because there is considerable evidence to show that they have a unique transphysical soul, which will not only survive bodily death,[65] but will also have high intellectual, moral, religious, aesthetic, and empathetic capacity through that soul, which is not able to be manifest through their brains. Current medical studies of a phenomenon called terminal lucidity indicate these high-functioning capacities in patients with severe atrophying of the cerebral cortex due to Alzheimer's disease, dementia, hydrocephalus, and serious mental developmental disabilities. These patients regained almost complete use of their intellectual, emotional, and spiritual functioning about one to six hours before death. This cannot be explained by their physical brain (which remained severely atrophied).[66]

---

[64] See Satan's speech in John Milton's *Paradise Lost* 1, described in Volume I, Chapter 6, of this Trilogy.

[65] See Volume II, Chapters 3 and 5, of the Quartet on the evidence for a soul from peer-reviewed medical studies of near-death experiences.

[66] See Michael Nahm and Bruce Greyson, "The Death of Anna Katharina Ehmer: A Case Study in Terminal Lucidity", *Omega* 68, no. 1 (2014): 77–87, http://journals.sagepub.com /doi/10.2190/OM.68.1.e. See also Michael Nahm and Bruce Greyson, "Terminal Lucidity in Patients with Chronic Schizophrenia and Dementia: A Survey of the Literature", *Journal of Nervous and Mental Disease* 197 (2009): 942–44; Michael Nahm, "Terminal Lucidity in People with Mental Illness and Other Mental Disability: An Overview and Implications for Possible Explanatory Models", *Journal of Near-Death Studies* 28, no. 2 (2009): 87–106; Michael Nahm, "Reflections on the Context of Near-Death Experiences", *Journal of Scientific Exploration* 25 (2011): 453–78; Michael Nahm et al., "Terminal Lucidity: A Review and a Case Collection", *Archives of Gerontology and Geriatrics*, 55, no. 1 (2012): 138–42, http://www .sciencedirect.com/science/article/pii/S0167494311001865?via%3Dihub; and Jesse Bering, "One Last Goodbye: The Strange Case of Terminal Lucidity", *Scientific American* (blog), November 25, 2014, https://blogs.scientificamerican.com/bering-in-mind/one-last-goodbye -the-strange-case-of-terminal-lucidity/.

If we assume that the transphysical soul is the true center of our self-consciousness, intellectual functioning, emotional functioning, and free choice, as well as our awareness of authentic love, morality, beauty, God, and transcendence (as shown in Volume II, Chapters 3–6, of the Quartet), and we further assume that every individual has a unique transphysical soul and that the cause of such a soul must itself be transphysical—that is, God (as shown in Volume II, Chapters 3–4, of the Quartet)—then we are all *equally* created in the image and likeness of God; we are created as transcendental beings called to eternal life by a unique, unrestricted spiritual being (i.e., God the Father) revealed by Jesus to be perfect unconditional love.

Humble-heartedness means threading the needle between false humility (underestimating and undervaluing our true transcendental and eternal nature) and self-idolatry (viewing ourselves as creator instead of creature). It means recognizing that we are all equally made in the image and likeness of God, but are not God, that we are all equally wonderfully made, but with imperfections and fallibility that can only be alleviated through the help of God. If we can integrate creature consciousness and our equality with all other individuals into our conscious and subconscious self-image, then we can inhibit exaggerating comparative advantages over others, and avoid the false pretention that we are *intrinsically* superior to them. The avoidance of this false view of self helps to avert the vanity of Norma Desmond (*Sunset Boulevard*), the greed of Gordon Gecko (*Wall Street*), the envy of Iago (*Othello*), and the pride of Macbeth (all of which are discussed in Volume I, Chapters 5–6, of this Trilogy).

Can sloth be averted by humble-heartedness? Inasmuch as sloth is based on a false humility that undervalues our true transcendental nature, self-worth, and meaning in life, and is also based on the hubris of believing that our lives are our own, and that we are not responsible to the One who has created us, then true humility can help us overcome sloth.

How do we cultivate this new self-image that affirms at once our transcendental nature, our equality with others, and our creatureliness before God? We must first be convinced of the truth of these three views of self, not only through rational evidence, but also through our faith in the teaching of Jesus Christ. Second, we must be vigilant about resisting the constant bombardment of counterpositions from almost every corner of the culture—such as, "You are better—or the best," "You are responsible to yourself alone," "You are the center not only of your world, but also the world of others," and "You deserve high praise and honor because you really are 'all that' and much more." Third, we must ask the Lord for help in our daily prayer to have His humility as well as the humility of the saints.[67]

I personally begin this prayer with Psalm 8, which contains the three truths of self—our transcendental nature, equality with others, and creatureliness before God:

> O LORD, our LORD,
> how majestic is your name in all the earth!
> You whose glory above the heavens is chanted
> by the mouth of babies and infants,
> You have founded a bulwark because of your foes,
> to still the enemy and the avenger.
> When I look at your heavens, the work of your fingers,
> the moon and the stars which you have established;
> what is man that you are mindful of him,
> and the son of man that you care for him?
> Yet you have made him little less than the angels,
> and you have crowned him with glory and honor.
> You have given him dominion over the works of your
>   hands;
> you have put all things under his feet,
> all sheep and oxen,
> and also the beasts of the field,
> the birds of the air, and the fish of the sea,
> whatever passes along the paths of the sea.
> O LORD, our LORD, how majestic is your name in all the
>   earth!

Humble-heartedness along with gentle-heartedness and compassion are the three virtues that Jesus associates most deeply with Himself (see below, Sections II.B.5 and II.B.6). In Matthew 11:28–30,

---

[67] This petition for humility can be significantly enhanced by the Ignatian Examen and affirmation prayers. See Chapter 6 of this volume.

Jesus explicitly identifies humbleness of heart and gentleness of heart with Himself:

> Come to me, all who labor and are heavy laden, and I will give you rest. Take my yoke upon you, and learn from me; for I am gentle and lowly in heart [i.e., humble of heart], and you will find rest for your souls. For my yoke is easy, and my burden is light.

Notice that these two virtues of humble-heartedness and gentle-heartedness are also the first and third Beatitudes, which point the way to our true dignity and fulfillment. The first Beatitude uses "poor in spirit" instead of "humble of heart" (as in Mt 11:29), but they are roughly equivalent in meaning. The same Greek word is used for "gentle" (*praeis* in Mt 5:4 and *praos* in Mt 11:29). The parallels between these first Beatitudes and the attributes Jesus identifies most closely with Himself show how important they are for imitating Jesus, resisting the deadly sins (mentioned throughout the rest of the Sermon on the Mount [Mt 5–7]), and staying on the path to salvation in Jesus Christ.

In the Parable of the Tax Collector and Pharisee (Lk 18:10–14), Jesus warns us of the consequences of failing to appropriate at least some measure of humble-heartedness in our hearts. The Pharisee's prayer (which Jesus indicates the Pharisee addressed *to himself*) produces no justification (readiness for salvation) because his pride and his belief in his capacity to justify himself blocks out the grace of the real God to do so.

> Two men went up into the temple to pray, one a Pharisee and the other a tax collector. The Pharisee stood and prayed thus with himself, "God, I thank you that I am not like other men, extortioners, unjust, adulterers, or even like this tax collector. I fast twice a week, I give tithes of all that I get." But the tax collector, standing far off, would not even lift up his eyes to heaven, but beat his breast, saying, "God, be merciful to me a sinner!" I tell you, this man went down to his house justified rather than the other; for every one who exalts himself will be humbled, but he who humbles himself will be exalted.

The Pharisee's pride prevents him from seeing the truth about both himself and the tax collector, the truth of the heart concerning

God and love—by allowing his ego to do the praying, he does not recognize the goodness and necessity of the tax collector's humble authenticity before God. As such, he does not recognize the absence of this virtue in himself, or his great need for God. He is quite alone in this self-image, without compassion, without truth, without a heart, and without God. If he cannot get over himself, he will never allow God to help him find the way to love.

All of us will want to examine ourselves in this regard, because without humble-heartedness, we are wide open to temptations of pride, contempt, and self-righteousness, which block the effects of faith and prayer in moving us toward Jesus' humble heart of love.

5. Gentle-Heartedness

As with humble-heartedness, Jesus associates gentle-heartedness with Himself (Mt 11:29) and ranks it among the top Beatitudes (Mt 5:5). We might ask how gentle-heartedness differs from humble-heartedness. In brief, humble-heartedness affirms the truth about oneself in relation to God and others, while gentle-heartedness affirms the goodness and lovability of others in their *weakness and fallibility*. Though gentle-heartedness incorporates many of the characteristics Saint Paul associates with love—patience and kindness as well as refraining from anger, boasting, jealousy, arrogance, and rudeness—it is still more fundamental, focusing not only on our conduct toward others, but on our interior empathy and appreciation for others amid comparative differences, faults, and failings. This strong empathy moves us to genuine care for them, which transforms impatience (with weakness and need) into appreciation of their lovability, giving rise to a desire to help them.

Gentle-heartedness begins with looking for the good news in the other (see Chapter 2, Section II.D.2.a). At any given moment, we can choose to look for the good news or the bad news, but we cannot do both at the same time. If we look for the bad news, which is oftentimes much easier to do, we open ourselves to feelings of irritation and impatience as well as thoughts about weakness, unkindness, and deficiencies, which close the door to empathy and genuine care. Alternatively, if we shift our focus to look for the good news—the little good things others try to do, the great good things to which they aspire, their gratuitous acts of kindness, their virtues and strengths, their unique lovability and delightful idiosyncrasies, and their transcendental desires for perfect truth, love, goodness, beauty, and home—we contextualize the bad news, opening the way to empathy and genuine care.

Gentle-heartedness goes beyond looking for the good news. It is a sublime expression of love because it continually attempts to put ourselves in the others' situations, and to see them through the unconditionally loving eyes of Jesus. The reader might be thinking, "How in the world would I know what Jesus is thinking and feeling while gazing upon a very irritating person?" We can get a pretty good idea by examining some of the passages given above about Jesus' love of sinners.

If you have twenty to thirty minutes devoted to daily contemplative prayer, take some of the Scripture passages given above about Jesus' love of sinners to that prayer, and contemplate the following questions: What do you think Jesus is thinking and feeling when the Samaritan woman (whose sins are well known to Him) approaches Him at Jacob's well (Jn 4:1–42)? Why do you think Jesus asks *her*—a Samaritan and a woman—for a cup of water? What do you suppose He is feeling and thinking when she is subtly insulting Him with her quips? Do you think He is bothered by this—or rather, does He see something good, lovable, and redeemable in her that supersedes her rudeness? Do you think that Jesus' gentle, persistent approach helped *her* to become His first Samaritan evangelist—bringing many in her town to believe in Him?

Let us now turn to the woman caught in adultery who is about to be stoned by religious authorities (Jn 8:1–11). What do you think Jesus was thinking and feeling about the woman who was caught in adultery (a very serious offense against God in first-century Judaism)? Notice that Jesus does not rush to judgment—not even when He is pushed to do so by the religious authorities. Instead, He seems to be dispassionate, bending down on the ground, nonchalantly writing in the dust. Why do you think He does this? When the religious authorities press Him about the teachings of Moses prescribing that the woman be stoned, why does He ask them to examine their own hearts first ("Let him who is without sin among you be the first to throw a stone at her" [v. 7])? Why do you think Jesus asks the woman the seemingly obvious question, "Has no one condemned you?" (v. 10). How do you think Jesus is looking at the woman when she is standing before Him? Given that He does not judge her in condemnation ("Neither do I condemn you" [v. 11]), do you think He sees in her a goodness, lovability, and mystery that supersedes her serious sin of adultery?

Let us now consider the tax collector, Zacchaeus (Lk 19:1–10). Recall that being a tax collector is an extremely serious sin in first-century Judaism, and that Zacchaeus is a *chief* tax collector, meaning that he is like a chief sinner among sinners. What do you suppose that Jesus is thinking and feeling about Zacchaeus when He sees that he has made the effort to climb the sycamore tree to see Him? Do you think He sees a "supersinner", or, rather, does He see in him a respect for fairness and the poor, which points to a goodness that supersedes his "supersinfulness"? Why do you think the first thing He says to Zacchaeus is, "Zacchaeus, make haste and come down; for I must stay at your house today" (v. 5)? Doesn't He know that the religious authorities in the crowd are going to jump to judgment out of a sense of scandal? Recall that table fellowship manifests close trust and friendship with another. What do you think that Jesus is trying to tell Zacchaeus about himself—and what do you think He is trying to tell the religious authorities about Zacchaeus? Why do you think that Jesus makes the adamant declaration, "Today salvation has come to this house, since he also is a son of Abraham" (v. 9)? Consider that the expression "son of Abraham" means being *accepted* by Israel's first forefather.

Now, if you have some additional time, try to ask yourself what Jesus is thinking and feeling about the following sinners whom He has defended, accepted, and brought into His company—Matthew, the tax collector whom He invites to be one of the Twelve (Mt 9:9–13); a woman who goes into the house of Simon the Pharisee to wash Jesus' feet with her tears and dry them with her hair (Lk 7:36–50); the good thief whom Jesus accepts into His Kingdom during His Crucifixion (Lk 23:39–43); and Saint Peter after his triple betrayal of Jesus (Jn 21:15–19). Readers may also want to review Jesus' parable about the father of the prodigal son (Lk 15:11–32).

Notice that in the case of all of these "sinners", Jesus never rushes to judgment and refuses to reduce these individuals (whom the authorities and others considered to be "deplorables") to a problem or the "bad news". Notice His penetrating vision that bores right into the heart of these seemingly "bad" individuals to find a goodness, lovability, and faith that He can defend and liberate. Jesus not only sees the good news in these others, but cares about them and their eternal well-being so profoundly that He endures not only the insults and anger of the religious authorities, but also their ongoing plot to destroy Him.

As the Pharisees focus on the *sins* committed by these individuals, Jesus focuses on the *goodness of the sinners*—the preciousness of each one of these uniquely good and lovable mysteries in the eyes of His Father (made in His image). This moves Him to call them out of the darkness into which they have wandered by inciting them to repentance. His awareness of their intrinsic goodness, lovability, and mystery is so profound that He is incapable of rejecting them. He sees them (in the midst of their sinfulness) as worthy of salvation, and so He goes out of His way to call, heal, and sacrifice Himself for them.

What can we learn from Jesus? When we encounter others, we will want to begin by looking for the good news in them, and then to take a closer examination looking for little glimmers of goodness and faith as well as the divine image in which they are created. This will help us look beyond superficial irritation. If we are particularly blocked to the good news or "obsessed" with weakness and irritating features, we might want to try the prayer "Lord, help me to look at this person as You look at him." Keep repeating the prayer, because, as you do so, you will notice the grace of the Holy Spirit— the grace of the compassion of Jesus—freeing you from the blocks and obsessions.

I have a very difficult time being gentle-hearted with enemies, particularly those who are trying to undermine me, the Lord, and the Kingdom of God. I can testify that this repeated prayer has worked wonders in freeing me from passionate resentments so that I can catch a glimmer of the good news that sparks an initial sense of empathy, which opens the door to gentleness and care.

We might be thinking to ourselves that this profound vision of the unique goodness, lovability, and divine mystery of enemies is beyond our capacity, and that it is easier for Jesus, who is, after all, the Son of God and who has divine power and insight. However, Jesus does not want us to take this "easy out" from this difficult mandate.

Instead, He calls us to imitate His Father's perfection in loving ene-mies: "You, therefore, must be perfect [in loving enemies], as your heavenly Father is perfect" (Mt 5:48).[68] He asks us to do this not only to be His light and face to our enemies, but also to help us become more like Him in love, which will ultimately bring us true spiritual freedom and joy. He is well aware that largess in gentleness and com-passion could be taken advantage of, or even used against us, for this sometimes happened to Him (e.g., Judas Iscariot [Jn 13:21–30], and the man He healed at the pool of Beth-za'tha [Jn 5:2–15]). Neverthe-less, most of the time Jesus' gentleness and compassion is greeted with gratitude. Whether this happens to us or not, the Lord asks us to trust that our kindness and compassion will lead to great good—for others, our communities, and ourselves.

I have developed a three-step method for finding the good news in (and engendering compassion for) those for whom I have little nat-ural empathy, including narcissistic and hostile individuals. All three steps are premised on my desire to be like Jesus, who does the same for me—and much more. First, I keep in mind the central insight about myself that I related at the end of Volume I of this Trilogy—"There but for the grace of God go I." This provides an opening for me to experience the other person's situation. Though we might be tempted to think that we are beyond hostility, dishonesty, and egregious displays of the deadly sins, I have come to realize in my own life that my propensity toward certain deadly sins is only a few degrees away from tragic characters such as Hamlet, Iago, or Mac-beth. Most of us have some degree of inclination toward fallibility and concupiscence—some stronger and some weaker. Some of us were fortunate enough to have good role models in our parents, strong religious upbringing, and outstanding education to help us contend with the deadly sins. But whether we have been so blessed or not, we cannot afford to think that we are beyond a fall and that we have overcome Satan. It is precisely this kind of spiritual pride that leads to the Pharisees' self-righteousness as well as the prophetic

---

[68] Notice that this teaching to "be perfect, as your heavenly Father is perfect" is the con-cluding instruction to a lengthy discourse on loving enemies (Mt 5:43–48). Hence, the per-fection to which Jesus calls us—the perfection of His Father—consists precisely in loving enemies.

warning given in the Book of Proverbs: "Pride goes before destruction, and a haughty spirit before a fall" (16:18).

If I can simply call to mind the truth that I am but a few degrees away from a fall, and give the Lord thanks for the graces He has given to help me avoid it, I can then begin to appreciate what others might have suffered or may be suffering—the anxieties and difficulties they may be facing in their minds, hearts, and lives. This moment of appreciation often leads to a crucial moment of empathy, which helps me stave off impatience, criticism, and judgment.

This empathy frees me for my second step—to say an appropriate spontaneous prayer that will allow God's grace to move my soul toward patience and kindness. If someone has unjustly offended me, I use the prayer "Lord, *You* are the just judge; please take care of this situation" (see below, Section II.B.7). If I am blocking the intrinsic goodness, lovability, and transcendent mystery of the other because of egocentricity or self-righteousness, then I use the simple prayer "Lord, help me to be like *You*, who sees the unique goodness, lovability and mystery of every immeasurably valuable person." If I am being impatient because I am obsessing about getting some tasks done quickly, I say a quick prayer for peace and then ask the Lord to act according to His timetable instead of my obsessive one.[69] These prayers frequently help me to back away from my obsessions and to restore my focus on the intrinsic unique goodness and transcendent mystery of the person before me. Gratitude for our good fortune and graces as well as remembering our vulnerability, and concupiscence, while asking the Lord to help us refocus on the intrinsic goodness and transcendence of others, can have remarkable effects if we allow them to mitigate our egocentricity, self-righteousness, and impatience.

We are now prepared to move into the third and final step: focusing on the intrinsic unique goodness, lovability, and transcendent mystery of the other (discussed above and in Chapter 2, Section II.D.2.a). I generally begin by focusing on the eyes that are the windows to the soul, not only to grasp the mood and disposition of others, but also to appreciate their seemingly limitless layers of interiority and the spiritual state of their souls.

---

[69] There is an explanation of a long list of spontaneous prayers in Appendix II (Section I) of this volume.

I then try to focus on the unique transcendent soul that stands behind the spiritual look within the eyes. When I do this, I have an experience of what I might call "spiritual empathy", soul speaking to soul, which produces not only respect, but a kind of reverence for the person standing before me. If I remain focused on the ineffable mystery before me in this state of spiritual empathy, it enables me to transcend not only the overtly bad news in the other, but also negative moods, and even the lifeless eyes of someone who is in a state of darkness. The uniquely transcendent character of every individual seems to shine through even the most disconsolate and foul expressions. As this occurs, I begin to approach what Jesus may have felt for egregious sinners and enemies—a reverence for their unique goodness and mystery, a sense of the difficulties in their lives that may have led to their current attitudes, and a desire to help them move from darkness into the light of their true dignity and destiny.

Does this work all the time? No, but if I remember the first two steps ("There but for the grace of God go I" and an appropriate spontaneous prayer), then this focus on the mystery of the other has the potential to contextualize the problems, insincerity, and hostility I might see. If this occurs, I can move to the next two subvirtues of love—compassion and forgiveness (see the next two subsections below).

Before proceeding, we should say a brief word about the ordering of the eight subvirtues of love. I chose this order because the earlier virtues seem to open the way to the later ones—at least in my life. My fundamental choice to put contributive (Level Three) and transcendent (Level Four) identity above materialistic-sensual (Level One) and ego-comparative (Level Two) identity freed me to pursue the other seven subvirtues of love. Without this choice, the virtue of love would have never "gotten off the ground". For me, a general transcendent identity was not enough. I desperately needed the example and teaching of Jesus, the power and love of the Holy Spirit, and the sacraments, guidance, and community of the Catholic Church, to move into deep gratitude, humble-heartedness, gentle-heartedness, and compassion so that I could express the fruit of these *interior attitudes*—these transformations into the heart of Jesus—in the *actions* of forgiveness and covenant love.

6. Compassion

"Compassion" refers to the interior state of feeling overwhelmed by sympathy for someone else's suffering. We can discern this meaning by analyzing its two constituent parts in Latin: *cum* (signifying "with") and *passio* (signifying "suffering")—hence, the composite meaning: "to suffer with". Compassion almost invariably leads to a decision to help the other, and, if possible, to relieve their suffering. These feelings of sympathy arise out of care for the other, which can be so strong that one is willing to sacrifice oneself to relieve another's suffering.

The origin of this care is connected with our sense of the intrinsic unique transcendent goodness, lovability, and mystery of the other (see the previous subsection), which makes the other "precious" in our eyes. There is almost a chain reaction that occurs when we sense this intrinsic unique transcendent mystery in a moment of spiritual empathy. We proceed almost immediately to a sense of the irreplaceable and inestimable preciousness of others, which causes us to care deeply for them. When others experience suffering, we cannot help ourselves; we are moved to deep feelings of sympathy for them, feelings that incite us to actions of help and protection to the point of self-sacrifice.

Jesus refers directly to this deep feeling of sympathy in the Parable of the Good Samaritan (Lk 10:25–37). When the Samaritan encounters the beaten man, he sees his plight and helplessness. Though the man (a Jew) is a traditional enemy of the Samaritans, the Samaritan still sees his intrinsic value and preciousness, and so feels that he deserves relief from the sad state to which he has been subjected. Jesus describes the Samaritan's feeling of sympathy for this precious other through a visceral sense of compassion, expressed by the Greek word *esplagchnisthē*. As we saw above (Section II.A.3), this term means "feelings of sympathy originating in the bowels, which were thought to be the seat of love and pity".[70] Gripped by these feelings of sympathy, the Samaritan goes to extraordinary lengths to relieve the plight of his Jewish victim—dressing his wounds, taking him to an inn, and paying for several days' provision.

Again, as we saw above, when Jesus encountered the widow of Nain leaving town in a funeral procession with her only son (Lk 7:11–17),

---

[70] See *Strong's Concordance*, s.v. "4697: splagchnizomai".

Luke uses the same word to describe Jesus' feelings, *esplagchnisthē*, a visceral feeling of sympathy for the suffering widow that moves him to raise her son from the dead immediately. The same visceral reference to compassion is used in the Parable of the Prodigal Son (Lk 15:11–32) to characterize the heart of the father when he sees his son returning from afar battered and reduced to the status of a slave (Lk 15:20). Recall that the father in this parable is Jesus' consummate revelation of His Divine Father's heart and essence—and that the prodigal son is His figurative representation of an egregious sinner who has violated almost every prescript of the Torah, while shaming his family, his country, and his election—as well as violating the statutes of purity. Jesus places the verb *esplagchnisthē* ("took pity" or "took great compassion") at the center of the parable to show the essential characteristic of His Father's heart and nature. When he sees his son's desperation and great need, he identifies with his suffering and deprivation completely and is moved to overlook all of the outrageous offenses that the son has committed to God, family, and the people of Israel. Any sense of just retribution for these offenses is reduced to insignificance in the father's unrestricted feelings of sympathy and love for his son who has suffered the consequences of his irresponsibility and sinfulness. The twofold implication is clear:

1. Jesus' heavenly Father and Jesus Himself are, at heart, unrestricted compassionate, forgiving, and redeeming love.
2. This is the kind of love to which we are called so that we will be like them in the Kingdom of Heaven.

Of course, we will fall short of reaching this noble call many times, and we will need to make recourse to the Lord's unrestricted compassionate loving forgiveness, as well as His grace, to reach this highest eternal dignity.[71] The Lord's grace will likely continue to help us after death in Purgatory until we become "little images" of unrestricted compassionate love.

Luke makes another important reference to compassion in his reformulation of Matthew's account of Jesus' admonition to "be perfect, as your heavenly Father is perfect" (Mt 5:48). Luke substitutes

---

[71] See Chapter 7 of this volume on forgiveness and the grace of reconciliation.

the word "compassionate" for Matthew's "perfect", to clarify Jesus' meaning for his Gentile audience: "be compassionate [*oiktirmones*], just as your Father is compassionate" (Lk 6:36, NLT). *Oiktirmones* has roughly the same meaning as *esplagchnisthē*, but does not refer specifically to the bowels (as the seat of love and pity). *Oiktirmones* refers to feelings and interior states as well as actions and behaviors—and means deep pity.[72]

Matthew also refers to mercy/compassion in a general sense in the fifth Beatitude in the Sermon on the Mount: "Blessed are the merciful [*eleēmones*], for they shall obtain mercy" (5:7). *Eleēmones* here refers to mercy in a general sense without making specific reference to deep feelings of sympathy for a suffering person.[73] According to John McKenzie, it has a twofold implication—compassion for the poor, suffering, and marginalized, and forgiveness of those who have offended us (see below, II.B.7).[74] Given the position of "mercy" within the Beatitudes and its centrality in the Gospel of Luke, we may conclude that it is one of the most important interior attitudes and virtues espoused by Jesus, essential to His view of love and essential to the heart of His Father. The perfection of this virtue within us will be our perfection (Lk 6:35) when we enter into the Kingdom of Heaven—and will be the source of our ultimate happiness, dignity, and unity with the three Persons of the Holy Trinity throughout eternity.

Given the importance of this virtue to our happiness, dignity, and eternal destiny, we will want to probe more deeply into how we can cultivate it through intention, through practice, and above all, through the grace of God. So how do we cultivate compassion? We may glean two indispensable components from the lives of Jesus and the saints. We have seen the first component several times in the foregoing subsection—to develop our capacity for spiritual empathy by attending to the good news in others, particularly their intrinsic unique goodness, lovability, and transcendent mystery. The second

---

[72] See *Strong's Concordance*, s.v. "3629: oiktirmón", https://biblehub.com/greek/3629.htm, as derived from *Strong's Concordance*, s.v. "3627: oiktiró", https://biblehub.com/greek/3627.htm.

[73] See *Strong's Concordance*, s.v. "1655: eleémón", https://biblehub.com/greek/1655.htm.

[74] See McKenzie, "Gospel according to Matthew", in Brown, Fitzmyer, and Murphy, *Jerome Biblical Commentary*, 2:70.

component is the natural fruit of the first—the desire to serve the suffering (e.g., sinners, the sick, the poor, the lonely, and the marginalized [see above, Section II.A.3]) to the extent that we can according to the gifts, time, and opportunity we have been given.

Let us consider each point in turn. We have already addressed the topic of developing spiritual empathy by focusing on the good news and transcendent mystery of the other, even amid the bad news (above in Section II.B.5). An additional observation may be made at this juncture: some personalities are more naturally adept at spiritual empathy than others. We don't have to look far to see the natural empathy of mothers for their children, the capacity to appreciate their unique goodness, lovability, and transcendent mystery amid occasional bad news. We can also see this gift in what some psychologists term "natural empaths", having the capacity to empathize and sympathize with others far beyond what their young age would warrant. Remarkable as these examples of natural empathy and spiritual empathy are, most of us are not "natural empaths", and when most of us look upon other people's children, we do not have the same level of natural or spiritual empathy as for our own.

So if we are not natural empaths, how might we best cultivate natural and spiritual empathy beyond what we have discussed above (in Section II.B.5)? Practice makes perfect. The more concertedly we focus on the good news, and keep searching for the transcendent mystery in the eyes of another amid the bad news, the more proficient we become at it. At first, we have to remember to do it, and when we do, we then have to concentrate on looking for these characteristics through the eyes and words of the other. Over the course of time, it becomes progressively more engrained in our subconscious mind, and eventually it becomes habitual, second nature, and we do not even have to think about it. As this occurs, we become "cultivated empaths", which opens the door to genuine compassion—not simply compassionate deeds done out of obedience to Jesus' command, but interior compassion (sincere feelings of sympathy for others in their suffering) in imitation of the heart and feelings of Jesus. At this juncture, we begin to see others as Jesus sees them, to see ourselves as Jesus sees us, and to see Jesus in every person we encounter, which characterizes the inner attitude of most of the saints.

We can adduce from the above the connection between love of neighbor, love of self, and love of God. We might notice in our own lives (or in the lives of the saints) that the more proficient we become at spiritual empathy and compassion for others, the more we understand (in our hearts) how Jesus sees them as well; and when this occurs, we also understand how Jesus sees *us*. This is a huge foundation for the development of our spiritual lives—the awareness that the Lord feels the same unrestricted and deep feelings of sympathy for us in our sinfulness and suffering that the father feels for his prodigal son, that Jesus felt for the widow of Nain, and that the Samaritan felt for his traditional enemy. If we appreciate this, even to a small degree, we begin to sense the magnitude of God's love for us, even in our sinfulness; and if we have some sense of this great love, then our confidence, trust, and hope in Him will dramatically increase, which frees us to love Him evermore deeply. As we live within the light of that love, we become more and more transformed in it, becoming more and more like Him, our beloved, and when this occurs, we want to be like Him, imitate Him, and show His compassion to those in need. This is the making of a saint.

We may now proceed to the second step—service to the needy and the suffering. It is not enough merely to think about serving others or to desire to serve others; we actually have to *do* it. If we do not take the plunge into actual service, we will never truly *experience* the lovability and transcendent mystery of someone who is in a state of need, whether it be spiritual or temporal needs, or whether we serve to strengthen others in faith and hope, support them in sickness or the dying process, or aid them in poverty or oppression. Furthermore, if we do not experience the suffering of a person whose lovability and transcendent mystery is real to us, then we will not sympathize with their need as we would sympathize with the need of our own children or spouse, and if we do not do this, then we will not *experience* (beyond mere abstraction) Jesus' feelings of sympathy for them, or for us in our need and suffering. Conversely, the opposite is true: real service to those for whom we empathize leads to ever deepening sympathy and compassion, and the greater our compassion and sympathy for them, the greater our recognition of Jesus' compassion for them and for us.

One last observation should be made: we cannot do everything for everybody, because we do not have unlimited skill sets, time, psychic energy, physical energy, or opportunity. Though it is always good to be in contact with those who are poor to get a sense of real desperation and need, we will probably want to focus our service in the areas where we have greatest opportunity and skill, and in times and in places that will conform with our family and work obligations. Remember, our primary obligation is to our family and to those whose needs are real and immediate in our lives. With respect to skill sets and opportunities, we will want to remember Paul's advice in 1 Corinthians 12:

> Now there are varieties of gifts, but the same Spirit; and there are varieties of service, but the same Lord; and there are varieties of working, but it is the same God who inspires them all in every one. To each is given the manifestation of the Spirit for the common good. To one is given through the Spirit the utterance of wisdom, and to another the utterance of knowledge according to the same Spirit, to another faith by the same Spirit, to another gifts of healing by the one Spirit.... All these are inspired by one and the same Spirit, who apportions to each one individually as he wills. (vv. 4–9, 11)

We may conclude by recalling (from Volume I, Chapter 5, of this Trilogy) the transformation of Ebenezer Scrooge, who finally takes the plunge of real compassion:

> "I don't know what to do!" cried Scrooge, laughing and crying in the same breath; and making a perfect Laocoön of himself with his stockings. "I am as light as a feather, I am as happy as an angel, I am as merry as a schoolboy. I am as giddy as a drunken man. A merry Christmas to everybody! A happy New Year to all the world. Hallo here! Whoop! Hallo!" ... "A merry Christmas, Bob!" said Scrooge, with an earnestness that could not be mistaken, as he clapped him on the back. "A merrier Christmas, Bob, my good fellow, than I have given you, for many a year! I'll raise your salary, and endeavour to assist your struggling family, and we will discuss your affairs this very afternoon, over a Christmas bowl of smoking bishop, Bob! Make up the fires, and buy another coal-scuttle before you dot another i, Bob Cratchit!" Scrooge was better than his word. He did it all, and infinitely more; and to Tiny Tim, who did NOT die, he was a second father. He became as good a friend, as good a master, and as good a man, as the good old city knew, or any other good old city, town, or borough, in the good old world.... His own heart laughed:

and that was quite enough for him. He had no further intercourse with Spirits, but lived upon the Total Abstinence Principle, ever afterwards; and it was always said of him, that he knew how to keep Christmas well, if any man alive possessed the knowledge. May that be truly said of us, and all of us! And so, as Tiny Tim observed, God bless Us, Every One![75]

7. Forgiveness

Forgiveness is mentioned more often in the Gospels than any other moral prescription. Jesus sees it as the condition necessary to alleviate strife and discord of every kind—and therefore it is the condition necessary for peace and the common good. The alternative to forgiveness is vengeance begetting vengeance and violence begetting violence.[76] The tendency of retribution to build on itself in ever-increasing layers of violence is difficult to interrupt without a deliberate act of forgiveness, which forsakes the claims to retribution that justice allows. As we saw with Hamlet, the desire for retribution or vengeance, no matter how justified, tends to escalate, leading ultimately to gross tragedies and even war (see Volume I, Chapter 6, of this Trilogy).

Jesus was aware that forgiveness could go far beyond interrupting the cycle of increasing vengeance and violence. He recognized its power to heal and edify not only the recipient, but also the giver, and in so doing, to build the foundation for a society based on the Golden Rule—a society that history has shown would be able to throw off the yoke of slavery, severe social stratifications, and entrenched inequities, creating the possibility of a common good far beyond human imagination. Today we see the power and effects of His vision of compassion and forgiveness that created the path out of the atrocities of Rome, as well as the abuses of slavery, the industrial revolution, and even global conflict. One remarkable example is the Marshall Plan after World War II. There was a great temptation to

---

[75] Charles Dickens, *A Christmas Carol* (London, 1843; Project Gutenberg, 2018), Stave 5, http://www.gutenberg.org/files/46/46-h/46-h.htm.

[76] The expression was first published in *The London Times*, November 4, 1834, and seems to have been derived from the passage in the Gospel of Matthew where Jesus tells Peter, who draws his sword and cuts off the high priest's servant's ear, "Put your sword back into its place; for all who take the sword will perish by the sword" (Mt 26:52).

repay the German people for the appalling atrocities committed to dozens of nations and millions of people during the Second World War. However, the formulators of the Marshall Plan remembered how the onerous Treaty of Versailles (after WWI) caused desperation and economic hardship to the German people, which led to the ascendency of the Nazis regime. So instead of submitting to the seemingly just prescriptions of retribution, General Marshall and his staff constructed a plan to rebuild (rather than repay) Germany and Japan. These plans led to not only prosperity for both nations (instead of crushing retribution), but also peace and prosperity for the world that benefitted from these nations' peacefulness and creativity. Instead of reliving the cycle of retribution and violence that led from the First to the Second World War, this plan of forgiveness and the Golden Rule allowed the world to recover, heal, and move forward.

How do we cultivate the interior attitude of forgiveness? Before exploring this, we need to make some important distinctions. First, forgiveness must be distinguished from excuse, because it is an act of mercy going beyond justice, while excuse shows why a particular action was within the bounds of justice, that it was not unjust and therefore does not require an act of mercy. When I tell you that I ran into your car because my brakes failed, and it is subsequently shown that in fact they did fail, this excuse shows that I did not intend to commit an injustice against you for personal gain or careless disregard. You will still want my insurance company's number to seek compensation, but you will not need to forgive me, and I will not need your act of forgiveness. Alternatively, if I run into your car because I was texting and did not notice you (careless disregard) or I intentionally damaged your car because I dislike you (intentional injustice), then you have the right to receive not only compensation, but also punitive damages for my intentional injustice or careless disregard. You could pursue those punitive damages or you could forgive me—that is, you could forsake your claims against me by an act of mercy that I do not in justice deserve. In sum, forgiveness is necessary when a person's actions are inexcusable and unjust, which makes forgiveness—the granting of an undeserved favor by a victim to a perpetrator—necessary. This favor consists in the victim forsaking his rights to justly deserved punitive damages to help the perpetrator recover and to avert the cycle of increasing vengeance and violence.

Two other distinctions may prove helpful. First, Jesus' view of love (*agapē*) goes beyond an external act of forgiveness (conferring the above undeserved favor on an unjust or careless perpetrator) to cultivating an interior attitude of concern or even care for that perpetrator (from which the act of forgiveness naturally follows). Jesus is certainly asking us to confer the external act of forgiveness on unjust perpetrators, but He is also challenging us to go even further—to be concerned about and even to care for the unjust perpetrator. Let's examine each of these acts in turn. How does Jesus justify asking us to forsake our claims to justice against those who have unjustly done us wrong? He does so by appealing to the fact that we are and have been the recipients of forgiveness by God for our unjust deeds toward others and God Himself. If God has shown us mercy countless times for our sins and misdeeds, then *we in justice* should show mercy to others for their misdeeds toward us. Thus, Jesus asks us to act mercifully toward our neighbor (by conferring acts of forgiveness) in order to act *justly* toward God (who has conferred on us countless acts of forgiveness and mercy).

After teaching us the Our Father in the Sermon on the Mount, Jesus adds the clarification that we *owe* others mercy out of *justice* to God for His mercy, "for if you forgive men their trespasses, your heavenly Father also will forgive you; but if you do not forgive men their trespasses, neither will your Father forgive your trespasses" (Mt 6:14–15). Jesus views our denial of forgiveness to others as a failure to give God what we owe Him in justice for His forgiveness of us. He illustrates this with the Parable of the Unmerciful Servant.

> Therefore the kingdom of heaven may be compared to a king who wished to settle accounts with his servants. When he began the reckoning, one was brought to him who owed him ten thousand talents; and as he could not pay, his lord ordered him to be sold, with his wife and children and all that he had, and payment to be made. So the servant fell on his knees, imploring him, "Lord, have patience with me, and I will pay you everything." And out of pity for him the lord of that servant released him and forgave him the debt. But that same servant, as he went out, came upon one of his fellow servants who owed him a hundred denarii [a mere fraction of what he owed his master]; and seizing him by the throat he said, "Pay what you owe." So his fellow servant fell down and pleaded with him, "Have

patience with me, and I will pay you." He refused and went and put him in prison till he should pay the debt. When his fellow servants saw what had taken place, they were greatly distressed, and they went and reported to their lord all that had taken place. Then his lord summoned him and said to him, "You wicked servant! I forgave you all that debt because you pleaded with me; and should not you have had mercy on your fellow servant, as I had mercy on you?" And in anger his lord delivered him to the jailers, till he should pay all his debt. So also my heavenly Father will do to every one of you, if you do not forgive your brother from your heart. (Mt 18:23–35)

For Jesus then forgiveness is only an act of justice toward God, though it is an act of mercy toward an unjust perpetrator. We owe this mercy to one another because we have already received and will continue to receive the far greater mercy of God. If we deny others forgiveness, then God is justified in denying forgiveness to us, because we owe it to Him in justice.

Jesus does not stop at mandating *acts* of forgiveness from us; He challenges us to go further—to grant forgiveness from the *heart*. Jesus is saying here that it is better to forgive others because we feel genuine concern and care (love) for them than to forgive them out of mere compliance to God's just command. Though it is good to obey God's just commands, it is much better to imitate the heart of the Father by genuinely loving the person who has unjustly sinned against us.

Jesus knows that this is a tall order, but nevertheless encourages us to reach for the higher motivation by an appeal to *gratitude* for the unconditional love that God shows to us. To illustrate this, we turn again to the Parable of the Prodigal Son (Lk 15:11–32), where Jesus manifests how God *genuinely feels* not only toward the prodigal son, but also by implication toward *us*. As we listen to the parable, He hopes that we will feel the same deep and unrestricted compassionate love of God for us that the father shows to his prodigal son. Jesus hopes that we will have the same reaction to this unrestricted love as Saint Ignatius Loyola, who is struck with amazement and gratitude that God could possibly love him in this way, love him like the prodigal son's father, and even more astoundingly, love him to the point of self-sacrificial death on a cross. Inasmuch as gratitude is the origin of love (as we saw above), then felt gratitude for the overwhelming and unconditional love of God for us in our sinfulness can move us to the sincere desire to love Him in return by imitating Him. Such imitation is not only the sincerest form of flattery, but also the sincerest form of love.

In his Contemplation to Attain Divine Love (at the end of the *Spiritual Exercises*), Saint Ignatius encourages retreatants to move from the recognition of God's love to gratitude for it and then to our loving response, which moves us to imitate Him. We might adapt this three-step process to the development of a forgiving heart as follows. First, we will want to recognize God's love for us, particularly in His Son's Incarnation, ministry, Eucharist, Passion, death, Resurrection, and gift of the Spirit, which are all sacrificial actions done not only to show us His unconditional love, but also to *establish* that unconditional love in our souls and in the world. We will then want to compare Jesus' love to that of His Father described in the Parable of the Prodigal Son (Lk 15:11–32). Notice that the sympathy and compassion of the father for his sinful son is identical to the felt sympathy and compassion that He has for us in our sinfulness.

Second, we will want to reflect in amazement on this unrestricted love of God, and consider that we are similarly loved by God. We will then want to accept this *undeserved* gift of love (of inestimable and eternal worth) and open ourselves to our natural response—*gratitude* that He sees us with such benevolence, affection, and compassion.

Third, consider where this gratitude is leading us: to love Him in return. But how? By the highest means we have available to us— imitating His love for us in our treatment and love of others. Moved by this desire to imitate Him in His love, we turn to the spiritual empathy arising out of the genuinely good news in the other. When we combine the glimpse of the unique goodness, lovability, and transcendent mystery of the other with our desire to imitate the Lord, who sees the fullness of that unique goodness and lovability, we are inspired to a new depth of love similar to that of Saint Francis, Saint Peter Claver, and Saint Teresa of Calcutta, among so many others.

When we surrender to God by imitating His forgiving love, we will be able to hand all our grievances (from a human offender) over to Him in trust, with a simple prayer: "Lord, You are the just judge; You take care of it." If you let the loving God take the burden of grievances against past injustice from you, then it becomes much easier to recognize the intrinsic unique lovable, good, transcendent mystery in the other, and to let the other be free of the burden of past mistakes.

One might object that forgiveness relieves people of the need to be responsible and accountable to others—it is just an "easy out" from adult accountability. A distinction must be made here between relieving contrite people of the burden of past mistakes versus allowing irresponsible people to remain unaccountable. Though Jesus felt genuine sympathy for all sinners, contrite or uncontrite, and forgave all contrite sinners, He also expected them to try to amend their lives. That is why He calls us to repent (*metanoia*—"turn your life around") when preaching about the Kingdom (Mk 1:15), why He tells His disciples to be responsible and vigilant like the five wise bridesmaids (Mt 25:1–13), and why, after forgiving the woman caught in adultery, He exhorts her to "go, and do not sin again" (Jn 8:11). Thus, Jesus is not providing an "easy out" from adult accountability, but rather a call to adult accountability through repentance. Yes, He provides an easy out for sinners from being held captive to past mistakes after expressing contrition, but this does not imply irresponsibility and nonaccountability into the future. By releasing us from captivity to past sins while holding us accountable to our future conduct, Jesus enables us to be truly free, free from imprisonment to the past, and free to pursue the light of truth and goodness in the future. It may take some time to become accustomed to living according to the example and heart of Jesus, but if we do, we will not only bring peace and reconciliation to situations of great injury, anger, and harm, but also bring the light and love of Christ to the world.

This last point merits deeper consideration. Genuine forgiveness of others in imitation of Jesus enables us to bring the healing power of Christ not only into our personal lives, but into the larger community and the world itself. When we forgive one another from the heart, we not only interrupt the cycle of increasing vengeance and violence; we bring greater peace and advancement to culture and social structures, as well as the light of divine wisdom and healing into the world.

Victor Hugo made this truth the central theme of his classic work *Les Misérables*. After being released from prison, Jean Valjean finds himself rejected by virtually everyone on the streets of Paris. When Bishop Myriel allows him to stay in his house, Jean "repays" him by stealing his silverware. He is caught by the police, who accuse him before Bishop Myriel, but Myriel refuses to accuse him, and instead indicates to Valjean that he has forgotten to take two silver candlesticks. The police accept the bishop's explanation, after which the bishop tells Valjean to sell the candlesticks and use the money to become a good man. Valjean returns to his old ways by stealing a coin from a twelve-year-old, but immediately repents, searches for the boy, but fails to find him. The boy accuses Valjean to the police, and his traditional foe, Javert, pursues him relentlessly until the end of the novel.

After repenting, Valjean repays the bishop's kindness again and again by taking on a life of virtue, compassion, and self-sacrificial good. Much of the time he performs his works of generosity and compassion at great risk to himself because by happenstance they reveal his identity to Javert, who never loses interest in bringing Valjean to "justice". At one point, Valjean hears that another man will be sent to prison because he has been mistakenly identified with him, and so he turns himself in to prevent the innocent man from serving in his place. After escaping, he continues his acts of self-sacrificial kindness and compassion, particularly to Cosette, the daughter of a woman who was fired from Valjean's factory (unbeknownst to Valjean). He rescues Cosette from wicked innkeepers and raises her as his own daughter after her mother dies. He also rescues Cosette's future husband, Marius, at the barricades, and even rescues his nemesis Javert from death as well. His act of mercy toward Javert has the same effect as Bishop Myriel's act of mercy toward him. Javert cannot bring himself to turn Valjean over to the authorities. After a lifetime of self-sacrificial struggle, Valjean dies a happy man with Cosette and Marius by his side, whom he has subsidized for a lifetime.

A single act of forgiveness and compassion by Bishop Myriel has led to countless acts of self-sacrificial compassion that positively transformed the lives of almost everyone touched by Valjean. The healing light and love of forgiveness and compassion spreads more readily throughout the human community than the darkness that incessantly tries to overtake it.

8. Chastity and Covenant Romantic Love

"Chastity" has been defined both proscriptively and prescriptively within the Christian tradition. Though the proscriptive definition

sets out the parameters of behavior with which this virtue is concerned, it does not reach the heart of the virtue—the interior attitude
that frees us to be faithful to charitable love in our sexual activity.
We will first examine the proscriptive definition of chastity and then
explore the prescriptive (positive) definition—the heart of chastity
integral to Jesus' ideal of the heart of love.

Jesus relies on the Deuteronomic and Levitical codes for the
underpinning of His proscriptive definition of chastity. These codes
prohibit "illicit sexual intercourse" (*porneia* in the Septuagint Greek
translation of the Old Testament). Acts of illicit sexual union (*porneia*)
include adultery (Deut 5:18; Lev 20:10), fornication, homosexual-
ity, intercourse with animals (see Lev 20:10–16), and sexual intercourse with close relatives (see Lev 18:6–18; 20:17–21).[77] Jesus adds
to this the following proscriptions: sexual intercourse with a divorced
man or woman (Mk 10:11) and unmarried sexual activity (implied
by *porneia* at the beginning of the list in Mk 7:21–22). This translation of *porneia* is discussed and justified more thoroughly in Volume
III, Chapter 2, of this Trilogy. For the moment, suffice to say that
porneia (illicit sexual acts) stands at the beginning of the list of sinful
acts in Mark 7:21–22. This list includes adultery (*moicheiai*—unlawful
married sexuality) and licentiousness (*aselgeia*). Inasmuch as *porneia* in
Mark's list probably has a distinct meaning from the other two sexual
terms in the list—adultery (unlawful married sexuality) and licentiousness (outrageous sexual conduct shocking to public decency[78])—we
might infer that *porneia* refers to illicit *unmarried* sexual conduct that is
more private or discreet than licentiousness. Saint Paul also implies a
distinction between *porneia* and *moicheiai* (adultery—illicit marital sex)
in his list in 1 Corinthians 6:9, further implying that *porneia* probably
refers to unmarried sexual acts.

When we combine the Deuteronomic and the Levitical codes
(upon which Jesus relied) with Jesus' explicit prohibition of sex with
a divorced man or woman and the implied prohibition of unmarried or premarital sex, the proscriptive parameters of chastity become
apparent. Jesus gives His reason for these proscriptions—namely, that
they run contrary to the purpose and proper use of sexuality ordained

---

[77] *Strong's Concordance*, s.v. "4202: porneia", BibleStudyTools.com, 2020, https://www
.biblestudytools.com/lexicons/greek/nas/porneia.html.

[78] See *Strong's Concordance*, s.v. "766: aselgeia", https://biblehub.com/greek/766.htm.

by the Creator (His heavenly Father) from the beginning of time; He implies that sexuality was created to strengthen marriage, procreate children, and create a secure and lasting family structure for the sake of all family members. The Gospels of Mark (10:6) and Matthew (19:4) report this teaching quite clearly, noting that Jesus refers back to the Book of Genesis (1:26–27; 5:2) to justify it:

> From the beginning of creation, "God made them male and female." "For this reason a man shall leave his father and mother and be joined to his wife, and the two shall become one flesh." So they are no longer two but one flesh. What therefore God has joined together, let not man put asunder. (Mk 10:6–9; cf. Mt 19:4–6)

Saint Paul expands on Jesus' rationale for proscribing illicit sexual acts by adding several reasons implied by Jesus' Incarnation and redemption:

- our integration into His Mystical Body through Baptism,
- the future glorification of our bodies given through His Resurrection, and
- His gift of the Holy Spirit.

In brief, Saint Paul asserts that the body is not meant for immorality, but for the Lord, and the Lord for the body (see 1 Cor 6:13). He justifies this by noting that we are to be raised in the same way that the Father raised Jesus (see 1 Cor 6:14).

Saint Paul goes further by implying that sexual immorality offends the Mystical Body of Christ, into which we have been integrated through Baptism and sins against the Holy Spirit, who dwells within that mystical embodiment:

> Do you not know that your bodies are members of Christ? Shall I therefore take the members of Christ and make them members of a prostitute? Never! Do you not know that he who joins himself to a prostitute becomes one body with her? For, as it is written, "The two shall become one flesh." But he who is united to the Lord becomes one spirit with him. Shun immorality. Every other sin which a man commits is outside the body; but the immoral man sins against his own body. Do you not know that your body is a temple of the Holy Spirit within you, which you have from God? You are not your own; you were bought with a price. So glorify God in your body. (1 Cor 6:15–20)

We may adduce from this why the above sexual acts—*moicheiai* (adultery, illicit sexual acts in marriage), *porneia* (illicit sexual acts outside of marriage), and *aselgeia* (licentiousness, outrageous sexual acts that offend public decency)—are proscribed by Jesus and later by Saint Paul. They cause us to sin against God's and Jesus' intention for us, against others, and against ourselves. The latter two sins against others and ourselves merit closer examination.

Why are illicit sexual acts sins against others and ourselves? As will be discussed in Volume III (Chapter 2) of this Trilogy, pressuring, inviting, or cooperating with others in illicit sexual acts can, and frequently does, undermine future marital commitment and relationship with the Lord. According to several studies done by the National Survey of Family Growth (a part of the Centers for Disease Control and Prevention's National Center for Health Statistics), the number of premarital partners is directly proportional to divorce rate, where zero premarital partners correlated with a 5 percent divorce rate, while those with ten premarital partners had a 35 percent divorce rate.[79] Furthermore, the number of premarital partners directly correlates with increased infidelity within marriage,[80] and cohabitation, counter to popular cultural mythology, leads to less marital satisfaction and higher divorce rates.[81]

What are the reasons for these significantly negative effects of premarital relationships? It seems that linking sexual activity to publicly committed love (from the beginning of dating experiences) reinforces the intrinsic dignity of and respect for both partners, the linking of sexuality to a single marriage commitment, and the linking of marital commitment with fidelity to God. These three factors correlate with satisfaction within marriage as well as low divorce rates.[82] Viewing

[79] See Nicholas Wolfinger, "Counterintuitive Trends in the Link between Premarital Sex and Marital Stability", Institute for Family Studies, June 6, 2016, https://ifstudies.org/blog/counterintuitive-trends-in-the-link-between-premarital-sex-and-marital-stability.

[80] See the statistics on infidelity by the National Opinion Research Center reported by Rebecca Lake, "Infidelity Statistics: 23 Eye-Opening Truths", May 18, 2016, CreditDonkey (website), https://www.creditdonkey.com/infidelity-statistics.html. See also the statistics compiled by David Atkins at the University of Washington, reported by Naomi Schaefer Riley, "The Young and the Restless: Why Infidelity Is Rising among 20-Somethings", *Wall Street Journal*, November 28, 2008, https://www.wsj.com/articles/SB122782458360062499.

[81] Galena K. Rhoads and Scott M. Stanley, *Before I Do: What Do Premarital Experiences Have to Do with Marital Quality among Today's Young Adults?* (Charlottesville, Va.: National Marriage Project at University of Virginia 2014), http://before-i-do.org/.

[82] Ibid.

it in reverse, sexual experiences unlinked to public familial commitment appears to decrease each partner's intrinsic dignity and respect for the other, disconnect sexuality from a single committed relationship, and diminishes the sacredness of the marital bond. As might be expected, extramarital relationships have even greater negative effects on marriages, families, and both partners.[83]

Premarital relationships and extramarital relationships also have a negative effect on both partners' faith life. Religiously inclined individuals engaging in illicit sexual conduct frequently feel tension between the teachings of Jesus and their sexual relationship. This often leads to a decline in their rapport with Jesus and attendance at church services. The longer the premarital/extramarital relationship lasts, the more detached they become from the Lord and the Church. Eventually they rationalize this distance from God and Church, making it difficult to rekindle them.

This distance from God and Church has significant negative psychological effects detailed by the American Psychiatric Association's 2004 study.[84] It also opens the door for the Evil One to tempt individuals toward greater sexual license, rationalization of vice,[85] and overt rejection of Christ and/or the Church, as in the fictional cases of Anna Karenina and J. Gatsby.[86] One might object that my introduction of the Evil One into this discussion is merely a subjective perspective. If the evidence for the reality of spiritual evil given in Volume I of this Trilogy is not enough to convince readers that the

---

[83] Researchers David Atkins and Elizabeth Allen calculate the odds of a divorce after a single act of infidelity to be about 50 percent. See Elizabeth Allen and David Atkins, "The Association of Divorce and Extramarital Sex in a Representative U.S. Sample", *Journal of Family Issues* 33, no. 11 (November 2012): 1477–93, www.researchgate.net/publication/258151224 _The_Association_of_Divorce_and_Extramarital_Sex_in_a_Representative_US_Sample. See also Robert Hughes Jr., "Does Extramarital Sex Cause Divorce?", *HuffPost*, August 8, 2012, https://www.huffingtonpost.com/robert-hughes/does-extramarital-sex-cau_b _1567507.html.

[84] See the summary of their findings in Chapter 3, Section V, of this volume. See Kanita Dervic et al., "Religious Affiliation and Suicide Attempts", *American Journal of Psychiatry* 161, no. 12 (December 2004): 2303–8, http://ajp.psychiatryonline.org/article.aspx?articleid=177228.

[85] Benjamin Le, "Cheaters Use Cognitive Tricks to Rationalize Infidelity", *Scientific American*, November 20, 2013, https://www.scientificamerican.com/article/cheaters-use -cognitive-tricks-to-rationalize-infidelity/.

[86] See Anna Karenina's fall from church, family, and virtue to decadence and suicide in Volume I, Chapter 5, Section III. See also J. Gatsby's decline, leading toward broken marriages, undermined friendships, and murder (in the same section).

Evil One is indeed present in the decline and fall of marriages, friend-ships, and individuals, it will be sufficient to note that infidelity and sexual jealousy are often the cause of domestic violence.[87]

As can be seen from the above studies, Jesus' prohibition of pre-marital and extramarital sex is prophetically and evidentially substan-tiated in our hypersexualized world. As Saint Paul and the Church indicate, these sexual sins are not victimless. They do real harm to our relationship with God, marriage, others, and ourselves. Hence, they are called "sins".

Can the above assessment of the proscriptive definition of chastity give us any insight into its prescriptive (positive) definition? It can, for the prescriptive definition arises out of the attitudes needed to avert the above harms to others, ourselves, and our relationship with God. As such, we might initially prescriptively define "chastity" as the virtue of trustingly following the Lord's intention for marriage and sexuality by seeking the good, God's will, and salvation for others to whom we are romantically attracted. We do this for the sake of our and others' psychological and relational well-being, spiritual life, and present or future marriage. Since this is the goal of Christian love (*agapē*), it is an essential subvirtue of love.

So what are the attitudes that avert harms to marriage and family as well as others, ourselves, and our relationship with God? First, for Christians, the attitude of gratitude and love for *His* redemption and salvation forms the foundation for obedience to His teaching. Yet, this gratitude and love is based on an even more fundamental attitude—strong faith that He is the Son of God. If we do not have strong faith that Jesus is the Son of God who came to us as Savior and Redeemer, we will have great difficulty feeling any kind of grat-itude or love for His Incarnation, complete self-sacrificial love on the Cross, and His gifts of the Holy Eucharist, the Holy Spirit, His Word, and the Church—and if we feel no gratitude or love for Him, we will probably view His and the Church's teaching on sexuality as an "out of touch" imposition by a moralistic, hypercontrolling, prudish Church. This worldview (devoid of faith) cannot move us to do much of anything—let alone something countercultural and self-sacrificial.

---

[87] Megan Gannon, "Domestic Violence Often Triggered by Jealousy", *Live Science*, August 1, 2012, https://www.livescience.com/22039-domestic-violence-often-triggered-by-jealousy.html.

It would be needless deprivation if some individuals ignored the sage, salutary, salvific teaching of Jesus for lack of evidence, for as we have explained in the Quartet, there is considerable contemporary scientifically validated evidence to substantiate reasonable and responsible belief in Jesus as the Son of God (see the summary of this evidence in the introduction to this volume). However, if we were aware of this evidence, but chose to ignore it (or ignore looking into it) because we could not be bothered to do so or did not want to be challenged by an "inconvenient truth", then we would have *culpably* deprived ourselves of the grace and salvation of Jesus. Why would we make such a choice? Is there a higher priority for us? If so, do we not want to challenge this prioritization for the sake of our souls, and to resist evil, pursue our highest dignity and destiny, and inherit eternal love and joy? The stakes are so high that we would be remiss indeed to take the chance of forfeiting our eternal lives (souls) even to gain the entire world (see Mt 16:26).[88]

If we responsibly look into the evidence for God, the soul, and Jesus, and cultivate strong faith in His divine Sonship, then gratitude and love for His Incarnation, His self-sacrificial death, and His gifts of the Holy Eucharist, the Holy Spirit, His Word, and His Church will almost naturally follow, because we will then know that Jesus has given us everything we need to inherit His eternal love and joy through our free will. This path to salvation will no doubt have many challenges and crosses, but if we follow Jesus' teaching as best we can through the inspiration of the Holy Spirit, avail ourselves of the sacraments (particularly the Holy Eucharist and Reconciliation), and participate in His Church, we will, through His unconditional mercy, be well on the way to His eternal salvation. As Saint Ignatius of Loyola might say, what other response could we have besides great gratitude and love?[89] We may now move to three attitudes of chastity built upon this faith, gratitude, and love:

---

[88] In Matthew 16:26, the phrase is "forfeits his life"—*psychēn*, which refers to everything we are, both temporally and eternally.

[89] In his second prelude of the Contemplation to Gain Love, Saint Ignatius states the intention of the contemplation: "to ask for what I want. It will be here to ask for interior knowledge of so great good received, in order that being entirely grateful, I may be able in all to love and serve His Divine Majesty." See *Spiritual Exercises*, "Contemplation to Gain Love", http://sacred-texts.com/chr/seil/seil35.htm.

1. The intention to please and serve the Lord according to His Word out of deep gratitude and love
2. The intention to focus on the highest dignity and destiny of others and to help them avoid the seductions of the Evil One and pursue salvation in Jesus
3. The intention to foster our own well-being by living up to our highest dignity and character, avoiding the seduction and influence of the Evil One, and remaining on the road to salvation

First, if we truly desire to please the Lord out of gratitude and love for the gift of salvation He has given us, we will have a strong sense of inauthenticity and aversion when tempted toward sins against chastity (defined above); the stronger our gratitude and love of the Lord (which comes from deep contemplative prayer-spiritual conversion [see Chapter 3]), the greater will be our sense of inauthenticity and aversion to images and thoughts running contrary to His loving will. Admittedly, some of these images and thoughts can be quite strong (see Volume I, Chapter 4), but the counter force presented by deep gratitude and love of the Lord can make them resistible. The more quickly and intentionally we juxtapose our deep love of the Lord to these images and thoughts, the greater our resistance to them, increasing the likelihood that we will be successful in acting according to our higher self (what Saint Paul calls "the new man" [Eph 4:22–24; Col 3:10]). In addition to deep spiritual conversion, we will explore two other important techniques for strengthening our "higher self" in both our conscious and subconscious mind in Chapters 5 and 6—the Ignatian Examen and Albert Bandura's visualization-affirmation technique. The key point to appreciate here is that deep gratitude and love of the Lord incite a strong desire to please Him, which, when quickly and intentionally juxtaposed to temptation, makes it resistible.

Let us move to the second attitude of chastity—compassionate care for others' well-being and salvation. If we focus on our neighbors' highest nature, dignity, and destiny (their salvation)—refusing to reduce them to anything lower, such as an object of lust, ego-satisfaction, or utilitarian advantage—then we can juxtapose this high focus quickly and intentionally to temptations to the contrary. If we truly love others as ourselves, then the very thought of leading others astray—that is, opening them to the Evil One and jeopardizing their salvation—will incisively counteract temptations to and fantasies of unchastity. When we combine this aversion to unchaste thoughts (out of care for the other) with our desire to please the Lord (out of love for Him), it forms a very powerful intrinsic resistance to unchastity.

We now move to our third attitude of chastity—the intention to live according to our highest dignity and character, to avoid the seductions of the Evil One, and to pursue our own salvation. As will be discussed in Chapters 5 and 6, we can sometimes regress from our higher self ("the new man") to our lower self ("the old man"). This can happen because of inattentiveness to our prayer lives or allowing ourselves to deviate from the Lord's teaching by succumbing to sensuality and/or egocentricity. Though the Lord will try to counteract this with feelings of spiritual emptiness, alienation, and loneliness—and even awaken us in the early hours of the morning to confront us with the jeopardy into which we have placed ourselves (see Chapter 3, Sections IV and V)—the Evil One will rush into the gap we have created between ourselves and the Lord, because he gets his best results when we are weakened.

In this spiritually weakened state, the first two attitudes of chastity (given above) are diminished in power and effectiveness, leaving us with only the more fundamental attitude and motivation of spiritual self-preservation. If we find ourselves in this weakened state, we should remind ourselves that succumbing further to unchastity will open the door to the Evil One's stronger temptations and deceits, which increase the gap between us and the Lord. This will lead ultimately to confusion, separation from the Lord and the Church, spiritual darkness, a habitual sinful lifestyle, and despair, all of which are orchestrated by the Evil One for the purpose of having us choose his "lifestyle and kingdom" instead of the Lord's.

The Lord will not leave us alone to choose Hell. As noted above, He will allow us to feel the spiritual emptiness, alienation, and loneliness we have produced by distancing ourselves from Him. He will also plant thoughts in the back of our minds, confront us in the early hours of the morning, and providentially conspire to have people or circumstances influence us. The more quickly we cooperate with the Lord's attempts to rescue us, the more easy will be the reversal of our digression into darkness. At this juncture, we will want to allow ourselves to feel the fear of the loss of our salvation and abhorrence toward the Evil One, who has captivated us, which will move us to reach out to the Lord for help and forgiveness. As noted in Chapter 3 (Section IV), we should complement this plea with the Sacrament of Reconciliation and with pledged first "small steps" to move out of our immediate jeopardy. If we progressively amplify our "small steps", the Lord will guide us out of our perilous situation. As He does so, we will want to activate our third attitude of chastity, the most basic one—the intention to live up to our highest dignity and character, to avoid cooperating with the Evil One, and to pursue salvation in Jesus. This moves us out of base fear and refocuses us on our highest dignity and our salvation. When this attitude of chastity becomes reasonably strong, we can again pursue the first two attitudes—pleasing the Lord out of gratitude and love, and intentionally caring for the well-being and salvation of others.

I have a shorthand way of reminding myself of the above three attitudes of chastity by means of three spontaneous prayers to the Lord in times of temptation and during my Examen Prayer:

- "Lord, I thank you and love you and want to please you by imitating you and your Mother in chastity."
- "Lord, reinforce my desire to focus on each person's highest dignity, well-being, and salvation, and never to reduce them to mere objects of gratification."
- "Lord, help me to seek my highest dignity and destiny by closeness to you and distance from our enemy, Satan."

Saint Ignatius' Examen Prayer is a great way to reinforce these three spontaneous prayers. It will be explained in Chapter 6 (Section II).

We will now turn our attention to two profoundly Christlike lifestyles arising out of this virtue of chastity:

1. The life of celibacy—chastity in imitation of Jesus and His Blessed Mother (Section II.B.8.a)
2. Married chastity—covenant romantic love in marriage as articulated by the Christian tradition (Section II.B.8.b)

a. The Life of Celibacy—Chastity in Imitation of Jesus and His Blessed Mother

Jesus has called some people to a vow of chastity—for example, priests, religious sisters and brothers, and laypeople who make public and private commitments to it. If we have received this call, in imitation of Jesus, then we will want to pursue the ideal of purity commensurate with our vocation. The rewards of this commitment are expressed not only in the total gift we can make of ourselves to the service of God and the Church, but also in the level of trust and example we can provide to the people with whom we work. One of the more remarkable blessings we receive from chastity is deep bondedness with the Lord in our prayer, the sacraments, and our work with His people. This closeness to the Lord has a way of purifying our hearts toward all the virtues, which transforms the authentic and charitable quality of our actions. It also animates us with a kind of transcendent confidence, peace, and above all, joy.

In order to receive these blessings, we must give ourselves more deeply to the Lord in prayer. If we lapse in this commitment to prayer, we will likely lose the blessings of chastity, find ourselves continuously tempted and distracted, and even feel frustrated with the vow itself.

As so many priests and religious have discovered, devotion to the Blessed Virgin Mary (particularly the Rosary) can be very helpful in living the vow of chastity and bringing us closer to the Lord through it. Those who have loved and prayed to Blessed Mary know well how her presence begins to imbue both our conscious and subconscious minds. Without our thinking about it, her chaste goodness and motherly love not only become present to us, but are the object of our desire. The more we incorporate Marian devotion into our contemplative lives,[90] the more we love and want to imitate her goodness, purity, and chastity—and the more we desire to be like her (and her Son), the easier it becomes to fight the many temptations against chastity presented by the culture. We will discuss this more fully in Chapters 5–6 with respect to being transformed into what Saint Paul calls "the new man".

---

[90] For an explanation of this, see Chapter 3 (Section III) of this volume.

Saint Francis de Sales describes the blessing of chastity as follows:

Chastity, is the lily of virtues, and makes men almost equal to angels. Nothing is beautiful but what is pure, and the purity of men is chastity. Chastity is called honesty, and the possession of it honor; it is also named integrity, and the opposite, vice and corruption. In short, it has its peculiar glory, to the fair and unspotted virtue of both soul and body.[91]

The vow of chastity brings us into communion with Jesus and His Mother through identification with them in our life's vocation. When we imitate them in their self-sacrificial desire to give up sexuality for the sake of exclusive commitment to the Lord and His Kingdom, we come closer to them, which enables us to become more like them in love. One of the Sisters of Life describes this as follows:

The vowed religious thus proclaims to the world that sacrificial love, selfless love, is possible. The purest love is seen in the life of Jesus, Crucified and Risen. Meditating on the lives of Jesus and Mary expands our hearts to attempt pure love; a love that is for others; a love that keeps nothing for oneself; a love that pushes the boundaries of our selfishness and fear.[92]

John Cardinal O'Connor captures the transformative spirit of vowed chastity, which liberates us to see and serve others as Jesus Himself:

The great gift of chastity, of celibacy, of vowed virginity, is a liberation, freeing you from looking merely at the externals; freeing you from the mere physical attractions or emotional attractions that you might experience; freeing you to see another person as made in the image and likeness of God; freeing you to love because in everyone, in every man, every woman, in every child, in every unborn infant, in every cancer-ridden patient in the hospital, in the most

---

[91] Saint Francis de Sales, "On the Necessity of Chastity", *On the Devout Life* 3, 12, in *St. Francis de Sales Collection* (London: Aeterna Press, 2016).

[92] Sister Bethany Madonna, S.V., "Chastity—Love without Limits", Sisters of Life (website), 2013, accessed July 2018, https://www.sistersoflife.org/vocations/chastity-love-without -limits (site).

handsome man, in the most beautiful woman, your heart reaches out in love because always what you see is the image of God. The vow of chastity, of virginity, of celibacy is not intended simply to be a restrictive vow, but a truly liberating vow. . . .

[No matter what the spiritual or temporal state of a person,] you see the Christ, and you love. And you are free to love. This is the great gift that God offers those in religious life. You can spend the rest of your life exploring it. It will always be a mystery, the mystery of love.[93]

b. Married Chastity—Covenant Romantic Love

Most of the faithful are not called to a vow of chastity, but to marriage and family and the romantic love that sustains it. Covenant romantic love (Level Three *eros* [see below]) is the ideal of romantic love as expressed by Christian tradition. Though Jesus did not specifically address the dynamics of romantic love, He was very explicit about the importance of chastity, the sinfulness of lust, and the permanence and exclusivity of marital commitment (Mt 5:31–32; 19:3–12 [explained above]).

Using this as a basis, the Christian tradition has developed a philosophy and theology of romantic love[94] that orients believers to its ideal, culminating in exclusive, deep, intimate, generative commitment, which is the ground of marriage and family. Along with temperance as well as respect and care for others and their salvation, pursuing this ideal of romantic love is integral to contending with the deadly sin of lust. Other more specialized measures will be needed if an individual is addicted to pornography or other forms of sexual gratification (detached from intimacy, generativity, and commitment).[95]

---

[93] John Cardinal O'Connor, "Address to the Sisters of Life", Sisters of Life (website), July 5, 1992, https://www.sistersoflife.org/vocations/chastity-love-without-limits (site discontinued).

[94] See, for example, C. S. Lewis, *The Four Loves* (New York: Harcourt, 1960), pp. 91–115.

[95] A simple Internet search will bring up a variety of reputable treatment options for pornography and other sexual addictions. These include diagnostics, therapy, group assistance, etc. There are several Catholic authors and speakers who address this topic. If their solutions prove ineffective because of an ingrained addiction, recourse to online help for pornography addiction may be the next step. For a Catholic program, visit the website of the Diocese of Fargo, "Breaking Free from Pornography", 2020, http://www.fargodiocese.org/breakingfree. If the problem continues to be intransigent, other in-person therapeutic or group solutions may be needed to prevent losing a sense of intimacy, generativity, and desire for commitment.

When we speak of romantic love, we are focusing on one of the four major kinds of love of which humans are capable—*eros* (romance), *storgē* (affection), *philia* (friendship), and *agapē* (charitable love that focuses on the good of the other without expectation of reward leading toward compassion, forgiveness, and self–sacrifice).[96] We might begin with a general description of *eros*, which is concerned with romance and romantic feelings. Romance is a complex phenomenon much broader than sexual feelings and satisfaction. It involves many dimensions of the psyche, including intimacy, generativity, the reception of generativity, anticipation of deep friendship and commitment, the perception of beauty, complementarity of function, anticipation of family, and a sense of adventure. Hence, *eros* has a very wide range of feelings and psychological engagement coming from both personal maturity and decisions about life's meaning.

In our discussion of happiness (see Appendix I of this volume), we indicate that a Level One or Level Two view of happiness/purpose tends to emphasize *personal* gratification and satisfaction of *self* while Level Three and Level Four tend to emphasize empathy, contribution, and transcendental purpose. Thus, a person who has a Level One or Level Two meaning in life (who is likely to be less personally mature) will have a more superficial view of *eros* than a person in Level Three and Level Four (who is more mature, and is open to an intimate, generative, and committed relationship).

In Volume I (Chapter 4, Section V) of the Quartet, we discussed "freedom from" and "freedom for", in which it was shown that individuals on Level One and Level Two are likely to have a view of "freedom from", which focuses on immediately attaining strong urges and desires, escaping constraint and commitment, "keeping options open", and resenting unreciprocated sacrifices. Conversely, individuals on Level Three and Level Four are likely to view freedom as "freedom for", which focuses on the most pervasive, enduring, and deep purpose in life—one that goes *beyond* self and makes a genuine contribution to family, friends, community, organizations, church, the Kingdom of God, and even the culture. In this view, constraint and commitment for the sake of achieving life's higher purpose is

---

[96] Ibid.

seen as worthwhile. Likewise, foreclosing options to pursue some truly good directions is deemed essential, and unreciprocated sacrifices are accepted and expected. Once again, these different views of freedom radically affect individuals' views of a romantic relationship, as well as the feelings coming from it.

We may now give a general profile of the focus and expectations for a romantic relationship in the perspectives of Level One-Two and Level Three-Four. As might be expected, the Level One-Two perspective of *eros* emphasizes what is more apparent, immediately gratifying, intense, and ego-fulfilling. Hence, its focus is predominantly on the sexual, beauty, gender complementarity, and romantic excitement and adventure. Furthermore, its expectations are fairly short-term and focused on immediate gratification, keeping options open, increased levels of romantic excitement, and avoiding commitments and unreciprocated sacrifices. As a consequence, it resists movement to Level Three-Four, and the intimacy and generativity intrinsic to them (discussed below in this section).

In contrast to this, a Level Three-Four perspective of *eros* focuses on making a difference beyond the self—and in mature individuals on making the most pervasive, enduring, and deep contribution possible. It is also open to empathy and care for others (in its quest to make an optimal positive contribution to the world). Though it does not abandon the dimensions of *eros* emphasized in Level One and Level Two (sexuality, beauty, gender complementarity, and romantic excitement), it contextualizes these desires within concomitant desires for intimacy, generativity, complementarity, collaboration, common cause, deep friendship, loyalty, commitment, and family. As noted above, a Level Three-Four perspective is not enough to bring about these desires; there must also be psychological stability and personal development and maturation. When these factors are co-present, the expectations of romantic relationships broaden and deepen. As a consequence, there is a willingness to foreclose options and to invest more fully in the romantic relationship (and ultimately to make this relationship exclusive). There is willingness to make the other a "first priority" in the expenditure of physical and emotional resources, which anticipates a lifelong commitment as well as unreciprocated sacrifices. The following chart summarizes the outlooks of both perspectives.

Level	Focus	Expectations
Eros (Romantic Love) Three and Four	Openness to the importance and inclusion of intimacy, generativity, complementarity, collaboration, common cause, deep mutual friendship, long-term commitment, and family (note: sexuality, beauty, and romantic excitement are still important, but contextualized by the above).	Pervasive, enduring, and deep meaning, foreclosing of options to secure "best option", mutually supportive communion, constraints for the sake of intimacy, depth, and commitment, unreciprocated sacrifice
Eros (Romantic Love) One and Two	The emphasis is on sexual feelings and gratification, beauty of the other, romantic adventure, excitement of the relationship, and control within the relationship.	Immediate and heightened gratification, fulfillment of the desire to be admired and loved, keeping options open, greater levels of excitement, and no unreciprocated sacrifices

When romantic relationships occur in Level Three-Four individuals who are stable and mature, the intimate friendship becomes deeper and deeper. As noted in Chapter 2 (Section II.D.1), when *philia* (friendship) is reciprocated, it tends to deepen and become more committed. When we commit more of our time, future, and physical and psychic energy to a friend, and that friend reciprocates with a deeper commitment to us, the friendship becomes closer, more supportive, more fulfilling, and more emotionally satisfying. When it is appropriate, this deep friendship can incite intimacy, generativity, and romantic feelings, which, in turn, can deepen the friendship even more—but now it is not just a deep friendship; it is an *intimate, romantic* deep friendship. This distinctive kind of friendship can continue to deepen until both parties are not only ready for, but desirous of, making the other their *number-one priority*. From a logical point of view, there can only be one number-one priority—everything else is a contradiction. Hence, the desire to make a deep intimate friend a number-one priority is tantamount to wanting an *exclusive* commitment, which cannot be given to anyone else.

Furthermore, this deep friendship anticipates a *lifelong* commitment in which the couple enters into common cause—that is, to do some good through their mutual efforts for the world *beyond* themselves. The most significant dimension of common cause for a couple who are intimately related (anticipating sexuality) is the creation of a *family*. Recall from above that love moves *beyond* itself; we seek to do the good for *the other*, the community, the world, and the Kingdom of God. Just as loving individuals move beyond themselves, so also loving couples move beyond themselves. Though it is very important that the couple have their "alone time" to develop their closeness, affection, generativity, and mutual support, it is likewise important that they do not *stay* within the relationship *alone*. A couple staring into each other's eyes can be as mutually self-obsessive as Narcissus looking at his image in the pool; they can simply fade away doing nothing else. This illustrates the need for intimate friendships to move from "*within* the relationship" to "*beyond* the relationship". The deeply committed romantic relationship cultivates a complementary and collaborative strength—a synergy to move beyond itself to make a positive difference through common cause. Family is the most fundamental aim of such a relationship. But there can be many other objectives as well—for community, church, culture, Kingdom of God, and so forth. Though the most fundamental objective—that is, family—must come first, it too must move beyond itself, to make a positive difference in ways that will not undermine its depth and cohesiveness.

In sum, the ideal of a Level Three-Four romantic relationship is to bring intimate friendship to its highest level—to make the intimate friend a number-one priority through an exclusive and lifelong commitment to enter into mutually supportive and collaborative common cause toward family and other positive objectives that will serve not only friends, but community, culture, church, and the Kingdom of God.

We can now see an inherent conflict between Level One-Two *eros* and Level Three-Four *eros*. The emphasis on beauty, adventure, and sexual feelings in Level One-Two *eros*, without the dimensions of generativity, friendship, and commitment, can incite individuals to be both sexually permissive and promiscuous. Sexual stimulation (including everything from sexual relationships to pornography) is

frequently addictive.[97] Sexuality can become an end ؛
when it does, romantic desires can only be accentuated by mu_
ual activity, more partners, or more excitement (amplified by aggres-
siveness, risk, and alcohol/drugs, etc.).[98] These activities can enhance
sexual addiction[99] and desensitize the individual to higher dimensions
of relationship and psychic satisfaction (e.g., intimacy, generativity,
collaboration, common cause, friendship, commitment, exclusivity,
and family).

Thus, the long-term practice of Level One-Two *eros* can become
addictive, callous, and aggressive[100]—leading to objectification
("thingification") of the other, "using" the other as an object of
gratification, and dominating the other for ego satisfaction. This can
lead to a state of mind in which intimacy, generativity, and mature
friendships are hard to recapture. The addictive quality of lower brain
activities can make it difficult to move from Level One-Two to Level
Three-Four happiness and meaning. The longer individuals reinforce
Level One-Two *eros*, the more difficult it will be for them to grow
in levels of maturity and development, and to seek genuinely intimate, generative, and exclusive romantic relationships. Hence, it is
difficult, if not impossible, to maintain and deepen marital and family
relationships with a narrow Level One-Two perspective and focus.
We will further examine this tension in our discussion of the "lower
self" ("old man") and "higher self" ("new man") in Chapters 5–6.

[97] Activation of the reward pathways (dopamine system) in the lower brain by sexual activity, pornography, aggression, and drugs all form memories and habits of pleasure
that can become gradually addictive. See Donald Hilton Jr., "Pornography Addiction—A
Supranormal Stimulus Considered in the Context of Neuroplasticity", *Socioaffective Neuroscience & Psychology* 3, no. 1 (2013): 1–18, https://www.tandfonline.com/doi/full/10.3402
/snp.v3i0.20767?scroll=top&needAccess=true. See also Frances Prayer, "What Drives a Sex
Addict? Is Sex Addiction about Love or an Insatiable Craving?", *Psychology Today*, October 7,
2009, http://www.psychologytoday.com/blog/love-doc/200910/what-drives-sex-addict.

[98] Both sexual activity and aggression activate reward pathways in the hypothalamus. There
is also evidence of interrelationship between sexual desires and aggression (even violence)
through the hypothalamus. See D. Lin et al., "Functional Identification of an Aggression Locus
in the Mouse Hypothalamus", *Nature* 470 (February 10, 2011): 221–26. See also Ewen Callaway, "Sex and Violence Linked in the Brain", *Nature News*, February 9, 2011, http://www
.nature.com/news/2011/110209/full/news.2011.82.html. If sexuality is connected to generative (higher cerebral) functions, it will likely mitigate the aggressive components originating
in the hypothalamus.

[99] See Hilton, "Pornography Addiction", pp. 1–18, and Prayer, "What Drives a Sex Addict?"
[100] See ibid.

Conversely, if we focus on the needs and goodness of the beloved who is the object of our romantic desire, and seek intimate, generative, common cause with him or her for the sake of exclusive and permanent commitment in marriage and family, then we will elevate our love from the desire for mere sexual or ego-gratification through a powerful empathetic union capable of creating life and doing immense good for the world. Focusing on this ideal requires at the very least a Level Three view of happiness and purpose, and preferably a Level Four view as well, for as noted in Chapter 2 (Section II.D.2), "The family that prays together, stays together."[101] This ideal not only helps us to enter into lasting marriages, but also helps to overcome lust—sexual/romantic gratification as an end in itself.

III. Conclusion

After reading the above eight subvirtues of Christian love (describing the ideal that Jesus set out for us), some readers might be thinking—as I would have in my younger years—"If this is the ideal of love, then I am doomed, because I will never be able to fully imitate it!" Please do not think this. Jesus anticipated that the vast majority of us would fall far short of this ideal, even with concerted effort, before we pass on to the next life; and so out of His unrestricted compassion and mercy, He provided a means for people like myself—quite unperfected in the above eight subvirtues—to move steadily toward salvation. Though He left us with many gifts to vouchsafe our salvation, three are of particular importance in the cultivation of the virtue of love:

1. An unrestricted act of merciful love (given in His Passion and death), to reconcile us and reinstate us on the path to salvation through the Sacrament of Reconciliation and our sincere contrition

---

[101] David Briggs (of the *HuffPost*) summarizes the five characteristics of deep, enduring, resilient, and nurturing marriages that are significantly enhanced by couples who practice a sacramental and spiritual life. This correlation is supported by four major longitudinal studies at seven universities—Florida State University, University of Georgia, Bowling Green State University, University of Auburn, East Carolina University, University of North Texas, and the University of Calgary. See David Briggs, "5 Ways Faith Contributes to Strong Marriages, New Studies Suggest", *HuffPost*, February 8, 2015, https://www.huffpost.com/entry/5-ways-faith-contributes_b_6294716.

2. The gift of the Holy Spirit, to guide us interiorly ⟍
   of love through continual conversion of the heart
3. The Church under the leadership of the successo⟍
   Peter, to nourish us with the sacraments, moral teach⟍
   tual devotion, intellectual reflection, and community ⟍

We have discussed all three of these gifts above in Chapters 1–3.

The first gift—Jesus' unconditional act of love—is not given in word and intention only, but also in action, particularly His Incarnation, Passion, and death. When Jesus suffered and died on the Cross, He did not leave a void in His place, but rather the spiritual presence of His love and compassion actualized through His self-sacrifice on the Cross. This unrestrictedly loving presence remains in the world in the Holy Eucharist, in His Mystical Body (the Church), and in the sacraments. Of particular importance is the Sacrament of Reconciliation. Jesus' self-sacrificial loving presence becomes felt and effective whenever we seek forgiveness through the Sacrament of Reconciliation, and when we sincerely ask for forgiveness for our sins, to be healed from our interior darkness, and to be brought into closer union with Him.

When we stray from the path to salvation, we can frequently feel the loss of that presence—like a profound emptiness—inciting us to come back to Him, and when we return to Him through the Sacrament of Reconciliation and sincere contrition, we frequently experience His healing and restoring presence. This was His intention when He set His face resolutely toward Jerusalem prior to His Passion. He followed through on this plan to bring His unrestrictedly loving presence into the world until it was completed with His dying breath. His unconditionally loving, forgiving, and healing presence gives hope to us who fail often in our pursuit of the ideal of love, for we know that He will never refuse our sincere contrition through the Sacrament of Reconciliation or through our act of contrition, which anticipates that sacrament. When He hears our sincere contrition, He unhesitatingly forgives us, heals us, and restores us to His favor. We will explain this in greater detail in Chapter 7.

The second gift—the indwelling of the Holy Spirit—also helps us in the pursuit of love, for the Spirit transforms our hearts into the heart of Jesus' Father whenever we use the name that Jesus gave us— Abba. Saint Paul expresses it this way:

For you did not receive the spirit of slavery to fall back into fear, but you have received the spirit of sonship. When we cry, "Abba! Father!" it is the Spirit himself bearing witness with our spirit that we are children of God, and if children, then heirs, heirs of God and fellow heirs with Christ, provided we suffer with him in order that we may also be glorified with him. (Rom 8:15–17)

As noted in Chapter 3, the Spirit inspires, guides, and protects us, while sharing the love of Christ and the Father with us. This not only brings confidence and peace in our adopted sonship but also God's loving perspective within our hearts. As such, the Spirit deepens the eight subvirtues of love addressed above in ways that words cannot express:

The Spirit searches everything, even the depths of God. For what person knows a man's thoughts except the spirit of the man which is in him? So also no one comprehends the thoughts of God except the Spirit of God. Now we have received not the spirit of the world, but the Spirit which is from God, that we might understand the gifts bestowed on us by God. And we impart this in words not taught by human wisdom but taught by the Spirit, interpreting spiritual truths to those who possess the Spirit. (1 Cor 2:10–13)

The third gift Jesus left us is the Church herself. As we have seen in Chapters 1–3, the Catholic Church established by Jesus is a complex reality with an interior and exterior dimension—a teaching authority, a source of sacraments, a community of support, a center of devotion and spiritual life, a center of service and help for the poor, and an inspirer of religious intellectual tradition. This remarkable, complex mediator of grace offers a myriad of benefits to help us appropriate a Christian moral life and stay on the path to salvation.

We very probably will not reach perfection in the eight subvirtues of love underlying spiritual and moral conversion before passing on to the next life, but we have a Savior who has given Himself completely to us so that when we sincerely ask for His mercy through the Sacrament of Reconciliation (and in acts of contrition anticipating that sacrament), we can be sure of it. We have also been given the Holy Spirit to inspire us interiorly and the Church to guide and protect us exteriorly, which gives the assurance that we can make progress in our spiritual and moral conversion if we but avail ourselves of the many gifts and graces offered to us through them. Progress may well be slow and our egos frequently intransigent, but the unrestricted mercy of Christ, the Holy Spirit, and the Church can break through even the most intransigent ego so long as we are willing to listen to and avail ourselves of the gifts we have been given by Jesus.

We might conclude with the poem by John Donne, who asks the Holy Trinity to batter his heart so that he may be transformed in the image of Christ:

> Batter my heart, three-person'd God, for you
> As yet but knock, breathe, shine, and seek to mend;
> That I may rise and stand, o'erthrow me, and bend
> Your force to break, blow, burn, and make me new.
> I, like an usurp'd town to another due,
> Labor to admit you, but oh, to no end;
> Reason, your viceroy in me, me should defend,
> But is captiv'd, and proves weak or untrue.
> Yet dearly I love you, and would be lov'd fain,
> But am betroth'd unto your enemy;
> Divorce me, untie or break that knot again,
> Take me to you, imprison me, for I,
> Except you enthrall me, never shall be free,
> Nor ever chaste, except you ravish me.[102]

By now it will be clear that deep spiritual conversion significantly enhances our appropriation of virtue (particularly the supreme virtue of love) and our moral conversion. We now proceed to Chapters 5 and 6, where we discuss the mutual complementarity of spiritual and moral conversion as well as four additional concrete steps of moral conversion (from Ignatian spirituality, contemporary psychology, and philosophy) that help to resist temptation and effect the transformation from the "old man" to the "new man".

---

[102] John Donne, "Holy Sonnets: Batter My Heart, Three-Person'd God", Poetry Foundation (website), 2020, https://www.poetryfoundation.org/poems/44106/holy-sonnets-batter-my-heart-three-persond-god.

Chapter Five

Moral Conversion and the "Higher Self"

Introduction

The *Catechism of the Catholic Church* succinctly summarizes the previous four chapters:

> It is not easy for man, wounded by sin, to maintain moral balance. Christ's gift of salvation offers us the grace necessary to persevere in the pursuit of the virtues. Everyone should always ask for this grace of light and strength, frequent the sacraments, cooperate with the Holy Spirit, and follow his calls to love what is good and shun evil.[1]

Our close connection with the heart of Christ that catalyzes the spiritual gifts of the inner Church gradually transforms us, conforming us ever more closely to the heart of Christ. Saint Paul speaks of this transformation as moving from the fleshly man to the spiritual man (Rom 8:5–11) and moving from the "old man" to the "new man" (Eph 4:17–24; Col 3:9–10). If we examine the context of the two passages from the Letters to the Colossians and the Ephesians, we can see how central this transformation process is in the thought of Saint Paul and his followers. Let us begin with the Letter to the Colossians:

> Put to death therefore what is earthly in you: immorality, impurity, passion, evil desire, and covetousness, which is idolatry. On account of these the wrath of God is coming. In these you once walked, when you lived in them. But now put them all away: anger, wrath, malice, slander, and foul talk from your mouth. Do not lie to one another, seeing that you have put off the old man [*anthrōpon*] with his practices and have put on the new man [*anthrōpon*], who is being renewed in knowledge after the image of his creator. (3:5–10)

---

[1] *CCC* 1811.

Notice that the Pauline author associates the "old man" with the deadly sins, which are oriented toward sensuality, baseness, and egocentricity. Note also how he associates the "new man" with the image of God, in which we are created. This suggests that we are created with both natures, but that the old or lower nature is dominant when we are young and spiritually immature, requiring substantial effort to make the higher nature (created in the image of God) emerge, grow stronger, and ultimately become preeminent. As we have seen in previous chapters, Saint Paul does not underplay the efforts that must be made to move from the lower self (old nature) to the higher self (new nature), because he himself experienced this struggle dramatically well into his Christian life (see Rom 7:17–20). Let us now turn to the Letter to the Ephesians:

> Now this I affirm and testify in the Lord, that you must no longer walk as the Gentiles [*ethnē*—"unbelievers"] walk, in the futility of their minds; they are darkened in their understanding, alienated from the life of God because of the ignorance that is in them, due to their hardness of heart; they have become callous and have given themselves up to licentiousness, greedy to practice every kind of uncleanness. You did not so learn Christ!—assuming that you have heard about him and were taught in him, as the truth is in Jesus. Put off the old man [*anthrōpon*] that belongs to your former manner of life and is corrupt through deceitful lusts, and be renewed in the spirit of your minds, and put on the new man [*anthrōpon*], created after the likeness of God in true righteousness and holiness. (4:17–24)

The Pauline author repeats the same themes as those mentioned in the Letter to the Colossians, associating the "old man" with sensuality, baseness, and egocentricity (the lower self) while associating the "new man" with the likeness of God—the higher self, created in His image. The author further implies that this "belief" in Jesus Christ is the pathway to move from our dominant lower self to the divine-like higher self. This "belief" includes trusting in Jesus' spiritual and moral teaching, participating in His Church (through the sacraments, community, service, and evangelization), and praying (see Chapters 2–3 of this volume).

These two passages also give an important clue about how to resist temptation through Christian faith. They imply that a most important step in moral conversion (beyond spiritual conversion and learning about virtue) is to replace "thinking with our lower self" (our "fleshly self" or "the old man") with "thinking through our higher self" (our "spiritual self" or "the new man"). This will be explained in detail below (Section III). For the moment, suffice it to say that Christians are not consigned to resisting temptation by using a mere act of the will—a "no" to temptation. We can empower this "no" by moving our thought process from our lower to our higher self.

Though the Catholic spiritual and moral tradition offers a variety of paths to move from spiritual conversion to moral conversion—such as those of Saint Augustine,[2] Saint John Cassian,[3] Saint Benedict,[4] Saint John Climacus,[5] Saint Thomas à Kempis,[6] and Saint

---

[2] Saint Augustine's *Confessions* (composed around A.D. 397) presents an implicit path from spiritual to moral conversion. By recounting his own path, Saint Augustine gave a kind of "prototype" to other spiritual writers who drew from its richness quite liberally. See Saint Augustine, *Confessions*, trans. and ed. Henry Chadwick (New York: Oxford University Press, 1991).

[3] Saint John Cassian was a highly influential monk who brought the ideas of the Desert Fathers to the West and was an important influence on Saint Benedict, the father of Western monasticism. He consolidated much of the thought of the Desert Fathers into a volume titled *Conferences of the Desert Fathers* (composed around A.D. 420), which became a manual for the training of the "inner man". It contains an early tractate on spiritual conversion and the path from spiritual conversion to moral conversion. See John Cassian, *Conferences*, Classics of Western Spirituality (Mahwah, N.J.: Paulist Press, 1985).

[4] Saint Benedict is the father of Western monasticism principally because his Rule (composed around A.D. 530) is simple and takes a middle path between ascetical individualism and community life. Though his Rule is mostly concerned with the organization of monastic life and the monastery itself, the prologue in Chapter 7 (on the Twelve Stages of Humility) was highly influential in prescribing a path from spiritual to moral conversion. See Saint Benedict, *The Rule of Saint Benedict*, ed. Timothy Fry, O.S.B. (New York: Vintage, 1998).

[5] Saint John Climacus wrote the very famous work *Ladder of Divine Ascent* around A.D. 610. It contains thirty chapters detailing spiritual conversion and the ascent from spiritual conversion to moral perfection. It was highly influential in the West and contains detailed descriptions of the virtues and the deadly sins. See Saint John Climacus, *The Ladder of Divine Ascent* (Mahwah, N.J.: Paulist Press, 1982).

[6] Saint Thomas à Kempis' classical work *The Imitation of Christ* (ca. 1420) is one of the most popular and well-disseminated books on Christian devotion and is still quite popular today. It emphasizes spiritual conversion, particularly devotion to the Eucharist, and the first part of moral conversion, detachment from the world. Its path to detachment is through withdrawing from the world and its vanities, then pursuing interior conversion through asceticism, good conscience, and following the divine will. See Saint Thomas à Kempis, *The Imitation of Christ* (New York: Image Classics, 1955).

Ignatius of Loyola—I will concentrate on the path recommended by Saint Ignatius of Loyola, not only because I am familiar with it as a Jesuit, but because I believe he had a genius for integrating spiritual depth (contemplation) with the practical matters of will and action to serve God, His Kingdom, His Church, and His people.

Though Saint Ignatius of Loyola was familiar with the works of Saint Augustine, Saint Benedict, and Saint Thomas à Kempis (as well as other works of spiritual devotion), he probably had only a sketchy acquaintance with them at the time he wrote *The Spiritual Exercises* in a cave outside of Manresa (Catalonia, Spain). The *Exercises* were developed through reflection on his meditation and prayer in a period of rigorous asceticism devoted to detachment from the world and moral conversion. Hence, they come more from his experience of relationship with the Lord in prayer than from reading other spiritual masters. This experiential background provided several advantages in helping others to deepen their conversion. First, he could speak not from somebody else's experience, but from his own, which enabled him to advise others confidently and practically about what might be helpful to them. Second, he could construct meditations that would be helpful for *both* spiritual conversion (deepening our relationship with Christ) and moral conversion (the hard discipline of developing aversion to the deadly sins and devotion to the virtues for the sake of Christ and His Kingdom). Third, it would enable him to set out unique practical guidelines for spiritual discernment, interpretation of consolation and desolation in prayer, and the snares of the Evil One that he believed would be part of most everyone's spiritual journey. Fourth, he could set out meditations and guidelines for *individual* (instead of communal—monastic) approaches to spiritual and moral conversion. As the reader may have surmised, these advantages are ideally suited for our time and culture, which highly values individuality, experience, and creativity.

I have taken the approach of presenting first spiritual conversion through the guidance of the Catholic Church (in Chapters 1–3) and then moral conversion (in this, the previous, and succeeding chapters). Saint Ignatius takes a more mixed approach in *The Spiritual Exercises*, blending spiritual and moral conversion. The First Week (of four weeks) of the *Exercises* is devoted almost entirely to the first level of moral conversion—a firm resolve to move away from serious sin (a life controlled by desires for the eight deadly sins, particularly greed, lust, vanity, and pride). The second through fourth weeks focus on spiritual conversion (through Ignatius' contemplations on the life of Christ), and blending them with explicit meditations and rules for moral conversion such as the Kingdom Meditation, the Two Standards, the Three Degrees of Humility, and the Three Kinds of Men. His instructions and rules to assist moral conversion include the General Examen, the Particular Examen, and three methods of prayer. The final contemplation (to attain divine love) and the rules for discernment of spirits are focused on synthesizing both spiritual and moral conversion.

These Ignatian insights into moral conversion can be fruitfully complemented by insights from philosophy and contemporary psychology. These additional insights provide an efficacious method for resisting temptation, reinforcing our higher self, and building an identity based on virtue and the image of Christ.

We may now proceed to a discussion of three preliminary aspects of moral conversion, followed by the first of four steps of the conversion process:

1. The Complementarity of Spiritual and Moral Conversion (Section I)
2. The Good Spirit and Evil Spirit during Moral Conversion (Section II)
3. The "Higher Self" and the "Lower Self" (Section III)
4. The First Step in Moral Conversion: Aversion to Sin and Devotion to Virtue (Section IV)

We will present the second, third, and fourth steps of the conversion process in the following chapter.

Evidently, deepening moral conversion will not be a steady upward improvement. There will be times of failure, distraction, and perhaps extended periods of inattentiveness to this challenging process. This will require the Lord's unconditional merciful love through the Sacrament of Reconciliation and prayer, which we will discuss in Chapter 7.

I. The Complementarity of Spiritual and Moral Conversion

Moral conversion—turning our hearts toward virtue and God's will through detachment from sensuality and egocentricity—presents a significant challenge. Saint Paul tells us that it is likely to be a struggle even for those dedicated to holiness (like himself) until the end of our lives. As we shall see, this does not mean that moral conversion will not become simpler and habitual over the course of time—for it certainly will. It means only that we must be vigilant until our dying day, ready to ask for forgiveness from the Lord of love when we fail and encounter setbacks. As we saw in Chapter 3, in the Letter to the Romans, Saint Paul proclaims in exasperation:

> I do not understand my own actions. For I do not do what I want, but I do the very thing I hate.... For I know that nothing good dwells within me, that is, in my flesh. I can will what is right, but I cannot do it. For I do not do the good I want, but the evil I do not want is what I do. Now if I do what I do not want, it is no longer I that do it, but sin which dwells within me. So I find it to be a law that when I want to do right, evil lies close at hand. For I delight in the law of God, in my inmost self, but I see in my members another law at war with the law of my mind and making me captive to the law of sin which dwells in my members. Wretched man that I am! Who will deliver me from this body of death? Thanks be to God through Jesus Christ our Lord! (7:15, 18–25)

Saint Paul wrote this passage when he was a mature Christian in A.D. 58, twenty-three years after his conversion in A.D. 35 and nine years before his martyrdom in A.D. 67. Even after twenty-three years, he was tempted by various deadly sins—though it is difficult to identify which ones they were beyond his self-disclosed sin of pride (see 2 Cor 12:7).[7]

[7] We should not jump to the conclusion that Paul was tempted by sins of the flesh because he uses the word "flesh" in 2 Corinthians 12:7. This is a technical term that Paul sets in contrast to "Spirit", and it means "an inclination toward sin of any kind". This might be sins of the flesh, ego-centricity (vanity or pride), anger, impatience, etc. See Joseph Fitzmyer, "The Letter to the Romans", in *The New Jerome Biblical Commentary*, ed. Raymond E. Brown, Joseph A. Fitzmyer, and Roland E. Murphy (Englewood Cliffs, N.J.: Prentice-Hall, 1990), p. 851.

Nevertheless, as the Pauline author implies in the Letter to the Ephesians cited above (Eph 4:17–24), we should continually try to replace the "old man" (our inclination toward the deadly sins) with the "new man" (our identification with Jesus and the virtues He espoused). As implied in the previous chapters, spiritual conversion frequently precedes moral conversion because the closer we are to Jesus in relationship and prayer (spiritual conversion), the more we will want to imitate Him in thought, word, virtue, and action (moral conversion). Yet, the relationship between spiritual and moral conversion is not that simple. As we become more proficient at resisting temptation and living the Christian virtues (moral conversion), we open the way to an even deeper relationship with the Lord through prayer and sacraments (deeper spiritual conversion), which, in its turn, opens the way to the final stages of moral conversion—conformity of our will to the Lord's, giving rise to complete self-offering to the Lord in evangelization and charitable service. Saint Ignatius truly appreciated this cycle of spiritual and moral conversion and formulated the *Spiritual Exercises* to inspire and complete it. Before addressing the very important practical topic of cultivating the higher self and resisting temptation, we will take a closer look at the complementarity between spiritual and moral conversion seen through the lens of Saint Ignatius' *Spiritual Exercises*. We will do this in two steps:

1. The Prioritization of Prayer and Discipleship (Section I.A)
2. The Cycle of Spiritual and Moral Conversion (Section I.B)

A. The Prioritization of Prayer and Discipleship

As noted many times in the foregoing chapters, moral conversion (detachment from sensuality and egoism, appropriation of virtue, and resistance to sin and temptation) is immeasurably supported by spiritual conversion (a close relationship with the Lord through sacraments, prayer, and discipleship). Saint Ignatius states this incisively at the beginning of the the First Week of the *Spiritual Exercises* in a meditation called Principle and Foundation:

> Man is created to praise, reverence, and serve God our Lord, and by this means to save his soul. And the other things on the face of the

earth are created for man and that they may help him in prosecuting the end for which he is created. From this it follows that man is to use them as much as they help him on to his end, and ought to rid himself of them so far as they hinder him as to it. For this it is necessary to make ourselves indifferent to all created things in all that is allowed to the choice of our free will and is not prohibited to it; so that, on our part, we want not health rather than sickness, riches rather than poverty, honor rather than dishonor, long rather than short life, and so in all the rest; desiring and choosing only what is most conducive for us to the end for which we are created.[8]

Saint Ignatius' priorities reflect the teachings of Jesus: "Seek first his kingdom and his righteousness, and all these things shall be yours as well" (Mt 6:33). Saint Ignatius wants the retreatant to go further: to understand what will be required in order to live for these priorities—namely, indifference to what might be called "the things of this world".

As we read Ignatius' words, particularly his example of indifference—"So that, on our part, we want not health rather than sickness, riches rather than poverty, honor rather than dishonor, long rather than short life"—we might at first be overwhelmed by its seeming impossibility. We might be thinking, "How could I possibly be indifferent to sickness, poverty, dishonor, and a short life?"

If we focus solely on this phrase, we fail to grasp the whole context in which it is said: the real meaning intended by Saint Ignatius. So what is the whole context? It is his first statement that the true end of our lives is to save our souls, to be saved by our loving God. To do this, we will want to follow God's will, which means praying (praising and reverencing) and discipleship (following and serving). He recognizes that there will be two huge obstacles to prayer and discipleship in our lives:

1. Undue attachment to created things
2. Spiritual evil (whom he refers to as "the evil one")

So what is Saint Ignatius asking of us? He is asking us first to prioritize our salvation (through prayer and discipleship) *above* any other

---

[8] See *Spiritual Exercises*, "First Week: Principle and Foundation", http://sacred-texts.com /chr/seil/seil07.htm.

created thing, even health, riches, honors, and a long life. He recognizes that if we truly prioritize our salvation (through prayer and discipleship) above everything else, we will direct everything else—health, riches, honors, and a long life—to the end for which we were created: eternal life with the Lord of unconditional love.

For Saint Ignatius, then, the first step in moving from spiritual to moral conversion is to subordinate all worldly pursuits, the pursuit of health, wealth, honors (ego-comparative advantage), and a long life, to prayer and discipleship for the Lord. This will enable us to continuously ask the question "Is my pursuit of health, wealth, etc., commensurate with my relationship with the Lord in prayer and my desire to follow Him?" Another way of asking this question is, "Is this particular pursuit interfering with my desire to pray and be a disciple of the Lord?" If so, then I should find a way to modify it so that it won't interfere with my salvation or the salvation of others whose lives I touch. Notice that Ignatius does not expect us to *stop* a particular pursuit that seems to be interfering with prayer or discipleship but only to modify the pursuit so that it ceases to interfere with our higher priorities.

B. The Cycle of Spiritual and Moral Conversion

Though fear is often thought to be the most powerful of all motivators, it is restricted by its negativity. It can produce a short-term jolt into action, but the negative state of mind it induces depletes and even exhausts us, so it loses its compelling quality over the long-term. Furthermore, fear will not bring us to the objective of spiritual and moral conversion that is *love* (see Chapter 4, Section II). The First Letter of John says this explicitly:

> In this is love perfected with us, that we may have confidence for the day of judgment, because as he is so are we in this world. There is no fear in love, but perfect love casts out fear. For fear has to do with punishment, and he who fears is not perfected in love. We love, because he first loved us. (4:17–19)

In view of this, we might legitimately ask, "If fear is such a poor long-term motivator of Christian conduct, then why did Saint Ignatius make recourse to it so pointedly in the First Week of the *Spiritual*

Exercises?" For two reasons. First, Saint Ignatius recognized that for people of the First Week (who are committed to Level One sensuality and materialism and Level Two ego-comparative advantage), an appeal to love would not work because they do not yet have an interest, let alone a cultivated desire, to be contributive or empathetic. He also recognized that this group was quite susceptible to motivation by fear, because the threat of losing eternal happiness—or being subject to eternal darkness and loneliness—implies pain and unhappiness incommensurate with Level One and Two objectives.

Nevertheless, Ignatius had no illusions about the long-term efficacy of fear as a motivating power, because he intended to use this motivation only for a short time—to help people move from the First Week (before spiritual and moral conversion) to the Second Week (the active pursuit of spiritual and moral conversion for love of God). When an individual moves to the Second Week, fear is less needed to motivate him because he is growing in gratitude and love of God. Yes, he continues to fear his spiritual enemy, the Evil One, but his thanks to the Lord for saving him from that enemy by His Incarnation, Passion, and death induces a love and confidence greater than fear. This love of the Lord substantially enhances his love of neighbor as explained in the previous chapter (Section II).

The transition from the First to Second Week is generally *not* punctuated and clear-cut. It is constituted by a phase (that could be quite lengthy) in which the believer can vacillate between motivation by fear and by love. As the believer deepens his spiritual conversion, he becomes more inclined toward motivation by love, at which point he becomes less motivated by fear, eventually ignoring it as a significant motivating influence. As this occurs, the believer grows in gratitude and love of the Lord, which opens upon even greater love of neighbor. We address this in the previous chapter's discussion of chastity (Section II.B.8), showing that deeper gratitude and love of God enables us to appropriate more fully the three noble intentions of chastity:

1. The intention to please and serve the Lord according to His Word out of deep gratitude and love
2. The intention to focus on the highest dignity and destiny of others and to help them avoid the seductions of the Evil One and pursue salvation in Jesus

3. The intention to foster our own well-being by living up to our highest dignity and character, avoiding the seduction and influence of the Evil One, and remaining on the road to salvation

The more one grows in thankfulness and love of the Lord (through spiritual conversion, particularly through the sacraments and contemplative prayer), the more deeply one will appropriate the intentions and attitudes of chastity that also apply to the other seven subvirtues of love. We apply these intentions to the other subvirtues below in Section IV. This foundational step in moral conversion (conforming our will to that of the Lord's) gives us freedom to resist temptation, act virtuously, and progressively detach ourselves from the fleeting things of this world. As we shall see, this reinforces our transformation from the lower self to the higher self.

How does the cycle of fear and love play out? When a believer first starts his spiritual journey, he is moved by a combination of the desire for salvation and a fear of losing it; but as he becomes more familiar with the Lord in spiritual conversion, he grows more aware of the Lord's presence in his life—and he notices that if he slackens his commitment to participation in the Church or violates basic moral precepts, he feels an acute sense of spiritual emptiness, alienation, loneliness and guilt, which moves him to recommit himself to Church participation and moral propriety.

Yet, the Lord is not content to leave the believer there. As noted in Chapter 3 (Sections IV–V), the Lord inspires thoughts in the back of the believer's mind, wakes him in the early hours of the morning to make strong suggestions, and sends people (frequently through Church participation) into his life to help him strengthen his conviction about His existence and presence, and the goodness and desirability of greater participation in the Church and deepened moral conversion. This might take several attempts, all of which might have some short-term effects. Frequently, the believer will discover that increased moral conversion has tremendous efficacy for his salvation, helping others to their salvation, and closer relationship with the Lord. If he makes this discovery, he will likely resolve to dedicate more of his life to religious participation, and to make an ever greater effort to resist temptation and sin. As he fortifies his resolve for the long-term, the Lord will come to him with greater consolation, and he will experience a heightened sense of the Lord's presence, peace, home, and love.

The believer's deepened resolve leads to an ever-widening cycle of spiritual and moral conversion—his greater Church participation leads to increased resolve to resist temptation, which leads in turn to greater love of the Lord. As the believer catches fire, he begins to resist temptation more concertedly, which in turn opens him to the love and blessings of God around him. This leads to a greater love of the One who loves and blesses him, which in turn leads him to ever greater resolve to resist temptation—and the widening cycle continues.

The hardest and most important part of the above cycle is the believer's initial decision to increase his resolve to resist temptation. Though he can use some of the tools mentioned in the next chapter (such as the Ignatian Examen, visualization, and affirmations) to help him in a positive way, he still needs to make resistance to temptation one of the *highest priorities* of his life, resolving to bring it into every part of his day. Extremely active people may be reticent to make such a firm resolution because they may think that it will take too much time or deplete psychic energy from the multiple commitments they have for work and family. However, this is really not the case. What is required is heightened awareness of one's vulnerability to the eight deadly sins and the temptations of the Evil One. This entails not only awareness of the sins one is most likely to commit, but also being aware of when the temptation toward that sin is beginning to arise during the day. This requires training ourselves to catch the first signs of temptation before our desire becomes significantly enkindled. The more quickly we catch the temptation, the more easily and quickly we can resist it.

Beginners will have a more challenging time resisting temptation even if they catch it quickly, because they have not yet made habitual the three above noble intentions (toward chastity and the other virtues). Recall the three noble intentions flowing out of spiritual conversion (listed above)—the intention to please the Lord, to focus on the highest dignity and destiny (salvation) of others, and to foster our own highest dignity and destiny (salvation). Inasmuch as beginners have not made these intentions habitual, they have to call them to mind when they are resisting temptation, which can be somewhat cumbersome and unsuccessful. However, as they repeatedly call these intentions to mind, they become more and more a part of their conscious and subconscious mind. This enables the believer to call forth these noble intentions quite powerfully at the moment a temptation occurs, which helps to overcome it successfully. Beyond repeating these intentions during times of temptation, there are four other ways of reinforcing them in our conscious and subconscious minds, which correspond to the four steps of moral conversion (explained below and in the next chapter):

1. Meditations to enhance aversion to the deadly sins and devotion to the virtues (see below Section IV)
2. Use of visualization and affirmations to condition the subconscious mind toward the higher self (see Chapter 6, Section I)
3. Use of Saint Ignatius' daily Examen to bring grace into our conversion process (Chapter 6, Section II)
4. Using spontaneous prayers and habits to solidify the higher self and moral conversion (Chapter 6, Section IV)

The strong integration of the three noble intentions in the conscious and subconscious mind can lead to a powerful reflex reaction when temptation occurs. The practiced believer can simply say the word "no" on catching the first glimpse of temptation, which can bring the thought, desire, and positive emotion of wanting to please the Lord, to vouchsafe the salvation of others, and to reach one's salvific dignity to the forefront of consciousness. As will be explained below, if the subconscious mind is imbued with these three noble intentions (what we will call the "higher self"), it will reinforce, rather than impede, the conscious mind's resistance to temptation.

The practiced believer is now in the midst of moral conversion. His conscious intention and subconscious motivation are integrated toward the Lord's will, and so the believer's will is becoming more and more conformed to the Lord's. Temptation is now easier to resist, because the believer's conscious and subconscious mind have integrated his higher self, and therefore they are strongly oriented toward the intentions to please the Lord, to seek the highest dignity and salvation of others, and to seek his own highest dignity and salvation.

Let us pause for a moment and consider three steps involved in resisting temptation:

- Saying no at the moment of temptation
- "Thinking with our higher self" (using the three noble intentions)
- Using spontaneous prayers to the Lord, the Blessed Virgin Mary, and Saint Michael to bolster the desires of our "higher self"

These three steps are explained more fully in the next chapter. For the moment, it is important to note only that the higher self is imbued with the fruits of spiritual conversion, which leads to the three noble intentions and the desire to appropriate virtue fully (especially the virtue of love) in one's whole mind (intellect), heart (affect/ emotion), and will. We will explain below that this entails bringing the higher self to both the conscious and subconscious mind.

Though the beginner will no doubt have to implement all of the above three steps to resist temptation successfully, the practiced believer will fuse the first two steps together, and so simply saying and willing "no" brings the noble intentions and desires of the higher self to bear against the temptation. When this is combined with a brief spontaneous prayer, temptation can frequently be resisted. How does this happen?

The frequent recollection of the three noble intentions (of the higher self) in the midst of temptation reinforces both the ideas and the loving emotion accompanying the ideas in both the conscious and subconscious mind. As noted above, these intentions, ideas, and emotions of the higher self can be furthered reinforced by the Ignatian Examen, visualization, and affirmations. After a while, the believer will notice that when he is resisting temptation—saying no to temptation— these ideas and emotions will *automatically* come to the forefront of consciousness the moment he says no. We might say that the believer's no is imbued with the felt intention to please the Lord, to seek the salvation of others, and to seek his own salvation—or stated negatively, the believer's no is filled with the heartfelt desire *not* to disappoint the Lord, *not* to undermine the highest dignity and salvation of others, and *not* to undermine his own salvation. Since his heart, mind, and will are set on these three intentions (his higher self), he will be well-disposed to resisting any temptation to the contrary.

Now let us return to the cycle of spiritual and moral conversion we were discussing above. If we become proficient in resisting temptation, then we will probably find ourselves drawn more to contemplative prayer and, like Saint Ignatius, moved more deeply by the Lord's consolation, both affective and spiritual, in that prayer.[9] At this juncture, a retreat becomes essential, and Jesuits would hasten to add, a silent retreat like the *Spiritual Exercises*. In Chapter 3 (Section III.C.3), we briefly addressed the importance of a retreat to catalyze our entry into the third stage of contemplative prayer. Retreats are needed for the silence (to listen to the Lord), spiritual exercises (to direct the mind and heart toward deeper spiritual and moral conversion), designated lengthy prayer times to be with the Lord, and individual direction from a person well-versed in the spiritual life (to sort out the ideas and emotions that well up within the silence). Saint Ignatius' *Spiritual Exercises* are ideally suited to deepen our spiritual conversion (after the first stage of moral conversion explained above) and to enter more deeply into the third stage of contemplative prayer. How does Saint Ignatius do this?

The *Spiritual Exercises* are divided into four weeks. As noted above, the First Week is devoted to moving the retreatant from a stage of premoral conversion to a state of genuine desire for that conversion. In the Second Week, Saint Ignatius asks the retreatant to meditate on scenes from the life and ministry of Jesus, paying special attention to His humble upbringing, His compassion for sinners, the sick, and the poor, and His relationship with His disciples. Though he does not mention the verse from John 15:12, his intention is to have the retreatant embrace the commandment "Love one another as I have loved you," out of deep gratitude and love for Jesus' redemptive presence for us. In the Third Week, Ignatius has the retreatant focus on each aspect of the trial, Passion, and death of Jesus, paying special attention to His self-sacrificial love for the

---

[9] As noted in Volume I (Chapter 1, Section III) of this Trilogy, the believer's progress in the spiritual life is generally reinforced by affective consolation through the Holy Spirit (see the quote by Ignatius about spiritual movements of the soul in the next section). However, as the believer progresses more deeply in the spiritual life to greater and greater intimacy with the Lord, the Lord may choose to purify him through a "dark night". This will decrease the believer's dependence on affective consolation and purify his love for God and neighbor. See Volume I, Chapter 1, Section III, of this Trilogy.

retreatant and the world. By doing this, Saint Ignatius facilitates the grace of the Holy Spirit to move the retreatant to *even deeper* gratitude and love for the Lord so that he will want to offer himself back to the Lord in humility, compassion, and service. In the Fourth Week, Saint Ignatius considers the Resurrection of Jesus and gives a final contemplation called "The Contemplation to Attain (or Gain) the Love of God". Again, his objective is to fill the retreatant with great gratitude for the gifts that he has been given—the creation of his body and soul, the beauty of the world around him, his redemption by Jesus, and his many personal gifts (family, friends, talents, and opportunities). He then asks the retreatant to consider what he would want to offer in return for this great love of the Lord, his God (explained below).

Some readers may be thinking that they do not have four weeks to give to a silent Ignatian retreat. Does this rule out the possibility of a silent Ignatian retreat with the movements of the four weeks of the *Spiritual Exercises*? Saint Ignatius anticipated this challenge, and devised a form of the exercises (called "The Annotation 19 Retreat") that can be accommodated to our everyday life. Though this is a remarkable method for facilitating deeper spiritual conversion and contemplative life, it misses the value of prolonged silence and lengthy periods devoted to contemplative prayer. For this reason, I would suggest that readers who cannot devote thirty days, but can devote three to eight days to a retreat, to investigate the shortened offerings available to them in their particular area.[10]

If readers dedicate time to one of the above retreats, they can expect a deepening of their contemplative prayer life, moving them into the third stage of contemplative prayer, particularly the prayer of companionship (see Chapter 3, Section III.C, of this volume). Remember, this deeper contemplative prayer is the foundation for deeper moral conversion that will ultimately facilitate a transition from the lower self to the higher self (see below Sections II–III).

---

[10] The following website (from the Loyola Institute of Spirituality) recommends contacting a Jesuit retreat house that offers such retreats in your area. It lists twenty-six retreat houses throughout the country that offer three- to four-day weekend retreats, eight-day retreats, thirty-day retreats, and "Annotation 19" retreats for everyday life. See https://www.ignatian spirituality.com/ignatian-prayer/retreats. This service is not limited to the United States, and similar websites may be found in many countries throughout the world.

Gratitude plays a central role in facilitating progress in the complementary process of spiritual and moral conversion given in the *Spiritual Exercises*. Assuming that the reader has moved beyond the First Week (the first stage of moral conversion leading to a sincere desire for deeper spiritual and moral conversion), Saint Ignatius suggests contemplations to intensify *gratitude*, which he knows will ignite the believer's love. He knew well (from his own experience) that increased resistance to temptation will lead to decreased influence of sensuality and egocentricity in the believer's life. This means that the believer will have to contend less with these obstacles to recognizing the blessings he has been given by God and others. Now profoundly aware of those blessings, the believer is primed to be filled with appreciation and gratitude leading toward deepened love. Saint Ignatius hopes the believer will reach this state of increased resistance to temptation followed by deepened gratitude and love of the Lord by the Third Week of the *Spiritual Exercises*, and so he spends an entire week on the Passion of our Lord, which ushers the retreatant into profound gratitude for Jesus' whole gift of Himself for our redemption. In the Fourth Week, Ignatius goes further, presenting contemplations on the Resurrection of Jesus, summing it all up with the Contemplation to Attain Divine Love. Here he leads the believer through the various kinds of blessings that will stimulate the believer's gratitude and love, telling him what to ask for:

> Second Prelude. The second, to ask for what I want. It will be here to ask for interior knowledge of so great good received, in order that being entirely grateful, I may be able in all to love and serve His Divine Majesty. The First Point is, to bring to memory the benefits received, of Creation, Redemption and particular gifts, pondering with much feeling how much God our Lord has done for me, and how much He has given me of what He has, and then the same Lord desires to give me Himself as much as He can, according to His Divine ordination. And with this to reflect on myself, considering with much reason and justice, what I ought on my side to offer and give to His Divine Majesty, that is to say, everything that is mine, and myself with it, as one who makes an offering with much feeling.[11]

---

[11] *Spiritual Exercises*, "Contemplation to Gain Love", http://sacred-texts.com/chr/seil/seil35.htm.

As the believer considers these blessings in the time and silence of the retreat, Ignatius hopes that he will be overwhelmed with gratitude and love, and will be moved to respond in kind: to love the Lord not merely in words and feelings, but also in action—the profound action of self-offering. So he proposes the following prayer, well known to every Jesuit, the Suscipe ("Take Lord, Receive"):

> Take, Lord, and receive all my liberty,
> my memory, my understanding,
> and my entire will,
> All I have and call my own.
> You have given all to me.
> To you, Lord, I return it.
> Everything is yours; do with it what you will.
> Give me only your love and your grace,
> that is enough for me.[12]

The believer's love of the Lord cannot help but intensify and deepen, which will in turn lead to greater resolve to resist temptation. This increased resolve arises out of the believer's deepened desire to love the Lord and to avoid separating himself from Him. As noted above, love is the strongest and most long-lasting of all motivations—going far beyond mere fear, rational desire, and stoic acts of the will. As the Song of Songs states, love is even stronger than its opposing counterpart—egocentricity—and stronger than death itself:

> Set me as a seal upon your heart, as a seal upon your arm; for love is strong as death, jealousy is cruel as the grave. Its flashes are flashes of fire, a most vehement flame. Many waters cannot quench love, neither can floods drown it. If a man offered for love all the wealth of his house, it would be utterly scorned. (8:6–7)

As the believer moves more deeply into this cycle of spiritual and moral conversion, he begins to transition from what the mystics call the purgative way to the illuminative way. Recall from our discussion

---

[12] "Suscipe", Loyola Press (website), 2020, https://www.loyolapress.com/our-catholic-faith/prayer/traditional-catholic-prayers/saints-prayers/suscipe-prayer-saint-ignatius-of-loyola.

of mysticism in Volume I (Chapter 1, Section III) of this Trilogy that this may entail a dark night of the soul. For those with a contemplative or monastic vocation, this dark night may last for a prolonged period, but for more active believers, such as Jesuits, these periods of purifying darkness from the Lord are generally shorter in duration. Indeed, Ignatius counsels those who are moving from this purgative to illuminative state to expect that consolation will soon return after this time of purification:

> **Seventh Rule.** The seventh: Let him who is in desolation consider how the Lord has left him in trial in his natural powers, in order to resist the different agitations and temptations of the enemy; since he can with the Divine help, which always remains to him, though he does not clearly perceive it: because the Lord has taken from him his great fervor, great love and intense grace, leaving him, however, grace enough for eternal salvation.

> **Eighth Rule.** The eighth: Let him who is in desolation labor to be in patience, which is contrary to the vexations which come to him: and let him think that he will *soon be consoled*, employing against the desolation the devices, as said in the Sixth rule.[13]

As the mystics indicate, the cycle of spiritual and moral conversion continues into the illuminative way. Though it may be punctuated by periods of aridity and "dark nights" (for the sake of purification), it is also filled with a remarkable capacity to resist temptation, divine consolation in peace, and a purified state of love directed not only toward the Lord, but also to His people—and this, after all, is the objective of the spiritual life—the road to sainthood.

II. The Good Spirit and Evil Spirit during Moral Conversion

The firm resolve to resist temptation in all its forms (whether it originates in us or through a malevolent spiritual power) is central to

---

[13] *Spiritual Exercises*, "Rules for Perceiving and Knowing in Some Manner the Different Movements Which Are Caused in the Soul" (italics added), http://www.sacred-texts.com /chr/seil/seil78.htm.

moral conversion and the subsequent deepening of spiritual conversion. Virtually every spiritual master recognized the importance of discerning the movements of spirits as one of the most difficult and essential dimensions of conversion.

In his consideration of temptation in the General Examen, Saint Ignatius recognized the need not only to empower resistance to temptation, but also to use this empowered resistance as quickly as possible—before a temptation captivates our thought, inflames our desire, and becomes difficult to resist at the moment of decision.[14] As we make progress in spiritual conversion, strengthening our resolve toward moral conversion, the Evil One intensifies his efforts to make us fall into one or more of the deadly sins, precisely because our initial successes at spiritual and moral conversion make us his adversary, distance us from his dark intentions, and open us to the inspiration and will of the Holy Spirit. As long as we are haplessly playing into the Evil One's intentions (what Saint Ignatius calls "people of the First Week"), the Evil One need only stoke the fires of our own misaligned desires; but once we decide to prioritize prayer, moral conversion, and discipleship above worldly pursuits (what Ignatius calls "people of the Second Week"), we become a real problem to the enemy of our human nature—Satan. Jesus warns us that this could occur at the very moment that we try to put our spiritual and moral house in order:

> When the unclean spirit has gone out of a man, he passes through waterless places seeking rest; and finding none he says, "I will return to my house from which I came." And when he comes he finds it swept and put in order. Then he goes and brings seven other spirits more evil than himself, and they enter and dwell there; and the last state of that man becomes worse than the first. (Lk 11:24–26)

Evidently, Jesus is not trying to discourage us from cleaning up our spiritual and moral households. So what is He saying? He is warning us that when we embark on the path to moral conversion by taking the first step of prioritizing prayer, moral conversion, and discipleship above all other things, we can be sure that our enemy, the devil, will

---

[14] See *Spiritual Exercises*, First Week, "Particular and Daily Examen", http://sacred-texts.com/chr/seil/seilo8.htm.

do everything he can to undermine and discourage us. He is almost like an obstreperous evil boarder at our home. When we evict him, he screams back at us, "How dare you!" The Evil One's disposition is hostility, and he will not hesitate to manifest this even when we are being protected by the Holy Spirit through our attempt to deepen our spiritual and moral conversion.

Make no mistake about it—the Holy Spirit will also intensify His efforts to inspire, guide, and protect us, particularly when we resolve to prioritize divine pursuits over all worldly concerns. Yet, the Holy Spirit will not undermine our freedom, and so He will allow the Evil One to continue tempting us and even to intensify those temptations. Yes, the Holy Spirit will also intensify His graces and inspirations, so much so that it can become like an overwhelming "first fervor". However, we must be alert—the Evil One will find ways to undermine our resolve to prioritize prayer, moral conversion, and discipleship, intending not only to set us back to where we were before, but also to discourage us, undermine our trust in God, and push us back even further than where we were before we embarked on the journey to deepen moral conversion.

Saint Ignatius addresses these movements of the Holy Spirit and the Evil One in people of the First and Second Week, showing how each spirit works within the souls of both groups:

> First Rule. The first Rule: In the persons who go from mortal sin to mortal sin [people of the First Week], the enemy is commonly used to propose to them apparent pleasures, making them imagine sensual delights and pleasures in order to hold them more and make them grow in their vices and sins. In these persons the good spirit uses the opposite method, pricking them and biting their consciences through the process of reason.[15]

Notice that Saint Ignatius divides the rules for spiritual movements into those of the First Week (premoral conversion) and those of the Second Week (trying to engage in moral conversion). The Holy Spirit and the spirit of the Evil One have opposite tactics for these two groups. For those in the First Week, the Evil One *encourages*

---

[15] *Spiritual Exercises*, "Rules for Perceiving and Knowing", http://sacred-texts.com/chr/seil/seil78.htm.

them in temptation, fills their imagination with greater seductions, and helps them formulate rationalizations to justify the conduct separating them from God, neighbor, and love. Conversely, the Holy Spirit tries to discourage them from their self-destructive course of action by enhancing the feelings of spiritual emptiness, alienation, and loneliness arising out of their separation from God and neighbor. After describing these differences for those in the First Week, Saint Ignatius proceeds to individuals in the Second Week (pursuing moral conversion):

> Second Rule. The second: In the persons who are going on intensely cleansing their sins and rising from good to better in the service of God our Lord [people of the Second Week], it is the method contrary to that in the first Rule [pertaining to the First Week], for then it is the way of the evil spirit to bite, sadden and put obstacles, disquieting with false reasons, that one may not go on; and it is proper to the good [spirit] to give courage and strength, consolations, tears, inspirations and quiet, easing, and putting away all obstacles, that one may go on in well doing.[16]

For individuals in the Second Week, the Holy Spirit and the spirit of the Evil One work in precisely the opposite way than they do for those in the First Week. The Evil One tries to cause disquiet and to use deceptions to undermine progress in spiritual and moral conversion. In later rules, Saint Ignatius explains the many deceptions of the Evil One for those in the Second Week. Frequently, the Evil One appears as "an angel of light" (2 Cor 11:14), making suggestions that *seem* good and pious, but in reality are exaggerations and partial truths meant to impede progress in moral conversion. Additionally, the Evil One appears as an accuser, trying to convince the progressing believer that the Lord is dissatisfied with everything that he is doing, disgusted with him, and indifferent to his salvation. Evidently, these are all lies intended to cause disquiet within the progressing believer with the objective of convincing him to quit the process of moral conversion or to despair (explained more fully in Volume I, Chapter 4, Section V, of this Trilogy).

[16] Ibid.

As we embark on our journey of deepened moral conversion, we must expect that the Evil One will resist our efforts by intensifying temptations, distracting us from prayer, and discouraging us, provoking both resentment and depression. To think otherwise would ignore not only the advice of Saint Ignatius, but Jesus Himself. In view of this, we should reflect on the determination of the Evil One in frustrating our efforts:

> Fourteenth Rule. The fourteenth: Likewise, [the Evil One] behaves as a chief bent on conquering and robbing what he desires: for, as a captain and chief of the army, pitching his camp, and looking at the forces or defences of a stronghold, attacks it on the weakest side, in like manner the enemy of human nature, roaming about, looks in turn at all our virtues, theological, cardinal and moral; and where he finds us weakest and most in need for our eternal salvation, there he attacks us and aims at taking us.[17]

As we become accustomed to recognizing our spiritual enemy and progress in resisting him, and his temptations and deceits, we will reengage the cycle of spiritual and moral conversion, and we will very likely find that our relationship with Christ (through the sacraments and prayer) has become quite close. We will also likely experience increases in affective consolation (punctuated by periods of affective desolation, described in Volume I, Chapter 4, Section V, of this Trilogy). This will lead to an intensification of our desire to serve Christ, His Kingdom, His Church, and His people. As we continue to follow the promptings of the Holy Spirit and our hearts, we will move toward the illuminative way through Ignatian mysticism (contemplation in action).

III. The "Higher Self" and the "Lower Self"

In the above discussion about resisting temptation, we noted that we could bring three forces to bear against it: saying no for the sake of Christ, "thinking with the higher self", and using spontaneous

---

[17] Ibid.

prayers. We said there that cultivating the higher self would empower our no to temptation substantially. We also noted that Saint Paul (see Eph 4:22–23; Col 3:9–10) and many other spiritual writers[18] recognized that we have two selves dwelling within us—a lower self and a higher self—and further recognized that we can develop and reinforce this higher self in order to resist temptation more easily and effectively.

As we shall see, temptation has great power over the thoughts and desires of the *lower* self, but has very little power over the thoughts and desires of the *higher* self (the virtuous, Christlike self). Thus, if we can develop and reinforce our higher self, and bring it to bear in times of temptation, we can disempower the temptations coming from both our imagination and from the Evil One. In order to explain this, we will discuss the four topics mentioned above (the higher self, visualizations and affirmations, the Ignatian Examen, and habits and spontaneous prayers) in this section and the next chapter.

What is meant by "the lower self" and "the higher self"? As noted above, Saint Paul's view of "the old man" and "the flesh" may be put into modern terminology as "the lower self" and his view of "the new man" and "the spirit" as "the higher self". At first glance, Saint Paul's idea of the old man and the new man may seem ambiguous or even confusing, but a proper explanation of them will reveal how efficacious they can be in resisting temptation and conforming ourselves to the image of Christ. Before discussing the role of Saint Paul's "new man" (the higher self) in resisting temptation, we must first explore the contemporary notion of "the self".

The term "self" has a rich recent history in both philosophy and psychology, but this is beyond the scope of our current investigation. For the moment, we will focus only on an aspect of the "self" that is pertinent to the topics of resisting temptation and self-transformation.

---

[18] See, for example, Saint Augustine, *Sermon* 64; see also Saint Augustine, *The Teacher* 1–3. The "new man" is also the underlying rationale for Saint Thomas à Kempis' approach to temptation in *The Imitation of Christ*. Saint Ignatius of Loyola has this clearly in mind in his meditations on the Two Standards, the Three Kinds of Men, and the Three Degrees of Humility (in the Second Week of the *Spiritual Exercises*). He seems to have discovered this independently of Saint Augustine and Saint Thomas à Kempis—through his own reading of the *Life of Christ* and his conversion experience in the Cave of Manresa. See *Spiritual Exercises*, "The Twelfth Day", http://sacred-texts.com/chr/seil/seil26.htm.

"Self" refers to the persona-personality-identity that our self-consciousness can appropriate to define itself. When it does so, the particular persona-personality-identity gives definition and character—conveying feelings, desires, character attributes, and thinking processes—to self-consciousness.[19] We are not indeterminate acts of self-consciousness without direction and focus, like Descartes' *Tabula Rasa* (blank tablet). We are born into the world with two "generic selves", sort of like "starter kits" that our self-consciousness can appropriate to focus our feelings, desires, character attributes, and thinking patterns. As we shall see, the lower self exerts considerable influence in children, adolescents, and the emotionally and spiritually immature. Though the higher self is present in these individuals, it can be easily overshadowed by the lower self. When individuals progress in emotional maturity, spiritual conversion, and moral conversion, the higher self is empowered and begins to exert influence over the lower self. As implied above, the process of empowering the higher self is increased considerably by the progressive interplay between spiritual and moral conversion.

A. The Lower Self and Higher Self as Natural and Essential

In Volume I (Chapter 1) of the Quartet (summarized in Appendix I of this volume), we spoke about several natural human powers connected with Levels One, Two, Three, and Four desires. We saw that the lower brain, limbic system, and biological instincts enable us to feel pleasure and pain, forming the basis for Level One (sensual-material) desires. We also discussed the power of self-awareness or self-consciousness to form our own "inner universe", and how this power stands at the foundation of our Level Two (ego-comparative) desires. We also saw how the powers of empathy and conscience

---

[19] See Daphna Oyserman, Kristen Elmore, and George Smith, "Self, Self-Concept, and Identity", in *Handbook of Self and Identity*, 2nd ed., ed. Mark R. Leary and June Price Tangney (New York: Guilford Press, 2011), pp. 69–104. See also Richard Ryan and Edward Deci, "Multiple Identities within a Single Self: A Self-Determination Theory Perspective on Internalization within Contexts and Cultures", in Leary and Tangney, *Handbook of Self and Identity*, pp. 255–46. Leary and Tangney, *Handbook of Self and Identity*, is widely recognized as the definitive fieldwork on self and identity.

focus our self-consciousness on love and the good, which forms the foundation of our Level Three (contributive and loving) desires. Finally, we discussed our five kinds of transcendental awareness manifest in the desires for perfect truth, love, justice/goodness, beauty, and home, which focus us on the sacred, the eternal, the highest forms of truth, love, and goodness, as well as our awareness of God (Level Four).

Now let us return to the two "generic selves"—the two "starter kits"—we are born with. We not only have the above powers and desires; we seem to have them self-organized into personas-personalities-identities that our self-consciousness can appropriate and use. A "persona" (a term used frequently in theater) designates the feelings, character attributes, desires, and thinking processes of a character that an actor is attempting "to play". This term can be applied to the "generic selves" we are born with, but the generic selves are more than this. They are potential dimensions of our psyches that are more than characters in a play. They are like potential personalities or identities that our free self-consciousness can appropriate. When it does so, the "selves" bring an affective and cognitive organizing framework to our self-consciousness that focuses us on certain feelings, desires, character attributes, and thinking processes. As the reader may have guessed, the "lower self" (the lower persona-personality-identity) is connected with Level One and Level Two desires, imagination, and thinking processes, while the "higher self" (the higher persona-personality-identity) is connected with Level Three and Level Four desires, imagination, and thinking patterns.

As noted above, infants and children have a strong lower self, and a weaker, unrefined, higher self. Though children are not sophisticated in their sensual desires and ego desires (Level One and Level Two), they can be quite strong in their unsophisticated desires—seeking sweets, playtime, and insisting on "having it their own way" (ego fulfillment).[20] This is not to say that children do not have a higher

---

[20] See Violet Kalyan-Masih, "Cognitive Egocentricity of the Child within Piagetian Developmental Theory", *Transactions of the Nebraska Academy of Sciences*, 1973, Paper 379, http://digitalcommons.unl.edu/cgi/viewcontent.cgi?article=1382&context=tnas. See also Jean Piaget, *The Child's Conception of Physical Causality* (New York: Harcourt Brace & Company, 1930), and Jean Piaget, *The Essential Piaget*, ed. Howard E. Gruber and J. Jacques Voneche (London: Routledge and Kegan Paul, 1977), p. 137.

self—for they have empathy for parents, siblings, and friends,[21] and a sense of nobility and guilt (associated with conscience),[22] and a strong unrefined natural sense of the spiritual and God.[23]

Throughout human history, sages and philosophers have advised parents to cultivate morality and piety in their children, which is particularly evident in Jewish Wisdom literature,[24] Plato,[25] and Aristotle.[26] These authors recognized the need to cultivate the desires and thinking patterns of the higher self (through education and the development of virtuous habits), because they tend to be weaker than the Level One and Level Two desires of the lower self (which gives immediate, surface apparent, and intense gratification). Children have to be pried away from these immediate and intense gratifications and taught the more pervasive, enduring, and deep benefits of the higher self—Level Three and Level Four desires (see Volume I, Chapter 3, of the Quartet). If they make the transition, they are likely to have a much higher quality of life that does considerable good for individuals and culture as well as the Kingdom of God.

As Saint Paul implies, there is a strong likelihood that we will be caught between the lower self (the "old man") and the higher self (the "new man") for a long period of time. As noted above, Paul experienced this double self for at least twenty-three years—and probably longer (see Rom 7:13–25 and the explanation below in Section III.B). The image of these two selves in conflict has been humorously portrayed in dozens of cartoons. I recall from my childhood a particularly vivid image of Fred Flintstone, who had a small figure of himself with a halo and wings standing above his right shoulder, and another small figure of himself with devil's horns and a tail above his

---

[21] See Jean Decety, Kalina J. Michalska, and Yuko Akitsuki, "Who Caused the Pain? An fMRI Investigation of Empathy and Intentionality in Children", *Neuropsychologia* 46, no. 11 (2008): 2607–14. For a summary of the results, see Steve Koppes, "Children Are Naturally Prone to Be Empathetic and Moral, University of Chicago Shows", *UChicago News*, University of Chicago Bulletin, July 11, 2008, https://news.uchicago.edu/article/2008/07/11/children-are-naturally-prone-be-empathic-and-moral-university-chicago-study-shows.

[22] See Robert Coles, *The Moral Life of Children* (New York: Atlantic Monthly Press, 1986).

[23] See Robert Coles, *The Spiritual Life of Children* (Boston: Houghton-Mifflin, 1990).

[24] Sir 6; 30; Wis 1–5.

[25] See Plato, *Meno, Phaedo*, and *The Republic* 6–7, which concern education in virtue, piety, and immortality.

[26] See Aristotle, *Nichomachean Ethics* 2, and *Politics* 7.

left shoulder. As he considered a mischievous deed, the two selves gave counsel, each according to his appropriate desires and thinking processes. Strange as it may seem, this portrayal is not far from the reality many of us experience when we are in that long developmental period where both selves seem to coexist on a quasi-equal level. Even though the higher and lower selves tug at our self-consciousness with seeming equality, one will win—and when it does, it will incite us to action.

Contemporary psychology has long recognized the distinction between the lower and higher personae-identities beginning with Sigmund Freud, who divided the psyche into three parts (which do not have physiological counterparts, but rather psychic personae-identities):

- The id, which is the primitive and aggressive persona seeking the satisfaction of basic needs, pleasures, and childlike egocentricity[27]
- The superego, which is the moral persona overseeing the aggressive and sensual persona (id). It comes from internalization of cultural rules through parental (and teacher) instruction and influence.[28]
- The ego, which is rational self-consciousness mediating between the id and reality, assuring that the sensual and aggressive dimensions of the id conform to reality[29]

Freud's "id" generally corresponds to the persona-identity of what we have called "the lower self", while his "superego" corresponds generally to the persona-identity of what we have called "the higher self". Some transactional psychologists refer to the "id" as "the child" and to the "superego" as "the parent". Though the characterization of "id" or "child" captures the Level One and Level Two desires of the persona we have called "the lower self", the characterization of "superego" or "parent" does not capture the richness of what the Christian philosophical-psychological tradition might call "the higher self".

With respect to the higher self, the Freudian and transactional analysis view puts emphasis on parent-teacher training of the superego,

---

[27] See Sigmund Freud, *The Ego and the Id* (New York: Courier Dover Publications, 2018), pp. 8–18.
[28] Ibid., pp. 19–33.
[29] Ibid., pp. 43ff.

while the Christian philosophical-psychological tradition puts emphasis on five faculties forming the higher self that can be influenced by (but not reduced to) parent-teacher training:

1. Conscience (which moves us naturally toward good and away from evil, and originates with God)[30]
2. Empathy (the capacity to bond with another person, which underlies self-giving love)[31]
3. The five transcendental desires for perfect truth, love, goodness, beauty, and home[32]
4. God's invitational presence to us in the numinous experience and intuition of the sacred[33]
5. The subconscious archetypal myth of the cosmic struggle between good and evil[34]

All of these higher faculties have their origin in God,[35] and form our Level Three-Four desires as well as the foundation for our higher self. Parental and teacher training can influence these five higher faculties, but these higher faculties are *intrinsic* to all of us, enabling us to be good, loving, and transcendent beings. Hence, we are born into the world with a higher self (grounded in these five higher faculties of the soul[36]), which forms the context through which we receive and interpret the teaching and training given to us by parents, religious authorities, and others. As such, the Christian philosophical-psychological view recognizes human beings to be transphysical and transcendental beings in relationship with God, which forms the foundation for free-will,[37] moral-loving transcendent consciousness, and a destiny beyond physical life and the physical universe.

[30] For a detailed explanation, see Volume II (Chapter 2, Section II) of the Quartet.

[31] For a detailed explanation, see Volume I (Chapter 1, Section IV) of the Quartet.

[32] For a detailed explanation, see Volume II (Chapter 4) of the Quartet.

[33] For a detailed explanation, see Volume II (Chapters 1 and 2) of the Quartet.

[34] For a detailed explanation, see Volume II (Chapter 2, Section III) of the Quartet.

[35] In Volume II of the Quartet, I show the transphysical nature of all of these faculties, implying their transphysical or transcendental origin (causation) and destiny (beyond physical life).

[36] For the evidence of these faculties' transphysical and transcendental nature, see the whole of Volume II of the Quartet.

[37] For an explanation of how these five faculties and self-consciousness ground human free will, see Volume I (Chapter 4, Section III) of this Trilogy.

Alternatively, the Freudian view of "superego" is limited to a physio-psychological reality that perforce arises mostly out of teaching and conditioning, implying a very limited or nonexistent view of freedom[38] and self-transcendence.[39] As such, Freud's view of human morality, love, nature, and destiny is quite limited in comparison to the Christian philosophical-psychological tradition, which leaves him and his followers open to underestimating life's purpose and undervaluing human worth and dignity (a recipe for cultural tragedy).

Let us now return to the conflict between the lower self and the higher self. A serious and profound portrayal of this conflict is given by J. R. R. Tolkien through the creature Gollum in *The Lord of the Rings*. His higher self (portrayed as the young man, Sméagol) feels pity for the hobbits and sympathy for their noble mission, but his lower self (portrayed by the old and withered Gollum) is mesmerized by his desire for and addiction to the power of the ring as well as his anger toward the hobbits. As he debates with himself, his facial and vocal expressions change from Sméagol to Gollum and back again. Ultimately, his lower self wins, and he resolves to betray the hobbits (who had in many ways become his friends) and to take the ring for himself. It is said that Tolkien actually wept as he created this scene, because every man (like Sméagol) has the capacity to reach his higher self and complete a noble mission, but so many (like Gollum) do not, preferring instead to lapse into their addictions to the deadly sins (the power of the ring).[40]

---

[38] Since Freudian analysis does not recognize intrinsic transcendental faculties (arising out of a transphysical soul), but only the moral conditioning of the ego, it implies that human beings are *determined* by their id and the conditioning of their superego. Since Freud held that the other dimensions of the psyche result from physical mechanisms and the unconscious, there is little room for human freedom. Human beings might think that they are free, but in reality, their behavior is determined by intrinsic physical processes, conditioning, and the unconscious. See James Daley, "Freud and Determinism", *Southern Journal of Philosophy* 9, no. 2 (June 1971): 179–89.

[39] Freud rejected transcendence beyond the physical-psychological world, which entailed denial of transcendent activity or power within the human psyche. See Sigmund Freud, *The Future of an Illusion*, trans. Gregory C. Richter (Ontario: Broadview Press, 2012), pp. 150–84.

[40] See J. R. R. Tolkien, *The Lord of the Rings, Part 2—The Two Towers* (New York: Del Rey, 1986), p. 366. Steven Winter recounts part of Gollum's inner conflict in "A Scene Which Caused Tolkein to Weep as He Wrote It", *Wisdom from* The Lord of the Rings (blog), December 15, 2015, https://stephencwinter.com/2015/12/15/a-scene-which-caused -tolkien-to-weep-as-he-wrote-it/#comments.

Plato illustrates how every human being (starting with the young) must manage the opposition between these two selves in his dialogue *Phaedrus*. He uses the image of a charioteer to indicate self-consciousness, an unruly winged horse to symbolize the lower self, and a noble winged horse to symbolize the higher self:[41]

> Of the other souls that which best follows a god and becomes most like thereunto raises her charioteer's head into the outer region, and is carried round with the gods in the revolution, but being confounded by her steeds she has much ado to discern the things that are; another now rises, and now sinks, and by reason of her unruly steeds sees in part, but in part sees not. As for the rest, though all are eager to reach the heights and seek to follow, they are not able; this one striving to outstrip that. Thus confusion ensues, and conflict and grievous sweat. Whereupon, with their charioteers powerless, many are lamed, and many have their wings all broken, and for all their toiling they are balked, every one, of the full vision of being, and departing therefrom, they feed upon the food of semblance.[42]

The charioteer who is able to give preeminence to the noble steed (the higher self) and can control the unruly steed (the lower self) will reach the realm of the gods, becoming like them. However, those who do not succeed in giving preeminence to the noble steed (the higher self) will allow the unruly steed to create confusion and turmoil in the soul. Ultimately, the turmoil and conflict hurts both steeds (laming and de-winging them), which renders the charioteer powerless. These individuals never reach the highest levels of enlightenment, purpose, fulfillment, and destiny—they are consigned to the world of the appearances (sensuality and egocentricity).

Though Plato did not have the benefit of Saint Paul's spiritual insights (e.g., the old man versus the new man) or the insights of contemporary psychology,[43] he had a remarkable intuition into self and personal identity as well as the higher and lower selves within each individual. As we shall see, this insight—complemented by Christian spirituality and the psychological insights into self, identity, and the subconscious

---

[41] See *Phaedrus* 246a–254e.

[42] Plato, *Phaedrus* 248a, trans. R. Hackforth, in *Plato: Collected Dialogues*, ed. Edith Hamilton and Huntington Cairns (Princeton, N.J.: Princeton University Press, 1961).

[43] See Leary and Tangney, *Handbook of Self and Identity*, esp. Oyserman, Elmore, and Smith, "Self, Self-Concept, and Identity", pp. 69–104.

mind—can lead us to a remarkably efficacious way of resisting temptation and transforming ourselves into the image of Christ.

B. Reinforcing the Natural Higher Self with Sacraments, Prayer, and Christian Practice

Saint Paul recognized that when we are baptized into the Mystical
Body of Christ—through which we receive the Holy Spirit—our
higher self is elevated by these two gifts (see Chapter 2, Section II.A
of this volume); however, he also recognized that the lower self (the
pull toward sensual desire and egocentricity) does not go away (see
Rom 7:13–25; explained below). He calls the lower self "the flesh"
and the higher self—enhanced by its participation in the Mystical
Body and the Holy Spirit through Baptism—"the spirit". Though
the enhancement of our higher selves (through the urgings and guidance of the Holy Spirit as well as communion with the saints through
Christ's Mystical Body) is quite powerful, it does not take away what
Saint Paul called "the flesh" (the lower self):

> Now if I [my free self-consciousness] do what I [my higher self] do
> not want, it is no longer I [my higher self] that do it, but sin which
> dwells within me [my lower self].
> So I find it to be a law that when I want to do right, evil lies close at
> hand. For I [my higher self] delight in the law of God, in my inmost
> self, but I see in my members [my lower self] another law at war with
> the law of my mind [my higher self] and making me captive to the
> law of sin which dwells in my members [my lower self]. Wretched
> man that I am! Who will deliver me from this body of death? Thanks
> be to God through Jesus Christ our Lord! So then, I of myself [my
> higher self] serve the law of God with my mind, but with my flesh
> [my lower self] I serve the law of sin. (Rom 7:20–25)

Later, Church Fathers called Saint Paul's "flesh", "concupiscence"
(the tendency to act unreflectively in accordance with the lower self
toward sensual pleasure and egocentricity).[44] Church tradition holds

---

[44] See Saint Augustine, "The Free Choice of the Will", in Fathers of the Church series,
vol. 59, *Saint Augustine: The Teacher, The Free Choice of the Will, Grace and Free Will*, trans.
Robert P. Russell, O.S.A. (Washington, D.C.: Catholic University of America Press, 1968),
pp. 63–241. See also Saint Augustine, *Confessions* 7.

that concupiscence does not go away after Baptism. However, the fruits of Baptism (the gifts of the Holy Spirit and participation in the Mystical Body) can help us significantly to resist the urgings of the lower self ("concupiscence") by making the higher self more preeminent—*if we cooperate* with those fruits in our thoughts and actions through spiritual and moral conversion.[45]

The gift of Baptism makes resistance to temptation and self-transformation toward the higher self more manageable—so also the Sacrament of Reconciliation and the Holy Eucharist (see Chapter 2, Sections I, II.A, and II.C; see also Chapter 7). We are not constrained to join what Plato called the fate of most people who fail to give preeminence to the noble steed over the unruly one (losing control and relegated to life in the lower realms). Baptism, the Sacrament of Reconciliation, the Holy Eucharist, and the other sacraments give, as it were, the noble steed (the higher self) a significant spiritual advantage—if we cooperate with and cultivate the fruits of those gifts through spiritual and moral conversion. This is why young children, after Baptism, can have significant spiritual experiences and insights. I will use my own experience to explain how these gifts of Baptism and the other sacraments enhance the higher self within me.

I recall from my youth the catechism classes that helped me prepare for my First Holy Communion, and the special day when I received the Lord for the first time. Though I was happy with all the attention given to me by family and friends on that day, I also had a deep interior conviction that this was spiritually significant and important to my salvation—and it brought me a joy, a spiritual joy, beyond the temporal joys of being the center of family and friends and receiving gifts. I suppose it was my first conscious spiritual awakening. My religion was always important to me, but after receiving my First Holy Communion, I became reflectively aware of the priority that God and religion should play in my life. I knew I was a different person—though I did not know how or why. Looking back on it, I would have to say that this event galvanized the *sensus fidei*—one of the gifts of my Baptism—within me (see Volume I, Chapter 1, of this Trilogy).

---

[45] For an explanation of concupiscence, its continued effects, and the grace of Baptism and the sacraments, see *CCC* 1264.

On that occasion, I received my first Catholic picture Bible, which offered other galvanizing religious experiences. I would gaze upon the pictures in that Bible as if I were entering into the scene and, after staring at it for a while, would have the same sense of how important God and my religion were to me—almost as if they were becoming best friends and even a part of my inner world. I loved reading other stories—and listening to Mrs. Paxton tell us stories in school and in the library. Though I entered into the scenes of these stories too, they did not have the same effect on me as the Bible picture and stories, for I did not want to make the characters or the ethos of those stories a part of my interior life—they were simply not that important. I knew that religion was more important to me than for many of my friends at school, but I did not think much more about it.

After receiving First Holy Communion, catechism classes became much more important. I really loved learning the faith even more than I loved arithmetic and other favorite subjects, and looked forward to Saturday mornings when my father would take us to church for those classes. After class (before our mothers picked us up) many of us would have discussions about the topics of the class, thinking through the implications of the little sayings we had memorized from our *Baltimore Catechism*. Several of us were able to advance the core teachings from the *Catechism* beyond anything discussed in class. We had a remarkable sense of the rightness and sacredness of these teachings as if we were being led to a truth beyond ourselves. I cannot attribute this sense of conviction and sacredness to mere schooling, because I did not go to a Catholic school. It simply took hold of me in a one-hour catechism class, a picture Bible, and Sunday Mass.

Many of my friends were non-Catholic and non-Christian. I grew up in Honolulu, where there was a considerable diversity of religions and first-generation Asian cultures. Though I loved the school I attended (because of wonderful friends and education), I looked forward to my Saturday morning catechism classes, to reengage in the theological ideas and discussions that animated me and my church friends.

In about the fifth grade, I became an altar boy and noticed a significant heightening of theological conviction and closeness to the Lord. I became close to my friends who were fellow knights of the altar. I really cared about my salvation, about Christ, the Church, Christmas, Easter, the New Testament readings I heard, and even the Masses I attended. I knew interiorly that these were important not only to my mother, but also to Jesus—and to me.

In about the sixth grade, my mother took us to a Good Friday service, and I was quite moved by the Passion account of Jesus; kissing the Cross; and receiving Holy Communion. I felt after the service that I was somehow saved, and that Jesus really cared about me—that His Passion and death were *for me*. I was in a state of consolation for the rest of the day—indeed for the rest of the Easter Triduum. When I told one of my fellow Mass servers about this, he said he had had a similar experience, so I decided to see if this was fairly commonplace at my secular school as well. It was not, and in fact, some of my buddies thought that I was getting "a little too religious". I thought to myself, "I can bring this matter up with fellow Mass servers, but I better refrain from talking about it with other people—they just don't seem to get it." In hindsight, I see the graces of my Baptism, the Holy Eucharist, the Sunday Masses, and the Sacrament of Reconciliation as progressively working on my interior life *and* my higher self. The more I progressed in my religion and spiritual practice, the more convinced I became about the importance of God, Jesus, and religion—from First Holy Communion, to the picture Bible, to the catechism classes, to serving at Mass, and in the Good Friday service.

My progress continued through the seventh and eighth grades. I wore my religious medals proudly and was quite willing to explain their significance to my friends at school, using them as an opportunity for evangelization—to convince my friends to take greater interest in God and religion. I never entered into a debate with someone of another religion, respecting their love for God and the spiritual life. However, I truly felt the need to tell those who were nonreligious about God and my understanding of the faith. I was amazed by the questions people asked, and I always seemed to have an answer that helped them. Half the time, I would think to myself, "I didn't know I knew that!" Again, the fruits of Baptism and the other sacraments were galvanizing my higher self, and I was becoming progressively more interested in God, the Church, theology, and prayer, as well as spreading and defending the faith. Like the Parable of the Talents

(Mt 25:14–30; Lk 19:12–28), the more I used what I had, the more I seemed to get—not only the *sensus fidei*, but also my sense of God's presence and love.

When I went to Punahou Academy in Honolulu (ninth through twelfth grades), I already had a reputation for being the "religion guy". I remember my friend saying to his friends, "If you have any questions about religion, just ask Spitzer." I was only too happy to provide answers that came partly from my education and partly from my rich religious interior life. In retrospect, I still think they were fairly good answers—definitely the Holy Spirit inspiring me. I also became a lightning rod for a few individuals who were antagonistic to religion (though some, I'm convinced, were really seeking to know God, but too afraid to admit it in public). They would always come up to me with a really sneaky question: "Well, God created Hell, didn't He?" to which I would say, "Of course." This would be quickly followed by, "Well, God knows everything in the future, doesn't He?" I knew where this was going, but I responded truthfully—"Yes." And then, they would try to tighten the noose: "Well, isn't it much worse to be in Hell for all eternity than to never have been born at all?" I would of course say yes and expect their conclusion: "What kind of a God do you believe in that would knowingly create a person who is destined to go to Hell for all eternity?" This led to a long excursus on human freedom, and why the person who goes to Hell has chosen it (because he believed it would make him happy). I read some of these responses from my mother's theology books, including some by Fulton J. Sheen and Frank Sheed. The nuanced philosophical mind of Sheed inspired my creativity and theological defense far beyond my natural abilities.

My last two years of high school were challenging because I was exposed to several works of atheistic existentialist literature for which I had not yet developed a proper philosophical response. Jean-Paul Sartre's *Nausea* (1938) and Albert Camus' *The Stranger* (1942) and *The Plague* (1947) really disturbed me. This disturbance was greatly enhanced by reading Elie Wiesel's *Night* (1960). I began to question my faith, looking for some proof for God—particularly a loving God as preached by Jesus—but was unable to find any from teachers or priests beyond brief references to proofs of Aquinas. Unfortunately, no one could direct me to the original texts of these proofs, so I was caught between a very strong *interior spiritual* conviction about God's existence, presence, and love on the one hand and some challenging *intellectual* questions and doubts on the other. Though I could not find the proof I needed in high school, I did not abandon my faith. In retrospect I would attribute this "little miracle" to the interior gifts (particularly the *sensus fidei* that I was given through my Baptism, reception of Holy Communion, and participation in the Church and evangelization).

Later in college I did discover several proofs of God from metaphysics and contemporary physics as well as an explanation for suffering given by C. S. Lewis in *The Problem of Pain* (1940). As I entered more deeply into intellectual conversion during those years, the gifts of the Holy Spirit became even more powerful. After some retreats and teaching a catechism class, I took off like a shot out of a canon into spiritual conversion. This led to my interest in the Jesuits and the priesthood—and along with it, my desire to pursue deeper moral conversion.

As I look back on those early years, I am left with one singular conviction—if I had not been baptized, had not regularly attended church (receiving Holy Communion), and had not entered into the life of prayer and defense of the faith, my "higher self" would be in a state of quasi-infancy, and as a result, I think my spiritual and moral conversion would have likewise been quite limited. Thinking back on Plato's analogy, I am sure that without my Baptism and practice of faith, I would be one of the charioteers that fell to the ground because I would not have been able to give preeminence to the noble steed and control the ignoble steed. I would have been lamed, de-winged, and living in the lower regions. This is what motivates me to continue my apostolate of evangelization and defense of the faith today—particularly the doctrine of infant Baptism and early reception of Holy Communion. I can't imagine where I would have been without them—no fire in my heart, no conviction in my soul, no confidence in a loving eternity, and a severely underdeveloped higher self.

Let us review for a moment where we have come. Like Saint Paul, Plato, Tolkien, and many contemporary psychologists and philosophers, I would contend that we have two selves, two personae (personalities–identities) that organize feelings, desires, character attri-butes, and thinking processes through which our self-consciousness intentionally acts (the lower self and the higher self). The lower self is organized around Level One desires for pleasure (coming from the limbic system and lower brain) and Level Two desires (coming from self-consciousness in combination with the limbic system). The higher self is organized around Level Three desires (arising out of our capacity for empathy and conscience) and Level Four desires (arising out of our five transcendental desires for perfect truth, love, goodness, beauty, and home). Initially, the two selves are generic, but the lower self is more powerful than the higher self. When children are encour-aged to develop their Level Three and Level Four desires (through empathy, moral education, and religious practice), their higher self begins to emerge—and if they mature in these practices through edu-cation, inspiration, and appropriation of virtue, the higher self will eventually equal and better the lower self. However, if little attempt is made to encourage Level Three and Level Four desires, the lower self will gain in power, causing it to overshadow the higher self. This can frequently lead to superficiality, addiction, the habitual practice of deadly sins, and even criminal behavior.

We noted above that both the lower self and higher self are nat-ural dimensions of the human psyche, and that the higher self can be enhanced through Christian Baptism, Holy Communion, and the practice of Christian faith. We also noted two corollary truths. First, if the higher self is not cultivated, the lower self (which is quite susceptible to temptation) will grow in influence and power. Second, even when we do cultivate the higher self, the lower self will persist for a significant period of time (coexisting as it were, with the higher self). However, the longer we continue to culti-vate the higher self, the stronger and more habitual it will become, while the lower self correspondingly diminishes in influence and strength. Though the sacraments, Church participation, and moral education can help initiate the process of spiritual and moral con-version (enhancing the higher self), they need to be complemented by other efforts to bring the higher self into a position of preem-inence, such as contemplative prayer, the appropriation of virtue through the three noble intentions, the resistance to temptation, and the progressive cycle of spiritual and moral conversion.

Even with these efforts, we might expect a considerable period of "being caught in the middle", similar to that described by Saint Paul, who experienced an increase in the "new man" for twenty-three years, but nevertheless continued to feel himself under the influence of the "old man", "the flesh". Saint Ignatius of Loyola understood well how powerful the influence of the lower self could be, particularly during the time of his Manresa experience, which moved him to develop the *Spiritual Exercises* and the General and Particular Examen. These two spiritual practices can accelerate our transition from mastery by the lower self to mastery by the higher self, enabling us to live in closer connection to the Lord and our neighbor, to help others in their spiritual and temporal need, and ultimately to share in the Lord's salvation forever. We will discuss the General and Particular Examen in the next chapter (Section II).

Thanks to some advances of contemporary psychology, particularly in the area of subconscious identity and self-efficacy, we have the opportunity to accelerate the process of strengthening the higher self even more. In the next chapter, we will discuss two contemporary techniques for enhancing the higher self from Dr. Albert Bandura—visualizations and affirmations. These techniques can be folded into the daily Examen for optimal effectiveness. If we practice all three of these techniques, they will galvanize and enhance the fruits of our spiritual conversion (relationship with Christ through the Church, in reception of the sacraments and practice of contemplative prayer) as well as the initial fruits of our moral conversion (our study of the deadly sins, our appropriation of virtue, and our resolve to resist temptation).

IV. The First Step in Moral Conversion: Aversion to Sin and Devotion to Virtue

The first step in moral conversion is to become emotionally involved in the appropriation of virtue and the shunning of vice. It is not enough to have knowledge of virtue and the deadly sins; we must also enkindle our desire for virtue and our aversion to the deadly sins. Inasmuch as emotion transforms thought into action, it is essential for creating the necessary self-motivation for moral conversion.

The reason we have made this emotional involvement in virtue the first step in the process of moral conversion is its necessity for motivating the other three steps:

- Using visualization and affirmations to condition the subconscious mind (Chapter 6, Section I)
- Using the Ignatian Examen to foster spiritual conviction and invoke the Lord's grace (Chapter 6, Section II)
- Using spontaneous prayers and cultivating habits to solidify our moral conversion (Chapter 6, Section IV)

If we lack the emotion, desire, and inner conviction to move these latter steps into action, we might try them once or twice, but without instant results, we are likely to drop them, delaying moral conversion. Moral conversion requires concerted effort, and sometimes, contending with the desires of the lower self and demonic temptation can be quite challenging. Yet if we have a strong desire to appropriate the twelve virtues (the four cardinal virtues and the eight subvirtues of love [see Chapter 4]), and a strong aversion to the deadly sins (because they hurt others and ourselves, open us to the Evil One's life of darkness, and jeopardize our salvation), we have a strong vested interest and motivation to work concertedly and sincerely on our visualizations, affirmations, Ignatian Examen, and spontaneous prayers. This will not only launch our effort into the domain of moral conversion, but also bring it ultimately to successful completion.

Recall that when we are thinking with our higher self, the *deadly sins* will produce fear and revulsion, but they will produce attraction and excitement when we are thinking with our lower self. Alternatively, the *virtues* will produce attraction and devotion when we are thinking with our higher self but will produce boredom and dislike when we are thinking with our lower self. When we are in the first stages of moral conversion, the higher self is weak by comparison with the lower self (even in individuals who have reached a high degree of spiritual conversion). This is probably why Saint Ignatius included the General and Particular Examen at the forefront of the *Spiritual Exercises*. He knew that it was not enough to participate actively in church, to receive the sacraments regularly, to be practicing the first and second stages of contemplative prayer, and to be serving and evangelizing for the Kingdom of Christ. As important as these spiritual activities are in building a relationship with the Lord and participating in the Church community, they have to be complemented by explicit consideration of the deadly sins, virtues, and moral teaching of Jesus if we are to make progress in imitating the heart of Christ. If we overlook transformation into the higher self and moral conversion, we leave ourselves open to the Evil One, to offending and hurting our neighbor, to undermining the very faith community we are trying to serve, and even to jeopardizing our eternal soul. This truth helps to explain what might be thought to be a perplexing assertion of Jesus:

> Not every one who says to me, "Lord, Lord," shall enter the kingdom of heaven, but he who does the will of my Father who is in heaven. On that day many will say to me, "Lord, Lord, did we not prophesy in your name, and cast out demons in your name, and do many mighty works in your name?" And then will I declare to them, "I never knew you; depart from me, you evildoers." (Mt 7:21–23)

Why would Jesus declare that some of His spiritually adept disciples who were prophesying, casting out demons, and doing miracles in *His* name are evildoers unfit for His Kingdom? Undoubtedly, for the same reason that Saint Paul declares:

> If I speak in the tongues of men and of angels, but have not love, I am a noisy gong or a clanging cymbal. And if I have prophetic powers, and understand all mysteries and all knowledge, and if I have all faith, so as to remove mountains, but have not love, I am nothing. If I give away all I have, and if I deliver my body to be burned, but have not love, I gain nothing. (1 Cor 13:1–3)

So how do we get the process of moral conversion and development of the higher self underway? How do we cultivate emotion and desire for the appropriation of virtue, particularly the virtue of love? How do we develop emotional aversion toward the deadly sins? The best way I have discovered for doing this is intentionally to associate the three motives for aversion (given below) with each of the eight deadly sins (see Volume I, Chapters 5 and 6, of this Trilogy) and intentionally to associate the three noble intentions with each of the twelve virtues (the four cardinal virtues and the eight subvirtues of love). I would suggest meditating on one deadly sin and one or two counteracting virtues each day throughout the week as a kind of "spiritual exercise". It may prove helpful to review the material on that deadly sin from Volume I (Chapters 5 and 6) and to review the material on the counteracting virtue(s) from the previous chapter. I would recommend you do the part on the deadly sins first, and then the part on the counteracting virtues. Repeat this exercise for as many weeks as necessary to increase fear and revulsion toward the deadly sins and devotion and attraction to the virtues.

First Part: Aversion and Revulsion toward the Deadly Sins. First, consider the three motives for aversion to sin mentioned above and in Volume I of this Trilogy:

1. Each deadly sin hurts others as well as our relationship with others.
2. Each deadly sin opens us to the influence of the Evil One and his deceits and seductions toward the way of darkness.
3. Each deadly sin undermines our capacity for love and our relationship with the Lord, thereby jeopardizing our salvation and our capacity to help others toward their salvation.

Recall what was said in Volume I (Chapters 4–6) that the Evil One will select the deadly sins to which we are most inclined; he will then tempt us and deceive us into believing that these sins will make us *truly* happy, and then after we have followed him along the way of darkness, he will either pull the rug out from under us in the hopes of causing despair, or suggest that we engage more deeply in the deadly sins with the objective of having us reject the Church and the Lord altogether. This is the usual pattern for the person in Saint Ignatius' "First Week of the Spiritual Life". He changes his methods for those in the "Second Week of the Spiritual Life" (see above, Section II).

We may now proceed to the formal part of the meditation. Select one of the deadly sins in the first column of the chart below, viewing it through the lens of the three above-mentioned motives for aversion to sin. Spend a few moments with the Lord, asking for His inspiration to move us to fear and revulsion at this sin.

Eight Deadly Sins	Counteracting Virtues
Gluttony	Temperance and prudence
Greed	Contributive-transcendental identity, and gratitude
Lust	Chastity, respect and care for others, and temperance
Sloth	Prudence, fortitude, and contributive-transcendental identity
Vanity	Contributive-transcendental identity, humble-heartedness, respect, and care for others
Anger	Forgiveness, compassion, and gentle-heartedness
Envy	Gratitude, justice, and compassion
Pride	Humble-heartedness, justice, and compassion

If you, for example, selected greed, ask the Lord for the grace to fear and recoil at what greed does to others and your relationship with others. Next, ask for the inspiration to fear and recoil at how greed opens you to the Evil One and his way of darkness. Finally, ask for the inspiration to fear and recoil at how greed undermines your relationship with Him and your salvation.

Second Part: Devotion and Attraction to the Virtues. Select one or two of the countervirtues connected with the deadly sin you have just considered. View them with the Lord through the lens of the three noble intentions listed below:

1. The intention to please and serve the Lord according to His Word out of deep gratitude and love
2. The intention to focus on the highest dignity and destiny of others and to help them avoid the seductions of the Evil One and pursue salvation in Jesus
3. The intention to foster our own well-being by living up to our highest dignity and character, avoiding the seduction and influence of the Evil One, and remaining on the road to salvation

As you begin your meditation, first ask the Lord to catalyze devotion for and attraction to the virtues for the sake of others and yourself, as well as for your salvation and theirs. Now, take a few moments with the Lord to first give Him thanks for His creation, redemption, guidance, protection, and help toward salvation. Next, proceed to the three intentions of the meditation. If, for example, you picked chastity, look at it with Him first through the lens of the first intention, asking for inspiration to see how the appropriation of this virtue would please Him and bring you closer to Him. Next, look at chastity with Him through the lens of the second intention, asking Him to inspire you as to how it helps you serve others and their salvation—how it gives you greater purity of motive and credibility, and how it immunizes you from using others and endangering their salvation. Finally, view chastity with Him through the lens of the third intention, asking Him to inspire you as to how this virtue helps you in the pursuit of your salvation, and immunizes you from the way of darkness proposed by the Evil One to jeopardize your salvation. Now say a prayer of thanksgiving for the graces given you during the meditation.

Since this meditation has several points, I would recommend that the reader photocopy it to take to prayer for two or three weeks. You need only photocopy from "First Part: Aversion and Revulsion toward the Deadly Sins" through the previous paragraph. As noted above, it will be helpful to repeat this meditation daily using a different deadly sin and a different virtue each day. If you believe that you could be further strengthened in your desire for virtue and revulsion toward the deadly sins, repeat the same set of exercises in subsequent weeks until you feel a strong devotion and firm conviction to appropriate the virtues as well as a strong aversion and revulsion to the deadly sins accompanied by a firm conviction to avoid them. Now proceed to the next three steps to moral conversion given in the following chapter:

- Using visualization and affirmations to condition the subconscious mind toward virtue
- Using the Ignatian Examen to integrate the virtues with your higher self, and to make the higher self preeminent in both your conscious and subconscious mind
- Using spontaneous prayers and habits to solidify the virtues within the higher self and to make the higher self preeminent in the conscious and subconscious mind

V. Conclusion

Moral conversion means replacing the lower self (what Saint Paul called "the old self") with the higher self ("the new self"), which is free to act according to the will and love of Christ. This new self is able to effectively resist temptation, seek Christ's will beyond one's own, and embrace virtue even at the cost of self-sacrifice. Though the higher self is incipiently present in us from our birth, the lower self tends to dominate it, requiring parental guidance and constraint.

The path to the higher self requires both spiritual conversion and moral conversion, which are interrelated with one another throughout our spiritual journey. It generally begins with our reception of the sacrament of Baptism, which is brought to life by the Holy Eucharist, Reconciliation, and religious education. When we receive these gifts of Christ through the Church, our higher self is awakened, and we desire to learn about the Lord and grow closer to him. These feelings motivate us to resist temptation, which can be quite strong as we move into adolescence. At this juncture, the desire for moral conversion becomes paramount. If we ignore it, making no attempt to pursue virtue and overcome the deadly sins, we will stagnate in our spiritual development.

A solid commitment to the sacraments, prayer, and devotion (spiritual conversion) are essential, but they need to be complemented by a moral conversion strategy. This strategy must go beyond the free decision of the conscious mind and include reorientation of the subconscious mind toward virtue and the higher self. Our first step is to intensify our desire for the three noble intentions—the desire to please the Lord, the desire to help rather than hurt our neighbor's well-being and salvation, and the desire to pursue our salvation while avoiding the seduction of our spiritual enemy. The second step is to embrace and pursue the virtues as the vehicle for actualizing the three noble intentions and avoiding the deadly sins in our lives. Yet we must ask, "How can we move our subconscious mind to embrace these noble intentions and virtues (within the higher self) so that it supports, rather than fights, our conscious desire for them?"

We must now turn in the next chapter to two major methods of subconscious transformation—affirmation prayers (based on the psychological insights of Dr. Albert Bandura) and the Examen Prayer (based on the spiritual insights of Saint Ignatius of Loyola). The combination of these two methods produces the vital step of reorienting the subconscious mind needed to make the higher self a reality. When we succeed, we are free to follow the will of Jesus Christ.

Chapter Six

Moral Conversion and Resisting Temptation

Introduction

In the previous chapter, we laid the groundwork for a process of moral conversion. We showed that full effectiveness of this process entails incorporating philosophical, theological, psychological, and spiritual wisdom and practice to incite aversion to sin and devotion to virtue. We further showed that this combination of methods would be needed to affect our conscious and subconscious minds as well as our transcendent souls. Also in the last chapter, we addressed the first step of moral conversion—meditation and prayer leading to aversion to the deadly sins and devotion to the virtues. In this chapter, we discuss three additional steps to moral conversion:

1. The second step of moral conversion: visualizations and affirmations, to influence the subconscious mind (Section I)
2. The third step of moral conversion: the Ignatian Examen, to incorporate grace (Section II)
3. The fourth step of moral conversion: spontaneous prayers and habits, to reinforce moral conversion (Section IV)

If we practice these four steps of moral conversion, we will pave the way for the ascendancy of a preeminent higher self, a strong appropriation of virtue (and aversion to vice), and a capacity to resist temptation effectively. As this process becomes increasingly solidified, the cycle of spiritual and moral conversion will continue, in which believers will draw quite close to the Lord, entering into a relationship with Him, which the mystics call "the illuminative way". As the experience of thousands of Jesuits indicates, this process leads to "the magis" ("the even more") in prayer and service to the Lord for His greater glory—the objective for which we were created.

I. The Second Step in Moral Conversion: Visualization and Affirmations to Condition the Subconscious Mind

Two insights from contemporary psychology can help us accelerate and enhance the development of our higher self:

1. The discovery of the subconscious mind
2. The use of visualization and affirmation to condition the sub-conscious mind

These techniques for self-efficacy can be used beyond the domain of developing and strengthening the higher self. They can, for example, help us overcome unnecessary inhibitions produced by fears, low self-image, self-loathing, and habitual patterns of low-efficacy (by changing our subconscious self-image). Though these topics are beyond the scope of this book, they can be fruitfully studied in the works of Dr. Albert Bandura and Lou Tice cited below. In this section, we will restrict ourselves to the topic of how to conform our subconscious self-image to the desires, character attributes, and thinking patterns of our higher self.

Some of the best work on enhancing self-efficacy through the conditioning of the subconscious mind has been thoughtfully set out by Stanford psychologist Dr. Albert Bandura. He has developed a generic process of enhancing self-efficacy.[1] Though he does not apply this work specifically to the area of resisting temptation, it can be easily adapted to this purpose by using it to explain the insights of Christian spiritual masters such as Saint Paul,[2] Saint Augustine,[3] Saint Thomas à

---

[1] See Albert Bandura, *Self-Efficacy: The Exercise of Control* (New York: W.H. Freeman, 1997).

[2] See Eph 4:22–23; Col 3:9–10.

[3] See Saint Augustine, *The Teacher* 1–3.

Kempis,[4] and Saint Ignatius Loyola.[5] In brief, Bandura's work explains in great depth the power of strong self-image, cultivating it in both the conscious and subconscious psyche, and using it to direct efficacious behavior. Lou Tice has popularized some of these insights, providing techniques to help appropriate strong subconscious self-image through visualization and affirmations.[6] I will give a brief summary of these findings and apply them to the specific challenge of resisting temptation. Three topics are germane to this discussion:

1. How Does Strong Subconscious Self-Image Work to Direct Behavior? (Section I.A)
2. Using Visualization to Cultivate a Christlike Subconscious Self-image (Section I.B)
3. Using Affirmations to Cultivate a Christlike Subconscious Self-Image (Section I.C)

A. How Does Strong Subconscious Self-Image Work to Direct Behavior?

We might begin by defining the subconscious mind. As most psychologists recognize, the conscious mind can attend to or focus only on a limited amount of perceptual and intelligible data at any given time, so much of the data of experience and memory is screened out of the purview of consciousness. However, not all of it is screened out of the active psyche. As hypnosis and various therapeutic techniques have revealed, the psyche can apprehend a considerable amount of experiential data on which consciousness is not focused and can retain this data in what might be called "subconscious memory". Hence, a person might have been involved in a serious accident and, when asked to describe what happened, give only a vague account

---

[4] See Saint Thomas à Kempis, *The Imitation of Christ* 3 and 4, in which Jesus is in dialogue with His disciple, instructing him on how to imitate Him in mind and heart.

[5] *Spiritual Exercises*, the second through fourth weeks. Saint Ignatius asks us to place ourselves in contemplations on the life of Christ, that we might become like Him through relationship with Him.

[6] See Lou Tice, *Smart Talk for Achieving Your Potential* (Seattle, Wash.: Pacific Institute Publishing, 2005).

of what transpired without significant details. However, under hypnosis, it is revealed that he apprehended and remembered far more about the accident than that on which the conscious mind focused.

Furthermore, the subconscious mind can introduce data and emotions into the motivational framework of an acting subject, mostly unbeknownst to him. For example, a person might see a car resembling the one that hit the family car when he was a little boy. Though he may be consciously unaware of the pain and fear he felt at the time, his subconscious mind may have appropriated and remembered it, associating it with that model of car. Later when the boy has become an adult, he might see a similar model of car and find himself trying to avoid it because of an almost unrecognized fear and anxiety.

Thus, we might say that the subconscious mind is an active part of the human psyche lying underneath the conscious psyche that attends to perceptual data, emotions, and other cognitional impressions that it remembers and associates with elements from a particular experience. When stimulated by those elements (e.g., subconsciously remembered data, emotions, and other impressions), the subconscious can introduce strong feelings (e.g., fear, anxiety, anger, guilt, and aversion) into the active psyche, affecting motivation and behavior not consciously chosen by an acting agent. These subconscious emotions can have deleterious effects on self-efficacy by blocking or interfering with our conscious rational choices. However, subconscious data and emotions can also be positive because they allow for creative associations giving rise to creative discoveries (called "the creative subconscious"). A positive subconscious self-image can also help direct our behaviors in positive ways, because as we shall explain, we move naturally (without effort) toward that subconscious self-image.

Some examples may prove helpful here with respect to a negative or nonefficacious self-image. We might think of the example of a golfer who is on the front nine holes of a challenging golf course and is effortlessly achieving par on every hole. He suddenly thinks to himself, "This is totally unlike me—I'm not anywhere near a par golfer." As Lou Tice would say, "Don't worry, your subconscious mind will take care of the incongruity between your performance and your negative self-image. At the eighteenth hole, you will be ten strokes above par (a poorer performance than before). You will have moved naturally and effortlessly toward your negative subconscious self-image—who you believe yourself to be."

We could give the opposite example as well. A golfer could be out on the front nine holes and be golfing at a very substandard level. If he does not panic in the midst of competition, he might think to himself, "I'm better than this." Frequently enough, his positive subconscious self-image will remove the negative impressions he feels about his past performance, and he will move naturally and effortlessly toward the higher range of his capability.[7]

Of course, a positive self-image will not allow us to perform better than our intrinsic capacities, but it frequently helps us to reach the high end of our capacities. Why so? Because a self-image that underestimates our true capacity can prevent us from reaching that capacity. It introduces feelings of doubts and anxiety into our motivational and behavioral framework, causing nervousness—what some call "choking"—while we are moving our plans into action. If we can remove those feelings of doubt and anxiety, by adjusting our self-image, before putting our plans into action, there is a strong likelihood that we will perform more efficaciously, on a higher level of quality, creativity, and productivity—quite naturally.[8]

I have known several people throughout my life who had excellent capacities for articulation and organization, but would tell me that they were "bad public speakers" or "suffered from writer's block". I recognized right away that this was not a problem of intrinsic capability, but rather with their self-image. Some teacher had told them in the first or second grade that they were not good speakers or writers, and they believed those teachers—so much so that they dutifully etched this self-image into their subconscious minds. Sure enough, every time they were called upon to do public speaking, they began to feel quite nervous—even feeling constriction in their throats and vocal chords, almost paralyzing them to the point of fainting. The same held true for people with supposed "writer's block". Like the "poor" public speakers, these people had experiences of having a great difficulty writing in the fourth or fifth grade. They remembered these experiences, thinking to themselves, "I just can't

[7] See Bandura, *Self-Efficacy*, pp. 36–61.
[8] Ibid.

write—nothing comes out." In the meantime, they became avid readers of both fiction and nonfiction, and proved themselves quite organized in their thought. Nevertheless, every time they sat down to write, their subconscious minds took care of it—nothing came out.

I have recommended Lou Tice's book *Smart Talk* to these individuals, particularly the sections on visualization and affirmations[9] (described below) to help them adjust their needlessly negative self-image. After working on this, I helped them break speech writing and prose writing into small achievable steps—and the result was amazing. Some of them became very creative and productive speakers and writers—not from an increase in intelligence or talent, but from simply removing the negative elements in their self-image. I have heard many testimonies from readers of Lou Tice's work who overcame "mathematics blocks" and "social blocks" through the same method.

The reader may be thinking, "Well, that's all great; but I don't have a problem with self-efficacy in golf, speaking, writing, mathematics, or social events. What does this have to do with the subject at hand—namely, resistance to temptation and becoming more virtuous?" As it turns out, subconscious self-image is just as important to character development (acquisition of virtue and resistance to temptation) as it is to efficacious use of talents and actualization of goals, because reinforcing our higher self by conscious choice alone is not enough. We have to complement our conscious choice to enhance our higher self with deliberate conditioning of our *subconscious* self-image. As the reader may by now have discovered, forming our *subconscious* self-image is not as simple as *consciously* choosing a particular self-image. The former entails changes to our previous subconscious self-image, which in turn requires conditioning the subconscious mind to a new self-image as well as repeated choice and action (explained below).

If we make a *conscious* choice to give preeminence to the higher self without reconditioning our *subconscious* self-image to conform to that choice, our subconscious mind will resist our conscious choice, and in the end, it will probably win. Why? Unfortunately our subconscious self-image has a "default drive" toward the *lower self*, coming from

[9] See Tice, *Smart Talk*, Chapters 1–3. See also Bandura, *Self-Efficacy*, pp. 79–159.

our childhood desires, pleasures, and experiences.[10] Even though we learn how to regulate the lower self in adulthood to become socially acceptable, the "lower self" still exerts considerable influence over our behavior because our subconscious self-image still continues to come from our childlike desires, pleasures, and experiences. As we shall see, if we do not recondition our subconscious self-image to conform to the higher self, it will keep its old propensities and resist the higher self in our beliefs and behaviors. Thus, if we are not to be continually hampered by the intrusion of the lower self when resisting temptation and appropriating virtue, we will have to make a concerted effort to change our subconscious self-image to match our conscious choice to emphasize the higher self. The work of Dr. Albert Bandura (and Lou Tice) on self-efficacy can be quite useful.

As noted above, if we do not reorient our subconscious self-image toward the higher self, allowing the lower self to have continued significance in our behavior, we can expect our bifurcated psyche to fail in many of its resolutions and to be unsuccessful in resisting temptation, particularly when we are lacking in psychic energy (e.g., when we are tired or stressed). Thus, the sooner we endeavor to reorient our subconscious self-image toward the higher self, the sooner we will have greater success in resisting temptations and completing our resolutions.[11]

As might be expected, a subconscious self-image oriented toward the higher self will have the opposite effect of our default drive (i.e., a subconscious self-image oriented toward the lower self), because it will reinforce our conscious choices to resist the deadly sins and act virtuously (in the image of Christ and the saints). When our

---

[10] Recall that Freudian psychologists would call the lower self the "id", which was later called "the child" by transactional psychologists. For Freud, the id works to satisfy *basic* urges, needs, and desires, operating on the pleasure principle that seeks Level One satisfaction, what is immediately gratifying, surface apparent, and intense in pleasure. See Sigmund Freud, *The Ego and the Id* (New York: Courier Dover Publications, 2018), pp. 8–18. For a summary, see Chapter 5 (Section III.A).

[11] Some individuals may successfully complete resolutions and resist temptations without changing their subconscious self-image toward the higher self, because they feel pressure from employers, social networks, family, and so forth. But this kind of success, due to fear and pressure, will probably be unsuccessful in the *long-term* because their subconscious self-image will continue to resist the higher self. Furthermore, fear and social pressure are exhausting, which motivates most individuals to free themselves from it in the long-term.

subconscious self-image has been strongly reconditioned toward the higher self, resistance to temptation can be significantly facilitated. All we really need to do is say to ourselves, "I am going to act according to my noble, virtuous, saintly, Christlike self," or some other similar expression such as, "I am going to act according to my loving, respectful, generous, saintly, Christlike self." As we shall see, our choice of wording for this expression should conform not only to the virtues to which we most naturally relate, but also to the virtues that resist the deadly sins to which we are most vulnerable. But we are getting ahead of ourselves here. For the moment, suffice it to say that the more strongly we associate our subconscious self-image with these virtues, the more quickly our simple declaration (that we are going to act according to our higher self) will become effective in resisting temptation.

Louis Pasteur said, "Chance favors the prepared mind." We might adapt this statement to our purposes by noting that "resistance to temptation and virtuous conduct favor the reconditioned subconscious self-image (toward the higher self)". Given its importance in moral conversion, we must now discuss how, according to Bandura and Tice, we can recondition our subconscious mind. They recommend two techniques:

1. Visualization (Section I.B.)
2. Affirmations (Section I.C)

Saint Ignatius' daily Examen can also be helpful in this process (Section II) as well as spontaneous prayers (Section IV). Let us begin with visualization.

B. Using Visualization to Cultivate a Christlike Subconscious Self-Image

Lou Tice summarizes the process of visualization in transforming our subconscious self-image as follows:

You will never accomplish all that you dream, but you will seldom accomplish anything that you don't envision first. So, think in terms of ideals; compare your ideals with your current reality; establish what you want; find models of what you want to become; and visualize yourself achieving your desired end result.[12]

We might infer a three-step process from this passage:

1. Find an ideal (virtue).
2. Find a model of this ideal.
3. Visualize yourself as having reached the ideal.

The first step may be accomplished by studying the table of deadly sins and counteracting virtues from the previous chapter (Section IV). Given that we cannot appropriate all virtues in a single attempt at visualization (because we have a limited amount of psychic energy and concentration), we will have to be strategic about selecting the virtues (what Tice calls "ideals") with which we want to start. How might we best do this? Recall what Saint Ignatius says about how the Evil One tempts us:

> Fourteenth Rule. The fourteenth: Likewise, [the Evil One], the enemy of human nature, roaming about, looks in turn at all our virtues, theological, cardinal and moral; and where he finds us weakest and most in need for our eternal salvation, there he attacks us and aims at taking us.[13]

If we are to avoid being spiritually attacked where we are weakest, we will have to counter the Evil One's strategy by cultivating the virtues that best help us to resist the deadly sins to which we are most vulnerable. For example, if we are most vulnerable to the sin of anger, we will want to start the process of visualization with the virtues of forgiveness, compassion, and gentle-heartedness (explained in Chapter 4, Section II). If we are most vulnerable to lust, then we would want to start the process of visualization with the virtues of chastity, respect and care for others, and temperance. If we are most vulnerable to the sin of pride, we will want to start with the virtues

---

[12] Tice, Smart Talk, p. 20.
[13] Spiritual Exercises, "Rules for Perceiving and Knowing in Some Manner the Different Movements Which Are Caused in the Soul", http://sacred-texts.com/chr/seil/seil78.htm.

of humble-heartedness, justice, and compassion. Now go back to the table in the previous chapter (Section IV) and identify the deadly sins to which you are most vulnerable, and then the counteracting virtues to those deadly sins. If you need additional explanation of those virtues, see Chapter 4, Section I (for the cardinal virtues) and Section II (for the subvirtues of love).

After you have studied the descriptions of the subvirtues on which you are focused, you are ready to proceed to Tice's second step—finding a role model who exemplifies this virtue and the subordinating virtues. Evidently, Jesus is the prime role model of every virtue, so we can use Saint Ignatius' technique of contemplating on scenes in the life of Christ in which Jesus exemplifies these virtues. There are multiple examples of Jesus' gentleness, respect, care, and compassion for sinners; His care for the sick, poor, and possessed; His total humility in offering Himself up as a sin offering and pascal sacrifice; His prayerfulness and complete confidence in the Father manifested throughout His ministry; and His chastity in promoting the sanctity of marriage and living and promoting celibacy. It might be useful to read one or more of the narrative versions of the life of Christ to get a better "feel" for how Jesus lived these virtues. There are several excellent ones, such as Fulton J. Sheen's *Life of Christ*;[14] Archbishop Alban Goodier's *The Public Life of Our Lord Jesus Christ*[15] as well as *The Passion and Death of Our Lord Jesus Christ*;[16] Romano Guardini's *The Lord*;[17] and Pope Benedict XVI's three-volume series *Jesus of Nazareth*.[18]

Some people may also benefit from finding a role model from among the many saints of the Catholic Church. Rather than trying to identify a saint who seems to exemplify a particular virtue or virtues,

[14] Fulton J. Sheen, *Life of Christ* (Garden City, N.Y.: Image Books, 1977; originally, New York: McGraw-Hill, 1953).

[15] Alban Goodier, *The Public Life of Our Lord Jesus Christ* (New York: P.J. Kenedy & Sons, 1944).

[16] Alban Goodier, *The Passion and Death of Our Lord Jesus Christ* (New York: P.J. Kenedy & Sons, 1944).

[17] Romano Guardini, *The Lord* (Chicago: Regnery, 1954).

[18] Pope Benedict XVI, *Jesus of Nazareth: The Infancy Narratives* (San Francisco: Ignatius Press, 2018); Pope Benedict XVI, *Jesus of Nazareth: From the Baptism in the Jordan to the Transfiguration* (San Francisco: Ignatius Press, 2008); Pope Benedict XVI, *Jesus of Nazareth: Holy Week; From the Entrance into Jerusalem to the Resurrection* (San Francisco: Ignatius Press, 2011).

I would suggest finding a saint or saints to whom you feel attracted or drawn, with whom you naturally identify. In my case, Saint Paul, Saint Augustine, Saint Thomas Aquinas, Saint Ignatius of Loyola, Saint Robert Bellarmine, Saint Peter Canisius, and Saint Thomas More (among the earlier saints) as well as Saint John Henry Newman and Venerable Fulton J. Sheen (among the more contemporary saints) have not only inspired me, but also attracted me—to the point of imitation. If you, the reader, identify with certain saints, you may want to read a good hagiography about them (see Chapter 3, Section VII, of this volume), then look at how they lived the virtues, and then proceed to Lou Tice's third step—visualization.

What does visualization entail? As you might expect, it is rather difficult to imitate the saints you most admire, since they lived in different times and cultures. So the point is not to visualize yourself imitating them in that time, but trying to visualize yourself having the same virtues that led to their holiness of life and effectiveness in the apostolate. We know in faith that these saints are interceding on our behalf *right now* within the Mystical Body of Christ, and so we should pray for their inspiration and intersession to become like them in prayer, discipleship, and above all, virtue. The more we read about these saints and pray for their intercession, the more lucidly we will be able to identify with their three noble intentions—to please the Lord out of gratitude and love, to respect and care for the good and salvation of others, and to seek their own highest character and salvation by following the teaching of Jesus and resisting their spiritual enemy. Now we can envision ourselves having not necessarily their talents, but their virtues. By doing this, we place ourselves in the same position as Saint Ignatius Loyola in the early part of his spiritual and moral conversion when he read a book on the life of Christ and another on the lives of the saints during his recovery from a severe injury that occurred at a battle in Pamplona (when he was a commander of a fort). He began to visualize himself being like these saints and desired to imitate them in virtue and discipleship. He describes this process in his own words:

> While perusing the life of Our Lord and the saints, he began to reflect, saying to himself: "What if I should do what St. Francis did?" "What if I should act like St. Dominic?" He pondered over these things in his

mind, and kept continually proposing to himself serious and difficult things. He seemed to feel a certain readiness for doing them, with no other reason except this thought: "St. Dominic did this; I, too, will do it." "St. Francis did this; therefore I will do it."[19]

Of course, we need not have the resolve of Saint Ignatius in order to obtain the benefits of visualization, but the more resolve we have, the more we will identify with our favorite saint, and the more we do this, the more our subconscious mind will appropriate the mentality of that saint. The more closely we subconsciously identify with this saint, the more we will naturally (and effortlessly) move toward his mentality, particularly his deep love of the Lord, his desire to serve Jesus, and the virtues springing from them—respect and care for others and their salvation, humble-heartedness, fortitude, temperance, chastity, forgiveness, and so forth. We might imitate Saint Ignatius in ruminating on what it would be like to have the faith and heart of our favorite saints. As we do this, we might find ourselves subconsciously appropriating their saintly mindset, precisely as Saint Ignatius did. The more we visualize ourselves emulating these saints, the stronger our subconscious identification will become, creating, as it were, "the new man" within ourselves.

We might think it presumptuous to view ourselves as saints, as already having a preeminent "saintly (higher) self". We might even believe it to be appropriately humble to say, "I am no saint", or "I am no saint yet." However, I believe those humble statements to be at least partially misleading, because, as noted in the previous chapter, we are all born into the world with a higher self—a transphysical *soul* inclined toward Level Three and Level Four desires.[20] The higher self may be weakly manifest in our conscious and subconscious mind,

---

[19] Saint Ignatius of Loyola, *The Autobiography of St. Ignatius*, ed. J. F. X. O'Conor, S.J. (New York: Benziger Brothers, 1900; Project Gutenberg, 2008), Chapter 1, https://www.gutenberg.org/files/24534/24534-h/24534-h.htm.

[20] Recall the evidence for the soul from Volume II of the Quartet. In addition to the evidence from near-death experiences, Gödel's proof, self-consciousness, and conceptual ideas, we showed that the awareness needed for our five transcendental desires (for perfect truth, love, goodness, beauty, and home) requires some form of *trans*physical agency (beyond physical processes). Thus, our five transcendental (Level Four) desires require a soul to be aware of their objectives. The powers of this transphysical soul belong properly to the higher self, and so also do the powers of empathy and conscience that give rise to Level Three desires.

but it is nevertheless quite present, awaiting the time of its ascendency through our moral conversion. As noted in the previous chapter (Section III), this ascendency can be initiated during our childhood through Baptism, continuous reception of the sacraments of the Holy Eucharist and Reconciliation, and active participation in the Church, but we cannot stop there. If we want to be proficient at resisting temptation, appropriating virtue, and imitating Christ, we must proceed to moral conversion—preferably through the four steps recommended in this and the previous chapter.

This means that every person has a "saintly self" in *potencia*, and every baptized and practicing Christian has a partially actualized "saintly" self. The more we practice our faith and deepen our spiritual and moral conversion, the more we strengthen our "saintly self", but we need not stop there. We can also work on conforming our *subconscious* self-identity to our saintly higher self by visualizations, affirmations, and spontaneous prayers.

Visualization is particularly effective in doing this, because it is almost natural to imitate someone we respect, admire, and have even grown to love. After all, imitation is the sincerest form of flattery. The more we study, admire, and love a particular saint, the more we begin to imitate him *in our subconscious mind*. Here's the problem—when we are reading a hagiography about someone we admire (and with whom we identify), we begin the process of subconsciously imitating him, but if we don't reinforce this admiration and love after we finish the hagiography, our subconscious imitation begins to fade.

The more we can visualize *ourselves* being like a particular saint in his love for God and desire to serve, the more we will naturally imitate him subconsciously. Imitating extraordinary love for God and desire to serve others (Level Three and Level Four desires) will naturally reinforce the "higher self" within our subconscious mind. The more we visualize ourselves loving and serving heroically, the more our subconscious mind will naturally imitate the desires of the higher self. It will also weaken the dominant grip of the lower self, which, as noted in the previous chapter, is stronger than the higher self in children, adolescents, and adults who have not chosen to do otherwise.

It seems that divine providence led Saint Ignatius of Loyola to do this quite naturally—without benefit of any insights from contemporary psychology—while he visualized himself imitating Jesus, the apostles, Saint Dominic, and Saint Francis in his hospital bed. Almost five hundred years later, his form of contemplation is being vindicated by insights from those relatively new disciplines.

Recall that grace builds on nature. So we might expect the Lord to add grace and consolation to this natural strengthening of the higher self. When we visualize ourselves imitating the mindset (the love and desire to serve) of the saints, we not only form our subconscious mind *naturally*; the Holy Spirit also takes the occasion to reinforce our love and desire through grace and consolation. This probably explains why Saint Ignatius was able to move from a dominant lower self to a dominant higher self so rapidly during his stay in the hospital. Recall that his transition was so profound that it led him to abandon his worldly goods, go to the cave outside of Manresa, and undergo a remarkably profound interior purification through his evolving method of spiritual exercises. In view of this, I recommend visualizing ourselves imitating the love and desire of the apostles (in Scripture) and our favorite saints. The Lord—and our subconscious mind—will not disappoint us.

This opens the way to Lou Tice's second recommendation for conditioning our subconscious mind toward our higher self—*affirmations*.

C. Using Affirmations to Cultivate a Christlike Subconscious Self-Image

Recall for a moment the reason we want to conform our subconscious self-identity to the character attributes of the higher self—to resist temptation. Recall our threefold process of resisting temptation:

1. Asserting no for the sake of Christ
2. Thinking, feeling, and acting with our higher self by recalling the three noble intentions given above and in the previous chapter—to please the Lord out of gratitude and love, to respect and care for the good and salvation of others, and to seek our own highest character and salvation by following the teaching of Jesus and resisting our spiritual enemy
3. Using spontaneous prayers to reinforce our higher self and our resistance to temptation

Recall from above that temptations appeal to the lower self and derive their power from it. The more influential the lower self is within our psyche, the more power temptation has over us. However, the more we cultivate our higher self (by conforming our subconscious identity to it and repeatedly acting through it), the more we will naturally use its higher thought processes, feelings, and character attributes. This will *disempower* the suggestions of temptations because the higher self has "little interest" in sensual and egotistical feelings, desires, and thoughts. Simply shifting from the thought processes of the lower self to those of the higher self—of the mature, noble, loving, faith-filled saintly self—greatly empowers our no to temptation because of the higher self's detachment from them.

Even if our lower self becomes initially engaged by a temptation, we can quickly dispel it by a voluntary shift to the mindset of the mature, noble, saintly, higher self, *if* our subconscious identity has made progress in appropriating our higher self by practicing visualizations, affirmations, the Ignatian Examen, and spontaneous prayers. As noted in Chapters 3–5, the effectiveness of all four of these practices is dependent on deep spiritual conversion through prayer, which opens us to the three noble intentions:

- To please the Lord out of gratitude and love
- To respect and care for the good and salvation of others
- To seek our own highest character and salvation by following the teaching of Jesus and resisting our spiritual enemy

The above strategy is the only one that will work over the long-term; for if we do not conform our subconscious identity to our higher self, we can only reject temptation by a *conscious* act of the will, which is continuously mitigated by our lower self's feelings, desires, and character attributes within our *subconscious* identity. Inasmuch as this scenario forces us to fight with ourselves continuously, it will make resistance to temptation a struggle with a very limited prospect of success.

So if we are to extricate ourselves from needless interior fighting (between the conscious and subconscious mind) and appropriate an easier, more successful method of resisting temptation, we will want to reinforce our higher self within our subconscious mind by every means possible. We have already explored the effectiveness of visualization for doing this, and contemporary psychology offers one more important tool—affirmations, on which we will now focus.

Lou Tice summarizes this technique as follows:

> Affirmation means the exercise of faith and belief in your inherent potential, imagined ideal, desired result, and set goal. You affirm them as if they were presently realized in your life. Affirmation applies to every step: You apply positive, proactive thinking to create vision, shift attitudes, see options, seize opportunities, expand comfort zones, and build teams and organizations.[21]

Using techniques derived from Dr. Bandura's work on self-efficacy,[22] Tice explains how to reinforce the ideals and models we have chosen for our new subconscious identity. The objective is to write a simple one-line statement about the ideal, model, or virtue (of the higher self) we want to reinforce subconsciously. Though our treatment of affirmations will focus solely on ideals that reinforce the higher self within the subconscious mind, we can use Bandura's techniques to reinforce other kinds of ideals—such as goals of performance, lifestyle, athleticism, and work performance. So long as the goals do not surpass our intrinsic physical, emotional, or intellectual capabilities, affirmations can reinforce them in our subconscious mind, which will help us to move naturally and almost effortlessly toward those goals. Since our focus is on cultivating the higher self in our subconscious mind, we will restrict our discussion of affirmations to this area.

Though Tice does not restrict the number of affirmations one can have, the limits of psychic energy and concentration will probably dictate that the first three or four affirmations will create a stronger impression on the subconscious psyche than additional ones beyond them. Before discussing how to use affirmations, we will want to discuss how they work and how to write them.

As Tice implies in the above passage, affirmations should be stated in the *present tense*, as if the desired ideal is already a reality. Though we will address this in more detail below, we must clarify one important

---

[21] Tice, *Smart Talk*, p. 3.
[22] See Bandura, *Self-Efficacy*, pp. 36–78.

aspect of Tice's assertion—namely, that we are not affirming a fiction about ourselves. You, the reader, might be a bit nervous about writing an affirmation stating a desired goal in the present tense—for example, "I love God and serve Him like Saint Ignatius of Loyola." You might want to say, "Well, that's not truthful; I don't have Saint Ignatius' love of God or his freedom to serve—right now. After all, this is my desired *ideal or goal*." Truthful as this may seem, it is also partially misleading.

Recall from our discussion of visualizing the mentality of the saints above, that baptized and practicing Christians already have a partially actualized "saintly higher self". We noted there that if we are reading about a particular saint—admiring his love of God and others—we are already in the process of imitating him in our subconscious mind. Hence, it is not untruthful to say that we already have within us Saint Ignatius' love and service of God. Our affirmation statement therefore is only *reinforcing* a truth about our higher saintly self that is already in the process of imitating Saint Ignatius. We may now give some simple rules for how to write affirmations, and then move to the topic of why they work.

There are two dimensions to writing an affirmation—first, selecting the content, and second, writing them in a first-person, positive, emotionally engaging way. We will begin with the first dimension—selecting content for the affirmation. We can focus the content of our affirmation on either a *person* we want to imitate or a *virtue* we want to appropriate. Since we do not want to write a negative affirmation (explained below), we will want to avoid selecting a person whose conduct we do not want to imitate—for example, "I am *not* like Adolf Hitler", or "I am *not* like Ted Bundy." For the same reason, we will want to avoid focusing on vices that we don't want to appropriate—for example, "I am *not* proud", or "I am *not* envious."

With respect to persons we want to imitate, we can profitably begin with the saints we most love and admire—and have already begun to visualize being like. When we write the affirmation, we may want to include a particular attribute of this saint as well. So, for example, we might write the following affirmations:

- "I am like Jesus in my gentleness of heart."
- "I am like Jesus in my sincere respect for others and their freedom."

- "I am like Jesus in my forgiveness of others after they have insulted or harmed me."
- "I am like Jesus in the chasteness of my heart and life."
- "I am like Saint Ignatius in my tireless commitment to build the Kingdom of God."
- "I am like Saint Ignatius in my commitment to prayer."
- "I am like Saint Peter Canisius in my desire to bring the truth of Christ to the world."
- "I am like Saint Thomas More in my fidelity to defend the Church even at the cost of my life."
- "I am like Saint Paul in my commitment to chastity and obedience to follow the example of Jesus."
- "I am like Saint Paul in my deep love of Christ and my desire to follow Him."
- "I am like Venerable Archbishop Fulton J. Sheen in my commitment to use every means possible to evangelize the world."

By associating a particular virtue with the Lord or a saint we admire or love, we create a natural affinity between that virtue and our subconscious mind. The more we repeat our affirmation, the stronger this affinity becomes, which has the benefit of strengthening both the virtue and the higher self within our subconscious mind. This strong subconscious self-image will prove invaluable for resisting temptation.

Beyond imitating the Lord or a saint we admire or love, there is another very powerful way to reinforce virtues and our higher self within our subconscious self-identity—namely, associating the virtue with our positive reason for wanting it—for example, "for the sake of building the Kingdom", "because I love the Lord", "in order to imitate the Lord I love", or for the three noble intentions: to please the Lord out of gratitude and love, to respect and care for the good and salvation of others, and to pursue our highest character and salvation by fidelity to the teaching of Jesus and resistance to our spiritual enemy. When we use this method, we will again want to concentrate on the virtues we need the most—particularly those contrary to the deadly sins to which we are most vulnerable. In view of this, you may want to return to the table of deadly sins and opposing virtues given in the previous chapter (Section IV) and select the virtues on which you want to concentrate. For example, if you are working on the deadly sin of anger, you will want to focus on the virtues of forgiveness, respect and care for others and their salvation, compassion, and so forth. Once you have made a selection, then you will want to write a positive present-tense affirmation associating this virtue with yourself along with your reason for wanting it. So, for example, if you are working on chastity, you might write the following:

- "I am chaste to respect others and their salvation."
- "I am chaste in imitation of Jesus, my Lord."
- "I am chaste to respect and care for my spouse and our family."
- "I am chaste to consecrate my sexuality to the Lord I love."
- "I am chaste to consecrate my sexuality to my spouse and family."
- "I am chaste to please the Lord I love."
- "I am a chaste person in the company of the Blessed Virgin Mary."
- "I am chaste because it is the right thing to do."

Some people prefer to associate a virtue with themselves by supporting it with a reference to their personhood, such as "I am a man who ..."; "I am a gentle-hearted person who ...; or "I am a patient woman who ... ". If this helps you to identify with a virtue, then try the following forms for your affirmations:

- "I am a chaste man to respect others and their salvation."
- "I am a man who is chaste to please the Lord I love."
- "I am a chaste man in imitation of Jesus, my Lord."
- "I am a woman who is chaste to respect my husband and our family."
- "I am a chaste woman to consecrate my sexuality to the Lord I love."
- "I am a chaste woman to consecrate my sexuality to my husband and family."

The objective is not only to reinforce the virtue in the subconscious mind, but also to associate the virtue with positive emotion, which frequently comes from a noble cause, a sense of integrity, admiration for a role model, love of Christ, and love of the Blessed Virgin or one of the saints.

Though Bandura and Tice do not give examples of affirmations with prayer content, I have found it *very* helpful to include prayer content in my affirmations. This has not in any way inhibited the conditioning of my subconscious mind, but rather enhanced it with both positive emotional content *and grace*. If readers have strong faith and a close relationship with the Lord (which frequently comes from dedicated time to contemplative prayer [see Chapter 3, Section III]), I would recommend including prayer content in your affirmations. Hence, you might rewrite the above sample affirmations as follows:

- "I am chaste to be like you, heavenly Father."
- "I am chaste for love of you, dear Lord."
- "I am chaste to be like you, Mother Mary."
- "I am chaste to be in your company, Saint Ignatius."
- "I am forgiving and patient to be like you, Lord Jesus."
- "I am forgiving and patient for love of you, dear Lord."
- "I am forgiving and patient to be like you, Mother Mary."
- "I am forgiving and patient to be in your company, Saint Ignatius."

I have found this particular phrasing of affirmations to be the most effective in my life for reconditioning my subconscious mind toward the higher self as well as for resisting temptation (see below in this section).

One last point should be mentioned to prevent a frequently made mistake. Since we want our affirmations to be stated in the present tense (explained below), we must avoid using the expression "I want to ..." in our affirmations. Phrasing the affirmation this way inadvertently pushes it into the future—at which point your subconscious mind does not interpret it as your *present* reality. So, for example, we will not want to say:

- "I *want* to be chaste to please the Lord I love."
- "I *want* to be gentle-hearted to be like Saint Francis."
- "I *want* to be humble for the sake of the Lord I love."

You will probably recognize the problem of phrasing the affirmation this way. By saying that you *want* a particular attribute, you are saying to yourself that you do *not* have that attribute now, which suggests to your subconscious mind that you are *not* a chaste person, a humble person, and so forth. This is precisely the opposite of what you *want* to do.

We may now consider the topic of how to write affirmations—and some additional pitfalls to avoid along the way. Recall the four essential points mentioned above:

1. Every affirmation should begin with "I", the first-person singular pronoun. Failure to use "I" will render the affirmation powerless to affect our subconscious identity.
2. Every affirmation should be phrased in the present tense—for example, "I am", "I am like", "I have". Any affirmation written in the future tense or as an aspiration or wish (e.g., "I want") will be powerless to affect our subconscious identity.
3. Do not introduce *negative* content into the affirmation—for example, "I am chaste to avoid being sinful," or "I do not want to be a pornography addict," or "I do not want to be like Adolf Hitler."
4. Associate the affirmation with an emotional (felt) motive for valuing it—for example, "To please the Lord I love" or "To consecrate myself to my wife and children" or "To respect others and their salvation". If you have a close relationship with the Lord, include prayer content in your affirmation, such as, " ... to be like You, my Lord."

Why do we want to write an affirmation as if it were present reality? Briefly, because our subconscious mind will do everything it can to identify with the present reality it believes itself to be. Recall that our higher self already exists within our mind, but may be recessive in comparison to our lower self in our subconscious mind when we begin the process of moral conversion. When we repeat an emotionally engaging affirmation in the first-person present tense, it appeals immediately to our higher self—calling it to the forefront of our subconscious mind. For example, if I repeatedly say to myself, "I *am* a chaste man to please the Lord I love and to edify the Church I desire to help," or "I am like Jesus in my chastity to be in His special service," I immediately bring my higher self to the forefront of both my conscious and subconscious mind (because these qualities belong properly to the higher self). When my subconscious mind feels the positive emotion associated with the saints and virtue in my affirmation, it begins the process of natural imitation. The more I repeat the affirmation with its positive emotion, the more I stimulate this natural process of imitation—reinforcing the virtue and my higher self within my subconscious mind.

When we reinforce a virtue and our higher self *as present realities* within our subconscious mind, our subconscious mind will join our conscious mind in resisting sin and our lower self (because they do not correspond to our present reality—virtue and the higher self). This gives us an automatic advantage when temptation presents itself (whether it originates from within us or from the Evil One). Recall that temptation appeals to the lower self and derives its power from it. Thus, if our subconscious mind identifies our present reality with our virtuous saintly higher self, it will automatically be either disinterested in or resist this temptation. Our conscious mind is now supported by our subconscious mind—instead of being undermined by it (when it was mired in the lower self).

For example, if my subconscious self-image is that I am chaste because of my love for the Lord, and I am being tempted away from that, my subconscious mind will introduce feelings of emptiness, alienation, and inauthenticity into my conscious psyche as I am entertaining a temptation that is opposed to its image of who I really am. These negative feelings arising out of believing that I am "out of sync" with my present reality can break the spell of temptation to resume my present reality—my virtuous saintly higher self.

We may now move to our next point about writing affirmations—avoiding any negative content. Why is this so important? We noted above that negative assertions are very difficult to maintain over the long-term, but affirmations are aimed precisely at the long-term, indeed, one might say, at a permanent term. For this reason alone, negative content in affirmations is unsuitable. Yet, there is an even more important reason for avoiding it in our affirmations. We do not want to ingrain the negative content we are trying to avoid in our subconscious self-image by implication. If we repeat to ourselves that we don't want to be an unfaithful person, it reinforces our concern or fear of being unfaithful in our subconscious mind, which implies that we believe ourselves to be capable of, if not tending toward, infidelity and unchastity. Ironically, trying to ingrain a negative motive in our subconscious mind strongly suggests that we are inclined in that direction at the present moment. Our subconscious mind will not miss the implication. Hence, putting negative content into our affirmations is tantamount to preparing our subconscious mind to fight against itself! The solution is simple: keep your affirmations positive; focus on your higher self, your ideals, and the Lord and saints you admire; and make these your present reality by writing your affirmations in the first-person present tense.

If you have a fairly good grasp of the above instructions for writing affirmations, I would suggest consecrating about three hours to the Lord—perhaps after Mass on a Sunday—to sit down and write a set of ten affirmations, bearing in mind the virtues you want to appropriate, the saints you want to imitate, and the positive emotional reasons for doing so. If you repeat these affirmations in your daily Examen (see below Section II)—or at another time every day—you will see the power of Bandura's theory of self-efficacy in your own moral conversion, which will make your efforts quite worthwhile.

Recall what was said above about grace building on nature. As with visualization, the Lord can infuse our affirmations with grace and consolation to help reinforce them. We can facilitate this infusion of grace through one of the following three methods:

- Adding prayer content to our affirmations, such as, "I am chaste to be like You, Lord" (see above in this section)
- Integrating our affirmations into Saint Ignatius' daily Examen Prayer (see below, Section II)
- Saying spontaneous prayers connected with our affirmations (see below, Section IV.A)

Before considering this, we will briefly address how to use our affirmations.

D. Using Affirmations

How do we use our affirmations? There are two main ways of doing so. First, repeat them several times per day—either within your daily

Examen or outside of it (see below, Section II). If you have included prayer content in your affirmations to the Lord, the Blessed Virgin Mary, or one of the saints, you may want to reinforce them by praying to them asking for their help and inspiration so that you might be like them in prayer, virtue, and zeal for the Kingdom. Now put yourself in the position of Saint Ignatius Loyola when he was convalescing in the hospital and consider what it would be like for you to act, pray, and embrace virtue like these role models. If you are practicing the Examen Prayer, you may want to insert your affirmations into it by adding a step to the prayer (see below, Section II).

The second way in which affirmations can be used is within the context of resisting temptation itself. Recall the three dimensions of resisting temptation given above—asserting no to temptation for the sake of Christ, appealing to your higher self, and reinforcing this with spontaneous prayers. We can use our affirmation to appeal to our higher self (the second dimension of resisting temptation) and also within the context of our spontaneous prayers (see below, Section IV).

Since our affirmations appeal to our higher self, we need do nothing more than repeat our affirmations to bring our higher selves to bear in the process of resisting temptation. Doing this appeals not only to our higher self, but also to the specific virtue that is opposed to the temptation being experienced. If our subconscious mind is already strongly conformed to our higher self (and its virtues), a simple statement of the affirmation will incite the subconscious mind to join the conscious mind to resist temptation successfully. Alternatively, if our subconscious mind is *not* yet strongly conformed to our higher self (and its virtues), the lower self may still be dominant in it—in which case our subconscious mind will act *against* our conscious mind's attempts to resist temptation. Affirmations are still exceedingly helpful in this eventuality, because they challenge the dominance of the lower self within the subconscious mind, which further mitigates the subconscious mind's engagement of the temptation. If the affirmation even temporarily disengages the lower self within the subconscious mind, it gives the conscious mind much freer rein to resist the temptation (without the opposition of the subconscious mind). This might provide the edge needed to resist a persistent temptation successfully. Successfully resisting the temptation might also reinforce the higher self (and its virtues) within the subconscious mind at the same time.

I have found that affirmations with prayer content, such as "I am chaste to be like You, Lord," are particularly helpful for resisting temptation, because they combine my appeal to the higher self with my love of the Lord and the grace He provides through my prayer. Bringing these three catalysts to consciousness not only helps to resist the temptation, but also to condition the subconscious mind. You may have to repeat this affirmation with prayer content several times before it begins to mitigate the momentum of temptation. You may also want to use an appeal to more than one holy agent in your affirmation, such as, "I am forgiving and patient to be like You, Heavenly Father, and You, Lord Jesus"—or "I am forgiving and patient to be like You, Lord Jesus, and you, Mother Mary."

In sum, repeating our affirmations at times of temptation is always likely to be helpful. If our subconscious mind is already conformed to the higher self, then a simple recitation of the affirmation might well dispel the temptation. Even if our subconscious mind is not conformed to the higher self, repeating our affirmation is likely to be quite helpful, for it could disengage a counterproductive subconscious mind, give an edge to our conscious mind in resisting temptation, and reinforce the higher self (within the subconscious) in the process.

We can also combine the first and second dimensions of our process for resisting temptation by simply using the phrase "I'm better than that" before we state our affirmation. Thus, if we are tempted toward pride, we might say something like, "I am better than that— humble-hearted like the Lord I love," or "I am better than that— humble-hearted to be like You, Lord Jesus." If we are being tempted toward lust, we might say something like, "I'm better than that— chaste for love of You, Lord Jesus."

One final observation should be mentioned here (and will be taken up in more detail below in Section III). When our subconscious mind becomes strongly conformed to our higher self (and its virtues), we will likely not have to use our affirmations in the process of resisting temptation anymore, because we can do this by taking a "shortcut", using one simple phrase—"I am better than my lower self—I am my higher self, to be like You, my Lord." Even if we have to repeat this phrase several times (during persistent temptations), our previous efforts at forming and using affirmations will very likely enable this one phrase to resist the temptation successfully. Generally, the more strongly conformed our subconscious mind is to our higher self, the less we have to repeat the above phrase. One or two recitations are sufficient to allow our strong higher self to emerge and disengage even the most persistent temptations.

It cannot be emphasized enough that the stronger our spiritual conversion—our loving connection with the Lord—the more effective our affirmations will be in forming our subconscious mind toward the higher self and resisting temptation. When we include prayer content in our affirmations, and our gratitude and love of the Lord is strong, our affirmations will be more effective, not only because of their strong emotional pull on the subconscious mind, but also because the Lord can infuse His grace into the process of self-transformation.

Our first two steps of moral conversion can be strengthened and amplified by the third and fourth steps. We will now consider the third step—the Ignatian Examen prayer.

II. The Third Step in Moral Conversion: The Ignatian Examen Prayer to Incorporate Grace

The Ignatian Examen Prayer is a short daily exercise (around ten minutes) that aims at moral conversion.[23] It is not meant to be implemented at the time we are resisting temptation, but rather at some regular time, normally toward the end of the day. When it is practiced faithfully, it has a cumulative effect that empowers the three dimensions of our technique to resist temptation—saying no for the sake of Christ, making recourse to the higher self, and spontaneous prayers. As noted above, our visualization and affirmations toward our new subconscious identity can be fruitfully integrated into this daily discipline.

---

[23] Father William Watson has written an excellent practical guide for laypeople (and another one for priests), introducing the Examen Prayer in a very concrete way, entitled *Forty Weeks*. He provides excellent specific meditations for a guided Examen Prayer experience over forty weeks. When completed, the reader can continue the Examen Prayer in the fashion recommended by Saint Ignatius of Loyola throughout the rest of his life. This fifteen-minute prayer can be exceedingly helpful in moral conversion, i.e., self-transformation and resistance to temptation. See William Watson, *Forty Weeks: An Ignatian Path to Christ with Sacred Story Prayer* (CreateSpace Independent Publishing Platform, 2014).

When Saint Ignatius developed this discipline in his *Spiritual Exercises*, he indicated that it consisted of five points:

First Point. The first Point is to give thanks to God our Lord for the benefits received.

Second Point. The second, to ask [for the] grace to know our sins and cast them out.

Third Point. The third, to ask account of our soul from the hour that we rose up to the present Examen, hour by hour, or period by period: and first as to thoughts, and then as to words, and then as to acts, in the same order as was mentioned in the Particular Examen.

Fourth Point. The fourth, to ask pardon of God our Lord for the faults.

Fifth Point. The fifth, to purpose amendment with His grace.

OUR FATHER.[24]

The First Point—the prayer of thanksgiving—may at first seem to be out of place with respect to the other four points, because it focuses on the positive blessings of the day (and our life), while the other four points focus on the temptations and sins of the day. As might be expected, it is not out of place, because Saint Ignatius is trying to help us toward moral conversion; and the first step of moral conversion is spiritual conversion (spiritual depth), which consists in recognizing the Lord's love for us and our response of love back to Him. As noted earlier, this love of the Lord is most incisively aroused by recognition of His blessings to us, which elicits profound gratitude. Saint Ignatius wants us to reflect about not only the blessings of the day, but also the blessings of our lives—our families, friends, community life, work life, and faith life—and the blessings of creation, particularly our unique souls, the blessings of redemption through the self-sacrificial love of Jesus, and the blessings of the Holy Spirit, who guides and animates us. As we recognize the love of God for us and all humanity, we cannot help ourselves—we are moved to love Him in return.

---

[24] *Spiritual Exercises*, "General Examen of Conscience to Purify Oneself and to Make One's Confession Better", under "Method for Making the General Examen", http://www.sacred-texts.com/chr/seil/seil09.htm.

This positive framework is essential to the rest of the Examen Prayer, because the objective of the Examen is not to beat ourselves up, to focus on our imperfections, and to feel a profound sense of self-alienation, but rather to desire to move beyond our temptations and sins by increasing resolve against temptation, strengthening our higher self in Christ ("the new man"), and freeing ourselves for greater love and service of the Lord and His Kingdom. We can deepen our experience of the First Point by preparing some lists of blessings we have received throughout our lives: the blessing of our immortal transphysical souls, made in the image and likeness of God; the blessing of our families, our many friends throughout life, our gifts and opportunities to make a positive difference and to see our and our family's well-being; the blessing of our faith and the Spirit's guidance into deeper intellectual, spiritual, and moral conversion; the blessing of our many opportunities to serve and be served throughout our lives; and so forth. This list may prove particularly helpful when we are drawing a blank about items for which to be grateful in the first step of the Examen Prayer. I have discussed this in more detail in Chapter 3 (Section III.A.3) of this volume and in Volume I (Chapter 9) of the Quartet.

We cannot stop at the First Point, because Points 2–5 (concluding with our firm purpose of amendment) are essential to the objective of the Examen Prayer—*moral conversion*. The reader will notice that Points 2–5 resemble the formula recommended for the Sacrament of Reconciliation, to incite true contrition for sin. Notice that this daily discipline is not a reflection, but rather, an intimate prayer grounded in our desire to love and imitate the Lord, who has loved us first. Let's examine each of the four recommended points:

- To ask the Lord for the grace to know our sins. Saint Ignatius assumes here that we have a desire to imitate the Lord and have sufficient trust in His merciful love, to examine our failings *with Him* to become *more like Him*.
- To ask account of our sins of thoughts, words, and deeds during the day. Notice that Saint Ignatius does not say "to *take* account", as if one were reflecting independently of the Lord, but rather, "to *ask* account", implying that we are looking at our day *with the Lord*, to better see and understand where we have entertained temptation and fallen short of imitating His loving heart. Saint

Ignatius is assuming here that we are at a sufficient stage of spiritual conversion to desire fervently to be like the Lord, who has blessed us and loved us.

- To ask pardon for the sins and failings we see. If we have examined our failings with the Lord, noticing where we might have separated ourselves from Him, hurt our neighbor, or opened ourselves to our spiritual enemy, we will likely experience a sincere sense of regret and contrition. When we feel this regret, we will want to express pardon for our sins, perhaps by using the incisive prayer of the tax collector in the Temple—"God, be merciful to me a sinner!" (Lk 18:13).
- To make a firm purpose of amendment with His grace. As with the Sacrament of Reconciliation, this purpose of amendment flows naturally from our feelings of regret and contrition. When we truly regret a past action, as incommensurate with the Lord's heart of love, it provides significant internal motivation to do better in the future for the sake of the Lord (and His Kingdom), others, and our salvation.

Should we stop at the Fifth Point? Since the objective of the Examen is to deepen our moral conversion, and the above-mentioned techniques of visualization and affirmations accomplish this objective by reinforcing the higher self in the subconscious mind, why wouldn't we want to integrate those points into our Examen along with spontaneous prayers? I can't imagine that Saint Ignatius would object to it, since he was in favor of using every legitimate tool to move the believer to spiritual and moral conversion. In view of this, I would recommend adding one point to Saint Ignatius' original five points (if I might be so presumptuous):

Sixth Point: Recite your affirmations about your ideals, models, and virtues, allowing them to affect you emotionally (see above, Section I.C).
Then say the Our Father to conclude the Examen.

By adding the above Sixth Point, we risk prolonging and overcomplicating this daily discipline to a point where individuals may begin to shrink from it; but I ask the reader seriously to consider running these risks and bearing patiently with the possible overcomplication that might initially come from it, because the benefits will be substantial. I do not want to imply that we abbreviate the first five points so that we can get to the additional point—quite the opposite. The sincerity with which we consider the first five points affects the efficacy and depth of the affirmations in the additional point. Hence, sincerely considering and expressing gratitude for the blessings of the day, creation, redemption, and our lives helps to deepen our love for the Lord, which in turn will deepen our desire to imitate Him. This not only will move us to contrition for our failings during the day, but will also inspire and empower our affirmations to be like the Lord.

Saint Ignatius was so convinced of the efficacy of this daily prayer for moral conversion that he told the Society of Jesus, "If we pray no other prayer, the Examen should be the one we pray." Given the importance of this discipline, it is essential to put it into practice. Saint Ignatius and many other spiritual masters have one rule in common: if you want to get something done, get started, even if it is not perfectly planned. I would recommend making a large-print, type-written copy of the above Six Points and clipping it into your prayer book or Breviary; then find a ten- to fifteen-minute period in the evening that you can routinely dedicate to this prayer—then, get started.

Don't worry about "not getting it right". You will improve over the course of time, if you faithfully engage in the Six Points of the prayer every evening. Some readers may want to start with Saint Ignatius' original Five Points for the sake of simplicity, and then add the Sixth Point after a month. With or without the additional point, the Examen Prayer should be considered a major part of the process of moral conversion, without which the effectiveness of that process would be seriously compromised and reduced. Recall that this prayer discipline is the critical point at which the Lord's inspiration, redemptive consolation, and grace are infused into the moral conversion process—and that makes all the difference.

III. A Brief Summary of Techniques for Conforming the Subconscious Mind to the Higher Self

Now let's review for a moment the various steps we have elucidated to resist temptation and solidify moral conversion. We might divide this task into two stages: a preparation stage and an implementation stage.

The *preparation stage* consists of three steps:

1. Reviewing the material on virtue (in Chapter 4) and doing one to two months of the recommended meditation to create aversion to deadly sins and devotion to the virtues (the first step in moral conversion [see Chapter 5, Section IV]).
2. Reinforcing our higher self in the subconscious mind through the techniques of visualization and affirmations (the second step of moral conversion to condition the subconscious mind to the higher self [see above, Section I]). There are two substeps in forming this new subconscious self-image:
   a. Selecting some role models such as Jesus, the Blessed Mother, or one or more saints, to help us with visualization of our new identity
   b. Writing several affirmations according to the three principles listed above—first-person present tense, positive content only, and associating it with motivations eliciting positive emotions
3. Learning some spontaneous prayers to help us during times of temptation—fourth step of moral conversion process (see below, Section IV)

The *implementation stage* has three major steps:

1. Repeating our affirmations several times per day. If feasible, we will want to integrate one of those times into our Examen Prayer (see above, Section II).
2. Reserving ten to fifteen minutes every evening to pray the Examen Prayer with the Lord, to bring inspiration, redemptive consolation, and grace into our moral conversion process (see above, Section II)
3. Resisting temptation by implementing the above three-step process—saying no for the sake of Christ, thinking with our increasingly strengthened higher self, and using spontaneous prayers (see above, Section I.C)

I might briefly note here that there are three very worthwhile prayer disciplines for moral conversion that can be undertaken on a daily basis, though they will bear fruit *whenever* we can make time in our busy schedules to accommodate them:

1. Mass, including daily Mass, when possible (see Chapter 2, Section I)
2. The Examen Prayer, daily for ten to fifteen minutes in the evening (see above, Section II)
3. Contemplative prayer, daily in the morning for fifteen minutes or more (see Chapter 3, Section III)

Spontaneous prayers for various needs (see below, Section IV and Appendix II of this volume) and prayers to the Holy Spirit for inspiration, guidance, and protection (see Volume I, Chapter 1, of this Trilogy) can be interspersed throughout the day in various contexts as needed.

I realize that some of these prayer disciplines are more readily accomplished by priests and religious, as well as laity who do not have significant parental responsibilities. Nevertheless, busy parents can benefit from very brief commitments to the above three prayer disciplines, because it will transform the quality of their marriage and parenting and form a foundation for slight gradual increases in prayer commitment as their children grow older. The Lord is very much aware of the demands placed on us by children and our workplace, and He rewards us richly for the time we can give Him in accordance with our availability. As the author of *The Cloud of Unknowing* taught, "The short prayer pierces the Heavens."[25]

IV. Fourth Step in Moral Conversion: Solidification through Spontaneous Prayers and Habits

Though the first three steps of moral conversion are highly effective in helping the higher self to become preeminent, they can be complemented by two other practices recommended by Christian saints from the inception of the Church:

1. Spontaneous prayers (Section IV.A)
2. Habits (Section IV.B)

[25] Anonymous, *The Cloud of Unknowing and Other Works*, trans. A. C. Spearing (New York: Penguin Classics, 2001), Chapter 38, p. 234.

A. Spontaneous Prayers

As noted above, spontaneous prayers—short, memorable, and easily repeatable prayers—are particularly important in bolstering our efforts to resist temptation. We might group them into two kinds:

1. Prayers asking for protection from temptation, particularly from the Evil One
2. Prayers expressing our desire to be like the Lord, the Blessed Virgin, or one of the saints

We will discuss each in turn.

Let us begin with prayers for protection from the Evil One, because these are the simplest to recall and repeat. I intentionally do not use complex prayers to ask for protection, because invoking the name of the Lord, the Blessed Virgin, or the saints is far more important than adding lots of words of petition. Recall the early Church's view of the power of the Spirit working through the *name of Jesus* in the Acts of the Apostles. The early Church soon discovered the same power by calling upon the name of the Blessed Virgin Mary as well as the names of the angels and saints, particularly Saint Michael (see Chapter 3, Section VII, of this volume). Invoking the name of Saint Michael the Archangel for protection from the Evil One goes back to the early Church, because of his prominent role in the defeat of Satan in the Book of Revelation (Rev 12:7–12), which harkens back to the Book of Daniel, in which Daniel has a vision of Saint Michael as the protector of Israel (Dan 10:13–21). Pope Leo XIII wrote the well-known prayer to Saint Michael as protection against Satan and other evil spirits after having a vision of demonic spirits surrounding Rome in 1880. He also wrote the prayer of Saint Michael in the Roman ritual of exorcism:

> Saint Michael the Archangel,
> defend us in battle,
> be our protection against the wickedness and snares of
>   the devil;
> may God rebuke him, we humbly pray;
> and do thou, O Prince of the heavenly host,

by the power of God, cast into hell
Satan and all the evil spirits
who prowl through the world seeking the ruin of souls.
Amen.

In view of the above, I recommend reciting and repeating the following three simple prayers when facing temptation, particularly those that seem to have a demonic origin or influence—such as temptations having an extraordinary vividness or force beyond self-originating desires or emotions:

- "Lord Jesus, please protect me."
- "Mother Mary, please protect me."
- "Saint Michael the Archangel, please protect me."

It is not necessary to add anything to these prayers beyond the simple invocation of the names of our protectors and the petition for protection, but if you, the reader, find it helpful, you might add the words "from this temptation" or "from the evil behind this temptation". Hence, you might pray the longer prayers:

- "Lord Jesus, please protect me from the evil behind this temptation."
- "Mother Mary, please protect me from the evil behind this temptation."
- "Saint Michael, please protect me from the evil behind this temptation."

I would recommend saying these prayers at least three or four times, particularly if you feel an overriding desire to sin, or you sense the emptiness, loneliness, and alienation that typically mark the Evil One's presence. I can personally attest to the fact that the Lord, the Blessed Virgin Mary, and Saint Michael do in fact come to our aide. They can break the grip of the Evil One and temptation and can restore a sense of equanimity and peace to our souls.

Powerful as these spontaneous prayers for protection are, they can also be complemented by prayers expressing our desire to be like the Lord or the saints. We might begin by giving some simple versions of this prayer:

- "Lord, help me to be like You—chaste in mind and heart (or gentle in mind and heart or humble in mind and heart)."
- "Mother Mary, help me to be like you—chaste in mind and heart (or gentle in mind and heart or humble in mind and heart)."
- "Saint Thomas Aquinas, pray that I may be like you—chaste in mind and heart (or gentle in mind and heart or humble in mind and heart)."

When temptation strikes, it is generally helpful to repeat these prayers three or four times to reinforce through grace our higher self and the virtues we have affirmed.

When we have just begun to reinforce our higher self in our subconscious mind, these spontaneous prayers may not be as effective as we would like, because the higher self in our subconscious mind is not very strong, and we may not yet have developed the habit of resisting temptation for the sake of Christ. Hence, a temptation to unchastity, vanity, or greed, or the emotion of anger, pride, and envy, might be quite powerful by comparison to the resistance we can muster against it. Do not get frustrated or discouraged by this, bearing in mind that every effort you make to use these prayers and resist temptation (along with continued visualization, affirmations, and the daily Examen) is reinforcing your higher self in your subconscious mind. As Saint Paul implies in Romans 7:13–25, moral conversion is a long process, requiring patience in ourselves and trust in the Lord's unconditional mercy, healing power, and grace. Discouragement and frustration are counterproductive and are most assuredly encouraged by the Evil One (see Chapter 5, Section II), who will do everything within his power to stop your progress in moral conversion. After a while, you will notice that your ability to fight off temptation will increase. Slowly but surely, your appeal to your higher self within your subconscious mind, in combination with spontaneous prayers, will have longer and more powerful effects, and eventually even the most persistent temptations will begin to fade in power and duration.

We must be careful to avoid overconfidence in our newly emerging higher self and its capacity to resist temptation, because the Evil One will look for ways to surprise us or discourage us (as described in Chapter 5, Section II). Recall the Lord's many admonitions to remain vigilant and persistent over the long-term: building our house on solid ground (Mt 7:24–27), buying sufficient oil for our lamps (Mt 25:1–13), and keeping our hearts open to His Word (Mt 13:1–9). Recall also the words of Peter regarding our spiritual enemy:

> Be sober, be watchful. Your adversary the devil prowls around like a roaring lion, seeking some one to devour. Resist him, firm in your faith. (1 Pet 5:8–9)

Though spontaneous prayers can be very effective in helping us to resist temptation while it is occurring, contemplative prayer also reinforces our moral conversion. This is why spiritual conversion is such an important foundation for moral conversion (see Chapter 3, Sections III–V, and Chapter 5, Section I). There are two other kinds of prayer that support our progress in the moral life that strengthen our spontaneous prayers in depth and efficacy:

- The prayer of thanksgiving at the beginning of the Ignatian Examen
- Prayers of forgiveness in times of transgression

I have discussed contemplative prayer in Chapter 3 (Section III) and the prayer of thanksgiving in the Examen Prayer (in this chapter, Section II). I will discuss prayers of forgiveness in Chapter 7 (Section I). At this point, the reader may want to review the three essential prayer disciplines for moral conversion discussed above in Section III—Mass, the Examen Prayer, and contemplative prayer. Remember, even if you do not have the recommended time to devote to these prayer disciplines, they will bear great fruit *whenever* you are able to accommodate them.

Finally, there is one prayer that is essential to fight temptations manifesting extraordinary demonic phenomena: deliverance prayers, and in cases of possession, exorcism. We have discussed exorcism in Volume I (Chapter 3, Sections IV–V) of this Trilogy. Though the scope of this book does not extend to deliverance ministry, there are some good resources for this ministry within the Catholic Church. The National Service Committee, a group of leaders in the Catholic Charismatic Renewal, offers several resources and hosts training programs in deliverance ministry.[26] The Catholic charismatic movement has approved and given guidelines for deliverance ministry in the International Catholic Charismatic Renewal Services Doctrinal Commission's book entitled *Deliverance Ministries*.[27] Some other excellent resources are books by Father Mike Driscoll,[28] Neal Lozano,[29] and Michael Scanlan.[30]

B. Using Habits to Reinforce the Higher Self

Socrates, Plato, and Aristotle recognized the power of habit to ease the force of "willpower" in making ethical decisions.[31] The Catholic philosophical and theological tradition recognized the importance of habits in the formation of virtues, and Saint Thomas Aquinas devoted an entire treatise to it in the *Summa Theologica*.[32] Though these great philosophers did not know about the subconscious mind or its role in the appropriation and use of habits, they were well aware of the power of repeated behavior to form proclivities toward future behavior. Repeated bad behavior leads to bad habits, which in turn lead to a future proclivity toward bad behavior, while repeated good behavior leads to good habits (virtues), which in turn lead to proclivities toward future good behavior. This insight has not changed for over twenty-four hundred years, with the notable exception of the discovery of the subconscious mind as the agency through which good

[26] For these resources, see the National Service Committee's website at www.nsc-charis center.org.

[27] International Catholic Charismatic Renewal Services Doctrinal Commission, *Deliverance Ministry* (National Service Committee of the Catholic Charismatic Renewal in the U.S., 2017).

[28] Father Mike Driscoll, *Demons, Deliverance, Discernment: Separating Fact from Fiction about the Spirit World* (El Cajon, Calif.: Catholic Answers Press, 2015).

[29] Neal Lozano, *Resisting the Devil: A Catholic Perspective on Deliverance* (Huntington, Ind.: Our Sunday Visitor Publishing, 2010).

[30] Michael Scanlan, T.O.R., and Randall Cirner, *Deliverance from Evil Spirits* (Ann Arbor, Mich.: Servant Books, 1980).

[31] See Plato, *Republic* 7, 518e; 10, 619c. See also Aristotle, *Nichomachean Ethics*. This classic, concerned with virtue ethics, speaks about good habit (virtue) in almost every book, starting with Book 1, Chapter 4.

[32] For the nature of habits, see *Summa Theologica* I-II, qq. 49–54; for the impact of habits on virtues, see *Summa Theologica* I-II, qq. 55–67.

and bad habits obtain their power to influence our behavior with minimum involvement from our conscious mind and will.

The above philosophers also recognized that the time to build virtuous habits is childhood, because when a good habit is formed, it will continue to build on itself throughout life. Therefore, good childhood training, good families, and good education is essential for using habits to reinforce the higher self throughout life. However, the question arises, "What happens to a person who did not receive good formation and education in his younger years?" Indeed, what happens to someone who received precisely the opposite, a reinforcement of materialism, sensual pleasure, ego–comparative advantage, and even the deadly sins themselves? Is this person consigned to a life of evil? After all, bad habits reinforce bad behavior into the future. How can we break the spell of such habits for even a little while so that good habits can have a chance to "get off the ground"?

By now the reader will know the answer. We can break the spell of bad habits and the lower self by using the fruits of spiritual conversion (particularly the grace coming from Baptism, Holy Communion, the Sacrament of Reconciliation, contemplative prayer, the Examen Prayer, and religious practice) as well as the techniques of Albert Bandura and Lou Tice (visualization and affirmations). The remarkable part of these graces and techniques is that they can transform a subconscious mind firmly entrenched in the lower self into one that is open and even receptive to the higher self. The more we practice these techniques, the more receptive we become to the higher self, and eventually we begin to act on it. As we begin to act on the higher self with greater frequency, good habits (virtues) begin to form. Slowly but surely, these virtues are reinforced in the subconscious mind, which ultimately leads to the preeminence of our higher self: moral conversion.

Habits are yet another indispensable arrow in the quiver of moral conversion. For those who from their youth were active in the Church and given good moral formation, habits can be lifetime agents of moral freedom and the higher self. However, they are not the whole answer. As most of us know, the lower self can still exert considerable power over us not only because of our youthful proclivities toward Level One and Level Two desires, but also because of concupiscence (the proclivity toward sensual pleasure and egocentricity, which is the damage of original sin). If we do not go beyond habits to counteract the influence of the lower self (which can emerge quite powerfully in adolescence), we could wind up like Saint Augustine, who allowed himself to be pulled ever more deeply and powerfully into the grip of sensual pleasure and egocentricity. Fortunately, he followed the impetus of the Holy Spirit (and the wisdom of Saint Ambrose) in seeking relief from his feelings of spiritual emptiness, alienation, and loneliness by entering and participating in the Catholic Church. The grace of the Lord worked very efficaciously with his openness to the Church. After his conversion—marked by his final acceptance of the need for moral conversion and his surrender to God to actualize it—habits took their natural course, forming him into the saint we know today.

Though Saint Augustine was able to undergo moral conversion through prayer, love of virtue, and mentorship by Saint Ambrose, today we can be greatly assisted by incorporating the Examen Prayer of Saint Ignatius and the techniques of Albert Bandura and Lou Tice, because these vehicles allow us intentionally to transform our subconscious mind in ways that would have greatly assisted Saint Augustine when he cried out to God, "Give me chastity and continency, only not yet."[33] Perhaps Saint Paul would have also benefitted from these vehicles when he exclaimed, "I do not understand my own actions. For I do not do what I want, but I do the very thing I hate" (Rom 7:15).

What might we now conclude about the important role of habits in fostering the "new man" (the higher self)? First, habits are indispensable for helping us *persevere* in our moral conversion (the preeminence of our higher self). They are also powerful in reinforcing moral conversion. For those raised in an active religious household with good moral formation, habits can take effect quickly and last throughout a lifetime. For those raised in a neutral or negative moral environment, habits can only become helpful after the spell of the lower self has been broken and the higher saintly Christlike mature noble virtuous self has been discovered and embraced. This will likely require concerted religious practice and prayer, particularly frequent Mass, contemplative prayer, and the Examen Prayer. As noted above,

---

[33] "The Confessions of Saint Augustine, Book VIII", in *The Confessions of Saint Augustine*, trans. Edward Bouverie Pusey, 1914, SacredTexts.com, http://www.sacred-texts.com/chr/augconf/augo8.htm.

this process can be greatly assisted by Bandura's techniques of visualization and affirmations.

Jesus spoke of perseverance as one of the key virtues of Christian life;[34] and as we might infer from the above, habits are quite important for persevering in virtue and religious practice, and so we must take them seriously. Though it can be a real struggle to get to the stage where habits can be useful (i.e., discovering the darkness, emptiness, and alienation of sin, embracing spiritual conversion and virtue, and breaking the spell of the lower self), habits can help us to persevere in fidelity to the Christlike self that is becoming our "new nature".

V. A Shortcut to Resisting Temptation

Let's return for a moment to resisting temptation. When our new subconscious self-identity is strong, we can use it effectively in the very first step of resisting temptation, saying no for the sake of Christ. If we have a strong proclivity toward the higher self, then we will instinctively feel the contrast between it and the call of temptation. This recognition enables us to take a shortcut in resisting temptation.

Recall that as we engage in the process of replacing the lower self with the higher self, we will probably enter an intermediary phase for a significant period of time (such as Saint Paul experienced for twenty-three years, between his conversion and the writing of Romans 7:15–25). During this period our lower self and higher self will likely be in a struggle with one another (as Saint Paul describes in that passage). Recall also that each self has a mode of thinking appropriate to the desires and objectives it seeks. The lower self continues to seek sensual and egotistical satisfactions (which has its own mode of thinking), while the higher self seeks faith, love (and its supporting virtues), and relationship with the Lord. The more we deepen our spiritual conversion and moral conversion (through the use of the Examen Prayer, affirmations, visualization, spontaneous prayers, and habits), the stronger and more preeminent our higher self becomes.

---

[34] Perseverance is explicitly mentioned as an important virtue, particularly in times of persecution (Mt 24:13). Being vigilant throughout one's life is a complementary virtue to it (Mt 24:42–44). Perseverance is one of the needed virtues for salvation in the Parable of the Sower (see Mt 13:1–23). Preparing for a lengthy journey and being vigilant on it is also emphasized by Jesus in the Parable of the Ten Virgins (Mt 25:1–13).

When our higher self becomes strong enough, we do not have to work very hard to choose it and allow it to do the thinking, because we are habituated to it. We are *consciously* aware that the higher self is noble and capable of high purpose, dignity, and destiny, and that our lower self seeks less noble objectives that are beneath us. Thus, our conscious and subconscious minds are working in tandem to pursue the objectives of the higher self.

This means that we need only do two things to resist temptation—even strong temptations:

1. Be aware that we are being tempted and therefore we are thinking with our lower self.
2. Reflectively choose (through rational self-consciousness) what we really want, the higher self, which entails thinking with that higher self.

If we can remember to associate temptation with our lower self, and choose what we really want (i.e., to think with our higher self), then the temptation is essentially defeated; for temptation only has power over us when we are thinking with our lower self. As noted above, when we intentionally switch to the higher self, temptation has very little power over us. Recall that when we think with the higher self, we bring to bear our relationship with the Lord that empowers the three noble intentions: to please the Lord out of gratitude and love, to respect and care for the good and salvation of others, and to seek our highest character and salvation by following the teaching of Jesus and resisting our spiritual enemy. These three noble intentions, when empowered within the higher self, can stave off temptation with a simple no.

The reader might be thinking, "This sounds too easy to be usable," but in point of fact it works exceedingly well when we have a strong sense of the higher self. Try it for yourself after you have done your affirmations and daily Examen for two or more months. The next time you are being tempted toward any of the deadly sins, simply use the following assertion to intentionally change the "self" who is doing the thinking: "I am better than my lower self, and I am thinking with my higher self—the mature, virtuous, Christlike self."

You do not have to use the above lengthy expression to bring your higher self to the forefront of self-consciousness. Once your higher self has become strong enough in your subconscious mind, you can use much shorter expressions that reflect the strength of your higher self. Some of the more effective ones I have used are the following:

- "I am more Christlike than that."
- "I am better than that—chaste to be like You, Lord Jesus."
- "I am better than that—forgiving and patient for love of You, Lord Jesus."

The affirmations incorporating prayer content (i.e., the last two examples given immediately above) are the most effective, because they not only bring our higher self into focus, but also bring to mind the positive emotional content of the prayer as well as the grace of God. I use these prayer affirmations every day, sometimes several times, and find them remarkably incisive and effective.

These affirmations can be so effective that the temptation could actually disappear before you bring spontaneous prayers to the Lord, the Blessed Virgin, or Saint Michael against it. Of course, spontaneous prayers can reinforce your intentional change from lower to higher self (from temptable self to virtuous self), but you may already be well on your way before the prayer leaves your lips. As implied above, the stronger your new subconscious self-identity, the faster and more effective your change from "thinking with the lower self" to "thinking with the higher self" will be, and you will be well on the way to imitating the Lord in thought, word, and action.

One last caution: we cannot afford to think that our lower self will simply disappear, for it can reemerge with remarkable strength if we are not *vigilant* about keeping the higher self in its preeminent place. Jesus,[35] Saint Peter,[36] Saint Ignatius,[37] and the whole Catholic

---

[35] "When the unclean spirit has gone out of a man, he passes through waterless places seeking rest; and finding none he says, 'I will return to my house from which I came.' And when he comes he finds it swept and put in order. Then he goes and brings seven other spirits more evil than himself, and they enter and dwell there; and the last state of that man becomes worse than the first" (Lk 11:24–26).

[36] "Be sober, be watchful. Your adversary the devil prowls around like a roaring lion, seeking some one to devour. Resist him, firm in your faith" (1 Pet 5:8–9).

[37] "Fourteenth Rule. The fourteenth: Likewise, [he Evil One] behaves as a chief bent on conquering and robbing what he desires: for, as a captain and chief of the army, pitching his camp, and looking at the forces or defences of a stronghold, attacks it on the weakest side, in like manner the enemy of human nature, roaming about, looks in turn at all our virtues,

spiritual tradition warn us that the Evil One will take advantage of *any* lapse in vigilance. It does not matter how preeminent our higher self has become. We have to remember to use it when unexpected and strong temptation arises. Hence, we will want to keep our "shortcut" technique ready at hand for the times when temptation (particularly through the Evil One) rears its ugly head. The Pauline author of the Letter to the Ephesians sums up our challenge as follows:

> For we are not contending against flesh and blood, but against the principalities, against the powers, against the world rulers of this present darkness, against the spiritual hosts of wickedness in the heavenly places. Therefore take the whole armor of God, that you may be able to withstand in the evil day, and having done all, to stand. Stand therefore, having fastened the belt of truth around your waist, and having put on the breastplate of righteousness, and having shod your feet with the equipment of the gospel of peace; besides all these, taking the shield of faith, with which you can quench all the flaming darts of the Evil One. And take the helmet of salvation, and the sword of the Spirit, which is the word of God. Pray at all times in the Spirit, with all prayer and supplication. To that end keep alert with all perseverance, making supplication for all the saints. (6:12–18)

VI. Conclusion

As Saint Augustine repeatedly implied in the *Confessions*, moral conversion is likely to be the last and most challenging stage of our spiritual journey toward purification and salvation.[38] The spiritual and psychological practices explained above—spiritual conversion, visualization, affirmations, the Examen Prayer, spontaneous prayers, and habits—will assuredly assist in this process by helping us to disengage temptation by appealing to our strong, noble, mature, virtuous, saintly higher self. At this point, we will have become what Saint

---

theological, cardinal and moral; and where he finds us weakest and most in need for our eternal salvation, there he attacks us and aims at taking us." *Spiritual Exercises*, "Rules for Perceiving and Knowing", http://sacred-texts.com/chr/seil/seil78.htm.

[38] See *Confessions* 8, which addresses his struggles with temptation, particularly concupiscence and the deadly sin of lust, after he had made significant progress in intellectual and spiritual conversion.

Ignatius called "people of the Second Week"—people with a st.
moral conversion and higher self.

Even in the midst of this important transition, the Lord warns us
that we can still fall prey to temptation either out of lapses in vigilance, assaults, and deceits of the Evil One or the reemergence of
the lower self. Saint Ignatius further warns us that the Evil One will
change his tactics to deal with our transformed "new nature". Since
we have become people of the Second Week who can readily and
successfully resist temptation, the Evil One will deemphasize overt
temptations to serious habitual sins, and place his emphasis on more
subtle schemes.

Recall from Volume I (Chapter 4, Section V) that for people of
the Second Week, the Evil One will move his attention to three
other approaches to weaken our new nature and undermine hope:

1. *Deceit*—disguising himself as an angel of light to make suggestions that seem pious, but will lead to decreases in faith, hope,
   and love
2. *Discouragement*—coming to the "new man" as "the accuser"
   (Rev 12:10), telling him that he is repulsive and disgusting to
   God, and that he should hate himself and run from God
3. *Spiritual pride*—telling the believer that he has completed the
   process of conversion, reaching the heights of sanctity by his
   own discipline and diligence, a position from which he can
   look down at others and see himself as indispensable and central
   to the whole order of salvation

Deep spiritual and moral conversion places the believer in a position to leave a legacy similar to canonized saints, which puts the Evil
One in a position of extreme disadvantage. He cannot make recourse
to his usual overt temptations, and if he is unsuccessful in undermining the "new man", the consequences for "his evil kingdom" will be
dire. Having few tactics left, he will use them with all his skill and
cunning—but we need not be afraid. We will have the inspiration,
guidance, and protection of the Holy Spirit and the teaching of the
Church to combat his wiles.

How do we listen more acutely to the Holy Spirit's wisdom than
the Evil One's deceits, accusations, and temptations to pride? First,

we must counteract the Evil One's deceits by recognizing the signs of his appearance as an angel of light (see Volume I, Chapter 4, Section V.C). Second, we must recognize the language and content of "the accuser" and counteract it with the Lord's true language of gentleness and love (see Chapter 3, Section IV.B, of this volume). Finally, we must keep careful watch over subtle hints of our "spiritual superiority to others", "importance to the Kingdom", and "spiritual accomplishments", using the above "shortcut" to resist these temptations to spiritual pride. Similarly, we should deflect any accolades about our so-called holiness and recall the truth about ourselves—"We are unworthy servants; we have only done what was our duty" (Lk 17:10).

If we maintain vigilance to our moral conversion, humility in our hearts, and discernment about the Evil One's deceptions, we will be well on the way to our salvation while helping others to the Kingdom of eternal love. This is precisely the end and dignity for which we were created.[39]

Even if we should fall or fail miserably, the Lord can save us from ultimate defeat through His unconditional love, if we faithfully and sincerely call upon His mercy and make a firm purpose of amendment to be faithful to His teaching by our best efforts. He gives us the vehicle for doing this through the Sacrament of Reconciliation and prayers of forgiveness, which will be discussed in the next chapter.

---

[39] See *Spiritual Exercises*, "First Week: Principle and Foundation", http://sacred-texts.com /chr/seil/seil07.htm.

Chapter Seven

God's Mercy and Reconciliation

Introduction

We are imperfect, and no matter how deep our moral conversion, we are unlikely to attain moral perfection in the image of Jesus before we pass from this life. Yes, the Lord will bring us to moral perfection and perfectly authentic love in Heaven through His grace assisting our free choices, but while we are on this earth, it is very likely that our love will fall short of perfection. Hence, we will always be in need of forgiveness, reconciliation, and moral healing. Our heavenly Father has always been perfectly aware of this, and He knew from all eternity that He would have to love and grace us into His loving perfection; so He chose from all eternity to send His Son into our midst, a mission freely and completely accepted by the Son to bring, teach, and demonstrate His forgiving, reconciling, and healing love. Therefore, it should come as no surprise that one of the central dimensions of Jesus' mission was to seek out and forgive sinners, to teach about His Father's unconditional love, and to demonstrate His own unconditional love in His Passion and death, which led to the redemption of the world.

I discuss this extensively in Volume III (Chapters 1–3) of the Quartet, and so I will not give an extensive summary of it here, but rather will limit myself to three important areas concerned with entering into the reality of the Lord's forgiving, reconciling, and healing love:

1. A review of Jesus' revelation of the heart of His Father in the Parable of the Prodigal Son (Section I)
2. The power of the Sacrament of Reconciliation (Section II)
3. Spontaneous prayers for forgiveness, reconciliation, and healing (Section III)

There are many other ways in which we can deepen our contrition and experience of healing, but these three are most central to the method and mission of Jesus and the Church.

I. The Father of the Prodigal Son

If we are to ask for forgiveness, reconciliation, and healing as Jesus has taught us and receive the unconditional mercy and love He intends to bestow on us, we must first understand the true nature of that intention and love and put our trust in it. Jesus' most incisive revelation of the Father's heart and unconditional love is clearly presented in His Parable of the Prodigal Son (Lk 15:11–32). I have given a more extended explanation of this in Volume III (Chapter 2, Section III.C) of the Quartet. Given its importance, I give a detailed summary of it here.

Three preliminary considerations should be made before retelling the parable as a first-century Jewish audience would have understood it. First, Jesus intends that the father in the story be a revelation of the heart of God His Father. The parable would be more aptly named the Parable of the *Father* of the Prodigal Son. Second, notice that the younger son has committed just about every sin imaginable according to the mindset of Second Temple Judaism (the religious context in which Jesus was living), and so he has absolutely no basis or merit for asking the father to receive him back into the household, even as one of the servants. Third, the older son in this story represents the Pharisees and those who are trying to remain righteous according to their understanding of the Jewish law; so we can see that Jesus has not abandoned them, but he desires to give them everything he has—so long as they come back into the house. Now we may retell the story as Jesus' audience would have understood it.

A father had two sons, the youngest of whom asked for his share of the inheritance. This would have been viewed as an insult to the father, which would have shamed both father and family (because the son is asking not only for the right of possession, but the right of disposal of the property that legally does not occur until the death of the father[1]). Nevertheless, the father hears the son's request and

---

[1] See Joachim Jeremias, *The Parables of Jesus* (London: SCM Press, 1972), pp. 128–29.

acquiesces to it. He divides his property and lets his son go. Remember, the father in the story is Jesus' revelation of God the Father.

The son chooses to go to a foreign land, probably a Gentile land, indicated by his living on a Gentile farm with pigs. Whether he started there or simply ended there is of little consequence. His actions indicate a disregard for (if not a rejection of) his election and his people, and a further shaming of the family from which he came.

The son then adds further insult to injury by spending his father's hard-earned fortune on dissolute living (violations of the Torah) in the Gentile land. This shows the son's callous disregard for (if not rejection of) God's law, God's revelation, and perhaps God Himself. Furthermore, he manifests his callous disregard for his people, the law, and God before the entire Gentile community, bringing shame upon them all.

Just when it seems that the son could not possibly sin any more egregiously, the foreign land finds itself in a famine. The son has little money left and is constrained to live with the pigs, which were considered to be highly unclean animals. The son incurs defilement not only from working with the pigs but actually living with them! He even longs to eat the food of the pigs, which would defile him both inside and outside. This reveals the son's wretched spiritual state, which would have engendered disgust on the part of most members of Jesus' first-century Jewish audience.

The son experiences a "quasi-change" of heart, not so much because of what he's done to his family, country, people, election, law, religion, and God, but because of the harshness of his condition ("How many of my father's hired servants have bread enough and to spare" [Lk 15:17]). He decides to take advantage of what he perceives to be his father's merciful nature by proffering an agreement to accept demotion from son to servant (even though it was the father's right to reject and even disown him altogether). The son then makes his way back home.

The father (who is the God-Abba figure in Jesus' parable) sees him coming while he is still on his way (possibly indicating that the father had been looking for him) and is so completely overjoyed that he runs out to meet him (despite the fact that the son has so deeply injured and shamed both him and his family). When he meets his son, he throws his arms around him and kisses him. The kiss is not only an act of affection, but also a sign of forgiveness.[2] The son's list of insults, injuries, and sins is incapable of turning the father's heart away from him. The father is almost compelled to show unrestrained affection toward him. The son utters his speech of quasi-repentance/quasi-negotiation: "Treat me as one of your hired servants" (Lk 15:19). Instead, the father tells the servants to get him a robe, which not only takes care of his temporal needs, but is also a mark of high distinction.[3] He then asks that a ring be put on his hand. Joachim Jeremias indicates that this ring is very likely a signet ring,[4] having the seal of the family. This would indicate not only belonging to the family, but also the authority of the family (showing the son's readmission to the family in an unqualified way). He then gives him shoes, which again takes care of his obvious temporal need, and inasmuch as they are luxuries, signifies a free man who no longer has to go about barefoot like a servant or slave.[5] He then kills the fatted calf (reserved only for very special occasions) and holds a feast. This is a further indication of the son's readmission to the family by being received at the festal family table.[6]

Jesus' audience probably felt conflicted (if not angered) by the father's "ridiculously merciful" treatment of his son, because it ignored (and even undermined) the "proper" strictures of justice. The father's love/mercy seems to disregard the justice of the Torah. This does not deter Jesus, because He knows that God the Father treats sinners, even the most egregious sinners, with a heart of unconditional love.

Jesus continues the story by turning His attention to the older son, who reflects a figure of righteousness (like the Pharisees) according to the Old Covenant. He has stayed loyal to his father, family, election, country, religion, law, and God. Furthermore, he has been an incredibly hard worker and seems to accept patiently the father's frugality toward him ("You never gave me a kid [goat]" [Lk 15:29]). Most of Jesus' Pharisaical audience probably sympathized with this older son's plight when the father demonstrated his extraordinary generosity to his younger son. By all rights, the father should have either rejected

[2] Ibid., p. 130.
[3] Ibid.
[4] Ibid.
[5] Ibid.
[6] Ibid.

or disowned the younger son, and if not that, he certainly should have accepted the younger son's offer to become a servant—but an unqualified re-admittance to the family appeared to be a great injustice to his loyal son.

The father understands the son's difficulty with his actions and goes outside literally to "plead" with his son, virtually begging him to come back into the house (an almost unthinkable humiliation for a father at that time, let alone God Himself). Though the older son expresses great anger and indignation ("You never gave me a kid [goat], that I might make merry with my friends. But when this son of yours came, who has devoured your living with harlots, you killed for him the fatted calf!" [Lk 15:29–30]), the father responds by literally giving him all his property, renouncing his right of ownership by saying, "All that is mine is [now] yours" (Lk 15:31).[7] He then gives him an explanation that did not fall within the mainstream interpretation of the law: mercy must take precedence over justice and love take precedence over the law, for that is the only way that the negativity of sin and evil can be redressed and overcome: "Your brother was dead, and is alive; he was lost, and is found" (Lk 15:32).

This parable coincides precisely with Jesus' address of God as Abba and His declaration of "love as the highest commandment", because the only way in which they can make sense together is through the logic of unconditional love in the heart of an unconditionally loving God.

I recommend that the reader review this retelling of the parable before going to the Sacrament of Reconciliation, to experience the Lord's unconditional mercy as Jesus and so many of the saints have described it.[8] Furthermore, I would ask the reader to share it with as many people as possible; for if people truly understand who God is and is not (e.g., "the angry god", "the terrifying god", "the payback god", "the disgusted god, "the stoic god", and "the domineering god"),[9]

[7] Ibid.
[8] Julian of Norwich (*Revelations of Divine Love*), Saint Margaret Mary (initiator of the Sacred Heart devotion), and Saint Faustina (initiator of the divine mercy devotion) have declared the unconditional love of the Lord as an integral part of their revelations by Him.
[9] For a complete description and scriptural response to these notions of God, see Volume IV (Chapter 2) of the Quartet.

they may more readily turn to Him in their need for mercy instead of running from a false caricature of Him coming from a demonic "accuser" or the recesses of their subconscious mind. If you, the reader, have appropriated Jesus' revelation of His Father in your heart, then proceed to Section II on the Sacrament of Reconciliation.

II. The Power of the Sacrament of Reconciliation

Jesus encourages individual prayers of contrition that He implied could lead to justification and salvation (see below, Section III), but He did not stop there. He provided a definitive, powerful, sacramental means of forgiveness, absolution, and healing through the Sacrament of Reconciliation (also known as the Sacrament of Penance). This sacrament provides definitive absolution from mortal sin (defined below in Section II.B) and imparts six powerful graces that help us in moral conversion (see Section II.C).

Virtually every saint from the twelfth century onward has testified to the importance of the regular reception of this sacrament in their ongoing process of moral conversion. Though the Church asks the faithful to avail themselves of the sacrament at least once per year,[10] we should seriously consider more regular reception of the sacrament, to avail ourselves of its six central graces so important to moral conversion.

We will begin our discussion with the origin of the sacrament by Jesus (Section II.A), then proceed to the theology and practice of the sacrament today (Section II.B), and then to a spiritual explanation of the six major graces of the sacrament (Section II.C).

A. The Origin of the Sacrament of Reconciliation: Jesus and the New Testament

The Sacrament of Reconciliation has its origin in the New Testament, in which Jesus clearly imparts the power to the apostles to forgive sins through the Holy Spirit after the Resurrection:

---

[10] CCC 2042.

Jesus said to them again, "Peace be with you. As the Father has sent me, even so I send you." And when he had said this, he breathed on them, and said to them, "Receive the Holy Spirit. If you forgive the sins of any, they are forgiven; if you retain the sins of any, they are retained." (Jn 20:21–23)

The meaning of this passage is clear: Jesus gave a universal power to forgive and retain sins to His apostles—"If you forgive the sins of *any*." Though the form under which this power is to be administered is not defined, it is evident that the apostles (and by implication their successors) are to be mediators of the divine power and authority of forgiveness. Since the power to forgive sins belongs to God alone,[11] the apostles must be mediators of the power of God, mediators of the power of the Holy Spirit, which Jesus has given them. As such, it is a specific sacramental power that is the ground of the Sacrament of Reconciliation that has been administered by the Church since its inception.

Jesus claimed to have this divine power within Himself, and to be the administrator of it by His own authority. In the Gospel of Mark, the Pharisees challenge Jesus to explain Himself when He claims to have the power to forgive a paralytic's sins:

When Jesus saw their faith, he said to the paralytic, "Child, your sins are forgiven." Now some of the scribes were sitting there, questioning in their hearts, "Why does this man speak this? It is blasphemy! Who can forgive sins but *God alone*?" (2:5–7; cf. Mt 9:2–3; Lk 5:20–21 [italics added])

The Pharisees assume that Jesus is blaspheming because they believe that the power to forgive sins is an exclusively divine power, which means that Jesus is claiming to possess divine power within Himself. Jesus confirms this moments later by saying:

"But that you may know that the Son of man has authority on earth to forgive sins"—he said to the paralytic—"I say to you, rise, take up your pallet and go home." And he rose, and immediately took up the pallet and went out before them all. (Mk 2:10–12; cf. Mt 9:6–7; Lk 5:24–25)

---

[11] The power to forgive sins belongs to God alone; see Ps 103:2–3; Is 43:25; Mk 2:5–7.

All we need do now is connect the dots: Jesus possesses the power and authority of God to forgive sins. He proves it through His miraculous cure of the man (Mk 2:12; Mt 9:7; Lk 5:25). He later confers that same divine power upon the apostles and their successors (Jn 20:21–23). The conferral of this divine power on the apostles is the foundation of the Sacrament of Reconciliation,[12] which the first- and second-century Church, believed to be the authentic proclamation of Jesus.[13]

There are three other passages confirming Jesus as the origin of the Sacrament of Reconciliation:

- Jesus' conferral of the power to bind and loose on the apostles (Mt 18:18)
- Jesus' conferral of the power to bind and loose on Peter, which also brings the authority to excommunicate (Mt 16:19)
- Paul's reference to the ministry of reconciliation (2 Cor 5:18–20)

Let us begin with Jesus' conferral of the power to bind and loose on the apostles:

> If your brother *sins* against you, go and tell him his fault, between you and him alone. If he listens to you, you have gained your brother. But if he does not listen, take one or two others along with you, that every word may be confirmed by the evidence of two or three witnesses. If he refuses to listen to them, tell it to the Church; and if he refuses to listen even to the Church, let him be to you as a Gentile and a tax collector. Truly, I say to you, whatever you bind on earth shall be bound in heaven, and whatever you loose on earth shall be loosed in heaven. (Mt 18:15–18)

This passage concerns the forgiveness of grave sins that need to be redressed within the community. There are three layers of potential

---

[12] The Church considers a sacrament to be a visible rite or sign of an invisible divine reality, the efficacious power of God for human salvation (grace). As can be seen from the above, the power to forgive sins is a divine reality helping us toward salvation that has been conferred on the apostles and their successors to be administered through the visible sign of their mediation. Hence, it is a sacrament originating with Jesus.

[13] This is stated in the *Didache* 4, 14; 14, 1 (written c. A.D. 95); *The Letter of Barnabas* 19 (written c. A.D. 95); Ignatius of Antioch, *Letter to the Philadelphians* 3 (written c. A.D. 105); and several later second- and third-century documents.

action—a personal one (v.15), a communal one (v. 16), and a juridical one ("tell it to the Church" v. 17). In the context of seeking a juridical solution, Jesus confers the power on the apostles to bind and loose on behalf of the whole Church. Thus, the power to bind is the power to impose a penance or exclude a member from the community, and the power to loose is the power to pardon (forgive) and readmit a member to the community. So again we see Jesus conferring not only the power to forgive sins on His apostles (as in Jn 20:21–23), but also the power to bind and loose by juridical sanction.

Far too much ink has been spilled on arguing whether Jesus would have been concerned with juridical sanctions and whether He would have used the term *ekklesia* (church [v. 17]), because it really does not matter whether Jesus used these terms or whether the apostolic Church interpreted His words to mean this. What matters is that the apostolic Church believed He meant this, and so put it into Scripture and action. This is sufficient to show that both the Sacrament of Reconciliation and the power of juridical sanction (conferred on the apostles and their successors) had their origin in Jesus.

We now turn to Jesus' conferral of the power to bind and loose on Peter. Note that the context of this conferral of authority is quite different from that of the apostles. The conferral concerned with the apostles is focused specifically on imposing penance and forgiveness of sins, while the conferral on Peter, as we shall see, is in the much broader context of Peter being the foundation of the Church and receiving the keys to the Kingdom:

> Simon Peter replied, "You are the Christ, the Son of the living God."
> And Jesus answered him, "Blessed are you, Simon Bar-Jona! For flesh and blood has not revealed this to you, but my Father who is in heaven. And I tell you, you are Peter, and on this rock I will build my Church, and the gates of Hades shall not prevail against it. I will give you the keys of the kingdom of heaven, and whatever you bind on earth shall be bound in heaven, and whatever you loose on earth shall be loosed in heaven." (Mt 16:16–19)

As explained in Chapter 1 (Section IV), the elements of this commissioning have their roots in Jesus. Furthermore, Jesus' commissioning of Peter as the foundation rock and His conferral of "the keys to the kingdom" give him the office and authority of prime minister[14] of the Church—that is, an office of supreme authority in place of the king (who is Jesus Himself). As noted in Chapter 1 (Section IV), Jesus created an office of supreme authority (as implied in the passage from Isaiah to which Jesus was likely referring),[15] and so the authority conferred on Peter is also given to the successors of Peter's office (see Chapter 1, Section V).

As with all New Testament passages, the meaning of any specific saying must be derived from the context in which it was said. So what does the "power to bind and loose" mean in this context? It means far more than the power to bind and loose given to the apostles (Mt 18:17–18) where that context reveals that their power is limited to imposing penance, forgiving sins, and imposing and remitting juridical sanctions. In the case of Peter, the context shows that his power to bind and loose is primary, heavenly, and absolute, like that of Shebna's and Eliakim's (Is 22:19–22). Peter's authority goes beyond that of Shebna's and Eliakim's inasmuch as Jesus grants him *heavenly* authority (to lead the Church) as well. Thus, we might say that there is an implicit conferral of the power to forgive sins and impose sanctions on Peter in Matthew 16:17–19, but that this is only a very small part of a much larger one—for the context reveals that Peter's power extends to the power to "rule" the Church in the place of Christ in every doctrinal and juridical way that may be required to carry out the charge of that office.

We now turn to a passage from Paul's Second Letter to the Corinthians that references "a ministry of reconciliation":

---

[14] Recall that Isaiah uses "keys to the kingdom" in the sense of "the power of prime minister (highest office) in the kingdom of Israel" in his oracle against Shebna, deposing him and elevating Eliakim to that office: "I will thrust you from your *office*, and you will be cast down from your station. In that day I will call my servant Eli'akim the son of Hilki'ah, and I will clothe him with your robe, and will bind your belt on him, and will commit your *authority* to his hand; and he shall be a father to the inhabitants of Jerusalem and to the house of Judah; and I will place on his [Eliakim's] shoulder the *key of the house of David*; he shall open, and none shall shut; and he shall shut, and none shall open" (Is 22:19–22; italics added). Notice that the power to bind and loose follows precisely upon the conferral of the keys to the kingdom of Israel, giving Eliakim the office of prime minister. See Chapter 1 (Sections IV and V of this volume).

[15] See previous note.

Therefore, if anyone is in Christ, he is a new creation; the old has passed away, behold, the new has come. All this is from God, who through Christ reconciled us to himself and gave us the ministry of reconciliation. (5:17–18)

Paul very likely means by "the ministry of reconciliation" the power to forgive sins conferred upon men. Jerome Murphy O'Connor states it this way:

> In the Divine plan human agents mediate grace. Paul cites and interprets a traditional formula which mentioned the initiator (God), the agent (Christ), and the means of reconciliation (forgiveness of sins).... Paul answers the question how, arising out of the present participle in the formula, by introducing the mediators, who make the action of Christ real to their contemporaries [i.e., human ministers of Reconciliation].[16]

As Murphy O'Connor implies, Saint Paul believes that Christ has imparted the authority to forgive sins on human beings, who are mediators of the grace of God actualized through Christ. He does not speak about a specific form in which this ministry is carried out, but refers to it as a "ministry". "Ministry" (diakonia) refers to a specific office within the Church,[17] and so we may infer that the ministry of reconciliation is not conferred on every Christian, but only on those who have been given that office by Church leaders—in this case, the apostles. This probably implies that the office of reconciliation extended to more than the apostles, and was conferred on prophets who later became presbyters and later priests.[18]

So what might we conclude about the origins of the Sacrament of Reconciliation and Jesus and the New Testament? There is

---

[16] Jerome Murphy-O'Connor, "The Second Letter to the Corinthians", in *The New Jerome Biblical Commentary*, ed. Raymond E. Brown, Joseph A. Fitzmyer, and Roland E. Murphy (Englewood Cliffs, N.J.: Prentice-Hall, 1990), p. 822.

[17] *Strong's Concordance* links diakonia to specific church offices in both the Old and New Testaments: "those who by the command of God proclaim and promote religion among men, of the office of Moses, of the office of the apostles and its administration, of the office of prophets, evangelists, elders etc." Blue Letter Bible (website), "Strong's G1248—diakonia", 2020, https://www.blueletterbible.org/lang/lexicon/lexicon.cfm?t=kjv&strongs=g1248.

[18] See ibid.

considerable direct evidence of the origin of this sacrament in Jesus, particularly in John 20:21–23 and also in Matthew 18:17–18 (which includes the power to impose and remit juridical sanctions). Though Matthew 16:17–19 (Peter's commission) implicitly addresses the power to forgive sins on Peter, it is really focused on Peter's primary and heavenly authority to "rule" the Church of Jesus Christ. Paul's Second Letter to the Corinthians (5:17–18) strongly implies an office of reconciliation (forgiveness of sins) given to the apostles, and through them, to others (probably presbyters) in the early Church. These references are sufficient to show that the Sacrament of Reconciliation is present in the New Testament and had its origins in Jesus Christ, who commissioned the apostles (and their successors) to carry it out in a specific ministry (*diakonia*).

The early Church followed the interpretation of John, Matthew, and Paul with respect to the ministry of giving Jesus' definitive forgiveness through the hands of the apostles and their successors. For example, the *Didache* (written around A.D. 95) implies confession (absolution) was available before Sunday Masses:

> Confess your sins in church, and do not go up to your prayer with an evil conscience. This is the way of life.... On the Lord's Day gather together, break bread, and give thanks, after confessing your transgressions so that your sacrifice may be pure.[19]

The *Didache* is ambiguous as to whether "confession of sins" refers to a general confession of sins and a general absolution before Mass or individual confession of sins. This is clarified later by Saint Ignatius of Antioch, who addresses the absolution of *serious* sins by the bishop through "penance":

> For as many as are of God and of Jesus Christ are also with the bishop. And as many as shall, in the exercise of penance, return into the unity of the Church, these, too, shall belong to God, that they may live according to Jesus Christ.... To all them that repent, the Lord grants forgiveness, if they turn in penitence to the unity of God, and to communion with the bishop.[20]

---

[19] See *Didache* 4, 14; 14, 1.
[20] Ignatius of Antioch, *Letter to the Philadelphians* 3; 8.

So how does one come back into communion with the bishop and the Church? Ignatius refers to this special means of reconciliation as "penance". It implies, as later Church Fathers indicate, a period of either public penance (for public sins) or private penance (for private sins), to make satisfaction for grave sins that would have alienated the penitent from the Church. It seems that this period of penance preceded absolution from the bishop, who had the power to restore the penitent to full communion with him, the Church, and Christ Himself.

Cyprian of Carthage (writing in about A.D. 250) clarifies the administration of the Sacrament of Reconciliation to an even greater extent, indicating that even individual confessions to priests (not simply to the bishop) are available for those who have committed minor to moderate sins:

> How much greater is the faith and more salutary the fear of those who, though bound by no crime of sacrifice or certificate, yet merely because they entertained such a thought, confess even this to the priest of God simply and contritely, and manifest their conscience to them. They lay bare the burden that is on their minds and seek treatment for their wounds, light and superficial as they are.[21]

The implication is that individual confession to a priest provides absolution for major sins as well as minor ones, as suggested by the phrasing "confess *even this* [a minor sin] to the priest".

A more complete explication of the history of the Sacrament of Reconciliation is given in CredibleCatholic.com.[22]

B. Theology and Practice of the Sacrament of Reconciliation Today

The *Catechism of the Catholic Church* describes the elements, form, minister, and theology of the Sacrament of Penance (Reconciliation).[23]

---

[21] Saint Cyprian of Carthage, *The Lapsed: The Unity of the Catholic Church*, Ancient Christian Writers, vol. 25, trans. Maurice Bevenot (Mahwah, N.J.: Paulist Press, 1957), p. 35.

[22] See Robert Spitzer, *Credible Catholic Big Book*, vol. 10, *The Sacraments, Part 2—Baptism, Confirmation, Reconciliation, Sacrament of the Sick, and Holy Orders* (Magis Center, 2017), CredibleCatholic.com, Chapter 3, https://www.crediblecatholic.com/pdf/M10/BB10.pdf #P1V10C3T2.

[23] See *CCC* 1422–98.

The *Catechism* affirms what the Church has practiced throughout the centuries: that the sacrament reconciles the penitent to *both* God and the Church. Thus, when absolution is given and the particular penance completed, the penitent is brought back into communion with both God and the Church. We now proceed to an explanation of the form of the sacrament and the three acts of the penitent.

There are three essential acts of the penitent that complement the actions of the priest within the sacrament: contrition, confession, and satisfaction. The first act, contrition (sorrow for sins), is part of the examination of conscience (before confession), the confession itself, and the doing of penance ("satisfaction"). The Church (since the Council of Trent) teaches that there are two kinds of contrition:

1. Perfect contrition—done out of love of God[24]
2. Imperfect contrition—done out of fear of damnation or punishment[25]

In the case of mortal sin (see the definition below), perfect contrition is sufficient for reconciliation with God, if it is accompanied by sacramental confession within a year. However, imperfect contrition *must* be accompanied by sacramental absolution to be effective in reconciling the penitent to God and the Church.

The need for the Sacrament of Reconciliation to complete the process of forgiveness (and restoration of communion with God) turns on the definition of mortal sin, which is given later in the *Catechism:*

> For a *sin* to be *mortal*, three conditions must together be met: "Mortal sin is sin whose object is grave matter and which is also committed with full knowledge and deliberate consent" (*Reconciliatio et Paenitentia* 17 § 12).... Mortal sin requires *full knowledge* and *complete consent.*[26]

The gravity of sin is defined by the Ten Commandments, though there are degrees of gravity among the sins and within each sin. For example, murder and adultery are graver than stealing or lying; and within stealing and lying, some offenses are venial (e.g., stealing pencils

---

[24] See ibid., 1452.
[25] See ibid., 1453.
[26] Ibid., 1857, 1859 (italics in original).

at work or harmlessly exaggerating one's merits), while others are grave (e.g., stealing a car or lying to hurt the reputation of another).

With respect to the second condition, sufficient knowledge means having a proper understanding that a particular action is not only sinful, but gravely sinful. In the case of certain sins, such as murder, theft, and adultery, it is assumed that most people who have reached the age of reason are by nature aware of the sinfulness and gravity of such actions. Knowing the sinfulness and gravity of other actions may require instruction and the formation of conscience. Without such instruction, the second condition of mortal sin may be absent, in which case it would not be mortally sinful.

The third condition is the most difficult to meet: complete consent of the will. It means not having any impediments to the free use of the will. Impediments may be external (such as being constrained, forced, or threatened to do something against one's will) or internal (such as strong passions or feelings,[27] strong unconscious motivations, psychological disorders,[28] addictions, deeply engrained habits, and strong situational fear, duress, and depression).[29]

Not infrequently, the above impediments to complete consent of the will are influential in the commission of certain grave sins, which would mitigate the mortal nature of the sin. In this case, the sin in question would not threaten the salvation of the penitent, and confession may not be *required* in order for complete reconciliation with God to be restored. However, one should try to make recourse to the sacrament as soon as possible, if such sins are committed. This will assure the penitent of absolution and impart the healing power of the sacrament as well.

Even if contrition occurs immediately after the commission of a sin, a good examination of conscience before confession can revive feelings of sorrow for having offended the God who has loved us

[27] According to the *Catechism of the Catholic Church*, "The promptings of feelings and passions can also diminish the voluntary and free character of the offense, as can external pressures or pathological disorders" (*CCC* 1860).

[28] Psychological disorders may include psychosis, schizophrenia, bipolar disorder, obsessive-compulsive disorder, and long-standing neuroses, among other disorders.

[29] The philosophical and psychological analysis of Paul Ricoeur is one of the most complete contemporary phenomenological and psychological assessments of both free will and its impediments. See Paul Ricoeur, *Freedom and Nature: The Voluntary and the Involuntary* (Chicago: Northwestern University Press, 1966).

so—as well as our neighbor who may have also been offended or hurt. The *Catechism* recommends the following sources for examination of conscience:

> The reception of this sacrament ought to be prepared for by an *examination of conscience* made in the light of the Word of God. The passages best suited to this can be found in the Ten Commandments [Ex 20:1–17], the moral catechesis of the Gospels and the apostolic Letters, such as the Sermon on the Mount [Mt 5–7] and the apostolic teachings (cf. Rom 12–15; 1 Cor 12–13; Gal 5; Eph 4–6).[30]

There are some excellent published works[31] and web resources[32] that give a summary and explanation of examination of conscience from the above Scripture passages. You might want to bring these to church, to focus and elucidate your examination of conscience.

The second act of the penitent is the actual confession of sins with a priest. The form may differ slightly from diocese to diocese or priest to priest, but the general form for the liturgy of the sacrament in the United States is as follows:

> In the Liturgy of Penance, the elements are ordinarily these: a greeting and blessing from the priest, a reading from Scripture, the confession of sins, the giving and accepting of a penance, an act of contrition, the priest's absolution, a proclamation of praise of God, and a dismissal.[33]

Each one of these elements is explained and illustrated in the *United States Catholic Catechism for Adults.*[34]

---

[30] *CCC* 1454 (italics in original).

[31] See, for example, George Aschenbrenner, *The Examination of Conscience* (Chicago: Loyola Press, 2007).

[32] The USCCB (the United States Conference of Catholic Bishops) has a free online reflection on the examination of conscience, which can be printed and used before confession; see http://www.usccb.org/prayer-and-worship/sacraments-and-sacramentals/penance /examinations-of-conscience.cfm. Father John Trigilio has also provided an examination of conscience based on the Ten Commandments; see "Sacrament of Penance: Examination of Conscience", EWTN.com, 2020, https://www.ewtn.com/catholicism/library/sacrament -of-penance-examination-of-conscience-9121. The Beginning Catholic website also provides a good examination of conscience based on the Ten Commandments and the precepts of the Church; see http://www.beginningcatholic.com/catholic-examination-of-conscience.

[33] *United States Catholic Catechism for Adults* (Washington, D.C.: United States Conference of Catholic Bishops, 2006), p. 265, http://ccc.usccb.org/flipbooks/uscca/files/assets/basic -html/page-265.html.

[34] See ibid., pp. 265–68.

Penitents should first confess to the priest all sins that they judge to be mortal, and then confess venial sins they remember after their examination of conscience. All adults should attempt to go to the sacrament at least once per year.[35] Penance services during Advent and Lent can be very helpful for recollection, examination, and contemplation, and can bring together members of the community to reinforce and pray for one another.

The third act of the penitent is the acceptance and completion of a penance (satisfaction for sins committed). Satisfaction may have two components:

1. Seeking to repair the damage of sin to our neighbor (e.g., payment for stolen goods, asking forgiveness for transgressions, correcting damage to someone's reputation, and so forth)
2. Some form of prayer or sacrifice to initiate the process of healing within the penitent and with the Lord

The *Catechism* states in this regard:

> The *penance* the confessor imposes must take into account the penitent's personal situation and must seek his spiritual good. It must correspond as far as possible with the gravity and nature of the sins committed.[36]

After the confession of sins and the imposition of a penance, the priest absolves the penitent from his sins by the following formula:

> God, the Father of mercies,
> through the death and the resurrection of his Son
> has reconciled the world to himself
> and sent the Holy Spirit among us
> for the forgiveness of sins;
> through the ministry of the Church
> may God give you pardon and peace, and I absolve
> you from your sins in the name of the Father, and of the
>   Son, and of
> the Holy Spirit. [Amen.][37]

[35] CCC 2042.
[36] Ibid., 1460 (italics in original).
[37] Quoted in ibid., 1449.

The ordinary form of the sacrament is individual confession and absolution (the liturgy of which was described above in this section). However, there are a few occasions in which general absolution can be administered. The *Catechism of the Catholic Church* summarizes it as follows, which is based on the Code of Canon Law:

> In case of grave necessity recourse may be had to a *communal celebration of reconciliation with general confession and general absolution*. Grave necessity of this sort can arise when there is imminent danger of death without sufficient time for the priest or priests to hear each penitent's confession. Grave necessity can also exist when, given the number of penitents, there are not enough confessors to hear individual confessions properly in a reasonable time, so that the penitents through no fault of their own would be deprived of sacramental grace or Holy Communion for a long time. In this case, for the absolution to be valid the faithful must have the intention of individually confessing their grave sins in the time required (cf. CIC, can. 962 § 1). The diocesan bishop is the judge of whether or not the conditions required for general absolution exist (cf. CIC, can. 961 § 2). A large gathering of the faithful on the occasion of major feasts or pilgrimages does not constitute a case of grave necessity (cf. CIC, can. 961 § 1).[38]

C. A Spiritual Explanation of the Six Major Graces of the Sacrament

There are six major graces associated with the Sacrament of Reconciliation (or Penance), which makes it a powerful vehicle for spiritual healing and the deepening of conversion toward the heart of Christ:

1. Definitive absolution for mortal and venial sins
2. Reconciliation with the Church
3. Spiritual solidification of a turning point in life
4. Healing of the interior damage and darkness of sinfulness
5. Graced resolve for continual conversion toward the heart of Christ
6. The peace of Christ

These were briefly explained in Chapter 2 (Section II.C).

---

[38] *CCC* 1483 (italics in original).

With respect to definitive absolution for mortal and venial sins, we must remember that God wants only what will bring us to our true dignity and fulfillment in His truth, goodness, and love, because He created us to experience the fullness of joy through the spiritual and transcendental powers that He gave us. Above all, He loves us and wants us to find our joy in His love, and giving our love to Him and others in the Kingdom. God cannot simply give us this life without our free acceptance of it and participation in it, because love must be borne out of freedom.

Recall from Volume I (Chapter 4, Section III) of this Trilogy that if love is to originate from within us (and not to be merely a robotic program from God), we have to *choose* it over the possibility of choosing "unlove" or "antilove". If we do not have the possibility of choosing to do something contrary to love, then we do not have the possibility of choosing love either, because love would be our only possible course of action, which means it would be programmed into us. Evidently, this means that we can choose actions that are at once contrary to God's will and contrary to our ultimate happiness and fulfillment.

Of course, at the time we choose something contrary to God's goodness and love, we don't think that it will be contrary to our happiness and fulfillment. Rather, we believe that going against God's will (His goodness and love) *will* make us happy and fulfilled, and so we ignore or rebel against God's goodness and love (manifest in the Ten Commandments and the Sermon on the Mount) and delude ourselves into thinking that we will find "true happiness" through vice or sin. We can stay on that path for a little while and turn back in repentance, or we can rationalize our actions and pursue a path contrary to God's goodness and love (contrary to His commandments and virtues), immersing ourselves in sensuality and egocentricity, power, domination, money, and even self-worship. If we choose the latter, we mire ourselves ever more deeply in the antitruth, antilove, and antigoodness of the Evil One, damaging our ability even to see the light, let alone follow it.

Even if we should remain on the path into darkness and sin, the falsity and destructiveness of this path will be revealed by our true nature (longing for companionship with God) as well as the Holy Spirit's grace and inspiration. If we persist along the path of darkness, we will begin to feel pangs of emptiness, loneliness, and alienation on a cosmic level (see Chapter 5, Section I.B), and if we allow ourselves to feel it, our conscience begins to weigh heavily (in guilt) against the destruction we have caused to our neighbor and ourselves (see Chapter 3, Section IV.B). At this juncture, we must *choose* to acknowledge the error and destructiveness of our ways, and to reconcile ourselves with both God and neighbor. If we do not, the Lord is likely to awaken us in the early hours of the morning and fill us with a profound sense of guilt and alienation, to call us back to companionship with Him (see Chapter 3, Sections IV.B and IV.C).

Recalling that God is not a stoic, angry, and vengeful critic and judge, but rather like the father of the prodigal son who Jesus addressed as Abba (see Section I above), we will want to return to Him who has been seeking us out like the shepherd of the lost sheep. This return can *feel* difficult or even impossible if we have been away from God or in a state of rebellion—and it is here that the Sacrament of Reconciliation is so important. In these circumstances, we need only swallow our pride—admitting our mistakes, failures, and destructiveness—and seek out a priest to receive the Sacrament of Reconciliation.

Since the sacrament has a set liturgy, we need not be confused or uncertain about how reconciliation will occur—or whether it will occur (so long as we are sincerely contrite and have a firm purpose of amendment). The form of the sacrament and the definitive absolution by the priest gives us a process and assurance of reconciliation with God, who has loved us unconditionally even in our sin. After finding a confessor, we will then want to obtain one of the above resources for the examination of conscience, and with a sincere desire to change, and regret for the harm caused to others, ourselves, and our relationship with God, proceed to the Sacrament of Reconciliation, trusting in the Lord's love, the definitive power of absolution, and the priest, who will mediate Christ's mercy and absolution. We will then want to satisfy the penance asked of us to complete the process of reconciliation.

The action of the priest and the definitiveness of absolution form a strong foundation upon which we can base certain hope in our resurrection and rebuild our lives after a period of darkness and wandering. This gift of definitive absolution is so powerful that I have seen it turn the lives of thousands of college students from a downward to an upward spiral, giving them not only a *feeling* of being restored to relationship with the Lord, but a resolve to reorient their lives toward God's goodness and will. I have been involved in many FOCUS conferences[39] where literally thousands of students will participate in the Sacrament of Reconciliation, some of them for the first time since their Confirmation. Some of them stand in line for hours to participate, but one feature is almost universal: they all have a renewed sense of hope and relationship with God, and they are resolved to maintain that new status as they return to their college campuses. I have also participated in dozens of reconciliation ceremonies at *agapē* retreats and Ignatian retreats at Georgetown University, Seattle University, and Gonzaga University. The experience of the students is essentially the same.

Will they fall again and get themselves into darkness? Many will, but their recollection of rediscovering the Sacrament of Reconciliation induces them to return to it and restore their relationship with God. I believe this sacrament has almost a miraculous effect on people who have wandered away from faith and religious commitment. It is so powerful, so assuring, and so definitive that it allows people who have fallen away to pivot radically and build their lives anew (see Chapter 3, Section IV.B). It is at once the foundation for forgiveness, restoration, healing, and conversion—the intention of Jesus Christ in giving men His authority and power to forgive sins for the life of the world.

The power and grace of definitive absolution also breaks the spell and hold of the Evil One over us. When absolution removes our sins, it also releases us from the bondage to Satan into which we have entered. This occurs even if we have been living a life of sin away from the Church for many years. As noted in Chapter 3 (Section IV.B), this special grace of the Lord to break our bondage to Satan should be accompanied by some resolutions to take "small steps" to move out of previous sinful habits. When we take these steps in conjunction with definitive absolution in the Sacrament of Reconciliation, we can get decent traction, because the power of Satan over us has been weakened by Christ's light and grace. This formidable

---

[39] FOCUS is the acronym for the Fellowship of Catholic University Students, which was founded in 1998 at Benedictine College in Atchison, Kansas.

combination of absolution and initial resolutions for moving out of sinful habits is indispensable for drawing closer to the light of Christ in our path toward moral conversion.

The second grace of the sacrament is reconciliation with the Church. You might be thinking, "I can see why this would be important if we undermine someone's faith, scandalized someone, or publicly apostatized, as might have been the case in the first three centuries of Christianity; but why would this be important in today's Church, where most penitents have not publicly undermined the Church or the Christian faith?" The key to understanding this is found in Saint Paul's declaration about the Church as the body of Christ:

> For just as the body is one and has many members, and all the members of the body, though many, are one body, so it is with Christ. For by one Spirit we were all baptized into one body—Jews or Greeks, slaves or free—and all were made to drink of one Spirit. For the body does not consist of one member but of many.... If one member suffers, all suffer together; if one member is honored, all rejoice together. Now you are the body of Christ and individually members of it. (I Cor 12:12–14, 26–27)

When we are baptized into the body of Christ (the Church), then we affect it for better or for worse. If we wander into spiritual darkness, emptiness, and alienation, it brings that darkness, emptiness, and alienation into the rest of the body. The Church does not feel it in the same way we do, but our darkness does cause the Church to suffer. This cannot be helped because we are loved by Christ, and if we are suffering from spiritual darkness, Christ feels our suffering and alienation, which is in turn communicated throughout His body— the Church. Our darkness sends a haunting vibration or whisper, a "suffering with" to every member of the body; and this "aching" will not be resolved until we begin to move out of the darkness and return to the One who loves us.

In the Sacrament of Reconciliation, Christ has given the Church and the ministers of the sacrament (the priests) the authority and power to lift the darkness and to restore peace to our aching souls. That is why the formula of absolution says, "By the ministry of the Church, may God grant you pardon *and peace*." The sacrament not only brings absolution and reconciliation with God (the first grace);

it also reunites us with Christ's body, lifts our alienation and darkness, and sends our restored light and peace to all of her members. Thus, when we go to confession, we not only do it to reconcile *ourselves* to God, but also to bring light and peace to the Church (Christ's body), which formerly felt our darkness and discord. Our participation in the Sacrament of Reconciliation then not only reunites us with Christ's body; it is also a gift and grace to the Church, with which we are reunited.

The third grace of the Sacrament of Reconciliation (spiritual solidification of a turning point in life) is yet another powerful grace of the Sacrament of Reconciliation. Many of us, including myself when I was younger, have allowed ourselves to buy into the culture's view of purpose, dignity, and destiny, rationalizing its seductions toward materialism, sensuality, and egocentricity. In so doing, we allowed the Evil One to get an increased grip on our hearts, predisposing us to his sophistries about the "goodness" of sin, and his suggestions about the naiveté and unjust rules and rigors of the Church. We also open ourselves to other deceits—for example, the justification of ethical violations and shortcuts, sexual indiscretions, greed, envy, anger, and pride. One can almost hear the refrain "Of course, we ought to be proud of our accomplishments", or "Of course, we deserve to indulge in the fruits of our labors", or "Of course, a little bit of anger is justified", or "She doesn't deserve that benefit in life—I do." As we skip lightly down the wide road of perdition, we will probably notice increased hostility to the Church as well as to her teachings and leaders; increased resentment toward Christ and the Church for impositions placed on us; and an increasing loss of the distinction between good and evil. We will also feel increased emptiness, loneliness, alienation, and guilt on a cosmic level, but we will not know the reason why. We will contrast freedom with obedience to God's law, rather than seeing obedience to God's law as freedom. At the same time we will find ourselves believing a new set of definitions for "goodness", "love", and "truth". We will then align ourselves with new friends who have little regard for Christ or the Church, even tolerating their insults and ridicule for the Lord of life (which we may have previously found intolerable).

Though the Lord always allows us to be free, He will not sit idly by, letting us sow the seeds of our own eternal destruction, and so

He will come with warnings. As explained in Chapter 3 (Section IV.B), this might take the form of some very disturbing dreams in which the Blessed Virgin Mary or some image of the Lord Himself is tearfully present. It may also take the form of thoughts in the back of our minds that we are in severe spiritual danger and must act quickly to avert potential disaster. These dreams and thoughts might be accompanied by an intensification of cosmic emptiness, loneliness, alienation, and guilt, provoking us to consider reconnecting with the Lord and the Church. It may also take the form of a family member or friend approaching us and saying, "You have really changed—and I'm worried about you!" Frequently, the Lord will wake us up at two o'clock or three o'clock in the morning, when the noise of the world is reduced and we are more open to His suggestions. He will then use some of the above methods to heighten our sense of spiritual jeopardy; our closeness to our enemy, Satan; and the downward path on which we are spiraling. His hope is that when we see the incredible danger of our situation, we will choose (in our freedom) to ask Him for help: "Lord, save me" (Mt 14:30). When we turn to Him with this request for His mercy, He will immediately suggest the need for repentance and to begin the process of resolving to change our deadly ways.

This is where the Sacrament of Reconciliation comes into play. Though it is incredibly important to ask the Lord for help and to resolve to do better in the future, *we* need more. We need an assurance of forgiveness that can only come from the definitive absolution that Jesus empowered His disciples (and their followers) to administer. Our sense of the Lord's forgiving love is faint by comparison to the graced restoration we receive through the power of absolution given by Jesus to his apostles and their successors (Jn 20:23). When we receive that definitive absolution, we have a certainty of being ontologically changed and restored. We are elevated from darkness and death into the light and life of God Himself. It is quite certain that Jesus intended to give this power to absolve sins definitively to His apostles not only because of the unconditional nature of His bestowal of that power on His disciples in John 20:23 ("any" [*tinōn*]), but also because of the same unconditional power to bind and loose given to the apostles in Matthew 18:18 ("whatever" [*hosa*]). Saint Paul also believed that he had been given the power to mediate the forgiving grace of Jesus Himself through his ministry of reconcilia-tion.[40] The early Church followed this interpretation of Saint Paul as well as John, Matthew, Mark, and Luke (see above Section II.A).

Given the origin of definitive absolution in Jesus, and the power of this gift to restore us to His Kingdom as well as our true need for it, it is difficult to understand why any Christian church would want to separate themselves from the ordained lineage of the apostles and their successors in administering this precious gift (as well as the gift of Jesus' Body and Blood in the Holy Eucharist). This provokes the question that I have asked since my collegiate years: If only for the gifts of the Sacrament of Reconciliation and the Holy Eucha-rist, why wouldn't everyone want to be Catholic? Why would anyone want to turn away these two most precious gifts that Jesus evidently intended to give us through the mediation of His apostles and their successors to the end of the age?[41]

Let us now return to the third grace of the Sacrament of Recon-ciliation (spiritual solidification of a turning point in life). In addition to the spiritual "reset" coming from definitive absolution, the Lord also provides additional grace to help us separate from our attachment to deadly sins and bondage to Satan. As the grace of sacramental con-fession takes hold, we can sometimes sense a weakening of Satan's grip on us, as well as a strengthening of the Lord's grip on us—similar to God snatching Goethe's *Faust* from the grip of Mephistopheles (the devil). As the priest administers absolution, we can almost feel the relief of not only having our sins wiped away, but also being res-cued from the master of darkness—a sense of true freedom, the free-dom from evil and its destructive promptings toward egocentricity, power, domination, and the eight deadly sins. As this occurs, we can almost sense the light of truth, goodness, and love peeking through once again, beckoning us to come into its perfect fullness.

The Lord anticipated that we would need still more—a solid onto-logical foundation on which to build our "turning point" into an

---

[40] See Jerome Murphy O'Connor's interpretation of 2 Corinthians 5:17–18, explained in Section II.A above.

[41] With respect to Jesus' intention to give us the gift of His real Body and Blood in the Holy Eucharist, see Chapter 2, Section I, of this volume. With respect to Jesus' intention to mediate the power of forgiveness through the apostles and their successors, see Section II.A above.

ongoing conversion. And here, the sacrament once again affords us what we truly need: supernatural grace pouring into our intention to turn our lives around (repent), giving it the security of God's acceptance of our repentance and assuring us that His gift of forgiveness and healing is supernaturally real. From this remarkable base, we can muster the creativity and resolve to formulate our "small steps" for pushing beyond the darkness into the light of Christ, "small steps" to initiate a daily prayer life, regular reception of the Sacrament of Reconciliation, and doable steps to avoid the sins to which we are most prone.

The reader might be thinking, "Really? Are you really saying that the Sacrament of Reconciliation does all this? Isn't a lot of this just your pious imagination?" I would not have made these claims if I had not known many others, including myself, who experienced all these graces given by Jesus to His apostles when He breathed the Holy Spirit upon them, saying, "If you forgive the sins of any, they are forgiven; if you retain the sins of any, they are retained" (Jn 20:23). Frankly, I could not have dreamt up these graces out of my pious imagination even if I had wanted to. Thank God they originated with the superabundant heart of Jesus Christ.

The fourth grace of the Sacrament of Reconciliation is healing. Spiritual wounds are similar to physical ones—as long as the wound is open and losing blood, healing cannot begin; and the longer the wound remains open, the weaker the body/soul becomes. The Sacrament of Reconciliation through the grace of definitive absolution stops the bleeding and seals the wound, enabling spiritual healing to begin. Thus, it provides the necessary initial healing of the soul, but goes further.

When we move into the domain of darkness, it affects not only our souls, but also our emotional health and our intellectual acuity. As many of us know, remaining in the darkness for an extended period (without the benefit of the Sacrament of Reconciliation) starts to affect our capacity for love. We grow more impatient, more insensitive, more angry, and more arrogant, and then we turn these emotions in on ourselves, producing a loss of joy and hope as well as a state of growing malaise, interior tension, and sometimes, depression.

Our emotional condition is not the only casualty of the Evil One's influence; so also is our intellect. We become increasingly uncertain about our core identity, becoming almost chameleon-like, to please whatever group we encounter. We find it increasingly more difficult to distinguish between good and evil, good and bad opinions, and rational and irrational thinking processes. As a result, we seem to be more muddled in our emotional and intellectual tone. When we break out of the grip of the evil one through the Sacrament of Reconciliation, the Lord provides the additional grace to rectify the emotional, psychological, intellectual, and spiritual damage done to us in the domain of darkness. Seizing on the openness of our hearts, the Lord begins gently to expose the sophistries we have embraced and the callousness and shallowness of our hearts, inciting us to choose His truth, goodness, and love in place of them. Obviously, He cannot make the choice for us, but He can make suggestions, inspire us, and enflame our desire for truly good ideals. Reinforced by the grace of the sacrament, we begin to move in the direction of His suggestions, gradually overcoming the darkness in which we were mired. As we become more accustomed to trusting and loving His guiding spirit, we willingly move toward His light of eternal truth and love.

As above, I make these claims on the basis of many testimonies, including my own, that tell the same story of renewed grace and goodness through this sacrament again and again. The power of this precious sacrament to heal is truly remarkable, and when we combine it with the healing power of the Holy Eucharist (see Chapter 2, Section I.C), it can cause a complete transformation of our souls and spiritual disposition.

The fifth grace of the sacrament (graced resolve toward continued conversion) reinforces our resolve to do better in the future, and this "graced" resolve is precisely what enables us to make progress in the spiritual life. The power of this grace provides a foundation for us upon which to build our continuing moral conversion. Saint Ignatius of Loyola thought that this grace of the sacrament empowered our daily General Examen (see Chapter 6, Section II), and so he recommended frequent confession for Jesuits. As we take small steps away from the darkness into the light, our souls, filled with the light, become stronger and healthier; that is, they are able to recognize wisdom and generate wisdom, recognize God's presence and connect with it, recognize the needs of others and respond to them, recognize pitfalls, dangers, and errors, and react to them—all of which enable us to love both God and neighbor more authentically and deeply. "Graced resolve" is healing of the highest order, because it leads to a purification of love that will define our relationship with God and one another forever.

Graced resolve blends the fruit of *our will* to do better (elicited by examination of conscience, contrition, and confession) with God's grace—the inspiration of the Holy Spirit to go toward and stay in the light of Christ. Thus, "graced resolve" initiates and perpetuates the purification of our desires, what Saint Paul called "putting off the body of flesh" (Col 2:11).

Purification of desire has two dimensions: becoming less attached to disordered desires (leading toward spiritual darkness and alienation) and having greater attachment to ordered desires (leading to the light, wisdom, and love of Christ). The "graced resolve" from the Sacrament of Reconciliation initiates and perpetuates both dimensions of purification of desire, because detachment from disordered desires and attachment to ordered ones is greatly enhanced by the interaction of the fruit of our will with the inspiration and grace of the Holy Spirit. Without willpower, resolve would be a fiction—there would be nothing for the Spirit to inspire. But once the Sacrament of Reconciliation has galvanized and fueled our resolve to do better, the Holy Spirit can act on that resolve and enhance its effects on our process of detachment and attachment by imparting spiritual consolation toward good desires and affective desolation toward disordered desires (see Chapter 3, Section IV.C). Inspired by consolation and informed by desolation, our resolve to detach from the desires of darkness and attach to the desires of light becomes much clearer and stronger than we could ever achieve on our own. We might say, then, that the Sacrament of Reconciliation galvanizes our resolve, which enables the Holy Spirit to inspire it in our process of purifying our desires to conform more and more with those of Jesus Christ's—that is, to imitate the heart of Christ.

The sixth grace of the sacrament (the peace of Christ) can occur immediately after receiving absolution and can grow in intensity as we progress in our moral conversion. In our discussion of the previous five graces, we noted that long periods of unrepentant sinfulness can produce self-alienation, cosmic emptiness and loneliness, and a loss of joy and hope. When we try to restore our sense of equanimity and peace by making recourse to nonsacramental means, such as counselors, friends, recreation, and the like, the discord seems to continue and even intensify. Yet when we make recourse to the Sacrament of Reconciliation, the opposite occurs: a sense of supernatural peace, "which passes all understanding" (Phil 4:7), breaks through the self-alienation and discord we could not dispel. Our spirits lift as if they are being drawn upward toward the Lord of joy and love (Jn 15:11–12). I have seen that sense of peace and renewed joy not only on the faces of thousands of young people at FOCUS conferences (see above), but also in the eyes of adult penitents who come to me for confession. The longer those individuals stayed away from the sacrament (and the Church), the more intense was the sense of relief, peace, and joy when they finally returned to it.

Once when I was working as a hospital chaplain, I encountered a man who was evidently angry at God, the Church, and me (for being associated with the Church). When I went into the hospital at the beginning of the day, I was given a list of all the patients who had indicated that their religion was Catholic. As with other patients, I popped into this gentleman's room and asked how he was doing. He looked up and said, "I don't need a priest, I don't need the Church, and I don't need to see you." I said, "Okay." However, something told me that this man really did want to see a priest. So the following day, I popped in on him again, and he said the same thing. I said, "Mind if I pop in tomorrow just to see how you are doing?" to which he responded, "You needn't bother, but suit yourself." I took this as a sign that he might eventually be willing to see me. So I repeated my visit for two more days with pretty much the same result. The following day, he looked up at me and asked, "Why are you so persistent?" I said, "Something inside me tells me that you would like to talk to me, that's all." He said, "Come to think about it, I am a little worried about the surgery I am having tomorrow. I'm told that it is fairly dangerous, and perhaps you could say a prayer." I said, "I would be happy to say a prayer *with you* right now." He then told me, "I don't think you would really like me. I have been away from the Church and involved in some pretty heavy things, and I think you would find me quite unlikeable." I responded, "I don't think you are unlikable at all, but more importantly, since your surgery is coming up early tomorrow, it might be good to go to confession and prepare your soul for whatever might happen." He asked me, "Do you really think I could be forgiven for everything I have done?" I responded, "Well, if you are sincere in your contrition and will try to avoid these sins in the future, the answer is most assuredly yes."

He then proceeded to his confession, and began to cry quite profusely throughout most of it. After receiving absolution, the look on his face was utterly transcendent. Prior to the sacrament, his eyes seemed dark and shallow, and as he looked up from the sacrament, they seemed filled with light, depth, and joy. After thanking me, he asked to say some prayers *with me*. His surgery was successful, but more importantly, the healing and restoration of his spirit was transformative unto eternity. Though this precious sacrament can be difficult, if we place our trust in the Lord who provided us with it, we too will find ourselves experiencing a peace beyond all understanding.

In sum, the six graces of the Sacrament of Reconciliation are a most powerful intervention into our souls and spiritual lives. It wipes away our sins, severs our bondage to the Evil One, lifts us out of his darkness, dispels his lies and seductions, begins the process of healing the damage to our spiritual, emotional, and intellectual lives, points the way to the light of Christ, infuses us with His resolve and truth, and brings us back to the path of salvation, catapulting us, as it were, toward our true spiritual home in Christ. If we Catholics truly knew the cosmic struggle between good and evil in which we are immersed, truly feared the deadliness and darkness of our spiritual enemy, Satan, truly appreciated the light and salvation given to us by Jesus Christ, and truly loved Him for it, we would not hesitate to seek out the Sacrament of Reconciliation several times per year—instead of balking at it. The more we know the deadliness of our enemy, the loveliness of Jesus Christ, and our extreme need for His grace to rescue us and keep us on the path to salvation, the more we would cherish this great sacrament given to the Church by Jesus. Indeed, it would be one of the key reasons we would love and never leave the Catholic Church. My hope is that every Catholic will know the preciousness of this gift, take advantage of it, seal it with the grace of the Holy Eucharist, and stay on the path to salvation until they truly experience the light of Christ in Heaven.

III. Spontaneous Prayers for Forgiveness, Reconciliation, and Healing

Though spontaneous prayers for forgiveness are an important way to reestablish our relationship with God after serious sin and moral failure (see below), the Church teaches that the Sacrament of Reconciliation is needed to absolve mortal sins—grave matter committed with sufficient knowledge and full consent of the will (no impediments to the free use of the will). Thus, when we believe we have sinned mortally, we must intend to go to confession (with sincere contrition and firm purpose of amendment) as soon as it is feasible. This will bring about not only definitive absolution from mortal sin, but also restoration to the Church, healing, and graced resolve, as explained above.

Spontaneous prayers can be quite helpful and efficacious prior to confession as well as after confession (as a means of continuing the healing and restoration process). Jesus encouraged short and sincere personal prayers of contrition that He said could lead to justification. One of the more striking examples of the powerful effect of these short prayers is found in the Parable of the Pharisee and Tax Collector (Lk 18:9–14). In contrast to the Pharisee's lengthy "prayer" of praise of himself, the tax collector stands in the back of the Temple, beats his breast, and sincerely prays the simple line, "God, be merciful to me a sinner!" (v. 13). Jesus says about this man's simple, sincere prayer, "I tell you, this man went down to his house justified [i.e., ready for salvation]" (v. 14).

We see the same act of forgiveness given to the prodigal son with his simple prayer to his father (signifying Jesus' Father): "Father, I have sinned against heaven and before you; I am no longer worthy to be called your son; treat me as one of your hired servants" (Lk 15:18–19). As we saw above (Section I), the father not only forgives the son with these simple words; he also restores him completely to the family and kills the fatted calf in celebration. We also see the same mercy offered to the good thief on the cross when he turns to Jesus and asks, "Jesus, remember me when you come in your kingly power," to which Jesus responds, "Truly, I say to you, today you will be with me in Paradise" (Lk 23:42–43). We might infer from this that Jesus (and His Father) honors a sincere plea for mercy (accompanied by a firm purpose of amendment), indicating true for-giveness and healing.

In view of this, we might wonder why the Church teaches the necessity for confession after committing a mortal sin when we have contritely prayed for forgiveness with a firm purpose of amendment.[42] There are three major reasons for this. First, the Sacrament of Rec-onciliation gives definitive absolution for sin, but we cannot be sure that spontaneous prayers for forgiveness *will in fact* bring about defini-tive forgiveness. Spontaneous prayers alone leave us open to perpetual uncertainty about how the Lord judges our prayer, contrition, and purpose of amendment. Since Jesus clearly gave the apostles the power to absolve sins definitively (see above, Section II.A) and the power to interpret definitively His teachings on sin, forgiveness, and sacramental powers (see Chapter 1, Sections IV–V), we can be sure of the defin-itive nature of absolution through the Sacrament of Reconciliation. In view of this, why would we want to endure uncertainty about our salvation by challenging the Church's teaching authority or the efficacy of the Sacrament of Reconciliation when these doctrines are so well-grounded in the teachings of Jesus? Why wouldn't we want to avail ourselves of the sacrament when it is so readily available?

Second, as noted above, the Sacrament of Reconciliation im-parts five additional graces that spontaneous prayers alone do not—restoration to the Mystical Body, solidification of a turning point in life, healing for the soul, graced resolve toward deeper conversion, and transcendent peace. As noted above (Section II.C), these graces are indispensable for our ongoing spiritual and moral conversion, and therefore for our salvation as well as the salvation of others we touch.

Third, when we decide to turn our life around after straying off the path to salvation for a considerable period of time, the Sacrament of Reconciliation proves invaluable as a definitive turning point (*metanoia*) in our moral lives. The grace of absolution is so powerful that it enables us to make a clean break from the past so that we can build our lives anew. This grace of *metanoia* (turning our lives around) imbedded in the sacrament of reconciliation lies at the foundation of the movement

---

[42] The Church teaches that even after perfect contrition we should strive to go to confes-sion for definitive absolution of our sins within one year. See *Catechism of the Catholic Church*, no. 1860.

of many saints from darkness into the light of Christ (see Chapter 3, Section IV.B).

So what might we conclude about the Sacrament of Reconciliation and the use of spontaneous prayers for forgiveness? First, if we believe that we have committed a mortal sin with full knowledge and complete consent of the will (see above, Section II.B), then we should make a sincere prayer of contrition and then resolve to go to the Sacrament of Reconciliation as soon as possible. The prayer of contrition could be the well-known Act of Contrition:

> O my God, I am heartily sorry for having offended Thee, and I detest all my sins because of Thy just punishments, but most of all because they offend Thee, my God, Who art all-good and deserving of all my love. I firmly resolve, with the help of Thy grace, to sin no more and to avoid the near occasions of sin, Amen.

Second, if we are trying to break a persistent habit of sin (such as that intimated by Saint Paul's "sins of the flesh" in Romans 7:15–25), then we will want to first avail ourselves of the Sacrament of Reconciliation (to receive the absolution and graces mentioned above) followed by recitation of many spontaneous prayers (in combination with the affirmations and Examen mentioned in the previous chapter) over the course of time.

Third, if we are uncertain about whether we have committed a mortal sin with sufficient knowledge and full consent of the will (no impediments to the free use of the will), we will want to recite the Act of Contrition and some of the spontaneous prayers (mentioned below) with a view to going to the Sacrament of Reconciliation as soon as it can be managed. During that confession, we will want to ask the priest about whether this sin is truly mortal—that is, whether it meets all three criteria mentioned above. This is crucial, because scrupulosity about the nature of our sinfulness can drive us toward despair and induce us to change our view of God from the loving Creator to the stoic, terrifying, indifferent, or "payback god" (see Volume IV, Chapter 2, of the Quartet). A good confessor (experienced in the spiritual life) can help us to form our conscience properly so that we can truly recognize the applicability of the three criteria of mortal sin while avoiding scrupulosity.

Let us now proceed to a brief consideration of some spontaneous prayers. These prayers can be quite helpful to prepare ourselves for the Sacrament of Reconciliation by helping us toward sincere contrition, trust in the Lord's love, and firm purpose of amendment. They can also help us after receiving the Sacrament of Reconciliation by supporting our acceptance of the Lord's forgiveness, His healing power, and His providential assistance to make good come out of whatever harm we may have caused. We will first consider prayers for forgiveness (Section III.A) and then prayers offering forgiveness (Section III.B).

A. Prayers for Forgiveness

Three complementary spontaneous prayers for forgiveness have proven quite helpful to me throughout my religious journey.

- "Lord, have mercy on me, a sinner."
- "Lord, I accept your forgiveness."
- "Lord, make good come out of whatever harm I might have caused."

We will consider these prayers in their interrelationship with one another.

The Lord's unconditional love makes the prayer of the tax collector in the Temple quite efficacious. In Jesus' parable, a tax collector, considered to be one of the very worst of all sinners, stood at the back of the Temple and sincerely prayed, "God, be merciful to me a sinner!" (Lk 18:13). As Jesus said, "This man went down to his house justified" (Lk 18:14), which means he was ready for salvation. Bearing Jesus' promise in mind, we can always use this prayer to petition the Lord sincerely for mercy and forgiveness with the assurance that He will hear and respond to us in the same way as He did for the tax collector.

We can sometimes run from the incredibly liberating prayer of the tax collector because we think that God will hold back His forgiveness until we are "a little more deserving" or "a little less weak" or "a little more perfect". Yet if we do this, we implicitly put conditions on the Lord's *un*conditional love, undermine our trust in His forgiveness, and condition the efficacy of the Sacrament of Reconciliation. So how might we overcome this tendency to limit the Lord's love so that we can make the Lord's forgiveness come fully alive in our hearts? We must truly *believe* that His love is unconditional in the same way Jesus portrayed it in the Parable of the Prodigal Son (Lk 15:11–32). How can we enhance our belief in this? I will illustrate my response through a story.

When I was in the novitiate (the first stages of Jesuit formation), I slipped into the habit of believing that God had not quite forgiven me for my sins. Though I had heard the Parable of the Prodigal Son and knew Jesus' address for the Father as "Abba", and I was aware of His admonition to forgive seventy times seven times (Mt 18:22) and tacitly aware of the implications of the Eucharist and the Passion (with respect to God's unconditional love), I would come away from my prayer of repentance with the hunch that God was saying, "I wish I could forgive you, but unfortunately your repentance was not quite right and there's still too far to go before you're perfect enough to be forgiven." Since I did not want to be caught short, I would pray what I would now call the worst of all possible prayers: "Don't worry, God. I'll get it taken care of, and when everything is fine, then I'll be able to ask You for forgiveness, and then You will really want to forgive me."

I had forgotten an important aspect about the spiritual life— namely, I *need* the Lord, especially to turn my life around. By putting so many limitations on God's love, mercy, and forgiveness, I had slipped into the worst of all possible spiritual attitudes (which is devilish, to say the least), for I had conditioned God's forgiveness on being "good enough", yet I could not be "good enough" without God's forgiveness and healing. The Father of the prodigal son was standing outside of me waving at me and trying to get my attention while I was busy turning Him into a stoic ogre who would not want to give me His attention because I was not good enough.

Fortunately, my novice master recognized the insanity of my position and pointed to the conundrum, asking, "What does God have to gain by having you keep Him on the outside of your life; why in the world would God not want to get into your consciousness and help you clean up what you perceive to be a mess?" It occurred to me that even if God were a pure pragmatist (which He is not), He would have nothing to gain by putting me into a position of zero progress and very probable regression. Since I was miserable, I readily assented to his point. He gave me the following advice, which I have maintained throughout my life: "When you ask for forgiveness, turn to God with the heart of a child who trusts unconditionally in his parents and say, "Lord, I accept Your forgiveness." What a relief! Since God's love is unconditional, I can accept His forgiveness with the full knowledge that it is His intention to set me free.

The recognition of God's unconditional love led me to a three-step process that readers might find useful for themselves. First, affirm that God really is Abba, that God really possesses the unconditional love of the prodigal son's father, that the divine Son really became incarnate and died in order to give Himself away unconditionally (in an act of unconditional love), and that the Holy Spirit is really working to effect that unconditional love within the world.

Second, affirm that God truly wants to forgive and heal you in order to work with you toward *metanoia*, and that God could have no other attitude because it would lead to the demise of the whole human race.

Third, given this, when you ask for forgiveness, when you say, "Have mercy on me, Lord, for I am a sinful person," *accept* His forgiveness—accept it as the prodigal son returning to his father's house; accept it with the heart of a child who truly believes that his parents want to forgive him even after he has "committed every imaginable offense". Put on the mind and heart of Saint Peter at the Sea of Tiberius after Jesus' Crucifixion when he hears John say, "It is the Lord!" (Jn 21:7). After denying Jesus three times, he dives into the water and swims to shore, convinced that Jesus has but one thing in store for him: His healing and forgiving love (Jn 21:7–9). I took my novice master's advice and I put on the heart of a child, and when I address Abba I say, "Have mercy on me, Lord, for I am a sinful man. And I accept Your forgiveness and invite You into the depths of my heart so that You may call me to transformation."

The Lord's forgiving and healing love also extends to the people we might have harmed by our attitudes or actions. If the harm is intentional, we need to ask those who are harmed for forgiveness, for in this one act of humility we can redress the cycle of resentment begetting vengeance, vengeance begetting violence, and violence giving rise to further violence.

In the midst of trying to clear up harms or even possible harms, we often find ourselves powerless. Sometimes we do not recognize the depth of the hurt we might have caused; sometimes we are not even sure if we caused a harm; sometimes we only realize that we might have caused a harm hours after perpetrating a possible harm; sometimes we feel powerless when others cannot talk to us. In all such cases there is a brief prayer that can prevent us from collapsing under the weight of our burden; a prayer that allows the grace of God (through the Holy Spirit) to work in the hearts of others, to effect eventual reconciliation and peace: "Lord, please make good come out of whatever harm I might have caused."

Many have been the times when I have found myself in such predicaments. Sometimes I am giving advice that I think will be quite fruitful, only to realize at three o'clock in the morning (when I wake up with startled lucidity) that I might have really "blown it". "Oh, no. That person might have taken the comment this way, or that other way, and may now be plunged into depression because of my idiocy.... Arghh!" I think to myself, "They probably won't want a call at three in the morning to hear my attempt to straighten out the matter." At times like these, the above prayer is quite helpful. When I pray it (in confidence and trust) I sense the Holy Spirit working in the hearts of people I may have offended or harmed, and I sense a peace arising out of that confidence. I frequently find that my confidence is confirmed when the "victim" comes up to me a few days later and says, "Father Spitzer, when you said X, I really took it in the wrong way. I thought you meant Y, which really disturbed me; but the next day I got up and I got a different insight into what you were saying, and now I realize that you meant Z, which has been really helpful." As I listen to this great miracle of the Holy Spirit, I think to myself, "Whew!" I feel like Mario Andretti on a speedway after avoiding a potentially deadly crash by a split second. I have no question about who was doing the driving.

B. Prayers Offering Forgiveness

Jesus teaches us to forgive one another from the heart, to forgive seventy times seven times (Mt 18:21–22), and to ask the Father to "forgive us our trespasses, as we forgive those who trespass against us" (Mt 6:12). It will probably come as no surprise that Jesus mentions this one prescription more often than any other commandment, injunction, or prescription in the New Testament. Why? Because, as noted above, violence begets violence, vengeance begets vengeance, resentment begets resentment, and the cycle will continue and grow so long as one of the offended parties does not let go. If one party does let go (forgives), the cycle frequently degenerates, and forgiving eventually turns into forgetting. Forgiving (the intention to let go of an offense intentionally and unjustly perpetrated against us) takes far less time than forgetting. My general rule is, for minor offenses, forgetting occurs at least six weeks after forgiving, and in the case of particularly egregious offenses, forgetting can take several years longer than forgiving.

In any case, one thing is clear: without forgiving, forgetting is impossible; indeed, the opposite occurs. The memory of an offense seems to mushroom in its proportions and emotional discharge. When I am in a "nonforgiving mood", I tend to exaggerate all the bad features of a memory, omit all the good features of the perpetrator, and attempt to construct a scenario whereby the demon-other has perpetrated the unforgivable—then I get *good* and mad. Without forgiveness, the reliving of a scenario seems to get worse with every retelling. The following prayer has helped me immensely in this regard: "Lord, You are the just Judge. You take care of it."

I remember the time I discovered this prayer. I had written a philosophical paper and a colleague criticized it behind my back. When I had publicly read the paper, I had given ample opportunity for questions and had even submitted the paper to selected individuals before reading it. This particular colleague said nothing. But a few days later, he was not only critical of the paper, but also of me. When someone called this to my attention, I was quite angry. Even after I had redressed the criticism in writing, I felt no relief. In fact, my anger began to grow. Every time I opened my Breviary, this person's face suddenly appeared. Instead of taking the hint from God, I chose to stew in my anger. Finally, it occurred to me that this was only hurting *me*, and furthermore, it might cause me to say something I would regret—so I had to face it.

I first tried to face it on my own, thinking, "Okay ... now I'm going to stop thinking about this and I'm going to forgive this person

from the heart," but every time I tried the "solo method"
myself having about one-half second of peace followed by an
burst of anger. I was quite helpless. Finally, it occurred to n
not let God help? So I said, "Okay, Lord, You're the just Judge.
You can see into the hearts of every human being. You understand
our history and our failings. You can effect reconciliation where
mere mortals cannot. Okay, You take care of him; in fact, You take
care of the whole situation, please." An unbelievable peace began
to come over me. By putting this person (and the past situation) into
God's hands, I allowed the Holy Spirit to work His reconciling love
through His infinite providence in my heart. In letting go (into *God's*
hands) I was eventually able to forget; and in the forgetting, I was able
not only to find peace, but also to even smile at and acknowledge
the person who had offended me. This is a powerful prayer, and I
have used it often. The immense reconciling love of the Holy Spirit
cannot be underestimated in its power to transform and bring peace.
This leads to the next prayer.

Jesus teaches, "Love your enemies, do good to those who hate
you, bless those who curse you, pray for those who abuse you" (Lk
6:27–28). Paul does the same by saying, "If your enemy is hungry,
feed him; if he is thirsty, give him drink" (Rom 12:20). In my life
and leadership positions, I have found no wiser advice. What at first
appeared to be virtually impossible, I have found to be not only possible, but efficacious and transformative. Throughout my career, I have
found myself in conflict with people (sometimes justifiably, sometimes not). I have seen how these conflicts can intensify in emotion
when people continue to think the worst about one another. These
emotions can become so heightened that there seems to be no way
of reconciling (or even communicating) with the parties in conflict.

When this occurs, I begin my campaign to pray for those who
feel extremely angered by me or are trying to harm me. I ask at least
three or four times a day that the Lord enter into their hearts, show
them His love, and bring them to Himself. The response is truly
remarkable; a great majority of the time, the person for whom I am
praying will show a marked decrease in hostility within days. Sometimes he displays an openness to compromise, and even manifests
understanding and compassion for both me and my position. This
connection between prayer and unexpected beneficial results occurs

so frequently, I recommend that people practice it not only to effect reconciliation, but also to see firsthand the power of prayer. Again, the power of the Holy Spirit to work through the hearts of intrinsically dignified human beings and to draw them toward the love for which they were created cannot be underestimated.

IV. Conclusion

As we have seen throughout this volume, the path of spiritual and moral conversion is filled with holes, bumps, curves, and reversals. Yet, there is never reason to give up or become discouraged because the Lord, through His Passion and Resurrection, has bestowed unconditional love upon the world for everyone to draw upon. Not only that; He has given us His very Body, Blood, Soul, and Divinity in the Holy Eucharist, the Sacrament of Reconciliation with definitive absolution for our sins, and His teaching about His and His Father's unconditional love. Given this, why would any of us give up hope or fall prey to discouragement? If *the Lord* does not grow weary hearing our incessant pleas for forgiveness, why would *we* grow weary asking for it? As Saint Paul asks:

> If God is for us, who is against us? He who did not spare his own Son but gave him up for us all, will he not also give us all things with him? Who shall bring any charge against God's elect? It is God who justifies; who is to condemn? Is it Christ Jesus, who died, yes, who was raised from the dead, who is at the right hand of God, who indeed intercedes for us? Who shall separate us from the love of Christ? Shall tribulation, or distress, or persecution, or famine, or nakedness, or peril, or sword? As it is written, "For your sake we are being killed all the day long; we are regarded as sheep to be slaughtered." No, in all these things we are more than conquerors through him who loved us. For I am sure that neither death, nor life, nor angels, nor principalities, nor things present, nor things to come, nor powers, nor height, nor depth, nor anything else in all creation, will be able to separate us from the love of God in Christ Jesus our Lord. (Rom 8:31–39)

Saint Claude de La Colombière, the Jesuit spiritual director of Saint Margaret Mary, who zealously promoted devotion to the Sacred

Heart, captured the spirit of hope embedded in Jesus' preaching an. Saint Paul's declaration in his prayer of hope and confidence to the Lord of love:

> My God, I believe most firmly that Thou watchest over all who hope in Thee, and that we can want for nothing when we rely upon Thee in all things; therefore I am resolved for the future to have no anxieties, and to cast all my cares upon Thee.
>
> People may deprive me of worldly goods and of honors; sickness may take from me my strength and the means of serving Thee; I may even lose Thy grace by sin; but my trust shall never leave me. I will preserve it to the last moment of my life, and the powers of hell shall seek in vain to wrestle it from me.
>
> Let others seek happiness in their wealth, in their talents; let them trust to the purity of their lives, the severity of their mortifications, to the number of their good works, the fervor of their prayers; as for me, O my God, in my very confidence lies all my hope. "For Thou, O Lord, singularly has settled me in hope" [Ps 4:10, Douay-Rheims]. This confidence can never be in vain. "No one has hoped in the Lord and has been confounded" [see Ps 30:2, Douay-Rheims].
>
> I am assured, therefore, of my eternal happiness, for I firmly hope for it, and all my hope is in Thee. "In Thee, O Lord, I have hoped; let me never be confounded."
>
> I know, alas! I know but too well that I am frail and changeable; I know the power of temptation against the strongest virtue. I have seen stars fall from heaven, and pillars of firmament totter; but these things alarm me not. While I hope in Thee I am sheltered from all misfortune, and I am sure that my trust shall endure, for I rely upon Thee to sustain this unfailing hope.
>
> Finally, I know that my confidence cannot exceed Thy bounty, and that I shall never receive less than I have hoped for from Thee. Therefore I hope that Thou wilt sustain me against my evil inclinations; that Thou wilt protect me against the most furious assaults of the evil one, and that Thou wilt cause my weakness to triumph over my most powerful enemies. I hope that Thou wilt never cease to love me, and that I shall love Thee unceasingly. "In Thee, O Lord, have I hoped; let me never be confounded."[43]

[43] "An Act of Hope and Confidence in God, by Saint Claude de la Colombiere", Catholic Saints.Info, accessed August 2, 2020, https://catholicsaints.info/an-act-of-hope-and-confidence-in-god-by-saint-claude-de-la-colombiere/.

Let us together with Saint Claude de La Colombière hope unceasingly in the Lord of unconditional mercy and love, for as he prayed, "I know that my confidence cannot exceed Thy bounty, and that I shall never receive less than I have hoped for from Thee."

CONCLUSION TO PART TWO

The Fruit of Spiritual and Moral Conversion: Love of God and Neighbor

The well-known writer on mysticism Evelyn Underhill noted that Christian mysticism was distinct from most other kinds of mysticism by the fact that the Christian mystic feels compelled to return to the world to love and serve in imitation of Christ.[1] In Volume I (Chapter 1, Section III) of this Trilogy, we gave a brief account of how Christian mystics enter into deeper spiritual and moral conversion through the dark night of the soul. Their intention is not only to purify themselves to love the Lord more deeply, but also to love their neighbor more deeply. The same holds true for people outside the monastery, who undertake moral conversion through the practical and familial demands and trials of being in the world. The first objective of our moral conversion is to purify our hearts of sensuality and egocentricity (the deadly sins) to gain protection from the Evil One and to attain deeper union with the Lord of life. This objective helps us to move concertedly toward our eternal salvation—and much more. It transforms not only our motives, but the quality of our actions, empathy, and prayers. Christ begins to shine through us—not just in our actions and words, but also in our eyes, our mannerisms, and the palpable spiritual peace and joy that we exude. As I was writing the previous sentence, I was not thinking of myself, but of some of my friends and colleagues who had reached a purity of heart that no good-willed person could deem inauthentic—"house mystics", former Carthusians, previously persecuted missionaries, and a remarkable Jesuit mentor at Georgetown University.

---

[1] See Evelyn Underhill, *Mysticism: A Study in the Nature and Development of Spiritual Consciousness* (New York: Renaissance Classics, 2012), p. 16.

As we deepen our moral conversion, the authenticity and purity of our love for others increases along with our love for God. This is the true nature of Christian spiritual conversion. Recall from Chapter 5 (Section I) that spiritual conversion leads to moral conversion, which leads to increased spiritual conversion, and in turn, to increased moral conversion in a widening spiral. Hence, the complementarity between spiritual and moral conversion leads not only to heightened love of the Lord and to our salvation, but also to deepened love of others (described in Chapter 4, Section II). This deepened love arises out of an unobscured appreciation of the unique goodness, lovability, and mystery of the other grounded in the tempering of our sensuality and egocentricity. It is, after all, egocentricity that obscures our appreciation of each person's uniquely lovable and transcendent mystery and that compels us to look for the bad news in them, and to exaggerate their problems. This obscured appreciation of others makes it quite difficult to see and appreciate others as Jesus did—and still does today. His vision of us, unobscured by ego, apprehends our unique goodness and lovability amid our imperfections. He so deeply empathizes with our goodness and lovability (amid our imperfections) that He wishes to move closer to us and to give more of Himself to us in affectionate and compassionate love. As we detach ourselves from our sensuality and egocentricity, we begin to see more clearly how genuine, beautiful, and deep His love for us is—and it almost shocks us and dazzles us, precisely as the mystics describe it. When we catch a deeper glimpse of His love through our moral conversion (which removes the obscurity of our sensuality and egocentricity from our spiritual vision), we are filled with a deep sense of spiritual peace and joy, His sublime holiness, and a sense of being perfectly at home in union with Him.

Now we can begin to understand Saint John of the Cross' exclamation in the living flame of love:

Since He is the virtue of supreme *humility*, He *loves you* with supreme humility and esteem and *makes you His equal*, gladly revealing Himself to you in these ways of knowledge, in this His countenance filled with graces, and telling you in this His union, not without great rejoicing:

"I am yours and for you and delighted to be what I am so as to be yours and give myself to you."[2]

The deeper our awareness of the love of Christ (occurring through the heightened spiritual vision of our moral conversion), the more we see others as He sees them, appreciate others as He appreciates them, and find them irresistible as He finds them to be irresistible. As a result, we cannot help ourselves—we begin to serve and love others as He serves and loves us. The purer our appreciation for the other, the more natural and effortless our service and love, entering into the very disposition and action of Jesus Himself. This is what the saints universally call "seeing others through the eyes of Christ." As we practice this love in imitation of Jesus, we bring His final commandment in the Gospel of John to fruition:

> This is my commandment, that you love one another as I have loved you. Greater love has no man than this, that a man lay down his life for his friends. (15:12–13)

As we deepen our spiritual vision of the Lord (through moral conversion), enabling us to see others through the eyes of Christ, we also see *ourselves* through the eyes of Christ. It is here that we are amazed by the depth of Christ's love for us even when we were completely unconverted. As our moral conversion and love deepen, He does not love us more, for He always loves us unconditionally. However, He is relieved and joy-filled, because we have moved away from the darkness, and there is less chance that we will be seduced by it. Now we are free to be led by Him into the fullness of His light and love. Saint Paul points to the fulfillment of this loving plan as follows:

> As it is written, "What no eye has seen, nor ear heard, nor the heart of man conceived, what God has prepared for those who love him," God has revealed to us through the Spirit. For the Spirit searches everything, even the depths of God. (1 Cor 2:9–10; quoting Is 64:4)

---

[2] Saint John of the Cross, "The Living Flame of Love", in *The Collected Works of St. John of the Cross*, ed. and trans. Kieran Kavanaugh, O.C.D., and Otilio Rodriguez, O.C.D. (Washington, D.C.: ICS Publications, 1979), p. 613 (italics added).

As we see ourselves as beloved through the eyes of Christ, we become overwhelmed with gratitude, and we respond naturally with love—not only in feeling and thought, but in action and service. This desire to serve the Lord with every fiber of our being is the objective of Saint Ignatius' final contemplation in the *Spiritual Exercises*, the Contemplation to Attain Divine Love. As noted previously, Saint Ignatius tells the retreatant to ask for the following grace:

> Second Prelude. The second, to ask for what I want. It will be here to ask for interior knowledge of so great good received, in order that being entirely grateful, I may be able in all to love and serve His Divine Majesty.[3]

The final objective of the *Spiritual Exercises* is to bring the retreatant to the point where he gives himself completely to the Lord in service. Now the question arises, how? What kind of service should I give to the Lord?

We might begin with the advice given by Saint Paul in 1 Corinthians 12—namely, to use the gifts that we have been given through the Holy Spirit:

> Now there are varieties of gifts, but the same Spirit; and there are varieties of service, but the same Lord; and there are varieties of working, but it is the same God who inspires them all in every one. To each is given the manifestation of the Spirit for the common good. To one is given through the Spirit the utterance of wisdom, and to another the utterance of knowledge according to the same Spirit, to another faith by the same Spirit, to another gifts of healing by the one Spirit, to another the working of miracles, to another prophecy, to another the ability to distinguish between spirits, to another various kinds of tongues, to another the interpretation of tongues. All these are inspired by one and the same Spirit, who apportions to each one individually as he wills.... Now you are the body of Christ and individually members of it. And God has appointed in the Church first apostles, second prophets, third teachers, then workers of miracles, then healers, helpers, administrators, speakers in various kinds of tongues. (1 Cor 12:4–11, 27–28)

---

[3] *Spiritual Exercises*, "Contemplation to Gain Love", http://sacred-texts.com/chr/seil/seil35.htm.

All of us have been given spiritual gifts to serve the Church in the ways that the Holy Spirit has designated for us. Saint Paul is encouraging us to know what our spiritual gifts are, and to find ways to use them in the service of the Church and the common good (see Volume IV, Chapter 7, Section II, of the Quartet). If you are at a point in your spiritual and moral conversion where you feel called to serve the Lord and the Church with generosity and faith, I would recommend first reaching out to a program such as the *Called and Gifted Discernment Process*, offered by the Catherine of Siena Institute, to get a better idea of your gifts and how to use them in the Lord's service.[4] Your best opportunity for service might be in the area of evangelization; catechesis; adult education; Bible studies; spiritual development; or service to the needy and sick, such as the Society of Saint Vincent de Paul and the many charities listed by Catholic Charities USA.[5] There are many other ministries and service organizations that you may want to consider, but the first place to make inquiries is through your parish and diocese. If you want to probe more deeply, you may want to consult with Catholic Charities USA. Once you have identified a possible way of serving the Church and the needy, take action—make a phone call and get involved. The Holy Spirit will lead you the minute you use your freedom to put your love into action.

Can we push our love and fervor to serve too far? Sometimes. Those who are deeply moved by the Lord to service (through spiritual and moral conversion) will probably try to serve the Lord with great fervor. Though Saint Ignatius would encourage them to follow their desires, he would also advise them to make their families their first priority and to care for their health, including psychological health (i.e., to preserve enough psychic energy to maintain self-control and the fruits of their moral conversion). Stress and overextension could lead to psychological problems, chronic fatigue, and even a loss of moral balance followed by a regression in moral life.

Recall what was said in Chapter 6 (Section VI) about the Evil One posturing as an angel of light. Since it is very difficult for him

---

[4] See their website at http://siena.org/called-gifted. For an assessment of your gifts for service, see SpiritualGiftsTest.com.

[5] See the website of Catholic Charities USA at https://www.catholiccharitiesusa.org/.

overtly to tempt a person who has undergone deep moral conversion, he must find another strategy to induce moral failure, discouragement, and despair. He does this by pushing a fervent individual to an extreme that will likely undermine his psychic energy, concentration, and psychological balance. He uses phrases like, "The Lord would be more pleased if you work harder, faster, and better: you are only working ten hours a day and seven days a week; there are far more serviceable hours left in the day. Show your love to the Lord by dedicating this additional time to Him." A fervent individual could easily run with this suggestion, only to find himself exceedingly tired, losing his concentration, feeling a bit "wobbly", and so forth. It then begins to occur to him that there is no relief in sight to regain his psychic energy, concentration, and affective balance. Without sufficient psychic energy and concentration, he no longer uses his higher cerebral faculties, but makes recourse to the functions of the lower brain—which gets him into trouble. The lower brain urges toward immediate gratification, which leads him to the doorway of the eight deadly sins. If the Evil One can push him into one of those doorways—just to get relief—the individual is likely to fall into a deep state of discouragement and regression.

So what is the solution? Try to be reflective about how much of yourself you can devote to serving the Lord out of love and fervor before you run out of psychic energy. Keep your eyes peeled for the following clues to when you are reaching your limits: a subdued desire to pray after significant progress in spiritual conversion, difficulties concentrating, feelings of being overwhelmed no matter how hard you work, difficulties finding psychic and physical energy in the morning before work, discouragement when facing the prospect of going to work (even though there is no stressful event on the calendar), difficulties curbing your sensual appetites and the images induced by the urges of the lower brain, a growing fatalistic attitude, and anxiety dreams. These symptoms may individually arise out of other causes, but if several of them begin to present themselves at the same time after significant spiritual and moral conversion, there is a strong likelihood that you are pushing your love and fervor too far and too hard, far beyond where the Lord would have you go to express them. You may be listening to the wrong spirit who is dedicated to burning you out, discouraging you, and undermining your spiritual and moral conversion. If this is the case, consult with a spiritual director, and above all, cut back on your service until you regain your psychic energy and affective balance.

Let us now return to the subject of fervor for service and love of neighbor arising out of spiritual and moral conversion. Bearing the above caveat in mind, we should not be surprised to find ourselves desiring greater commitment to the service of God and neighbor as spiritual and moral conversion deepen, even service that is exhausting, troubling, and punctuated with daily crosses. It may seem paradoxical to desire something that is difficult and painful, but when we are moved by gratitude and love of the Lord for all He has given us (especially the promise of eternal salvation), which is the fruit of deepening spiritual and moral conversion, we experience a sublime joy in the midst of painful service. The joy comes from our love of the Lord and His people as well as our imitation of His way of the Cross. Though this joy of loving the Lord through imitation and service is mixed with the Cross in this life, it is filled with the knowledge and hope that it will be brought to fulfillment in our eternal life with Him. Saint Paul synthesizes these two seemingly opposed states of soul by noting:

> Indeed I count everything as loss because of the surpassing worth of knowing Christ Jesus my Lord. For his sake I have suffered the loss of all things, and count them as refuse, in order that I may gain Christ and be found in him, not having a righteousness of my own, based on law, but that which is through faith in Christ, the righteousness from God that depends on faith; that I may know him and the power of his resurrection, and may share his sufferings, becoming like him in his death, that if possible I may attain the resurrection from the dead. (Phil 3:8–11)

Recognizing that he has been made righteous by Jesus, and the likelihood of his Resurrection, Saint Paul considers it an honor to share in the sufferings of Christ, who has given him the lasting gift of inestimable worth: eternal love. In this context, we can almost feel Paul's sublime joy arising out of his honor to share in the sufferings of Christ. The greater his effort to serve the Lord and His people, and the greater the risk of the Cross, the greater the honor and joy of service.

Saint Gregory of Nyssa expresses the same synthesis of self-sacrificial love with honor and joy in his homily on the Book of Ecclesiastes:

> As no darkness can be seen by anyone surrounded by light, so no trivialities can capture the attention of anyone who has his eyes on Christ. The man who keeps his eyes upon the head and origin of the whole universe has them on virtue in all its perfection; he has them on truth, on justice, on immortality and on everything else that is good, for Christ is goodness itself.... People are often considered blind and useless when they make the supreme Good their aim and give themselves up to the contemplation of God, but Paul made a boast of this and proclaimed himself a fool for Christ's sake. The reason he said, *We are fools for Christ's sake* was that his mind was free from all earthly preoccupations. It was as though he said, "We are blind to the life here below because our eyes are raised toward the One who is our head." And so without board or lodging he traveled from place to place, destitute, naked, exhausted by hunger and thirst. When men saw him in captivity, flogged, shipwrecked, led about in chains, they could scarcely help thinking him a pitiable sight. Nevertheless, even while he suffered all this at the hands of men, he always looked toward the One who is his head and he asked: *What can separate us from the love of Christ, which is in Jesus? Can affliction or distress? Can persecution, hunger, nakedness, danger or death?* In other words, "What can force me to take my eyes from him who is my head and to turn them toward things that are contemptible?" He bids us follow his example: *Seek the things that are above*, he says, which is only another way of saying: "Keep your eyes on Christ."[6]

The fruit of spiritual and moral conversion is great gratitude and love of Christ, and the fruit of great gratitude and love of Christ is the desire to serve Him (even at great cost). This desire to serve—this honor and joy of service—leads to great love of neighbor by opening us to see our neighbor through Christ's eyes while seeing Christ in our neighbor. As Jesus and all the saints tell us, this paradoxical freedom, desire, honor, and joy of self-sacrificial love leads not only to *our* salvation, but also to the salvation of those we touch. Jesus expresses this movingly in the Gospel of John:

---

[6] Saint Gregory of Nyssa, "Homily on Ecclesiastes", Homily 5, *Patrologia Graeca*, vol. 44, trans. *Liturgy of the Hours* (Totowa, N.J.: Catholic Book Publishing, 1990).

These things I have spoken to you, that my joy may be in you, and
that your joy may be full. This is my commandment, that you love
one another as I have loved you. Greater love has no man than this,
that a man lay down his life for his friends. (15:11–13)

In His last discourse to His disciples, Jesus presents the paradox of
joy and self-sacrificial love standing at the heart of His teaching. At
this point in His ministry, the apostles are ready to hear it, having
experienced deep spiritual and moral conversion in His presence.
He begins by telling them the reason for His teaching, that His joy
may be theirs and their joy complete. He then sums up His teaching
in a single commandment, "Love one another as I have loved you,"
indicating that the highest possible love is to give up one's life for
one's friends. The implication is clear: those who sacrifice themselves
completely for love of God and neighbor will experience joy in this
life and complete joy in the life to come.

It takes great faith to throw ourselves into this paradox of joy and
self-sacrificial love, but Gregory of Nyssa (in the above passage) gives
us a clue to doing it: keeping our eyes fixed on the teaching and
example of Jesus (our Emmanuel, our "God with us"), which in turn
focuses us on goodness itself:

The man who keeps his eyes upon the head and origin of the whole
universe [Jesus] has them on virtue in all its perfection; he has them
on truth, on justice, on immortality and on everything else that is
good, for Christ is goodness itself.[7]

Saint Gregory here gives us a concise summary of spiritual and moral
conversion; for spiritual conversion is none else than fixing our gaze
upon the one we love—Christ Jesus—in order to follow Him, and
moral conversion is none else than following the example we see as
we fix our gaze on Christ Jesus—"Virtue in all its perfection . . . truth,
justice, immortality and everything else that is good." If we follow
Him in faith, His joy will be ours, and our joy complete.

Saint Ignatius of Loyola knew and lived this paradox well, expressing it in the Suscipe, discussed in Chapter 5.

---

[7] Ibid.

Take, Lord, and receive all my liberty,
my memory, my understanding,
and my entire will,
All I have and call my own.
You have given all to me.
To you, Lord, I return it.
Everything is yours; do with it what you will.
Give me only your love and your grace,
that is enough for me.[8]

Saint Ignatius said repeatedly that love is best manifest through service and action, and so he composed a complementary prayer to ask for the grace to serve with great generosity, love, freedom, honor and joy:

Lord Jesus, teach me to be generous.
Teach me to serve you as you deserve,
To give and not to count the cost,
To fight and not to heed the wounds,
To toil and not to seek for rest,
To labor and not to seek for reward,
Except that of knowing that I do your will.
Amen.[9]

Saint Paul, Saint John, Saint Gregory of Nyssa, and Saint Ignatius of Loyola were no strangers to the hardships of following Jesus Christ in times and places of extreme difficulty. Yet all of them, indeed all the saints, were bathed in the honor and joy of serving the Lord they loved, imitating "Christ [who] plays in ten thousand places, / Lovely in limbs, and lovely in eyes not his / To the Father through the features of men's faces."[10]

---

[8] "Suscipe", Loyola Press (website), 2020, https://www.loyolapress.com/our-catholic-faith/prayer/traditional-catholic-prayers/saints-prayers/suscipe-prayer-saint-ignatius-of-loyola.

[9] Saint Ignatius of Loyola, "To Give and Not to Count the Cost", IgnatianSpirituality.com, 2020, https://www.ignatianspirituality.com/19060/to-give-and-not-to-count-the-cost.

[10] Gerard Manley Hopkins, "As Kingfishers Catch Fire", Poetry Foundation (website), 2020, quoting Gerard Manley Hopkins, Poems and Prose, Penguin Classics (New York: Penguin Books, 1985), https://www.poetryfoundation.org/poems/44389/as-kingfishers-catch-fire.

This paradox of joy amid the Cross is but a pale glimmer of the eternal ecstasy prepared by the Lord for those who love Him. As Jesus showed through His own Resurrection, the faithful may expect a transformation of their physical bodies into a glorious, spiritual, powerful, imperishable, and awesome reality similar to His own risen body (see 1 Cor 15:42–55; 1 Jn 3:2) and to be brought to a state of peace, joy, and glory in which all suffering will cease and every tear be wiped away (see Rev 21:4). They may expect to be completely freed from the influence of spiritual evil and purified in love and sacredness (Rev 21:1–27). They may expect to see and be seen by all the blessed through the eyes of love unobscured by egocentricity and base sensuality (see 1 Jn 4:8–12) and to be invited to the banquet of the communion of saints, where they will encounter not only the great canonized saints but all the unheralded ones along with the Father, Son, and Holy Spirit themselves (see Lk 13:29). They may expect to be surrounded by the whole created world liberated from its futility into the glory for which it was created (see Rom 8:18–23).

In sum, the faithful may expect joy upon joy, the joy of loving perfectly and being loved perfectly, the joy of being in perfect communion with all the blessed and the Persons of the Trinity themselves, the joy of being transformed into the glorious image of the risen Christ, the joy of being surrounded by the whole of creation brought to its proper state of glory, the joy of being free from sin and evil, and the joy of being brought to eternal fulfillment in intellect, affect, goodness, and sacredness. They may expect an ecstasy so profound that time itself will stand still at the moment they are swept into enormous bliss—and it will last forever.

Just a pipe dream? Hardly! As we have shown in Volumes II and III of the Quartet, the evidence for Jesus' Resurrection and gift of the Holy Spirit is quite compelling, including thousands of verified accounts of transphysical consciousness after bodily death from peer-reviewed medical studies of near-death experiences; the scientific investigation of evidence for the Resurrection regarding the Shroud of Turin; and the scientific investigation of contemporary validated miracles associated with Mary, the saints, and the Eucharist; as well as historico-exegetical studies of the New Testament—not to mention the new evidence for God from contemporary physics and philosophy. And if this is not enough, simply look within yourself to your own yearning for ultimacy, your own experience of the numinous and sacred, your own sense of conscience, and your own desire for perfect truth, love, goodness, beauty, and home—your desire for communion with truth itself, love itself, goodness itself, beauty itself, and being itself. Simply consider your own resonance with the prayer of Saint Augustine:

> For Thou has made us for Thyself and our hearts are restless until they rest in thee.[11]

---

[11] *Confessions* 1, 1.

Appendix I

A Summary of the Four Levels of Desire/Happiness

The four levels of desire (happiness) have been mentioned several times throughout this book. I have given a detailed explanation of this philosophical–anthropological model in Volume I of the Quartet. This appendix is only a brief summary of that volume, to give readers sufficient knowledge to read the present volume.

Level One is the desire for externally stimulated or physical pleasures and possessions (e.g., a bowl of linguini or a new Mercedes e-Class with leather upholstery).

Level Two is ego-gratification coming from increases in status, admiration, achievement, power, control, winning, and so forth, and generally entails a comparative advantage, such as, "I am more intelligent than you", or "I have more prestige or esteem than you", or "I have a higher position and make more money than you", or "I have achieved more than you." These comparative advantages can lead to fixation and extremely negative emotive conditions (see below).

The third level of happiness moves in the opposite direction of Level Two. Instead of trying to be better than others, Level Three seeks to contribute to others. It invests our gifts and energy in the world around us by making an optimal positive difference to the world (e.g., to family, friends, organization, community, church, culture, and Kingdom of God) with our time, talents, energy, and our lives. It is actualized through our actions and our presence to others (spending time with and listening to them). It occurs most powerfully through *agapē*—love without expectation of return; love for the sake of the beloved (see Chapter 4, Section II).

Level Four is the desire for the ultimate, unconditional, and perfect in truth, love, goodness, beauty, and being. People of faith identify perfect and unconditional truth, love, goodness, beauty, and being with God, and so Level Four, for people of faith, is the desire for God. It is the fullest expression of our nature, dignity, and destiny.

The above four levels of desire (happiness) are summarized in the diagram on the next page.

As one moves *up* the four levels of desire, one attains more pervasive, enduring, and deep purpose in life. For example, Level Three and Level Four purpose have a much greater effect in the world (more *pervasive*) than a Level One or Level Two purpose (which is restricted to *self*-benefit). Similarly, Level Three and Level Four purpose *endure* much longer than Level One or Level Two purpose. Level Four purpose even endures unto eternity. Finally, Level Three and Level Four purpose are *deeper* (utilizing our higher powers of creativity, intellection, moral reasoning, love, and spiritual awareness) than Level One or Level Two purpose. If efficacy in life is determined by the pervasiveness, endurance, and depth of our actions, then the higher we move up the levels of desire, the greater the effectiveness of our lives.

The only "down side" to this ascendancy of effectiveness and purpose in life is that we have to delay gratification, look beneath and beyond the surface of life, and give up some degree of intensity. It is clear that Level One is immediately gratifying, surface apparent, and intense, while Level Four frequently requires nuance, education, subtlety, delay in gratification, and detachment from intensity. Thus, the spiritual life is marked by a trade-off, in order to attain universal and eternal effects arising out of our self-transcendent powers of truth, love, goodness, beauty, and being; we frequently have to give up some degree of immediate gratification, intensity, and surface apparentness.

This "trade-off" marks one of the most difficult challenges of the spiritual life, for it is not easy to let go of what is so easily and intensely satisfying. Yet, it is worth it, for the move to Levels Three and Four fills us with higher purpose, more enduring (even eternal) effects, and awakens the highest, most sophisticated powers within us. Far more than this, Level Four introduces us to a deep relationship with the unconditionally loving God (which helps us become like Jesus in love and joy through spiritual and moral conversion [see Chapters 2–7]). Thus, Level Four simultaneously actualizes our humanity and spiritual life.

Four Levels of Desire/Happiness

4

Ultimate or Unconditional Purpose

Objective: Seek and live in ultimate Truth, Love, Goodness, Justice, and Being (Platonic transcendentals).

Characteristics: Seeing the unconditional, unrestricted, perfect, eternal in above transcendentals. Can come from pursuit of transcendentals or faith/God/religion. Optimal pervasiveness, endurance, and depth.

3

Contributive (Ego-out)

Objective: Optimize positive difference in the world. (The world is better off for my having lived.) Comes from "doing for" and "being with".

Characteristics: More pervasive (positive effects beyond self), enduring (lasts longer), and deep (using highest creative and psychological powers). Can come from generosity, magnanimity, altruism, love.

2

Comparative (Ego-in)

Objective: Shift locus of control to self (ego) and gain comparative advantage in status, esteem, power, control, winning, and success.

Characteristics: Intense ego-gratification (sense of progress, superiority, and esteemability). If dominant, then fear of failure, ego-sensitivity, ego-blame/rage, self-pity, inferiority, suspicion, resentment.

1

Physical/External Stimulus

Objective: The pleasure or material object itself (nothing beyond this).

Characteristics: Immediate gratification, surface apparent, and intensity of stimulus. No desire for common, intrinsic, or ultimate good.

Any of the levels of desire can become dominant, and when one of them does, it becomes our purpose in life and our identity. We can only be *ultimately* satisfied by a Level Four identity, because our desire for the unconditional and perfect in truth, love, goodness, beauty, and being can never be satiated by what is conditioned or imperfect. Inasmuch as God is the one and only Being that can be perfect truth, love, goodness, beauty, and being (see Volume II, Chapter 4, of the Quartet), then only God can bring us to true fulfillment and happiness. This is borne out in the study of the American Psychiatric Association showing that nonreligiously affiliated people have significantly higher rates of depression, impulsivity, aggressivity, familial tensions, substance abuse, and suicides.[1]

Most of us do not come to this insight intuitively, but rather through the school of hard knocks. We obsess upon the material/physical world (Level One) and the ego/comparative world (Level Two) because they are so immediately gratifying, intense, and surface-apparent. It is hard to loosen our grip on them, even in order to pursue what is more pervasive, enduring, and deep; even to pursue what is eternal, perfect, and unconditional; even to pursue the ultimate fulfillment of our being. Thus, most of us move through a series of trials and tribulations that manifest the pain of overinvesting in what is beneath our ultimate dignity and nature. The most popular overinvestment in our culture is the one directed at Level Two, and so I will illustrate it here. I have written extensively about other overinvestments in Volume I of the Quartet.

Level Two (ego-gratification) is almost always linked to comparisons. In order to shift the locus of control from the outer world to the inner world, I must constantly ask myself, "Who's achieving more? Who's achieving less? Who's making more progress? Whose making less? Who's winning? Who's losing? Who's got more status? Who's got less status? Who's more popular? Who's less popular? Who's got more control? Who's got less control? Who is more admired? Who is less admired?" Notice that these questions are not linked to a pursuit of the truth or to a contributive mentality, or to

[1] See Kanita Dervic et al., "Religious Affiliation and Suicide Attempt", *American Journal of Psychiatry* 161, no. 12 (December 2004): 2303–8, http://ajp.psychiatryonline.org/article.aspx?articleid=177228.

an ultimate meaning of life. One is using these comparative questions to obtain identity. Thus, one is literally living for a Level Two answer to these questions and is therefore treating these comparative characteristics as *ends in themselves*. Hence, one is not achieving in order to contribute to family, colleagues, or the culture; one is achieving as an end in itself, as if achievement gives life meaning. Similarly, one is not seeking status in order to have the credibility to do good for others or even the Kingdom of God. One is simply seeking status as an end in itself. The same holds for winning, power, control, and so forth.

Notice further that Level Two is not bad. Indeed, quite the opposite. The desire for achievement leads to progress in civilization. The desire for respect leads to credibility, confidence, and self-respect. The desire to win leads to competitiveness and the seeking of excellence. Even the desire for power can be used for good purposes. So what's the problem? The problem is not Level Two, but living for Level Two *as an end in itself*. When we do this, then achievement leads to compulsive "getting ahead", instead of "a good beyond the achievement". Seeking respect leads to pandering after admiration. Power sought as an end in itself corrupts—and absolute power sought in itself corrupts absolutely.

A variety of consequences follows from this narrow purpose in life: one may feel emptiness arising out of "underliving life". The desire to make a positive difference (or even an *optimal* positive difference) to family, friends, community, organization, colleagues, church, culture, and society (Level Three) goes unfulfilled. We begin to think that our life doesn't really make any difference to the world or to history— "the world is not better off for my having lived." To make matters worse, our desire for the ultimate (in truth, love, goodness, beauty, and being, i.e., God) is also unfulfilled. Though we long for the ultimate with all our heart, our obsession with Level Two precludes the pursuit of Level Four. Again, our spirit reacts with a profound sense of emptiness, a sense of underliving life, a more and more poignant awareness that "I am wasting the little precious time I have in this world."

Furthermore, a large array of negative emotions begins to accompany this emptiness. Most of these emotions arise out of a fixation on comparative advantage. Since a dominant Level Two identity treats status, admiration, power, control, winning, and so forth as ends in themselves, it is compelled to seek comparative advantage as its fulfillment. This fixation requires not only that we progress more and more (in status, power, winning, etc.), but also that we have *more* of it than Joe, Sue, Frank, and Mary. When we do not have more, when we are not better than others, we profoundly believe that our lives are either stagnant or slipping away. We feel a profound diminishment in self-worth and success. And so we begin to feel jealousy, a malaise about life, inferiority, loneliness, frustration, and even a terrible sense of self-pity and resentment.

We might respond that these negative emotions do not befall the dominant Level Two *winner*, for to the victor go the spoils. While it is true that winners do receive significant ego-gratification, the above-mentioned emptiness still follows in its wake. Furthermore, such winners are obliged to increase in their Level Two successes, because they cannot attain any sense of progress without doing so. If they do not continually increase in their successes, they experience the same kinds of malaise, inferiority, jealousy, frustration, and self-pity as nonwinners.

Moreover, these winners contract a peculiar disease—namely, the desire to be overtly admired. When perceived inferiors do not acknowledge the winner's superiority (and their own inferiority by comparison), the winner feels tremendous resentment. "You have not given me the accolades I deserve. And furthermore, you are actually treating yourself as my equal—who do you think you are? It's outrageous." This peculiar disease has another aspect that Saint Augustine well recognized—namely, contempt. Dominant Level Two winners can't help it. They really do feel that their lives are worth more than other people's lives, and so they either project contempt or (if they are more enlightened) they are patronizingly condescending ("That's a nice *little* project you did there"). In the end, such winners cannot afford to fail; if they do, those whom they have treated with contempt will ravage them.

Furthermore, a winner's self-image cannot tolerate being embarrassed in front of inferiors ("Spitzer, you pronounced the word 'spectroscopy' improperly three times. I cannot believe that a person of your caliber would make such a mistake." I go to my room, close the door, and play that excruciating tape over and over again in my mind until I want to do myself physical harm, for the physical pain would be so much better than ... "I can't believe I made that mistake in public. Aaarrgghh!"). Dominant Level Two winners also feel the need to blame others for all their failures (because, in principle, they cannot fail).

In sum, winners better be perfect; but then again, they can't be altogether perfect. So winners must construct a huge façade and then protect it; but then again, they cannot construct a façade impenetrable enough to keep observant inferiors at bay. So dominant Level Two winners better be prepared for contempt, resentment, blame, anger, debilitating ego-sensitivities, and above all, loneliness—for no one (except Mother Teresa, and maybe their own mothers) will want to be around them for any other reason than sheer necessity. The reason I know all these things is because I have struggled and continue to struggle with these negative emotions (from both winning and losing). Nevertheless, I can attest that Level Three (contributive/love) and Level Four (transcendent/spiritual life) help immeasurably to diminish the pain, emptiness, and obsession of a dominant Level Two identity. Indeed, as will be seen, the spiritual life can break the grip of a dominant Level Two identity and usher in a life of sublimity in God.

We can begin the process of extricating ourselves from the problems of Level One and Level Two dominance by intentionally moving to Level Three (contributive) identity. As explained in Volume I (Chapters 3–5) of the Quartet, this can be facilitated by explicitizing how we can optimize our contribution to family, friends, workplace, community, church, Kingdom of God, culture, and if we are so fortunate, even society—and then devoting ourselves to fulfilling these objectives. We can also facilitate our Level Three transition by looking for the good news in others and adjusting our view of freedom (toward "freedom for" rather than "freedom from").

Though these solutions can certainly help us break the spell of Level One and Level Two dominance, they are unlikely to be successful without the help of prayer and grace. Furthermore, Level Three identity (without Level Four) will not ultimately satisfy us. Without faith, prayer, and grace, we will feel the absence of God and ultimate fulfillment in Him—feeling a sense of cosmic emptiness, alienation, and loneliness, giving rise to the debilitating conditions explained by the American Psychiatric Association study mentioned above.[2] Additionally, without grace and prayer, we will be more vulnerable to the Evil One's temptations toward the deadly sins, potentially jeopardizing our salvation. If we are to avoid these major problems, pursue our highest purpose in life, and concertedly pursue the path to salvation, we will want to move toward Level Four—that is, faith and relationship with the Lord.

In Volume III of the Quartet, we explain why Jesus Christ is the highest and most fruitful way of pursuing Level Four (faith) identity. Jesus revealed that love is truly the most positive and creative power we possess and that it is the highest virtue, leading toward the highest purpose of life. If we affirm these truths about love for ourselves, we will know in our hearts that Jesus possesses the key to ultimate purpose in life. We then explain that Jesus' definition of love, His teaching about His Father's unconditional love, and His demonstration of unconditional love in His life and Passion point to Him as the definitive self-revelation of God, and even to His being *Emmanuel*—"God with us". After examining the evidence for His Resurrection in glory, gift of the Holy Spirit, and miracles by His own authority as well as the power of the Holy Spirit today and the contemporary scientifically validated miracles connected with Him (e.g., with respect to His Mother, the Eucharist, and the saints),[3] we concluded that it is both reasonable and responsible to have faith in Him as the Son of God.

In Catholic and Christian religious faith, "living on Level Four" means desiring the unconditionally loving, good, truth-filled, and salvific will of the unconditionally loving God manifest in Jesus Christ. As we have seen throughout this volume, bringing this desire to fruition entails spiritual and moral conversion. We not only have to know the teaching of Jesus (as interpreted by the Church); we must also engage in spiritual conversion—that is, participate in the Church community (Chapter 1) and the sacraments (Chapter 2), and develop a relationship with the Lord in contemplative prayer (Chapter 3). Beyond this, we must engage in moral conversion—trying to appropriate virtue to avoid the deadly sins (Chapter 4) and facilitate the ascendency of

---

[2] Ibid.

[3] This evidence is explained thoroughly in Volumes II and III of the Quartet as well as in the appendix to Volume I of this Trilogy. For a brief review of the evidence and its sources, see the Introduction to this volume.

the higher self (the "new nature/man") in our conscious and subconscious mind (Chapters 5 and 6).

Slowly but surely, Levels Three and Four begin to replace the deep attachment to Levels One and Two, bringing with them a decrease in jealousy, fear, anger, egocentricity, self-pity, contempt, inferiority, superiority, ego-sensitivity, and so many other debilitating emotive states. In their place, Level Four (arising out of a deep relationship with the unconditionally loving God) brings peace, inspiration, zeal, hope, a remarkable efficacy in life, and above all, love (even progress toward unconditional love). In sum, as we progress in Level Four identity through spiritual and moral conversion, we will notice greater freedom to love (in imitation of Christ); greater capacity to resist temptation; greater faith, hope, and love; more intimate communion with the Lord; a greater sense of purpose, dignity, and eternal destiny; and as a result, greater assurance toward salvation and deeper happiness.

As will by now be clear, the most effective way of moving from Levels One and Two to Levels Three and Four is through God's grace, and the most effective way of allowing God's grace to work in us is through the Catholic Church, spiritual conversion, and moral conversion.

Appendix II

Spontaneous and Common Prayers

Introduction

The following prayers can be quite helpful in daily life, and in initiating a life of contemplative prayer (see Chapter 3, Section III). We will treat three kinds of prayer:

1. Spontaneous Prayers (Section I)
2. Psalms for Daily Prayer (Section II)
3. Popular Catholic Devotional Prayers (Section III)

I. Spontaneous Prayers

Spontaneous prayers are short, effective, "easy to remember" vehicles for grace in daily life. If we are to avail ourselves of the grace that God wants to give us, we should have a variety of these at hand for use in times of trial, forgiveness, temptation, and so forth. I will speak of two groups of spontaneous prayers in this appendix:

1. Prayers in Times of Trial, Suffering, and Anxiety (Section I.A)
2. Prayers of Gratitude and Abandonment to Divine Providence (Section I.B)

Recall that spontaneous prayers for forgiveness and offering forgiveness are treated in Chapter 7 (Section III) of this volume.

A. Prayers in Times of Trial, Suffering, and Anxiety

The first and most important prayer here is "Help". We oftentimes forget it because we think it is too easy, or that God would not respond

533

to something that simple; but if God really is Unconditional Love, and God not only hears us but wants to help us in our time of need, then the prayer "Help" should be more than sufficient to incite the heart of God toward a myriad of unexpected graces. This prayer can be further (and beneficially) specified by a variety of other prayers. I will here mention only six of them that have been very important in my own life.

The Hail Mary. This prayer has been not only a foundational contemplative prayer, but also one of galvanizing grace in times of trouble. Our Blessed Mother's consoling presence seems to be evoked (along with her help) during the most desperate of times. This prayer, when repeated, opens upon a consolation filled at once with familial strength, a mother's understanding, and the assistance for a "child not fully in control". It seems to activate a providence (a conspiracy of grace) that betokens a mother's request of her son, much like the Wedding Feast at Cana (Jn 2:1–12).

Countless have been the times when it has come naturally to my mind, inviting me to repeat it. Countless, too, have been the times when that repetition has led to increasing peace of mind and clarity of thought. It always seems to give me courage—the courage to do what is right, to face adversaries, to move ahead with unpopular plans, and to bear the possibility of defeat bravely. Jesus intended that His family be our family, and that His Mother be our Mother (Jn 19: 27); and so we can believe that she would do for us everything she would do for Her Son—particularly comforting us, interceding for us, and being protectively present to us. Speaking from experience, in my times of need, I have never been disappointed by her. For a detailed explanation of Marian devotion, see Chapter 3, Section VI.

"Lord, make optimal good come out of this suffering." Sometimes trials turn into suffering, and sometimes suffering has neither speedy relief nor obvious meaning. At these times, it is essential to ask for the Lord's help to optimize the good in suffering (good for oneself, good for others, good for the community, and even good for the Mystical Body of Christ). Suffering can be debilitating and depressing, if we do not see any good coming from it. However, if we recognize a good in suffering for ourselves, others, the culture, the community, and even the Mystical Body of Christ, suffering can become not only meaningful, but an invaluable companion in the life of grace, virtue, and salvation. The above prayer has helped me to invoke the Lord's blessings upon my suffering (and to recognize that blessing) in the deepest ways.

When I first became aware of the onset of a serious eye problem six months before my ordination to the priesthood, I was completely baffled. Fortunately, I knew that God's providential love would be operative in this challenge throughout the rest of my life. In that faith, I began to pray, "Lord, do not waste one scintilla of this suffering. Make some good come out of it for me (a change in life direction, a deepening of faith and love, a protection from other adversity), for others (a zeal for Your Kingdom, a desire to help others, an empathy with those in need, and an eagerness to serve the Kingdom), for the culture, and for the community. Lord, please *optimize* the good that can come from this suffering." The Lord has certainly answered this prayer, for He has deepened my sense of gratitude for what I *do* have; He has helped me to see that every day and every moment counts in manifesting His love and presence; He has made me far more circumspect about what matters and doesn't matter; and He has deepened my appreciation for the Beatitudes and the love intrinsic to them. I frankly cannot imagine what my priesthood or apostolic zeal would be like without my challenge. But I do know this: it would be less, much less.

"Lord, snatch victory from the jaws of defeat." This prayer is essential when a situation has grown out of control with so many possibilities for increasingly bad results that we cannot keep track of them. We all experience these situations where problems seem to be compounded again and again. It begins with one or two things going wrong and then something else—perhaps with the family or friends—and then something at work goes wrong, and then when you're leaving work in a completely dilapidated condition you get a flat tire, and people are screaming at you, "Get out of the way!" These scenes happen to just about everyone—including those living in a monastery.

This little spontaneous prayer has the capacity to move me from *self*-reliance to trust in the Lord's "conspiracy of providence". I sometimes repeat it by saying, "Lord, *You* snatch victory from the jaws of defeat. *You* use your wisdom and power to untangle this web of problems—I'm going to remain in the background for the moment." When I say this, I find that my first fatal error—believing that *I* have to resolve all problems—is mitigated. It seems that the Holy Spirit reaches into my consciousness and gives me enough peace to let go of my obsessive need to solve the entangled web of problems all by myself—right now.

"Lord, I offer it up." One of the great mysteries of Christian life is that our suffering can (with Christ's) help in the redemption of others. This is best explained in Jesus' final words on the Cross, reciting Psalm 22:1—"My God, my God, why have you forsaken me?" (Mt 27:46). Jesus, here, was not referring only to the first line of that psalm, but rather to the psalm in its entirety. When we read the psalm, we notice a man who is going through a set of trials uncannily similar to Jesus' own sufferings on the Cross—but more importantly, that the psalmist is not discouraged by the trials being suffered. He has a deep trust and confidence that God will use His sufferings not only for the good of the community around Him, but also to bring all the nations to Himself in the future. Thus, when Jesus recited the words, "My God, my God, why have you forsaken me," He moved beyond the note of lamentation (in the first line) to a sublime confidence that the Father would effect universal salvation through His suffering. Jesus' Passion is His free gift of self—that is, His unconditional love. When Jesus was dying on the Cross, He created a "gift of self"— that is, an unconditional love (as scapegoat, as Paschal Lamb, and as Blood of the covenant)—which He intended to give to the Father to shower down upon mankind so that all the nations might come into His Kingdom of unconditional love.

We can imitate Christ in our own limited ways by presenting our sufferings to the Father as a "gift of self" (love) for the Father to shower down upon mankind as a grace to strengthen and unify the Mystical Body of Christ. Every moment of suffering is a potential for a gift of love (grace) to be given to mankind and specific individuals in their need—for the salvation of souls, for reparation for sins, for assistance in Purgatory, for the Church throughout the world, and so forth. All we need do to convert suffering into grace for the world is to *offer it up* to the Father as our gift of self.

When I was a child, I would complain to my mother about various things that had gone wrong at school, and she would say, very matter-of-factly, "Offer it up." My general reaction was, "I'm always offering it up, and no resolution seems to come from it." It only occurred to me years later that the offering was not intended to be a *direct* benefit to *me*, but rather a benefit for the world and the Kingdom, which would eventually become my life's purpose and passion. By offering up my sufferings to God, I turn it into self-sacrifice—into gift of self, which Jesus taught is "love for the life of the world". When I offer my suffering as a self-offering (act of love) to the Father, and ask Him to make it a source of grace for those who need it, I know that He will do this just as He did it for His Son. In this way, the negativity of suffering turns into the positivity of self-offering, love, and grace. My mother used to say, "Mothers know everything." In this particular case, that was true.

"I give up, Lord. You take care of it." Sometimes life gets out of control. No matter how hard we try to obviate freefall or to figure ourselves out, life's circumstances seem to get the better of us. It is at these moments that I recommend the above prayer, which I have put to great use throughout my life.

I recall my discovery of this prayer in Rome back in 1980. I had been sent to the Gregorian University to take all of my theology classes in Italian. I went to Italy two months early without any background in Italian, to attain "fluency". I was reasonably confident after studying the language in Perugia for two months that I would be able to understand my classes. My first class on the first day was an exegesis class on the Gospel of Matthew taught by an intelligent Cuban professor who spoke Italian faster than the Italians. I was not able to understand 25 percent of what he was saying, and began to panic. I kept thinking to myself (in my unqualified ignorance) that I was going to "go down". What would I say to my Provincial? To my classmates? "Here I am, back in the United States. I couldn't understand anything and I flunked out." Needless to say, I began to feel considerable discomfort. Realizing that circumstances were quite out of my control, I muttered, "I give up, Lord. You take care of it!" When I said this it seemed like steam came out of my ears. A pressure was relieved by simply giving it over to the Lord, who could providentially bring some good out of my predicament. As a matter of fact, He did. The moment this prayer enabled me to calm down, I became content with understanding partial sentences and concepts. I could then begin to make sense out of the general line of thought, which in turn built my confidence, and in turn enabled me to understand more. As the semester progressed, I began to understand far more of what the professor was saying and eventually made it to the final exam, where the professor gave two or three choices of questions for various passages of Scripture. I was able to choose questions that pertained to the last parts of the course, thereby hiding my inadequate understanding of the first part. In the end, I did quite well. (Thank You, Lord!)

Evidently, much of that success is attributable to my *natural* gradual appropriation of the Italian language and exegetical method, but much of it, in my opinion, was due to the composure and openness to the content as well as the Lord's grace, induced by my trust in the Lord of love. That trust was galvanized through the above simple prayer: "I give up, Lord. You take care of it."

"Lord, push back the foreboding and darkness." Foreboding is a complex phenomenon. Some of it can come from feelings of anxiety and depression that our conscious or unconscious psyche projects into the future—so it is internally, psychologically induced. To those, who like myself, are not materialists, there is another side to foreboding—a genuine premonition about darkness or evil in the future. I am uncertain about the cause of such premonitions—whether they are a warning from God, harassment from an evil spirit, or a kind of psychic protention (intrusion) into an impending future. They could be the result of two or three of these causes. Whatever the cause, I believe that foreboding is not completely psychological, and that it does portend some kind of future darkness. I believe this for the simple reason that most of the times I experience it, something dark does in fact happen a few days later. It contains not only a sense of darkness, but powerlessness toward the darkness, and resembles the descriptions of it by prophets (like Jeremiah, Ezekiel, and Isaiah)—mythologists (like Thomas Malory and J. R. R. Tolkien) and litterateurs (like Sophocles and Shakespeare).

When these premonitions are accompanied by feelings of powerlessness and anxiety, I refuse to entertain them. I give them over to the Lord immediately by saying the simple prayer, "Lord, push back this darkness and foreboding." I even use my hands to gesture pushing back against something palpable while I repeat the prayer: "Lord, push it back." Since I'm fairly sure that something dark or harmful is about to happen to me, I also use this follow-up prayer—"Lord, take care of the dark situation that is about to befall me—please protect me and minimize the harm that may come to me." I frequently repeat that prayer until the foreboding begins to subside. Most of the time, the foreboding *does* subside. It does so in stages—first, it loses its bite and intensity, then it gradually weakens, and finally after some time, a sense of normalcy or even consolation occurs. I can think of only a few occasions when the sense of normalcy-consolation did not occur—though the sense of foreboding decreased considerably.

B. Prayers of Gratitude and Abandonment to Divine Providence

"Thank You!" This is one of the most important prayers for all followers of Jesus, because it anchors us in the real truth of life—namely, that we have been blessed and loved by God and will continue to be so, even in the midst of setbacks and misfortune. When we are grateful for our blessings, we take nothing for granted. However, when we are ungrateful, we take most everything for granted, resenting the Lord for giving us less than others and making life comparatively difficult. A life of resentment leads to anger, envy, and detachment from God, which ultimately incites profound unhappiness and even despair. As virtually every saint tells us, simple prayers of gratitude to the Lord—even in times of challenge and suffering—can dispel anger, envy, and depression through close connection with the One who is using our suffering to lead us to salvation. Gratitude also dispels the power of the deadly sins (and therefore the Evil One) and ushers us into a life of contemplation. A good way to pray this brief prayer profoundly is to recall first our supernatural blessings—for example, our transcendent and eternal soul, our redemption by Jesus, and the gift of the Holy Spirit and the Church to guide us—and then our natural blessings (e.g., our family, friends, education, talents, and opportunities, and even such things as the beauty of nature, music, and architecture). As we review these blessings, we need only say,

"Thank You," because this one simple word/idea—this one simple prayer—connects us with both God and His love through His blessings. An excellent way of preparing to make this prayer profoundly is to create your personal "Book of Gratitude". I explain this in Chapter 3 (Section III.A.3) of this volume.

As noted in Chapter 6, Saint Ignatius of Loyola grounded his Examen Prayer in the prayer of gratitude. He also formulated his final contemplation in the *Spiritual Exercises*, called the Contemplation to Attain Divine Love, on the basis of giving God thanks for both the supernatural and natural blessings in life. When we give God sincere thanks for our blessings, His love becomes apparent, which enables us to *trust* Him—even in times of suffering. This trust, in turn, enables us to hope in our future, look for His guidance, recognize His providential hand, and see the potential for good—to us, others, the Church, and the world—that can come from our suffering. By saying this simple prayer sincerely and frequently, we will find consolation in our suffering, experience a deep sense of God's personal love for us in the past and present, and encounter God's grace pulling us ever more deeply and firmly into His eternal salvation.

"Thy loving will be done." In my view, the most important spontaneous prayer of all is "Thy loving will be done." Jesus teaches us this prayer in the Our Father (Mt 6:10) and uses it Himself during His Agony in the Garden (Mt 26:42). Since that time, it has become a centerpiece of Catholic and Christian spiritual life. It can be used in times of fear, temptation, anger, trial; indeed, it may be substituted for all the spontaneous prayers given above. If you cannot remember any other prayer, default to this one.

Why? Because the will of God is optimally loving, optimally good, optimally just, and optimally salvific; and when the will of God is working through you, you become an instrument of God's optimally loving, good, just, and salvific will in the world—you become the agent of a legacy that will last into eternity, an agent for the Kingdom of God manifest on earth and perpetuated for eternity. There could be no more worthy purpose for living than this, which is why this prayer can make good come out of the harms we may have caused and the trials we endure, can calm us in the heat of anger, can help us in times of temptation, and can bring salvation out of every seemingly negative course of events. If we give our problems over to God by praying, "Thy loving will be done," He will bring good for us, others, the community, the culture, and His Kingdom out of the most bizarre, tragic, desolate, angering, hurtful, fearful, tempting, and confusing dimensions of our lives. In His loving and efficacious will, there is peace—a peace beyond all understanding (Phil 4:7). I say this prayer at least twenty-five times a day, and I find the all-loving will of God and the immense providence of the Holy Spirit to be unbelievably efficacious and transformative.

There is only one thing to remember. We cannot have the wrong attitude about God or His will when we say this prayer. If we forget that God is Abba, the Father of the prodigal son, the Father of Jesus the Beloved One, and Unconditional Love itself, then we will start attributing antithetical qualities to Him, such as stoic indifference, competition with us, getting even with us for past offenses, anger and retribution, lack of forgiveness and mercy, unkindness, and boastfulness. These false characterizations of God, which run contrary to the hymn to love in 1 Corinthians 13, serve only to undermine our relationship with the unconditionally loving God—not because *He* withdraws, but because *we* no longer trust Him enough to let Him near. (For a detailed explanation of these false notions of God, see Volume IV, Chapter 2, of the Quartet.)

There is another consequence of the above false characterizations of God. We not only view *Him* as uncaring and untrustworthy, but also His *will*. Instead of seeing His will as focused on optimizing love, goodness, and salvation, we imagine it as a sword of Damocles ready to drop on our necks in some capricious fashion. When we believe that God's will is harmful or capricious, we cannot bring ourselves to ask for it; instead, we run for cover. We have all heard the jokes about the capricious God who tries to convince some "poor sap" to let go of a tree limb on a cliff only to let him fall to his death. If we let these jokes (and the attitude of "Murphy's Law" underlying them) become pervasive in our minds and hearts, we will likely deprive ourselves of the most powerful, spontaneous prayer the Lord has given us.

I had an experience of this in my first month at the Jesuit novitiate. We were given the Suscipe prayer of Saint Ignatius (cited in previous chapters) to say at our final prayers:

Take, Lord, receive all my liberty, my memory, my understanding, and my entire will. Whatsoever I have or hold, You have given to me. I give it all back to You. Dispose of it wholly according to Your will. Give me only Your love and Your grace, and that's enough for me, and I ask for nothing more.

As can be seen, this is an enlarged and eloquent way of saying, "Thy loving will be done."

Unfortunately, when I first came to the novitiate I had not appropriated (in either my mind or heart) the unconditional love, goodness, justice, and salvation intrinsic to the will of God. As a result, I prayed this prayer in what now appears to me to be an incredibly humorous (but at the time, fearful and painstaking) way. I began by saying, "T-t-take, L-Lord, receive all my liberty (but I really like my liberty, so don't destroy it if I give it to You; on second thought, I'll take it back for safekeeping); m-m-my memory (but You gave me a good memory, and I really need it, and I really use it, so please don't destroy it if I give it to You; on second thought, I'll take it back for safekeeping); m-m-my u-understanding (but You gave me a fine intellect and I really use it, so please don't destroy it if I give it to You—I think I'll take it back for safekeeping).... Whew! I made it through that prayer and I'm still intact." This clearly was not the intention of Saint Ignatius, who probably would have been mystified by the sheer panic I was experiencing in giving myself over to God's will.

This prayer takes on a completely opposite significance when we remember that God's will is to bring optimal love, goodness, justice, and salvation out of every aspect of our actions. When we remember this, the prayer "Thy loving will be done" becomes an instant conduit for God's love and grace to work *in* us and *through* us.

Some readers may be thinking, "If God's will is truly optimally loving, good, and salvific, then why do we have to ask for it?—Why doesn't He just simply do the good that He truly wants to do?" The answer lies in a simple word: "freedom". God will always respect our freedom, and therefore our choice to have Him work in us and through us. If we do not ask for His loving will to be done, He cannot go through with it without violating our freedom.

When we remember God's loving and salvific will, this little prayer can provide us with His peace, strength, insight, and love, making all the gifts of the Holy Spirit come alive in us. At this juncture, our thoughts, actions, and operations become an instrument for His optimally loving, good, just, and salvific purposes.

I use this prayer in times of fear, loss, deprivation, temptation, anger, and guilt, implying that it can be substituted for all the other spontaneous prayers mentioned above. Of course, those other prayers have a special kind of efficacy for us, because they focus on specific needs in specific situations. Nevertheless, if we cannot remember those other prayers in a moment of fear or suffering, we will probably be able to remember the prayer of Jesus Himself—"Thy [loving] will be done."

I recommend that readers use these prayers to get started on the life and adventure of transcendent grace, purpose, and happiness. They will be both an indispensable support and a passageway to even deeper faith and prayer. When you feel called to a deeper relationship with the Lord, I would recommend returning to Chapter 3 (particularly Sections III–VI), and integrating the above prayers into the contemplative life explained there. Above all, I recommend participating in weekday Mass as often as possible, bearing in mind the graces of the Eucharist described in Chapter 2 (Section I) and cultivating a habit of going to the Sacrament of Reconciliation at least once every two months, attending to the graces explained in Chapter 7 (Section II).

II. Psalms and a Canticle for Daily Prayer

I have selected the following psalms and canticle as a "starter kit" for those not accustomed to the Breviary or the *Magnificat*. The psalms are well known, addressing a variety of prayer intentions—prayers of praise, forgiveness, petitions, examination of conscience, and thanksgiving. The canticle, the Song of the Three Young Men, is from the Book of Daniel (3:58–88, 56). It is a hymn of praise and thanksgiving to God, sung by the three Jewish youths Hananiah, Azariah, and

Mishael, whose lives were miraculously spared from being thrown into a fiery furnace, the penalty for not obeying the commandment to bow down and worship a golden image of the Babylonian king Nebuchadnezzar (see Dan 3:1–23).[1]

Psalm 8

O LORD, our Lord,
how majestic is your name in all the earth!

You whose glory above the heavens is chanted
by the mouths of babies and infants,
you have founded a bulwark because of your foes,
to still the enemy and the avenger.

When I look at your heavens, the work of your fingers,
the moon and the stars which you have established;
what is man that you are mindful of him,
and the son of man that you care for him?

Yet you have made him little less than the angels,
and you have crowned him with glory and honor.
You have given him dominion over the works of your hands;
you have put all things under his feet,
all sheep and oxen,

and also the beasts of the field,
the birds of the air, and the fish of the sea,
whatever passes along the paths of the seas.

O LORD, our Lord,
how majestic is your name in all the earth! [Amen.]

---

[1] Note that in the referenced Daniel passage, Hananiah, Azariah, and Mishael are mentioned by their Babylonian names: Shadrach, Abednego, and Meshach, respectively.

Psalm 23

The LORD is my shepherd, I shall not want;
he makes me lie down in green pastures.
He leads me beside still waters;
he restores my soul.
He leads me in paths of righteousness
for his name's sake.

Even though I walk through the valley of the shadow of death,
I fear no evil;
for you are with me;
your rod and your staff,
they comfort me.

You prepare a table before me
in the presence of my enemies;
you anoint my head with oil;
my cup overflows.
Surely goodness and mercy shall follow me
all the days of my life;
and I shall dwell in the house of the LORD
for ever. [Amen.]

Psalm 51

Have mercy on me, O God,
according to your merciful love;
according to your abundant mercy
blot out my transgressions.
Wash me thoroughly from my iniquity,
and cleanse me from my sin!

For I know my transgressions,
and my sin is ever before me.
Against you, you only, have I sinned,

and done that which is evil in your sight,
so that you are justified in your sentence
and blameless in your judgment.
Behold, I was brought forth in iniquity,
and in sin did my mother conceive me.

Behold, you desire truth in the inward being;
therefore teach me wisdom in my secret heart.
Purge me with hyssop, and I shall be clean;
wash me, and I shall be whiter than snow.
Make me hear joy and gladness;
let the bones which you have broken rejoice.
Hide your face from my sins,
and blot out all my iniquities.

Create in me a clean heart, O God,
and put a new and right spirit within me.
Cast me not away from your presence,
and take not your holy Spirit from me.
Restore to me the joy of your salvation,
and uphold me with a willing spirit.

Then I will teach transgressors your ways,
and sinners will return to you.
Deliver me from bloodguilt, O God,
O God of my salvation,
and my tongue will sing aloud of your deliverance.

O Lord, open my lips,
and my mouth shall show forth your praise.
For you take no delight in sacrifice;
were I to give a burnt offering, you would not be pleased.
The sacrifice acceptable to God is a broken spirit;
a broken and contrite heart, O God, you will not despise.

Do good to Zion in your good pleasure;
rebuild the walls of Jerusalem,
then you will delight in right sacrifices,

in burnt offerings and whole burnt offerings;
then bulls will be offered on your altar. [Amen.]

Psalm 103

Bless the LORD, O my soul;
and all that is within me,
bless his holy name!
Bless the LORD, O my soul,
and forget not all his benefits,
who forgives all your iniquity,
who heals all your diseases,
who redeems your life from the Pit,
who crowns you with mercy and compassion,
who satisfies you with good as long as you live
so that your youth is renewed like the eagle's.
The LORD works vindication
and justice for all who are oppressed.
He made known his ways to Moses,
his acts to the people of Israel.
The Lord is merciful and gracious,
slow to anger and abounding in mercy.
He will not always chide,
nor will he keep his anger for ever.
He does not deal with us according to our sins,
nor repay us according to our iniquities.
For as the heavens are high above the earth,
so great is his mercy toward those who fear him;
as far as the east is from the west,
so far does he remove our transgressions from us.
As a father pities his children,
so the LORD pities those who fear him.
For he knows our frame;
he remembers that we are dust.

As for man, his days are like grass;
he flourishes like a flower of the field;

for the wind passes over it, and it is gone,
and its place knows it no more.
But the mercy of the LORD is from everlasting to everlasting
upon those who fear him,
and his righteousness to children's children,
to those who keep his covenant
and remember to do his commandments.

The LORD has established his throne in the heavens,
and his kingdom rules over all.
Bless the LORD, O you his angels,
you mighty ones who do his word,
hearkening to the voice of the word!
Bless the LORD, all his hosts,
his ministers that do his will!
Bless the LORD, all his works,
in all places of his dominion.
Bless the LORD, O my soul! [Amen.]

Psalm 139:1–18, 23–24

O LORD, you have searched me and known me!
You know when I sit down and when I rise up;
you discern my thoughts from afar.
You search out my path and my lying down,
and are acquainted with all my ways. Even before a word is on
        my tongue,
behold, O LORD, you know it altogether.
You beset me behind and before,
and lay your hand upon me.
Such knowledge is too wonderful for me;
it is high, I cannot attain it.

Where shall I go from your Spirit?
Or where shall I flee from your presence?
If I ascend to heaven, you are there!
If I make my bed in Sheol, you are there!

If I take the wings of the morning
and dwell in the uttermost parts of the sea,
even there your hand shall lead me,
and your right hand shall hold me.
If I say, "Let only darkness cover me,
and the light about me be night,"
even the darkness is not dark to you,
the night is bright as the day;
for darkness is as light with you.

For you formed my inward parts,
you knitted me together in my mother's womb.
I praise you, for I am wondrously made.
Wonderful are your works!
You know me right well;
my frame was not hidden from you,
when I was being made in secret,
intricately wrought in the depths of the earth.
Your eyes beheld my unformed substance;
in your book were written, every one of them,
the days that were formed for me,
when as yet there was none of them.
How precious to me are your thoughts, O God!
How vast is the sum of them!
If I would count them, they are more than the sand.
When I awake, I am still with you. . . .

Search me, O God, and know my heart!
Try me and know my thoughts!
And see if there be any wicked way in me,
and lead me in the way everlasting! [Amen.]

*Song of the Three Young Men: Canticle from
the Book of Daniel (3:58–88, 56)*

Bless the Lord, all works of the Lord,
sing praise to him and highly exalt him for ever.

Bless the Lord, you heavens,
sing praise to him and highly exalt him for ever.
Bless the Lord, you angels of the Lord,
sing praise to him and highly exalt him for ever.
Bless the Lord, all waters above the heaven,
sing praise to him and highly exalt him for ever.
Bless the Lord, all powers,
sing praise to him and highly exalt him for ever.
Bless the Lord, sun and moon,
sing praise to him and highly exalt him for ever.
Bless the Lord, stars of heaven,
sing praise to him and highly exalt him for ever.
Bless the Lord, all rain and dew,
sing praise to him and highly exalt him for ever.
Bless the Lord, all winds,
sing praise to him and highly exalt him for ever.
Bless the Lord, fire and heat,
sing praise to him and highly exalt him for ever.
Bless the Lord, winter cold and summer heat,
sing praise to him and highly exalt him for ever.
Bless the Lord, dews and snows,
sing praise to him and highly exalt him for ever.
Bless the Lord, nights and days,
sing praise to him and highly exalt him for ever.
Bless the Lord, light and darkness,
sing praise to him and highly exalt him for ever.
Bless the Lord, ice and cold,
sing praise to him and highly exalt him for ever.
Bless the Lord, frosts and snows,
sing praise to him and highly exalt him for ever.
Bless the Lord, lightnings and clouds,
sing praise to him and highly exalt him for ever.
Let the earth bless the Lord;
let it sing praise to him and highly exalt him for ever.
Bless the Lord, mountains and hills,
sing praise to him and highly exalt him for ever.
Bless the Lord, all things that grow on the earth,
sing praise to him and highly exalt him for ever.

Bless the Lord, you springs,
sing praise to him and highly exalt him for ever.
Bless the Lord, seas and rivers,
sing praise to him and highly exalt him for ever.
Bless the Lord, you whales and all creatures that move in the
    waters,
sing praise to him and highly exalt him for ever.
Bless the Lord, all birds of the air,
sing praise to him and highly exalt him for ever.
Bless the Lord, all beasts and cattle,
sing praise to him and highly exalt him for ever.
Bless the Lord, you sons of men,
sing praise to him and highly exalt him for ever.
Bless the Lord, O Israel,
sing praise to him and highly exalt him for ever.
Bless the Lord, you priests of the Lord,
sing praise to him and highly exalt him for ever.
Bless the Lord, you servants of the Lord,
sing praise to him and highly exalt him for ever.
Bless the Lord, spirits and souls of the righteous,
sing praise to him and highly exalt him for ever.
Bless the Lord, you who are holy and humble in heart,
sing praise to him and highly exalt him for ever.
Bless the Lord, Hananiah, Azariah, and Mishael,
sing praise to him and highly exalt him for ever....
Blessed are you in the firmament of heaven
and to be sung and glorified for ever. [Amen.]

III. Popular Catholic Devotional Prayers

The following prayers, like the above psalms and canticle, represent
a selection of prayers produced by saints of the Catholic Church
throughout the ages. They address similar themes to those mentioned
in the psalms as well as the themes of protection from evil, help
toward salvation, help in fulfilling God's will, and help in inspiring
hope, peace, and love.

Prayer of Saint Augustine

Late have I loved you, O Beauty ever ancient, ever new, late have I loved you! You were within me, but I was outside, and it was there that I searched for you. In my unloveliness I plunged into the lovely things which you created. You were with me, but I was not with you. Created things kept me from you; yet if they had not been in you they would not have been at all. You called, you shouted, and you broke through my deafness. You flashed, you shone, and you dispelled my blindness. You breathed your fragrance on me; I drew in breath and now I pant for you. I have tasted you, now I hunger and thirst for more. You touched me, and I burned for your peace. [Amen.][2]

Prayer of Saint Patrick

I arise today
Through the strength of heaven;
Light of the sun,
Splendor of fire,
Speed of lightning,
Swiftness of the wind,
Depth of the sea,
Stability of the earth,
Firmness of the rock.

I arise today
Through God's strength to pilot me;
God's might to uphold me,
God's wisdom to guide me,
God's eye to look before me,
God's ear to hear me,
God's word to speak for me,
God's hand to guard me,
God's way to lie before me,

[2] *Confessions* 10, 27, quoted in the Office of Readings on Saint Augustine's feast day (August 28), in *The Liturgy of the Hours*, copyright © 1973, 1974, 1975 by International Commission on English in the Liturgy Corporation, http://www.liturgies.net/saints/augustine/readings.htm.

God's shield to protect me,
God's hosts to save me ...
Afar and anear,
Alone or in a multitude...

Christ shield me today ...
against wounding....
Christ with me, Christ before me, Christ behind me,
Christ in me, Christ beneath me, Christ above me,
Christ on my right, Christ on my left,
Christ when I lie down, Christ when I sit down,
Christ in the heart of every man who thinks of me,
Christ in the mouth of every man who speaks of me,
Christ in the eye that sees me,
Christ in the ear that hears me.

I arise today
Through a mighty strength ...
of the Oneness
Of the Creator of creation. [Amen.][3]

Prayer of Saint Francis of Assisi

Lord, make me an instrument of your peace:
where there is hatred, let me sow love;
where there is injury, pardon;
where there is doubt, faith;
where there is despair, hope;
where there is darkness, light;
where there is sadness, joy;

O divine Master, grant that I may not so much seek to be
    consoled as to console,
to be understood as to understand,
to be loved as to love.

[3] "Lorica of Saint Patrick", *Catholic Online*, August 2, 2020, https://www.catholic.org /prayers/prayer.php?p=1770.

For it is in giving that we receive,
it is in pardoning that we are pardoned,
and it is in dying that we are born to eternal life.

Amen.[4]

Prayers of Saint Thomas Aquinas

Prayer before Mass

Almighty and everlasting God,
behold I come to the Sacrament of Thine only-begotten Son,
our Lord Jesus Christ:
I come as one infirm to the physician of life,
as one unclean to the fountain of mercy,
as one blind to the light of everlasting brightness,
as one poor and needy to the Lord of heaven and earth.
Therefore I implore the abundance of Thy measureless bounty
that Thou wouldst vouchsafe to heal my infirmity,
wash my uncleanness,
enlighten my blindness,
enrich my poverty and clothe my nakedness,
that I may receive the Bread of Angels,
the King of kings, the Lord of lords,
with such reverence and humility,
with such sorrow and devotion,
with such purity and faith,
with such purpose and intention
as may be profitable to my soul's salvation.
Grant unto me, I pray,
the grace of receiving not only the Sacrament of our Lord's
    Body and Blood,
but also the grace and power of the Sacrament.
O most gracious God,

---

[4] "Peace Prayer of Saint Francis", Loyola Press (website), 2020, https://www.loyolapress
.com/catholic-resources/prayer/traditional-catholic-prayers/saints-prayers/peace-prayer-of
-saint-francis/.

grant me so to receive the Body of Thine only-begotten Son,
our Lord Jesus Christ,
which He took from the Virgin Mary,
as to merit to be incorporated into His mystical Body,
and to be numbered amongst His members.
O most loving Father,
give me grace to behold forever
Thy beloved Son with His face at last unveiled,
whom I now purpose to receive under the sacramental veil
   here below.

Amen.[5]

Prayer for after Mass

I give thanks to Thee, O Lord, most holy,
Father almighty, eternal God,
that Thou hast vouchsafed,
for no merit of mine own,
but out of Thy pure mercy,
to appease the hunger of my soul
with the precious Body and Blood of Thy Son,
Our Lord Jesus Christ.
Humbly I implore Thee,
let not this holy Communion
be to me an increase of guilt unto my punishment,
but an availing plea unto pardon and salvation.
Let it be to me the armour of faith
and the shield of good will.
May it root out from my heart all vice;
may it utterly subdue my evil passions
and all my unruly desires.
May it perfect me in charity and patience;
in humility and obedience;
and in all other virtues.

[5] "A Prayer before Mass (by St. Thomas Aquinas)", CatholicSay.com, accessed August 4, 2020, https://catholicsay.com/a-prayer-before-mass-by-st-thomas-aquinas/.

May it be my sure defence
against the snares laid for me by my enemies,
visible and invisible.
May it restrain and quiet all my evil impulses,
and make me ever cleave to Thee
Who art the one true God.
May I owe to it a happy ending of my life.

And do Thou, O heavenly Father,
vouchsafe one day to call me, a sinner,
to that ineffable banquet, where Thou, together with Thy Son
    and the Holy Ghost,
art to Thy saints true and unfailing light,
fullness of content,
joy for evermore,
gladness without alloy,
consummate and everlasting happiness.
Through the same Christ our Lord.

Amen.[6]

Prayers of Saint Ignatius Loyola

Anima Christi

Soul of Christ, sanctify me.
Body of Christ, save me.
Blood of Christ, inebriate me.
Water from the side of Christ, wash me.
Passion of Christ, strengthen me.
O Good Jesus, hear me.
Within your wounds hide me.
Permit me not to be separated from you.
From the wicked foe, defend me.

---

[6] "A Prayer for after Mass (by St. Thomas Aquinas)", *Catholic Online*, accessed August 4, 2020, https://www.catholic.org/prayers/prayer.php?p=2025.

At the hour of my death, call me
and bid me come to you
That with your saints I may praise you
For ever and ever. Amen.[7]

Suscipe

Take, Lord, and receive all my liberty,
my memory, my understanding,
and my entire will,
All I have and call my own.
You have given all to me.
To you, Lord, I return it.
Everything is yours; do with it what you will.
Give me only your love and your grace,
that is enough for me. [Amen.][8]

Prayer of Saint Thomas à Kempis

I offer up unto You my prayers and intercessions, for those especially who have in any matter hurt, grieved, or found fault with me, or who have done me any damage or displeasure. For all those also whom, at any time, I may have vexed, troubled, burdened, and scandalized, by words or deeds, knowingly or in ignorance; that You wouldst grant us all equally pardon for our offences against each other. Take away from our hearts, O Lord, all suspiciousness, indignation, wrath, and contention, and whatsoever may hurt charity, and lessen brotherly love. Have mercy, O Lord, have mercy on those who crave Your mercy, give grace unto them that stand in need thereof, and make us such as that we may be worthy to enjoy Your grace, and go forward to life eternal. Amen.[9]

---

[7] "Anima Christi", IgnatianSpirituality.com, 2020, quoting from *Finding God in All Things: A Marquette Prayer Book* (Milwaukee: Marquette University Press, 2009), https://www.ignatian spirituality.com/ignatian-prayer/prayers-by-st-ignatius-and-others/anima-christi/.

[8] "Suscipe", Loyola Press (website), 2020, https://www.loyolapress.com/our-catholic-faith /prayer/traditional-catholic-prayers/saints-prayers/suscipe-prayer-saint-ignatius-of-loyola.

[9] "Prayer for Others", CatholicSaints.Info, accessed August 2, 2020, https://catholicsaints .info/prayer-for-others/.

Prayer of Saint Francis de Sales

O my God, I thank you and I praise
you for accomplishing your holy
and all-lovable will without any regard for mine.
With my whole heart,
in spite of my heart,
do I receive this cross I feared so much!

It is the cross of Your choice,
the cross of Your love.
I venerate it;
nor for anything in the world
would I wish that it had not come,
since You willed it.

I keep it with gratitude and with joy,
as I do everything that comes from Your hand;
and I shall strive to carry it without letting it drag,
with all the respect
and all the affection which Your works deserve.

Amen.[10]

Prayer of Saint Claude le Colombière

My God, I believe most firmly that Thou watchest over all who hope
in Thee, and that we can want for nothing when we rely upon Thee in
all things; therefore I am resolved for the future to have no anxieties,
and to cast all my cares upon Thee.

   People may deprive me of worldly goods and of honors; sickness
may take from me my strength and the means of serving Thee; I may
even lose Thy grace by sin; but my trust shall never leave me. I will
preserve it to the last moment of my life, and the powers of hell shall
seek in vain to wrestle it from me.

[10] "An Act of Abandonment", *Catholic Online*, accessed August 2, 2020, https://www
.catholic.org/prayers/prayer.php?p=518.

Let others seek happiness in their wealth, in their talents; let them trust to the purity of their lives, the severity of their mortifications, to the number of their good works, the fervor of their prayers; as for me, O my God, in my very confidence lies all my hope. "For Thou, O Lord, singularly has settled me in hope" [Ps 4:10, Douay-Rheims]. This confidence can never be in vain. "No one has hoped in the Lord and has been confounded" [see Ps 30:2, Douay-Rheims].

I am assured, therefore, of my eternal happiness, for I firmly hope for it, and all my hope is in Thee. "In Thee, O Lord, I have hoped; let me never be confounded."

I know, alas! I know but too well that I am frail and changeable; I know the power of temptation against the strongest virtue. I have seen stars fall from heaven, and pillars of firmament totter; but these things alarm me not. While I hope in Thee I am sheltered from all misfortune, and I am sure that my trust shall endure, for I rely upon Thee to sustain this unfailing hope.

Finally, I know that my confidence cannot exceed Thy bounty, and that I shall never receive less than I have hoped for from Thee. Therefore I hope that Thou wilt sustain me against my evil inclinations; that Thou wilt protect me against the most furious assaults of the evil one, and that Thou wilt cause my weakness to triumph over my most powerful enemies. I hope that Thou wilt never cease to love me, and that I shall love Thee unceasingly. "In Thee, O Lord, have I hoped; let me never be confounded." [Amen.][11]

Gerard Manley Hopkins

Pied Beauty

Glory be to God for dappled things—
For skies of couple-colour as a brinded cow;
For rose-moles all in stipple upon trout that swim;
Fresh-firecoal chestnut-falls; finches' wings;
Landscape plotted and pieced—fold, fallow, and plough;
And áll trádes, their gear and tackle and trim.

[11] "An Act of Hope and Confidence in God, by Saint Claude de la Colombiere", CatholicSaints.Info, accessed August 2, 2020, https://catholicsaints.info/an-act-of-hope-and-confidence-in-god-by-saint-claude-de-la-colombiere/.

All things counter, original, spare, strange;
Whatever is fickle, freckled (who knows how?)
With swift, slow; sweet, sour; adazzle, dim;
He fathers-forth whose beauty is past change:
Praise him. [Amen.][12]

Prayer of Saint Thérèse of Lisieux

O my God!
I offer Thee all my actions of this day for the intentions and
    for the glory of the Sacred Heart of Jesus.

I desire to sanctify every beat of my heart, my every thought,
    my simplest works, by uniting them to Its infinite merits;
    and I wish
to make reparation for my sins by casting them into the
    furnace of Its Merciful Love.

O my God! I ask of Thee for myself and for those whom I
    hold dear, the grace to fulfill perfectly Thy Holy Will, to
    accept for love of Thee the joys and sorrows of this passing
    life, so that we may one day be united together in heaven
    for all Eternity.

Amen.[13]

Prayer of Saint John Henry Newman

Dear Jesus,
help me to spread Your fragrance everywhere I go.
Flood my soul with Your spirit and life.
Penetrate and possess my whole being so utterly

---

[12] "Pied Beauty", Poetry Foundation (website), 2020, quoting Gerard Manley Hopkins, *Poems and Prose*, Penguin Classics (New York: Penguin Books, 1985), https://www.poetry foundation.org/poems/44399/pied-beauty.

[13] "A Prayer Written by Saint Therese", SaintTherese.com, accessed August 3, 2020, http://www.sainttherese.com/a-morning-prayer-written-by-saint-therese/.

that my life may only be a radiance of Yours.
Shine through me and be so in me that every soul I come in
    contact with
may feel Your presence in my soul.
Let them look up and see no longer me but only Jesus!
Stay with me and then I will begin to shine as You shine,
so to shine as to be a light to others;
the light, O Jesus, will be all from You; none of it will be
    mine:
it will be You, shining on others through me.
Let me thus praise You in the way You love best:
by shining on those around me.
Let me preach You without preaching, not by words, but by
    my example,
by the catching force, the sympathetic influence of what I do,
the evident fullness of the love my heart bears to You.
[Amen.][14]

Prayer of Saint Teresa of Calcutta

Heavenly Father,
you have given us the model of life
in the Holy Family of Nazareth.
Help us, O Loving Father,
to make our family another Nazareth
where love, peace and joy reign.
May it be deeply contemplative,
intensely eucharistic,
revived with joy.
Help us to stay together in joy
and sorrow in family prayer.
Teach us to see Jesus in the members of our families,
especially in their distressing disguise.
May the eucharistic heart of Jesus

[14] "The Prayer Radiating Christ", *Catholic Online*, accessed August 2, 2020, https://www
.catholic.org/prayers/prayer.php?p=1862.

make our hearts humble like his
and help us to carry out our family duties
in a holy way.
May we love one another
as God loves each one of us,
more and more each day,
and forgive each other's faults
as you forgive our sins.
Help us, O Loving Father,
to take whatever you give
and give whatever you take with a big smile.

Immaculate Heart of Mary,
cause of our joy, pray for us.

St. Joseph, pray for us.
Holy Guardian Angels,
be always with us,
guide and protect us.

Amen.[15]

Prayers to Mary

The Angelus

V. The Angel of the Lord declared unto Mary.
R. And she conceived of the Holy Spirit.
Hail, Mary, full of grace,
the Lord is with thee.
Blessed art thou among women
and blessed is the fruit of thy womb, Jesus.
Holy Mary, Mother of God,
pray for us sinners,
now and at the hour of our death. Amen.
V. Behold the handmaid of the Lord.
R. Be it done unto me according to thy word.

---

[15] "Prayer for Our Family #3—Mother Teresa of Calcutta", *Catholic Online*, accessed August 2, 2020, https://www.catholic.org/prayers/prayer.php?p=695.

Hail Mary ...
V. And the Word was made flesh.
R. And dwelt among us.
Hail Mary ...

Let us pray: Pour forth, we beseech thee, O Lord, thy grace into our hearts; that we, to whom the Incarnation of Christ, thy Son, was made known by the message of an angel, may by his Passion and Cross be brought to the glory of his Resurrection. Through the same Christ, our Lord. Amen.[16]

The Memorare

Remember, O most gracious Virgin Mary, that never was it known that anyone who fled to thy protection, implored thy help, or sought thy intercession, was left unaided. Inspired by this confidence I fly unto thee, O Virgin of virgins, my Mother. To thee do I come, before thee I stand, sinful and sorrowful. O Mother of the Word Incarnate, despise not my petitions, but in thy mercy hear and answer me. Amen.[17]

Hail, Holy Queen (the Salve Regina)

Hail, Holy Queen, Mother of Mercy,
our life, our sweetness and our hope. To thee do we cry,
poor banished children of Eve.
To thee do we send up our sighs,
mourning and weeping in this valley of tears.
Turn then, most gracious advocate,
thine eyes of mercy toward us,
and after this our exile
show unto us the blessed fruit of thy womb, Jesus.
O clement, O loving,
O sweet Virgin Mary. [Amen.][18]

---

[16] "Basic Prayers: Essential Catholic Prayers", United States Conference of Catholic Bishops (website), accessed August 2, 2020, from *Catholic Household Blessings and Prayers*, rev. ed. (Washington, D.C.: United States Conference of Catholic Bishops, 2007), https://www.usccb.org/prayer-and-worship/prayers-and-devotions/prayers/basic-prayers.

[17] Ibid.

[18] Ibid.

Prayer to Saint Michael

St. Michael the Archangel,
defend us in battle.
Be our defense against the wickedness and snares of the Devil.
May God rebuke him, we humbly pray,
and do thou,
O Prince of the heavenly hosts,
by the power of God,
thrust into hell Satan,
and all the evil spirits,
who prowl about the world
seeking the ruin of souls. Amen.[19]

Litany—The Divine Praises

Blessed be God.
Blessed be His holy Name.
Blessed be Jesus Christ, true God and true Man.
Blessed be the name of Jesus.
Blessed be his most Sacred Heart.
Blessed be his most Precious Blood.
Blessed be Jesus in the most holy Sacrament of the altar.
Blessed be the Holy Spirit, the Paraclete.
Blessed be the great Mother of God, Mary most holy.
Blessed be her holy and Immaculate Conception.
Blessed be her glorious Assumption.
Blessed be the name of Mary, Virgin and Mother.
Blessed be Saint Joseph, her most chaste spouse.
Blessed be God in his angels and in his saints. [Amen.][20]

---

[19] "Prayer to St. Michael the Archangel", EWTN.com, accessed August 2, 2020, https://www.ewtn.com/catholicism/devotions/prayer-to-st-michael-the-archangel-371.
[20] "Basic Prayers: Essential Catholic Prayers", https://www.usccb.org/prayer-and-worship/prayers-and-devotions/prayers/basic-prayers.

BIBLIOGRAPHY

Allen, Elizabeth S., and David C. Atkins. "The Association of Divorce and Extramarital Sex in a Representative U.S. Sample". *Journal of Family Issues* 33, no. 11 (November 2012): 1477–93. www.research gate.net/publication/258151224_The_Association_of_Divorce _and_Extramarital_Sex_in_a_Representative_US_Sample.

Ambrose. *"On the Mysteries" and the Treatise on the Sacraments by an Unknown Author*. Edited with introduction and notes by J. H. Strawley and translated by T. Thompson, B.D. New York: Macmillan, 1919. http://oll.libertyfund.org/titles/ambrose-on-the-mysteries -and-the-treatise-on-the-sacraments.

Anonymous. *The Cloud of Unknowing and Other Works*. Translated by A. C. Spearing. New York: Penguin Classics, 2001.

———. *Didache*. Translated by M. B. Riddle. From *Ante-Nicene Fathers*. Vol. 7, edited by Alexander Roberts, James Donaldson, and A. Cleveland Coxe. Buffalo, N.Y.: Christian Literature Publishing, 1886. Revised and edited for New Advent (website) by Kevin Knight, 2020. http://www.newadvent.org/fathers/0714.htm.

Aquinas, Thomas. *The Summa Theologica of St. Thomas Aquinas*. Translated by Fathers of the English Dominican Province. Vols. 1–3. New York: Benziger Brothers, 1947.

Aristotle. *The Basic Works of Aristotle*. Edited by Richard McKeon. New York: Modern Library, 2001.

Aschenbrenner, George. *The Examination of Conscience*. Chicago: Loyola Press, 2007.

Augustine. *Confessions*. Translated and edited by Henry Chadwick. New York: Oxford University Press, 1991.

———. "The Confessions of Saint Augustine, Book VIII". In *The Confessions of Saint Augustine*. Translated by Edward Bouverie Pusey, 1914. SacredTexts.com. http://www.sacred-texts.com/chr /augconf/aug08.htm.

———. "The Free Choice of the Will". In Fathers of the Church series, vol. 59, *Saint Augustine: The Teacher, the Free Choice of the Will*,

Grace and Free Will, translated by Robert P. Russell, O.S.A., pp. 63–241. Washington, D.C.: Catholic University of America Press, 1968.

———. *The Literal Meaning of Genesis (*De Genesi ad litteram*).* Translated by John Hammond Taylor, S.J. Vol. 2. Mahwah, N.J.: Paulist Press, 1982.

Bandura, Albert. *Self-Efficacy: The Exercise of Control.* New York: W. H. Freeman, 1997.

Beale, Stephen. "Just How Many Protestant Denominations Are There?" *National Catholic Register*, October 31, 2017. https://www.ncregister.com/blog/just-how-many-protestant-denominations-are-there.

Bearison, David J. *The Edge of Medicine: Stories of Dying Children and Their Parents.* New York: Oxford University Press, 2012.

Belmonte, Charles. Commentary to "Letter of St. Ignatius of Antioch to the Romans". In *Faith Seeking Understanding.* Metro Manila, Philippines: Cobrin Publishing, 2012. http://fsubelmonte.weebly.com/letter-of-st-ignatius-of-antioch-to-the-romans.html.

Benedict. *The Rule of Saint Benedict.* Edited by Timothy Fry, O.S.B. New York: Vintage, 1998.

Benedict XVI, Pope. *Jesus of Nazareth: From the Baptism in the Jordan to the Transfiguration.* San Francisco: Ignatius Press, 2008.

———. *Jesus of Nazareth: Holy Week; From the Entrance into Jerusalem to the Resurrection.* San Francisco: Ignatius Press, 2011.

———. *Jesus of Nazareth: The Infancy Narratives.* San Francisco: Ignatius Press, 2018.

Bergson, Henri. *Duration and Simultaneity: Bergson and the Einsteinian Universe.* Translated by Leon Jacobson. Manchester: Clinamen Press, 1991.

Bering, Jesse. "One Last Goodbye: The Strange Case of Terminal Lucidity". *Scientific American* (blog), November 25, 2014. https://blogs.scientificamerican.com/bering-in-mind/one-last-goodbye-the-strange-case-of-terminal-lucidity/.

Bethany Madonna, Sister, S.V. "Chastity—Love without Limits". Sisters of Life (website), 2013. https://www.sistersoflife.org/vocations/chastity-love-without-limits (site discontinued).

Betz, Johannes. "Eucharist". In *Sacramentum Mundi*, edited by Karl Rahner, 2:257–67. London: Burns & Oates, 1968. Accessed July 1, 2018.

Boekraad, Adrian J., and Henry Tristram, eds. *The Argument from Conscience to the Existence of God according to J. H. Newman* [with the text of an unpublished essay by Newman, entitled "Proof of Theism"]. Louvain: Editions Nauwelaerts, 1961.

Briggs, David. "5 Ways Faith Contributes to Strong Marriages, New Studies Suggest". *HuffPost*, February 8, 2015. https://www.huff post.com/entry/5-ways-faith-contributes_b_6294716.

Butler, Alban. *Butler's Lives of the Saints*. 2nd ed. 4 vols. Edited by Herbert J. Thurston and Donald Attwater. New York: Christian Classics, 1956.

Callaway, Ewen. "Sex and Violence Linked in the Brain". *Nature News*, February 9, 2011. http://www.nature.com/news/2011/110 209/full/news.2011.82.html.

Cassian, John. *Conferences*. Classics of Western Spirituality. Mahwah, N.J.: Paulist Press, 1985.

Chadwick, Henry. "The Early Christian Community". In *The Oxford Illustrated History of the Christian Church*, edited by John McManners, pp. 21–61. New York: Oxford University Press, 2001.

Chapman, Dom John. "St. Cyprian on the Church and the Papacy". In *Studies on the Early Papacy*. Port Washington, N.Y.: Kennikat Press, 1971. Reprinted with a brief introduction on Philvaz.com. http://philvaz.com/apologetics/num44.htm.

Chesterton, G. K. *The Autobiography of G. K. Chesterton*. San Francisco: Ignatius Press, 2006.

―――. *St. Francis of Assisi*. New York: Image, 2013.

―――. *St. Thomas Aquinas: The Dumb Ox*. CreateSpace Independent Publishing Platform, 2012.

Christianica Center. *Scriptural Rosary*. Glenview, Ill.: Christianica Center Publishing, 1989.

Chrysostom, John. "Homily 24 on First Corinthians". Translated by Talbot W. Chambers. From *Nicene and Post-Nicene Fathers*, 1st series. Vol. 12, edited by Philip Schaff. Buffalo, N.Y.: Christian Literature Publishing, 1889. Revised and edited for New Advent (website) by Kevin Knight, 2020. https://www.newadvent.org /fathers/220124.htm.

Ciszek, Walter, S.J. *He Leadeth Me: An Extraordinary Testament of Faith*. New York: Image, 1973.

―――. *With God in Russia*. San Francisco: Ignatius Press, 1997.

Clement of Rome. "The First Epistle of Clement to the Corinthians". Translated by Charles H. Hoole, 1885. *Early Christian Writings* (website), 2020. http://www.earlychristianwritings.com/text
/1clement-hoole.html.

Climacus, John. *The Ladder of Divine Ascent.* Mahwah, N.J.: Paulist
Press, 1982.

Coles, Robert. *The Moral Life of Children.* New York: Atlantic
Monthly Press, 1986.

———. *The Spiritual Life of Children.* Boston: Houghton-Mifflin, 1990.

Colombière, Claude de la. "An Act of Hope and Confidence in God,
by Saint Claude de la Colombiere". CatholicSaints.Info. Accessed
August 2, 2020. https://catholicsaints.info/an-act-of-hope-and
-confidence-in-god-by-saint-claude-de-la-colombiere/.

Connolly, Donald F. X. *Family Prayer Book.* Melville, N.Y.: Regina
Press, 1967.

Conwell, Joseph. *Contemplation in Action: A Study in Ignatian Prayer.*
Spokane, Wash.: Gonzaga University Press, 1957.

Cornwall, Marie, Stan L. Albrecht, Perry H. Cunningham, and Brian
L. Pitcher. "The Dimensions of Religiosity: A Conceptual Model
with an Empirical Test". *Review of Religious Research* 27, no. 3
(1986): 226–44.

Covey, Stephen. *The 7 Habits of Highly Effective People: Powerful Lessons in Personal Change.* Miami: Mango Publishing, 2017.

Cyprian of Carthage. *The Lapsed: The Unity of the Catholic Church.*
Ancient Christian Writers, vol. 25, translated by Maurice Bevenot.
Mahwah, N.J.: Paulist Press, 1957.

Daley, James. "Freud and Determinism". *Southern Journal of Philosophy* 9, no. 2 (June 1971): 179– 89.

Davies, W.D., and Dale C. Allison. *International Critical Commentary.*
Vol. 2, *Matthew 8–18.* New York: T&T Clark, 1991.

Decety, Jean, Kalina J. Michalska, and Yuko Akitsuki. "Who Caused
the Pain? An fMRI Investigation of Empathy and Intentionality in
Children". *Neuropsychologia* 46, no. 11 (2008): 2607–14.

Dervic, Kanita, Maria A. Oquendo, Michael F. Grunebaum, Steve
Ellis, Ainsley Burke, and J. John Mann. "Religious Affiliation
and Suicide Attempt". *American Journal of Psychiatry* 161, no. 12
(December 2004): 2303–8. http://ajp.psychiatryonline.org/doi/abs
/10.1176/appi.ajp.161.12.2303.

Dickens, Charles. *A Christmas Carol*. London, 1843. Project Gutenberg, 2018. http://www.gutenberg.org/files/46/46-h/46-h.htm.

Diocese of Fargo (website). "Breaking Free from Pornography", 2020. http://www.fargodiocese.org/breakingfree.

Dominican Sisters of Saint Cecilia Congregation. *A Short Guide to Praying as a Family: Growing Together in Faith and Love Each Day*. Charlotte, N.C.: Saint Benedict Press, 2015.

Donne, John. "Holy Sonnets: Batter My Heart, Three-Person'd God". Poetry Foundation (website), 2020. https://www.poetry foundation.org/poems/44106/holy-sonnets-batter-my-heart -three-persond-god.

―――. "Meditation XVII". In *Devotions upon Emergent Occasions Together with Death's Duel*. University of Michigan Press, 1959; Project Gutenberg, 2011. http://www.gutenberg.org/cache/epub /23772/pg23772.txt.

Doran, Robert M. "What Does Bernard Lonergan Mean by 'Conversion'?" LonerganResource.com, 2011. http://www.lonerganre source.com/pdf/lectures/What%20Does%20Bernard%20Lonergan %20Mean%20by%20Conversion.pdf.

Driscoll, Mike, Father. *Demons, Deliverance, Discernment: Separating Fact from Fiction about the Spirit World*. El Cajon, Calif.: Catholic Answers Press, 2015.

Dunn, James. *Jesus and the Spirit: A Study of the Religious and Charismatic Experience of Jesus and the First Christians as Reflected in the New Testament*. Philadelphia: Westminster Press, 1975.

Eisenberg, Ronald. *What the Rabbis Said: 250 Topics from the Talmud*. Santa Barbara, Calif.: ABC-CLIO, 2010.

Eliade, Mircea. *The Myth of the Eternal Return: Or Cosmos and History*. Princeton, N.J.: Princeton University Press, 1971.

―――. *The Sacred and the Profane: The Nature of Religion*. New York: Harcourt Brace Jovanovich, 1987.

Flannery, Austin, O.P., ed. *Vatican Council II: The Conciliar and Postconciliar Documents*. New rev. ed. Collegeville, Minn.: Liturgical Press, 2014.

Francis de Sales. "On the Necessity of Chastity". *On the Devout Life*. In *St. Francis de Sales Collection*. London: Aeterna Press, 2016.

Freud, Sigmund. *The Ego and the Id*. New York: Courier Dover Publications, 2018.

————. *The Future of an Illusion*. Translated by Gregory C. Richter. Ontario: Broadview Press, 2012.

Fuller, Reginald H. *The Formation of the Resurrection Narratives*. New York: Macmillan, 1971.

Gallagher, Timothy M., O.M.V. *An Ignatian Introduction to Prayer: Scriptural Reflections according to the Spiritual Exercises*. New York: Crossroad Publishing, 2007.

————. *Meditation and Contemplation: An Ignatian Guide to Praying with Scripture*. New York: Crossroad Publishing, 2008.

Gannon, Megan. "Domestic Violence Often Triggered by Jealousy". *Live Science*, August 1, 2012. https://www.livescience.com/22039 -domestic-violence-often-triggered-by-jealousy.html.

General Council of Trent: 1545–1563. From *The Canons and Decrees of the Sacred Ecumenical Council of Trent*. Edited and translated by J. Waterworth. London: Dolman, 1848. Papal Encyclicals Online. Last updated February 20, 2017. http://www.papalencyclicals.net /councils/trent.htm.

Goodier, Alban. *The Passion and Death of Our Lord Jesus Christ*. New York: P.J. Kenedy & Sons, 1944.

————. *The Public Life of Our Lord Jesus Christ*. New York: P.J. Kenedy & Sons, 1944.

Gray, Timothy. *Peter: Keys to Following Jesus*. San Francisco: Ignatius Press; Greenwood Village, Colo.: Augustine Institute, 2016.

————. *Praying Scripture for a Change: An Introduction to Lectio Divina*. West Chester, Penn.: Ascension Press, 2009.

Gregory of Nyssa. "Homily on Ecclesiastes". Homily 5, *Patrologia Graeca*. Vol. 44. Translated by *Liturgy of the Hours*. Totowa, N.J.: Catholic Book Publishing, 1990

Guardini, Romano. *The Lord*. Chicago: Regnery, 1954.

Hampsch, John. *The Healing Power of the Eucharist*. Welland, Ontario: Servant Book Publications, 1999.

Hardon, John A., S.J. *The History of Eucharistic Adoration: Development of Doctrine in the Catholic Church*. Oak Lawn, Ill.: CMJ Marian Publishers, 2003. http://www.therealpresence.org/archives /Eucharist/Eucharist_017.htm.

Harrington, Daniel J. "The Gospel according to Mark". In *The New Jerome Biblical Commentary*, edited by Raymond E. Brown, Joseph A. Fitzmyer, and Roland E. Murphy, pp. 596–629. Englewood Cliffs, N.J.: Prentice-Hall, 1990.

Heiler, Friedrich. "The History of Religions as a Preparation for the Cooperation of Religions". In *The History of Religions*, edited by Mircea Eliade and J. Kitagawa, pp. 142–53. Chicago: Chicago University Press, 1959.

Hilton, Donald L., Jr. "Pornography Addiction—A Supranormal Stimulus Considered in the Context of Neuroplasticity". *Socioaffective Neuroscience & Psychology* 3, no. 1 (2013): 1–18.

Hopkins, Gerard Manley. "As Kingfishers Catch Fire". Poetry Foundation (website), 2020, quoting Gerard Manley Hopkins, *Poems and Prose*. Penguin Classics. New York: Penguin Books, 1985. https://www.poetryfoundation.org/poems/44389/as-kingfishers-catch-fire.

Hughes, Robert, Jr. "Does Extramarital Sex Cause Divorce?" *HuffPost*, August 8, 2012. https://www.huffpost.com/entry/does-extramarital-sex-cau_b_1567507.

Ignatius of Antioch. "Ignatius to the Ephesians". In *The Apostolic Fathers*, translated by J.B. Lightfoot and J.R. Harmer, 1891. *Early Christian Writings* (website), 2020. http://www.earlychristianwritings.com/text/ignatius-ephesians-lightfoot.html.

————. "Ignatius to the Philadelphians". In *The Apostolic Fathers*, translated by J.B. Lighthouse and J.R. Harmer, 1891. *Early Christian Writings* (website), 2020. http://www.earlychristianwritings.com/text/ignatius-philadelphians-lightfoot.html.

————. "Ignatius to the Romans". In *The Apostolic Fathers*, translated by J.B. Lightfoot and J.R. Harmer, 1891. *Early Christian Writings* (website), 2020. http://www.earlychristianwritings.om/text/ignatius-romans-lightfoot.html.

Ignatius of Loyola. *The Autobiography of St. Ignatius*. Edited by J.F.X. O'Conor, S.J. New York: Benziger Brothers, 1900; Project Gutenberg, 2008. https://www.gutenberg.org/files/24534/24534-h/24534-h.htm.

————. *A Pilgrim's Journey: The Autobiography of Ignatius of Loyola*. Rev. ed. Translated by Joseph N. Tylenda, S.J. San Francisco: Ignatius Press, 2001.

————. *The Spiritual Exercises of St. Ignatius of Loyola*. Translated by Elder Mullan. New York: P.J. Kennedy & Sons, 1914. SacredTexts.com. https://sacred-texts.com/chr/seil/index.htm.

————. "Suscipe". Loyola Press (website), 2020. https://www.loyolapress.com/our-catholic-faith/prayer/traditional-catholic-prayers/saints-prayers/suscipe-prayer-saint-ignatius-of-loyola.

————. "To Give and Not to Count the Cost". IgnatianSpirituality
.com, 2020. https://www.ignatianspirituality.com/19060/to-give
-and-not-to-count-the-cost.

International Catholic Charismatic Renewal Services Doctrinal
Commission. *Deliverance Ministry*. National Service Committee of
the Catholic Charismatic Renewal in the U.S., 2017.

Irenaeus. *Against Heresies*. In "Catholic Biblical Apologetics: Post-
Apostolic Fathers of the Church", edited by Robert Schihl and
Paul Flanagan. FreeRepublic.com, 2010. http://www.freerepublic
.com/focus/religion/2476599/posts?page=1.

Isaacs, Craig. *Revelations and Possession: Distinguishing Spiritual from
Psychological Experiences*. Kearney, Neb.: Morris Publishing, 2009.

Jeremias, Joachim. *The Eucharistic Words of Jesus*. London: SCM Press,
1966.

————. *New Testament Theology*. Vol. 1. London: SCM Press, 1971.

————. *The Parables of Jesus*. London: SCM Press, 1972.

Johanny, Raymond. "Ignatius of Antioch". In *The Eucharist of the
Early Christians*, translated by Matthew J. O'Connell, pp. 48–70.
New York: Pueblo, 1978.

John of the Cross. "The Living Flame of Love". In *The Collected
Works of St. John of the Cross*, edited and translated by Kieran Kava-
naugh, O.C.D., and Otilio Rodriguez, O.C.D., pp. 569–649.
Washington, D.C.: ICS Publications, 1979.

Josef, Linda. "Healing through Communion", March 1, 2006.
https://sidroth.org/articles/healing-through-communion/.

Jungmann, Josef. *The Mass: An Historical, Theological, and Pastoral Survey*. St. Paul, Minn.: North Central Publishing, 2006.

Justin Martyr. *First Apology*. Translated by Marcus Dods and George
Reith. From *Ante-Nicene Fathers*. Vol. 1, edited by Alexander
Roberts, James Donaldson, and A. Cleveland Coxe. Buffalo,
N.Y.: Christian Literature Publishing, 1885. Revised and edited
for New Advent (website) by Kevin Knight, 2020. https://www
.newadvent.org/fathers/0126.htm.

————. *Second Apology*. Translated by Marcus Dods and George
Reith. From *Ante-Nicene Fathers*. Vol. 1, edited by Alexander Rob-
erts, James Donaldson, and A. Cleveland Coxe. Buffalo, N.Y.:
Christian Literature Publishing, 1885. Revised and edited for New
Advent (website) by Kevin Knight, 2020. http://www.newadvent
.org/fathers/0127.htm.

Kalyan-Masih, Violet. "Cognitive Egocentricity of the Child within Piagetian Developmental Theory". *Transactions of the Nebraska Academy of Sciences*, 1973. Paper 379. http://digitalcommons.unl .edu/cgi/viewcontent.cgi?article=1382&context=tnas.

Kempis, Thomas à. *The Imitation of Christ*. New York: Image Classics, 1955.

Klein, Dianne. "The Visions of Dying Children Seem to Bring God Alive". *Los Angeles Times*, April 22, 1990. http://articles.latimes .com/1990-04-22/local/me-518_1_fewer-children.

Koester, Helmut. "The Great Appeal: What Did Christianity Offer Its Believers That Made It Worth Social Estrangement, Hostility from Neighbors, and Possible Persecution?" *Frontline*. New York: WGBH Educational Foundation, 1998. pbs.org/wgbh/pages/front line/shows/religion/why/appeal.html.

Komp, Diane M. *Images of Grace: A Pediatrician's Trilogy of Faith, Hope, and Love*. Grand Rapids, Mich.: Zondervan, 1996.

Koppes, Steve. "Children Are Naturally Prone to Be Empathetic and Moral, University of Chicago Shows". *UChicago News*, University of Chicago Bulletin, July 11, 2008. https://news.uchicago.edu /article/2008/07/11/children-are-naturally-prone-be-empathic-and -moral-university-chicago-study-shows.

Lake, Rebecca. "Infidelity Statistics: 23 Eye-Opening Truths". Credit Donkey (website), May 18, 2016. https://www.creditdonkey.com /infidelity-statistics.html.

Le, Benjamin. "Cheaters Use Cognitive Tricks to Rationalize Infidelity". *Scientific American*, November 20, 2013. https://www .scientificamerican.com/article/cheaters-use-cognitive-tricks-to -rationalize-infidelity/.

Leary, Mark R., and June Price Tangney, eds. *Handbook of Self and Identity*, 2nd ed. New York: Guilford Press, 2011.

Lelen, J. M. *Pray the Rosary*. Totowa, N.J.: Catholic Book Publishing, 1999.

Lewis, C. S. *The Abolition of Man*. New York: HarperCollins, 1974.

———. *The Four Loves*. New York: Harcourt, 1960.

———. *Surprised by Joy: The Shape of My Early Life*. New York: Harcourt, Brace, Jovanovich, 1966.

———. *Surprised by Joy: The Story of My Early Life*. New York: HarperCollins, 1955.

Lin, D., M. Boyle, P. Dollar, H. Lee, E.S. Lein, P. Perona, and D.J. Anderson. "Functional Identification of an Aggression Locus in the Mouse Hypothalamus". *Nature* 470 (February 10, 2011): 221–26.

Lonergan, Bernard. *Method in Theology*. Edited by Robert M. Doran and John D. Dadosky. Vol. 14 of *The Collected Works of Bernard Lonergan*, edited by Frederick E. Crowe and Robert M. Doran. Toronto: University of Toronto Press, 1990.

———. *Verbum: Word and Idea in Aquinas*. Edited by Frederick Crowe and Robert M. Doran. Toronto: University of Toronto Press, 1967.

Low, Robbie. "The Truth about Men and Church". *Touchstone: A Journal of Mere Christianity*, June 2003. http://www.touchstonemag.com/archives/article.php?id=16-05-024-v#ixzz4RjWtmadF.

Lozano, Neal. *Resisting the Devil: A Catholic Perspective on Deliverance*. Huntington, Ind.: Our Sunday Visitor Publishing, 2010.

Luce, Clare Boothe, ed. *Saints for Now*. San Francisco: Ignatius Press, 1993.

Mazzoleni, Danilo. "Ancient Graffiti in Roman Catacombs". EWTN.com, 2020. From *L'Osservatore Romano*, February 9, 2000. https://www.ewtn.com/catholicism/library/ancient-graffiti-in-roman-catacombs-1642.

McKenzie, John L. *Dictionary of the Bible*. New York: Macmillan, 1965.

———. "The Gospel according to Matthew". In *The Jerome Biblical Commentary*, edited by Raymond Brown, Joseph A. Fitzmyer, and Roland E. Murphy, 2:62–114. Englewood Cliffs, N.J.: Prentice-Hall, 1968.

Meier, John P. *A Marginal Jew: Rethinking the Historical Jesus*. Vol. 1, *The Roots of the Problem and the Person*. New York: Doubleday, 1991.

———. *A Marginal Jew: Rethinking the Historical Jesus*. Vol. 2, *Mentor, Message, and Miracles*. New York: Doubleday, 1994.

Merton, Thomas. *Seven Storey Mountain*. New York: Harcourt, 1998.

Miller, Charles. *Together in Prayer: Learning to Love the Liturgy of the Hours*. Eugene, Ore.: Wipf and Stock Publishers, 2004.

Murphy-O'Connor, Jerome, O.P. "The First Letter of Paul to the Corinthians". In *The New Jerome Biblical Commentary*, edited by

Raymond E. Brown, Joseph A. Fitzmyer, and Roland E. Murphy, p. 822. Englewood Cliffs, N.J.: Prentice-Hall, 1990.

Nahm, Michael. "Reflections on the Context of Near-Death Experiences". *Journal of Scientific Exploration* 25 (2011): 453–78.

―――. "Terminal Lucidity in People with Mental Illness and Other Mental Disability: An Overview and Implications for Possible Explanatory Models". *Journal of Near-Death Studies* 28, no. 2 (2009): 87–106.

Nahm, Michael, and Bruce Greyson. "The Death of Anna Katharina Ehmer: A Case Study in Terminal Lucidity". *Omega* 68, no. 1 (2014): 77–87. http://journals.sagepub.com/doi/10.2190/OM.68.1.e.

―――. "Terminal Lucidity in Patients with Chronic Schizophrenia and Dementia: A Survey of the Literature". *Journal of Nervous and Mental Disease* 197 (2009): 942–44.

Nahm, Michael, Bruce Greyson, Emily Williams Kelly, and Erlendur Haraldsson. "Terminal Lucidity: A Review and a Case Collection". *Archives of Gerontology and Geriatrics* 55, no. 1 (2012): 138–42. http://www.sciencedirect.com/science/article/pii/S0167494311001865?via%3Dihub.

Newman, John Henry. *Apologia Pro Vita Sua*. Edited by Maisie Ward. Eugene, Ore.: Wipf & Stock, 2017.

―――. *An Essay in Aid of a Grammar of Assent*. Notre Dame, Ind.: University of Notre Dame Press, 2013.

Nouwen, Henri. *The Road to Daybreak: A Spiritual Journey*. New York: Doubleday, 1988.

O'Brien, Kevin, S.J. "Ignatian Contemplation: Imaginative Prayer". In *The Ignatian Adventure*, pp. 141–42. Chicago: Loyola Press, 2011.

O'Connor, John Cardinal. "Address to the Sisters of Life". Sisters of Life (website), July 5, 1992. https://www.sistersoflife.org/vocations/chastity-love-without-limits (site discontinued).

Origen. *On Prayer*. Translated by William A. Curtis. Tertullian.org, 2008. http://www.tertullian.org/fathers/origen_on_prayer_02_text.htm.

Ott, Ludwig. *Fundamentals of Catholic Dogma*. Rockford, Ill.: Tan Books, 2009.

Oyserman, Daphna, K. Elmore, and G. Smith. "Self, Self-Concept, and Identity". In *Handbook of Self and Identity*, 2nd ed., edited by Mark Leary, pp. 69–104. New York: Guilford Press, 2011.

Parboteeah, K. Praveen, Martin Hoegl, and John B. Cullen. "Ethics and Religion: An Empirical Test of a Multidimensional Model". *Journal of Business Ethics* 80, no. 2 (June 1, 2008): 387–98.

Pascal, Blaise. *Pensées*. Translated by W. F. Trotter. New York: E. P. Dutton, 1958.

Pennington, Basil. *Lectio Divina: Renewing the Ancient Practice of Praying the Scriptures*. New York: Crossroad Publishing, 1998.

Perrin, Nicholas. *Jesus the Temple*. Ada, Mich.: Baker Academic, 2010.

Piaget, Jean. *The Child's Conception of Physical Causality*. New York: Harcourt Brace & Company, 1930.

————. *The Essential Piaget*. Edited by Howard E. Gruber and J. Jacques Voneche. London: Routledge and Kegan Paul, 1977.

Pieper, Josef. *About Love*. Chicago: Franciscan Herald Press, 1974.

————. *The Four Cardinal Virtues*. South Bend, Ind.: University of Notre Dame Press, 1966.

Plato. *Plato: The Collected Dialogues*. Edited by Edith Hamilton and Huntington Cairns. Princeton, N.J.: Princeton University Press, 1961.

Prayer, Frances. "What Drives a Sex Addict? Is Sex Addiction about Love or an Insatiable Craving?" *Psychology Today*, October 7, 2009. http://www.psychologytoday.com/blog/love-doc/200910/what-drives-sex-addict.

Rhoads, Galena K., and Scott M. Stanley. *Before I Do: What Do Premarital Experiences Have to Do with Marital Quality among Today's Young Adults?* Charlottesville, Va.: National Marriage Project at University of Virginia, 2014. http://before-i-do.org/.

Ricoeur, Paul. *Freedom and Nature: The Voluntary and the Involuntary*. Chicago: Northwestern University Press, 1966.

Riley, Naomi Schaefer. "The Young and the Restless: Why Infidelity Is Rising among 20-Somethings". *Wall Street Journal*, November 28, 2008. https://www.wsj.com/articles/SB122782458360062499.

Robinson, James M., and Helmut Koester. *Trajectories through Early Christianity*. Philadelphia: Fortress, 1971. Reprint, Eugene, Ore.: Wipf & Stock, 2006.

Rossini, Connie, and Dan Burke. *The Contemplative Rosary with St. John Paul II and St. Teresa of Avila*. Irondale, Ala.: EWTN Publishing, 2017.

Ryan, Richard, and Edward Deci. "Multiple Identities within a Single Self: A Self-Determination Theory Perspective on Internalization within Contexts and Cultures". In *Handbook of Self and Identity*, 2nd ed., edited by Mark Leary, pp. 225–46. New York: Guilford Press, 2011.

Scanlan, Michael, T.O.R., and Randall Cirner. *Deliverance from Evil Spirits*. Ann Arbor, Mich.: Servant Books, 1980.

Seligman, Martin. *Learned Optimism: How to Change Your Mind and Your Life*. New York: Vintage Books, 1990.

Senior, Donald, ed. *The Catholic Study Bible*. New York: Oxford University Press, 1990.

Sheen, Fulton J. *Life of Christ*. Garden City, N.Y.: Image, 1977. Originally, New York: McGraw-Hill, 1953.

Spitzer, Robert. *Christ versus Satan in Our Daily Lives: The Cosmic Struggle between Good and Evil*. San Francisco: Ignatius Press, forthcoming.

———. "A Contemporary Metaphysical Proof for the Existence of God". *International Philosophical Quarterly* 59, no. 4 (December 2019): 427–66.

———. "A Contemporary Thomistic Metaphysical Proof of God". MagisCenter.com, July 25, 2016, https://magiscenter.com/a-contemporary-thomistic-metaphysical-proof-of-god-with-a-response-to-richard-dawkins-the-god-delusion/.

———. *Credible Catholic Big Book*. Magis Center, 2017. Credible Catholic.com. https://www.crediblecatholic.com.

———. "Definitions of Real Time and Ultimate Reality". *Journal of Ultimate Reality and Meaning: Interdisciplinary Studies in the Philosophy of Understanding* 23, no. 3 (September 2000): 260–76.

———. *Finding True Happiness: Satisfying Our Restless Hearts*. San Francisco: Ignatius Press, 2015.

———. *Five Pillars of the Spiritual Life: A Practical Guide for Active People*. San Francisco: Ignatius Press, 2008.

———. *God So Loved the World: Clues to Our Transcendent Destiny from the Revelation of Jesus*. San Francisco: Ignatius Press, 2016.

———. *The Light Shines on in the Darkness: Transforming Suffering through Faith*. San Francisco: Ignatius Press, 2017.

———. *New Proofs for the Existence of God: Contributions of Contemporary Physics and Philosophy*. Grand Rapids, Mich.: Eerdmans, 2010.

———. "Philosophical Proof of God: Derived from Principles in Bernard Lonergan's Insight". MagisCenter.com, July 25, 2016. https://magiscenter.com/philosophical-proof-of-god-derived-from-principles-in-bernard-lonergans-insight/.

————. *The Soul's Upward Yearning: Clues to Our Transcendent Nature from Experience and Reason.* San Francisco: Ignatius Press, 2015.

————. *Ten Universal Principles: A Brief Philosophy of the Life Issues.* San Francisco: Ignatius Press, 2011.

Spitzer, Robert, and James Sinclair. "Fine-Tuning and Indications of Transcendent Intelligence". In *Theism and Atheism: Opposing Arguments in Philosophy*, edited by Joseph Koterski, S.J., and Graham Oppy, pp. 331–63. New York: Macmillan Reference, 2019.

Stein, Robert H. *Jesus, the Temple and the Coming Son of Man: A Commentary on Mark 13.* Downers Grove, Ill.: InterVarsity Press, 2014.

Stoddard, John L. *Rebuilding a Lost Faith: By an American Agnostic.* Rockford, Ill.: Tan Books and Publishers, 1990.

Teresa of Avila. "Let Nothing Disturb You". Order of Carmelites (website), 2020. http://ocarm.org/en/content/let-nothing-disturb-you.

————. *St. Teresa of Avila: Her Life in Letters.* Translated by Kieran Kavanaugh, O.C.D. Notre Dame, Ind.: Christian Classics, 2018.

Thérèse of Lisieux. *The Story of a Soul.* Translated by Thomas N. Taylor. Burns, Oates, and Washbourne, 1912; 8th ed., 1912; Project Gutenberg, 2009. http://www.gutenberg.org/cache/epub/16772/pg16772-images.html.

————. *The Story of a Soul.* Translated by Thomas N. Taylor. Teddington, U.K.: Echo Library, 2006.

————. *The Story of a Soul: The Autobiography of the Little Flower.* Edited by Mother Agnes of Jesus. Translated by Michael Day. Charlotte, N.C.: TAN Books, 2010.

Tice, Lou. *Smart Talk for Achieving Your Potential.* Seattle, Wash.: Pacific Institute Publishing, 2005.

Tittle, C.R., and M.R. Welch. "Religiosity and Deviance: Toward a Contingency Theory of Constraining Effect". *Social Forces* 61, no. 3 (1983): 653–82.

Tolkien, J.R.R. *The Lord of the Rings, Part 2—The Two Towers.* New York: Del Rey, 1986.

Toynbee, Arnold. "Christianity and Civilization". In *Civilization on Trial.* New York: Oxford University Press, 1948. http://www.myriobiblos.gr/texts/english/toynbee.html.

Trigilio, John. "Sacrament of Penance: Examination of Conscience". EWTN.com, 2020. https://www.ewtn.com/catholicism/library/sacrament-of-penance-examination-of-conscience-9121.

Turner, J. H. *The Institutional Order.* New York: Addison-Wesley Educational Publishers, 1997.

Underhill, Evelyn. *Mysticism: A Study in the Nature and Development of Spiritual Consciousness.* New York: Renaissance Classics, 2012.

United States Catholic Catechism for Adults. Washington, D.C.: United States Conference of Catholic Bishops, 2006. http://ccc.usccb.org /flipbooks/uscca/#264.

Vanauken, Sheldon. *A Severe Mercy.* New York: HarperCollins, 1987.

Viviano, Benedict. "The Gospel according to Matthew". In *The New Jerome Biblical Commentary*, edited by Raymond E. Brown, Joseph A. Fitzmyer, and Roland E. Murphy, pp. 630–74. Englewood Cliffs, N.J.: Prentice-Hall, 1990.

von Rad, Gerhard. *Old Testament Theology.* Vol. 2, *The Theology of Israel's Prophetic Traditions.* London: Westminster John Knox Press, 1965.

Watson, William. *Forty Weeks: An Ignatian Path to Christ with Sacred Story Prayer.* CreateSpace Independent Publishing Platform, 2014.

Waugh, Evelyn. *Edmund Campion: A Life.* San Francisco: Ignatius Press, 2012.

Weaver, G. R., and B. R. Agle. "Religiosity and Ethical Behavior in Organizations: A Symbolic Interactionist Perspective". *Academy of Management Review* 27, no. 1 (2002): 77–97.

Wendon, John. "Christianity, History, and Mr. Toynbee". *The Journal of Religion* 36, no. 3 (July 1956): 147.

Wild, Robert. "The Pastoral Letters". In *The New Jerome Biblical Commentary*, edited by Raymond E. Brown, Joseph A. Fitzmyer, and Roland E. Murphy, pp. 893–94. Englewood Cliffs, N.J.: Prentice-Hall, 1990.

Wolfinger, Nicholas. "Counterintuitive Trends in the Link between Premarital Sex and Marital Stability". Institute for Family Studies, June 6, 2016. https://ifstudies.org/blog/counterintuitive-trends-in -the-link-between-premarital-sex-and-marital-stability.

Wright, N. T. *Jesus and the Victory of God.* Minneapolis: Fortress Press, 1996.

———. *The Resurrection of the Son of God.* Minneapolis: Fortress Press, 2003.

Zammit, Victor, and Wendy Zammit. *A Lawyer Presents the Case for the Afterlife.* White Crow Books, 2013.

NAME INDEX

Abednego (Azariah; biblical figure), 543, 544n1

Adam (biblical figure), 136

adultery, woman caught in (biblical figure), 331, 338–39, 355

Agle, B.R., 276n7

Agnes of Jesus, 254n48

Akitsuki, Yuko, 404n21

Alacoque, Margaret Mary, 118, 253, 473n8, 508

Allen, Elizabeth, 360n83

Allen, Woody, 83

Allison, Dale C., 51n18, 57, 58, 59

Ambrose of Milan, 109, 462

Amos (biblical figure), 562–63

Anscombe, G.E.M., 276

Saint Anthony, 253

Aquinas. *See* Thomas Aquinas

Aristotle, 276, 285, 289, 296–97, 404, 460

Aschenbrenner, George, 484n31

Atkins, David, 359n80, 360n83

Augustine of Hippo
Confessions, 254n48, 325n58, 380n2, 462n33, 466, 522n11, 552n2
on contempt, 528
Contra Mendacium, 284n20
The Free Choice of the Will, 409n44
on inner Church and prayer life, 239, 252, 253, 254n48, 264, 265
lower self and higher self, experience of, 462
Merits and Remission of Sin, and Infant Baptism, 124nn59–60
on moral conversion, 380, 381, 401n18, 409n44
on outer Church (sacraments and the Mass), 124–25, 135n68, 140

Prayer of Saint Augustine, 522, 552
The Teacher, 401n18, 409n44, 425n3
on virtue[s], 284n20, 289, 324–25
visualization-affirmation and, 425, 434

Azariah (Abednego; biblical figure), 543, 544n1

Bandura, Albert, 284, 363, 416, 423, 425–26, 428n7, 429n9, 430, 431, 439, 443, 446, 461, 462, 463

Barnabas (biblical figure), 64, 159, 476n13

Bartimaeus (biblical figure), 312–13

Beale, Stephen, 36n1

Bearison, David J., 238

Bellarmine, Robert, 434

Belloc, Hilaire, 265

Belmonte, Charles, 70

Benedict of Nursia, 22, 186, 253, 329n60, 380, 381

Benedict XVI (pope), 188, 433

Bennetts, Geni, 237–38

Bergoglio, Jorge (now Pope Francis), 42, 102

Bergson, Henri, 93n7

Bering, Jesse, 333n66

Sr. Bethany Madonna, 367n92

Betz, Johannes, 89–90n3, 91, 92, 93

Blackburn, Simon, 293n33

Saint Bonaventure, 252, 265

Bosco, John, 253

Bridget of Sweden, 253

Briggs, David, 146n71, 374n101

brother of the Prodigal Son (biblical figure), 472–73

Bultmann, Rudolph, 58

Burke, Dan, 206n19

SUBJECT INDEX

Page numbers with an italic *t* appended indicate a table. Personal names, with the exception of the Father, Jesus Christ, the Holy Spirit, and the Evil One, will be found in the separate **Names Index**. Specific biblical citations are listed in the separate **Biblical Citations Index**.

Catholic, as reason for being, 263, 493, 498
Church, reconciliation with, 132, 490–91
commission of sin[s], 482–83
confession of sins, 484–85
conscience, examination of, 483–84
continued conversion, graced resolve for, 133, 263, 495–96
contrition, perfect and imperfect, 482–84
definitive absolution offered by, 131, 486, 487–90, 492–93, 494, 499, 500
Eucharist, prior to reception of, 108
Evil One, severing bondage to, 263, 487, 489, 491–94, 495, 498, 509
father of the Prodigal Son and, 470–74
forgiveness/healing as grace of, 131, 133, 487–90, 494–95, 499, 500
graces of, 131–34, 486–98, 500
habits, breaking, 501
Holy Orders and power of, 158, 163
individual versus general absolution, 486
moral conversion, as path to, 22, 23, 24, 225
necessity of, 499–502
New Testament origins and early Church practice of, 474–81
penance, acceptance and completion of, 485
"prayer block", breaking, 199–200
priestly participation in, 166, 167, 168, 169
regular reception of, 474
reinforcing natural higher self through, 410
saints on, 474

school of the cross, awakening to guilt and awareness of past failings in, 229–30
spiritual peace as grace of, 133–34, 490–91, 496–98
spontaneous prayers for, 502–8
temperance and, 287–88
theology and practice of, 481–86
turning point in life, solidification of, 132, 491, 493–94, 500–501
unconditional act of love, Jesus' gift of, 374–75
religiosity/religious affiliation
illicit sexual conduct and, 360
mental health, correlation with, 239, 526, 529–30
universality of conscience and religiosity, 21–22, 33–34
willingness to be ethical/unethical and, 275–76
religious conversion. *See* spiritual conversion
Republic (Plato), 177n1, 276, 278–79, 289, 290n30, 404n25, 460n31
respect and care for others, 319t, 330–32, 420t
Resurrection of Jesus, 299
retaliation/retribution/vengeance, 305, 350
romantic/sexual love. *See* chastity; *eros*; Marriage
Rome
catacombs, 205, 251–52
letter of Ignatius of Antioch to Church of, 39, 40, 66, 69–71, 72, 75
Rosary
in contemplative life and prayer, 182, 183, 197, 198, 204–7, 211, 212, 216
as Marian devotion, 244, 245, 247, 251
Trinity and, 205
virtue, cultivating, 327, 328, 366
Rule of Saint Benedict, 380n4

BIBLICAL CITATIONS INDEX